GRAND STRATEGY

VOLUME V

August 1943–September 1944

by

JOHN EHRMAN
Sometime Fellow of Trinity College, Cambridge

James Ramsay Montagu Butler

LONDON: 1956
HER MAJESTY'S STATIONERY OFFICE

First published 1956

PUBLISHED BY HER MAJESTY'S STATIONERY OFFICE
To be purchased from
York House, Kingsway, LONDON, W.C.2 423 Oxford Street, LONDON, W.1
P.O. Box 569, LONDON, S.E.1
13a Castle Street, EDINBURGH, 2 109 St. Mary Street, CARDIFF
39 King Street, MANCHESTER, 2 Tower Lane, BRISTOL, 1
2 Edmund Street, BIRMINGHAM, 3 80 Chichester Street, BELFAST
or from any Bookseller

Price £2.2.0 net

Printed in Great Britain under the authority of HER MAJESTY'S STATIONERY OFFICE
by Charles Birchall & Sons Ltd., Liverpool and London.

HISTORY OF THE SECOND WORLD WAR

UNITED KINGDOM MILITARY SERIES

Edited by J. R. M. Butler

The authors of the Military Histories have been given full access to official documents. They and the editor are alone responsible for the statements made and the views expressed.

THE FIRST QUEBEC CONFERENCE, AUGUST 1943

Back row, left to right: Field Marshal Dill, General Ismay, Air Chief Marshal Portal, General Brooke, Admiral Pound, Admiral Leahy, General Marshall, Admiral King.

Front row, left to right: Mr. Churchill, Mr. Roosevelt.

CONTENTS

APPENDICES

MAPS

END PAPERS

ILLUSTRATIONS

The Frontispiece is reproduced by courtesy of the Keystone Press Agency, Plate VI by courtesy of the Sport and General Press Agency, and Plate VII by courtesy of 'Life' Magazine. The other Plates are Crown Copyright, and have been selected with the help of the staff of the Imperial War Museum, where they are housed.

EDITOR'S PREFACE

IT HAS BEEN explained in the preface to other volumes of this history that the work has been planned in accordance with a Government directive 'to provide a broad survey of events from an inter-Service point of view'. Throughout this book the word 'military' is used to cover the activities of all three fighting Services.

This volume is the fifth of a series of six on Grand Strategy, or the central direction of the war. The series is intended to supplement and provide the background for the volumes devoted to the several campaigns and special aspects of the war, such as the War at Sea, the Defence of the United Kingdom and the Strategic Air Offensive, just as from another point of view those volumes supply the background for the present series.

Grand strategy is concerned with both purely military strategy and politics; some overlapping into both these fields has been unavoidable, but the intention has been to leave the story of operations and local strategy to the volumes assigned to them, and not to trespass further either in this direction or in that of political and diplomatic history than is necessary to explain how the war was conducted from the centre at the highest level.

The present volume opens with the Anglo-American Conference at Quebec in August 1943, at which the Allied offensive for the winning of the war was planned. It closes with the check sustained by this offensive a year later, and will shortly be followed by the final volume, Volume VI, which continues the story to the surrenders of Germany and Japan.

Apologies are due to the reader for the appearance of the last volumes of a series before the first, but it seems more sensible to publish at once the volumes now ready than to keep them in storage pending the completion of those which precede them in time. It may perhaps be pleaded that Volume V begins at a recognizable starting-point to a new, and largely self-contained, period of the war.

The breach of chronological order results from the decision, which may itself require apology, to entrust the volumes on Grand Strategy to a number of different hands. The excuse must be that any other plan would have entailed still longer delay.

Our narratives are based mainly on official sources, to which we have been allowed full access: particularly on the voluminous telegrams, memoranda and minutes preserved in the Cabinet Office and other Departments. Among these Sir Winston Churchill's papers are of outstanding importance. Besides archives in official custody we have been allowed to use a wealth of private diaries and correspondence, as well as to consult orally many of the principal actors. To all who have helped in this way, and to their representatives, we express our thanks.

Apart from these primary sources, we have drawn largely on the work, published and as yet unpublished, of our colleagues of both the military and civil histories, and on the narratives, monographs and summaries prepared by the Service historical sections, under Rear Admiral R. M. Bellairs, Brigadier H. B. Latham and Mr. J. C. Nerney. We have also benefited greatly by the arrangements made with the official historians of the United States and of Commonwealth countries for an exchange of information and of draft histories.

For help in the presentation and interpretation of enemy documents we wish to thank Mr. B. M. Melland and Colonel G. T. Wards and their staffs. The maps have been prepared under the experienced direction of Colonel T. M. Penney.

As has been stated with respect to earlier volumes, the historians have not normally included references to documents not open to public inspection; since our references could not be checked, one of the main reasons for doing so was absent; full references are, however, printed in a confidential edition which should be available to students whenever the archives are opened. This policy has raised the question whether we should include references to published sources in these volumes. To do so is open to the objection that, where both unpublished and published sources have been used, the reader may be misled into thinking that the text relies solely on the published authorities referred to. Nevertheless we have thought it better to depart as little as possible from the usual practice, and have accordingly included references to important published sources; the reader should understand however that the sources mentioned are not necessarily the only ones we have used. Further, while not specifically referring to sources not open to the public, we have indicated the nature of the authority for statements of fact and opinion when there seemed special reason for doing so.

In accordance with the recognized British constitutional principle, the historians have not held themselves free to reveal individual differences of opinion within the War Cabinet nor to lift the veil of Civil Service anonymity. We have felt bound, also, to respect the requirements of military 'security'.

The Editor would like to acknowledge his personal obligations to the members of his Advisory Panel, Vice-Admiral Sir Geoffrey Blake, Lieutenant-General Sir Henry Pownall, Air Chief Marshal Sir Guy Garrod and Lieutenant-General Sir Ian Jacob, and to Mr. A. B. Acheson of the Cabinet Office.

J.R.M.B.

INTRODUCTION

THE LAST TWO VOLUMES of this series on grand strategy, written by one author, are concerned with one main theme. For the period which they cover, from August, 1943 to August 1945, was the period of the Allied strategic offensive—of the final offensive in Europe and of the first (and as it proved, final) phase of the combined offensive in Asia and the Pacific. The volumes thus deal with two separate wars, in both of which, however, large Allied forces were engaged continuously in operations whose respective places within the grand design had to be carefully considered, and constantly adjusted, in the light of the available resources and of the developments themselves.

The plans for the strategic offensive were designed at the first Quebec Conference in August, 1943; and the results, at least for Europe, followed their intentions with remarkable accuracy for almost a year, and never departed significantly from the pattern they had established. But this was not brought about without constant modification of detail, and occasionally of principle, natural enough when events were moving rapidly and on a majestic scale. It is the purpose of the two volumes to follow the development of the plans in relation to the events.

As in other parts of this series, operations are accordingly treated in outline; and since these volumes precede the relevant parts of the histories of the campaigns, I cannot pretend that such detail or such conclusions as appear should be taken as finally authoritative. Both are subject in due course to correction by those qualified to provide it. Nor does the account seek to describe , in due proportion, the contributions of the different Services. It would indeed be otiose, if not impossible, in a brief outline of conjunct operations, to follow the parts played respectively by land, sea and air forces; and since those operations mostly served campaigns by land, the emphasis has fallen mainly on the movements of the armies, which of course depended in varying degrees on support from the sea and air.

But there is a more fundamental disproportion in these volumes between the space devoted to the great conjunct operations on the one hand and to operations at sea and in the air on the other. This is dictated by the stage which the war had reached. The British and American strategic offensive rested directly on the basis of maritime power, and included great bombing campaigns against Germany and later against Japan. But essential as both these factors were to final success, neither in this period occupied the foreground of British strategic thought as did the campaigns by land. Maritime superiority, gained by the combined efforts of sea and air forces, was by now a fact in the West—challenged on occasions, never to be taken for granted, and at times emerging as an immediate issue, but in general forming the background to the plans for the offensive; while the bombing of Germany, which formed an important element of those plans, was also by now pursuing its own course largely in the background of strategy, and emerged as a strategic issue at different times as that course affected, or was affected by, the conjunct operations. The progress and significance of the air campaign in Europe, highly important as it was, can therefore best be examined on such occasions, and the detail of the operations, which occupied the central planners only from time to time, need seldom occupy us.

A similar result for British strategy occurred, for different reasons, in the Far East. For most of this period, British operations against Japan were confined to Burma; and although there was much speculation in London on the nature of the effort to be put into the Pacific, it remained speculation until a late stage, and the Americans' great operations by sea and air in that theatre, which decided the fate of Japan, need not be followed at any length. In both East and West, therefore, British strategic thought was concerned more with campaigns involving the three Services in combination than with independent operations by sea and air; and this narrative must follow the same pattern.

But the space devoted to the campaigns themselves must in turn vary considerably on different occasions. For while an account of grand strategy can aim at describing them only in outline, the relation of operations to plans in this period demands a more detailed description of the former on some occasions than on others. It is sometimes impossible, for instance, to explain the precise interaction of the strategy for the Mediterranean with that for north-west Europe, without following closely the course of the battles in Italy; or to understand the British strategy for the Far East without a detailed knowledge of the topography of, and operations in, Burma. The space devoted to local events therefore varies with their significance in the larger pattern.

It is perhaps surprising at first sight that the greater space should be devoted to the smaller campaigns. Plans for, and operations in, north-west Europe, which set the pace and provided the climax for the Allied strategy in 1944, can normally be followed only so far as is necessary to know what is going on, and to appreciate their effects. It is the Mediterranean and south-east Asia which, throughout that year, claim most attention. But this is not so surprising when the nature of planning in general, and of the current conditions in particular, is considered. For by the later stages of a successful war, strategic thought may well concentrate chiefly on the marginal campaigns. The main stroke, which decides the pattern, has been designed, and is being prepared or executed. The function of planning is now to see that it is supported, or is not endangered, by necessary operations elsewhere. This applies the more strongly if there is no great preponderance of force. In 1943, it was thought that the main stroke, in north-west France, could be undertaken provided that opposition was kept within specific limits. The burden of strategic thought therefore fell on those measures, principally in the Mediterranean and in the air, which alone could achieve that end; and the limitations of force and of material which demanded such a strategy, naturally provided the obstacles to its success. Similarly, the necessary offensive in south-east Asia, and—as far as a British history can determine—the campaigns in the Pacific, were limited by the prior demands of Europe. In these circumstances, the lesser undertakings often attracted, and must now receive, the greater attention.

The story that emerges is intricate and sometimes complex, and it must be followed at some length. The shifts and changes of argument, as events distort and restore the pattern, are too frequent for a series of selected occasions either to illuminate the intervals or to account satisfactorily for the length of the discussion on some of the plans. Planning is in any case likely to be more complex in a period of offense than in a period of defence or of preparation. But an important reason for tracing its detail closely in this instance, arises from the fact that the fluctuations were often caused by a shortage of critical material, which forms the connexion between the two wars against Germany and against Japan, and whose consequences, involving comparatively small forces and quantities whose significance however was considerable, can be appreciated only by close examination. In both East and West we can therefore appreciate the course of the debates only by seeing each step against the background of resources, within whose iron limits the actors moved. In the West, in addition, we must cover a wider field, for the course of operations on the Continent, from France to the Balkans, raised diplomatic problems which reacted upon strategy, and whose course must therefore be followed, in proportion to their effect, with that of the campaigns.

It has accordingly proved necessary to devote two volumes to this phase of the war: the first covering the period from August, 1943 to September 1944, the second from October, 1944 to August, 1945. Although not greatly unequal in chronology, the two parts are unequal in length. For the first is concerned with the settlement of the strategy which endured throughout the second, and with its execution in the period of greatest complexity. The dividing line, however, is clear, at least for the British. For a distinction must be drawn at this point between the position of the British and that of the Allies. The last two years of the war have generally been seen as the period of inevitable victory, in which the long period of preparation and increasing production, made possible by a maritime strategy, reaped its due reward. Neither Germany nor Japan, in that order, could hope to withstand the pressure of the Allies' superiority in men and material. But such a view disregards one important factor, which modifies the perspective. If victory was inevitable, for the British it must also be reasonably swift. The limits of their war effort were by now compelling, and its tempo could not be sustained indefinitely. If they were to maintain their full contribution and to keep their place within the Alliance, the war in Europe must therefore end in 1944. In the summer of 1943, as Sir Winston Churchill has remarked, 'the danger which faced the United Nations was no longer Defeat but Stalemate'.[1] A year later, the danger to the British was not Stalemate but Delay.

This theme gives a unity to the period covered by this volume—a period whose limits are marked by the two Allied conferences at Quebec. In August 1943, the first Quebec Conference settled the strategy for the defeat of Germany. In September 1944, that strategy had been so far successful that the second Quebec Conference opened in the immediate hope of a German surrender. Three weeks later, when it had closed, that hope had disappeared. Thereafter, the war in Europe proceeded to its inevitable but protracted end, postponing further the full offensive against Japan which had necessarily been curtailed in 1944. The delay did not affect the capacity of the Allies to achieve final victory; but it affected the capacity of the British to maintain their effort any longer at its peak.

This difference in background fostered a certain difference in outlook that already existed between the two great Western Allies. And since these volumes are concerned largely with the relations between them, they are concerned largely with this difference. There has been no attempt to conceal the resulting disagreements; but I hope they have not been exaggerated. For there is perhaps always a danger that disagreement, which may breed discussion, will bulk larger than agreement in an account of this sort; and where the disagreements, as sometimes here, were profound, the danger is disproportionately greater. It is therefore as well to remember that the area of consent remained larger than the area of dispute, and that even when the partners differed they remained close partners. For the Anglo-American Alliance, in the last resort, must be accounted a remarkable success. The very frankness of the discussions, perhaps without parallel between allies, argues a close association that was also unparalleled. On no occasion, moreover, did the deadlock remain unbroken. One or other of the allies always gave way, or both reached a compromise favourable to one, before it was too late. Such an association may be contrasted with the periods of silence, punctuated by sudden demands

[1] *Closing the Ring* (1952), preface.

or complaints or as sudden concessions, which the Western Allies experienced in their dealings with the Russians.

Place names in this volume follow official practice. I have referred to individuals by the styles they held at the time—e.g., Mr. Churchill, General Eisenhower, Mr. Eden—and, where I have omitted prefixes, have tried to combine courtesy with convenience. Promotions in rank, where relevant, are given in an appendix.

I wish to thank all those who, by research, information, or comment on the text, have helped in the production of the book: the wartime Ministers, Chiefs of Staff and commanders, staff officers, and officials; the historians and staff of the United Kingdom Official Histories, Military and Civil; the members of the Advisory Panel of the Official Military Histories; the staffs of the Records and Historical Sections of the Cabinet Office, and of various Departments; and the historians in Commonwealth and Allied countries. It is, I think, worthy of record that, despite the novel nature of these volumes on grand strategy in the writing of official history, no Department or individual has asked me to censor or to alter anything of substance; nor has there been any obstacle to quoting the documents from which I have wished to quote. Her Majesty The Queen has graciously given permission for certain documents to be reproduced; and Ministers, the Secretary of the Cabinet, Departments, and the United States Government have given similar permission where required. Certain cypher telegrams have been paraphrased for security, but without affecting their substance or sense. Otherwise, quotations have been shortened, as shown in the text, only when I have considered a passage irrelevant or redundant. Where I reproduce substantial extracts from Sir Winston Churchill's unpublished Minutes and telegrams, as distinct from the full text, the full relevant text is given in an appendix: where the quotation is of one of his Minutes or telegrams already published, in whole or in part, in his memoirs, I refer for comparison to the volume concerned. Otherwise, I have cited publications where they contain statements or quotations not already available in the documents I have used.

I owe two special words of thanks: to my editor, Professor J. R. M. Butler, who has borne the ultimate responsibility for the work throughout; and to my principal Research Assistant, Miss Jean Dawson, who not only provided much information on detail, but also wrote several of the long studies on which sections of the book are based. I have been fortunate in being able to call, over a period of some years, on her industry, scholarship and judgment.

November, 1955

CHAPTER I

STRATEGY AND SUPPLY IN THE AUTUMN OF 1943

(i)

Outline of Strategy

BETWEEN 9th and 17th August, 1943, two large delegations, from Britain and from the United States, assembled in Quebec. The British included the Prime Minister, the Foreign Secretary, and the members of the Chiefs of Staff's Committee. The American delegation contained the President, the American Chiefs of Staff, Mr. Harry Hopkins, and later the Secretary of State, Mr. Cordell Hull. Other high officers and officials, and ample staffs, attended the principals. On the 17th, the sixth Anglo-American conference of the war opened, under the code name of the 'Quadrant' Conference.[1]

Its purpose was to design, on the foundations laid by its predecessors over the past eight months, a full offensive strategy in Europe and a limited offensive strategy in the Far East. The emphasis between the two wars had been defined in January 1942, when the two Governments agreed—as they confirmed, after some debate, a year later—that the defeat of Germany should precede the main attack on Japan. Their 'over-all strategic concept' was accordingly given as follows at 'Quadrant':

> '. . . 3. In co-operation with Russia and other Allies, to bring about at the earliest possible date the unconditional surrender of the Axis in Europe.
>
> 4. Simultaneously, in co-operation with other Pacific Powers concerned, to maintain and extend unremitting pressure against Japan with the purpose of continually reducing her military power and attaining positions from which her ultimate surrender can be enforced. The effect of any such extension on the over-all objective to be given consideration by the Combined Chiefs of Staff before action is taken.
>
> 5. Upon the defeat of the Axis in Europe, in co-operation with other Pacific Powers, and if possible with Russia, to direct the full resources of the United States and Great Britain to bring about at the earliest possible date the unconditional surrender of Japan.'

[1] For code names, see throughout this volume Appendix I below.

In the West, the Allies were now preparing to embark on the first stage of the final attack on Germany. Over the past year, her conquests had been brought abruptly and dramatically to an end, and she had in turn been pressed back with heavy losses in the east and in the south.[1] In August 1942, the German army stood in the suburbs of Leningrad and Stalingrad, in the Caucasus some 130 miles from the Caspian Sea, and, in North Africa, within sixty miles of the Nile delta. By August 1943, it had been ejected, with the Italians, entirely from North Africa, was fighting in Sicily, and in Russia had been forced back slightly in the north, appreciably in the centre from the areas of Moscow and Voronezh, and far in the south from Stalingrad and the Caucasus to the Sea of Azov and the west bank of the Don. In all of these operations probably half a million men had been killed, and at least as many again had surrendered or were missing. The tide had turned, Germany was now on the defensive, and the Allies were gathering strength for her encirclement. But the task remained formidable. 'Festung Europa', despite a marked weakness in the south, was a reality; the German army, hard pressed and declining in quality though it might be, remained a disciplined and effective force embracing some three hundred divisions and supported by a still formidable, though progressively unbalanced, air force; and large tracts of territory lay in every direction between the Allies and the Reich. The Russians at their nearest point were over three hundred miles from the eastern German frontier; while the Western Allies had still to gain a foothold on the mainland of Europe. Somewhere, at some time, the reconquest of the Continent must begin with the first British or American soldier wading ashore out of the sea; and while experience in North Africa had shown that such a venture could succeed, it had shown equally vividly, and in less critical conditions, the obstacles to success.

But while the main effort lay ahead, the Western Allies could look with satisfaction on three clear gains over the past year, without which it could not have been envisaged. First, they had recently won a great victory in the Atlantic, and for the first time since the autumn of 1940 were masters of that ocean. Between August, 1940 and March 1943, merchant shipping was sunk at a steadily increasing rate, and faster than it could be replaced. In 1940, 3,990,000 gross tons of shipping were lost, in 1941 4,330,000 tons, and in 1942 7,800,000 tons; and of these totals, the North Atlantic accounted for 1,810,000 tons, 2,420,000 tons and 5,480,000 tons respectively.[2] Over the same period, more U-boats were built than were destroyed. By March 1943, the danger to survival was as great as in April, 1917. The sinkings in January and February had been very serious, while the enemy's submarine

---

[1] See Front End-paper.
[2] All to the nearest ten thousand tons.

fleet continued to grow in numbers and confidence. In January, 1943 there were 212 U-boats and in March 250, of which at least one hundred were always at sea, highly trained in a type of warfare whose terms they dictated. But over the next two months a series of counter-measures appeared, which had been in preparation for some time. Very long-range aircraft, based on Iceland and Newfoundland, now closed the gap, and enabled air, as well as surface, escort and support to be given to the convoys throughout their passage; more escorts, with more ample training, were available for close defence; and there was a notable improvement in both seaborne and airborne radar. The results were decisive. In March 1943, 477,000 tons of merchant shipping were sunk in the North Atlantic, and twelve U-boats; in April, 245,000 tons and fifteen U-boats; in May, 165,000 tons and forty U-boats; in June, 17,000 tons and seventeen U-boats; in July, 123,000 tons and thirty-seven U-boats. These figures tell a tale of successful defence followed by highly successful attack. In June and July, when the U-boat packs had been seriously harried along the convoy routes, aircraft and escort groups carried the war to the Bay of Biscay, through which the marauders entered and left their ports. The offensive was successful, and by the autumn larger escort groups, with more effective support from the air, were able to subdue and often to destroy the individual U-boats that alone could now reach the convoys. Their task was made the easier, after September 1943, by the use of facilities in the Azores which the Portuguese Government then granted to the Allies. In the last quarter of the year, fifty-three U-boats were sunk, while the losses in the North Atlantic dropped to 146,000 tons. Meanwhile new construction was steadily rising, and in October 1943, for the first time, the British and American combined merchant fleets were larger than at the beginning of the war.

In the second half of 1943, the Battle of the Atlantic therefore gave no immediate cause for anxiety. This was indeed fortunate, for the next eight months demanded a heavy flow of men and material from the United States to the British Isles. The reinforcement of the British army in the United Kingdom by American troops had been planned in the spring of 1942, as a necessary condition for an invasion of north-west Europe. But the programme ('Bolero'), owing partly to intervening commitments in North Africa and partly to administrative inexperience, had only recently begun to approach the estimates. In May 1943, indeed, only one American division was in England, instead of five as originally designed; and while the figures improved in the autumn, a strenuous effort would clearly be needed throughout the forthcoming winter and spring, which must not however encroach on the normal imports on which the life of Britain depended. The defeat of the U-boats was not the only factor involved in meeting this demand; but it was an essential factor, without which the rest could scarcely be controlled. The invasion of Europe in 1944 would not have been possible without the success in the Atlantic in 1943.

Apart from the Battle of the Atlantic, Allied sea power was adequate to meet most of the tasks demanded of it in the West. A substantial Allied Fleet dominated the Mediterranean at the beginning of August, 1943. The Italian navy had long confined its activities to submarine attack, and even this had diminished notably over the past year. Convoys passed freely through the area, and the assault on Sicily in July could be undertaken with every prospect of countering serious opposition at sea. The earlier danger from the air, which had once crippled the Mediterranean Fleet, had also largely disappeared, thanks to the superiority of the Allied air forces and the invasion of Sicily.

In the north, the British Home Fleet, to which an American squadron was attached, pursued its two familiar tasks: the prevention of raids by German heavy ships or cruisers into the Atlantic, and the protection of the convoys to northern Russia, when they were resumed after having been stopped in March, 1943 by a shortage of escorts and the longer daylight. The effective German surface fleet was by now very small—one heavy battleship, the *Tirpitz*, one 'pocket battleship,' the *Admiral Scheer*, one battle-cruiser, the *Scharnhorst*, four cruisers and twenty-one destroyers; but of these, the *Tirpitz* and *Scharnhorst*, with one cruiser and twelve destroyers, were concentrated in Norwegian fjords, and at that point of vantage could not be ignored. The position, however, was transformed by the end of the year. At the end of September, in reply to the Russians' requests, it was decided to resume the convoys to the Arctic, given the appropriate facilities on arrival; and on the 22nd, as a preparatory measure, British midget submarines attacked the *Tirpitz* at anchor in Norway. The battleship was heavily damaged, and put out of action for some months. On Boxing Day, H.M.S. *Duke of York* sank the remaining German battle-cruiser, the *Scharnhorst*, which attempted to attack a convoy. The Home Fleet's superiority thereafter was complete, and although the northern convoys were still harried by submarine and aircraft, they had no longer to fear a serious surface attack, while the main strategic problem of preventing the escape of German heavy ships from their home waters was virtually removed. Throughout 1944, the Allied Fleets in the north and south of Europe were therefore able to support the main operations without difficulty, and indeed largely unopposed.

The war in the air was also moving in favour of the Allies. In 1940, the British had hastened and expanded the programme for a large force of heavy bombers, which had been started before the war. Their operations were designed originally as part of the 'indirect strategy' of bombing, blockade and subversion which emerged after Dunkirk; and alone survived the disappearance of that strategy after the United States entered the war. But the bombers, ordered in a period when an invasion of Europe was not in prospect, could be produced only in time to serve as the indispensable preparation and adjunct to invasion. In 1941 and 1942, the figures lagged behind the estimates, while the air authorities' estimates of the results exceeded the figures. In 1941, some 3,300 heavy and medium bombers were produced, as against a forecast in October, 1940 of some 5,100: in 1942, some 5,400 as against a forecast in December, 1941 of some 7,200.[1] Experience soon showed, moreover, that a bombing campaign raised highly complex problems of tactics, direction and intelligence, which had not been encountered before and were far from easy to solve. It was not a question here of winning a number of important battles over a part of the enemy's forces, but of exhausting a whole system of defence and thereafter of destroying a Great Power's capacity to wage war. The achievement of the air offensive's object, 'the progressive destruction and dislocation of the German military, industrial and economic system, and the undermining of the morale of the German people to a point where their capacity for armed resistance is fatally weakened', was accordingly difficult to attain in the period before the necessary conditions could be provided.

In 1943, these conditions were being, but had not yet sufficiently been, gained. On the one hand, British production had got into its stride, operational experience had improved the design of aircraft, equipment and tactics, and, after some discussion on the best use of their forces, the Americans were ready to participate in an agreed programme of operations. At the Casablanca Conference (the 'Symbol' Conference) in January of that year, a 'combined bomber offensive' was sanctioned, in which the Americans were to concentrate mainly on attacks by day, largely upon 'precision targets', while the British were responsible for those by night on large industrial centres. The 'primary objectives' of the campaign were specified as the submarine yards and bases, the aircraft industry, transportation and oil, with 'other targets in enemy war industry' last in priority. The Americans where possible favoured attacks on the later stages of production, concentrating at first on motor, rubber and aluminium plants, and later on the fighter aircraft industry. The British, as in 1942, devoted their greatest efforts to the cities of the Ruhr, where the high concentration of production at all stages offered a unique combination of targets and an opportunity to disrupt the life of a large population. They began with Essen in the spring, and Hamburg in the late summer, of 1943. The destruction from this combined offensive was great, the experience was new for the Germans on such a scale, there was a marked fall in the production of rubber, coal and iron, and a certain dislocation of transport.

But, on the other hand, this fall in production was in most cases

[1] Figures to the nearest hundred.

later reversed, while the pursuit of the programme placed a considerable strain on the Allied air forces. A factor in the first development, and a cause of the second, was the steady rise in production of the enemy's fighter aircraft, which despite repeated Allied attacks, and new technical means of baffling the German defences, remained a formidable opponent throughout the year. The Americans' daylight attacks incurred increasingly heavy casualties in the summer and autumn, forty-five aircraft out of 338 being lost on one occasion over Stuttgart, sixty out of 291 on another over Schweinfurt; and losses at night, though not so high, also remained considerable. This opposition was partly the cause, as its maintenance was a result, of the fact that the Allies' combination in the air was in practice still far from complete. For while co-operation grew in the course of 1943, the British and American programmes still remained largely separate from each other, and each moreover often ignored the priorities which had been laid before it. Despite its growing magnitude, therefore, the offensive lacked the consistent concentration which experience was to prove necessary for success.

The activities of the German fighters indeed caused an important modification of the original plan. In June 1943, the Allied bombing authorities decided to postpone their ultimate object of destroying the enemy's economy, and to concentrate, particularly in the daylight attacks, on the preliminary object of destroying his fighter air force. As the new plan ('Pointblank') recognized:

> '. . . *If the growth of the German fighter strength is not arrested quickly, it may become literally impossible to carry out the destruction planned* . . . Hence the successful prosecution of the air offensive against the principal objectives is dependent upon a prior (or simultaneous) offensive against the German fighter strength.'

While the final object remained the same, the intermediate object therefore claimed first priority. It was impossible to tell how soon either could be achieved. But while the strategic air offensive had so far failed to achieve the results anticipated for it, its progress was nevertheless laying the foundations for a superiority in the air which was later to secure the essential conditions for the main invasion of the Continent.

The third gain over the past year lay in the Mediterranean. In the course of 1940, Italy's entry into the war forced the British into a campaign in that area, which however they expected to lead in time to her complete defeat; in 1941, the Germans increased the dangers and the opportunities of the campaign, when they decided to weaken Britain by a combination of bombing her towns and of defeating her army in the Middle East; and in November 1942, the Allies' invasion of Algeria and Morocco, undertaken as the result of a separate process, confirmed and increased the attention which both sides were paying to the southern theatre. The outcome now seemed about to realize, in different circumstances, the original British object. The campaign in North Africa from October, 1942 to May 1943, and the subsequent attack on Sicily launched on 10th July, brought the Fascist régime to the point of collapse. On 19th July, Mussolini attended Hitler at the Villa Feltre near Rimini, to receive further demands for men and material which he was unable either to counter or to meet; on the 24th, the Fascist Grand Council voted, in his presence, for a transfer of power to the Monarchy; and on the 25th he was arrested. His successor, Marshal Badoglio, at once announced that the war would continue; but it seemed likely that an overture would soon be made, and this in fact came early in August. By the time that the 'Quadrant' Conference began, it seemed reasonable to suppose that Italy would surrender, and possibly would transfer allegiance, within the next few weeks.

The consequences could not yet be judged, for both the German and the Allied measures would depend on the event itself and on the manner of its accomplishment. Meanwhile, the Allies prepared to assault the Italian peninsula as soon as fighting ended in Sicily, so as to assist or exploit the surrender of the Italian Government. But whatever ensued, an experienced force of twenty divisions,[1] assured of Allied superiority in the air and of Allied control at sea, would be available for operations up the peninsula itself or to east or west. Italy's surrender, indeed, would mean the first break in the Germans' defence of Europe, and should enable the British and Americans, in easier circumstances, to gain that foothold on the Continent which was the object of their strategy for 1944.

The main lines of that strategy, following the design sketched tentatively at the Casablanca Conference in January, had been adumbrated at the Anglo-American conference in Washington in May, 1943 (the 'Trident' Conference). The Allies then agreed to aim over the next year at four distinct objects, none of which, in view of the state of the resources, was given priority over the others. First, they should secure control in the Atlantic. Secondly, they should pursue the strategic air offensive against Germany. Thirdly, they should mount an operation from the United Kingdom, 'with target date 1st May 1944', 'to secure a lodgement on the Continent from which further offensive operations can be carried out.' This would require a force of twenty-nine operational divisions by that date. Fourthly, they should conduct operations in the Mediterranean, after the capture of Sicily, 'to eliminate Italy from the War and to contain the maximum number of German forces.'

This pattern was confirmed at 'Quadrant' in greater detail, in the light of the intervening developments. Success at sea, in the air, and in

[1] After allowing for withdrawals from the theatre, and for garrison duties.

the Mediterranean now defined their relations to the cross-Channel attack (operation 'Overlord'), the plan for which had itself been produced in July. This suggested that an assault could be launched on 1st May, 1944 against north-west France, provided that certain conditions, on which the British insisted, were observed. The German air force must have been substantially reduced beforehand, facilities must be devised to sustain the operations in France without the use of a great port for at least three weeks, and the opposition on land must be kept, at different stages over a period of three months, within specified limits. If these conditions could not be assured, an assault in northern Europe, possibly on Norway (already studied as operation 'Jupiter'), might have to be considered as an alternative. The cross-Channel operation, in fact, which in May, 1943 had not been accorded priority over the other targets for the coming year, in August demanded their direct support. The strategic air offensive had already, for its own purposes, been adjusted in that direction. Now, strategy in the Mediterranean was given a more definite rôle following the defeat of Italy. The containment of the necessary German forces might demand a complementary assault on the south of France: it would certainly demand a diversionary campaign beyond France which the forces already in the southern theatre could best provide.

The balance between the various tasks was determined in the Combined Chiefs of Staff's Final Report at 'Quadrant', dated 24th August, which may indeed be regarded as the blue print for the final offensive in Europe. For, with remarkably few modifications, the design remained the same until the Western Allies were nearing the frontier of Germany; and the modifications themselves arose only from the necessity to relate intervening developments to its purpose.

'. . . 7. The following operations in execution of the over-all strategic concept are agreed upon:

THE U-BOAT WAR

8. (a) *Progress Report*

We have had encouraging reports from the Chiefs of the two Naval Staffs regarding the U-boat war. We have approved recommendations made by the Allied Submarine Board which should result in further strengthening our anti-U-boat operations. The Board has been directed to continue and expand its studies in search of further improvements.

(b) *Facilities in the Azores Islands*

The facilities of the Azores Islands will be used for intensified sea and air operations against the U-boats. . . .

THE DEFEAT OF THE AXIS IN EUROPE

9. We have approved the following operations in 1943–44 for the defeat of the Axis Powers in Europe:

THE BOMBER OFFENSIVE

10. The progressive destruction and dislocation of the

German military, industrial and economic system, the disruption of vital elements of lines of communication, and the material reduction of German air combat strength by the successful prosecution of the Combined Bomber Offensive from all convenient bases is a pre-requisite to 'Overlord' (barring an independent and complete Russian victory before 'Overlord' can be mounted). This operation must therefore continue to have highest strategic priority.

OPERATION 'OVERLORD'

11. (a) This operation will be the primary United States-British ground and air effort against the Axis in Europe. (Target date the 1st May, 1944). After securing adequate Channel ports, exploitation will be directed towards securing areas that will facilitate both ground and air operations against the enemy. Following the establishment of strong Allied forces in France, operations designed to strike at the heart of Germany and to destroy her military forces will be undertaken.

(b) There will be a balanced ground and airforce build-up for 'Overlord', and continuous planning for and maintenance of those forces available in the United Kingdom in readiness to take advantage of any situation permitting an opportunistic cross-Channel move into France.

(c) As between Operation 'Overlord' and operations in the Mediterranean, where there is a shortage of resources, available resources will be distributed and employed with the main object of ensuring the success of 'Overlord'. Operations in the Mediterranean Theatre will be carried out with the forces allotted at 'Trident', except in so far as these may be varied by decision of the Combined Chiefs of Staff.

12. We have approved the outline plan of General Morgan for Operation 'Overlord' and have authorised him to proceed with the detailed planning and with full preparations.[1]

OPERATION 'JUPITER'

13. In case circumstances render the execution of 'Overlord' impossible it may be necessary to consider 'Jupiter' as an alternative. Plans for this operation, with particular reference to an entry into Southern Norway, should therefore be made and kept up to date.

OPERATIONS IN ITALY

14. (a) First phase. The elimination of Italy as a belligerent and establishment of air bases in the Rome area, and, if feasible, further north.

(b) Second phase. Seizure of Sardinia and Corsica.

(c) Third phase. The maintenance of unremitting pressure on German forces in Northern Italy, and the creation of the conditions required for 'Overlord' and of a situation favourable

[1] See p. 22 below.

for the eventual entry of our forces, including the bulk of the re-equipped French Army and Air Force into Southern France.

OPERATIONS IN SOUTHERN FRANCE

15. Offensive operations against Southern France (to include the use of trained and equipped French forces) should be undertaken to establish a lodgement in the Toulon-Marseilles area and to exploit northward in order to create a diversion in connection with 'Overlord'. Air-nourished guerrilla operations in the Southern Alps will, if possible, be initiated.

AIR OPERATIONS

16. (a) Strategic bombing operations from Italian and Central Mediterranean bases, complementing 'Pointblank'.

(b) Development of an air ferry route through the Azores.

(c) Air supply of Balkan and French guerrillas (see paragraph 17 below).

OPERATIONS IN THE BALKANS

17. Operations in the Balkan area will be limited to supply of Balkan guerrillas by air and sea transport, to minor Commando forces, and to the bombing of strategic objectives.

GARRISON REQUIREMENTS AND SECURITY OF LINES OF COMMUNICATION IN THE MEDITERRANEAN

18. Defensive garrison commitments in the Mediterranean area will be reviewed from time to time, with a view to effecting economy of force. The security of our lines of communication through the Strait of Gibraltar will be assured by appropriate dispositions of our forces in North-West Africa, so long as there remains even a remote possibility of the Germans invading the Iberian Peninsula.

EMERGENCY RETURN TO THE CONTINENT

19. We have examined the plans that have been prepared by General Morgan's staff for an emergency operation to enter the Continent [operation 'Rankin']. We have taken note of these plans and have directed that they be kept under continuous review, with particular reference to the premises regarding the attainment of air superiority and the number of troops necessary for the success of these operations.'

The offensive against Japan had reached a less advanced stage, in August 1943, than the offensive against Germany. It had only recently got under way in some theatres, it had not yet started in others, and the targets lay in the outer ring of the Japanese conquests. The shape of the offensive was indeed still determined by the enemy's initial successes, from December, 1941 to June 1942, which had carried him north-east to the Aleutian Islands, south-east to the islands of Guam and Wake and beyond the Marshalls to the Gilberts, south to the Bismarck Archipelago, the northern half of New Guinea and the

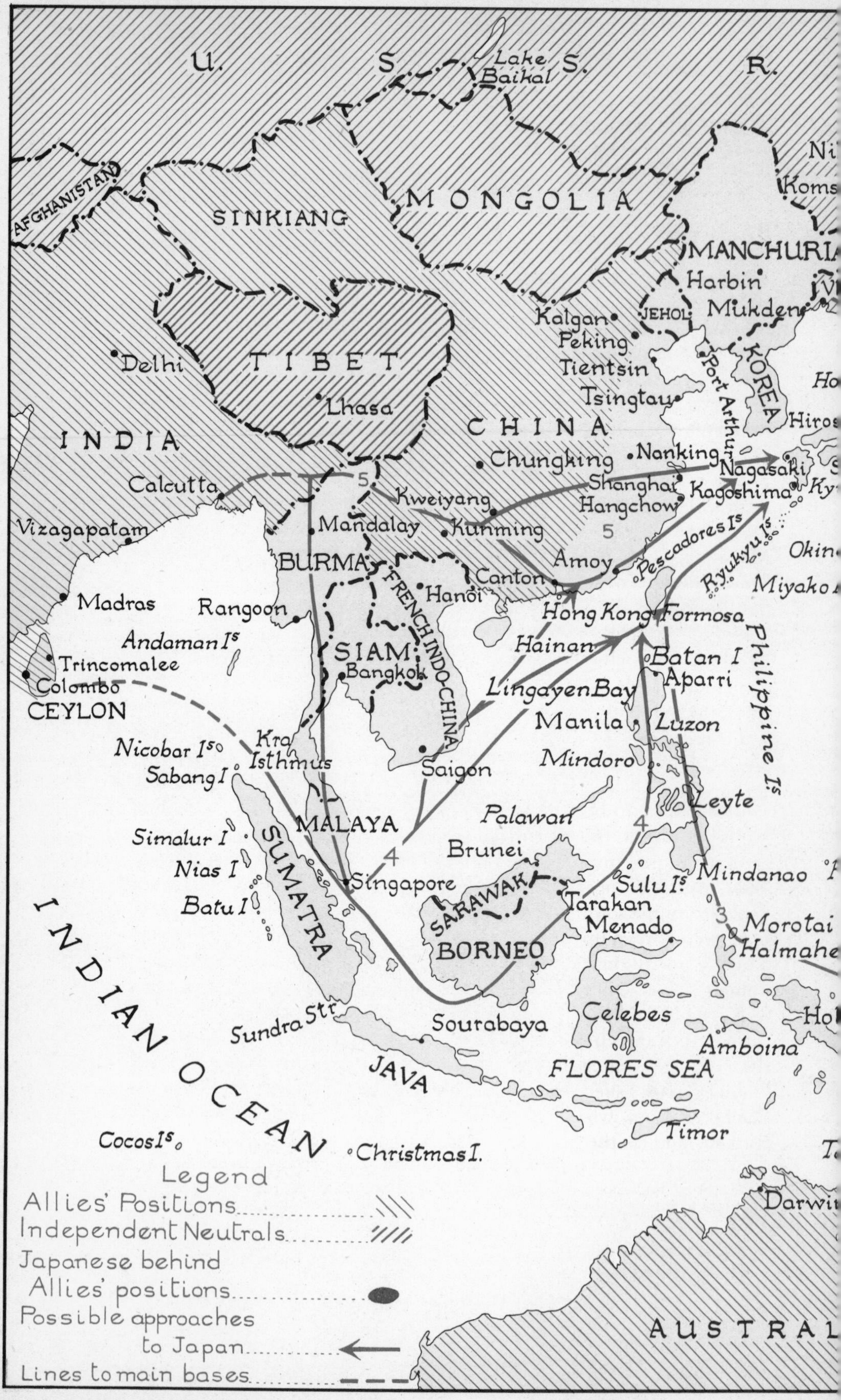
U. S. S. R.
Lake Baikal
AFGHANISTAN
SINKIANG
MONGOLIA
MANCHURIA
Harbin
JEHOL
Mukden
Kalgan
Peking
Tientsin
Tsingtau
Port Arthur
KOREA
TIBET
Delhi
Lhasa
INDIA
CHINA
Chungking
Nanking
Nagasaki
Shanghai
Hangchow
Kagoshima
Calcutta
Kweiyang
Vizagapatam
Mandalay
Kunming
BURMA
Amoy
Pescadores Is
Ryukyu Is
Canton
FRENCH INDO-CHINA
Hanoi
Madras
Rangoon
Hong Kong
Formosa
Andaman Is
Hainan
Trincomalee
SIAM
Bangkok
Batan I
Aparri
Colombo
CEYLON
Lingayen Bay
Philippine Is
Manila
Luzon
Nicobar Is
Kra Isthmus
Mindoro
Sabang I
Saigon
Palawan
Leyte
MALAYA
Simalur I
SUMATRA
Brunei
Nias I
Singapore
Mindanao
Sulu Is
SARAWAK
Batu I
Tarakan
Menado
Morotai
INDIAN OCEAN
BORNEO
Celebes
Sundra Str
Sourabaya
Amboina
JAVA
FLORES SEA
Timor
Cocos Is
Christmas I.
AUSTRAL
Legend
Allies' Positions
Independent Neutrals
Japanese behind Allies' positions
Possible approaches to Japan
Lines to main bases

Solomon Islands, and south-west to the Netherlands East Indies, to Malaya and northern Burma, to French Indo-China and to Hongkong. In China he stood, south of the conquered province of Manchuria, along a line to the west of the Peking-Canton railway.[1]

By the autumn of 1943, the Americans and Australians had regained the initiative throughout the Pacific. In the north, indeed, the counter-attack had already come to an end. The Japanese had occupied the islands of Kiska and Attu, off the Alaskan peninsula, as the last of their conquests in June, 1942. This move offered a direct, if minor, threat to the American continent itself, and in January, 1943 the Americans began to prepare for the reoccupation of the islands. In May they landed in Attu, in August in Kiska, and by the winter the Aleutians were safe. But distance and weather, and the prospect of heavy commitments further south, deterred the Americans from following their advantage further on this front.

The main attacks fell in the central and south-west Pacific. In the central Pacific, the Japanese, by the capture of Wake and Guam, had soon removed the threat to their own mandated territories in the Marshalls, Carolines and Marianas, and in turn were able to threaten American movements further east. At the same time, their conquests in the Philippines, in New Guinea and in the islands immediately to the eastward—from Rabaul in New Britain to Guadalcanal in the Solomons—threatened Australia and completed the defensive semi-circle guarding the sea lanes from the Netherlands East Indies and south-east Asia to Japan. By the end of 1942, the Americans and Australians had begun to weaken the perimeter of those defences. The great naval battles of the Coral Sea and Midway regained freedom of movement at either end of the line, enabling the Allies in the south-west and in the central Pacific to begin their separate offensives in the second half of 1943. By August, the forces in the central Pacific comprised six American operational divisions, and a large Fleet; while thirteen American and Australian operational divisions, with two lesser Fleets, were deployed in the south and south-west. In August and September 1943, plans were drawn up for the forces in the centre to begin a series of out-flanking operations upon the chain of island groups; and after a preliminary bombardment of Wake, the first series of landings took place in November on the Gilberts. Over the same period, the Allies were turning the tables in the south-west. Thanks again to their command of the sea, they entered the central Solomons between August and October, established a naval and air base in October in the northern Solomons from which to threaten the Japanese concentration at Rabaul, and in the last four months of 1943 began to push up the

---

[1] See Front End-paper, and Map 1. For a chronological comparison between events and plans in Europe and those in the Far East throughout this volume, see Appendix XI below.

northern coast of New Guinea, where they had been fighting for over a year, with a series of outflanking sea- and airborne assaults.

These offensives from the east found no counterpart on the mainland of Asia. The Americans had been engaged for a year in establishing a supply line to China by air from bases in northern India, which fed partly the Chinese armies and partly the American air force in that area. But while the best use of this supply, and the rôle of China in an offensive strategy, were under keen debate, the immediate commitment was still to hold the enemy to his line west of the Peking-Canton railway. To the south-west, the British and Japanese lay, in an uneasy stalemate, along the frontier of India and Burma. A Japanese attempt to enter India had been defeated in the autumn of 1942, and a British attempt to advance into Burma had failed in the spring of 1943. But plans were now under way for a fresh British offensive into Burma in November, after the end of the south-west monsoon, coupled with a seaborne assault across the Bay of Bengal. For this purpose, naval and air reinforcements were being prepared, new methods of jungle warfare and training had been devised, and in August the Allies decided to set up a new Command for south-east Asia, separate from that of India.

The prospect of a general offensive against Japan in 1944 did not enable the Combined Chiefs of Staff to determine its pattern in August, 1943. The fact that the different offensives were in an early stage, or were still preparing, had made it unnecessary so far to allocate priority to one line of attack over the other, particularly as some of the resources were limited by the prior claims of the war in Europe. On the other hand, this very limitation made an early allocation of priority desirable to establish a successful pattern. This perhaps applied particularly to the British, whose resources for the Far East were particularly slender, and whose theatre in south-east Asia offered sharply contrasting possibilities which might have to be settled, within the context of the general strategy, during the next few months. As we shall see, the problems were in fact being discussed in London and in Washington before the 'Quadrant' Conference began; but they did not yet demand close discussion between London and Washington, and the Combined Chiefs of Staff were content, in their Final Report, to promulgate the separate plans for the separate theatres in the Far East over the next six months.

'. . .THE WAR AGAINST JAPAN

Long-term Strategy

20. We have made a preliminary study of long-term strategy for the defeat of Japan and are of the opinion that the following factors require particular emphasis:

(a) The dependence of Japan upon air power, naval power,

and shipping for maintaining her position in the Pacific and South-East Asia.

(b) The consequent need for applying the maximum attrition to Japan's Air Force, Naval Forces, and shipping by all possible means in all possible areas.

(c) The advantage to be gained and the time to be saved by a more extensive use of the superior air resources at the disposal of the United Nations,[1] both in the strategic field and in conjunction with operations on land.

21. We consider that great advantage may be obtained, by modern and untried methods, from the vast resources which, with the defeat of Germany, will become available to the United Nations. We have in mind:

(a) A project rapidly to expand and extend the striking power of the United Nations air forces in China as well as of the ground troops for their defence by employing the large numbers of load-carrying aircraft available to open an " air road" to China.

(b) The employment of lightly equipped jungle forces dependent largely upon air supply lines.

(c) The use of special equipment to enable the superior power of the United Nations to be deployed in unexpected and undeveloped areas.

22. From every point of view operations should be framed to force the defeat of Japan as soon as possible after the defeat of Germany. Planning should be on the basis of accomplishing this within 12 months of that event. Decisions as to specific operations which will insure a rapid course of events must await further examination on the lines indicated above.

23. The deployment of forces and the operations to be undertaken in the war against Japan must be in accord with the overall objective and strategic concept. . . .

24. We are agreed that the reorientation of forces from the European Theatre to the Pacific and Far East should be started as soon as the German situation, in our opinion, so allows.

25. The principle has been accepted that the forces to carry out operations from the East, including the South-West Pacific, shall be provided by the United States, and for operations from the West by Great Britain, except for special types not available to Great Britain which will be provided by the United States. The employment of Dominion forces will be a matter of discussion between all Governments concerned.

Specific Operations, 1943–44

26. We have found it impracticable during 'Quadrant' to arrive at all the necessary decisions for operations in the war against Japan in 1943–44. We therefore propose that, as soon

[1] The term used to embrace the Allied nations in combination.

as the necessary further examinations have been made, a Combined Chiefs of Staff Conference should be held wherever may be most convenient, unless agreement is reached through the ordinary channels. There are, nevertheless, certain decisions which we feel able to make at once.

Operations in the Pacific, 1943–44

27. We approve the proposals of the United States Chiefs of Staff for operations in the Pacific in 1943-44 as follows:

28. The seizure and consolidation of the Gilberts preparatory to a further advance into the Marshalls.

29. The seizure of the Marshall Islands . . . preparatory to a westward advance through the Central Pacific.

30. The capture of Ponape preparatory to operations against the Truk area.

31. The seizure of the Eastern Carolines . . . and the establishment of a fleet base at Truk.

32. The capture of the Palaus, including Yap.

33. The seizure of Guam and the Japanese Marianas.

34. Consideration of operations against . . . the Kuriles.

35. The seizure or neutralisation of eastern New Guinea . . . including the Admiralty Islands and Bismarck Archipelago. *Rabaul is to be neutralised* rather than captured.

36. An advance along the north coast of New Guinea . . . *by step-by-step airborne-waterborne advances*.

37. To carry out operations for the capture of Upper Burma in order to improve the air route and establish overland communications with China. Target date mid-February, 1944.
It is recognised that the extent of these operations is dependent upon logistic considerations as affected by recent floods.

38. To continue preparations for an amphibious operation [in south-east Asia] in the spring of 1944. . . .

39. To continue the preparation of India as a base for the operations eventually contemplated in the South-east Asia Command.

40. To continue to build up and increase the air routes and air supplies to China, and the development of air facilities, with a view to:

(a) Keeping China in the war.
(b) Intensifying operations against the Japanese.
(c) Maintaining increased United States and Chinese Air Forces in China.
(d) Equipping Chinese ground forces.

41. We have decided that our main effort [in south-east Asia] should be put into offensive operations with the object of establishing land communications with China and improving and securing the air route. Priorities cannot be rigid and we

therefore propose to instruct the Supreme Commander in formulating his proposals to regard this decision as a guide, and to bear in mind the importance of the longer term development of the lines of communication.

. . . 46. The vigorous and effective prosecution of large-scale operations against Japan in South-east Asia, and the rapid development of the air route through Burma to China, necessitate the reorganisation of the High Command in the Indian Theatre. It has, therefore, been decided that the Command in India should be divided from the operational Command in South-east Asia . . .'

(ii)

Outline of Command

The offensive strategy was served by, and reflected in, a system of Anglo-American command which by this time was highly developed. Its apex may be observed at the first Plenary Meeting of the 'Quadrant' Conference; for the participants then comprised the machinery, and most of the personalities, with which we shall be mainly concerned. The attendance was as follows:

GREAT BRITAIN

The Prime Minister and Minister of Defence (Mr. Winston S. Churchill)
The Secretary of State for Foreign Affairs (Mr. Anthony Eden)
The Chief of the Imperial General Staff (C.I.G.S.) (General Sir Alan Brooke)
The First Sea Lord and Chief of the Naval Staff (Admiral of the Fleet Sir Dudley Pound)
The Chief of the Air Staff (C.A.S.) (Air Chief Marshal Sir Charles Portal)
The Head of the Joint Staff Mission in Washington (Field Marshal Sir John Dill)
The Chief of Combined Operations (Vice-Admiral Lord Louis Mountbatten)
The Chief of Staff to the Minister of Defence (Lieut.-General Sir Hastings Ismay)

UNITED STATES

The President (Mr. Franklin D. Roosevelt)
The Chief of Staff to the President (Admiral William D. Leahy)
The Chief of Staff of the Army (General George C. Marshall)
The Commander-in-Chief, U.S. Fleet and Chief of Naval Operations (Admiral Ernest J. King)
The Commanding General of the Army Air Forces (General Henry H. Arnold)
Mr. Harry Hopkins

These two delegations comprised the two active war-making bodies of the Western Allies. As Commander-in-Chief of the Armed Forces of the United States, the President was advised by the committee of the Joint Chiefs of Staff, formed in February, 1942 of the professional heads of the Army and Navy and of the Army Air Forces, to whom his own Chief of Staff was later added as chairman; and as sole Chief Executive, constitutionally free to summon whatever advice he chose, and under no obligation to consult a Cabinet with joint responsibility, he conducted grand strategy almost entirely through it. Subject, within the limits of the Constitution, to his judgment alone, its members indeed acted as the supreme military executive, forming the complement in the military sphere to the President's personal conduct of politics and diplomacy. High in these personal counsels, and acting as an unofficial but potent emissary of the President throughout the United States Government and the Alliance, was the sixth American representative at the meeting, Mr. Harry Hopkins. The Joint Chiefs of Staff remained the same throughout the last two years of the war: Hopkins' influence became intermittent after a long bout of ill-health beginning early in 1944.

The Joint Chiefs of Staff, set up soon after the United States entered the war, had taken their form largely from British example. The British Chiefs of Staff consisted of the professional heads of the three Services, to whom was added in 1940 the Chief of Staff to the Minister of Defence, and in 1942, as an extra member 'whenever major issues are in question and also when . . . any special matter in which he is concerned [is] under discussion', the Chief of Combined Operations. The C.I.G.S. and the C.A.S. remained the same throughout the last two years of the war. Admiral of the Fleet Sir Dudley Pound resigned as First Sea Lord from ill-health on 19th September, 1943, being replaced on 4th October by Admiral of the Fleet Sir Andrew Cunningham; and Admiral Lord Louis Mountbatten, who at the end of August, 1943 was appointed as Supreme Allied Commander in south-east Asia, was succeeded as Chief of Combined Operations in October by Major-General R. E. Laycock.[1] Thereafter there was no change. The Chiefs of Staff were served by a series of sub-committees, each consisting, like themselves, of officers in the relevant posts of the Service Departments, sometimes sitting with members of other Government Departments. Of these the most important were the Joint Intelligence Committee, which included the three Directors of Intelligence, and the Joint Planning Staff, composed of the three Directors of Plans. Each part of the organization employed a small special staff.

But the British Chiefs of Staff, though providing the pattern for their American colleagues, occupied a specific and subordinate position within the British Government that had no parallel in the United

[1] See Appendix III(A) below.

States. They formed in fact an integral part of the Cabinet committee system, and were collectively responsible to the War Cabinet itself through the Minister of Defence, a post occupied since the summer of 1940 by the Prime Minister. He was assisted in his responsibilities by the War Cabinet's Defence Committee, itself divided into (Supply) and (Operations). The Defence Committee (Operations), under the chairmanship of the Prime Minister and Minister of Defence, contained the Lord President of the Council, the Secretary of State for Foreign Affairs, the Minister of Production, the three Service Ministers, and the four regular members of the Chiefs of Staff's Committee. The War Cabinet itself consisted at the end of September, 1943 of the Prime Minister and Minister of Defence, the Lord President of the Council, the Secretary of State for Foreign Affairs, the Chancellor of the Exchequer, the Minister of Labour and National Service, the Minister of Production, the Secretary of State for the Home Department, and, until December 1943, the Minister of State Resident in the Middle East. The Minister of Reconstruction, a post created in November 1943, was added at that date to the body.[1]

The Defence Committee, by its composition, thus adequately represented the War Cabinet in military affairs, assisted by expert advice; and particularly between 1940 and 1942, it acted largely for it in the direction of strategy. The War Cabinet retained general supervision and control, but exercised its normal functions more in the fields of civil and diplomatic affairs, and in their relation to strategy, than in the field of strategy itself. The Cabinet, as distinct from the War Cabinet, disappeared, although some Ministers not in the War Cabinet were known as 'Ministers of Cabinet rank'. All papers were War Cabinet papers; all committees were War Cabinet committees; and the office for conducting their business was known as the Offices of the War Cabinet and Minister of Defence.

The constitutional position of the British Chiefs of Staff must be borne in mind throughout this volume, the more so as in practice it was seldom necessary to recall it. For throughout the war strategy was determined increasingly by this single committee, guided and supported by the Prime Minister. Even in Mr. Chamberlain's Administration, when the state of the war and personal preference were more favourable to traditional forms, the Service Ministers, of whom Mr. Churchill was then one, had questioned its excessive authority. The advent of Churchill as Prime Minister and Minister of Defence, heralding a more vigorous and knowledgeable political direction of strategy, and an exceptionally close association between himself and the Chiefs of Staff, proved decisive. The War Cabinet had already delegated its military authority to the Defence Committee; by 1943 the Defence Committee, though still meeting frequently and cognizant of all major

[1] For Ministerial appointments throughout this volume, see Appendix II below.

developments, had delegated much of its immediate authority to the Prime Minister and the Chiefs of Staff, for whom it acted increasingly as a court of appeal rather than as a supervisory body. The appearance of the Joint Chiefs of Staff, after the entry of the United States into the war, as the supreme military authority subject to the President, further stimulated a development which had itself been largely responsible for the stimulant. It was the Chiefs of Staff, not the Defence Committee, who thereafter controlled the hierarchy of military subcommittees in London and their offshoots in Washington. The Ministerial body, unlike its civil counterpart the Lord President's Committee, developed no directly subordinate agents; the professional body was responsible for the normal co-ordination and review of military affairs within the British Government and between the British and the Americans. As the Prime Minister consolidated his supremacy within the War Cabinet, and as liaison with Washington became intimate and continuous, the Chiefs of Staff emerged collectively as the decisive Committee in the making of strategy.[1]

Both sets of Chiefs of Staff thus derived their power directly from their Heads of Government. The same authority sanctioned their combined responsibility as the Combined Chiefs of Staff. When the United States entered the war, some organ had to be devised which would serve the Alliance as the Supreme War Council had served the British and the French in 1939/40. Events in the Far East soon led to the formation *ad hoc* of an executive committee composed of the American and British Chiefs of Staff, the former organized for the first time as the Joint Chiefs of Staff; and at the end of February 1942, the President proposed its perpetuation and extension to cover all Allied theatres of war. When the main spheres of responsibility had been settled, the Combined Chiefs of Staff were formally established in March.[2]

The purpose of the Committee demanded continuous meetings and consultation. The two sets of Chiefs of Staff themselves could naturally meet only on occasions; and since the headquarters of the combined organization were set in Washington, the Joint Staff Mission which the British had earlier established there served as the normal representative of the British Chiefs of Staff. Its head, until his death in November 1944, was Field Marshal Sir John Dill, formerly C.I.G.S., who was given the right to attend full meetings of the Combined Cheifs of Staff. The Combined Chiefs disposed of sub-committees on the lines

---

[1] More detailed examination of this and other aspects of the central machinery in the last two years of the war, is reserved for the concluding chapter of the next, and final, volume in this series.

[2] It is necessary to stress, at this point, the difference between 'Joint' and 'Combined', for the terms will appear often throughout this volume. 'Joint' always applies to inter-Service committees of one nationality, 'Combined' to Anglo-American (usually inter-Service) committees. Of the three Chiefs of Staff's Committees, the British were called simply the Chiefs of Staff, the Americans were called the Joint Chiefs of Staff, and the combination was called the Combined Chiefs of Staff.

of those serving each of the constituent bodies, the two most important of which were the Combined Intelligence Committee and the Combined Planning Staff. The British element on these sub-committees formed a separate staff from those in London, working under the Joint Staff Mission in Washington.

The organization of the Combined Chiefs of Staff, evolved by the necessity to control forces of different nations operating within a single theatre, in time reacted upon the theatre Commands; and by the middle of 1944, a common pattern had been established with local variations. But this had not come about by the autumn of 1943, and the structure of the Commands then differed according to tradition, experience or circumstance. The division of theatres between the two nations, following the President's suggestion, was made in March, 1942. The Allies then agreed to allocate responsibility for the day to day conduct of the war in the Pacific and China to the Americans, in the rest of Asia and the Mediterranean (later the Middle East) to the British, and in the rest of Europe and in the Atlantic to the two nations sharing control.[1] By this arrangement, the Combined Chiefs of Staff exercised a 'general jurisdiction over grand strategic policy' in all areas, while the Joint Chiefs of Staff exercised 'jurisdiction pertaining to all matters of operational strategy' in the American theatres and the British Chiefs of Staff in the British theatres. The more direct control of the Combined Chiefs of Staff over theatres of combined responsibility, was secured by different means in the different circumstances set by each.

The pattern of command in the areas controlled by the Americans differed from that in the areas controlled by the British. In the Pacific, the Americans set up two theatres, the Pacific Ocean Areas, itself divided into North, Central and South Pacific Commands, and the South-West Pacific Area.[2] In the summer of 1943, the South Pacific Command, although remaining under the control of the Pacific Ocean Areas, was placed under the strategic direction of the South-West Pacific Area when its operations entered that theatre. The commanders were then Admiral Chester Nimitz in the Pacific Ocean Areas, and General Douglas MacArthur in the South-West Pacific. With the title in each case of Commander-in-Chief, each was in fact a Supreme Commander,[3] alone responsible for his theatre to the Joint Chiefs of Staff, and the immediate superior of the Service commanders. Nimitz's forces were entirely American, and the emphasis was on the sea and its air: MacArthur commanded Americans and Australians,

[1] See Rear End-paper.
[2] See Rear End-paper.
[3] MacArthur was in fact sometimes addressed as such at the end of 1943.

the latter indeed in greater strength than the former, and the Services were more evenly balanced in his theatre. Each of the Commanders-in-Chief continued to command directly the forces of his own Service.

On the mainland of Asia, the Americans exercised no direct jurisdiction over the China theatre, in which they recognized Generalissimo Chiang Kai-shek as the Allied commander. In view of the paucity of their forces, and the uncertainty of their plans for the area, this was not surprising; and the arrangement was circumvented rather than altered when circumstances later demanded.

The British system, in India and in the Middle East, was in contrast to that in the Pacific. Command in both theatres was exercised by three Commanders-in-Chief in committee[1] forming a body of equals, although in both cases the land commander was recognized as the leading member, co-ordinating the problems of the three Services and normally representing the theatre to the Chiefs of Staff. This system of command by committee, which sought, as in former wars, to reconcile with the demands of conjunct operations the traditional lines of responsibility from Department to commander, had hitherto proved satisfactory for operations when the forces were predominantly of one nationality. But it had not as yet been troubled by the problems of controlling Allied forces on a basis of equality, or of making adequate provision within the theatre for Allied administration and diplomacy.

The other areas of active operations fell to the combined command of both Allies. In the autumn of 1943, there were four such Commands: in the Atlantic, over the air forces bombing Germany, in the western Mediterranean, and, in skeleton, for the invasion of north-west Europe. Command in the Atlantic was simple, following the nature of the campaign. Naval interests were paramount, and the operations were strategically defensive. In both the British and American areas of responsibility[2] they were therefore conducted by the naval Departments, which did not account directly to the Combined Chiefs of Staff. The Chief of Naval Operations in the United States directed the campaign through the Commander-in-Chief of the U.S. Atlantic Fleet, the Admiralty in Britain through the Commander-in-Chief, Western Approaches.

Control of the strategic air forces against Germany followed a pattern similar in some respects, but with significant differences. All of the forces were still based on the United Kingdom, and the Combined Chiefs of Staff therefore exercised authority through the agency of the British Chief of the Air Staff, who directed the activities of the two forces involved, the British Bomber Command and Eighth U.S. Army Air Force. As in the Atlantic, operations were thus controlled by a single Service; but, as was not the case in the Atlantic, forces of the

---

[1] See Appendix III(B) below.

[2] See Rear End-paper.

two nations came under the strategic direction of one authority, who was himself directly responsible to the Combined Chiefs of Staff. As an offensive weapon, hitherto in its own right and prospectively within the pattern of the strategic offensive, the long-range bombers against Germany were kept closely under review; and as their operations were extended to cover southern as well as northern and central Europe, and as the European Commands themselves developed, the form of the air Commands was involved increasingly in that development.

The European Commands were already developing in the two remaining theatres of operations, one actual and one potential. The Command in the western half of the Mediterranean had been formed in August, 1942 to control the Allied Expeditionary Force for the invasion of North Africa (operation 'Torch'). It was then placed under an American Commander-in-Chief, Lieut.-General Dwight D. Eisenhower, with an American deputy and an American Chief of Staff, the land and air forces remaining under their separate national commands. But when in February, 1943 the British Eighth Army reached Tunisia from the east, to work in close touch with the Allied forces by then operating west of Tunis, the Command was reorganized.[1] Eisenhower, promoted to General, remained Commander-in-Chief of the Allied Forces, but with a single Commander-in-Chief of all Allied ground forces in a newly-created Fifteenth Army Group (General Sir Harold Alexander); with a single Commander-in-Chief of all Allied naval forces (Admiral Sir Andrew Cunningham, succeeded in October, 1943 by Admiral Sir John Cunningham); and with a single Commander-in-Chief of all Allied air forces (Air Chief Marshal Sir Arthur Tedder), who also controlled all air forces in the adjacent Middle East Command. The Chief of Staff remained American (Major-General Walter Bedell Smith).[2] It seems later to have been assumed, although it was never laid down, that Alexander was also deputy to the Commander-in-Chief of the theatre. General Eisenhower was served by his own administrative and diplomatic staffs, but made use for planning and intelligence of the existing combined committees of the Service Commanders-in-Chief.

This organization, although it remained unique in all its aspects to the Mediterranean, may be said to have set the pattern for the European version of the Supreme Command. For the first time in British experience, apart from a short-lived experiment in the Far East early in 1942, a single commander was interposed between the Chiefs of Staff and the Service Commanders-in-Chief; for the first time in either British or American experience, he was not directly in command of any forces, but on the other hand exercised direct control over the machinery for diplomacy and administration within his theatre.

---

[1] See Rear End-paper.

[2] See Appendix III(B) below.

The system reflected the combined responsibility of the Combined Chiefs of Staff, from which it derived authority and on which it conferred greater reality.

Since the commander for 'Torch' was American, the Combined Chiefs of Staff agreed in the summer of 1942 that the Command should receive their instructions through the agency of the Joint Chiefs of Staff; and this held good after the reorganization in February, 1943. The same type of arrangement, though in this case the channel of communication was British, was specified for the organization in Britain which was preparing for the invasion of north-west Europe. Plans for this undertaking had been entrusted first to the British Joint Planning Staff, and later, from January, 1942 to April 1943, to a committee of commanders in the United Kingdom known as the Combined Commanders. But in January, 1943 the Western Allies agreed to appoint in due course a Supreme Commander 'for a re-entry to the Continent', and in the meantime a Chief of Staff 'for the control, planning and training for cross-channel operations in 1943.' In March, the British nominated for the second post Lieut.-General F. E. Morgan, and in April his appointment was confirmed as Chief of Staff to the Supreme Allied Commander (Designate), or Cossac as it was henceforth known. He was provided with a small British and American planning staff, and was instructed to submit his plans to the British Chiefs of Staff, with whom the American Commanding General, European Theatre of Operations would act for the Joint Chiefs of Staff. The outline of the Command was thus laid in accordance with the pattern in the Mediterranean; but, unlike his fellows in other theatres, the potential commander was known, even at this stage, as the Supreme Allied Commander.

These arrangements have referred, at each level, to the British and Americans alone. For there was in fact no comparable machinery between the United Kingdom and the rest of the British Commonwealth, or between the British and Americans and their European allies. Although there was a continual exchange of information between the nations of the Commonwealth, and particularly between each of them and London, no consultative or executive body existed for the direction of combined military affairs. Instances arose during the war of a Commonwealth officer holding a senior appointment in a British hierarchy; but the consultations with Commonwealth Governments on the employment of their forces under British command did not lead to any development of machinery, but indeed, in their progress and results, rather reflected its absence.[1] This was not surprising.

[1] E.g., the discussions on the Australian forces in the Middle and Far East in 1941/42; and see pp. 474 and 482-3 below.

The Imperial War Cabinet in the First World War had functioned only for a short time, and then only intermittently; and the subsequent growth in stature of the Commonwealth nations did not support the establishment of a combined military staff. The emphasis was on liaison rather than on formal organization; and that was maintained in the Second World War by the permanent representatives of the Commonwealth countries in London, by visits from Commonwealth Ministers (culminating in the Prime Ministers' Conference of May, 1944),[1] by constant communication through the Dominions' Office, and on occasion by representatives of a given nation attending for a period meetings of the British War Cabinet. Nor perhaps was a highly-developed organization necessary in the later stages of the war. The substitution within the British Government and the Anglo-American Alliance of a mainly professional for a mainly political War Council, may have rendered otiose, as it rendered inconvenient, an effective Imperial War Cabinet or even an Imperial Chiefs of Staff's Committee. The Combined Chiefs of Staff alone were capable of handling professionally the large and varied problems affecting Allied strategy outside Russia; and the military interests of Commonwealth nations were handled, not unsatisfactorily, by representatives in or representations to London or Washington, while the British Prime Minister normally kept Commonwealth Prime Ministers informed of major developments of policy. One notable exception to this rule was provided by the South African Prime Minister, Field Marshal Smuts, whom the War Cabinet, and Mr. Churchill in particular, regarded as the elder statesman of the Commonwealth, and who often proferred and was asked for advice on strategy. But Smuts' influence was due to history and to personal qualities; and his position indeed derives its unique importance by contrast with that obtaining elsewhere.

There was also no question at any time of a larger Allied War Council embracing the European allies apart from the Russians. All were exiles from their countries and—except for the French—their territories, for whom Britain provided refuge and support. Their forces were placed, with their own commanders and mostly owing allegiance to their Governments in London or Cairo, under British or Allied command, and the Governments themselves were consulted and informed as occasion arose. Londoners in those days saw the troops and representatives of many nations, and the British Government exercised a hospitality and an influence not unlike that which it had exercised in the Napoleonic Wars.

In their different ways, the Commonwealth, China and the exiled European allies thus occupied a marginal, though in some cases an important, position within an alliance that centred on the British and

---

[1] See p. 332 below.

Americans. The Soviet Union constituted an equal and virtually independent ally in the war against Germany. Although potentially of decisive strategic importance, there could as yet be no connexion between the operations of the Russians and of the Western Allies, and liaison was confined to ensuring the due arrival of supplies to the former from the latter, through convoys to the Arctic and through Persia. The form and extent of this aid were decided by the Anglo-American Missions, under Lord Beaverbrook and Mr. Averell Harriman, which visited Moscow in September, 1941; thereafter, it was handled in Washington by a Soviet Purchasing Commission and in Moscow through the agency of the British and American Military Missions, which in the late autumn of 1943 were headed by Lieut.-General Sir Giffard Martel and Major-General John R. Deane respectively. These Missions existed also to report on the progress of the war in Russia, and to handle the exchange of information on strategy and material between the Allied Governments. But in practice they received little information on plans or even on events, while the exchange of information on material, regulated in the case of the British by the Anglo-Russian Alliance signed in London in May 1942, was honoured, at least in Moscow, more in the breach than in the observance. Apart from the Missions, there was no regular contact with Russian officials, and only two visits by the Russian Foreign Minister, M. Molotov, had given the Western world a glimpse of the higher hierarchy.

Effective contact with Russia relied, in fact, entirely on the Heads of Government. Following the successful precedent of his telegrams to President Roosevelt, Mr. Churchill had opened a similar correspondence with Marshal Stalin on the eve of the German invasion of Russia; and spasmodic and often disappointing as this was, it was responsible for such results as had been achieved and for the communication of the Russians' ideas on strategy. The President followed suit when the United States entered the war, although until the second half of 1943 he left the initiative mainly to the Prime Minister. But as the prospect of the main offensive in the West approached in the course of that summer, the Western Allies felt, and the Russians acknowledged, the need for consultation. The Prime Minister had visited Moscow once, in August 1942; but the absence of effective machinery, reflecting in part the impotence of all Russian authorities but the very highest, now confirmed the desirability of a further meeting with Stalin of which Roosevelt and Churchill were in any case convinced. In August, 1943 they opened negotiations; meanwhile, they continued to regard the Soviet Union, as they had done from the start, with a mixture of expectation, caution and bewilderment which they hoped, in different degrees, might yet provide the material for a closer alliance to be forged by circumstances and the anticipated meeting.

(iii)
Supply

When the enemy's conquests were halted towards the end of 1942, in the Caucasus, in North Africa, and along the northern frontier of Burma, the last prospect of a strategic connexion between Germany and Japan, already faint, disappeared. Thereafter, the sole connexion between the two wars remained, for the British and Americans, that of supply. In the middle period of the war, from early in 1941 to the summer of 1943, the limits of strategy had been determined largely by the limits of production, confining the possibilities to a preliminary offensive on the fringe of enemy territory in the West, and to a series of holding operations and limited attacks in the Far East. By the autumn of 1943, that strategy, and production itself, were ready for the fuller offensive designed at Quebec; and on 26th August the Combined Planning Staff submitted a detailed report to the Combined Chiefs of Staff on the relation of means to ends.

The Combined Planning Staff examined the resources under seven headings: ground forces, naval forces, air forces, assault shipping, critical items, shipping, and oil. We may first take the armed forces themselves. Naval forces, of which no detailed figures were given, were reported to be adequate for all operations with the possible exception of those from India, and without allowing for a possible assault on the south of France. Otherwise, the limiting factor for naval operations seemed likely to be men; and the Planners noted, after their otherwise not unsatisfactory conclusions, that 'no additional operational requirements for British naval personnel, over and above that at present planned up to 1st May, 1944, can be met, except at the expense of some other operational undertaking.'

Requirements for ground forces were calculated at 137 divisions, of which 135 (50 British and British-controlled, 49 American, 12 Australian and New Zealand, 11 French and 13 Chinese) were reported likely to be available. But both forecasts were subject to serious qualifications. First, the provision of enough forces for the Pacific depended on the accuracy of plans that were acknowledged to be provisional, and on a successful reorganization of Australian and American formations, pending the end of the war in Europe, that had still to be carried out. Secondly, the forecasts assumed that operations in the Mediterranean would conform to the forces soon to be available in that theatre, which would be reduced by November, 1943 from thirty-six to twenty-nine Allied divisions, when three British and four American operational divisions had been transferred to the United Kingdom for 'Overlord'. No further reinforcement was planned thereafter from British or American sources; and the Mediterranean was in fact accepted, in the distribution of manpower, as a wasting asset—an assumption which its strategic rôle over the next few months might prove embarrassing.

This embarrassment was likely to affect south-east Asia; for the provision for that area was vague and rather optimistic. The estimates both of requirements and of availability allowed for a large Chinese force that had still to appear; while the estimate of availability relied further on a reorganization of British divisions which had not yet taken place. The Combined Planning Staff could therefore only say, in concluding its report on the ground forces, that 'searching investigations are proceeding to determine if the forces required for operations in Northern Burma can be found by the target date of mid-February 1944.'

The provision of air forces met the requirements in rather the same way as that of the ground forces. The 11,400 British and American aircraft deemed likely to be available in the United Kingdom, were considered adequate for all operations from that base over the first half of 1944; air operations in the Mediterranean would conform to the 4,100 aircraft available; there might be some 1,700 aircraft in south-east Asia, where again no detailed requirements for Burma were forecast, although some shortage of transport aircraft was envisaged; and some 3,900 aircraft in the Pacific, where there might be a shortage of land-based planes. Subject to these exceptions and provisions, the Planners concluded that 'the air resources required to meet the operations specified in this paper are available'.

But the armed forces represented, as it were, the finished product of supply; and to see the true position, we must examine the material from which they were formed. This in turn may be done by examining the main strategic shortages, as felt or envisaged towards the end of 1943. The equipment of the forces themselves was on the whole remarkably satisfactory. The Combined Planning Staff noted that there was still a shortage of certain 'critical items', such as radar and radio equipment, vehicles of various sorts, and equipment for handling cargo; but none was of the order, or indeed of the type, to affect strategic plans. A more serious difficulty lay in a potential shortage of high-grade aviation fuel, which would have to be carefully watched over the coming year. But it was hoped that increased production, and a wider use of lower-grade fuel than had been practised hitherto, would overcome this obstacle. The dangers to the 'Quadrant' strategy were indeed of a different order: not a lack of equipment for the forces, but a possible lack of mobility; not the capacity of the Allied effort, but the varying capacities of the different allies.

Four main shortages threatened to limit the offensive strategy: merchant shipping, assault shipping, transport aircraft, and, in the case of the British, men. The first two were included as specific problems in the Combined Planning Staff's report at Quebec.

A shortage of merchant shipping had been one of the main preoccupations in both London and Washington since the winter of 1941/42; and indeed remained so, despite a marked improvement in the supply and use of ships, throughout the war. In the second half of 1943, the danger, though contained, seemed still to threaten, for the improvement was too recent to be fully accepted, and neither its own implications nor those of an offensive strategy were as yet entirely clear. As recently as May 1943, the highest British authorities had concentrated specifically on shipping as the most pressing limit on strategy. It was at that time, to the Prime Minister, 'the measure of all our operations'; to the C.I.G.S., 'the stranglehold on all our operations'; while to the First Lord of the Admiralty, it 'will, and does indeed already restrict our whole offensive strategy'. Taking the British position alone, it is not difficult to see the reasons for this attitude. The rate of sinkings in the Atlantic had only just begun to decline, and new construction still lagged behind the losses and the demands. In the first three months of 1943, over twice as much British tonnage was sunk as was built, and the merchant fleet, over 17 million tons at the outbreak of war, now amounted, apart from foreign vessels on charter, to some 13½ million tons. Meanwhile the demands for shipping were expanding. The import programme of the United Kingdom, long a residuary legatee, was now an irreducible commitment; for during the first quarter of the year imports had reached the lowest point of the war, stocks had been seriously raided, and it was now necessary to safeguard the country against such depletions in the future. The trade and industry of the Commonwealth and of other overseas countries, necessary to the Allied cause, had to be sustained; a task which in many cases now demanded increased shipments to ward off dangerous crises. And lastly, the prospect of the strategic offensive raised a growing demand for ships on military operations, and for the support of troops overseas. While this was not the first occasion, therefore, on which a world war had been fought, the tasks were on a scale never before imagined.

It was thus not surprising that all of the British budgets for shipping throughout 1943 should have shown an estimated deficit for the next six months, which on occasion was calculated at between 2½ and 3 million tons. But grave though this deficit was for an island whose life depends on the sea, it did not reflect the true position for British strategy, or even for Britain herself. Since the entry of the United States into the war, a combined strategy had been conceived as having the support of combined resources; and in 1943, as a result of higher production and a lower rate of loss, the American merchant fleet for the first time exceeded the British and became the largest in the world. Without in any way releasing their control, the authorities in Washington provided shipping services from this fleet in various ways for their allies: by handing over vessels for the duration of the war, by carrying British military cargoes, and by carrying imports to Britain herself. Altogether, their measures of direct assistance to the British amounted to some 20 per cent of their own dry-cargo tonnage in 1943.

The fact that the Americans thus aided the British did not necessarily mean that there was American shipping to spare over all demands. In May 1943, the Combined Shipping Adjustment Board reported that there was a 'not unmanageable [Allied] deficit', and apart from a temporary, and in a sense unreal, surplus in August,[1] deficits, 'manageable' or 'unmanageable', were reported thereafter at the start of every Allied conference until Germany was defeated. The planners, therefore, never indulged in that assumption. American aid was given not because all American needs already seemed to have been met, but because the maintenance of the British Isles and of certain mainly British forces overseas at certain times, were regarded by the President and the Joint Chiefs of Staff as necessary objects, enjoying a given priority, of the Allied strategy.

To meet the full demands of this strategy until the middle of 1944, three things were necessary: more ships suitable to the various tasks, their efficient use, and their precise and flexible allocation. As we have seen, the ships were coming from the British and American yards—enough, as it was thought, to meet all demands by the summer of 1944, and on the whole in the right proportion of types. The four main categories of merchant shipping were troopships, dry-cargo ships, tankers and coasters. Troopships—or 'personnel shipping' as it came to be called—had proved the main shortage from early in 1941 to late in 1942. But improvements in the accommodation of men and in the use of the ships themselves, and some increase in their number, overcame the worst difficulties by the beginning of 1943, and although the programme remained 'very tight' in the second half of that year, it was generally recognized by the spring that the bottleneck was no longer 'personnel' but cargo shipping. This had in fact accounted for the bulk of the new construction from 1942. But production of general cargo shipping was complicated by that of two special types of vessel—tankers and coasters—which an offensive strategy demanded. There were enough large tankers by the summer of 1943 to meet existing demands, and new construction, set on foot in the previous year, was thought likely to prove equal to the extra load in 1944. But there remained a real need for smaller tankers, particularly to supply newly-established beach-heads and bases, which the current state of the plans

---

[1] See p. 31 below.

both for Europe and for the Far East made it difficult to estimate at all exactly. Coastal shipping, other than tankers, was also in great demand from the middle of 1943, particularly in preparation for 'Overlord' and for operations in south-east Asia. Both demands were met in the event, partly by new construction in the year before 'Overlord', partly by improved management of the shipping itself. But their satisfaction did not relieve the bulk of the demands for general cargo shipping; and the production of new vessels, significant and in the end decisive as it was, was a process whose results could not be felt immediately.

Meanwhile, the effect of the tonnage at the Allies' disposal could be increased by greater efficiency in the use of existing ships. The British authorities had for long been seeking to enlarge the carrying capacity[1] of the ships they controlled, and by 1943 had succeeded in many respects; and the American civilian shipping authorities—although faced with greater administrative difficulties[2]—could also record some success in their pursuit of the same object.

It was equally necessary for the Allies to allocate their ships effectively to the different tasks, which in turn meant the construction of Allied shipping budgets. But here the problems confronting the British and the Americans differed greatly from each other. In the first place, the trading positions of the two countries were by no means the same. The British, unlike the Americans, had always to meet their three main sets of demands—imports, the needs of overseas countries, and military operations—none of which could be increased without serious risk to the others. The interdependence of these demands, moreover, raised peculiar technical difficulties for a British shipping budget, for the greater part of British shipping was employed on voyages which took the vessels half or the whole way round the world, and in the course of which they met a large variety of different needs. The formulation of British estimates for an Allied shipping budget thus involved problems which did not affect the Americans, whose ships for the most part were employed in voyages backwards and forwards between two points.

But there was a further difficulty in the construction of Allied shipping budgets, caused by the difference between the organizations for controlling shipping in Britain and in the United States. Long before the summer of 1943, the Ministry of War Transport in London, linked to the industry by recruitment from its ranks and by the practice of collaboration in two wars, had gained the experience necessary to its task, and complete control over the allocation of British ships to military and civil purposes once the programmes of demands had been settled between Departments. The American system, on the other

---

[1] For a discussion of the meaning of this term see C. B. A. Behrens, *Merchant Shipping and the Demands of War* (H.M.S.O., 1955), pp. 18-20.

[2] See p. 30 below.

hand, was not so well fitted to tackle the same problems. Neither the shipping industry nor the U.S. War Shipping Administration had the same experience as their British counterparts in working with the other, the industry could not produce the combined experience of the British shipping lines, and the structure of American administration did not support close liaison between its component parts. As a result there was a clear division of responsibilities between the War Shipping Administration and the Service Departments in Washington, which contrasted with the practice in London. Once ships had been allocated to the Service Departments, the War Shipping Administration found it almost impossible to retain or regain any control over them, and in constructing the shipping budgets it was in no position to scrutinize the demands of its military colleagues. This was the more important because the Americans, unlike the British, had large strategic commitments in the Pacific, where the rôle of shipping raised problems not experienced elsewhere, and where the American Chiefs of Staff exercised sole control, on behalf of the Allies, over operational strategy.[1]

It was perhaps thus scarcely surprising that the shipping authorities in London and Washington should have been slower than other Allied authorities to construct combined budgets, or that those budgets, when constructed, should often have been subject to sudden and considerable amendment. The results were to be seen in the process of estimating shipping at the three Anglo-American conferences between May and December, 1943. When the Allies met at Washington in May, they had for the first time at their disposal separate British and American budgets, each showing a deficit. The figures suggested that the British would be short by some 800,000, the Americans by $1\frac{1}{2}$ to $2\frac{1}{2}$ million, tons; and the Allied deficit might thus amount to between $2\frac{1}{4}$ and $3\frac{1}{4}$ million deadweight tons for the second half of the year—a figure which must alter the whole strategic programme for that period.

The military and civilian shipping authorities thereupon examined the figures afresh. They had already taken into account (though as it turned out conservatively) a decline in losses in the Atlantic, so that they could derive no further solace from that quarter. The most likely source of improvement lay, in the British view, in curtailing the Americans' prodigality both in plans and in the use of their ships. For the British suspected—rightly, as it was later proved—that, even accepting the current rate of equipment for American operations,[2] American tonnage was employed wastefully throughout all theatres and particularly in the Pacific, and that the Americans' practice of planning for unlikely contingencies added unnecessarily to their estimates for tonnage. An inflated demand was thus, in British eyes,

[1] See p. 19 above.

[2] See p. 50 below.

imposed upon an extravagant practice; and as a result, strategy was being endangered by 'a deficit in ships which existed on paper but not in fact'. The difficulty for the British was to know how to remove it.

The consequences are instructive. The problem was left until late in the conference, so that time was short when it was tackled. The British began, for the sake of the example, by writing off their own deficit of 800,000 tons—a gesture which they appreciated must probably curtail supplies to the Indian theatre. They then, on the morning of 22nd May, proposed a reduction to the Americans. The discussion continued throughout that day, but without agreement; and at 3.30 a.m. on the 23rd, the American military authorities, who set the pace for their delegation, asked the civilians to make a combined forecast of shipping to the end of September, 1944 by 9 a.m., when the Combined Chiefs of Staff were due to meet. In these strange circumstances, the Minister of War Transport and his advisers, and their American counterparts, re-examined the figures; and by 6.45 a.m., the American civilian shipping authorities were able to produce more realistic requirements, which reduced by almost a third the initial demands of their military colleagues.

Such was the basis for the Combined Staff Planners' assertion at the 'Trident' Conference, that shipping 'deficiences are small, but if properly spread over all the programs concerned the effect will not be unmanageable'. A shortage of between $2\frac{1}{4}$ and $3\frac{1}{4}$ million tons was reduced to a shortage of $\frac{3}{4}$-$1\frac{1}{4}$ million tons within a few days, and mainly within a few hours. The first impact of combined planning on the material had demonstrated the extent to which unsatisfactory administrative arrangements in the United States could affect the difficulties of controlling this inherently difficult problem.

The pendulum continued to swing in the later months of the year. At the 'Quadrant' Conference, despite an estimated British deficit, American estimated surpluses showed for the first time a favourable position for the Allies. The Combined Staff Planners were therefore able to report that 'a careful operation of cargo shipping should enable us to meet all essential commitments'. To this, however, the British Minister of War Transport and the head of the U.S. War Shipping Administration added a cautionary rider, that further demands might arise from current plans which had not been taken into account.

The rider proved to have been wise; for by November, 1943 the spectre of a shipping shortage had reappeared. When the British and American shipping authorities met again at Cairo in the middle of that month, it was in 'an atmosphere of the deepest statistical gloom'. No unfavourable development had occurred since the 'Quadrant' Conference: no great losses had been encountered in the Atlantic, new construction was slightly greater than forecast, and the strategic plans themselves had not altered. How, then, was it possible for the position so to have changed in this short time? The answer was provided in part by the demands of 'Overlord', which though not greater than in August had now been studied in greater detail by the shipping authorities, with a consequent appreciation of what was involved. But the principal reason for the apparently sharp change of fortune lay, as before and as was to happen again, in the difficulty of calculating the true position and of making reliable estimates from it. This indeed was proved, as at Washington in May, by the outcome at Cairo. For after starting with a substantial British deficit for the first half of 1944, and only a small American surplus, the authorities managed, after long and vigorous debate again centering on the demands and practices of the American Services, to convert the total deficit into a small favourable balance. The Combined Staff Planners were accordingly able to report that 'examination of personnel and cargo shipping position indicates our ability to support approved naval and military operations.' This reversal, however, seemed as strange to the Combined Chiefs of Staff as its predecessor between the conferences. The sudden appearance of large deficits, and their equally sudden disappearance, appeared to rest on such arbitrary calculations and such uncertain hypotheses that it was difficult for the uninitiated to have much confidence in the results.

The figures produced at the conferences are therefore of limited value. They illustrate the difficulties of the British, faced with commitments they could not wholly meet and with an administrative machine in Washington which they could not greatly affect; and point the comparison—gradually turning into a contrast—between their position and that of their ally. But as a record of the Allied position, their interest lies as much in the light they throw on the answers as in the answers themselves. This very uncertainty, however, which attended calculation, had its effect on strategic thought. It cannot be said that a shortage of merchant shipping prevented any operation from being undertaken during the last two years of the war. Nor can it be said that it limited strategy by preventing the transfer of resources from one theatre to another, or by so shaping plans in advance that operations demanding excessive shipping were not adopted or were not seriously considered. Those operations that were vetoed during this period were vetoed for other reasons; and while a major transfer of resources, for instance from the Mediterranean to the United Kingdom, was impossible for lack of shipping, it was not in any case desirable for strategic reasons. It might perhaps be argued that, even if there were enough ships available for military purposes, more ships might have spared the Western Allies the worst effects of the shortage of assualt shipping, which proved the real embarrassment during this period.[1] But this argument is unreal, for the shortage of assault shipping

[1] See pp. 33-8, 51-2 below.

itself sprang partly from the necessity to concentrate on building merchant ships, and their escorts, until well into 1943. Nevertheless, if a lack of merchant shipping did not affect strategy in the event after the summer of 1943, that does not mean to say that it disappeared from strategic thought. Operations did not suffer. But the British at least were well aware until the end that their own war economy and the economies of many other countries might suffer unacceptably from an extravagant allocation of ships to operations; and both British and American Chiefs of Staff continued to be bewildered, until almost the end, by the fluctuations in the combined Allied estimates for shipping presented to them. Thus, whether or not the fear of a shipping shortage may have been justified on a specific occasion, the strategic authorities remained fearful; and while the disappearance of the deficit on further investigation preserved strategy, it did not relieve the strategists. The fluctuations in the estimates were too great, past experience was too serious, and the possible effects of faulty allocations and mismanagement were too grave, for the Combined Chiefs of Staff ever to forget them; and a shortage of shipping accordingly remained a shadow, and occasionally a vivid fear, until the last few months of the war, a continuing potential danger whose extent appeared the more alarming because its causes, though finally appreciated, could never be entirely mastered.

If a shortage of merchant shipping seemed to remain a potential threat, a shortage of assault shipping was the most immediate and obvious danger to an offensive strategy throughout the last two years of the war. As General Marshall stated in 1945,[1] it was 'to plague us to the final day of the War in Europe.' As Mr. Churchill put it later, thinking specifically of the most critical type of this shipping,[2] 'In this period in the war all the great strategic combinations of the Western Powers were restricted and distorted by the shortage of tank landing-craft for the transport . . . of vehicles of all kinds. The letters 'L.S.T.' (Landing Ship, Tanks) are burnt in upon the minds of all those who dealt with military affairs in this period.' The shortage was expressed differently from that of merchant shipping. Whereas the latter was apt to fluctuate at short notice and on a considerable scale, suddenly causing or reducing deficits of a million tons or more, deficits of assault shipping remained marginal but persistent, often involving a small group of ships and craft whose numbers seemed insignificant, but which, obstinately surviving all efforts to reduce them, governed the actions of forces far larger than themselves.

This shortage of assault shipping is perhaps not surprising when the

[1] *The War Reports of General of the Army George C. Marshall . . .* (New York, 1947), p. 154.
[2] *Closing the Ring*, p. 226.

nature of the task is considered. The combination of problems affecting assaults on a large scale, across the Channel, across the Mediterranean, across the Indian Ocean and in the Pacific, was entirely new in the experience of war, and could not be fully appreciated until the first of such ventures had been launched. Preparations for 'amphibious operations', as they were known in the contemporary jargon, had begun almost immediately after the evacuation of Narvik; but they necessarily envisaged raids rather than invasion, and derived largely from the small experiments of the First World War, modified by intervening Staff exercises and adjusted to meet later types of equipment. It was not until the decision to invade North Africa in 1942 that the scale and nature of the new task became apparent; and by that time, other commitments had absorbed a large proportion of the facilities needed to produce the special vessels required. Over the last half of the war, demands on assault shipping were therefore being formulated at the same time that the programme of construction, itself complicated by other priorities, was getting under way.

As was the case with merchant shipping, these demands covered all of the major theatres of war. At Quebec, indeed, no less than four sets of landings of varying dimensions were devised for the next nine months. The demands on assault shipping were calculated by the Combined Planning Staff,[1] which reported that:

> '. . . 11. There will be sufficient landing ships and craft for approved operations in 1943 and until the summer of 1944. Landing ships and craft will, however, be the bottleneck limiting the full scope of assault in the approved operations, both in the Pacific and the Atlantic.[2] [Our figures] are made out on the assumption that landing craft will be sent from the Mediterranean to 'Overlord', so as to arrive by the 15th December, 1943, and assault ships by the 1st March, 1944.
>
> 12. To provide sufficient landing craft after the summer of 1944, an acceleration and increase in the present British and United States assault shipping and landing craft programs is necessary, probably at the expense of cargo ship and escort production and certain Army items.'

This appreciation proved, and indeed appeared at the time as, somewhat optimistic. In the first place, it made assumptions for the theatres of lower priority which might be difficult to fulfil. The withdrawal of a large proportion of the assault shipping from the Mediterranean defined limits to the campaign in that theatre which must affect the course of operations themselves not so rigidly defined, and whose precise consequences, in the fluid conditions then obtaining, could not as yet be foreseen. Similarly, the small allocation of assault

---

[1] For the figures, and the estimated rates of casualties and serviceability, see Appendix IV below.

[2] 'The Atlantic', in this connexion, meant Europe.

shipping to the Indian theatre failed adequately to meet the possibility, raised in the plans and by the creation of a fresh Command for south-east Asia, of an assault on the coast of Burma which might demand considerable resources. These secondary, but most important, commitments proved the main source of difficulty in the event. But even on the assumption that they could be met, the main operation in Europe seemed likely still to be short on the existing programme of construction. Early in June 1943, Cossac[1] had been given an estimate of the assault shipping on which he should count for the invasion of northern France in May 1944, and the plan of July had been based on its validity. But in fact the estimate was not satisfactory in itself, nor seemed likely to be realized. The numbers of ships and craft which it promised might prove adequate to a given weight of assault, but the proportion of the different types bore little relation to the needs, and seriously handicapped certain necessary tasks. The composition of the assault fleet was thus not ideal; and its production in any case soon raised grave misgivings. Early in August 1943, the First Sea Lord warned his colleagues that the L.C.T. promised in June could not be made available, and by the end of the month the British had come to the conclusion that there must be an appreciable deficit in L.S.T. and L.C.I. as well.

The British concentrated initially on the shortage of L.C.T., because the supply of landing craft was their main responsibility in the programme of assault shipping. Landing craft were small vessels, varying according to type from twenty or thirty to seven or eight hundred tons, simple in design and mostly easy to build; unlike landing ships, which were either converted merchant vessels or—as was more convenient for carrying tanks and vehicles—specially constructed ships of some 2,000 tons (5,000 tons when loaded), demanding the same facilities and skill in construction as other types of ship. The limitations on these facilities, and the early conception of the rôle of assault shipping, led the British to concentrate on the smaller craft, which could be built at first in yacht- and boat-yards, and, after the development of prefabrication on a large scale in 1941, in factories connected not at all with the sea. The British shipyards were in fact not troubled by the programme of assault shipping until late in 1943. For when, in the spring of 1942, the Western Allies appreciated the necessity for a larger programme and for larger vessels, they agreed that the British should concentrate as before on the smaller types of landing craft, while the Americans should provide the bulk of the landing ships as well as a proportion of the landing craft. Thereafter, the British were in the habit of noting, on their balance sheets of demand and supply, that 'it would be necessary to ask the Americans' to meet the larger deficits that arose.

[1] See p. 22 above.

In the spring of 1943, it was generally accepted that there could hardly be too many landing ships and craft; for the larger the assault fleet, the more powerful could be the individual assault and the more flexible the strategy. But the combined programmes of production had so far failed to respond to the demands. In Britain, the target for the year May, 1942 – May, 1943 was set finally at 1,168 craft, and in the event 1,099 were produced from 1st June to 1st June. But in the spring of 1943, despite the obvious need and the fact that production was rising,[1] the new annual programme was settled at only 1,050 craft. The trouble lay partly in the higher priority still enjoyed by the programme of merchant shipping and naval escorts, which prevented landing craft from being built in the shipyards; and partly in the fact that the capital equipment of the factories and small yards had by now virtually reached its limit, so that the existing means of production could not be greatly increased or improved.[2] Meanwhile, the larger American production had encountered difficulties. In April 1942, when the Combined Chiefs of Staff were considering the possibility of landing in France in 1943, a programme had been approved for the construction of 12,000 ships and craft within twelve months, and in July this was placed at the head of the list of priorities. But the obstacles inherent in a new programme, combined probably with an initial lack of interest among the Joint Planners and in the Navy Department, prevented the target from being realized or even approached; and in November, when landings in North Africa had replaced the possibility of a landing in France the next year, the programme dropped to twelfth place among the priorities. The result was to be seen in the monthly figures of production, which delined from a peak of 106,000 tons of assault shipping in February, 1943 to 51,000 tons in July.

The position was thus unsatisfactory when the offensive strategy was promulgated in August. The deficits as they were then estimated to stand for 'Overlord' on 1st May, 1944, amounted in the case of L.S.T. to 64 per cent of the ships available, in the case of L.C.T. to 77 per cent, and in the case of L.C.I. (L) to 31 per cent. The British calculated that their programme of construction alone might have to be increased by at least 72 per cent, and possibly by much more. Moreover, they had not enough men to man the larger assault fleet for which the programmes were now striving. At the end of August 1943, in contrast to the Combined Planning Staff, the Ministry of Production therefore reported that:

> '. . . The deficiencies in landing-craft and crews stand now, and are likely to stand in the spring and early summer of 1944,

[1] See the figures in Duncan Hall, *North American Supply* (H.M.S.O., 1955), p. 401.
[2] See the figures *loc. cit.*, p. 401.

between us and a landing in North-West Europe, although all other equipment on a requisite scale should be available. . . .'

The British began to tackle these problems immediately after 'Quadrant'. Construction of assault shipping was still limited by the War Cabinet's decision in March 1943, 'to build as many landing-craft as possible without undue interference with other essential requirements'. But in the second half of August, the Prime Minister called for an increase in the assault lift for 'Overlord' of at least 25 per cent, and during September and October the Ministries of Supply and Production, the Admiralty and Cossac laboured to meet such part of the demand as lay within their compass. The extra men for the assault fleet were found by transferring soldiers and airmen to the navy, and by breaking up the only division of Marines, hitherto earmarked for the landings. The programme of construction caused more trouble. It must involve, for the first time, the use of the shipyards; and various obstacles at once appeared. The Defence Committee (Supply) decided to go ahead, as it turned out without undue disturbance. But even so, the British programme could not be expanded significantly. In 1942, 546 landing-craft had been produced; and in the first half of 1943, when the main expansion took place, 765. But production then declined slightly to 691 in the second half of that year; and only 770 craft of all sorts were produced in the first six months of 1944. British construction in this sphere had in fact very nearly reached its limit in 1943, and could no longer seriously tackle the demand by itself. The bulk of the deficit, in ships or craft of all sorts, must be reduced either by modifying the 'Overlord' plan or by an increase in American production.

But any modification of the 'Overlord' plan was likely to demand more, and not less, assault shipping. Towards the end of September 1943, Cossac was asked to state his lowest needs for a three- and for a four-divisional assault lift. The result was a report on the shortcomings of the existing arrangements, and a request for a further eighteen L.S.T., 251 L.C.T. and seventy-three craft of other types over what had already been allocated to a three-divisional assault, or for thirty-nine more L.S.T., 389 more L.C.T. and a large number of other craft if the assault was to be by four divisions. These figures were examined over the next few weeks, and at the end of October the Defence Committee (Supply) concluded that the deficit for a three-divisional assault might be reduced, principally by adjustments in loading and sailings, to five L.S.T. and 221 L.C.T. A four-divisional assault was thought to be out of the question.

Most of this deficit, together with any that might arise from operations in the Pacific, must be met by the Americans. As a result of the position disclosed at Quebec, their production of assault shipping was again raised in September, 1943 to the head of the priorities, and in the event, where some 6,900 assault ships and craft appeared in 1942 and some 17,000 in 1943, some 14,300 were produced in the first six months of 1944. But in August, 1943 there seemed to be two possible obstacles to the use of this increased production for 'Overlord'. First, the surplus of new construction over the earlier estimates might not be felt before April 1944, so that in order to fit, train and assemble the assault fleet by May it would still be necessary to transfer ships and craft from the Mediterranean, over a period when the campaign there would be acting as an essential preliminary to 'Overlord'. Secondly, the British could not rely on checking the allocation of new construction between Europe and the Pacific, an area on which they were not commonly kept informed in detail. A forecast had been produced at Quebec; but events might demand its adjustment, and although much that would go to the Far East was not designed for the shorter passages in Western waters, and although the peculiar problems of assembly and serviceability could not be judged accurately from London, the British felt uneasily that they might not be able, in this critical case, to scrutinize the problem as a whole, as experience had taught them to be necessary when supply seemed in danger of failing demand.

Such, then, was the state of the calculations when the first stage of the offensive opened on the mainland of Europe, and almost immediately raised new problems to throw the existing plans into confusion, and to threaten not only the capacity of the improved programme of construction, but the strategy for the intervening months on which the success of 'Overlord' itself might depend.

The provision of transport aircraft was not a strategic factor of the same magnitude or persistence as that of assault shipping; but occasionally in Europe, and constantly in Asia, it had a similar effect. Air transport was not fundamental to the Allies' tasks in 1944, as sea transport was fundamental. But it was a potent adjunct to both land and seaborne operations, proving vital to the first stage of 'Overlord', to the whole course of the campaign in Burma, and to the support of China; and its distribution at times aroused discussion of strategic priorities as sharp, though not as serious, as that aroused by the landing ships and craft.

The shortage of transport aircraft mainly affected the British; for it was the British theatre of South-East Asia that imposed an extra, partly unforeseen but necessary burden upon a programme of production that was otherwise largely adequate, and that lay largely outside their control. The British had built no transport aircraft during 1939 and 1940, and in October of the latter year had arranged to receive from the United States such as they might need. This agreement, modified on each occasion in detail, was reaffirmed after the United States entered the war, in January, June and December of 1942 and in the following July. It was not in fact until the beginning of 1943 that the British decided to start building transport aircraft themselves, and the decision did not relieve them of their dependence on American supplies.

These in turn depended first on the domestic allocation of priorities, and secondly on the subsequent allocation of production between the two allies. Air transport always enjoyed adequate priority in the United States, and by the end of 1941 output was rising steadily. Early in 1943, the average monthly rate of production (which again rose in the course of the year) was over five hundred transports; and in 1944 it rose to an average of eight hundred, before declining to around six hundred in 1945. These figures moreover represented a steady if slight increase in the percentage of the whole American production of aircraft to the end of 1943: under 5 per cent in January 1942, 7 per cent in January 1943, and just under 8 per cent in November.

In August 1943, the number of transports available seemed moreover not inadequate to the demands. The Combined Planning Staff noted at Quebec that there would be a shortage, on existing calculations, of 270 transports for 'Overlord', and that the capacity of the air ferry to China should be increased. But 'Overlord' could probably draw to some extent on the Mediterranean, where the proportion of transports to air strength was high, and it was specifically stated that the volume of air support to China was restricted by the state of the bases in northern India and not by the number of aircraft available.

But the position was not in fact so favourable as these calculations suggested. The estimates proved not to be complete, and the extra demands in the event fell mainly on the partner least fitted to meet them. The needs of 'Overlord' in its various stages were to grow beyond the provision made for them at Quebec; so was the support of China, once the bases were ready in India; and above all, operations in Burma were to demand air transport on a new scale for the land forces. This last development gave rise to peculiar difficulties. For not only did it occur in the theatre where the greatest expansion (on behalf of China) was already anticipated, so that the local competition for aircraft was fierce and immediate: it affected the British almost entirely, and thus pointed a problem of distribution which could not easily be resolved.

For in south-east Asia, the Americans' strategic interests were not identical with those of the British, and they were the less inclined to spare resources, whether from their own transport to China or from other theatres of combined responsibility, for a campaign of low strategic priority. This underlined the weakness of the British position, already demonstrated over the past two years. Their allocation of transports had in fact been not ungenerous. In 1941, they received 9 per cent of the American production; in 1942, 7 per cent; and in 1943, almost 11 per cent. But the earlier figures did not meet the promises, while the higher figure in 1943, which in the event exceeded the promise, was reached only after renewed demands in the summer of that year. The British in fact had been dissatisfied with the position since the beginning of 1942, when the entry of the United States into the war necessarily limited the flow of aircraft and munitions to their allies. Throughout that and much of the following year, new arrangements had constantly to be made and amended, as the needs first of one partner and then of the other demanded. In July 1943, it was finally settled that the Americans should send the British 550 transport aircraft over the year, and 715 in the first half of 1944; and early in 1944, the second figure was raised to 744.

The course of the negotiations, protracted and complex as they were, illustrated the difficulties attending allocations of material when one nation was solely responsible for production. The British argument rested on the fact that, wherever the aircraft might be produced, they were designed to serve a common cause in which the British bore at least a proportionate share. The Americans, on the other hand, bore the burdens of production and distribution in a period of constantly changing priorities and of a rapid expansion of their armed forces. Each partner had his case; but the British were necessarily in the weaker position, and in the winter of 1942/43 they decided to start producing transport aircraft for themselves. The first three appeared in June, 1943; a further 206 by the end of December; and 476 in the first half of 1944. But a large proportion of these aircraft went to meet the increased demands of 'Overlord', leaving the pressing needs of south-east Asia to be filled almost entirely by American production. Thus, the theatre that depended most upon transport aircraft was—alone of the theatres of active operations—a British theatre, and the British relied almost entirely for its satisfaction on an ally whose distribution of such aircraft they had already disputed unsuccessfully, and whose strategic views in this case differed from their own. In such circumstances, it was not surprising that this largely unforeseen disturbance to the programme should have proved unwelcome to its authors, and should have caused sharp debate, constantly on the use of the aircraft in Asia, and at times on their loan from other theatres of higher priority.

The three dangers to strategy we have so far discussed, relate to transport of men and material. The fourth is of a different order. It was a shortage of manpower itself.

This shortage affected the British far more than it affected the Americans. A lack of merchant or assault shipping, or of transport aircraft, were matters for consideration equally in Washington and in London. But, despite inevitable shortages in different sectors as the national mobilization got under way, American manpower towards the end of 1943 seemed equal to its share of the strategic demands, and, provided that it was efficiently distributed, likely to remain so over much of the following year. It was otherwise in Britain, where the limits of population both determined and reflected the limits of the war effort, and affected strategic thought. By the autumn of 1943, the effects could be seen plainly.

At the outbreak of war, the main problem relating to manpower lay in the speed rather than in the extent of its mobilization. But in order to avoid a repetition of the experience of the First World War, when production had been seriously hampered by the indiscriminate enlistment of skilled men into the armed forces, in August, 1939 the Minister of Labour was placed in charge of a Ministry of National Service, empowered to reserve certain types of labour. Later, in order to correlate departmental demands for the War Cabinet, an existing Cabinet organ—at first the Production Council, afterwards the Production Executive—undertook to present to the Lord President of the Council a periodical review of manpower, which until late in 1942 covered a span of twelve months and thereafter one of twelve or eighteen months. In November 1943, these reviews became the responsibility of two Manpower Committees, one consisting of officials, the other of Ministers under the chairmanship of Sir John Anderson, who in this as in some other fields continued as Chancellor of the Exchequer to fulfil the duties with which he had earlier been connected as Lord President.

The first of the eighteen-month budgets appeared in December 1942, covering the period mid-summer 1942 to December, 1943. At the earlier date, the armed forces amounted to some 4,092,000 men and women, and the labour force of the country to some 22,056,000, out of a population of 48,400,000. The navy disposed of some 525,000 men and women, the army of some 2,593,000, and the air force of some 961,000. A further 13,000 women were in the nursing services for the forces. The budget of December, 1942 provided as follows for further allocations, which the Production Executive agreed should be reviewed in the following spring.

	Earlier demands	*Allocations approved*
	(In thousands)	
Navy and Admiralty (Supply) . .	+ 509	+ 434
Army and Ministry of Supply . .	+ 957	+ 351
Air Force and Ministry of Aircraft Production (M.A.P.)	+1,075	+ 750
Civil Defence		— 75
Miscellaneous	+ 135	+ 116
Total	+2,676	+1,576

By the spring of 1943, the Service Departments had considered the implications of the strategy agreed at Casablanca in January. As a result, each raised its claims on those of the previous December. The army asked finally for an extra 183,000 men and women, the navy for an extra 40,000, and the air force for an extra 145,000. But while the Services were preparing these demands, the Minister of Labour presented a review of manpower which seriously prejudiced their chance of acceptance. In May, 1943 he reported that, despite cuts in some sectors of industry, the demands of the armed forces could now be met only at the expense of manpower in munitions. This conclusion marked the turning point in the development of the national mobilization. For, as had not been the case hitherto, expansion of any sector in the war economy, or of any of the armed forces, could now take place only at the expense of other sectors or forces. The point was soon underlined by the Lord President, in a report to the War Cabinet at the end of June. The latest demands from all sources for 1943 amounted to no less than 1,912,000 men and women, of whom 912,000 had still to be found within the year. In addition, the Government must provide for the replacement of normal wastage in industry, which for the first time was now exceeding the annual intake spared from mobilization for the Services. The country was in fact approaching the point of diminishing returns. Meanwhile, the Lord President thought that only 414,000 men and women could be found for the Services and munitions, to meet the outstanding demand of 912,000.

A long discussion ensued in the War Cabinet on these reports. By scrutinizing the Services' numbers severely, by allowing for a progressive reduction in air and civil defence as the enemy's attacks diminished, and by adjustments between the munitions' Departments, Ministers were able to reduce the remaining demand for the year from 912,000 men and women to 510,000, leaving a deficit, over the 414,000 available, of 96,000. The War Cabinet, however, still considered this unacceptable, and after further examination approved a revised allocation on 22nd July.

	Allocations December 1942	Allocations suggested by Departments spring 1943 (In thousands)	Allocations July 1943
Navy and Admiralty (Supply)	+ 434	+ 483	+ 450(240)[1]
Army and Ministry of Supply	+ 351	+ 528	+ 345(—40)
Air Force and M.A.P.	+ 750	+ 749	+ 570(215)
Other essential industries and services	+ 116	+ 152	+ 120(70)
Total	+1,651	+1,912	+1,485(485)

The estimated deficit for the rest of the year was therefore 71,000 (485,000-414,000) excluding civil defence. But further adjustment followed, when it was decided finally to cut the numbers in civil defence by 90,000 in the second half of 1943; and there was thus finally an estimated national surplus of 19,000—slightly less than one normal division.

The estimates, however, were bettered in the event. In March 1944, the Minister of Labour reported that by the end of 1943 the armed forces and munitions had received some 1,700,000 men and women since July, 1942. The distribution of these results, moreover, favoured those originally favoured by the allocations: those allowed an increase, together received a greater increase; those due to be cut, suffered a greater cut.

At the end of 1943, the population of Britain was thus nearing the limit of its capacity to support the Allied offensive. The Government had been able in the past year still to increase the size of its forces, until they reached the unpredecented figure (after allowing for wastage) of some 4,800,000 men and women, or just over 10 per cent of the population. At the same time, it had slightly increased the labour force of the country. But this had been achieved, after allowing for the normal fresh intake, only by cutting civil defence and by reducing labour substantially in 'non-essential' industries, a process which could not be carried much further without a serious—possibly a dangerous—decline in the standard of living. The Government was therefore faced by the prospect of conducting the main offensive against Germany and Japan over a period when greater casualties and further demands must lead, after a period of uneasy equilibrium, to a reduction in the war effort. If the country was to play its part, and to keep its place, within the Alliance, it could be only by the most careful and ingenious distribution of its resources, and if the war against two enemies did not last for too long.

[1] Numbers in brackets are those expected over the rest of the year.

These problems confronted the War Cabinet even while it was debating the allocations to the end of 1943. As early as July of that year, the Departments were advised to have their preliminary estimates ready in September for the period 1st January, 1944 – 30th June, 1945. By the third week in October 1943, the Services had produced their demands. All again asked for more: the navy for 288,500 men and women, the army for 346,000, the air force for 158,000; and all added a quota of civilian labour to serve their needs. The total came to some 920,000 men and women. At the same time, munitions and allied industries asked for an increase of 240,000, so that the grand total amounted to a further 1,160,000.

These demands were scarcely surprising, in view of the size of the task ahead and of an almost certainly higher rate of wastage in the armed forces. But they bore no relation to the position, as the Minister of Labour reported it towards the end of October, 1943. 'By the end of this year', he stated, 'the mobilization of the nation will be practically complete'. The amenities of the civil population, severely rationed in most commodities, could not be reduced further, and industry, already harassed and interrupted by blackout and bombing, was now faced by a greater gap than before between normal intake and wastage. '. . . *Even if no one is called up for the Forces* a decrease in the labour force in munitions in 1944 is an inevitable fact which one must face.' The deficit in 1944 might in fact amount to 1,310,000 men and women: 1,160,000 needed for the forces and industry, together with a decline of 150,000 in industrial manpower. From these figures, the Minister concluded that the situation in 1944 posed an entirely new problem for manpower, which demanded an examination of the subject from a new point of view.

This argument was accepted by the Prime Minister, and on 1st November he circulated an important Minute, in which he mentioned, for the first time as of practical significance, the possibility of a 'double ending' of the war.[1]

> '. . . 4. Thus, the problem is no longer one of closing a gap between supply and requirements. Our manpower is now fully mobilized for the war effort. We cannot add to the total; on the contrary, it is already dwindling. All we can do is to make within that total such changes as the strategy of the war demands.
>
> If we had to carry on the war against Germany and Japan for several more years, the scale of our war effort in terms of manpower would have to decrease progressively. This fact had not been taken into account by the Departments in estimating their requirements. We have now reached the point at which it must be taken into account. For the question how we should use our manpower in 1944 depends on what assumption we are prepared to make about the duration of the war with Germany.

[1] See Appendix X below for the complete text.

5. There seem to be two broad alternatives:

(a) We can assume, *for the purpose of our man-power plans*, that our maximum effort must be made in 1944, and that Germany will be defeated by the end of that year. On this assumption we could (after allowing for the munitions and men required for the war against Japan) cut back substantially the requirements for munitions which could not be delivered until after 1944 and for men who could not be trained in time to fight in 1944. We could also cut down the training organisations and ancillary formations which would otherwise be kept up to the strengths required if the Forces were to be maintained at their present level after 1944. All Departments could be directed to concentrate on the measures necessary to bring our greatest striking power to bear in 1944. On this basis the present man-power demands for the Forces and munitions could be substantially reduced.

(b) Alternatively, we can say that our man-power plans must be based on the assumption that war with Germany will continue well beyond the end of 1944. In that event we must face the fact that our Forces and munitions industries have been built up to levels which it is impossible for us to maintain over a prolonged period. And we must plan now for a progressive reduction in the scale of our effort. Unless it can be assumed that this shrinking process could be applied equally to all claimants, it would be necessary to determine on what other principles the cuts should be apportioned.

6. Whichever of these alternatives is now chosen, if the war with Germany continues after the end of 1944 we shall have to rely increasingly on United States resources to make up for the declining scale of our own effort. Our choice between these two alternatives will, however, determine the form which this American assistance must take. If we have chosen alternative (a), we shall have unbalanced our war effort and shall have to look to the United States to provide a larger proportion of the equipment for our Forces. If, on the other hand, we have chosen alternative (b), the additional help from the United States will have to come in the form of more fighting units with their equipment.

7. The Departments' estimates of requirements have not yet been subjected to the usual detailed scrutiny; but it is not thought that the broad issues set out above would be materially affected by any process of paring and pruning. It is suggested, therefore, that before work is started on a detailed scrutiny of the figures, Ministers should decide whether our Man-power Policy for 1944 is to be based on either of the two alternative assumptions set out in paragraph 5, or on some different assumption.'

Four days later, the Prime Minister called a special meeting of Ministers and the Chiefs of Staff, to consider policy and to improve the administrative machinery. As a result, they decided to adopt his first alternative, that Germany would be defeated by the end of 1944, and to set up the Manpower Committees which have already been mentioned. The Official Committee met almost at once. Its first task was to define more closely the implications of the Prime Minister's phrase, 'maximum effort in 1944'; and after some debate, this was taken to mean that

> 'We should apply the maximum impact on Germany in 1944 while fulfilling, so far as they are already planned to be fulfilled in 1944, our agreed contribution to operations against Japan. This must include the development and initial production of certain types of ships, aircraft and weapons specially designed for the Japanese war. But unless otherwise directed, the Official Committee would not regard the assumption that Germany will be defeated by the end of 1944 as meaning that more men must be recruited for the Services during 1944 simply to shorten the interval between the end of the war against Germany and the peak of our deployment against Japan.'

On this basis, the Committees produced a report for the War Cabinet in the last week of November. They recommended that the armed forces should be increased in 1944 by 284,000 men and women, distributed as follows:

	First half of 1944	*Second half of* 1944	*Total*
		(*In thousands*)	
Navy:	+ 28	+ 30	+ 58
Army:	+137	+ 25	+162
Air Force:	+ 35	+ 25	+ 60
Women's Nursing and V.A.D.	+ 3	+ 1	+ 4
Total	+203	+ 81	+284

Of the men for the air force, 17,000 should be so trained that they could be used in 1945 either by the air force or by the navy.

These allocations, which cut the Services' demands by almost 70 per cent, were not however expected to produce larger forces by the end of 1944. When normal wastage and casualties had taken their toll, it was estimated that the Services would then have some 124,000 fewer men and women than at the end of 1943.

To provide an increase for the armed forces of 284,000, the labour force must be further reduced. The Manpower Committees proposed cuts in civilian manpower of 309,000 over the whole of 1944.

The War Cabinet considered the report on 1st December, 1943. All of the Service and supply Departments agreed to accept the allocations—the air force with the proviso that it must probably ask for more women in the second half of 1944—apart from the Admiralty, which stressed its probable responsibilities in preparing for a greater effort in the Far East before the end of the war in Europe. The War Cabinet therefore decided to transfer outright to the navy from the air force the 17,000-odd men whom the Manpower Committees had recommended should be trained by the air force for both purposes. Otherwise, it approved the proposals, and instructed the Manpower Committees to review their figures for the second half of the year in May, 1944.

All of these shortages, actual or potential, have one feature in common. All illustrate, to a greater or lesser extent, the dependence of Britain on American supplies for the British war economy. That this must be so had been appreciated by the end of 1941, when British production could no longer be expected fully to meet British demands, or fully to support the British share in an Allied strategy. As co-operation improved over the next two years, the Government was able accordingly to concentrate increasingly on certain products, leaving others to the greater partner; and 'by 1944 reliance on American supplies went so far as to enforce what amounted to a division of labour between the war industries in the two countries.'[1] Some of the results may be seen in the following table, of the production of munitions of all kinds for the British Commonwealth.[2]

Supplies of munitions for the British Commonwealth: percentages from each source. (Calculated by value in dollars).

From	1939 (*Sept.-Dec.*) *and* 1940	1941	1942	1943	1944	1945 (*first half*)	*Total*
U.K.	90·7	81·8	72·6	62·4	61·2	66·1	69·5
Canada	2·6	5·2	8·6	8·8	8·9	10·0	7·9
Eastern Group (mainly Australia, New Zealand, India, South Africa)	1·1	1·5	1·9	1·9	1·2	1·7	1·6
Purchases in U.S. . .	5·6	9·1	4·7	2·4	1·5	1·2	3·7
Lend-Lease from U.S. . .	—	2·4	12·2	24·5	27·2	21·0	17·3

This is not of course to say that the British did not meet their share of the common effort. Their contribution, man for man, was not surpassed by any of their allies. While the Americans disposed of a larger navy and air force by the beginning of 1944, the British continued to field more divisions until the middle of that year; and the balance between the forces and their supply was moreover maintained remarkably well until the closing stages of the war. The mobilization and control of labour and material remained unequalled, as far as can be ascertained, by any other nation, and a greater cut was accepted in the

[1] M. M. Postan, *British War Production* (H.M.S.O., 1952), p. 228.

[2] Duncan Hall, *North American Supply*, p. 428.

standard of living than had been accepted in the First World War. The results moreover often exceeded the expectations, and accounted for a higher percentage of the combined Anglo-American programmes than had been anticipated in the agreements. At the same time, British material went, in fair proportion, in reciprocal Lend-Lease to the Americans;[1] to equip all of the forces raised by the Commonwealth; and to Russia, where the burden of delivery fell mainly on British forces. But when the magnitude of the effort has been properly recognized, it remains true to say that without the American supplies, particularly in 1943 and 1944, 'the most essential preparations for the offensive employment of the British forces and for their needs in battle would have had to be sacrificed; indeed the whole programme of Britain's war effort and the scale of her combatant action would have had to be radically recast.'[2]

For by 1944, as the discussions on manpower made clear, British production was falling in some fields in order to rise in others. The results for strategy were at first masked by the very increase in the size of the armed forces which was responsible for the process; and, viewed from the offices of the Combined Planning Staff, the British contribution reached its peak in 1944. More divisions, and a larger navy and air force, were then actively employed than had ever been employed before. But behind this great effort lay a strained and increasingly unbalanced economy. Production of some war stores continued to rise, notably of aircraft of all sorts.[3] But this increase was at the expense of other war-stores, only some of which were no longer needed in greater quantities. Naval construction did not materially diminish, for construction of aircraft carriers, submarines and escorts offset the decline in that of other types, and moreover the conversion of ships for the Far East in many cases notably improved their performance. But the building of merchant vessels, and production of munitions, had passed their peak by 1944. The former, indeed, reached its highest point in the third quarter of 1942; the production of shells and bombs in the last half of that year; the production of guns and small arms in the first half of 1943; of wheeled and armoured vehicles (including tanks) in its second quarter; and of small arms' ammunition, radar and searchlights in its last quarter. The general decline, mitigated by the action taken on the formula that Germany would be beaten in 1944, was still relatively slight in the first half of that year. But the uneasy equilibrium could not be maintained thereafter; and it is against the background of a contracting British economy that we must follow the development of Allied strategy, and of the British views upon it, in the last two years of the war.

---

[1] Hall, *loc. cit.*, pp. 285-6, 432-3, 481.

[2] Postan, *loc. cit.*, p. 228.

[3] See *Statistical Digest of the War* (H.M.S.O., 1951), Table 130.

(iv)

Data for an Offensive Strategy

The Allies' strategy for Europe from the early summer of 1943 was probably that best calculated to defeat Germany: certainly, neither the British strategy between Dunkirk and the end of 1941, nor the Americans' strategy in 1942, had been likely to lead to such a result. But by the autumn of 1943, the compromise between them had placed the two nations in a reasonable posture to launch their main assault in conjunction with the Russians, and the plans adopted for 1944 provided a reasonable prospect of success.

But this strategy, borne simultaneously with heavy commitments in the Far East, was expensive in men and material. As we have seen, the British could not fully support their commitments. The question therefore arises, how was the ratio established between supply and effective strength, and could it have been modified? If we take the land forces alone, some figures, illustrating different aspects of the problem, are worthy of remark. In May 1944, when the American army (excluding its air force) would consist of some $5\frac{3}{4}$ million men and the British army of some $2\frac{3}{4}$ million, the two nations, with the British Commonwealth, expected to dispose of ninety-five divisions in the theatres of war. This was not a large proportion of the numerical strength, even allowing for the high numbers allowed by the Planners for a British division, including all arms and support, in the different theatres—38,000 in the Mediterranean, 56,000 in south-east Asia, and 40,000 for 'Overlord'. The demands on equipment and transport were also high. In the first two days of 'Overlord', an armada of over 4,000 assault ships and craft carried seven divisions and their supplies across the Channel; two months later, over 1,500 assault ships and craft enabled three divisions to land in southern France. Such figures pose an obvious question. Was the Western Allies' strength in battle disproportionately low in relation to the effort that went to produce it?

The question of the proportion of 'teeth' to 'tail' was one which constantly troubled the Prime Minister, not least in the last two years of the war. But he never received a satisfactory reply, and perhaps he never could. For while the question was plain, it raised implications whose complexity made a single answer difficult if not impossible. It is indeed often hard to find not only an answer, but the data on which an answer could be based. For such data derive from accepted standards of calculation, whose validity in turn depends on the relations between planning and material. When these are uncertain—and they were sometimes uncertain during our period—it is perhaps as useful to examine the reasons, and to see the results for the calculations, as to discuss the calculations themselves. This chapter does not therefore seek to provide an answer to the question, but only to suggest some of the factors involved, and some of the implications for planning which may be borne in mind in the ensuing narrative.

Some of these factors bore equally on both allies, some on one more than on the other. In the first place, there was the legacy of strategic thought, which provided the starting point for fresh experience. The development of material, and reflection on the First World War, had led to a general assumption by 1939 that the advantage normally lay strongly with the defence, even if not to such an extent as some theorists suggested. This assumption—whose appearance invariably annoyed the Prime Minister—continued to inform strategic thought throughout the war, although after the dramatic results gained by the Germans' tactical air forces some of the more extreme conclusions from it disappeared in the summer of 1940. To the Western Allies, numbers were therefore insufficient in themselves; and much emphasis was laid on material, which as a result itself consumed manpower. The increase of mechanization and of armour since the First World War, and the growing complication of weapons, had already swollen the size of the 'tail' behind the lines. It now tended to grow further as new offensives set new problems for technique.

These problems were increased by the variety of the campaigns, some of which proved more expensive than others for men and material. Neither the Middle East nor India, for instance, could provide an adequate industrial base for modern war, and each therefore consumed large numbers of men in uniform on tasks that could be performed elsewhere by civilian labour. Each again, with the Pacific, lay far from the areas of production and assembly, and was expensive in shipping; and each posed difficult problems for material in conditions of weather and terrain more adverse than those in north-west Europe. The effects were felt beyond the theatres themselves. Scales of equipment and tactical experience which had served a specific purpose, tended to be absorbed into a common usage and theory for which they might not be altogether suited, and to influence practice in other theatres to which they might be irrelevant.

Another factor to be considered is the national background of the forces involved. Its results can be exaggerated, as perhaps in the case of the Americans; but, if not easy to assess precisely, they can nevertheless be important. For instance, the Americans' belief in their technical supremacy had a significant effect both on strategic thought and on its execution, while their widespread enjoyment of a high standard of living was partly responsible for a quantity of equipment which others might find extravagant, but which, in their case, may have been at the least a stimulant and at the most a necessity.

The same result might appear from another cause. If the Americans were affected by a high standard of living, the British were affected by the consciousness of limited strength. Again, it is possible to exaggerate the results on a particular campaign. But they were most important for strategic thought, and for the shape of the production programmes. Current conditions, seeming to confirm past experience, led the British to favour a flexible strategy based on command of the sea and air, and thus on particular types of material. It also led them, like the Americans but for this different reason, to rely on a high standard of preparation and equipment for their operations. Thus the very limits of the British strength tended to support a large and varied production which in turn must limit that strength, and to seek to overcome by a particular combination of strategy and supply the familiar disadvantage in a Continental war when the Continent was held by the enemy.

Factors such as these make it difficult to calculate an exact ratio of supply to effective strength; but their combination ensured that it would be high. Theory and experience alike urged, wherever possible, a substantial preponderance of force for the attack, and tended to raise the standards of preparation and equipment for what must in any case have been expensive operations. The fact that the operations must prove expensive, but that the limits of expense were hard to ascertain, had its effect on planning. To attack simultaneously in four widely separated areas threw a heavy burden on the Staffs, demanding close liaison between those in the theatres and at the centre and, so far as possible, common standards of calculation. Liaison was good, for the structure of the Combined Chiefs of Staff made possible a common pattern of Joint Planning Staffs, mostly in close touch with the central authority. But liaison could not by itself provide a common basis for measurement, particularly when a variety of experience and circumstance was aggravated by the knowledge that cuts could be made. The central planners often found that they could not reduce demands without questioning the foundations on which the demands had been assembled. The result was to increase their tendency—already liable to occur in a period of several simultaneous offensives—to intervene too closely in local planning, and sometimes arbitrarily to revise accepted criteria of measurement when conditions seemed to insist.

It was unfortunate that the most important type of material, in the period before 'Overlord' was launched, should have been peculiarly susceptible to such treatment. The Prime Minister once remarked, in one of the ensuing crises,[1]

> 'The whole of this difficult question only arises out of the absurd shortage of L.S.T's. How it is that the plans of two great empires like Britain and the United States should be so much ham-strung and limited by a hundred or two of these particular vessels will never be understood by history.'

---

[1] See *Closing the Ring*, p. 454.

The difficulties of planning with landing ships and craft seem indeed to have been exceptional. It was not only that the numbers were limited in relation to the tasks, but that there was no agreed standard by which to measure their effectiveness. The only guide to their performance in large operations lay in the experience of invading North Africa, where conditions differed in many respects from those likely to be encountered later. Important figures—of loading, of serviceability, of casualties—were thus liable constantly to be revised as pressure increased; and it was possible, as we shall see, to produce a series of different estimates from the same material within a matter of days. At a time when the Western Allies were committed to a series of seaborne assaults, some directly related to each other, launched in widely separated areas and apparently with no reserve of assault shipping, this statistical uncertainty was of the greatest importance. For it pointed to a significant contradiction, never overcome and perhaps never fully appreciated, between the end and the means. The offensive strategy, as envisaged by the Western Allies, was both flexible and precise, a combination, inherent in the proper exploitation of maritime strategy, which derives its particular force from the limitations of strength. But such a strategy depends on a close control of its material, and in this case the essential material seemed not amenable to close calculation. The greater the obstacles encountered in operations, and the greater the need for flexibility, the more difficult therefore it might be to adapt this material to the purpose; and the story of assault shipping in 1944 provides a striking example of the results that may follow from a failure, by no means evitable, to accompany an appropriate strategy with the appropriate means for its execution.

CHAPTER II

'OVERLORD' AND THE MEDITERRANEAN, AUGUST–NOVEMBER, 1943

(i)

The Conditions for 'Overlord'

AT THE END of July 1943, the enemy's power in Europe, battered though it was and due within a month to receive a severe blow, remained formidable to attack from the sea. But the main opponents in the west were disposed curiously at a tangent to each other. The Axis and its satellites disposed of 390 divisions (300 German), of which 216 (200 German) faced the Russians, and seven (excluding miscellaneous formations) remained in Germany itself. Of the other 167 divisions, the Germans accounted for ninety-three; and of those ninety-three, sixty-four lay north of the Alps. The immediate defence of southern Europe was entrusted to the other twenty-nine, with sixty-six Italian and eight Bulgarian and Croat divisions. This marked inequality of German strength, at a time when the fighting outside Russia was entirely in the south, was offset to some extent by a greater allocation of air support to the south than to the north. Of the 6,300 German aircraft available, 2,400 were on the Eastern Front and 1,700 in Germany. For the rest, there were 200 aircraft in Norway and Denmark, 800 in France and the Low Countries, and 1,200 in Italy and south-east Europe. Thus, even excluding the Italian air force of some 1,300 planes, Italy and the Balkans claimed more Axis aircraft (and particularly bombers and fighters) than France and Scandinavia. The dispositions of the Western Allies were markedly different. Most of their operational strength by land was concentrated in the Mediterranean, and even in May, 1944 they planned to have twenty-four divisions there compared with thirty-six (not all immediately available for operations) north of the Alps. But on the other hand, their air strength already lay mainly in the north, and was planned decisively to outstrip that in the south over the coming months.[1]

---

[1] See p. 26 above.

These dispositions reflected different solutions to the same problem. The Germans had to defend, the British and Americans to invade, a Continent whose areas of assault must lie within range of the existing Allied bases. The design for the attack derived its pattern from the acceptance of the plan for 'Overlord'. Studies for a return to the Continent had naturally been composed since the ejection of the British from France in 1940, at first by the Joint Planning Staff and from January, 1942 to April, 1943 by the Combined Commanders.[1] Their investigations, varying with the changing conditions of the war, had produced valuable results; and indeed in three papers in February and March, 1943 they adumbrated with remarkable accuracy, although on a different and hypothetical basis, many of the final decisions of January and February, 1944. But such inquiries, pursued by a group of commanders without a specific staff or a definite allocation of resources, could only produce a series of deductions from a combination of probabilities. More precise guidance, and a more direct responsibility, were needed before the studies could become plans. Both were furnished in the first half of 1943. The agreement to appoint a Chief of Staff to the Supreme Commander (Designate) was followed at the 'Trident' Conference by the decision to invade the Continent on 1st May, 1944, with a force initially of seven infantry and two airborne divisions, supported in the ensuing campaign by a further twenty divisions. By the beginning of June 1943, a single planning authority was thus established with the essential data at his disposal.

The plan itself appeared on 30th July, 1943, five days before the British party sailed for the 'Quadrant' Conference. Like his predecessors, and indeed like all who plan for conjunct operations, Cossac had to reconcile a number of divergent factors; for the choice of the area of assault depended on a particular combination of offensive and defensive qualities. As a base for the subsequent offensive, it must be judged as it were in retrospect, by the shape of the later campaign. Its position must conform to the final object, and both its position and the hinterland must favour the attacker when the relative state of the forces had been assessed. But this assessment was itself affected by the extent to which the assault could be maintained. The size of the force in the first phase, and the rate of its subsequent reinforcement, meant that it must either have access to a port or group of ports, or must land where it could be sustained for a given time until ports were available. During that period, moreover, the assault area must be capable of defence. Its position, and the facilities for the rapid development of airfields, must allow full scope to the Allied superiority in the air; and the terrain, while in due course favouring an attack inland, must provide immediately for an adequate local defence.

[1] See p. 22 above.

The area finally selected would therefore represent the best compromise to be found between a number of competing demands. The Combined Commanders had concentrated on two possible areas on the north coast of France; and Cossac, after reviewing the whole coastline of Europe from Norway to Spain, soon confirmed their choice. The alternatives in France were the Pas de Calais, between Gravelines and the river Somme, and the Caen-Cotentin area, including the Cotentin peninsula with Cherbourg and the coast immediately to the eastward as far as the river Orne. The Pas de Calais seemed attractive at first sight. It had beaches of suitable capacity, though not all sheltered from the prevailing wind, and air cover was easily maintained. But these advantages brought their own disadvantages, for the coast was known to be strongly defended and was within easy reach of the Germans' main air concentrations. It was better suited, moreover, to a raid than to an invasion. The harbours in the area could not themselves sustain the forces required, while the necessary deployment to east or west, towards the great ports of the Scheldt or of the Seine, involved an awkward movement to the flank along the enemy's front, and across a series of important obstacles.

The Caen-Cotentin area presented an almost complete contrast. Unlike the Pas de Calais, it lay far from the Allied air bases, and involved a more open sea-passage. But, unlike the Pas de Calais, it provided two great ports, Cherbourg and Le Havre, in or close to the area. There were several suitable beaches, some well sheltered from the prevailing wind; the defences by land were much weaker than those to the east; and while the Allied airfields were distant, so were those of the enemy. But the advantages of the area did not apply equally to all of its parts, and there were in fact three possible courses to consider. The assault could be made on the Cotentin peninsula alone, or partly on the Cotentin peninsula and partly in the Caen sector to the east, or in the Caen sector alone. A landing on the peninsula would probably lead to the early capture of Cherbourg, the goal of any operation in the area. But it had few other advantages for attack or defence. The country favoured neither the rapid development of airfields nor the rapid deployment of troops, and although the peninsula could be easily defended across its neck from the enemy's counter-attacks, the enemy for the same reason could seal off the attackers while he reinforced the neighbouring coasts against further assaults. Operations in the peninsula could not in fact stand on their own. They demanded a complementary attack from the flank, and thus simultaneous landings in the Caen sector to the east. This second course suffered from two disadvantages. First, and most important, it seemed doubtful if an attack from the flank would succeed in its object, for the two sectors were divided by a broad belt of marsh and intersecting streams. Secondly, in the summer of 1943 there seemed unlikely to be enough assault shipping for the seven available divisions, all of which were thought to be necessary if the two assaults were to succeed. Cossac therefore favoured the third possibility, of a landing in the Caen sector alone. The defences were known to be light, there were beaches of suitable capacity, and the terrain favoured both an immediate local defence by land and air and a subsequent advance.

But while the Caen sector seemed the most suitable in which to land, it was not ideal. Its main disadvantage lay in the nature of the 'beach exits'. There were three large beaches which could be used for the assault; but from the lie of the land, it was estimated that only some 12,100 vehicles could pass through them within twenty-four hours. This constituted the transport for three assault divisions, and thus, irrespective of the amount of shipping available, defined the weight of the initial attack in that area from the sea. The only means of adding to its weight was to land simultaneously west of the marshes, which Cossac did not wish to do for the geographical reason already given. He therefore proposed to pass two 'follow-up' divisions, and all further reinforcements during the first phase, through the three beaches, whose 'exits' would by then have been enlarged. This programme demanded a rapid expansion of the bridgehead, to accommodate the larger forces; and for this purpose Cossac intended to drop two airborne divisions, promised him at the 'Trident' Conference, a few miles inland on the day of assault, with orders to capture certain strongpoints and the town of Caen itself. After consolidating the perimeter, the combined force would begin to move slowly south by the end of the first week. In the second week, a part of the force would strike to the west, round the base of the marshes and up the Cotentin peninsula to Cherbourg, which it was hoped would fall within a fortnight of the initial landings. By that time, eighteen divisions with five tank brigades would have landed in, and passed through, the assault area.

The limitations of the initial assault defined strictly the circumstances in which it could take place. Cossac insisted that three conditions must be fulfilled for the plan to stand a reasonable chance of success. First, facilities must be devised which would enable a force of up to eighteen divisions to be maintained in the assault area, without any other assistance in the initial phase and with little assistance for a further two to three months while the captured ports were restored. The methods which were finally adopted for this purpose will be mentioned in a later chapter.[1] Secondly, the strength of the Germans' fighter aircraft available for north-west Europe must be severely reduced by the date of the assault. The measures taken to achieve this

[1] See Chapter VIII, section I below.

end are again described elsewhere.[1] Thirdly, the opposition on land must not exceed a given figure during the first nine days of the operation, nor must it be reinforced beyond a further figure for the first two months of the campaign. Cossac estimated these figures as follows. First, the existing defences in the area chosen for the assault, which were thought to be manned by some three 'static' divisions, must not be strengthened between July, 1943 and May, 1944. This postulated an effective scheme of deception, so as to achieve surprise. Secondly, the defences must not be reinforced by more than three 'active' divisions, of which one might be armoured, on D-day itself; by more than five 'active' divisions, of which two might be armoured, on D + 1 or D + 2; and by more than nine 'active' divisions, of which four might be armoured, by D + 8. Cossac submitted, as the most convenient formula through which to express these results under the various possible circumstances, that the enemy's reserve in France and the Low Countries should not be allowed to exceed twelve German mobile field divisions on D-day.[2] Thirdly, the Germans should not be in a position to transfer to France from other fronts in Europe more than fifteen divisions of the first quality during the first two months of the campaign.

In these circumstances, it seemed to the British that 'Overlord' was to be regarded as only one, even if the most important, of the operations to be undertaken in Europe; for only by action on other fronts could Cossac's demands be fulfilled. But such operations in turn must not attract Allied forces which might otherwise be devoted or added to 'Overlord' itself. A careful balance must be struck, often in circumstances of considerable complexity, between the various possibilities. It was on this question that the main argument turned for the rest of 1943.

---

[1] See Chapter VIII, section II below.

[2] This calculation represented an average to cover varying possibilities. 'Depending on how the various deterrents . . . were to function, there might well be fifteen German mobile field divisions in France on D-day of which only half a dozen could ever arrive near Caen. There might be a total of only ten such divisions available in the country, but five of these might be stationed within easy reach of our landing beaches.' Stalin's remark at Teheran, in November 1943, referring to the twelve divisions, 'What if there are thirteen?', did not therefore apply. (See Lieut.-General Sir Frederick Morgan, *Overture to Overlord* (n.d., but 1950), pp. 162-3.)

(ii)

The Rôle of the Italian Campaign

The only theatre in which these large diversionary operations could be sustained was the Mediterranean. The Western Allies in August, 1943 were already containing in that area, by engagement and threat, some twenty-nine German divisions and some 1,200 German aircraft; the Allied forces in the theatre could not themselves be effectively reduced for several months after the seven divisions had been removed for 'Overlord',[1] thanks to the limitations of ocean shipping; and it was in any case doubtful if the ports and facilities of Britain—the only European alternative—could sustain operations other than those already allotted to them for the summer of 1944. There was therefore no reasonable alternative to developing the necessary campaign in the south.

From August to December, 1943 there were three possible areas in the Mediterranean in which large operations might be staged: in southern France, with or without the earlier occupation of Sardinia and Corsica; in Italy, with or without the complementary occupation of Sardinia and Corsica; and in the Balkans, whether approached from the Adriatic, from the Aegean, or from the Adriatic and Aegean.[2] The choice between these possibilities was not static. It varied with the varying situations that arose in the second half of 1943. It is in fact necessary to examine the possibilities on five separate occasions during this period: in the middle of August, on Italy's surrender on 8th September, in the last week of September, in the middle of October, and towards the end of November. Their interaction may best be appreciated, before we turn to the strategy which it suggested, by a tour of the three areas in succession.

On the morning of 3rd September, 1943, exactly four years after Britain had entered the war, British troops from Sicily landed at Reggio di Calabria, on the toe of Italy and of the mainland of Europe. On the morning of the 9th, American and British troops from Sicily and North Africa landed at Salerno, some 150 miles to the north. These operations consumed all of the available assault shipping, and the bulk of the active divisions in Sicily and North Africa. They therefore committed the Allied effort to Italy for the immediate future.

The Allies had been seriously contemplating the invasion of Italy since May 1943, although the decision was not taken until late in July.

---

[1] See p. 25 above.

[2] See Map II, facing p. 57.

Throughout this period, the arguments remained the same. The object of operations in the Mediterranean was to place the Allies in such a position that by May, 1944 they were containing, and would contain for at least another three months, the necessary number of German divisions to enable 'Overlord' to succeed. This strategy would moreover ensure that the period before May, 1944 would be actively and adequately filled. Its objects would be achieved most effectively if Germany's allies in the south could be detached from her, and if the campaign struck at a vital point in her southern defences. The Italian peninsula seemed to provide the best answer initially to both demands. An invasion of Italy was the most likely course to drive the Italian Government out of the war, and, if carried out in sufficient force, would constitute a danger to the German position in the south that could not be ignored. Apart from a loss of prestige which the Germans could ill afford in the Mediterranean, it would directly threaten an important industrial area, and would open air bases to the Allies whence to bomb southern Germany and south-east Europe. These results should follow in Italy itself; but a successful invasion might also have important effects elsewhere. It might remove from the war the Italian divisions outside Italy, mostly in the Balkans; and, though this would be a matter for consideration, might even in due course open the way to the southern approaches to the Reich. Whether or not the Allies decided to pursue all of these consequences, the Germans could reasonably be expected to assume that they might. They could therefore be counted on not to abandon Italy prematurely to her fate, and thus to assist the Mediterranean Command to carry out part of its function as defined at Quebec.

These strategic advantages had to be weighed against serious operational disadvantages. The terrain of Italy does not favour attack from the south: indeed only the Byzantine general Belisarius in the sixth century had succeeded in reaching the north, after landing, like the British in 1943, at Reggio di Calabria. The southern provinces themselves are poor and undeveloped, marshy on the coasts and mountainous inland; and the mountains continue, in an unbroken and intricate mass, up the centre of the peninsula as far as the Lombard plain. Rivers and streams water the rocky valleys, quickly flooding in the winter rains and providing further obstacles to an advance. Transverse communications are poor, and the main roads in the centre pass steeply and circuitously from north to south. The main traffic, however, avoiding this slow and difficult route, follows the plains which lie along both coasts; but except in the neighbourhood of Foggia in the east, and of Rome and Pisa in the west, these stretch inland for only a few miles, and like the mountain valleys are often subject to winter floods, as the swollen rivers descend from the central range. Military operations must therefore commence on one or both flanks of the mountains, and must either continue along them in virtual independence of each other, or proceed into the mountains themselves against formidable natural obstacles. Only flanking attacks from the sea can relieve the difficulties of a frontal advance.

There was thus a danger in 1943 that a large effort might be compressed into a narrow front, where the defence held great advantages over the attack, and where in consequence the enemy might contain the Allies instead of the Allies containing the enemy. This risk, however, was acceptable for the early stages of the campaign, even if, as was hoped, it was not offset by favourable political developments. A more serious immediate danger lay in the strain which the separate lines of advance must impose on administration and supply, and in particular on the severely rationed shipping fleet available to the theatre. The complex and uncertain political situation, moreover, which might ease the initial operations, might add to these administrative demands, to the extent of interfering with the subsequent campaign. In contrast, the enemy enjoyed not only interior lines of communication, as was inevitable, but communications able to sustain a larger force than he would in fact wish to deploy. The facilities of northern Italy could maintain probably sixty divisions, although the Germans would probably not concentrate more than thirty; while there was a number of defensible positions in the centre and south, all served by road and rail from the north. Nevertheless, the Allies concluded that on balance the disadvantages could be countered and might be outweighed by the advantages: by their command of the sea and air, by the choice of action which they enjoyed from the possession of the offensive, and by the political uncertainty throughout the theatre which, in the absence of a central reserve, now haunted the Germans.

A campaign in Italy, of course, looked to the immediate rather than to the distant future. If it went well, the Allies would have to develop further operations, from Italy, designed in different and more favourable circumstances to meet the same purpose as the original invasion. Such operations would then be consequences of, and not alternatives to, the initial campaign. Meanwhile, the case for that campaign was strengthened when it was compared with the alternatives.

There was no question as yet of attacking the south of France, until much nearer the date for the main attack in the north.[1] A more serious possibility lay in an attack on Sardinia and Corsica. This had already been considered and rejected as an alternative to the attack on Sicily; but its apparent advantages persisted in new circumstances. The islands could probably be taken without great difficulty; their capture, threatening both western Italy and southern France, would not compromise the Allies' continued flexibility of manoeuvre; and it would add a further success to an already successful year. But these were in

[1] See pp. 104-5 below.

fact secondary advantages, or not advantages at all. Possession of the islands would not comply with the directive for the theatre, neither compelling Italy to surrender nor engaging German troops. In so far as it affected the German dispositions, indeed, it would tend to keep divisions in the south of France which the Allies wished to attract elsewhere. The operations, moreover, might be brief, forcing the Allies either to undertake fresh operations thereafter which could otherwise have been undertaken earlier, or, more probably, to reorganize and reconsider their plans, thus allowing the enemy a welcome respite from attack. Finally, the islands might be secured without further ado by the successful invasion of Italy. Their capture could thus not be seriously considered as an alternative to that operation.

A more important alternative to Italy—in General Alexander's words, 'the best alternative available'—lay in an attack on the Balkans. Its advantages were seen clearly by the Germans. Domination of south-east Europe, long an aim of German governments, provided the Reich with essential raw materials and offered a useful sanctuary for some war industries subject to bombing from the west. The grain, oil and minerals of the north, the timber and copper of the south, and the chrome, copper and other minerals of Turkey to which the enemy thus had access, formed an integral part of his war economy. But this economic domination involved him in a difficult diplomatic task. The political climate of south-east Europe, notoriously unstable, was exceptionally sensitive in war, and would at once be violently disturbed by an Allied incursion into the Balkans. Finally, this delicate and vital area offered a classic means of approach to the Reich; for no natural obstacle divides Germany and Austria from the eastern plains, as the Alps divide them from Italy. Thus, a Russian advance—and the Russians were advancing—combined with an invasion from the Mediterranean by the British and Americans, must prove a serious, and might prove a decisive, threat, not only to south-east Europe but to Germany herself, once the Western Allies had penetrated the crust of the mountains in the south of the Balkan peninsula. In the opinion of the German High Command, 'domination of the Balkans as an integral part of the Fortress of Europe is decisive from the point of view of winning the war for tactical, military-political and economic reasons'.

This appreciation was reflected in the Germans' dispositions and plans for Italy and south-east Europe. Early in July 1943, when they had six German divisions and one brigade in Italy and Sicily, they had twelve German divisions and two brigades (with five satellite divisions under German command) in south-east Europe and the Greek islands. Hitler himself had been expecting the Allies to invade south-east Europe at some point since May 1943, and the High Command shared his view from June. The invasion of Sicily in July did not seriously disturb this belief, and indeed one of the reasons for the Germans' defence of the island was to deny to the Allies for as long as possible a base in the west for a subsequent Balkan campaign. As the Italian Government grew steadily less effective, and as German suspicions of its intentions increased, the High Command's main preoccupation remained the defence of the south-east, then so largely in the hands of its ally. Plans for seizing control in Italy were accordingly subordinated, throughout the first three weeks of July, to similar plans for the Balkans. Throughout this period, the Germans moved troops to the south-east, negotiated with the Italians for a reorganization of command, and tried to bolster up the governments under their protection. As late as 21st July, Hitler placed Field Marshal Erwin Rommel in command of a new Army Group designed to defend Greece and the Aegean islands; and it was only on the 25th, when Mussolini fell from power, that the plans for Italy gained an immediate precedence. Even then, the Germans continued to reinforce south-east Europe as well as Italy, until at the end of August it held some eighteen German divisions; and again at the end of September, when the first stage of the Italian campaign was over, their thoughts reverted to its defence. It was not until November that they abandoned their belief in an immediate Allied invasion of the Balkans; and then it was merely to postpone the anticipated date until the following spring.

But the advantages of such a move at this stage were less apparent to the Allies than to the Germans. In the first place, a campaign in south-east Europe was not calculated, like a campaign in Italy, to lead to Italy's surrender; and if it did not, it would not remove from the war the Italian forces in that area, or transfer their allegiance to the Allies. Secondly, while operations in Italy might not lessen the Germans' fears for the Balkans, operations in the Balkans must lessen their fears for Italy, allowing them to use the facilities of the peninsula as a base for south-east Europe, and to maintain unimpaired the existing system of control over both areas. Thirdly, it would commit the Allies initially to an even more difficult terrain, with worse communications, than that of Italy, and to a more difficult approach. As Alexander later remarked, in order to invade the Balkans from the south it would have been necessary either to assemble a substantial force of aircraft carriers, or, for the sake of air cover, to break into the outer ring of islands from Crete to Rhodes; while the subsequent operations in difficult country might often have demanded complementary landings from the sea, which the promised removal of assault shipping from the Mediterranean might well have rendered impossible. Operations against the Balkans in the summer of 1943 must therefore have been launched either from the south, which would have consumed the available resources and thus have precluded an invasion of Italy; or from the south and west in conjunction with an invasion of Italy, which itself could then have been only on a minor scale. But, as we have already seen, the invasion of Italy was considered essential; and, as we shall now see, it had to be undertaken on a scale that rendered the second alternative impossible.

For while the Allies at no stage wished to disperse their limited effort, the exact margin of strength available for the rest of the Mediterranean was finally settled by the strength required for the main operation. This in turn was dictated by a combination of geographical and diplomatic considerations in August, 1943.

As the Mediterranean Command surveyed the Italian scene in the summer, the prospects for invasion were not particularly encouraging.[1] The limiting factor to any assault by this stage in the war was always taken as air cover, and from his personal experience in France and Burma Alexander was not likely to neglect it. There was no possibility of providing that cover by sea, for there was no possibility of getting the necessary aircraft carriers from other theatres. It must therefore be provided by land-based fighters. If the Spitfire was taken as the standard, this gave an operational limit of 180 miles. The arc of a circle of that diameter, constructed on Messina in the north-east corner of Sicily, cut the Italian coast in the Gulf of Salerno, and again at a point on the Gulf of Taranto some fifteen miles west of Taranto itself. Naples and Taranto, the two great prizes in southern Italy, thus lay just outside the justifiable range of direct assault. The force for the attack was moreover uncertain until the campaign in Sicily was well under way. The first plans were therefore conservative, confined to landings by two British Corps in Calabria at the beginning of September and October respectively, with complementary attacks on Sardinia by an American Corps and on Corsica by a French division. But these plans were soon extended, as the fighting in Sicily and an uncertain political situation in Italy seemed to veer in favour of the Allies. In the middle of July, the first had progressed well enough for the commanders in the Mediterranean to consider a series of more ambitious possibilities in the 'toe' and 'heel' of the peninsula; but when Mussolini fell on the 25th, they decided that they might legitimately risk a greater prize. On the 27th, they ordered Major-General Mark Clark, commanding Fifth U.S. Army in North Africa, to prepare plans for an assault on the port of Naples 'with a view to preparing a firm base for further offensive operations'. Such a task would demand the use of resources still contained in Sicily, which were unlikely to be available before the middle of August. Its target date was therefore given as 7th September, the first day of the period in the ensuing month when the moon would be most suitable.

[1] See Map V, facing p. 270.

The operation against Naples (operation 'Avalanche') now took precedence of the earlier possibilities. Its details were worked out over the next three weeks. The assault was to be launched against the Gulf of Salerno, some twenty-five miles south of Naples and at the extreme limit of air cover. This fact, and the uncertain political situation which made the operation possible, decreed that it should be mounted in strength. The attacking force was composed of the British 10th and the American VI Corps,[1] consisting together of three infantry divisions with a tank battalion and commandos, to be reinforced after three days by one armoured and two infantry divisions. Part of an American airborne division was also designed to be dropped from Sicily to the north of Naples, to prevent the arrival of reinforcements for the enemy. The landing would be covered from the sea by a substantial British naval force, while aircraft from Sicily and from the carriers already available would provide air cover until a base was established on the mainland.

These forces were to sail from North Africa and Sicily in an armada of some three hundred assault ships and craft. The size of the assault determined the shape of the complementary operations, to be chosen from those already tabled. The end of the campaign in Sicily would soon release one (13th) British Corps. At the end of July, General Sir Bernard Montgomery, commanding the British Eighth Army, was accordingly ordered to use it against Calabria as early as possible in September. Another (5th) British Corps, in North Africa, was held in reserve for a later and complementary attack on Calabria.

These plans were confirmed by the theatre commanders at a conference on 16th August, the day before operations in Sicily ended, and were approved by the Combined Chiefs of Staff on the 18th. A bare three weeks thus remained in which to prepare an enterprise to which the Allies were now irrevocably committed. The preparations could not but attract the attention of the enemy, and their success therefore depended on the achievement of strategic surprise or on the exploitation of a favourable political situation. But the political uncertainty, which had hitherto favoured the Allies, now, by its continuation, militated against them. The Italians secretly opened negotiations for surrender on 15th August. But the impulse came chiefly from the General Staff, now resigned to defeat but eager to mitigate the consequences by transferring the Italian forces to the victor. Such a plan, while offering to the Allies a greater eventual advantage than a mere act of surrender, presented a greater immediate disadvantage. The transfer of forces, to be effective, must be concerted with the invasion itself, and the Italians were therefore anxious to know the Allies' intentions in detail. But the Allies, concerned for security and aware that

[1] Throughout this volume, in order to distinguish them, British Corps will be given in Arabic, and American in Roman, figures.

PLATE I. MEDITERRANEAN COMMANDERS

Back row, left to right: Air Chief Marshal Tedder, Admiral John Cunningham, General Alexander, General Bedell Smith.

Front row, left to right: General Eisenhower, Mr. Churchill, General Wilson.

their plan was not such as further to embolden the Italians, refused to comply, and the negotiations accordingly hung fire. It was not until 3rd September that the plenipotentiaries signed the military terms of surrender in Sicily, and not until the evening of the 8th that Marshal Badoglio could be induced to announce them publicly from Rome. Even then, the uncertainty of his intentions, and the manner of his final decision, were such that most of the Italian forces failed to respond.

Meanwhile, the Allies were well aware that the military situation was turning against them. The Germans were known to be reinforcing their six divisions in Sicily and Italy. In the course of July, their High Command prepared plans for disarming the Italians and for deploying German divisions in their place, for seizing control in Rome, and for guaranteeing communications with Germany and with the east. As has been seen, these were given precedence over similar plans for the Balkans after the 25th, and the preparatory deployment then got under way. Two divisions were withdrawn from southern France, and a new Army Group, consisting of some eight divisions from other fronts, was concentrated secretly near Munich for the occupation of northern Italy. This last force was placed under the command of Rommel. Meanwhile, German reinforcements for Sicily were halted, preparations made to evacuate the German troops already on the island, and the four divisions in central and southern Italy held ready to disarm and take over the Italians. By 3rd September, the deployment was complete. The eight divisions from Germany were in northern Italy, forming Army Group B; and another eight divisions (the six already in central and southern Italy and in Sicily, plus the two withdrawn from France) were in central and southern Italy, forming, with one and a half German divisions already in Sardinia and Corsica, Tenth Army under Field Marshal Albert Kesselring, the German Commander-in-Chief in the South.

But while the enemy was thus prepared for the Allies, he over-estimated their strength and in consequence misjudged their plan of campaign. While in fact they looked immediately no further than Rome and its airfields, he was prepared to retreat at once to the line Massa Carrara-Pesaro, across the Apennines to the north of Florence. He was even prepared, at the worst, to pull back to the line of the Po; at best, he hoped to stand on a line Grosseto-Perugia-Ancona, through the Apennines to the south of Lake Trasimene. All such plans, of course, ceded Rome in the course of the retreat.

The Allies were well informed of these movements and intentions. They therefore decided to adhere to their existing plans. An alternative to 'Avalanche' was indeed considered on 24th August, whereby Fifth Army would land in the 'heel' of Italy to capture the ports of Taranto and Brindisi. But this operation, it was thought, could not be carried out before 21st September, and in any case seemed unduly cautious. On 3rd September, accordingly, the earlier plan was put into effect. Montgomery's 13th Corps crossed the narrow Straits of Messina to Reggio, while on the same day the first of the convoys for Salerno sailed from North Africa. The rest followed over the next four days. On the evening of the 8th, they joined company off the Gulf of Salerno. As they headed towards the land, the troops, like the Italians and the Germans, learned that Italy had surrendered.

The invasion of Italy was thus set on foot before the surrender was announced. By then, there was little left with which to exploit the occasion. When the plenipotentiaries signed the military terms on 3rd September, the Allied commanders surveyed the possibilities that remained to their Command. The most fruitful gains seemed to lie in the western Balkans, and in some of the Ionian and Aegean islands. But these all lay outside their province, in the Middle East Command[1]; the bulk of their assault divisions and assault shipping was engaged; and an unknown commitment in Italy lay ahead. An important target, moreover, and the means for its capture, lay closer to hand. Once fighting began near Reggio and Salerno, no German troops were likely to remain within striking distance of the Gulf of Taranto. It therefore seemed possible that the port of Taranto itself, whose immediate capture had not hitherto been envisaged, might be taken unopposed. A spare airborne division was already assembled in North Africa, awaiting passage to England as one of the seven divisions for 'Overlord' and meanwhile, thanks to lack of transport aircraft and shipping, apparently condemned to idleness. The navy managed at short notice to provide for its embarkation and cover, and on 2nd September the division occupied Taranto without a fight. Two divisions, already held at Alexander's disposal, were then withdrawn, one from Sicily and one from the Middle East, and were put into the port. Meanwhile, 13th Corps' progress in Calabria had removed the necessity for 5th Corps' subsequent attack[2]. The force at Taranto was accordingly placed under 5th Corps' headquarters, which, with 13th Corps, formed Eighth Army on the mainland. Thus, on 9th September, 13th British Corps (two divisions) was moving through Calabria, 5th British Corps (soon to be three divisions) was in Taranto, and Fifth Army (one British and one American Corps, comprising some three divisions in the assault, and another three to follow up) was landing at Salerno.

The uncertainties of the final events surrounding the Italian surrender prevented its purpose from being achieved. The armed forces in

---

[1] See Rear End-paper.

[2] See p. 64 above.

Italy received no warning of their Government's intentions, and the result was a fatal apathy and disorganization. Only the Fleet observed the terms of surrender to the Allies: the land and air forces found themselves surrendering instead to the Germans. The Germans indeed moved so fast near Rome and in the south that by 10th September they had disarmed all the Italian divisions, and could turn, without fear of interference, to face the Allies at Salerno. This was the easier since the American airborne division, designed to impede the enemy's reinforcement of that area,[1] had first been kept in reserve to assist the Italians near Rome and then, in the final confusion, held inactive in Sicily. The landings were therefore contested, and some very hard fighting ensued. It was not until 16th September, by which time four German divisions were opposing eight Allied divisions in the beachhead, that the enemy withdrew as a result of the frontal pressure, combined with the threat from Eighth Army in the south.

But the end of the battle, as so often, was followed by a sudden retreat. By 20th September, Fifth Army was pushing towards the north, while Eighth Army had crossed the central mountains and was moving up the eastern plain. By the end of the month, Eighth Army had reached and captured the plain of Foggia, with its important group of airfields; and on 1st October Fifth Army entered Naples. In the same period, the Germans withdrew from Sardinia and Corsica, where local guerrillas and, in Corsica, French forces from North Africa were soon active.

Towards the end of September, the prospects therefore seemed bright; and Eisenhower and Alexander issued their instructions for the winter. The former, on the 26th, ordered the Allied forces in Italy to secure air bases in the area of Rome as their next objective. The latter, on the 21st, had already envisaged a comprehensive plan based on this immediate intention. The operations were divided into four phases. The first was the consolidation of the line Salerno-Bari. This was already almost complete. The second was the capture of Foggia, and the capture and employment of Naples. This was to be complete within the next few weeks. The third phase aimed at securing Rome with its airfields, and the road and rail junction of Terni to the north. This, it was hoped, would be complete before the end of the year. The last phase was to end in the capture of Arezzo, Florence and Leghorn. Plans for the last two phases were to be flexible, and were to take full advantage of opportunities for sea- and airborne attack.

The success of these plans depended on the Germans' reaction; for the weight and speed of the offensive were not such in themselves as to command events. The timing of the third phase was based on the assumption that the enemy still intended to withdraw under pressure to a line in the northern Apennines, contesting Rome and its environs

---

[1] See p. 64 above.

only in the course of the retreat. In these circumstances, Alexander's immediate superiority would gain the necessary results before the true balance of forces was redressed. But if the Germans were able to delay the advance, and to contest the 'waist' of Italy until the weather broke towards the end of October, the inherent flaws in the Allies' position would become apparent.

By the middle of October, it seemed possible that this would be the case. For the course of the fighting early in the month, and intelligence received between the 8th and the 10th, suggested for the first time that the Germans had changed their plan of campaign. As both Armies pressed forward from Foggia and Naples, they encountered a stronger and more confident resistance. We now know, indeed, that as early as 15th September Kesselring expected the Allies to pause after capturing Foggia, which was regarded as the gateway to the Balkans. The German High Command accepted this assumption, and decided to fight as long as possible in central Italy, so as to upset further moves before the winter. It accordingly ordered Tenth Army to retreat gradually into the Apennines, and deployed Army Group B in the north to counter possible Allied landings in Liguria or Istria. These movements were complete by 28th September. Tenth Army, despite an almost complete lack of air support, managed to withdraw intact across the Campanian plain, and was then able to yield more slowly, and in controlled order, a series of defensible mountain positions; and on 6th October, Kesselring submitted to the High Command that he should not retreat, as he had hitherto been prepared, to the line Grosseto-Perugia-Ancona, but should stand for as long as possible in suitable positions south of Rome. He suggested as the first of these, the line river Garigliano-Monte Cassino—river Sangro.

The High Command itself had already reached the same conclusion. On 4th October, the Fuehrer issued a directive for the winter to the Italian Commands, and on the 6th to the Command in the Balkans.

> 'The enemy', he informed Kesselring, 'may be expected to direct his main operation against the south-east area from Italy, possibly with the assistance of forces from Africa. It cannot yet be determined whether he will cross from southern Italy into Albania, Montenegro and southern Croatia, or whether he will first try to push further north in order to create a base in central Italy from which to attack northern Croatia and Istria.'

He ordered the German Tenth Army to fight a delaying action to the line Gaeta-Ortona, which it should hold with five divisions and two in reserve, while the rest guarded the coasts in the rear and around Rome. Army Group B would meanwhile organize the defence of northern Italy, paying particular attention to the Ligurian coast. If the Allies showed signs of transferring the weight of their forces to the Balkans, Kesselring should plan an attack on Apulia. A further directive defined the Germans' 'Winter Position',[1] from the mouth of the Garigliano in the west, along that river and the upper Volturno, past Monte Cassino at the foot of the Liri valley, through the Apennines and along the river Sangro to the Adriatic. At the end of September, Kesselring began to construct its defences in a series of positions in depth, with two forward lines (the 'Gustav' and 'Bernhard' positions), the second of which hinged on the main line at Cassino.

Throughout October the enemy gradually withdrew, under severe pressure from both Fifth and Eighth Armies. In the east, Eighth Army took the port of Termoli early in the month, and then fought its way forward slowly across the Trigno and Biferno to the Sangro, whose southern bank it reached in the first week of November. In the west, Fifth Army forced the Volturno, and after stubborn fighting in the mountains to the north of the Campanian plain, stood in the first week of November on the southern bank of the Garigliano, as far as Monte Cassino. At the beginning of November, five German divisions, with two in reserve, faced Fifth Army, and two German divisions opposed Eighth Army. Work on the Winter Position was still far from complete; but the nature of the terrain and the advent of bad weather powerfully assisted the defence, and committed the Allies to a frontal attack in the most unpromising conditions. The German preparations for the winter were completed in the course of November by a redistribution of command, whereby Kesselring took over the whole of the Italian theatre, as Commander-in-Chief, South-West and Army Group C. The new Army Group consisted of the Tenth Army and a new Army, the Fourteenth, comprising the eight divisions of the former Army Group B. Rommel was transferred to a command in north-west Europe. The Germans' balance of strength between Italy and the Balkans, and the totals involved, showed how the situation had changed in the past two months. Whereas early in July they had had some six divisions in the Italian zone and approximately twelve in south-east Europe, the figures were now some twenty-five and twenty-four respectively.

The developments in October at once affected the Allies' plans, and on the 21st—exactly a month after he had issued his first instructions for the winter[2]— Alexander presented a further appreciation. This showed the position in Italy to be in an interesting, and indeed a critical, state for the Allies. Whereas in mid-September there had been thirteen Allied and some eighteen German divisions in the country, at the end of October there were eleven Allied and some twenty-five German divisions. The initial intention, to contain as many Germans as possible, was thus being amply fulfilled, but to a degree which was now bringing its own anxieties. Two results might arise from the

[1] The German word was 'Winterstellung'.

[2] See p. 67 above.

enemy's strategy for the winter. First, he might stand strongly on the defensive for several months, weakening his opponents enough in that time for him to reduce his forces in Italy before the Allies invaded north-west France. Secondly, he might stage a local offensive, aimed for instance at the recapture of Naples, which if successful would gain him a welcome respite, and if unsuccessful would probably send him back only into the Winter Position. It was therefore essential not to relax pressure throughout the winter. As Alexander remarked, 'if we can keep the enemy "on his heels" until [the spring of 1944], we shall be certain of retaining in Italy the divisions already there; we might even draw still more into the theatre, while still keeping him sufficiently off-balance to be unable to seize the initiative from us; finally, if he were to launch a great counter-offensive next spring, we should welcome it . . .'

On this appreciation, Alexander developed a plan of campaign. The revised German strategy had its weak spots, the most pronounced of which was the necessity to defend Rome and its environs. Not only was the capital the focus of communications from the north, but its loss, after the line had apparently been stabilized to the south, would represent a more serious diplomatic defeat than would have been the case from the earlier German plan. A direct attack on Rome from the sea, moreover, would now threaten the enemy's rear. He was thus likely to respond in force to the combination of movements involved in such an operation. The ensuing battle might indeed decide the fate of Italy, and exhaust a large measure of the enemy's strength in southern Europe. Alexander therefore proposed a general offensive, starting in November, for the capture of Rome and its communications. In the east, he intended to establish Eighth Army on the high ground north of Pescara, whence it could turn south-west, along one of the few good transverse roads in central Italy, to Avezzano and Rome. Fifth Army would meanwhile aim due north at Rome along the only suitable approach, the valley of the Liri. The first stage here would be to force the dominating position of Monte Cassino. Each of these attacks was to be assisted if possible by a seaborne assault, in the east by a brigade group, and in the more sensitive western sector by at least one division with armour. The western assault was considered essential to the success of Fifth Army's frontal attack. Eisenhower accepted the appreciation, and approved the plans, on 24th October.

As Alexander pointed out, the new proposals did not depart from the earlier plan of campaign, but only affected its timing. But this was enough to throw into relief difficulties which had been inherent in the invasion itself. These centred on, and were expressed by, a shortage of assault shipping, needed not only for the landings on both coasts of Italy but for the reinforcement of the formations already in the peninsula. Neither demand was new. Landings from the sea had always been designed as part of the campaign, while supply and reinforcement had of course been under way since September. But the turn of events in October produced a definite demand for seaborne assaults, as an integral and indeed an essential element in the revised timetable, at a time when the administrative tasks, already in some difficulties, were being complicated by new burdens.

The problem of immediate supply had been largely solved by the beginning of October. The sea routes to Taranto and Brindisi, the ports themselves and their communications, were by then organized for the maintenance of Eighth Army, itself by then moving at a slower pace; while in the west, Fifth Army was supplied adequately from Sicily through harbours in the Gulf of Salerno. Naples itself was put into working order by the middle of October, to sustain the operations in the west. A more serious problem was that of reinforcement. At the beginning of October, the Mediterranean Command planned to have some 13½ divisions in Italy by the middle of the month, and some 18½ by February, 1944. This was a slow rate of reinforcement; but at the end of October it was not certain that it could be maintained. On 21st October, Alexander calculated that whereas the Allies had expected to put 1,300 vehicles a day into Italy, they were in fact putting in only 2,000 a week, and that only fourteen to fifteen divisions would be in the country by the end of December, and a further two by February, 1944. While Eisenhower did not accept these figures, he was no more inclined than Alexander to underrate the difficulties. The trouble lay largely in two independent commitments, both enjoined on the theatre—one not without the support of its Commander-in-Chief—by the Combined Chiefs of Staff.

The first commitment lay in the necessity to withdraw seven divisions (three British, four American) from the theatre by the end of November 1943, to return to the United Kingdom for 'Overlord', due in the following May. Of these seven divisions, one was armoured and one airborne, all were active and experienced formations, and three were engaged in the fighting in Italy in September. The Mediterranean Command had thus to allow not only for the loss of seven good divisions available for immediate use, whose place would be taken in due course by French divisions still forming or equipping in North Africa, but for the withdrawal of three of them from the current battle. Two divisions had indeed disappeared for this reason by the last week in October.[1]

The second commitment was, as it were, the reverse of the first. While divisions were being withdrawn, the Command was enjoined to put into Italy as soon as possible a substantial force of bombers. For one of the principal reasons for the invasion of Italy, particularly to the

[1] See p. 69 above.

Americans, had been the prospect of bombing Germany and her satellites from the south. Not only could the Allies then reach fresh targets, but the harassed German defences could be subjected to a greater and more continuous strain, while the air forces in Britain were correspondingly relieved. A strategic air force in Italy was accepted at Quebec as an integral part of 'Pointblank',[1] and the consequent movement of aircraft enjoyed the high priority accorded to that campaign. In September 1943, there were six groups of heavy bombers in the Mediterranean, consisting of some 250 aircraft. Their transfer from North Africa began towards the end of the month, when the airfields near Foggia were captured, and was designed to be complete by the end of October. In the same period, half a reconnaissance group and two fighter groups were to be moved to Italy. This commitment, which of course supported the immediate needs of the campaign as well as 'Pointblank', made a considerable demand on shipping in the early days of the invasion. But the Americans, increasingly anxious to reduce the heavy casualties suffered by their Eighth Air Force from Britain, decided in October to take further advantage of the new base in the south, and to redistribute their bombers in different proportions between the United Kingdom and Italy. They therefore announced that they proposed to replace Eisenhower's existing Twelfth U.S. Army Air Force (consisting of six heavy bomber groups, fifteen fighter groups and one reconnaissance group) by a new Fifteenth U.S. Army Air Force, which by the end of March, 1944 was to consist of twenty-one heavy bomber groups, seven long-range fighter groups and one reconnaissance group. Of these, twelve bomber groups, four fighter groups and the reconnaissance group were to be in Italy by the end of December, 1943. The planned expansion of Eighth U.S. Air Force in the United Kingdom would be reduced accordingly. The shipping required for the twenty-one heavy bomber groups alone amounted to rather more than that required for two divisions of troops, while their maintenance demanded nearly as much shipping as that of Eighth Army. Whatever its strategic advantage, the move was therefore likely to prove an embarrassment to the Italian campaign. As the authorities immediately responsible for that campaign, the British Chiefs of Staff at once raised this argument, and pointed out to the Americans that until the armies had reached Rome, the air forces could not in any case be usefully employed. There was indeed a real danger that the bombers sent from the United States to North Africa might have to stay there unused for some months, whereas if they were sent to Britain, as hitherto planned, they could be used almost at once against Germany. In the event, the Americans had their way over the distribution of the air effort,[2] but the commanders in the theatre meanwhile

[1] See p. 6 above.

[2] See pp. 196-7 below.

decided to bring the aircraft into Italy more slowly, transferring the first six bomber groups alone by the end of 1943. Even so, the move threw a heavy strain on shipping.

This strain fell particularly on assault shipping, so much more economical than cargo shipping in the transport of vehicles and armour. But in the third week of October, the Mediterranean was due to lose 80 per cent of its L.S.T. and L.S.I., and two-thirds of its landing craft, within the next six weeks. The programme for the L.S.T. was as follows:

British: 12 to leave for the United Kingdom on 12th November,
12 on 22nd November,
16 on 2nd December,
16 on 12th December.
Total 56.

American: 12 to leave for the United Kingdom on 2nd November,
12 on 12th November,
24 on 22nd November (all dates approximate).
Total 48.

The new pressure for reinforcements, and for landings on the coasts of Italy, thus came at a time when the necessary ships and craft were destined to be removed.

On 31st October, General Eisenhower accordingly telegraphed to the Combined Chiefs of Staff. The 'critical factor' in the theatre's plans was now the fate of the assault ships and craft, which were required to reinforce formations already in Italy, to prepare for a landing or landings behind the enemy's lines with at least one division, and to help move bombers from North Africa. On the current programme, they could complete the first of these tasks by 15th December, but not the second or third in their entirety. If, however, all of the fifty-six British L.S.T., and twelve of the American, could be held in the Mediterranean until 15th December, they could complete their first task, mount an assault with one division, and transfer approximately one-third of the six bomber groups to Italy. If they could be held until 5th January, 1944, they could complete the whole programme, sailing thereafter to arrive in Britain between the last week in January and the end of February.

> 'I am not certain', Eisenhower ended, 'what effect the two alternatives described would have on 'Overlord', but I am very sure that the success of our operation in this area will have a great effect on 'Overlord' and a greater on 'Pointblank.' Therefore, while I am reluctant to repeat my previous request for delay in returning L.S.T.'s to the United Kingdom the enormous value to us of being able to use these additional L.S.T.'s for a comparatively short period beyond the time

> originally scheduled for their return is so impressive from our local viewpoint that I have decided after consultation with my senior commanders again to present these facts for your consideration. Should later developments show that some of our proposed Amphibious operations are impracticable or can be executed on a smaller scale, to speed up return of corresponding craft, you can depend on me.'

Alexander's estimate of the situation had alarmed the authorities in London, already unhappy about the coming withdrawal of assault shipping from the Mediterranean. On 26th October, the British Chiefs of Staff had indeed informed their American colleagues that they intended to let Eisenhower keep his British L.S.T. 'for the time being'. His message of the 31st was therefore sympathetically received. On 4th November, the Chiefs of Staff again telegraphed to Washington, mentioning no date for the return of the L.S.T. from the Mediterranean, but urging that Eisenhower should be allowed free use of such assault shipping as he needed for the vigorous prosecution of his operations. Otherwise, in their view, 'we shall be faced with a long drawn-out campaign involving a series of frontal attacks at heavy cost'. On the same day, the Prime Minister telegraphed to the President on the same lines. The Americans, who were affected by the fate of twelve L.S.T. compared with the British fifty-six, agreed without delay that the sixty-eight ships should stay in the theatre, but suggested 15th December as the determining date; and the Combined Chiefs of Staff informed Eisenhower accordingly on 6th November.

The commanders in the Mediterranean had thus gained a respite. But, as Eisenhower had pointed out, the difference between 15th December and 5th January might mean the difference between partial and complete success. Alexander repeated this argument on 6th November to the C.I.G.S., concluding that Eisenhower must therefore postpone either the seaborne assaults or the transfer of the strategic air force to Italy. On his own calculation, the L.S.T. must stay in the Mediterranean until 15th January—ten days later than the date given by Eisenhower—if both objects were to be achieved. Eisenhower telegraphed in the same sense to the Combined Chiefs of Staff. The British Chiefs of Staff had not taken the date of 15th December as final, nor did they anticipate that the Joint Chiefs of Staff would do so. On 7th November, the C.I.G.S. accordingly instructed Alexander in private to plan on the assumption that the L.S.T. would stay in the Mediterranean until 15th January. The Chiefs of Staff meanwhile approached their American colleagues in the same sense.

On 8th November, Eisenhower was therefore able to issue a fresh directive for the winter.[1] After reaffirming the object given earlier, the capture of the area of Rome, he specified three immediate tasks: the

[1] See p. 67 above.

reinforcement of the Allied land forces and of the air forces required for their support; the completion of the transfer of six heavy bomber groups to Italy by the end of 1943, followed by the introduction of other groups according to the circumstances; and the prosecution of operations designed to secure the general line Civitavecchia-Terni. On the same day, Alexander issued his directive for the third object. Fifth Army, whose strength had been drained first at Salerno and more recently by hard fighting in the mountains, was ordered to pause and regroup. Meanwhile, Eighth Army was to gain possession of the transverse road from Pescara to Avezzano. When that had been achieved, Fifth Army would attack up the Liri valley to Frosinone, some forty miles south of Rome. At that point—as it was hoped, at the turn of the year—a seaborne landing would be made to the south of Rome, directed on the Alban Hills. Eighth Army would receive the bulk of the air support in the first phase, and Fifth Army thereafter. On 13th November, Fifth Army paused to regroup, and the first phase began in the attack on the main Winter Position.

(iii)

The Consequences in the Eastern Mediterranean

The course of the fighting in Italy set the pattern further east. We have seen how in August, 1943 the authorities in the theatre had considered the eastern as an alternative scene of action to the central Mediterranean. Thereafter it figured as a complement. In September, the prospects seemed bright. The Allies now held ports and airfields along the southern Adriatic coast of Italy; thirty-two Italian divisions had been removed from the Balkan scene after Italy's surrender; and the southern Balkans themselves, as a result, were in a ferment. The British, within whose Middle East Command the whole of this area fell, had two reasons to exploit the favourable situation. First, continued unrest in south-east Europe would contain German divisions in the immediate future which might otherwise be sent to other fronts, probably to Italy or Russia. But secondly, success in Italy at any time before May, 1944 would leave an interval when other pressure must be applied in support of 'Overlord', which might well prove possible only in the south-east. The question, therefore, for the British at this time was how to bring the greatest immediate pressure to bear on this area, within the strict limits imposed at Quebec on strategy and resources, and with the possibility of greater continuous pressure proving necessary within the next few months. Their choice of action depended on a particular combination of local military and diplomatic factors.

There were three possible areas in south-east Europe in which to conduct operations, separately or in combination: Yugoslavia, Greece, and the Aegean. At the end of September 1943, Yugoslavia might seem at first sight to have offered most. The Germans were in an awkward, possibly a dangerous, position; while the British for the first time exercised some influence over the Yugoslavs. To appreciate the exact position, we must retrace our steps to the spring of 1941.

When the Germans invaded Yugoslavia in April of that year, they provided a new context for the traditional rivalries within the modern State, which centred on the ancient division of the country between Serbs and Croats. The Royal Yugoslav Government, composed mostly of Serbs, fled with the young King Peter to Cairo, whence they removed later to London; and the invaders established in its place a puppet Administration under the Serbian Nedic. Two main movements of resistance soon coalesced: the Serbian 'Cetniks' under Draza Mihailovic, an officer of the Royal Yugoslav Army; and the Croat 'Partisans' under Josep Broz, the Secretary-General of the illegal Yugoslav Communist Party, who in orthodox style adopted the prosopopoeia of Tito ('The Hammer'). The Cetniks were first in the field. Like their predecessors in the wars against the Turks, from whom they took their name, they represented the spirit of militant Serb nationalism, which had so often defied the invader and had placed a Karageorgevic on the throne of Yugoslavia to serve the destiny of his race. But the very success of their efforts, which in the past had turned the Serbs' resistance into revolution, now made of it a potentially conservative movement. As heirs to the ruling element, the Cetnik leaders were concerned to preserve their provinces from the worst excesses of the conqueror, and to subdue pretentions from the Croats which might threaten the former balance of power. These objects could best be achieved by the establishment and preservation of organized bands, designed to harry but not as yet to challenge the occupying powers, and to repel or subdue such Croat rivals as might emerge. To the Germans and Italians, opposition of this calibre was not likely to prove very serious. Whether indeed there would be opposition depended chiefly on the activities of the Croats; and Mihailovic was in fact led, by the logic of his case and despite his own conception of honour, to compromise both with Nedic and with the Italians against whom he had taken up, and remained in, arms.

The position of the Partisans was essentially simpler. As Croats, they had less power to retain; as Communists, fewer scruples to observe. The Communist Party, which provided the Croat guerrillas with their direction and organization, seems not to have emerged as a movement of resistance as quickly as the Cetniks. At any rate, it was not until the late summer of 1941, after Germany had declared war on Russia, that its activity was such as to bring it equally into prominence. But once it set to work, it soon produced results. The Partisan leaders had a continuous experience of secret obstruction since the party had been outlawed in 1921, and their activities were limited by consideration for the people whom they affected only to the extent that this might influence the attainment of their goal. It was thus not surprising that their followers soon became a serious nuisance to the enemy. Nor was it long before they were also embroiled with the Serbian guerrillas, in a struggle for power whose complex ramifications were in the true tradition of Balkan warfare.

The Western Allies at first knew little of either movement. But in the summer of 1941 Mihailovic attracted their attention and sympathy. This was partly the result of the favour with which he was naturally regarded by the exiled Royal Yugoslav Government, which gave him its blessing as leader of the Yugoslav forces, appointed him *in absentia* Minister for War, and promoted his cause in London. But it was also because the authorities in London themselves approved of his methods, in contrast to those of the Partisans. The British Government—or rather the agent of the British Government in these matters, the Special Operations Executive (S.O.E.)—was always anxious to restrain the subversive movements in Europe from activities which would lead to their premature destruction. Their rôle, according to S.O.E., was rather to organize a common front, and secretly to build up a disciplined force whose operations could be connected at a later stage directly with those of the Allies. S.O.E.'s objects were thus always the same: to reconcile the racial or political groups on which resistance normally concentrated, and which were often hostile to each other, and to bring them effectively under the common authority of a British Command. The consequences for Yugoslavia were clearly stated in August, 1941 by the Minister then in charge of S.O.E., Dr. Hugh Dalton, in terms which held good for the Executive's policy over the next two years.

> 'The Yugoslavs [i.e., the exiled Royal Yugoslav Government], the War Office and we are all agreed that the guerrilla and sabotage bands now active in Yugoslavia should show sufficient active resistance to cause constant embarrassment to the occupying forces, and prevent any reduction in their numbers. But they should keep their main organization underground and avoid any attempt at large scale risings or ambitious military operations, which could only result at present in severe repression and the loss of our key men. They should now do all they can to prepare a widespread underground organisation ready to strike hard later on, when we give the signal.'

This was certainly not the policy of the Partisans.

Mihailovic therefore continued, for over a year, alone to enjoy the support of the British, despite warnings of the possible dangers of such a course which the first British observers sent from Yugoslavia. These reports maintained that Mihailovic's position was one on which no Allied plan could rely, and that there was little hope of reconciling him with the Partisans. The British nevertheless did their best in 1942 to bring about such a reconciliation, for which they tried to enlist Russian sympathy. But by the autumn, the position had to be reviewed. Support could no longer be confined to the Cetniks. The Partisans were by now a powerful force, perhaps of over 100,000 men, which was fighting the enemy at least as effectively as the Serbs; while the British influence with Mihailovic was not particularly great, owing to the small scale of supplies sent to him. Throughout the winter of 1942/43 a long debate took place in London on the policy to be adopted. Different interests held different views; but in the spring of 1943, it was decided to maintain support of Mihailovic in view of the possible advantages for the future, but also to establish immediate contact if possible with the Partisans, and from that new basis to work once more for a truce between the movements. During the next three months, the policy of 'equal assistance' was put into effect. Mihailovic himself was warned, at the end of March 1943, that the British would withdraw their support unless he ceased to collaborate with the Italians and with Nedic, unless he stopped fighting the Partisans, and accepted strategic direction from the British Middle East Command through British liaison officers. After considerable negotiation, the Cetniks accepted these terms, and in July agreed to observe a truce with the Partisans. Meanwhile, in April and May Croat and British liaison parties were dropped into Partisan territory; and at the end of May Captain F. W. Deakin was dropped, with a small party, into Montenegro, to act as liaison officer at Tito's headquarters.

Deakin's arrival marked a turning point in the relations between the British and the Partisans. Four months later, the British representation with Tito was further strengthened. The Foreign Office and the Chiefs of Staff now wished to establish a Military Mission with both movements, consisting in all of some fifty officers; and in the middle of July, 1943 the Foreign Secretary suggested that Lieut.-Colonel Fitzroy Maclean, a former member of the Foreign Office and then Member of Parliament for Lancaster, should act as 'political' adviser to the Mission to Tito. Later in July, the Prime Minister intervened to suggest that Maclean should himself lead the Mission, which he regarded as of more diplomatic than military significance. 'What we want,' he then remarked,[1] 'is a daring Ambassador-leader with these hardy and hunted guerrillas.' Maclean was accordingly given the rank of Brigadier, and dropped in September near Tito's headquarters in Bosnia. The

[1] See *Closing the Ring*, pp. 411-12.

Military Mission to Mihailovic was strengthened at the same time. Late in September, Brigadier C. D. Armstrong reached Cetnik headquarters from Cairo.

The Missions did not arrive entirely empty-handed. Between June, 1941 and June 1943, few British supplies had reached either Mihailovic or Tito. Twenty-three tons of material were dropped in that time to the Cetniks, and $6\frac{1}{2}$ tons to the Partisans. The paucity of the supplies followed warnings from the British observers that they would be used by both sides largely against each other; but it was due also to the shortage of aircraft, at a stage in the war when resistance in Yugoslavia seemed to be of only indirect consequence to the Allies' operations. The growing effectiveness of the Partisans, and the developments in the Mediterranean campaign, led the Prime Minister and the Chiefs of Staff in June, 1943 to reconsider the problem. As a result, thirty-two bombers were placed at S.O.E.'s disposal in the Mediterranean, capable, with their other commitments, of delivering some 150 tons a month to Yugoslavia; and it was agreed that the rate of supplies should if possible be increased thereafter to a level of some five hundred tons a month by September, 1943. The results were disappointing at first, owing mainly to the lack of effective liaison with the Partisans. Even after the bombers had been increased in July to the promised thirty-two, at which figure the force stood until the spring of 1944, the volume of airborne supplies to both movements in the third quarter of 1943 rose only to 144 tons. But adequate air supply was at least now available, if the occasion, or relations with Tito, demanded or allowed of its use.

Despite the small scale of the supplies, British influence in Yugoslavia was thus growing when Italy surrendered on 9th September, and the situation was suddenly transformed. The events of the next few weeks swung the balance finally in favour of the Partisans against the Cetniks.[1] They also created an extremely difficult position for the Germans. At the time of Italy's capitulation, the Partisans, though now perhaps some 150,000 strong, were still confined mainly to the mountains of Bosnia and Croatia, and lacked arms and equipment. But the removal of fifteen Italian divisions gave them an opportunity which they were quick to seize. Within a fortnight, they disarmed at least six of these divisions, and enlisted the support of two more with their equipment. At the same time, they descended on the areas within their reach which the Italians had garrisoned. In the north, they entered Italy itself on 15th September, seizing the province of Istria and the mountains between Trieste and the Austrian frontier; and at the beginning of October surrounded Zagreb, threatening the main railway thence to Belgrade. In the west, they occupied the town of Split and much of the adjacent territory, and then moved to the islands off

[1] See Map II, facing p. 57.

the Dalmatian coast, in most of which they established garrisons. In the centre, they extended and tightened their control throughout Bosnia and Croatia; and in the south moved into Montenegro, where they attracted to them many of Mihailovic's followers. By the beginning of October, the Partisans had increased their numbers by between 60,000 and 80,000, had captured enough Italian equipment to make them for the first time a serious military proposition, and had gained control, in varying degrees, of over half of Yugoslavia. By the end of that month, Maclean reported that they disposed of twenty-six divisions, comprising some 220,000 men. The Cetniks had also increased the area of their control at the Italians' expense, and had captured some arms and equipment. But their conquests and booty were smaller than those of the Partisans, and in the race for territory and equipment they soon found themselves again involved in clashes with Tito, in which they were usually worsted. Thereafter, the Cetniks declined steadily in importance compared with their rivals, even when the latter were again hard pressed and unable to hold their own against the occupying power.

At the end of September 1943, when the campaign in Italy was going well, developments in Yugoslavia could thus be regarded for the first time as of strategic significance. The British therefore did what they could to help the guerrillas. S.O.E. in Cairo called urgently for an increase in supplies, and, thanks largely to the personal support of the Prime Minister, naval coastal forces were diverted to help the bombers in their task. As a result, some 2,050 tons of material were landed by naval craft, mostly on the islands, in the last quarter of the year, although only 125 tons were dropped in the same period by the bombers allocated to S.O.E.

This support followed a pattern first laid down two months before, and confirmed while the support itself was being provided. On 12th July, in the course of a survey of Mediterranean strategy, the British Joint Planners had examined the possibilities open to the Allies on the assumption that Italy would soon collapse. Three courses of action then seemed to offer: operations in the Balkans 'either through a bridgehead in the Durazzo area or via Turkey', operations in northern Italy to occupy the area Milan-Turin, and operations in the Iberian peninsula. Of the Durazzo bridgehead, the Planners remarked:

> '[Its] establishment . . . would enable us to increase our assistance to the Resistance Groups and so extend German internal security commitments; we could also threaten Germany with the loss of vital raw materials. Possession of airfields in the Balkans and Turkey would enable us to increase interference with German resources especially Roumanian oil supplies.
>
> The diversion of German divisions to meet the increased threat in the Balkans would indirectly contribute to the success

> of 'Overlord', but the denial of raw materials would not exercise an immediate effect on the German war economy. Nor could we hope for a decisive success in the Balkans in time to influence the cross-Channel invasion of the Continent, and we might well find ourselves involved in an exhaustive and indeterminate campaign. At the same time the collapse of Italy will enable us to give a greater degree of assistance to guerrillas in the Balkans even without establishing a bridgehead at Durazzo.'

From this analysis, the Planners concluded that if Italy collapsed, operations in the Balkans should be subsidiary to those against northern Italy 'as resources permit; we should, in any case, increase the degree of assistance to guerrillas to the greatest possible extent'.

This strategy held good throughout the autumn; and as the scene in Yugoslavia changed, in September and again in October, the choice for the Allies lay not between invasion and assistance but between the different forms of assistance, and principally between a bridgehead or bridgeheads on the one hand, from which to organize agents, advice and supply, and on the other supply by sea and air alone. The question was first raised as an immediate issue on 9th September. The Prime Minister then pointed out, in a survey of the Mediterranean scene,[1] that 'it should be possible to open quite soon one or more good ports on the Dalmatian coast, enabling munitions and supplies to be sent in by ship, and all forces that will obey our orders raised to good fighting condition . . . For the moment the utmost efforts should be put forth to organize the attack upon the Germans throughout the Balkan peninsula and to supply agents, arms and good direction.' The Chiefs of Staff agreed at once with this object, but were not yet certain of the best means to achieve it, and were careful to stress that it must 'not, in any way, prejudice our main effort in Italy. We must guard against being drawn into a fresh campaign with inadequate forces.' The Prime Minister in turn agreed on the 14th that this must not be allowed; but he feared lest the support should fall short of the opportunity, and therefore remained eager to seize some ports across the Adriatic. 'Although we cannot fight a Balkan campaign ourselves we ought to use enough force to stimulate others to do it.' But the Chiefs of Staff preferred to confine the support to sea and air forces alone, rather than to send British troops ashore; and so the matter rested for the next few weeks.

The interest of this brief debate lies in the light it throws on the nature and the limitations of the British policy for Yugoslavia in 1943, at the time of its greatest promise. For early in October conditions again changed for the worse. The turn of events in Italy settled the immediate issue of a bridgehead, and made it neither possible nor

---

[1] See *Closing the Ring*, p. 121.

desirable to venture beyond the peninsula itself. The Germans' decision to stand south of Rome contained all of the available Allied strength in the Mediterranean Command. It also promised to commit the Germans themselves ever more heavily. There were now no Allied forces, however small, to spare for Yugoslavia; for the same reason, there was now no need to spare them. 'Campania and Latium were far enough from France'.[1]

By the middle of October, moreover, the position in Yugoslavia itself was changing for the worse. The scale of the Partisans' success in September forced the Germans to take it seriously. In the last week of the month, they attacked in strength in Istria and along the Dalmatian coast. These operations were largely successful. The Partisans retreated out of Istria, and ceded many of their coastal possessions in Dalmatia, including the town of Split. The enemy then embarked on a major campaign, known to the Partisans as the Sixth Offensive, but on a greater scale than its predecessors. A force of fifteen German divisions began preliminary operations in October and November in Slovenia and Macedonia, and in the Adriatic islands. By the beginning of December, it had driven the Partisans back into the central mountains, and had ejected them from all but two of the islands. From December, 1943 to February, 1944 the campaign continued in Bosnia. But the Germans then found, as they and the Italians had found before, that it was impossible to crush the guerrillas on their own ground, particularly when they had been so greatly reinforced in the interval; and in March, 1944 they gave up the attempt. The Partisans lived to fight again, and with a considerable accession of strength; but their period of success was over, and, in the changed conditions throughout the Mediterranean, could not be expected immediately to revive.

There was thus no question during September or October of Allied troops entering Yugoslavia from the central Mediterranean. There was equally no question at any time of their doing so from the eastern Mediterranean, under the aegis of the Middle East Command. For while that Command was responsible for the area east of the Adriatic, it possessed neither the forces nor the lines of communication to meet its responsibilities. In their absence, it devoted its attention to more rewarding possibilities elsewhere; and in fact by the end of September it had already committed its small resources, together with those that could be spared from the Mediterranean Command, to another area.

The second possible area for operations, and the alternative to Yugoslavia on the mainland, was Greece. In the autumn of 1943 this offered few strategic advantages, and some serious diplomatic

[1] Alexander's phrase.

disadvantages. The only occasion, indeed, on which the British considered landing in Greece during this period, was forced upon them, not by any strategic purpose, but by a political situation which might otherwise threaten their strategy elsewhere.

As far as the British were concerned, this situation resembled in many ways the political situation in Yugoslavia. In both cases the effective guerrillas were divided by political—though not in Greece by racial—antagonism, and in both the British Government was obliged to maintain relations simultaneously with an exiled Government and with a movement of resistance that was hostile to it. But there were two important differences. First, whereas in Yugoslavia the British had begun by supporting the royalist Mihailovic, in Greece they were committed from the start to the support of republican forces under Communist leadership. Secondly, whereas in Yugoslavia there was no connexion between the exiled Government and the Communist Partisans, in Greece the exiled Government had been brought into contact with the Communist guerrillas by September, 1943.

The Greek political problem was inherited from before the war. In 1936, King George II of the Hellenes returned from an exile which had lasted since 1923. But his reappearance failed to resolve the Parliamentary deadlock that had occasioned it, and before the end of the year he was obliged to dissolve the Chamber and to confer emergency powers on the Minister for War, General John Metaxas. No further election was held before the Italian attack on Greece in October, 1940 confirmed Metaxas in his position as dictator; but that did not mean that the political bitterness had diminished.

This was indeed confirmed over the next three years. Metaxas died in January, 1941. In April, the successful German attack drove the King and his Government from Greece to Crete, and in May from Crete to Cairo and thence to London. The constitutional question, therefore, changed from the King's position and policy in Greece to the advisability and the manner of his return. Its solution was not made the easier by subsequent cabals among the exiles, which bore little relation to events in Greece, or even to much of the feeling among the free Greek forces and the influential Greek colonies in Egypt. Meanwhile, in Greece itself the royalists soon lost ground. Within a few months of the British evacuation, scattered movements of resistance arose in different parts of the country, each of which, from the beginning, bore a political impress. Of the early groups, two of the most effective were royalist; but these were crushed or scattered before the winter, and while others arose later, they were unable to organize a national resistance under royalist direction.

For by the winter of 1941 a more powerful, republican organization had appeared, which became known as E.A.M. This movement claimed to be an alliance of independent republican Socialist bodies, formed for the purpose of resisting the occupying powers and thereafter of ensuring for the country a free constitutional choice of the form of government. In the spring of 1942, it formed a military organization, E.L.A.S. But both E.A.M. and E.L.A.S. were in fact a façade for the real intentions of the parent movement. E.A.M. had originally been set up by, and its organization was in the hands of, the Greek Communist Party (K.K.E.), whose aims it and its forces pursued consistently and with considerable success; and within two years of E.A.M's foundation, most of the more moderate Socialist leaders ceded from it and went into opposition.

By the spring of 1942, E.A.M. had enlisted a widespread and genuine support for its resistance to the enemy; had established on that basis an efficient organization, on the orthodox system of the 'cell', throughout the country; and had eliminated most of the guerrilla bands which refused to join it. Two movements alone remained hostile and independent. The first, the conservative and republican E.K.K.A., fielded no armed force until March 1943, and thereafter survived rather than challenged the attentions of E.A.M. until March 1944, when its leader was murdered and the movement fell apart. The second organization, E.D.E.S., proved to be an altogether tougher affair. Its political fortunes were at first guided by a group of republican politicians in Athens; its military organization was in the hands of General Zervas, whose strength lay in his native province of the Epirus, where he fought both E.L.A.S. and the occupying powers with some success. As E.A.M. grew stronger, Zervas turned increasingly towards the King, and in March 1943, when he dissociated himself from the group in Athens, he declared himself a royalist. But his influence had by then been outstripped by the republican organization, and the geographical position of the Epirus limited his activities to a strategic backwater. In 1943, the Zervas part of E.D.E.S., although well-organized and active, thus could not rival E.A.M. either as an influence in the country or as a significant element of resistance to the occupying powers.

The British reappeared on the Greek scene in October 1942, when a small party, responsible to S.O.E. in Cairo, was dropped to organize the destruction of the main railway line from the north to the Piraeus, as part of the plan for interrupting supplies to the Mediterranean before the Alamein campaign. Its leader was Colonel E. C. W. Myers, its second in command Lieut.-Colonel the Hon. C. M. Woodhouse. The success of the operation led S.O.E. to keep the party in Greece as a British Military Mission, by which name it was henceforth known. Myers and Woodhouse, while relying on Zervas for the most resolute support, soon appreciated that they must also co-operate with E.L.A.S. if they were to achieve any serious result. Following the accepted pattern of S.O.E. policy, they accordingly set about the task of co-ordinating the different movements in some form of alliance. Meanwhile, the Military Mission undertook a series of operations against supplies and communications, and in June 1943, as part of the plan of deception before the invasion of Sicily, staged a comprehensive series of attacks, with help from the guerrillas other than E.L.A.S., on the railways to the north. This was a great diplomatic, as well as a military, success. For the nature of the operations convinced E.A.M., as it convinced the Germans, that the Allies contemplated an invasion of Greece, and thus inclined them more readily to fall in with the British wishes. After a period of intricate negotiation, Myers succeeded in obtaining general consent in July to a 'National Bands Agreement', providing for a common front between the guerrillas, governing their relations within and between different areas, and setting up a joint headquarters with their representatives under the British Military Mission, which in turn was to be recognized by all as the agent of the British Middle East Command. Neither of the main guerrilla opponents, nor the British Military Mission, was under any illusion about the Agreement. Nor did its conclusion entirely stop the fighting between the movements. But it served to patch up a quarrel, and temporarily to arrest internecine fighting, that seemed otherwise bound to grow; and in August 1943, when Myers was summoned to Cairo for discussion, he decided to take advantage of the recent lull by bringing with him six representatives of the now allied guerrillas for the inspection of the outside world. In that month, the Allies and the Greeks in Cairo were thus brought face to face for the first time with the principal Greeks inside Greece.

The meeting came at a dramatic moment. In March 1943, after a mutiny by the Greek forces in Egypt, the British had induced the exiled Royal Greek Government to leave London for Cairo. Once there, it was reshaped to reflect more accurately than hitherto the Socialist republicanism of so large a sector of the Greek world; and early in July, the King himself promised publicly that the Government would resign on its return to Greece, and that a free election for a Constituent Assembly would then be held within six months. These moves, combined with those in Greece itself, were promising. But on 6th July the Greek forces in the Middle East mutinied for a second time, and although they were soon brought under control by British forces, the exiled Government was naturally alarmed and its new unity endangered. Its confidence was further shaken within the next few weeks, after a report had been received from E.D.E.S. in Athens on the position inside Greece. It was into this disturbed and excited atmosphere that Myers stepped with his guerrilla leaders.

The delegates from the mountains were dominated by the contingent from E.A.M., who knew where they stood and what they wanted. In the prevalent bewilderment, they were soon able to influence events. At first, indeed, it seemed possible that they would induce the Cabinet in Cairo to prevent the King from returning to Greece until a plebiscite had been held. But as their demands grew, the exiles closed their ranks, and early in September the British were able to press for the return of the guerrillas to Greece. They finally departed in the middle of the month, leaving behind them a shaken Cabinet and an unresolved constitutional question to which a satisfactory answer now seemed remote.

The political crisis had impressed the British as well as the exiled Greeks. For while the reports of the Military Mission and of S.O.E. had told of the dominating position of E.A.M., the movement's full force and importance could be gauged only by personal experience. It was not, and never had been, part of the Allied strategy in the Mediterranean to stage operations by land in Greece. But in the middle of September, 1943 it seemed possible that the course of the campaign in Italy, combined with the effect of the Italian surrender in the Balkans and the apparent threat to the mainland from operations which the British were now conducting in the Aegean,[1] might lead the Germans to withdraw to the north of Greece, or possibly out of Greece altogether. In that event, there would almost certainly be civil war, and almost certainly E.L.A.S. would win. The British would then be faced with a Communist Government in Greece, and an exiled King in Cairo to whose support they were committed at least until he was settled in Athens. A diplomatic defeat of this nature might have serious strategic, as well as diplomatic, results. A victorious E.A.M. was unlikely to accept further supervision from an Allied Command, or to collaborate effectively with its liaison officers. Strategy in the Mediterranean (which might prove to be of the utmost importance in the spring of 1944) must then allow for this uncertainty in a significant, possibly a vital, area, and for the possibility of its extension. E.A.M's victory might, for instance, encourage ambitions in Tito which would embarrass the Western Allies; at the least it would weaken the British position throughout the Balkans and the Middle East. The British were thus led at this point, as a consequence of possible developments elsewhere, to consider unwillingly whether they should not put troops into Greece. On 12th September, the C.I.G.S. raised the issue.

> 'At present all discussions concerning the liberation of Greece and the holding of a free plebiscite are based on the assumption that an Allied Force will, sooner or later, be invading Greece, and that a large number of troops would be available to maintain law and order. While it may be expedient so to tell the Greeks, and correct to plan on this assumption, it is in fact contrary to our present strategy. Clearly if Greece is liberated as

[1] See p. 93 *et seq.* below.

a result of an Axis withdrawal, we shall be forced to provide sufficient troops to further the present policy of His Majesty's Government. This would involve us in a military commitment of at least two divisions, since a weaker force might land us in an embarrassing position vis-à-vis the resistance groups, who were by force of arms alone carrying considerable sway in the country when it had been liberated. The provision of these divisions may well prove impossible unless we are to detract from the main effort in the Central Mediterranean. In consequence it raises the question as to whether the present policy of His Majesty's Government is indeed practical, or, if there can be no reversal of policy, whether it can, in fact, be carried out without the assistance of occupying troops. I am of the opinion that this matter should be urgently considered by the Foreign Office.'

After some discussion, the Foreign Office decided that a military force must be sent to Greece if the Germans withdrew, to forestall the probable course of events. The Foreign Secretary therefore recommended that the necessary troops should be reserved for the purpose, if possible the two divisions of which the C.I.G.S. had spoken. At the end of September, the Prime Minister agreed with the Foreign Office on this 'essentially political question'.[1] But it was soon clear that he differed from other authorities on the nature of the force to be employed. In contrast to the 50,000 men for whom the Foreign Office had called, he envisaged a force of 5,000 men with armoured vehicles, organized to contend only with riots in and around Athens, and intended to stay only until those had been quelled. 'There is no question of our going there on any other condition.' The argument, however, was soon overtaken by events. Whatever its nature, the British force must enter Greece either from Italy, in shipping diverted from the Italian campaign, or from the south, through islands already occupied by the Allies. By the middle of October, neither approach was possible. Nothing could be spared from Italy, and the Aegean remained in the possession of the enemy. These events, which robbed the Allies of the initiative, enabled the Germans to stand fast. They showed no sign of withdrawing from Greece; and there was accordingly no further talk of armed intervention. From October, 1943 the British turned their efforts to the political sphere, in a series of attempts to bring the King and the exiled Government closer to the moderate elements inside Greece.

The fighting in Greece itself broke out, in limited form, even while the British were debating its probability. Throughout September, E.A.M. awaited the arrival of the Allies, when it intended to seize power. For this purpose, E.L.A.S. quickly disarmed the Italians after their surrender, retaining their equipment despite the efforts of the

[1] See *Closing the Ring*, p. 475.

British Military Mission to take charge. At the beginning of October, the moment seemed to have come. The Allies were then attacking the Aegean islands, and to the Greeks the anticipated invasion seemed about to take place. Clashes had occurred since August between the rival movements. On 8th October, E.L.A.S. attacked E.D.E.S. in strength, and within the next few days a regular campaign developed. The British at once stopped all supplies to E.L.A.S., and supported E.D.E.S. as far as they could. The B.B.C., and the Prime Minister in the House of Commons, denounced E.A.M. and its forces; and as the Germans did not withdraw, and as Zervas continued to resist with British arms and equipment, E.L.A.S. was forced to pause. After two months' fighting E.A.M. decided to shelve its plans, and in the middle of December both sides asked for the mediation of the Allied authorities. But before a truce could be arranged, Zervas launched a sudden attack on his opponents, in the hope of recovering lost ground before it was too late. Further fighting ensued, and it was not until early in February, 1944 that an armistice was signed. Throughout the late autumn of 1943 and the winter of 1943/44, there was therefore no question of the British intervening in Greece, but only in Greek affairs.

The third possible area of operations in the south-east lay in the Aegean. Of the many islands which stretch between the Greek and Turkish shores, from Samothrace and Thasos to Rhodes, Scarpanto and Crete, the Dodecanese were strategically the most important in 1943, and Rhodes was the most important island in the Dodecanese.[1] As long as they remained, with Crete, in the possession of the enemy, they protected the Aegean Sea and the approach to south-east Europe. But conversely, their capture opened the passage to the north, and the prospect of controlling a vital area. The sea and air base of Rhodes, with the sea base of Leros and the complementary air base of Cos, could dominate the sea communications round Greece, and from Greece to the north, and could provide the necessary facilities for the air bombardment of communications throughout the Balkans. The consequent pressure might indeed, at best, force the Germans to withdraw from Greece; at the least, it should contain substantial German forces which might otherwise be moved elsewhere. These results, moreover, might well be gained, when Italy surrendered, at less cost and with fewer disadvantages than any significant result on the mainland. At the beginning of September 1943, the enemy had one German and one Italian division in Crete, and one German and two Italian divisions scattered throughout the Aegean islands and in Rhodes. Provided, therefore, that the Italian garrisons followed the lead of their Government, the German force in the Dodecanese should offer little

[1] See Inset to Map II, facing p. 57.

serious danger to an assault from the Middle East; while there were no diplomatic implications such as had to be considered in Greece or Yugoslavia. As an element in the immediate strategy, the capture of the Dodecanese had much to commend it. But it had another, and potentially greater, significance. It might bring Turkey into the war.

Such a prospect was not to be ignored. It would at once place at the Allies' disposal a group of air bases from which to bomb Greece, Rumania and Bulgaria while the air forces from Italy bombed Hungary, Austria and southern Germany. It would also bring an estimated forty-six Turkish divisions into the reckoning, although these must depend on the Allies for much of their equipment. It would transfer to Allied control the passage of the Dardanelles and Bosphorus, whose neutrality, governed by the terms of the Montreux Convention, then inevitably favoured the Germans; thus depriving the enemy in Greece of supplies from Rumania and the Danube valley, and, if the Russian campaign prospered, enabling British and American supplies to be carried in bulk to southern Russia (as they could not be carried by the existing route through Persia), instead of to the Arctic by the expensive northern convoys. Finally, the Turkish alliance would further upset the Germans' delicate balance of forces throughout Europe, threatening them with a new and formidable campaign on their most sensitive flank. The capture of the Dodecanese might indeed appear to them as the prelude to a revivified 'Dardanelles'.

By September 1943, the nature of the connexion between the Aegean and Turkey had been defined with some precision. For the possibility of Turkey's entry into the war was by no means new, and had been studied seriously in London and Ankara since January. The supply of equipment and technicians, which had been under way on a modest scale since before the war, now continued at a faster rate. From January to May 1943, some £16,000,000 worth of equipment, other than petrol, was carried to Turkey from the Middle East; and the traffic continued thereafter on a comparable scale. These supplies formed the background to a more ambitious series of negotiations. From the end of January, when the Prime Minister and the C.I.G.S. visited Turkey, the Turks were aware that the Allies might later ask them to enter the war; and when the campaign in North Africa drew to a close, and new and varied possibilities opened in the Mediterranean, the critical moment seemed to approach. In the middle of April, the British Ambassador informed the Turkish Prime Minister that 'a day would come when I should most certainly come to him and say that by joining us he could assist greatly in shortening the war. That day would probably not be till September, it might be later—but it would come.'

The British, indeed, had already prepared their plans for this contingency, and in the middle of April, 1943 the Commanders-in-Chief,

Middle East discussed them in detail with the Turks at Ankara. In the event of Turkey entering the war, British support would be given in four separate phases, each of the last three phases following directly on the completion of its predecessor.

First Phase: The provision of twenty-five R.A.F. squadrons, mainly fighters, with A.A. artillery to protect the airfields. The provision of three anti-tank regiments.

Second Phase: The provision of a further twenty-five R.A.F. squadrons, with the necessary A.A. artillery for the defence of their airfields.

Third Phase: The provision of two heavy A.A. regiments, two light A.A. regiments, and a further two anti-tank regiments.

Fourth Phase: The provision of two armoured divisions.

The whole plan was known by the name of 'Hardihood'.

The connexion with the Aegean was clear at this stage. In the words of General Sir Henry Maitland Wilson, the Commander-in-Chief of the land forces in the Middle East, 'it was the opinion of the British Staff that these two [armoured] Divisions could not be maintained in Turkey until the port of Izmir [Smyrna] had been opened. It was, therefore, essential to open the Aegean.' For this purpose, the British and the Turks discussed plans for capturing Rhodes, Cos and some of the neighbouring islands.

The British Ambassador's forecast proved to be correct, though not in the circumstances nor at the date that had been envisaged. This had seemed unlikely in the summer of 1943. For the Turks, who had appeared complaisant in the spring, in June and July were more reluctant to favour the British. Events, indeed, were not going as they had hoped. Turkish foreign policy, which the British had long supported, rested on the maintenance of a balance of power in eastern Europe. It therefore favoured the traditional type of negotiated peace, which would diminish Germany's influence before Russia's influence could be unduly exalted. Such an outcome seemed possible early in 1943, and it then behoved a prudent Turkey so to arrange her affairs that she was present as a victor at the peace table. But the subsequent Allied successes seemed increasingly likely to sustain the revolutionary policy of 'unconditional surrender' which had been announced at Casablanca, and the consequent disappearance of a balance in eastern Europe. The Turks, afraid of an undisputed Russian domination of the Balkans, now shrank from an undue loss of strength in a war whose objects they by no means wholeheartedly approved; while the British, thanks to the same developments, were less certain that they could spare the forces for a Turkish alliance. As the plans for Italy developed during August, the Joint Planning Staff reported that phase I of 'Hardihood' could not be carried out without a withdrawal of troops then employed in the central Mediterranean, while the execution of phase II would involve the withdrawal of aircraft soon to be used in 'Pointblank'. At the same time, the Middle East Command was asked to keep all but one of its operational divisions in reserve for the Mediterranean Command. The Chiefs of Staff accordingly concluded in the middle of August that Turkey should not be asked as yet to join the Allies, but should be pressed instead to adjust her neutrality in certain respects which would favour their immediate interests. The Prime Minister readily agreed to this more modest demand, and the Allied Governments accordingly stated at Quebec that the time was not ripe for Turkey to enter the war on their side, and that she should meanwhile be asked only to interpret the Montreux Convention more strictly, to stop supplies of chrome to Germany, and to allow the British to make the first preparations for 'Hardihood'. Meanwhile, the Allies would 'continue to supply such equipment as we can spare and as the Turks can absorb.'

One of the contributory arguments advanced by the Planners for Turkey's continued neutrality, was that the state of the resources in the Middle East would no longer allow of operations against the Dodecanese, as a necessary preliminary to phase IV of 'Hardihood'. The possibility of such operations had been studied since the end of July 1943, when Italy seemed likely soon to surrender. The connexion with Turkey was stressed from their first mention, when the Prime Minister raised the subject on the 27th.

> 'I suppose that the Planners are all keyed up with plans for taking over Rhodes on the assumption that the Italians ask for an Armistice.
>
> What is the composition of the garrison of Rhodes, German and Italian? We ought to get there quite quickly if it is humanly possible, as I need this place as part of the diplomatic approach to Turkey.'

On 1st August, General Wilson independently suggested the same operation, but stressed the need for an early decision if the Germans were to be forestalled.

The state of the resources lent weight to Wilson's concern. For thanks to their recent orders, the commanders in the Middle East now disposed only of one fully equipped active division, with a few landing ships and craft; while of their eight L.S.T., five were held in the Middle East temporarily and were intended for the Indian Ocean. The need for a quick decision, however, only stimulated the Prime Minister. 'Here', he remarked at once,[1] 'is a business of great consequence to be thrust forward by every means.' He asked that all supplies to Turkey should be stopped at once 'for the emergency', and the ships held instead for operations in the Aegean; and that assault groups should be prepared, based if necessary on formations other than divisions. The Chiefs of Staff agreed that the prize was worth the

---

[1] See *Closing the Ring*, p. 181.

risk. They accordingly instructed the Middle East to hold the landing ships destined for India until further notice, to stop supplies to Turkey, and to ask General Eisenhower (subject, as they took care at once to explain, to the existing order of priorities) for such assault shipping as might be needed and as he could spare from the main operations. The commanders in the theatre thereupon composed a plan for the capture of Rhodes on Italy's surrender ('Accolade'), using one infantry brigade and one armoured regiment, with a parachute battalion and two Special Service squadrons. This involved the loan from the Mediterranean Command of two L.S.T. and six storeships, four squadrons of long-range fighters and some transport aircraft, and one parachute battalion and the two Special Service squadrons. Eisenhower agreed to supply the troops; but in the uncertain situation then prevailing in Italy, and with the plans for Salerno under way, he felt himself unable to release the ships or aircraft. The plan had accordingly to be modified on the assumption that the Italians in Rhodes would co-operate to the full; and while the preparations went forward, the commanders now felt less confidence in the outcome. By the end of August, however, their hopes had been entirely removed. On the 21st, the Combined Chiefs of Staff at Quebec ordered the five landing ships held temporarily in the Middle East, plus a headquarters ship and three cargo ships, to leave at once for south-east Asia, where new and more ambitious operations had just been approved. On the 26th, the one operational division was put under orders for the central Mediterranean;[1] and on the 31st the commanders in the Middle East accordingly informed the Chiefs of Staff that any variant of 'Accolade' was now impossible, and that operations must be confined to raids on a small scale, sabotage by S.O.E. in the Balkans, and, if conditions offered and ships were available locally at the time, an unopposed entry into Rhodes and Crete.

Such was the position when the Italian surrender was broadcast on 8th September. The occupation of the Dodecanese could now be achieved only by bold action and bluff. But it was not unreasonable in the circumstances to hope that this might meet the case. The commanders in the Middle East therefore informed the Chiefs of Staff on the 7th that they intended to send small Special forces to Castel Rosso and Rhodes, as soon as Italy surrendered, to persuade the Italians to disarm the Germans. Meanwhile, they would prepare a force of one tank battalion with supporting troops, and two squadrons of fighters, to follow a successful issue in Rhodes, and such small parties as they could spare for other islands. 'We can see', they added, 'no further way to assist or exploit surrender in our area.'

These landings of course were a gamble, and unless Rhodes could be occupied, a risk. But there was much to gain, and the British Chiefs

[1] See pp. 66, 91 above.

of Staff, with the Americans' concurrence, at once sanctioned the plans. The Prime Minister added his own flavour to the decision in a telegram to Wilson on the 13th.[1]

> 'The capture of Rhodes by you at this time with Italian aid would be a fine contribution to the general war. Let me know what are your plans for this . . . This is a time to think of Clive and Peterborough and of Rooke's men taking Gibraltar.'

But the Germans had in fact already forestalled the move. At the end of August, when considering more urgently the measures to be taken in the event of an Italian surrender, the High Command had been unable to decide whether or not to evacuate the Dodecanese. But the uncertainty was caused by the danger of their isolation rather than by any lack of appreciation of their value. Hitler himself, indeed, seems to have regarded operations in the Aegean at this time in much the same light as Churchill, as a dangerous threat to the mainland and as a powerful inducement to Turkey to join the Allies. He was accordingly inclined to favour holding Rhodes, the key to the position. Military opinion eventually supported him, although partly because evacuation seemed in any case impossible in the face of British sea power; and on 9th September, the German division in Rhodes was ordered to resist all attacks, from whatever quarter. That night, a small British party was dropped on the island, and made contact the next morning with the Italian authorities. Throughout the 10th, the latter considered the advantages of joining the Allies; but meanwhile the Germans were preparing their measures, and on the 12th, after a short and stubborn fight, the Italians found themselves deprived of control. The British party, no longer able to influence events, quickly withdrew, and by the 13th Rhodes was entirely in German hands.

Despite this grave disappointment, the British concentrated as fast as possible in the islands to the north. A small party landed in Cos, and another in Leros, on the night of 13th/14th September, a third party was put into Samos on the 14th, and others landed in Lissos, Patmos, Furni and Icara. The British garrisons in Cos and Leros, and in Castel Rosso, were then reinforced as far as resources allowed. By the 17th, a force of 250 men had been put into Castel Rosso, a force of 400 men and eight fighter aircraft into Cos, and a force of 400 men into Leros. Cos and Leros were to be further reinforced, the first to a target of 2,100, the second to a target of 1,100 men. All reinforcements were to be carried in destroyers, using Turkish territorial waters for the purpose.

The eventual fate of these islands, however, must depend on the fate of Rhodes; and as soon as they were secured, the British returned to the problem of its capture. In the third week of September, the Middle East Command composed a new plan for an assault on the

[1] See *Closing the Ring*, p. 101.

island in the second half of October. The forces were even now comparatively light: at least four long-range fighter squadrons, small airborne formations, one division (to be found from the holding forces and reserve in the Middle East) and a part of one armoured brigade, to be carried and sustained by three landing ships, some landing craft, and ten cargo ships of various types. Some of the land and air forces, and almost all of the shipping, must come, as before, from the central Mediterranean. The British accordingly informed the Americans of the new plan, and asked them to agree that the Mediterranean Command should if possible supply the deficit. The Prime Minister took care again to stress the limited nature of the demands. On 25th September, he telegraphed to General Eisenhower:[1]

> '(1) As I have been pressing for action in several directions, I feel I ought to place before you the priorities which I assign in my own mind to these several desirable objectives:
>
> (2) Four-fifths of our effort should be the build-up in Italy. One-tenth should be our making sure of Corsica (which will soon finish) and in the Adriatic. The remaining tenth should be concentrated on Rhodes. This, of course, applies to the limiting factors only. These, I presume, are mainly landing-craft and assault-shipping with naval craft.
>
> (3) I send this as a rough guide to my thoughts only because I do not want you to feel I am pressing for everything in all directions without understanding how grim are your limitations.'

On the 26th, Eisenhower agreed to spare the armoured brigade and most of the shipping, with a group of troop-carrier aircraft for the small supporting formations. The commanders in the Middle East thereupon decided to stage the attack (still known as 'Accolade')[2] on 23rd October.

An essential part of the revised plan lay in the retention of Cos and Leros, which were now as necessary to the capture of Rhodes as its capture was necessary to their preservation. But while 'Accolade' was being considered, the Germans launched an assault on Cos, as the first of a series designed to expel the British garrisons. It began on 3rd October: the island fell on the 4th. The British now expected an attack on Leros, whose defence was correspondingly more important than before. Reinforcements were put in as fast as possible: naval units and long-range fighters were sent from the central Mediterranean, and air and sea patrols were organized to the north of Rhodes. But with the loss of the one island, and the threat to the other, the British feared that the troops already assigned to 'Accolade' would not prove strong enough for the purpose. On 7th October, the Prime Minister raised the matter with the President, in a series of telegrams

[1] See *Closing the Ring*, p. 134.

[2] See p. 92 above.

which stated clearly and precisely the British object in the Aegean, and its relation to the main operations.[1]

'1. I am much concerned about the situation developing in the Eastern Mediterranean. On the collapse of Italy we pushed small detachments from Egypt into several of the Greek islands, especially Cos, which has a landing ground, and Leros, which is a fortified Italian naval base with powerful permanent batteries. We then risked it in the hope that the Italian garrison which welcomed us would take part in the defence. This hope appears vain and Cos has already fallen except for some of our troops fighting in the mountains. Leros may well share its fate. Our enterprises against Rhodes have not yet proceeded.

2. I believe it will be found that the Italian and Balkan peninsulas are militarily and politically united and that really it is one theatre with which we have to deal. It may, indeed, not be possible to conduct a successful Italian campaign, ignoring what happens in the Aegean. The Germans evidently attach the utmost importance to this eastern sphere and have not hesitated to divert a large part of their straitened air force to maintain themselves there. They have to apprehend desertion by Hungary and Rumania and a violent schism in Bulgaria. At any moment Turkey may lean her weight against them. We can all see how adverse to the enemy are the conditions in Greece and Yugoslavia. When we remember what brilliant results have followed from the political reactions in Italy induced by our military efforts, should we not be short-sighted to ignore the possibility of a similar and even greater landslide in some or all of the countries I have mentioned? If we were able to provoke such reactions and profit by them our joint tasks in Italy would be greatly lightened.

3. I have never wished to send an army into the Balkans, but only by agents, supplies and commandos to stimulate the intense guerrilla prevailing there. This may yield results measureless in their consequence at very small cost to main operations. What I ask for is the capture of Rhodes and the other islands of the Dodecanese. The movement northward of our Middle East Air Forces and their establishment in these islands, and possibly on the Turkish shore, which last might well be obtained, would force a diversion on the enemy far greater than that required of us. It would also offer the opportunity of engaging the enemy's waning air power and wearing it down in a new region. This air power is all one, and the more continually it can be fought the better.

4. Rhodes is the key to all this. I do not feel the present plan of taking it is good enough. It will require and is worth at least up to a first-class division, which can, of course, be replaced by static troops once the place is ours. Leros, which for the moment

[1] See *Closing the Ring*, pp. 186-8.

we hold so precariously, is an important naval fortress, and once we are ensconced in this area air and light naval forces would have a most fruitful part to play. The policy should certainly not be pursued unless done with vigour and celerity requiring the best troops and adequate means. In this way the diversions from the main theatre would only be temporary, while the results may well be of profound and lasting importance.

5. I beg you to consider this and not let it be brushed aside and all these possibilities lost to us in the critical months that lie ahead. Even if landing craft and assault ships on the scale of a division were withheld from build-up of 'Overlord' for a few weeks without altering the zero date it would be worthwhile. I feel that we may easily throw away an immense but fleeting opportunity. If you think well, would you very kindly let General Marshall see this telegram before any decision is taken by the Combined Chiefs of Staff.'

The President answered on the 8th.

'. . . I do not want to force on Eisenhower diversions which limit the prospects for the early successful development of the Italian operations to a secure line north of Rome.

I am opposed to any diversion which will in Eisenhower's opinion jeopardise the security of his current situation in Italy, the build-up of which is exceedingly slow considering the well-known characteristics of his opponents, who enjoy a marked superiority in ground troops and Panzer divisions.

It is my opinion that no diversion of forces or equipment should prejudice 'Overlord' as planned.

The American Chiefs of Staff agree.

I am transmitting a copy of this message to Eisenhower.'

This did not satisfy the Prime Minister. He replied later on the same day:[1]

'I earnestly pray that my views may receive some consideration from you at this critical juncture, remembering how fruitful our concerted action has been in the past and how important it is for the future.

2. I am sure that the omission to take Rhodes at this stage and the ignoring of the whole position in the Eastern Mediterranean would constitute a cardinal error in strategy. I am convinced also that if we were round the table together this operation could be fitted into our plan without detriment either to the advance in Italy, of which, as you know, I have always been an advocate, or to the build-up of 'Overlord', which I am prepared faithfully to support.

3. . . . We know that the enemy is withdrawing to the north [in Italy] fighting rearguard actions and carrying off booty; we

[1] See *loc. cit.*, p. 189.

cannot yet tell whether it is in October or November that we can occupy Rome; but it is certain that we shall not come in contact with the main German forces at the top of the leg till December, or even later, and we certainly have control of the rate of advance.

4. There is therefore plenty of time to produce a division for the conquest of Rhodes and restore it to the battle-front in Italy before we reach the German fortified line.

5. We must find some means of resolving these difficulties and making sure of what is the right thing to do. I am willing to proceed to Eisenhower's Headquarters with the British Chiefs of Staff immediately, if you will send General Marshall, or your personal representative, to meet me there, and we can then submit the results of a searching discussion to you and your Chiefs of Staff. We can be there Sunday afternoon [10th October].'

Knowing the effect which the mention of 'Overlord' would have in Washington, he sent a further note the same evening:[1]

'I should have added that my estimate of the effect on 'Overlord' to which I referred is limited to a delay of about six weeks in sending home nine landing-craft which were to have started from the Mediterranean this month, nearly six months before they would actually be needed for 'Overlord'. There ought, I think, to be some elasticity and a reasonable latitude in the handling of our joint affairs.

2. The Quebec decision to send four landing-ships with the craft they carry from the Eastern Mediterranean to the Bay of Bengal also for training purposes has turned out ill. This decision should have been reviewed in the light of the new circumstances opened by the surrender of Italy. Unhappily this was not done, and in consequence the Middle East was stripped bare at a moment when great prizes could be cheaply secured.'

The President, however, remained unconvinced.

'I have received your [two telegrams of the 8th] and given personal consideration to the points you make. I have given careful thought to them and so has the Staff. I am concerned about the possibility of our armies suffering a reverse by the action of an enemy with superior forces except by air, under a commander of proved audacity and resourcefulness. This applies especially to the absolute safety of the line we hoped to gain in Italy.

With a full understanding of your difficulties in Eastern Mediterranean, my thought . . . was that no diversion of force from Italy should be made that would jeopardise the security of

---

[1] See *loc. cit.*, pp. 189-90.

the allied armies in Italy, and that no action toward any minor objective should prejudice the success of 'Overlord'.

We have almost all the facts now at our disposal on which to judge the commitments probably involved in the Rhodes operation. As I see it, it is not merely the capture of Rhodes but it must mean of necessity and it must be apparent to the Germans, that we intend to go further. Otherwise Rhodes will be under the guns of both Cos and Crete.

I was in accord with obtaining whatever hold we could in the Dodecanese without heavy commitments, but the present picture involves not only a well-organised, determined operation, but a necessary follow-through. This in turn involves the necessity of drawing for means, largely shipping and air, not ground troops, from some other source which inevitably must be Italy, 'Overlord', or possibly Mountbatten's amphibious operation. The problem then is are we to enter into a Balkan campaign starting with the southern tip, or is there more to be gained, and with security, by pushing rapidly to the agreed upon position north of Rome. It appears to me that a greater Allied threat against the Balkans is implied in this than by a necessarily precarious amphibious operation against Rhodes with a lack evident to the enemy of the necessary means for the follow-through. Strategically, if we get the Aegean Islands, I ask myself where do we go from there and *vice versa*, where would the Germans go if for sometime they retained possession of the islands?

As to the meeting you propose for Sunday in Africa, this would be in effect another meeting of the Combined Chiefs of Staff necessarily only involving a partial representation and in which I cannot participate. Frankly I am not in sympathy with this procedure under the circumstances. It seems to me that the issue under discussion can best be adjusted by us through our C.C.S. set-up in better perspective than by the method you propose. We have most of the facts and will soon have the results of the Conference scheduled for tomorrow in Tunis.'

Churchill had now to bow to this decision, which he viewed with open reluctance.

The conference on 9th October, which Roosevelt had mentioned, was attended by all interested parties, except for Churchill himself: by the First Sea Lord from London, by Eisenhower and his three British commanders in the Mediterranean, and by the commanders in the Middle East. Eisenhower informed the Prime Minister of the result on the same evening.

'1. All present fully agreed with your conclusions as to great advantages to be attained by successful 'Accolade' and resources were examined in earnest effort to accomplish it. We sincerely regret that current situation in Italy, aggravated by drastic changes of the last forty-eight hours of which you are fully aware,[1] does not permit, at this moment, diversion necessary to successful 'Accolade'.

2. Every conclusion submitted in our report to C.C.S. was agreed unanimously by all Commanders-in-Chief from both theatres. It is personally distressing to me to have to advise against a project in which you believe so earnestly but I feel I would not be performing my duty if I should recommend otherwise. All Commanders-in-Chief share this attitude.'

The Prime Minister was bitterly disappointed by this result. At first, indeed, unconvinced by the sudden intelligence from Italy, he was disposed to press his argument further. But as Eisenhower's message was followed by others, from the First Sea Lord, from Alexander and from Wilson, he was forced to recognize that all agreed, and that he alone, without Roosevelt's support, could not hope to sway the decision. This fact was moreover confirmed by a visit which Mr. Eden paid to the Middle East a few days later *en route* for a conference with his American and Russian colleagues in Moscow. The British accordingly turned to consider what was now a dangerous and discouraging situation. With no immediate prospect of capturing Rhodes, but with every sign that the enemy would contest the other islands, they faced a difficult and possibly an expensive task with strictly limited resources. On the other hand, their garrisons had not yet been attacked, the operations might extend the Germans as well as themselves, and until the issue was decided some at least of the original advantages remained. Even a handful of small and scattered bases could support a programme of raids, gun-running and intelligence which the enemy might find it difficult either to ignore or suppress. Indeed, his very sensitiveness to attack, which had provided the difficulties, provided the incentive. All British authorities therefore agreed that if possible the northern islands should be held. The local commanders did not hesitate; the Chiefs of Staff supported them; and the Prime Minister agreed with both. On 10th October he telegraphed to Wilson, on hearing that he intended to fight for Leros:[2]

'. . . Cling on if you possibly can. It will be a splendid achievement. Talk it over with Eden and see what help you can get from the Turk. If after everything has been done you are forced to quit, I will support you, but victory is the prize.'

This support involved the acceptance of a new factor, which Mr. Churchill recognized in his message. For it was now generally appreciated that the islands could scarcely be held without the active assistance of the Turks. 'We came to the conclusion', Wilson informed the

---

[1] See p. 68 above.

[2] See *Closing the Ring*, p. 193.

Prime Minister on the 10th, 'that the holding of Leros and Samos is not impossible, although their maintenance is going to be difficult and will depend on continued Turkish co-operation. . . . Must stress . . . that goodwill of Turkey must be bolstered up by every possible means . . .' The Turks had indeed already given valuable help. They did not challenge British warships proceeding through their waters, and throughout September ferried supplies to the garrison on Samos. The commanders in the Middle East now wished them, as a first step, to extend their services by carrying supplies from Samos to Leros, and to agree to receive and pass on British troops who might later be forced to leave the islands.

By the end of October, however, these demands had grown. Despite continuous operations by air forces from both the Middle East and Italy, the constant patrols and supply of the islands were taking a heavy toll of ships. From 9th September to the end of October, five destroyers and two submarines were lost and four cruisers and two destroyers damaged. These losses could no longer be accepted, particularly as sterner fighting presumably lay ahead. But the necessary air support could never be effective from bases so far removed from the scene of operations; and on 29th October, the Chiefs of Staff informed the Prime Minister that either Leros must be reinforced and sustained entirely by submarine, or some six squadrons of fighters must be operated from landing strips in south-west Anatolia within the next three weeks. This second course might lead to some hard bargaining with the Turks; they therefore suggested that if possible the Russians should be associated with the British request. It was in these unforeseen circumstances that the British now made their promised request for assistance to the Turks. Whereas the capture of the Dodecanese had originally been designed to precede action by Turkey, action by Turkey was now required to secure possession of the Dodecanese.

The Chiefs of Staff's suggestion that the Russians should be approached was apposite and timely. For on 19th October a meeting of the three Allied Foreign Ministers had begun in Moscow, at which policy towards Turkey was discussed. The British attitude was that of August, as modified by events in the Aegean: to bring Turkey into the war as soon as other commitments allowed, and meanwhile to persuade her to grant the military facilities that were needed at once. The Russians went further. Calculating that a belligerent Turkey would contain some ten German divisions, they wished her to declare war on Germany by the end of the year. The Americans, on the other hand, fully aware of the diversion of resources which might follow such a step, preferred Turkey to remain neutral, and meanwhile to lease the necessary airfields and communications to the British provided that she made no excessive demands for material in return. While the three

Governments thus disagreed, the difference between the British and the Russians was a tactical difference, which might moreover be solved if they presented a bold front in common. Mr. Eden therefore consented to the Russians' demands the better to sustain his own, and on 2nd November the two Foreign Ministers signed the following protocol.

> '1. The two Foreign Secretaries think it most desirable that Turkey should enter the war on the side of the United Nations before the end of 1943 in order that she may take her part with the United Nations in hastening the defeat of Hitlerite Germany in which Turkey and other freedom-loving states are interested.
>
> 2. The two Foreign Secretaries agree that it should be suggested to Turkey on behalf of the United Kingdom and Soviet Governments at the earliest possible date to be agreed upon between them that she should enter the war before the end of 1943.
>
> 3. The two Foreign Secretaries agree that Turkey should immediately be asked to give all possible aid to the United Nations by placing facilities at Turkish air bases at the disposal of the Allied Forces and providing such other facilities as the two Governments may be agreed upon are desirable.'

The Americans were not associated with this statement. On 5th November, the President informed the Prime Minister that his Government agreed to its terms, provided that no British or American resources were committed to the eastern Mediterranean which in the opinion of the responsible commanders were necessary for 'Overlord' or for operations in Italy. At the British suggestion, he later consented to substitute the Combined Chiefs of Staff for the responsible commanders, and the memorandum was then presented in this form to the British and the Russians.

The Turks agreed at the beginning of November to meet the Allied representatives in Cairo, and on the 4th Mr. Eden left Moscow to represent the three Powers. The talks began on the 5th, the Turks being represented by their Foreign Minister, M. Numan, the Secretary-General, M. Acikalin, and the Secretary to the Foreign Minister, M. T. Menemençoğlu. They continued until the 8th. While the Turks were sympathetic to the Allies' demands, they were naturally cautious of committing themselves without military and diplomatic guarantees. They feared immediate German reprisals on their western territories, and subsequent Russian ambitions in south-east Europe; and accordingly demanded adequate military protection from the first danger, and adequate diplomatic support to limit the second. The diplomatic deterrent, however, was for the moment less serious than the military. For while the Turks appreciated the advantages that might result from joining the Allies, they were determined not to do so unless they could be reasonably sure of immunity from a German attack. This fear of the Germans' reaction extended to the immediate as well as to the further Allied request; and M. Numan made it perfectly clear that he could not cede the air bases in Anatolia without the same guarantees of British protection as would be provided if Turkey declared war. On the evidence at their disposal, the British thought these fears greatly exaggerated. The Germans, in their view, could spare neither aircraft nor troops for a further campaign, and even if (as the British thought unlikely) they declared war on Turkey before Turkey declared war on Germany, they would be unable to inflict serious damage on her western territories. The British delegation was therefore not prepared to promise any stage of 'Hardihood'[1] in return for the use of the air bases in Anatolia. Neither side would move from its position; and on 7th November the Turks finally stated that their 'refusal for the bases was definite'. They added, however, that they would consider further the Allies' larger proposal.

Negotiations proceeded accordingly in Ankara during November. But despite continuous changes of emphasis, the position remained essentially the same. The Turks insisted, and the British denied, that Germany was strong enough to attack in force as soon as they entered the war. The Turks accordingly demanded a force of forty R.A.F. squadrons in Turkey when war was declared: the British offered seventeen squadrons and thirty A.A. batteries. While the Turks accepted on 15th November the principle of 'co-belligerency', it proved impossible for the protagonists to compromise on these requirements sufficiently to decide on any course of action. By the third week in the month, neither side had moved.

By that time, the lack of air bases in Turkey had had its effect on the operations in the Aegean. On 12th November, after several changes of plan, and one false start which was thought to have cost them some 550 men drowned by British naval patrols, the Germans' long-awaited attack on Leros began. By then, the navy had reinforced the garrison by three British infantry battalions, while the artillery remained in the hands of the Italians. The attacking force consisted of one German combat group, of some 4,000 men. Severe fighting ensued. Destroyers managed to reinforce the island with the equivalent of another battalion from Samos, and spasmodically to interrupt German supplies. But the enemy's control of the air enabled him to bomb the garrison continuously, and to drop airborne troops; and Leros fell on the evening of the 16th. Of the 5,000 British on the island, some 2,000 were casualties and many more were taken prisoner. The Germans lost 1,100 men. The garrisons on the other islands were now entirely cut off. On 10th November, the Germans occupied Lissos, Patmos, Furni and Icara, and Samos was evacuated three days later. The garrison on

[1] See p. 90 above.

Castel Rosso withdrew on the 27th. Some 1,000 men were saved in all from the different garrisons, at the cost of one destroyer sunk and another two damaged.

In the third week of November, the gamble seemed therefore to have failed. The Turks, while sympathetic, were clearly unwilling to enter the war without complete military, and possibly diplomatic, security; the Aegean was again in German hands; and the Americans had shown themselves opposed to any diversion of forces to the area. These difficulties, which might have deterred the local commanders and the Chiefs of Staff, stimulated the Prime Minister. In his view, while much had so far gone wrong, neither the case for operations in the Aegean, nor the possibility of their success, had finally disappeared. The negotiations with Turkey were still open; and the small resources necessary for the Aegean might still, though not immediately, be found. The more he considered the larger scene, the more indeed Mr. Churchill favoured these operations. Once Rome fell in the New Year, the stalemate in Italy might end; but there were still no plans for that contingency outside the peninsula itself. Meanwhile the enemy was disengaged elsewhere, and large Allied forces were locked in the central Mediterranean. If the Aegean went by default, we might lose the initiative throughout the theatre in the vital months before 'Overlord' was launched. Five days after Leros fell, he therefore returned to the subject of Rhodes.[1]

> 'The centre point of my thought is the capture of Rome at the beginning of January and the capture of Rhodes at the end. The former is already provided for. For the latter two requisites are necessary:
>
> First, a declaration of war by Turkey and the use of the Turkish bases;
>
> Second, a good British Division to be landed at the first wave, to be backed up and followed by [an] Indian as the second wave. Landing ships and craft will be required therefore on the scale of a Division. These divisions need not be fully equipped with transport, etc., on account of the small distances over which they have to operate and the fact that the 8,000 Germans will be pinned down to key points. How much landing craft will be needed? Where can it be obtained? . . .'

These questions set the stage for further discussion between the Allies.

This discussion turned on resources, and particularly on the essential assault shipping. Before we can proceed to it, we must therefore consider the last possibility in the Mediterranean, whose demands in the event were to complicate the argument.

[1] See *Closing the Ring*, pp. 598-9.

We have already seen that operations against southern France were not contemplated as taking place until 'Overlord' itself was about to be launched.[1] At that stage, however, they might play a significant part in the design. Operations elswehere in the Mediterranean could contain German divisions which might otherwise reinforce those in France; but the divisions already in central and southern France must themselves be contained, if they were not to reinforce those in the north. The Combined Chiefs of Staff accordingly decided at Quebec that:

> 'Offensive operations against southern France (to include the use of trained and equipped French forces) should be undertaken to establish a lodgment in the Toulon and Marseilles area to exploit northward in order to create a diversion in connection with 'Overlord'. Air nourished guerrilla operations in the Southern Alps will, if possible, be initiated.'

On 24th August, they asked General Eisenhower to submit an outline plan for such operations by 1st November, using the resources in the Mediterranean of which he had already been informed.

Eisenhower's report appeared on 27th October. In contrast to his later attitude, it was cautious and not entirely favourable. He began by reviewing the 'strategic consideration'. The projected assault was only a small part of the comprehensive scheme by which the necessary conditions for 'Overlord' would be produced by May, 1944. It could not be considered in isolation from plans for the rest of the Mediterranean, for the Germans could always transfer forces from one part of the coastline to another unless they were engaged or threatened effectively. But these plans were themselves still uncertain, and until they developed further the effect of a threat to, or an assault on, southern France could scarcely be measured exactly. Either might in fact produce the opposite effect to what was intended, leading the Germans to reinforce generally in France instead of diverting strength from northern France.

Eisenhower then turned to the conditions for an assault, which seemed to him likely to depend on the state of affairs in Italy. If the Allies stood on or south of a line Pisa-Rimini at the time the operation was to take place, it would have to be launched and maintained by sea. If however they had gained possession of the Lombard plain, it might be launched and maintained partly by sea and partly by land. The strength of the Allied assault shipping in the Mediterranean made it unlikely that an attack by sea could be launched with more than one division, followed immediately by two brigade groups; and reinforcement would be slow unless an adequate port could be seized and worked at the outset. Eisenhower therefore proposed that the Combined Chiefs of Staff should approve preparations for alternatives: if

[1] See p. 60 above.

the Allies had gained the Lombard plain, for an attack on southern France; if not, for a threat to that area. In either case, the measures should not be applied before the period immediately surrounding 'Overlord', so that the enemy did not concentrate too much strength too soon, which could be transferred to northern France in the early days of the main invasion.

This report, which was shown to Cossac,[1] did not meet with his unqualified approval. In his view, Eisenhower was confusing two separate tasks: first, to contain enough German divisions outside France for the enemy to have only a limited mobile reserve in that country for two months after 'Overlord' was launched;[2] secondly, to contain in the south of France a part—as he estimated, two divisions—of that reserve on the day that 'Overlord' was launched. These tasks were complementary, and Eisenhower's help was necessary to both. Cossac therefore submitted, as did Eisenhower, that the maintenance of an effective threat to the south of France, whether by deception or attack, should be accepted forthwith as an essential part of the 'Overlord' design; but, unlike Eisenhower, he doubted if deception alone would in fact suffice.

Cossac's comments appeared on 3rd November. The British Joint Planning Staff was inclined to accept his arguments, although it did not wish to prejudge the issue. It recommended therefore that Eisenhower should submit operational plans as soon as possible for each of his alternatives; and after a brief correspondence, the Combined Chiefs of Staff informed him on 12th November that they approved his report as a basis for further planning.

(iv)

The British and American Strategies

As the British surveyed the Mediterranean scene throughout this period, from early in September to the third week in November, they were driven to conclude that it could be neither appraised nor exploited adequately within the context of the strategy approved at Quebec. The precise effects of the Italian surrender, in the different areas within the theatre, could not then have been foreseen; but the decisions that had then been taken now seemed, in their combination, irrelevant to changing conditions. As the Germans managed to

---

[1] See p. 22 above.

[2] See p. 57 above.

stabilize their fronts, in Italy, in the Balkans and in the Aegean, the British chafed increasingly at the limitations to which they were subjected.

As early as 9th September, on the day after Italy surrendered publicly, the Prime Minister raised with the President the new possibilities in the south. On the assumption that Naples and Rome would soon be taken, he inquired what was then to be done. In his view, the Allies should proceed to the presumed main German line south of the Lombard plain, where they should stand and themselves construct defensive positions. Thereafter, they should use the air power from central Italy to the fullest extent as part of 'Pointblank', and should nourish the guerrillas throughout the Balkans, possibly through one or more captured ports on the Dalmatian coast. 'When the defensive line across Northern Italy has been completed, it may be possible to spare some of our own forces assigned to the Mediterranean theatre to emphasise a movement North and North-Eastward from the Dalmatian ports.'[1] Sardinia and Corsica should also be captured, and the implications of a favourable move by Turkey should be studied by the two Governments. These general suggestions were of course soon overtaken by events; but they showed a desire to take advantage of an uncertain situation which must be reconciled with decisions taken before that situation had arisen.

But the British ideas were not expressed openly during September. It was indeed only when the initial fluid situation had disappeared, owing partly, as they argued, to the limitations imposed by the 'Quadrant' strategy, that the authorities in London protested against that strategy, and proposed an alternative which by then could be more precise. The process began in the middle of October. On the 14th, the Chiefs of Staff informed the Prime Minister that they were suffering from 'a feeling of uneasiness . . . that the rigidity imposed by the 'Quadrant' decisions on our military dispositions is hampering the proper exploitation of our successes in the Mediterranean'. On the 19th, the Prime Minister accordingly asked them to embark on a study of the situation in that theatre, with particular reference to the resistance to Germany which was growing throughout the Balkans. On the same day, he held a Staff Meeting which discussed the position. All agreed that the operations hitherto conceived might fail to contain the necessary forces in the south, before and during the first three months of 'Overlord'. Even if they succeeded in the earlier period, the danger still remained; for there was no plan of containment for the summer, to prevent a later concentration by the enemy against the forces that would then have landed in northern France. If both dangers were to be avoided, the connexion between the two campaigns must be

[1] See *Closing the Ring*, p. 121.

re-examined. Strategy in the Mediterranean must be more flexible, and the date of 'Overlord' itself should not be considered sacrosanct. The Staff Meeting agreed that the Chiefs of Staff should study the problem afresh, and that if necessary the British should press for a further conference with the Americans.

Such a conference was in fact already under consideration, but in a different context. Since early in August, Churchill had been urging the desirability of a tripartite meeting with the Russians, and during 'Quadrant' he and Roosevelt tried to bring it about as a conclusion to that conference. The pressure of the German offensive, which was then in full swing, prevented Stalin from leaving Russia; but he in turn suggested a meeting of a 'Military-Political Commission' in Moscow, to discuss various diplomatic problems that were awaiting settlement and to pave the way for a later meeting between Heads of Governments. This suggestion bore fruit in the tripartite Conference of Foreign Ministers in Moscow from 19th to 30th October, and its success, combined with renewed pressure from the Western Allies, led to detailed negotiation during the autumn for the subsequent meeting. Towards the end of September, the three Powers agreed to meet at Teheran, possibly in the middle of November; and despite the Prime Minister's anxiety for an earlier date, and the President's preference for a more accessible place whence to conduct that business as Head of the State which constitutionally enjoined on him a narrow time limit, both time and place survived the subsequent correspondence.

It was in this context that Churchill mentioned to Roosevelt, on 23rd October, the new factor which had been discussed at the Staff Meeting on the 19th.[1]

> '. . . 3. November 15 would be ninety days from the beginning of 'Quadrant'. In these ninety days events of first magnitude have occurred. Mussolini has fallen; Italy has surrendered; its Fleet has come over; we have successfully invaded Italy, and are marching on Rome with good prospects of success. The Germans are gathering up to 25 or more Divisions in Italy and the Po Valley. All these are new facts.
>
> 4. Our present plans for 1944 seem open to very grave defects. We are to put 15 American and 12 British Divisions into 'Overlord' and will have about six American and 16 British or British-controlled Divisions on the Italian front. Unless there is a German collapse Hitler, lying in the centre of the best communications in the world, can concentrate at least 40 to 50 Divisions against either of these forces while holding the other. He could obtain all the necessary forces by cutting his losses in

[1] See *Closing the Ring*, pp. 277-9.

the Balkans and withdrawing to the Save and the Danube without necessarily weakening his Russian front. The disposition of our forces between the Italian and the Channel theatres has not been settled by strategic needs but by the march of events, by shipping possibilities, and by arbitrary compromises between the British and Americans. The date of 'Overlord' itself was fixed by splitting the difference between the American and British view. It is arguable that neither the forces building up in Italy nor those available for a May 'Overlord' are strong enough for the tasks set them.

5. The British Staffs and my colleagues and I all think this position requires to be reviewed, and that the Commanders for both fronts should be named and should be present. In pursuance of 'Quadrant' decisions we have already prepared two of our best divisions . . . now in Sicily, for transfer to 'Overlord'. Thus they can play no part in the Italian battle to which they stood so near, but will not come into action again for seven months and then only if certain hypothetical conditions are fulfilled which may very likely not be fulfilled. Early in November a decision must be taken about moving landing craft from the Mediterranean to 'Overlord'. This will cripple Mediterranean operations without the said craft influencing events elsewhere for many months. We stand by what was agreed at 'Quadrant' but we do not feel that such agreement should be interpreted rigidly and without review in the swiftly-changing situations of war.

6. Personally I feel that if we make serious mistakes in the campaign of 1944, we might give Hitler the chance of a startling come-back. Prisoner German General von Thoma was overheard saying " Our only hope is that they come where we can use the Army upon them". All this shows the need for the greatest care and foresight in our arrangements, the most accurate timing between the two theatres, and the need to gather the greatest possible forces for both operations, particularly 'Overlord'. I do not doubt our ability in the conditions laid down to get ashore and deploy. I am however deeply concerned with the build-up and with the situation which may arise between the thirtieth and sixtieth days. I feel sure that the vast movement of American personnel into the United Kingdom and the fighting composition of the units requires to be searchingly examined by the Commander who will execute 'Overlord'. I wish to have both the High Commands settled in a manner agreeable to our two countries, and then the secondary Commands which are of very high importance can be decided . . . My dear friend, this is much the greatest thing we have ever attempted, and I am not satisfied that we have yet taken the measures necessary to give it the best chance of success. I feel very much in the dark at present, and unable to think or act in the forward manner which is needed. For these reasons I desire an early Conference. . . .'

He also addressed a personal telegram to General Marshall, asking him to study the message to the President. 'We are,' he stated,[1] 'carrying out our contract, but I pray God it does not cost us dear.'

These fears increased towards the end of October, when Alexander's report on Italy was received.[2] The necessity to retain assault shipping and troops in the Mediterranean whose movement had earlier been agreed, provided a further and immediate example of the dichotomy between plans and reality. 'This is what happens', remarked the Prime Minister to Mr. Eden[3], 'when battles are governed by lawyers' agreements made in all good faith months before and persisted in without regard to the ever-changing fortunes of war'. The British, as we have seen, reacted vigorously to the danger, and carried the Americans with them in their immediate proposal for the assault shipping.[4] But while it was possible to agree on the immediate battle, in an area to which the Allies were already committed by plan, the simultaneous developments in the Aegean showed how differently they viewed the context of that battle and of the Italian campaign. While the Americans regarded the request for the assault shipping as of immediate and purely local significance, the British saw in the American view the most immediate example of an attitude which threatened the strategy for Europe as much as the battle for Rome. At the same time that they were engaged on the local issue, the British Chiefs of Staff were therefore preparing their recommendations for future strategy, to which, in their view, that issue was the necessary prelude.

Their conclusions appeared on 11th November.

''OVERLORD' AND THE MEDITERRANEAN OPERATIONS

Aide-Mémoire

For some time past it has been clear to us, and doubtless also to the U.S. Chiefs of Staff, that disagreement exists between us as to what we should do now in the Mediterranean, with particular reference to the effect of future action on 'Overlord'. The point at issue is how far what might be termed the "sanctity of 'Overlord' " is to be preserved in its entirety, irrespective of developments in the Mediterranean theatre. This issue is clouding the whole of our future strategic outlook, and must be resolved at [Cairo].

2. At the outset we must point out that since the decisions taken at 'Quadrant', there have been major developments in the situation. The Russian campaign has succeeded beyond all hope or expectations and their victorious advance continues. Italy has been knocked out of the war; and it is certainly not beyond the

---

[1] See *loc. cit.*, p. 220.

[2] See pp. 69-70 above.

[3] See *Closing the Ring*, p. 258.

[4] See p. 74 above.

bounds of possibility that Turkey will come in on our side before the New Year. In these changed conditions, we feel that consideration of adjustments of, if not actual departures from, the decisions taken at 'Trident' and 'Quadrant' is not only fully justified but positively essential.

3. Nevertheless, we emphasise that we do not in any way recoil from, or wish to side-track, our agreed intention to attack the Germans across the Channel in the late Spring or early Summer of 1944, or even earlier if 'Rankin'[1] conditions were to obtain. We must not, however, regard 'Overlord' on a fixed date as the pivot of our whole strategy on which all else turns. In actual fact, the German strength in France next Spring may, at one end of the scale, be something which makes 'Overlord' completely impossible and, at the other end, something which makes 'Rankin' not only practicable, but essential. Consequently, to assume that the achievement of a certain strength by a certain date will remove all our difficulties and result in shortening the duration of the war is entirely illusory. This policy, if literally interpreted, will inevitably paralyse action in other theatres without any guarantee of action across the Channel.

4. With the Germans in their present plight the surest way to win the war in the shortest time is to attack them remorselessly and continuously in any and every area where we can do so with superiority. The number of places at which we can thus attack them depends mainly on the extent to which they are stretched. Our policy is therefore clear; we should stretch the German forces to the utmost by threatening as many of their vital interests and areas as possible and, holding them thus, we should attack wherever we can do so in superior force.

5. If we pursue the above policy we firmly believe that 'Overlord' (perhaps in the form of 'Rankin') will take place next summer. We do not, however, attach vital importance to any particular date or to any particular number of Divisions in the assault and follow-up, though naturally the latter should be made as large as possible consistent with the policy stated above. It is, of course, valuable to have a target date to which all may work, but we are firmly opposed to allowing this date to become our master, and to prevent us from taking full advantage of all opportunities that occur to us to follow what we believe to be the correct strategy.

6. In the light of the above argument, we submit the following proposals for action in the Mediterranean:

(1) *Unification of Command*

Unification of Command in the Mediterranean . . . is an essential and urgent measure which should be put into effect

---

[1] Plans for an emergency return to the Continent, in the event of a German weakening or collapse. See p. 10 above.

irrespective of any other decisions taken about this theatre.

(2) *The Italian Campaign*

The offensive in Italy should be nourished and maintained until we have secured the Pisa-Rimini Line.

(3) *Yugoslavia, Greece and Albania*

Our policy should be to place on a regular military basis and to intensify our measures to nourish the Partisan and irregular forces in these countries. If necessary, we might form a limited bridgehead on the Dalmatian or Albanian Coasts.

(4) *Turkey*

We should bring Turkey into the war this year.

(5) *The Dardanelles*

We should aim to open the Dardanelles as soon as possible.

(6) *The Balkans*

We should undermine resistance in the Balkan States and do everything possible to promote a state of chaos and disruption in the satellite Balkan countries.

7. If the above measures necessitate putting back the date upon which the forces agreed to be necessary for 'Overlord' will be available in the United Kingdom, this should be accepted, since it does not by any means follow that the date of the invasion of France will be put back to the same extent.

8. To sum up, our policy is to fight and bomb the Germans as hard as possible all through the winter and spring; to build up our forces in the United Kingdom as rapidly as possible consistent with this; and finally to invade the Continent as soon as the German strength in France and the general war situation gives us a good prospect of success.'

On 12th November, the Prime Minister minuted on this document 'I cordially agree'. After further debate between themselves and with Alexander and Churchill, the Chiefs of Staff decided to omit from paragraph 6(3) the last sentence ('If necessary, we might form a limited bridgehead on the Dalmatian or Albanian Coasts'), which referred to a now improbable event and might cause misapprehension of their policy. With that single omission, the paper was submitted to the Americans as the official British case.

It is important to be clear on this. Much was said at the time, and has since been written, on British, and particularly on Churchillian, strategy in the Mediterranean during this period, which is misleading not only for the period but for the same problem in later periods. For it seems often to have been assumed that the strategy was static, and was held for the same reasons throughout the last phase of the European war, in 1945 as in 1944 and in 1944 as in 1943. This of course could never have been so. Plans for the different areas within the theatre, as for any other area of operations, depended on circumstances and resources, which did not remain constant on the three main occasions—in the autumn and early winter of 1943, in the late summer and autumn of 1944, and in the winter of 1944/45—on which they were considered. Each must therefore be examined separately, and not as part of a continuous and unchanged policy.

For the impression of a static policy has been created largely by reading later developments into the earlier scene. It has often been asserted—and despite the evidence to the contrary, seems still to be widely believed—that the British, either under Churchill's influence or through him as their spokesman, wished in the second half of 1943 to develop a campaign in the Balkans towards the north, if necessary at the expense of 'Overlord', for strategic or diplomatic reasons, or for a combination of both. Whatever may have been the case later, this was not so at that time. There was, in the first place, no real difference of opinion between the Prime Minister and the Chiefs of Staff as to what should be done. Churchill's policy in 1943 was not that of Lloyd George in 1916. Whatever his dreams—and there were dreams[1]—when faced with the realities he saw well enough the impossibility of a Balkan campaign involving substantial British or American forces; and while he was undoubtedly more enthusiastic than the Chiefs of Staff or their Planners over a policy in the Aegean that all acknowledged to be necessary, there was no need or occasion for him to urge on them a course of action which they adopted without serious hesitation from the first. The issue in the eastern Mediterranean, in the autumn and winter of 1943, was not in fact whether the Allies should land in force on the mainland of south-east Europe, but whether they could and should bring Turkey into the war. Strategy, like politics, is the art of the possible. British plans centred on the Aegean, where in their view a limited force could produce the greatest effect in support of the main strategic object, and not on operations by the Allies on the mainland for which none of the necessary conditions existed. So far as 1943 is concerned, the Balkan campaign with substantial Allied forces is a myth.

This may indeed be seen when the British strategy is compared with that held at the time by the only advocate of a Balkan campaign. Since the end of the 'Quadrant' Conference, Field Marshal Smuts had chafed at the policy for 1944, which seemed to him inadequate for a great Alliance in the fifth year of war. On 9th September, he outlined his alternative to Churchill. The Western Allies should at once capture the Dodecanese, support the guerrillas in Yugoslavia 'by two or four Divisions . . . and thus . . . build up an important Balkans front against German line on Danube and Sava', and thence devote their attention

[1] See Appendix VI below.

to Italy and the Balkans instead of 'now adopting cross-Channel plans'. Those plans 'should be slowed down or put into temporary cold storage while bombing campaign is intensified to prepare for eventual military knockout'. Such a policy was similar to that which the British have often been alleged to have held at this time. It is interesting, therefore, to note the terms of the Prime Minister's immediate reply.[1] '. . . There can be no question whatever of breaking arrangements we have made with the United States for 'Overlord'. . . . I hope you will realise that British loyalty to 'Overlord' is keystone of arch of Anglo-American co-operation. Personally I think enough forces exist for both hands to be played and I believe this to be the right strategy.'

This attitude held good over the next two months, in the course of which Smuts visited London in an effort to influence the decision. But his advocacy merely clarified the impossibility of his case. Whatever form they might take, the British regarded operations in the Mediterranean as a necessary complement to 'Overlord'; Smuts, on the other hand, regarded 'Overlord' as at best a complement to operations from the Mediterranean. He sought to reverse the 'Quadrant' strategy, and to re-examine its foundations: the British were concerned rather to modify those of its provisions which in their view were now likely adversely to affect the rest.[2]

It was the more important, therefore, that any modification in policy should accord with the available resources. As it was, the British argued, the existing policy was wasting resources which could otherwise be used profitably in support of a modified policy. The campaign in Italy was hanging fire, and operations in the Aegean were starved of the necessary troops; but divisions remained idle in North Africa and Sicily, awaiting their transfer to England for an operation in some six months' time. The fate of the Dodecanese hung in the balance, and with it that of Turkey; but the necessary assault shipping was engaged partly in ferrying an air force to Italy for which the airfields did not yet exist. The guerrillas in Yugoslavia needed arms; but the Command in charge of the operations was not in charge of the bases, and had not provided most of the resources. Divided authority and an unplanned future were undermining the proper use of the resources which would determine the future.

The British calculated that these difficulties could be overcome, and the relation between strategy and resources set on a proper footing, by the application of the three immediate remedies which they had proposed for the Mediterranean. The revision of command, desirable for the better conduct of affairs across the Adriatic and in the Aegean,

---

[1] See *Closing the Ring*, p. 116.

[2] For a consideration of three statements by Mr. Churchill which might seem at first sight to invalidate this argument, see Appendix VI below.

would create an authority which, for the first time since the invasion of North Africa, could see the theatre as a whole. The devotion of one-sixth of Eisenhower's resources to the capture of the Dodecanese,[1] would secure the base in the east necessary to a more flexible strategy with limited forces. Finally, the retention in the theatre until mid-January of all L.S.T. needed for the next stage of the Italian campaign, would give the Allies the opportunity, which the earlier withdrawal of the vessels might easily remove, of providing the foundation for such a strategy throughout the theatre.

The key to the whole design lay indeed in a readjustment to the programme for assault shipping. If the sixty-eight L.S.T. in the Mediterranean, due to leave for England on 15th December, left on that date, the campaign in Italy might stagnate and fester, the Mediterranean scene would then finally harden, and—unless assault shipping were diverted and held from the Far East—the Germans would have ample time to redistribute their forces before 'Overlord' took place in May. If, on the other hand, those L.S.T. remained in the Mediterranean for another month, there seemed every chance that the needs of Italy would be met, and that the Allies would be advancing rapidly north of Rome. This in turn would free at least part of the assault shipping that remained, with certain types of ocean shipping capable of supporting seaborne assaults but then engaged on ferrying men and supplies to Italy, for minor but damaging operations based on the Aegean islands, and for feints and support of the guerrillas elsewhere, before it was called on to take part in any operation that might be approved in direct support of 'Overlord'. It would also enable any assault shipping that might have to be loaned from the Far East early in 1944, to return there by the spring.

The revised programme would moreover have an effect, at first perhaps unwelcome but probably beneficent, on 'Overlord' itself. The British Chiefs of Staff calculated, early in November, that it must postpone the date for that operation by six to eight weeks, possibly until 1st July, 1944. But while this introduced a different date from that already agreed, and would shorten the campaigning period available before the winter, it would provide at least a month's extra production of assault shipping, still a limiting factor to the size of the assault, and would to the same extent ease the burden on 'Bolero', which was still causing anxiety.[2] If therefore the Allies could agree to delay 'Overlord' until about 1st July, 1944, the Chiefs of Staff believed that the strategy for Europe, and the preparations for 'Overlord' itself, could be set on a proper footing: if not, the Mediterranean campaign might enter a blind alley, 'Overlord' might thereby be endangered, and, in those

---

[1] See p. 94 above.

[2] See p. 3 above.

circumstances, new conditions might be set for the British effort in the Far East.

It will be asked why this argument for the Mediterranean, which was stated clearly enough, should, then and later, have been misinterpreted. The answer is that it was an argument peculiarly liable to misunderstanding, for it was of the type which seeks to avoid one course of action by following another apparently very like it. A precise allocation of forces between Italy and the eastern area, and allowing of little margin for error, was intended to provide a complement to the Italian campaign; it could also be regarded as intended to provide an alternative. Operations in the Aegean were designed to stimulate unrest in the Balkans without an Allied landing in force on the mainland; they could also be taken, by friend as well as by foe, for a prelude to such a landing. To the British, the strength of their case was precisely that a minor readjustment of forces was best calculated to achieve a major disturbance. Such an argument would be accepted, and might be understood, only by those who started from the same strategic assumptions, and thus could credit it with the objects it professed and not with those which it seemed so narrowly to avoid.

But by the autumn of 1943, the Mediterranean had already become the focus for a significant difference of thought between the British and the Americans, which throughout the alliance, often mitigated with skill and wisdom by the authorities whom it affected, informed their common strategy. To the British, nurtured and confirmed in the experience, and largely governed by the forms, of maritime warfare, strategy implied an economy of effort, best achieved, if circumstances allowed, by a careful distribution of strength between a number of complementary targets. Such a mode of warfare was pragmatic, for it must develop largely as opportunity offered; and the British placed a correspondingly high value on strategic flexibility, in preference to a rigid adherence to a long-prepared plan. To the Americans, on the other hand, strategy implied concentration of effort, in the Napoleonic sense. Unused to long wars against numerically superior Continental powers, and rightly confident in their application of ingenuity to unparalleled strength, they had no need for or experience of the devious approach. Their strategic resource and tactical boldness, the former already displayed in the Pacific, the latter soon to be displayed in north-west Europe, were accordingly exercised in the service of a single strategic target and of a single well-prepared design; and they were quick to note and to fear any sign of an apparent dispersal of force, or of a departure from plans already agreed.

The Americans thus disliked the 'side-shows' which to the British were an inherent element of warfare; and the Mediterranean had always seemed to them to bear all the marks of the 'side-show'. 'Every division sent into the Mediterranean,' an American official historian has remarked of the Joint Chiefs of Staff's position, 'was a division lost for the main battle'.[1] 'The Mediterranean', Marshall informed a meeting of the Combined Chiefs of Staff in Washington in May 1943, 'was a vacuum into which America's great military might could be drawn off until there was nothing left with which to deal the decisive blow on the Continent.' Thus, where the British feared that 'Overlord' would fail without larger diversionary operations in the south, the Americans feared that those operations would grow so large that 'Overlord' would fail. When the British asserted that 'Overlord', even if postponed, remained the main assault, the Americans replied that the diversions were already claiming the larger forces. As they surveyed the developments in the Mediterranean in 1943, the Joint Chiefs of Staff saw how landings in North Africa had been followed by an assault on Sicily; how an assault on Sicily had led to the invasion of Italy; and how the invasion of Italy was now leading to proposals for action in the eastern Mediterranean. What, they asked themselves, was to prevent such proposals in turn from demanding new forces for new possibilities? Large operations, it seemed to them, might be launched in the name of 'Overlord', whose success might then depend on reinforcements necessary to 'Overlord'. In these circumstances, the devotion to 'Overlord' which the British claimed, seemed to them suspiciously like lip-service.

This suspicion was the stronger because the Americans, unlike the British, were now actively on the offensive in both of the separate wars, against Germany and against Japan, whose only connexion to the Allies lay in their demands on resources; and while the European war enjoyed the higher priority, both had to be carried on. Strong pressure in the country, and a natural inclination arising from the same causes as that pressure, impelled the Joint Chiefs of Staff to devote as much of the American effort as possible to the campaigns in the Far East; and they were the more sensitive to demands for the Mediterranean which in their view might not only prove unnecessary but, by endangering 'Overlord', might force the diversion of Allied resources from the war against Japan, probably from the Pacific and possibly also from south-east Asia. However well justified this attitude may have been, it led to a curious position in the Mediterranean itself. Both British and Americans agreed that the necessary diversionary operations must take place in that theatre. But the suspicion with which they viewed the possible consequences of those diversions, led the Americans to suspect rather than to welcome certain manifestations of their success. A campaign in Italy was necessary, and must be

---

[1] Gordon A. Harrison, *Cross-Channel Attack* (1951), p. 96.

vigorously pursued. But victory before the late spring of 1944 would leave a hiatus which must still be filled. Neither partner of course contemplated a stalemate, and the Americans certainly did not consider its implication. But if the problem was not posed for Italy, it could scarcely be avoided for the area to the east. At times in October and November 1943, the Joint Chiefs of Staff seemed to dislike the thought of an Allied landing at any point to the east of Italy almost as much as the Germans; and while the British welcomed the confusion in south-east Europe, the Americans regarded the British attitude with increasing alarm.

The Americans, in fact, feared the shadow, rather than the substance, of the British proposals. Fearing the shadow, they tended to neglect the substance. The programme of the British Chiefs of Staff was designed to maintain an increasing threat in the south until an approximate date, without an increase of force. The Joint Chiefs of Staff saw it as the prologue to an indefinite increase of force which might indefinitely postpone that date. In these circumstances, it proved difficult to appraise the merits of the immediate case. Political considerations may have further confused an issue which was already misconceived; certainly the President himself at this time seems to have feared the effect on opinion in the United States of an entanglement in the Balkans at the expense of operations in northern France. But such considerations—and it is unlikely that they were significant as yet—could not have arisen had not the strategic argument allowed. A week before the conference at Cairo began, Marshall told Roosevelt and Hopkins, at a meeting of the Joint Chiefs of Staff, that 'the British might like to "ditch" 'Overlord' now in order to go into the Balkans'; and according to the American official history, 'the prospects of mounting 'Overlord' as planned could not have seemed very bright to the Joint Chiefs of Staff as they travelled to Cairo for the first conversations with the British . . .'[1]

Misunderstanding, as is not unusual, brought a certain resentment. The Americans suspected that the British, with their talk of the necessary conditions for 'Overlord', were trying to return to the position they had held before the Quebec Conference, when a decision on 'Overlord' awaited confirmation. They attributed, in fact, to London the policy advocated by Smuts. Always sensitive to a departure from earlier agreements, they accordingly came to Cairo in a state of some moral indignation. The British for their part were annoyed at an attitude which they considered to be unjustifiable, and almost certain to reintroduce to the debate familiar but irrelevant prejudices. But if the misunderstanding was deep, the irritation was not; and despite some misgivings in the weeks before the conference, at Cairo itself the

---

[1] Harrison, *loc. cit.*, p. 122.

principals were patient and the atmosphere was soon cordial. There was disagreement and criticism; but the consequences were too important, the alliance was too close and its balance still too even, and the protagonists themselves were too experienced, for a solution not to be found which would again at least postpone, and at best might resolve, the issue of their differences.

The disagreement on strategy was reflected in a problem of command that had also to be settled at the conference. On 2nd November, the British Chiefs of Staff informed Washington of their recommendations for the Mediterranean Command, to which they alluded in their paper of the 11th.[1] They stressed the difficulties which were produced by the inevitable delay in referring matters affecting two Commands to the Combined Chiefs of Staff—a delay which recent events had shown might be serious.

> '. . . 3. We therefore consider', they continued, 'the time has come for one Commander to be made responsible for all operations in the Mediterranean and suggest that Commander-in-Chief, Allied Forces, should now assume responsibility for operations in following areas in addition to those already in his command: Greece, Albania, Yugoslavia, Bulgaria, Rumania, Hungary, Crete, Aegean Islands and Turkey. Commanders in Cairo would be under his orders for these operations, but would remain responsible to British Chiefs of Staff for operation of Middle East Base and for all matters pertaining to those parts of present Middle East Commands situated in Africa, Asia and Levant (except Turkey), and should continue to receive political guidance from Minister of State Resident in Middle East in respect of those responsibilities.
>
> 4. Such reorganization would ensure that operations in Mediterranean are regarded as a whole and would empower Commander-in-Chief to transfer forces from one part of area to another in order to take advantage of fleeting opportunities. Consider this particularly desirable in view of possible opportunities in Balkans and effect operations in that theatre might have on main operations in Italy. . . .'

The Joint Chiefs of Staff were not unsympathetic to these proposals, in so far as they affected the domestic hierarchy within the theatre. But they also impinged on a problem outside the theatre with which the Americans were already concerned, and which, starting from a question of personalities, had by this time led them to consider the structure of command throughout Europe.

When Churchill and Roosevelt had agreed that the Supreme

[1] See pp. 109-11 above.

Commander for 'Overlord' should be an American, the obvious choice to the authorities in Washington seemed at first to be General Marshall. He alone was considered to possess the necessary influence and strength to see the plan through to completion in London; and, in the President's opinion, he particularly deserved the immortality which the greatest command ever held by an American would, if successful, confer upon the holder. Marshall was accordingly told that he would be given the post, and began secretly to make his arrangements. But a problem remained which in the event was to lead to a different result. For if Marshall was considered to be virtually indispensable to 'Overlord', he was also considered to be indispensable as Chief of Staff of the Army. There was indeed no question at any time of his being replaced in that office; instead, it was contemplated that he would remain Chief of Staff, while an Acting Chief of Staff, probably General Eisenhower, would be appointed in Washington in his absence. But this solution, not unnaturally, failed to satisfy the other American Chiefs of Staff. Admiral King, in particular, objected to an arrangement which would increase rather than mitigate the ill effects of Marshall's absence, by creating a likely source of confusion between him and Washington. Rumours of the problem soon spread in the Pentagon, and the discussion became entangled in the politics of the capital. It was alleged that Marshall was being removed to Europe as the victim of a dispute with Roosevelt or Churchill, or with the powerful and suspect Harry Hopkins. In September 1943, accusations appeared in public, in normally authoritative papers, and were eagerly seized on by the German propaganda. The excitement began to die down towards the end of the month, as fresh news invited fresh speculation; but it left a legacy which could not be ignored in selecting the commander and in defining his command.

It was against this background that the authorities in Washington began to consider a revision in the structure of command, which would secure Marshall's appointment to 'Overlord' without the attendant political odium. A possible solution seemed to offer in the creation of a new Supreme Command, to embrace not only the forces for the main invasion, but all Allied forces in Europe apart from the Russians. Such an appointment would not imply demotion for its holder: on the contrary, it was of unexampled range and magnitude. There seems to have been some such speculation in the middle of September; certainly the rumours were strong enough towards its close to elicit an anxious telegram of inquiry from Churchill to Hopkins. But nothing was heard officially throughout October.

Whatever its political advantages, the idea of the new Command could not hope to survive discussion as a political panacea alone; and while it remained a project dear to the President, it did not in fact run counter to the strategy of the Joint Chiefs of Staff. A Supreme

Commander for Europe, devoted to the conception of 'Overlord' and disposing of the resources for 'Overlord' and the Mediterranean, might prove decisive in preventing that departure from the Quebec strategy which the Americans suspected would soon be proposed. He was equally well placed to control directly the converging air operations which were now possible from north and south, and which must soon be related directly to his own operations. Nor was the pattern of authority itself uncongenial to the Joint Chiefs of Staff. They regarded it as the logical extension, over an area that had now become indivisible, of that theory of Supreme Command which they normally preferred to the alternative of a committee of Commanders-in-Chief. While, therefore, they were not themselves responsible for the idea, the Joint Chiefs of Staff were likely to appreciate its merits.

But at the beginning of November, the President had still not come out into the open; and while he would doubtless have done so within the next fortnight, before the delegates left for Cairo, the occasion was in fact provided by the British proposals for the Mediterranean Command. When, on 5th November, these were considered in Washington, Admiral Leahy read a statement of 'his own views' to his colleagues which they had not heard as a body before. This turned out to be the proposal for a European Supreme Command which had been rumoured in September, and which presumably now had the official support of the President. As Leahy remarked, it ran counter to the British recommendations; and the British at once reacted strongly to it. The Chiefs of Staff informed their colleagues that proper control in the Mediterranean was an urgent operational necessity, which could not await the discussion of a different solution that was in any case likely to be 'entirely unacceptable'. The Prime Minister, for his part, asked Dill to inform Leahy immediately that he would never consent to such an arrangement while he remained in office.

The strength of the British objection derived from an accepted principle which Leahy's proposal seemed to contravene, and whose maintenance at this time seemed essential to the maintenance of the British strategy for Europe. If the appointment was to be effective, it must conflict with the authority of the Combined Chiefs of Staff, which had proved both successful and constitutionally viable. In whatever terms his powers were defined, a 'Supremissimo' of the type suggested must either arrogate to himself functions hitherto denied to a Supreme Commander, or must subside into a nominally impressive but in fact redundant position in the chain of responsibility. Neither result was acceptable to the authorities in London. Neither, in their opinion, would work in practice, and both, in their different ways, would threaten the established machinery of Allied agreement and control, over a period in which the British were particularly anxious to retain their full and accustomed share in the formulation and supervision of Allied strategy in Europe. For the force of the British objection reflected not only a difference of principle on the structure of command, but its bearing on the complementary strategic difference that was about to be debated; and it accordingly served warning, on the eve of the Cairo conference, of the determination with which the British strategy would be pressed.

CHAPTER III

BRITISH STRATEGY IN THE FAR EAST, AND THE FORMATION OF THE SOUTH-EAST ASIA COMMAND, AUGUST–NOVEMBER, 1943

(i)

The Strategic Conditions

A STUDY OF THE WAR in the Far East in 1944 has little in common with a study of the war in Europe. Not only are the conditions for strategy and the processes of strategic thought entirely different in each case, but at first sight there is a marked contrast between the success of planning in the West and, for Britain, the frustration of planning in the war against Japan. In Europe, 1944 was a year of great achievement, leading, despite the failure of its initial promise, to final and complete victory in 1945. In the Far East, 1944 was distinguished, so far as the British were concerned, by a limited offensive on the western perimeter of enemy territory, while in London a succession of ambitious plans failed to mature and a prolonged and stubborn debate on the object of strategy took place at the very centre of Government.

The reasons for this apparent contrast are not hard to find. In the first place, the two wars had reached different stages at the beginning of 1944. The discussions on the strategy against Japan are comparable, not with those on 'Overlord' and the Mediterranean which proceeded at the same time, but with the discussions on the strategy against Germany which occupied 1942 and 1943; while the slowly mounting offensive in south-east Asia towards the end of 1944, and even during 1945, may be measured not against the final thrusts at the heart of Germany but against their preliminaries on the fringe of enemy territory during 1943 and early in 1944.

The war against Japan was moreover fought under peculiar difficulties. Throughout the story there are three factors to which the events must constantly be related: the geography of the theatre and its effect on the area in which the British operated, the state of their supplies, and the divergent interests of the Allies. Unlike Germany,

Japan lay far from her enemies and could be approached only by sea and air. There were five possible lines of approach, some of which could and obviously would be attempted simultaneously.[1] First, Japan could be attacked from the north: from the Kuriles with advanced bases in the Aleutians and rear bases in the United States, and from Russia, with bases in her Maritime Provinces. But such attacks, whatever their form, must depend for their success at least in part on Russian intervention, which was not to be expected until the end of the war with Germany, and could not in any case affect Japan in her weakest point, her dependence on sea communications to the south. An attack from the north could therefore be regarded only as the culmination of a general offensive whose preliminaries must be developed elsewhere. Secondly, Japan could be approached through the central Pacific, where the groups of islands—Marshalls, Gilberts, Carolines, Marianas and Bonins—provided advanced and intermediate bases for a maritime assault upon the Home Islands staged from Pearl Harbour and fed from the west coast of the United States. Thirdly, an offensive could be developed from the south-west Pacific, with Australia as the main base, through New Guinea and if necessary the Celebes and Dutch Borneo to the Philippines, and thence to Formosa and the Home Islands themselves. A fourth thrust could be developed from south-east Asia, with India as the base, through Burma, Malaya and the Netherlands East Indies to the Philippines and Formosa, or to Indo-China and Formosa, or to Indo-China and China. Lastly, Japan could be attacked from China, supplied for this purpose by air from the Pacific, or by air or land from Burma and India, or best of all by sea from a recaptured port such as Canton or Hong Kong.

In 1943, the Americans advanced along two of these possible lines, in the central and south-west Pacific; and their success towards the end of the year brought them to a position where they would soon have to decide which was to be their main and which their complementary assault on the inner Japanese defences. The alternatives, with their administrative implications, were indeed then under debate in Washington. The possibilities in Asia, however, did not seem as yet to be so clear. It was a cardinal factor in American policy that China must be kept in the war. But whether she should be regarded as an element in the combined assault upon Japan, and if so in what capacity, had not yet been determined. The state of the country in 1943 did not encourage too ambitious a plan. After seven years of sporadic but ruinous warfare, unoccupied China was scarcely in a position to do more than stay alive. The structure of administration, never strong, had largely collapsed. Chiang Kai-shek's government retained from Chungking its jurisdiction over the central and southern provinces, and the Generalissimo himself had indeed theoretically improved his

[1] See Map I, facing p. 11.

position in September, 1943 by his election to the Presidency and by his nomination as Head of the State. But the central government exercised only a nominal control. The traditional independence of the local governors was by now unassailable; risings continued throughout the provinces, even, in 1943, in the normally amenable Szechuan; and towards the end of the year the familiar rumours were heard of rebellion in the Kuomintang itself. At the same time, matters had almost come to a head with the Communists, who virtually controlled northern China and who were regarded by several foreign observers as potentially better material than the disorganized forces of the central government. Throughout the year, several of the Generalissimo's best divisions blockaded the Communist areas, and in July open civil war seemed possible. The danger was averted, largely owing to criticism from abroad; but at the end of 1943 there seemed little likelihood of the 'recalcitrant members of the family', to use the Government's official description, being reconciled to their self-styled parents.

Meanwhile the country continued as best it could in the face of appalling poverty. To the familiar pestilences of flood and locust was added the wartime taxation in kind, levied indiscriminately and with excess by the local governors and generals, and administered by their officials with the traditional corruption. But while the burden on the peasant was immense, the benefit to the Government remained small. No national budget had been published since 1937, but it was estimated that in 1943 China's expenditure was more than double her income. Inflation became steadily worse, and efforts to control prices proved entirely inadequate. By December 1943, the level of the wholesale price index in Chungking was more than twice as high as in January and two hundred times as high as in 1937. The production of war material, despite able technicians, was almost completely hamstrung by this lack of financial control. As a result, the Chinese soldier was, by western standards, almost incredibly ill-armed, ill-clothed and ill-fed. Starving and apathetic, and bringing to the campaigns of the twentieth century many of the habits of the Middle Ages, he lived on the countryside as far as possible and where possible evaded or compromised with the enemy. By 1944, indeed, despite the enormous paper strength of the Nationalist forces, their resistance was at best spasmodic, and the country was saved from overt defeat only because the Japanese already had most of what they wanted and were prevented by their other efforts from acquiring the rest.

But so long as China continued to resist, she remained an asset to the Western Allies: at the least, as a sponge to soak up Japanese resources, and as a guarantee against an unchallenged Japanese dominion on the mainland which might survive even the reduction of the Home Islands; at best, as a potential base for offensive operations against the enemy. The British, with only a slight strategic interest in the Chinese theatre, and doubtful of the Generalissimo's capacity to stage an offensive, were content simply with his continued resistance; the Americans, whose more direct strategic concern was supported by a traditional affection, were prepared to foster him in a more active rôle. There were three ways in which this might be done. First, the Chinese armies could be improved by American training and strengthened with American equipment until they were capable of staging a campaign to drive the enemy to the sea. Alternatively, their limitations could be accepted, and they could be used to contain the enemy while American tactical air power increasingly harassed his communications and forced him to abandon large areas of the country. Thirdly, the Americans could establish a strategic air force in China to bomb the approaches to Japan and the Home Islands themselves. The third possibility was not seriously considered until towards the end of 1943, and its fate will be discussed in another chapter.[1] But it was an addition rather than an alternative to either of the other possibilities. Each of these possibilities demanded entirely different efforts and supplies; and American policy in China was determined by the fact that in the circumstances it was impossible to pursue them simultaneously.

For the volume of American supplies to China was governed by the state of the communications. The successive Japanese conquests in the Philippines, in the Netherlands East Indies, and in Malaya and Burma, had quickly isolated her from her allies by land and sea, and when the Burma Road from Mandalay to Chungking was cut in 1942, all normal communication ceased. The British and Americans thereupon considered new routes, of which the most promising seemed to be the pack road through Tibet and the route by sea, road and rail from Karachi through eastern Persia and the Turksib railway to Sinkiang. But all such plans failed, either for physical or diplomatic reasons, and the Western Allies were forced in the event to rely entirely on the air route from India over the Himalayas, involving a passage of exceptional difficulty. The main American effort in Asia during 1942-3 therefore turned on the establishment of this air ferry. Its organization was confided to a new American China-Burma-India (C.B.I.) Theatre, which was set up in June, 1942 to embrace all activities in support of China. Under its aegis, material and technicians were provided to help the British India Command in building or modifying the necessary airfields and in improving their communications. The transport aircraft themselves were organized as a Wing of the world-wide U.S. Air Transport Command, which, with Tenth U.S. Army Air Force in India, itself reserved for the support of China, came under the direction of Major-General George E. Stratemeyer, commanding all American air forces in the C.B.I. Theatre. The theatre also included

[1] See Chapter XI, section III below.

certain Chinese troops who were placed under American control, and were training in India. Its commander was Lieut.-General Joseph B. Stilwell, and at the end of 1943 a Deputy Commander, Major-General Daniel I. Sultan, was appointed with an office in New Delhi.

The target for the capacity of the air ferry was set at 10,000 tons a month in May, 1943. By December, seven new airfields had been built in Bengal and Assam, while the American Air Transport Wing in India had grown to fifteen squadrons, with a total of 196 planes. Where in the first quarter of 1943 they had delivered some 1,700 tons of supplies to China, in the last quarter they delivered some 8,000 tons, and almost 14,500 tons in the first quarter of 1944. The direct British contribution to China over the same period was on a much smaller scale—186 tons in the last quarter of 1943, and 91 tons in the first quarter of 1944.

When every ton of supplies had thus to be carried to China by air, every ton had to be used to the best advantage. With a total monthly capacity for most of 1943 beneath that of a single medium-sized cargo ship, the air ferry could not hope simultaneously to nourish the Chinese armies and to build up an American tactical air force in China. A choice was necessary between the alternatives. It was rendered the more difficult by the acrimonious support which each received from its American protagonist within the theatre itself.

The land view was represented by Stilwell, the air view by Major-General Claire Chennault. Chennault had been in China since 1937 in the service of the Chinese Government, with a group of American volunteers who together made up the American Volunteer Group, or 'Flying Tigers' as they came to be known. Operating mainly from bases in Hunan and Yunnan, he concentrated on the Japanese communications by sea and river, and had evolved a technique of air fighting which, despite his scanty resources, brought him considerable success. When the China-Burma-India Theatre was formed, his force was brought under direct American control, and was later renamed Fourteenth U.S. Army Air Force, Chennault himself remaining in command under the orders of Stilwell, as Commanding General of the new theatre.

The two generals differed radically on the strategy to be adopted in China. Chennault, on the basis of his experience, pinned his faith on air power to paralyse the enemy's heterogeneous communications in China and to harass those with Japan. Stilwell, who had been military attaché in China before the war, strove for a regenerated Chinese army, with American officers and material, which at the least would absorb increasing Japanese opposition, and at best might drive through to Canton and inflict a major defeat upon the main Japanese armies in Asia. In consequence, the two men disagreed over the scale, the type and the destination of the supplies. Chennault wished to reserve them entirely for Fourteenth Air Force, and to see the air ferry enlarged as fast and as far as possible. Stilwell, while equally anxious to reserve the bulk of the supplies, though for the Chinese army, did not believe that the air ferry alone could ever meet his demands. He therefore wished to reopen land communications with China by driving a road from India to the old Burma Road, over ground then held by the Japanese. These differences, after smouldering for some months, were finally aired at the Washington Conference in May, 1943; and after some debate, and to Stilwell's intense disappointment, Chennault was given the priority in supplies. This, however, by no means closed the question. Stilwell continued to strive for his own objects, while a powerful section of the American Government, which was attracted by his strategy for China, encouraged his efforts to reopen the land communications through Burma so as to relieve the burden on the air.

The Americans' plans directly affected, and were affected by, the British; for whatever was done in China depended on India and Burma, where the C.B.I. organization lay across British territory and the only British strategic theatre in the Far East. At the end of 1943, all of Burma except parts of the northern and western mountains was held by the Japanese. The nature of American aid to China, whether of Chennault's or of Stilwell's devising, therefore depended on the plans for the campaign in Burma, which in turn were burdened with the effects of competing interests and policies.

For the interests of the Allies in south-east Asia were by no means the same. Their differences were masked at first by the necessity for freeing the approaches to India's north-eastern frontier, involving the clearance of a part of northern Burma on which both were agreed. But thereafter they diverged. The British, whose effort in the Far East must, at least initially, be anchored to the Indian base, looked from that base to the south-east, where the Japanese armies lay and where the reconquest of British territory in Burma, Malaya and Singapore was a cardinal object of policy. Beyond Singapore, again, lay the rich islands of the Netherlands East Indies to be restored to the Dutch, and eventually the Pacific itself wherein the British effort might hope to be effectually deployed. The British therefore looked from Burma towards the south, and in the north favoured Chennault's strategy to Stilwell's more ambitious design. But such a policy did not appeal to Americans of any party, who were not impressed by the strategic value of a campaign leading directly away from Japan, and were not interested in, nor particularly favoured, the restoration of a British order in south-east Asia which many had long been accustomed to disparage. It was to keep China in the war, and not to assist 'British imperialism,' that they were in India and northern Burma; and the shortest route to China lay in the north. As has been well said by an American, 'In Eisenhower's command, harmonious and whole-hearted co-operation was possible because British and American objectives could be summed up in one word—"Berlin". In South-East Asia, on the other hand, the British and Americans were fighting two wars for different purposes, and the Kuomintang Government of China was fighting a third war for purposes largely its own.'[1]

These fundamentally divergent interests might have been pursued independently had either the geography or the supplies permitted. Unfortunately, they did not. The peculiar conditions in Burma, and the shortage of material, demanded some compromise between them. To understand its exact nature, we must pause therefore at this point to examine the first factor in some detail.

The country and climate of northern Burma, where the Allies had perforce to begin their advance, were among the worst for that purpose in the world.[2] Following the frontiers of India, Burma and China, the mountains describe an unbroken arc from west to east, with the great Indian valley of the Brahmaputra lying to the westward, the permanent snows of Tibet and China to the north, and to the east a long series of mountain ranges until the lower land is reached around Chungking. Inside the arc, bounded by its eastern and western arms, lies the narrow plain of Burma stretching southward to the sea. At the end of 1943, the British lay along the Indo-Burmese frontier and in the extreme north of Burma, among the mountain ranges which run for over five hundred miles in a south-westerly direction from the undefined Chinese border to the province of Arakan by the Bay of Bengal. Between these mountains, or hills as they are called in deference to their greater neighbours to the north, there is little variation except of height: from 2-8,000 feet in the Patkais, around 5,000 feet in the northern Nagas and 2,000 further south, from 6-11,000 feet in the Chin Hills, and finally dropping from some 3,000 feet to 1,000 in Arakan before the hills debouch into the coastal plain. Heavily forested in and near the valleys, and covered by trees and scrub to the peaks, they rise abruptly, often from narrow rivers and streams which are converted into raging torrents in the rains, in a confused series of ridges bearing little relation to the main axis of the range as visualised from a map. Ephemeral streams drain many of their sides, soon disappearing in the dry weather and as soon swelling into rivers in the rains. The surface of the hills themselves, of jungle earth or shale, makes passage on foot at any time arduous and in the south-west monsoon almost impossible for man or beast.

[1] Robert E. Sherwood, *The White House Papers of Harry L. Hopkins*, (1949) II, p. 776.
[2] See Map III.

In Arakan, the narrow coastal plain, only the northern part of which was occupied by the British at this time, is bounded to the east by the spine of the Mayu Range, a series of steep, jungle-clad ridges sharing the characteristics of the mountains further north. The plain itself is largely swamp and paddy with some grass and tangled wood, interspersed by tidal creeks or 'chaungs'. These waterways provide almost as great a military obstacle as the hills and jungle elsewhere. Though forded with ease at low water, at high tide they enjoy a rise and fall of up to eight feet, and in the rains are swollen by floods which the mud banks often fail to contain.

All of this country is sparsely inhabited, and at the end of 1943 it boasted only one major road, that from Dimapur through Kohima to Imphal. There were a major and some secondary roads in northern Arakan; but secondary roads in Burma do not correspond to those in western Europe, and traffic in some cases was possible only at certain times of the year. The only other communications lay in the primitive tracks, such as that through the mountains south of Imphal, or from Myitkyina to Bhamo or from Bhamo to Indaw, which themselves were rare enough and which in the south-west monsoon quickly reverted to the jungle and the flood. The Allies, in fact, were required to move and sustain large bodies of men, equipped for modern war, over country much of which until then had been traversed only by the most intrepid explorers, with no local means of overcoming the lack of communications and only the inadequate facilities of Assam for transporting them from India and beyond.

On the eastern arm of the arc, the road to China, which was one of the possible targets of any Burmese campaign, also lies through high and tortuous country. From Mandalay in the plains it passes northeastward through the foothills to Lashio and thence, in an ever more northerly direction, across the mountainous frontier to the peaks which stretch eastwards, at heights of 5-10,000 feet, for a desolate six hundred miles to Kunming and Kweiyang beyond. Thence it runs down again to the river capital of Chungking. A branch had also been constructed from Bhamo to Wanting near the border, for a length of some hundred miles. The only immediate alternative to this road, which in places is almost impassable, lay in the journey by air across the northern mountains, later to be widely known as 'the Hump', which formed the curve of the arc between the Indo-Burmese ranges and the approaches to the China Road. This meant traversing in most weathers and for long periods at a time ranges of 12-15,000 feet or more, before the terminal was reached at Kunming.

The Burmese plain to the south, lying between the mountains on either side, was held at the end of 1943 by the Japanese. From the delta on the Bay of Bengal south of Rangoon, northward through Prome, Mandalay and Katha to Bhamo in the foothills north of

Lashio, its main feature is the Irrawaddy, with the chief tributary of the Chindwin forming a western boundary against the Chin and Naga Hills, and lesser streams intersecting the country to provide a network of water communications. A main railway line runs from Rangoon through Mandalay to Myitkyina, with branches in the south to Moulmein and Prome and in the north to Monywa and Lashio, and there is a number of secondary roads radiating between the Irrawaddy and the main road from Mandalay to Rangoon. To the west, in the Japanese part of Arakan, with its base in the seaport of Akyab, are the rivers of Mayu and Kaladan which allow of water transport. The enemy thus occupied interior lines of communication, in country which gave him the advantage of his opponents in concentrating and maintaining considerable forces.

The climate of Burma is controlled by the two monsoons, the north-east from November to February or March, the south-west from May to October. In the north-east monsoon it is fine and dry with occasional light rain; in April and May the temperature rises amid thunderstorms; and from May until October the south-west monsoon, or 'the monsoon' as it is generally known, brings heavy cloud and rain. The effect is worst on the coast, where there is an occasional rainfall of up to fifteen inches a day with frequent falls of three to five inches in the Irrawaddy delta and Arakan, and an average of over one inch a day for the whole area. This decreases in the central plain north of Magwe, where there is a relatively dry belt and where the climate in general is less severe; but the wet belt begins again in the hills, although the average rainfall is lower than on the coast, averaging approximately one inch in three days.[1] The consequent humidity combines with a high temperature to impose a severe strain on the human body, particularly below 5,000 feet, and it is accordingly at this time of year that there is most disease. Dysentery, scrub typhus and malaria abound, the latter particularly at either end of the monsoon.

Above 5,000 feet, the effect of the weather is chiefly one of extreme discomfort to men living in the hills and subjected to a constant downpour of rain upon jungle and mountain tracks. All movement becomes difficult, for the soft mountain surface is subject to constant landslides, and in consequence military operations until the recent war have always followed a close season throughout the summer. Air operations, too, are affected during this period by the heavy cloud which often stretches in an unbroken mass, containing dangerous air pockets, from some 300 to some 12,000 feet, and occasionally to 30,000 feet and more. Its nature may be gauged by the fact that during the last two years of the war few cases were reported of an aircraft entering such cloud and re-emerging. It was often difficult to fly above it, to fly beneath it in the mountains was hazardous, and to circumvent it meant severely to

[1] For comparison, the average rainfall in London is two inches a month over the year.

limit the length of the flight. To campaign between spring and winter, therefore, meant to face in the coastal plain a muddy, flooded swamp in hot and humid weather and with one of the worst malarial rates in the world, and in the hills a series of precipitous and wooded slopes, up crumbling tracks and across swollen rivers, with the possibility of a high rate of disease among the soaked and weary troops, and only limited opportunities for their support and maintenance by air.

These topographical and climatic conditions had their effect not only on the campaigns themselves, but also on the attitude in which they were approached by the theatre Command and in London. Within the theatre, much effort was devoted to the improvement of existing methods of warfare, and where possible to the introduction of new methods by which to overcome the obstacles of weather and terrain; but at the same time, and particularly under a Supreme Commander who had recently been Chief of Combined Operations, such obstacles led to a long series of plans designed not to overcome but to avoid the difficulties by seaborne operations elsewhere. These plans were of more than local significance, for once the war in Burma spread beyond the immediate campaign in the north the whole direction of the British effort in south-east Asia was brought into question; and thus alternatives which appeared of tactical interest to the local commanders, often evoked a debate on strategy in London and Washington.

This close connexion between tactics and strategy was fostered by the state of the supplies. Lack of material was the governing factor for the British in the Far East during the last two years of the war. Throughout 1944 and the first quarter of 1945, European operations claimed first priority, with effects on south-east Asia whose severity was increased by the constant uncertainty of the allocations. There was little to spare; and what there was, was sometimes suddenly withdrawn. 'This overriding factor', as Admiral Mountbatten later stated, 'condemned our strategy [in south-east Asia] to being planned against a background of perpetual uncertainty about higher policy'.

In these conditions, the effect of the smallest reinforcements or withdrawals was sometimes of critical importance. The presence or absence of a single division of troops, or of a single squadron of transport aircraft or a flotilla of landing craft, might decide between alternative operations. Much of our narrative, indeed, will deal with the disposal of small but marginal forces whose size alone would not justify their mention. Some of these forces—most of the air transport, and the Chinese divisions in the north—were under American control; and their employment, reacting so directly on the divergent Allied interests, was itself complicated by the fact of this divergence.

The difficulties produced by these conditions were repeated in a wider sphere. Confronted by the obstacles to the reconquest of Burma, and thus of the territories to the south, the Chiefs of Staff seriously considered the possibility of transferring the main British effort from south-east Asia to the Pacific, leaving only the necessary force in northern Burma to ensure the protection of India and of the supplies to China. There were indeed good military and diplomatic arguments in favour of such a course. A contribution to the Pacific campaigns provided a more direct contribution to the defeat of Japan than did a campaign on the mainland of Asia, whatever its merits in containing, and possibly defeating, a substantial Japanese force; while the diplomatic advantages of victory in south-east Asia could be balanced by other advantages—of a more direct connexion with Australia and New Zealand, of a greater parity with the Americans in the formulation of strategy in the East, and of the respect of the Japanese themselves—to be expected from the presence of British forces in the Pacific. But despite its attractions, the prospect in fact evoked the same type of problem as it was designed to avoid. Whatever their destination, only small British forces could be sent to the Far East before the end of the war in Europe; and in the Pacific, as in south-east Asia, the allocation of small forces was complicated by the choice of the interests they were designed to serve. For granted that the main British effort was devoted to the Pacific, it was by no means clear in which area it should lie: whether in the south-west in conjunction with the Australians and MacArthur, where a balanced force of all arms could perhaps be employed, or in the central Pacific with the American Fleet, where the main blow seemed more likely to fall but where the British share was less likely to be noticed or credited. The difficulties were aggravated by the fact that the Americans had themselves not decided on the shape of their final offensive, so that to commit the main effort of the British Empire to one or other of the assaults—and the preparations were quite different for each—was hazardous and possibly premature. The problem in the Far East, the Prime Minister remarked on one occasion when reviewing the allocation of resources, lay in 'the making of a key fitted to open a particular lock'. It was often complicated by the difficulty of first deciding on the pattern of the lock itself.

These conditions obtained until the end of war against Japan, although the reasons for them had partly disappeared some three months before that event, with the reconquest of Burma in May, 1945 and with the simultaneous surrender of Germany. The great obstacle to success in south-east Asia was then removed, and new resources were released for both Asia and the Pacific. But these resources were themselves limited by the demands of peace, instead of war, in Europe; while the new plans were in any case overtaken by events before their results could be observed. The British achievement in the Far East was thus confined, even in the last phase of the war, to the pattern prescribed by earlier circumstances which by then had largely disappeared.

It was perhaps not surprising, although it was unfortunate, that in these circumstances the British case should not have been appreciated in the United States; for, in the words of one American observer, 'the Chinese . . . and the British . . . were dealing with a situation whose complexity was far beyond anything in American experience'.[1] It proved difficult to bring home to the authorities in Washington, with their eyes on the main operations in the Pacific, that campaigns which were not of decisive importance might raise questions of supply, organization and diplomacy which themselves were important, and that a considerable expenditure might be needed for even a modest return. This difficulty was aggravated by the very weakness from which it sprang. In Europe, where each nation deployed a comparable strength until the middle of 1944, both exercised an equal responsibility for strategy, and the machinery for consultation at all levels supplied a genuine demand. In the Far East, where the Americans' superiority in strength was accompanied by their possession of the decisive theatres with purely American commands, the British could claim little right to share in the formulation of strategy, and the appropriate machinery suffered correspondingly. In all the circumstances of the case, it is indeed a tribute to the amity which had developed between the Allies in other fields that so high a degree of mutual forbearance and co-operation should have survived in the Far East throughout the last two years of the war.

Such were the conditions for British strategy against Japan in 1944. They go far towards explaining the length and the inconclusiveness of the discussions it aroused. The British troops in Burma, and indeed most of the British in the Far East, were firmly of the impression that they were forgotten. In fact, their affairs were discussed in London with as much attention as, and probably more passion than, those of any other theatre of war. But the very volume of the papers which remain indicates the complexity and uncertainty of the debate; and after a time, it is impossible not to feel that the protagonists despaired of a satisfactory conclusion. When the consequences were so disproportionate to the resources available, and were so largely governed by the action of others, the arguments easily became hypothetical, and there is often an air of unreality which is absent from the discussions on European strategy. The difficulties may have been exacerbated by the fact that the problems of the Far East were unfamiliar in the light of the Japanese conquests, and by the fact that they imposed an extra strain upon men who had already borne heavy responsibilities for four years and who were simultaneously preoccupied with the anxieties of in-

[1] Henry L. Stimson and McGeorge Bundy, *On Active Service in Peace and War* (New York, 1947/8), p. 534.

vasion and victory in Europe. This impression is perhaps strengthened by the difficult circumstances under which the strategy was debated. With some 5,000 miles between London and India, there could be little personal contact, and the telephone, the interview and the conference—the staple of planning the West—had to yield to the telegram and the letter. The inevitable disagreements and misunderstandings thus appear—and because of this, sometimes were—more important, and certainly more prolonged, than might otherwise have been the case; and in such circumstances the occasional missions from the Far East which endeavoured to mitigate the consequences were themselves not always successful. But these obstacles merely aggravated a problem whose causes lay elsewhere. It was because the British operations against Japan demanded larger resources than could be given, and not because they took place far from home, that planning encountered such difficulties throughout 1944, and that the prolonged debate in London failed so conspicuously to dispel the legend in south-east Asia of 'the forgotten war'.

(ii)

The Formation of the South-East Asia Command

The South-East Asia Command (S.E.A.C.) was the formal product of the 'Quadrant' Conference, its objects and organization being defined in the Combined Chiefs of Staff's Final Report of 24th August, 1943. This stated that there would in future be separate Commands in India and in south-east Asia, that the latter would include Burma, Ceylon, Siam, the Malay Peninsula and Sumatra,[1] that the Viceroy of India would resolve any 'day-to-day' differences that might arise between the two Commands, and that the South-East Asia Command would be placed under a British Supreme Allied Commander, with an American deputy, three Service Commanders-in-Chief, and a Principal Administrative Officer. All business between the Combined Chiefs of Staff and the Supreme Commander would pass through the British Chiefs of Staff, who 'would exercise jurisdiction over all matters pertaining to operations', while the Combined Chiefs of Staff retained 'a general jurisdiction over strategy' for the theatre, and over the allocation of American and British resources between it and the Chinese theatre.

The Report dealt in some detail with the positions of the Deputy Supreme Commander and of the American forces in the theatre, both of which offered peculiar features.

[1] See Rear End-paper.

'. . . 52. General Stilwell will be Deputy Supreme Allied Commander of the South-East Asia Theater and in that capacity will command the Chinese troops operating into Burma and all United States air and ground forces permitted to the South-East Asia Theater.

53. The operational control of the Chinese forces operating into Burma will be exercised, in conformity with the over-all plan of the British Army Commander, by the Deputy Supreme Allied Commander or by his representative, who will be located with the troops.

54. The operational control of the 10th U.S. Air Force[1] will be vested in the Deputy Supreme Allied Commander and exercised by his air representative located at the headquarters of the Air Commander-in-Chief.

55. General Stilwell will continue to have the same direct responsibility to Generalissimo Chiang Kai-Shek as heretofore. His dual function under the Supreme Allied Commander and under the Generalissimo is recognised.

56. The organisation and command of the United States Army and Navy Air Transport Services in the South-East Asia area will remain under the direct control of the Commanding General, United States Army Air Forces, and of the Commander-in-Chief, United States Fleet, respectively, subject to such supply and service functions as may be by them delegated to the Deputy Supreme Allied Commander. Requests by the Supreme Allied Commander for the use of United States troop-carrier aircraft for operational purposes will be transmitted to the Deputy Supreme Allied Commander.

57. Requests for the use of surface transportation capacity in and through India, or for development involving construction for the air route to China, will be passed through the Supreme Allied Commander in order that they may be related, as regards priority, to his requirements before being placed on the Commander-in-Chief, India.'

On 25th August, the appointment was announced of Admiral Lord Louis Mountbatten as Supreme Allied Commander.

The Report and the communiqué represented the result of two months' discussion between the British and the Americans. Although not falling within the chronological scope of the present volume, this must be followed in some detail, for it adumbrated with remarkable precision the issues, both of strategy and of organization, which were raised during the first year of the South-East Asia Command, and which cannot otherwise be seen in their true perspective.

The formation of the Command was first seriously considered in the spring of 1943, between the Casablanca Conference of January and the Washington Conference of May. At Casablanca, the Allies had

[1] See p. 126 above.

decided to start an offensive in northern Burma designed to protect the bases of the air supply line to China, which were being steadily extended in Assam. Limited operations had already just begun in Arakan for the recapture of Akyab as a base for further operations on the flank, and in their Final Report at the conference the Combined Chiefs of Staff recommended an immediate limited advance in Assam to gain bridgeheads for future operations, and in November, 1943 a major offensive, to be known as 'Anakim,' for the reconquest of Burma. In view of the resources which this last operation would require, its details were to be reviewed in July. At the end of January 1943, a mission including Field Marshal Dill and General Arnold flew to south-east Asia to see the conditions and to judge the prospects for themselves. Early in February they obtained from Chiang Kai-shek the reassuring news that Chinese forces in Yunnan and Assam would co-operate in the main advance after the monsoon, so long as air cover was provided, and a few days later they settled with Field Marshal Sir Archibald Wavell, then commanding in India, the main outlines of the offensive. It was on an ambitious scale. In the first phase in November 1943, ten Chinese divisions, estimated at 100,000 men, would advance from western Yunnan towards Mandalay, while Stilwell's two Chinese divisions advanced from Ledo to Myitkyina and three British divisions moved from Assam towards Mandalay; in the second phase, in December, these operations would be reinforced by assaults on the coast of Arakan; in the third phase, in January 1944, there were to be seaborne and airborne assaults upon Rangoon itself. 'Anakim', in short, which was the first coherent plan for the recapture of Burma, included all the ingredients of the later operations for the same purpose in 1944-5.

But at the time, with inadequate communications for the Assam front and with the preparations for an offensive barely begun, the responsible commanders considered the plan too ambitious. By the end of April 1943, it was clear that this was indeed the case. The operations which had begun in Arakan at the beginning of the year had so far gone badly, and malaria and typhus had taken their familiar toll. The troops were not yet ready to fight an important campaign, while the necessary communications could not apparently be ready in time. Nor were supplies coming forward as had been expected. Wavell calculated that 'Anakim' required a monthly shipment to India of 183,000 tons from March 1943, and during March and April only 60-70,000 tons a month were delivered. This had already delayed the operation, so that there was little chance of its being completed before the onset of the monsoon in 1944. Wavell, supported by his naval and air commanders, therefore recommended at the end of April that 'Anakim' should be cancelled, that a limited advance should instead be undertaken in north-west Burma, and that the main emphasis should fall on the training of the troops, the improvement of the communications, and the expansion of the capacity of the air route to China.

Granted that the theatre's figures were correct, such a strategy was hard to dispute; and at the Washington Conference in May the British took their stand upon it. The Americans, however, while acknowledging the difficulties, were inclined to be critical of the way in which they were being faced, and still wished to open land communications with China. The Final Report of the Combined Chiefs of Staff represented a compromise between the two points of view. First priority was given to building up the capacity of the air route to China to 10,000 tons a month by the early autumn of 1943. At the same time, air operations against the enemy in Burma were to be increased. On land, there was to be an advance from Assam into Burma via Ledo and Imphal at the end of the 1943 monsoon, 'in step with an advance by the Chinese from Yunnan'. This was designed to contain as many Japanese as possible, to cover the air route to China, and to act as 'an essential step towards the opening of the Burma Road'. There were also to be seaborne operations to capture Akyab and Ramree Island, while Japanese sea communications with Burma were to be interrupted as far as possible. Finally, administrative arrangements were to continue in India for 'an operation about the size of 'Anakim'.'

The compromise was clearly in favour of the British strategy for Burma, and of the complementary American 'air', as opposed to 'land', strategy for China. But the British were no happier than the Americans about the causes of these decisions. The Prime Minister in particular had been uneasy for some months about the apparent lack of vigour which he detected in the Command, and he was confirmed in his impression when Wavell visited London in April. The very difficulties which the Commander-in-Chief then stressed made it the more necessary to conduct the operations with energy and imagination, and fresh ideas seemed unlikely without a change of personalities. Wavell, after his experiences, seemed a tired man. At the same time, his qualities and his knowledge of India were of the greatest value. The post of Viceroy of India was due to be refilled in the summer; in the circumstances, the Commander-in-Chief was a possible candidate for the appointment, and in June the Prime Minister recommended his name to the King. The problem of his successor as Commander-in-Chief then became the most immediate subject in the discussion of Far Eastern affairs.

The choice of a suitable commander could not be divorced from the wider question of the future nature of the Command. The satisfactory conduct of the campaign in south-east Asia depended on more than a change of personalities, for the personalities themselves had to be judged by the part for which they were designed, and new men might do better in new rôles. The existing organization could certainly be improved. Since February 1942, operations in Burma had been the responsibility of the India Command; and while such an arrangement could possibly be defended when they were directly concerned with the protection of the frontier, it was less defensible when they moved, as they were designed to do, ever further from Indian territory and the orbit of Indian strategy. Nor was such an appendage of advantage to the strained resources of the India Command itself, an organization burdened with large and complicated responsibilities over a wide area. The problem had already engaged the attention of the Secretary of State and the Viceroy, and in April, 1943 Mr. Amery proposed a possible solution in a memorandum to the Prime Minister. The time had come, he suggested, 'for the appointment of a Commander-in-Chief for South-East Asia, in supreme command of all Allied forces from . . . India, eastwards up to whatever may be the eventual junction with MacArthur's advance from Australia north-westwards'; and for this purpose he proposed that the powers granted to Wavell early in 1942, for the first, short-lived Allied Command in the Far East,[1] should be resuscitated 'in a possibly more limited form'. As the responsible Minister for India, however, he urged that 'even without the same control over Allied forces. . . the case for the separation of the planning and direction of the South-East Asia campaign from the Indian Command holds good'.

The proposals of a new and separate Command, with a Supreme Commander rather than with three Service Commanders-in-Chief in committee—an arrangement of which Mr. Amery wrote that he doubted if 'the system of a co-equal trinity is really the best for working purposes in the terrestrial sphere'—were both soon adopted. The former was finally decided by the middle of June 1943, and in the following weeks the main features of the relations between India and the new Command, and many of the latter's domestic details, were settled by the Prime Minister and the Chiefs of Staff.

While these discussions were proceeding in London, the principles of Allied co-operation in south-east Asia were being raised with Washington. At the 'Trident' Conference, Churchill had privately disclosed to some of his hosts that the British might be setting up a new Command in the area, and on 13th June he raised the matter officially in a telegram to the President. The subsequent negotiations were concerned with five points: the boundaries of the Command; the relation of the Supreme Commander to the forces under him, to his deputy, and to the Combined Chiefs of Staff; and the nomination of the Supreme Commander himself.

The first of these subjects was easily decided. The existing boundaries of the India Command, outside India itself, were taken as the basis for

[1] See p. 21 above.

S.E.A.C., the only notable alteration being the transfer of Indo-China to the Chinese theatre. Siam, however, was also recognized later, by 'gentleman's agreement' in October 1943, as falling within the Chinese sphere, the South-East Asia Command retaining the right to employ troops there, to gather intelligence, and to hold any land it might gain from the enemy.

It was upon the three questions of the relations between the Supreme Commander, his subordinates and his superiors that the weight of the discussion fell. Each affected the other, and each was affected by the same differences of opinion between the Allies; as those differences did not end with the birth of S.E.A.C., neither did the arguments which first appeared in the months of gestation.

It was obviously desirable that the Supreme Commander should have complete control of all operational forces allotted to his theatre; and in a memorandum of 15th June, which was accepted by the British Chiefs of Staff, the Prime Minister had defined these as the Eastern Fleet in so far as it was required for 'combined operations', parts of the Army in India, R.A.F. groups in India and Ceylon, and Tenth U.S. Army Air Force. On 28th June, in a telegram to the President, he added to the list such Chinese troops on the Ledo Road as might cross the Burmese frontier. These proposals at once raised their difficulties. Tenth U.S. Air Force was designed to increase the American programme of aid to China and to act as a reserve for Chennault, and it was for these purposes that it had been placed in British territory. Its allegiance was to Washington, and its direction in the hands of the Commanding General of the American C.B.I. Theatre. Similarly, the two Chinese divisions on the Ledo Road, and any Chinese force that might in future be added to them, were at the disposal of Chiang Kai-shek and under the supervision of the same American authority. Neither force was likely to be surrendered to the direct command of an Englishman. A solution to both difficulties was thought to have been found in the personality of the Deputy Supreme Commander, whose qualifications seemed, at least to the Joint Chiefs of Staff, to offer the best possibility of reconciling the divergent claims of three nations.

In his telegram to the President of 13th June, the Prime Minister had suggested that the Deputy Supreme Commander of the new theatre should be an American, and to his compatriots the obvious choice for the post seemed to be General Stilwell. In view of the positions he already held, as Commanding General of the American forces in the C.B.I. Theatre, as Lend-Lease Administrator for China, and as Chief of Staff to the Generalissimo, he could hardly indeed have been ignored. With such qualifications, it seemed to the U.S. War Department and the Joint Chiefs of Staff that his appointment to the post of Deputy Supreme Commander in the new organization offered the best chance of safeguarding American interests in the

China-Burma-India Theatre, and of reconciling them with the British plans for a South-East Asia Command. On 30th June, the President accordingly proposed that Stilwell should 'command, under the Supreme Commander, all ground and air forces at present under him in the South-East Asia theatre and such additional American and Chinese forces as may in the future be made available.' At the same time, he was to preserve his independent relations with Chiang Kai-shek, 'for upon [this] relationship . . . will depend the positive action by the Chinese in operations against Burma'.

Stilwell's many responsibilities, which constituted his claim to an appointment in yet another capacity, were as likely to lead to confusion. For this reason, the British Chiefs of Staff did not take kindly to the President's suggestion, and reserved their approval until they had a chance to discuss the arrangement with the Joint Chiefs of Staff at Quebec. The latter, and in particular General Marshall, soon made clear both the importance and the limitations which they attached to it. In reply to the argument that a multiple command and a multiple allegiance would lead to difficulties, Marshall remarked at one point that:

> 'General Stilwell's function as Deputy Supreme Commander would be limited, since his other functions would occupy the majority of his time. It must be his major task, and that not an easy one, to ensure not only that the Chinese forces played their part in the operations, but also that, to the maximum extent possible, the Fourteenth Air Force[1] should co-operate in operations in Burma. It must be remembered that politically, all United States forces in China, or in the South-East Asia Command, were regarded as being there for the sole purpose of supporting China, and therefore a system must be evolved whereby, while retaining this political principle, the maximum support could be obtained for operations into Burma'.

To secure the essential support of the Chinese, he argued on another occasion, Stilwell needed the standing of Deputy Supreme Commander. After this, appreciating the advantages to be gained from the arrangement, and relying upon the possibility that adjustments to it could be made on the spot in the light of experience, the British agreed to the proposal with little delay.

The light of experience, as it turned out, did not shine favourably on the arrangement. Stilwell's tenure of office was marked not by any adjustment of the initial difficulties, but by their early and continued growth. Later apologists of both sides have prolonged the argument, and, as in similar cases in both the First and Second World Wars, the issue has been confused by the personality of the main protagonist. 'Vinegar Joe' Stilwell, a hero to his men, an embarrassment to his colleagues, and often the despair of his superiors, was indeed the bull

[1] See p. 127 above.

in the China shop. In view of his reputation for outspokenness and intolerance, the confidence which his superiors placed in him for this peculiarly difficult post may perhaps seem strange. But it was shared by many whose judgment must command respect, including General Marshall and Mr. Stimson, to whom the war in Burma 'unfolded principally as the saga of Joe Stilwell, fighting heroically against overwhelming odds.'[1] In one sense, certainly, their confidence was not misplaced. Stilwell was a good watchdog of American resources and, as he saw them, of American interests; and the War Department, unimpressed by British achievements in Burma, was perhaps not sorry to know that a figure of his calibre was at hand. In the past two years, moreover, the tide had swung his way. He was perhaps the most prominent of that group of American officers who knew and believed in the Chinese soldier, and—of great importance to a government committed to the support of China—he was prepared to put his belief to the test; and he had already achieved an unexpected success in inducing the Chinese to train some of their troops in India, where they were fed and clothed by the British, and paid and equipped by the Americans. But these achievements were largely irrelevant to the tasks which Stilwell now assumed, and whose complexity both he and his superiors in Washington underrated. Able, confident and forceful in command of a Corps in the field, in other capacities he was out of his depth; and his shortcomings were the more serious because of the emotional temper which he brought to the support of his strictly limited ability, and which, like other not dissimilar figures, he persisted in mistaking for toughness. In consequence, he could never refrain from attributing motives, and dismissed all opposition, whatever its cause, as the result of malevolence or stupidity.[2] If Stilwell was the only man through whom the Americans and Chinese were prepared at the time to entrust their resources to the British, he was perhaps the man least fitted to succeed in that particular task.

The British Chiefs of Staff were well aware of Stilwell's peculiarities, and it may be asked why they consented to his appointment. The answer is that there was nothing else for them to do. Once the strategy of 'Trident' had been adopted, British and American plans were too closely related for either party to ignore the intentions of the other. It was to the interests of both to set up an Allied Staff in south-east Asia and, following the pattern which had emerged unofficially in North Africa,[3] a Deputy Supreme Commander of the opposite nationality to his superior. The ensuing difficulties were inherent in the situation, and indeed while they were undoubtedly aggravated by Stilwell's personality, they did not disappear with his removal in October, 1944. In

[1] Stimson and Bundy, *loc. cit.*, p. 532.

[2] General Stilwell's diary had been published under the title of *The Stilwell Papers* (1949).

[3] See p. 21 above.

these circumstances, the British could scarcely resist their allies' nomination to an appointment which they had been the first to propose, and where they were on weak ground. They accordingly decided to accept it, but to demand in return a virtually unilateral control of the theatre, such as the Americans enjoyed in the Pacific. The decision to accept the unwelcome appointment must therefore be seen in the light of the determination to retain sole operational jurisdiction over the area.

The British Chiefs of Staff fought hard for the acceptance of their views on this point. Working on the North African model with which they were familiar, they had originally submitted that the Supreme Commander should be responsible to the Combined Chiefs of Staff for planning and executing operations; but almost immediately they revised the formula to follow what they called the MacArthur model, whereby the Combined Chiefs of Staff exercised only a 'general jurisdiction over grand strategic policy' and over the allocation of forces and raw materials, while the Joint Chiefs of Staff exercised 'jurisdiction over all matters pertaining to operational strategy', and issued all instructions to the Supreme Commander on behalf of the Combined Committee. The Americans, with their responsibility for China, would not however accept this proposal, and the President telegraphed that he 'could agree . . . only to this command relationship following the Eisenhower pattern, with the British Chiefs of Staff designated as the agency for the Combined Chiefs of Staff charged with the issue of instructions to the Supreme Commander'.[1]

The two points of view were now clear, and throughout the rest of June and July each side adhered firmly to its formula. So anxious were the British Chiefs of Staff to retain sole operational control over the area, that they were prepared in return to concede to the Combined Chiefs of Staff a similar direct control over the allocation of resources to China and to the South-East Asia Command itself; but the President and his advisers remained devoted to the alternative pattern of command, arguing that its adoption would facilitate the later integration of strategy, and therefore of command, in south-east Asia and the south-west Pacific. The question was still open when the British set sail for Quebec in August; but, after some discussion at the conference, their formula was adopted together with the Americans' recommendations for the Deputy Supreme Commander.

It remained to choose the Supreme Commander himself. The Prime Minister was determined that 'the opportunity should be taken of gripping the whole situation and injecting new vim into all proceedings', and it was these qualities in the commander which determined the search. Here again the candidate had to be acceptable to the Americans, and when the British party left for Quebec the choice was

[1] See pp. 19-22 above.

still open. On the voyage, however, Churchill came to favour the idea of Lord Louis Mountbatten, a name which had been first suggested to him at the end of May, and once again by Amery. The Chiefs of Staff, and most of the Ministers in London whom he consulted, approved; the President and his advisers were agreeable; and on 24th August the Combined Chiefs of Staff drew up the terms of the communiqué which on the following day announced Mountbatten's appointment.

The complementary command in India had already been filled by the re-appointment in June of General Sir Claude Auchinleck as Commander-in-Chief, India; and in October the British representation in China, now of greater importance than before, was strengthened by the appointment of Lieut.-General Adrian Carton de Wiart as personal representative in Chungking of the Prime Minister and of the Supreme Commander. The senior commanders and staff of the new theatre were chosen within the next few weeks as follows:

Deputy Supreme Commander.
Lieut.-General Joseph B. Stilwell (U.S.)
Commander-in-Chief, Eastern Fleet.
Admiral Sir James Somerville (Br.)
Commander-in-Chief,
Eleventh Army Group,
General Sir George Giffard. (Br.)
Commander-in-Chief, Air Forces,
South-East Asia Command.
Air Chief Marshal Sir Richard Peirse (Br.)
Principal Administrative Officer.
Lieut.-General J. W. Wheeler. (U.S.)
Chief of Staff to the Supreme Commander.
Lieut.-General Sir Henry Pownall. (Br.)

The background to this organization was reflected in the positions of the three Commanders-in-Chief, which in two cases differed significantly from those of the corresponding commanders in the European theatres. Of the three, the only 'Allied' commander was the Commander-in-Chief, Eastern Fleet, who was given control over units of the U.S. Navy when within the area of the South-East Asia Command. But he was also the only one to suffer from a dual allegiance. When defending sea communications or operating against the enemy's Fleet he was responsible, like all naval commanders, to the Admiralty: when tackling shore targets or affording direct support to the army, he came under the orders of the Supreme Commander. The interpretation of these responsibilities—common to all naval commanders within Supreme Commands—was to cause a good deal of uncertainty for almost a year between Admiral Mountbatten and Admiral Somerville.

The Air Commander-in-Chief, who had formerly been Air Commander-in-Chief, India, brought with him all British air forces throughout India, Burma and Ceylon, apart from a few Indian Air Force squadrons for the defence of north-west India. He was responsible for all air operations in the Command, including those at sea, and for the development of India as a base for operations and supply. But he was not given control over Tenth U.S. Air Force, which in November, 1943 accounted for almost one-third of the operational aircraft in the Command. This force, which came under the control of Major-General Stratemeyer,[1] took its orders from the Supreme Commander through his deputy General Stilwell, who also commanded Stratemeyer directly for certain purposes. From the start, Mountbatten considered such a division of responsibility embarrassing and potentially dangerous; and in December 1943, after representations to the Combined Chiefs of Staff, he amalgamated the two Commands under Peirse, who was made Allied Air Commander-in-Chief, with Stratemeyer as his second-in-command. The Joint Chiefs of Staff, however, in a memorandum of 7th January, 1944, reserved the right to dispose of units of Tenth U.S. Air Force whenever they considered it necessary.

On land, again, the Commander-in-Chief was not an 'Allied' commander. The Prime Minister had originally wished the Supreme Commander to deal direct with his army formations; but it was eventually agreed to set up an Eleventh Army Group, whose commander controlled the forces not under the Commander-in-Chief, India. It consisted of the new British Fourteenth Army, commanded by Lieut.-General W. J. Slim, the Ceylon Army Command, some garrisons in the Indian Ocean, and certain Nepalese troops. It also exercised general supervision over the preparation of forces in India for operations in the South-East Asia Command. This organization, however, was incomplete in one important respect, for it excluded the American[2]-Chinese force in the north, whose activities were directly related to those of the British on other fronts. Their small but important front formed a separate command, later known as the Northern Combat Area Command (N.C.A.C.), which was commanded by Stilwell in his capacity of Commanding General, C.B.I. Theatre, and for which, in his capacity of Deputy Supreme Commander, South-East Asia Command, and by courtesy of Chiang Kai-shek, he was directly responsible to Mountbatten. The military hierarchy was thus seriously upset; for as Deputy Supreme Commander, Stilwell was senior to the Commander-in-Chief, Eleventh Army Group and to the commander of Fourteenth

[1] See p. 126 above.

[2] The only American ground forces in the South-East Asia Command at this time were penetration groups, containing some 2,000 men, which were known as 'Galahad' Force. In the autumn of 1944, these were increased to a strength of some two British brigades, and the main part was then known as 'Mars' Task Force.

Army, while as an operational commander of some three divisions, on a front adjoining that of Fourteenth Army, his activities were those of a subordinate. As Mountbatten was not willing to assume direct responsibility for one section of the front himself, a temporary solution was reached in November 1943, with the approval of the Prime Minister, the President and the Generalissimo, whereby Stilwell agreed to place himself and his forces under the operational control of General Slim until they reached Kamaing, north of Myitkyina. They were then to revert to the direct control of the Supreme Commander. This arrangement applied specifically to Slim alone, and the extraordinary compromise, which in the event worked quite well, was not given any publicity.

The new Supreme Commander left England by air on 2nd October, and arrived in Delhi on the 7th. The situation which greeted him was not encouraging. His Command, apart from a strip of territory along the Chin Hills and in Arakan, and the island of Ceylon, was in the hands of the enemy, who in places was still within the frontier of India. The Japanese land forces, which with the air forces were commanded by Field Marshal Count Terauchi operating under the orders of Imperial General Headquarters in Tokyo, consisted at the beginning of November, 1943 of some seven divisions in Burma, as against six British divisions with local formations and the American-Chinese force of some three divisions[1] in the north. The Japanese strength was in the region of 135,000 men, with a further 215,000 in Malaya and Siam from whom they could draw several divisions for Burma. The British reserves for the South-East Asia Command, which were concentrated in India, consisted of four divisions and a special force which Major-General Orde Wingate was raising to conduct, on a larger scale, the long-range penetrations of the enemy's lines which he had initiated successfully in 1943.

On land, there was little to choose between the two forces. The superiority in strength which the Allies enjoyed was offset by the interior lines of communication and the dispositions of the Japanese, and, on past record, by their superiority in jungle warfare.

In the air, the South-East Asia Command disposed of some seven hundred operational aircraft in fifty-five squadrons, of which some five hundred aircraft were British and British-controlled. The enemy had under three hundred combat aircraft on his forward airfields, with reserves based on Siam and the Netherlands East Indies. The discrepancy in strength was again largely offset by the general superiority of the Japanese to the British fighters. Spitfire squadrons, however,

---

[1] A Chinese division consisted in theory of some 12,500 men.

were on the way, and the first were used in November in Arakan. Their activities on that front at the end of 1943 and early in 1944 marked the first stage in the achievement of air superiority, without which Burma could not have been regained.

Of the fifty-five Allied squadrons in the Command in November 1943, five consisted of transport aircraft. All other transports, reserved for the supply of China, came under separate American command, and the five squadrons themselves had to be shared between India and Burma. When India's needs had been met, only one could be counted as always available for the campaign. Although this number increased by the end of the year, no further reinforcements were expected immediately thereafter, and in the case of the British for some time. But in addition to this force, and following a promise made by General Arnold to Mountbatten in August, a specially-equipped air unit, consisting of some 250 aircraft of various types and known as No. 1 Air Commando, arrived from the United States at the end of 1943 for the support of the long-range penetration groups.

At sea, the Japanese dominated the Bay of Bengal, with a small force of cruisers and minor units. The British Eastern Fleet, based on Trincomalee in Ceylon, was largely dispersed over the wide area of the Command, cruising and convoying and repairing in African waters. Some units, also, were loaned to the Mediterranean or to home waters. The only forces at its effective disposal, other than coastal craft and escort vessels, were one cruiser squadron and one submarine flotilla. But preparations were being made at Trincomalee to receive reinforcements, and in January, 1944 the base was ready for a Battle Squadron, including three battleships and two fleet aircraft carriers, which arrived at the end of the month.

The most satisfactory features of the new Command, therefore, lay behind the lines, in the Spitfires and the Battle Squadron on their way from England, in No. 1 Air Commando on its way from America, in the new wharves and dock buildings in Trincomalee and the new airfields and expanding communications in Assam, in the long-range penetration groups training in India, and in the jungle training schemes and improved medical facilities throughout the area. Some of these activities were now increased. Important sectors of the communications in Assam were placed under military control, and with American help their capacity was increased by over 50 per cent within a year; the air supply of the long-range penetration groups was given a high priority—thanks largely to the advocacy of Wingate, whose sombre and unorthodox personality had fired the imagination of Prime Minister and public alike—with results which were to prove of value to Fourteenth Army as a whole; and medical improvements were introduced by which the ratio of sick to wounded dropped from 120:1 in 1943 to 20:1 in 1944, and to 6:1 by the end of the war. The malaria rate alone, which in 1943 was 84 per cent of the army's whole strength, dropped to 13 per cent by 1945.

Meanwhile, the Command in India was straining the limited facilities of the sub-continent, at a time of political and economic uncertainty, to prepare a base for twenty divisions, with capacity for five more in transit, for 154 R.A.F. squadrons and thirty shore-based naval air squadrons, and for more escorts and small units of the Fleet. By the winter of 1943, the effort that was being put into the area seemed to bode great things.

(iii)

A Strategy for Burma

On 23rd October, Admiral Mountbatten received his first directive from the Prime Minister, as recommended by the British Chiefs of Staff. The first paragraph referred to the arrangements already agreed for the form of the Command. The paragraphs affecting future operations ran as follows.

> '. . . 2. Your prime duty is to engage the Japanese as closely and continuously as possible in order by attrition to consume and wear down the enemy's forces, especially his air forces, thus making our superiority tell and forcing the enemy to divert his forces from the Pacific theatre—and secondly, but of equal consequence, to maintain and broaden our contacts with China. both by the air route and by establishing direct contact through Northern Burma *inter alia* by suitably organized air-supplied ground forces of the greatest possible strength.
>
> 3. You will utilise to the full the advantage of the sea power and air power which will be at your disposal, by seizing some point or points which
>
> (a) induce a powerful reaction from the enemy, and
>
> (b) give several options for a stroke on your part in the light of the enemy's aforesaid reaction.
>
> For this purpose, in making your proposals for amphibious operations in 1944, you will select the point of attack which seems best calculated to yield the above conditions, and will execute the operation approved. You will also prepare plans for the second phase of your campaign in 1944 contingent upon the reaction extorted from the enemy.
>
> 4. At least four weeks before your first major amphibious operation you will be furnished by His Majesty's Government with a Battle-Fleet to be based on Ceylon sufficient in strength to fight a general engagement with any force which, in the opinion of His Majesty's Government, it is reasonable to suppose the

Japanese could afford to detach from the Pacific. The Eastern Fleet will for this purpose be equipped with at least 10 escort carriers as well as with such armoured fleet carriers as may be available.

5. You will proceed to form, as resources come to hand, a combined striking force or circus which will be available as the foundation of whatever amphibious descent is eventually chosen. This force should consist of the aircraft carriers to provide air support, secondly of an in-shore squadron for coastal bombardment, and further of the necessary transports, assault ships and landing craft of various classes. You will arrange, in conjunction with the Commander-in-Chief, India, for the preparation and training of the forces required by you for the special task of making opposed landings from the sea and of thus establishing bridgeheads at which reinforcements not trained for the above special work can be safely and continuously landed. You will specify such requirements for making artificial harbours, airfields, and floating runways as you may think necessary and as are within the bounds of possibility at the dates involved.

6. You will, at the earliest moment, report your plans, dates and requirements, bearing in mind the advantages of speed.'

The main difference between this and earlier instructions lay in the emphasis on seaborne assaults. Mountbatten was thus able, unlike his predecessors, to consider a series of related operations by land and sea with which to further the objects defined in paragraph 2 of the directive. On land, he had at his disposal a plan for a winter offensive which General Auchinleck had produced in September.[1] This provided for an advance on the central front to a line Indaw-Katha with three divisions, supplied by twenty-three squadrons of transport aircraft and supported by a complementary and diversionary advance by the Chinese troops from Yunnan. In Arakan, operations were to be mounted against Akyab. Depending as it did upon a force of transport aircraft which the theatre did not possess, and upon the highly problematical co-operation of the Chinese, the success of the main plan seemed far from certain. Mountbatten's first action, nine days after his arrival in Delhi, was therefore to fly to Chungking in order to see Chiang Kai-shek. As a result, he was assured that after January, 1944 the Chinese would advance from Ledo under Stilwell and from Yunnan, provided that local air supply was guaranteed and that a seaborne operation, supported by an adequate Battle Fleet, was carried out as part of the operations. Chiang Kai-shek, indeed, reluctant to weaken the vital province of Yunnan and constantly assailed by intrigue, sought in the latter demand an obvious assurance that the Western Allies meant business. Mountbatten, fresh from talks with the Chiefs of Staff, was able to hint that such an operation would be

[1] See Map III, facing p. 129.

forthcoming; and the arrival of the Prime Minister's directive in the following week, suggesting that the Generalissimo's demand would be met, saw the beginning of detailed planning for the winter offensive by land.

The shape of the seaborne operation had still to be decided. Mountbatten had left London with one possibility in his pocket, the Prime Minister's personal plan for a major attack on the northern tip of Sumatra. This operation, known successively as 'Culverin' and 'First Culverin'[1], was to haunt the stage for over a year. Its object at this point was to make the best use, with the limited forces available, of the dry season of 1944. For this purpose the Prime Minister considered it essential to avoid a major campaign on the central front in Burma, where, in his own words, 'going into swampy jungles to fight the Japanese is like going into the water to fight a shark'.[2] Instead of putting the main effort into a frontal attack in difficult and disease-ridden country, he proposed to hold the line in Arakan, to penetrate behind the Japanese with Wingate's forces so as to join the Chinese in the north, and to exploit the length of the coastline to the south with the troops and shipping now reserved for the assault on Akyab and Ramree. The Allies would thereby create a situation in which the enemy would be forced to guard against a number of probable threats along his flank and against his main bases. If northern Sumatra were then occupied 'as far down south as was necessary to develop . . . a heavy scale of air attack against enemy bases and airfields within range', the Allies should obtain a strong reaction from the enemy, including perhaps a withdrawal of forces from Burma, for a comparatively small expenditure of effort; would gain a useful air base within range of Singapore; and, most important, would have established the necessary preliminary conditions for a flexible strategy based on the resources already available from India. The precise steps to be taken immediately after 'Culverin' remained uncertain: 'we might go on to Malaya, we might reinforce Northern Sumatra to cause the Japanese further annoyance, or if it paid us, we might even withdraw from it'. But in any case the Allies should be able to exploit a favourable situation in 1944, rather than allow valuable time to be consumed in an inevitably slow and hard fought campaign 'against the grain' of the mountains from the north. If his views were accepted, and the forces redisposed accordingly, Churchill calculated that operations in

[1] 'Culverin' was originally designed to cover an operation against northern Sumatra and Malaya. The Prime Minister then turned to the idea of an operation against the northern tip of Sumatra alone, which he christened 'Junior Culverin'. He then expressed the wish that it should be called 'Culverin'. This led to confusion, and in August, 1943 he decided to call the reduced operation 'First Culverin', retaining 'Culverin' for the more ambitious plan. In practice, both 'Culverin' and 'First Culverin' continued to be used indiscriminately for the attack on northern Sumatra alone, although theoretically—and in practice occasionally, as on pp. 159-60 below—they were distinguished from each other.

[2] See *The Hinge of Fate* (1951), p. 702.

northern Burma should occupy from February to June 1944, and 'Culverin' the months of May and June. On this basis, as he said in August 1943, the operation 'is . . . the largest diversionary action open to us with the forces available in 1944'. Always sensitive to the threat of a deadlock on land, and averse to an excessively rigid programme for the more distant future, the Prime Minister wished to initiate in south-east Asia a campaign which bore his favourite hall marks of audacity, economy and flexibility.

The plan was first produced at the Washington Conference in May, 1943; but in view of the meagre resources then available, the Combined Chiefs of Staff persuaded Churchill that its consideration must be postponed. But it reappeared in a more detailed form at Quebec, when the Prime Minister developed its advantages at some length. Mountbatten was also attracted by the plan at this stage, and when he left London, fresh from his last talks with Churchill, he felt that 'you are as right about 'Culverin' as you were about 'Torch',[1] but [I] fear you will find it difficult to persuade all the others'. 'The others', indeed, were entirely opposed to the operation. The British Chiefs of Staff agreed with the Prime Minister that success in the north depended on a complementary seaborne attack upon the enemy's flank; but they differed from him in their assessment of what any northern advance must involve. To regain enough ground from which to protect the bases for the air route to China, as well as to reopen land communications, they argued that it was necessary to reconquer the whole of northern and central Burma down to the port of Rangoon and the line of the Irrawaddy. Wingate's operations offered no firm line on which to stand, nor would they secure the bases and the permanent communications on which any offensive must rely. It was impossible, as the Chiefs of Staff then saw it, to supply a whole front continuously from the air. From Rangoon ran the roads and the railway which were so badly needed, while the port itself was the Cherbourg of Burma, whose capture they considered as essential ultimately to the nourishment of Mountbatten's operations as was Cherbourg's ultimately to those of Eisenhower. But before Rangoon could be attacked, an advanced base was needed nearer to the target than Chittagong; and it was for this reason, and to rest the flank more securely on the sea, that they suggested seaborne assaults on Akyab and Ramree. They admitted that these operations would occupy the dry season of 1943/44, and that Rangoon itself could not be captured before the following dry season at the end of 1944. But once the port had been gained, the Allies could command that flexibility which the Prime Minister desired, for they could then either extend operations into southern Burma or could bypass it to stage a major attack upon Singapore in March, 1945. 'Culverin', on the other hand, had little to recommend it. Its specific

[1] See p. 21 above.

purpose was to gain an air base from which to bomb Singapore—at best a minor advantage at this stage; while its implications had not been, and from the circumstances could not be, assessed with any precision, and their vagueness might well endanger the purposes for which they had been proposed. 'If we go for Sumatra [in 1944], we shall not only prejudice the possibility of subsequent operations to recapture Singapore, but by abandoning the proposed operations in Burma we shall surrender that flexibility'.

The Americans opposed 'Culverin' for different reasons. They disagreed with the British Chiefs of Staff that the major effort must wait until March 1945, but they disagreed entirely with the Prime Minister that that effort should lie in the south. The President, in particular, felt strongly that 'Culverin' would divert British resources from the main object of reopening communications with China, and that it was heading in the wrong direction, away from the shortest route to Japan. At Quebec, therefore, Mr. Churchill's efforts received little reward. They were on that account only redoubled.

Mountbatten's first acquaintance with 'Culverin' was at Quebec, when he and Wingate were ordered at short notice to produce an estimate of the forces required. When he came to study its implications on the spot, he was soon forced to modify his appreciation. For on closer examination, the forces originally allotted appeared inadequate for the task. Even before the local planners and commanders had studied the problem, the figures had risen substantially from those given at Quebec, and on 6th October the Joint Planners in London estimated that the operation would require, over and above the resources which would then be available in the theatre, naval ships and aircraft whose removal would severely hamper trade protection early in 1944, some 1,000 to 1,500 sailors earmarked for the assaults on the south of France and 'Overlord', 'personnel shipping' engaged in the Pacific and Atlantic, assault shipping wanted for operations in Europe, and land forces which, though probably available in time, would leave no reserve in India other than armour. The initial landings would moreover have to take place in March or early in April 1944, owing to the weather in the area under review, and not in May as the Prime Minister had proposed; and the timetable of supply from other theatres would therefore have to be revised. If the operation was to proceed, in fact, it could be only with American help, and the Chiefs of Staff accordingly inquired if this was likely to be forthcoming.

The Prime Minister was annoyed by the heightened demands. If they were accepted, he remarked on 23rd October, 'the Operation is killed stone dead', and he therefore preferred not to move until he had heard from Mountbatten. But the responsible commanders in south-east Asia, in the absence of the Supreme Commander in Chungking, had already informed the Chiefs of Staff that they could not carry out

'Culverin' with the resources at their disposal; and despite the Prime Minister's insistence—'There is only one Operation worth considering and we ought not to confuse the issue', he minuted on an alternative proposal early in November—the Chiefs of Staff over the next three weeks were considering other possibilities. 'Culverin' had at least shown the advantages of going further afield, and on 29th October they informed the British Joint Staff Mission in Washington that they had decided to abandon the assault on Akyab and Ramree in favour of an attack upon the Andaman Islands. This they considered the most promising operation possible within the resources allowed at Quebec. It would not offer advantages comparable to those arising from the capture of northern Sumatra; but it would provide a useful advanced base for reconnaissance and, later, preparation for further attacks to the south, and would force the enemy to guard against several unknown threats to his flank. On 10th November Mountbatten agreed with this appreciation, and by the third week of the month, with 'First Culverin' now scrapped, the Command had produced a comprehensive plan for the dry season of 1943/44. It consisted of seven related operations:

(a) A seaborne operation to capture the Andaman Islands (operation 'Buccaneer').
(b) An advance with one Corps along the Arakan coast and the Mayu Peninsula, leading eventually to the capture of Akyab.
(c) An advance with one Corps on the central front across the Chindwin river.
(d) An advance by Stilwell's three divisions on the northern front.
(e) An advance by the Chinese force in Yunnan (known as the 'Y' force) to Bhamo and Lashio, to secure the Chinese end of the Ledo road.
(f) Operations in support of (d) and (e) by Wingate's long-range penetration forces.
(g) Airborne operations to capture Indaw, on the railway from Mandalay to Myitkyina (operation 'Tarzan').

It was important to obtain early approval for these operations, and accordingly Mountbatten asked leave to attend the forthcoming conference in Cairo, at which the Chinese would be present for the first time. When he left Delhi, he was prepared to press for a decision.

CHAPTER IV

THE DECISIONS FOR 1944: I, CAIRO AND TEHERAN, NOVEMBER–DECEMBER, 1943

(i)

Cairo: The Problems Considered

THE CAIRO CONFERENCE (the 'Sextant' Conference) began on 22nd November, and continued until the 26th. Large British and American delegations attended its various meetings, and a Chinese delegation, headed by Chiang Kai-shek, was present in Cairo throughout. The British and Americans, with smaller staffs, then left for the conference with the Russians at Teheran (the 'Eureka' Conference), which lasted from 28th November to 1st December. On 2nd December they reassembled in Cairo, where 'Sextant' was resumed on the 3rd, lasting until the 7th.

The meeting with the Russians formed the central episode of the conferences, in importance as in time. Its prospect dominated the first, as its results governed the second, phase of 'Sextant'. But the precise relation between 'Sextant' and 'Eureka' appeared somewhat differently to the British and to the Americans, and some difference of opinion thus arose over the arrangements for the earlier meeting. The Americans' proposals arose partly from policy, and partly from the personal attitude of the President. For while the Prime Minister had first sustained the correspondence with Stalin for a meeting, Roosevelt may be regarded, in a particular sense, as its sponsor. 'Eureka' to him was indeed of crucial importance, for it provided the greatest challenge and the greatest opportunity that had yet faced the foreign policy of the United States, in its transition from isolationism to an active intervention in world affairs. This revolution, as Mr. Roosevelt appreciated, could be a success only if the new policy preserved the moral basis of its predecessor. The same ideals of disinterestedness and impartiality, which had been expressed by isolationism, must now serve its antithesis. An obvious consequence followed. American participation in Europe meant American arbitration in Europe, providing in the eyes of its authors a moral balance as the British supremacy had provided a balance of power. The forthcoming conference would for the first time allow, and indeed demand, the exercise of this new responsibility, in concert with two great European powers whose own traditions and interests did not coincide. Roosevelt was therefore determined that the meeting with Stalin should succeed, and convinced that he must be the medium of its success. This conviction, the natural reflection of a policy which had been generally beneficial to the British, in this case produced unwelcome consequences for them. For in accordance with his theory, the President was particularly anxious not to appear to 'gang up'[1] on the Russians, by holding long preliminary conversations before the Western Allies reached Teheran. At first, indeed, he had envisaged a tripartite conference, followed by a conference of the Combined Chiefs of Staff and preceded only by a brief meeting between the British and the Americans to compose agenda and plans. When this proved impossible, he sought to preserve his aims by other means: by proposing an opening date for 'Eureka' which would limit the length of the first stage of 'Sextant' to about three days, and by suggesting that a Russian military observer should attend the preliminary conference.

The President's proposals conformed to military policy; for an early meeting with the Russians was most agreeable to the Joint Chiefs of Staff. In the middle of November 1943, they placed the greatest emphasis for 1944 on the Pacific and on 'Overlord', to which a seaborne operation in south-east Asia and operations in the Mediterranean were regarded as auxiliary. One important proviso, however, had to be made. While the Joint Chiefs of Staff were anxious to preserve the inviolability of 'Overlord', they were not sure that they could do so. They expected the British to oppose it; and they were uncertain of the Russians' views. They had indeed received the impression in October that the Russians might accept the British argument for a larger campaign in the Mediterranean, even if this involved a postponement of 'Overlord'. In view of the long-standing clamour for a 'second front', and of subsequent developments, this may seem strange. But the possibility had recently received some support. During the Foreign Secretaries' conference in Moscow, Mr. Eden had informed Stalin, on instructions from London, that 'Overlord' might have to be postponed for a short while, if operations in the south demanded the retention of some of the necessary assault shipping in the spring. The Russians however took this calmly, and indeed remarked on the necessity for prosecuting the campaign in Italy with vigour. The Americans therefore concluded that recent successes had enabled the Russians to consider a more immediate measure of help from the Western Allies, and might lead them to demand at Teheran a larger effort in Italy and possibly even an invasion of the Balkans from the south. If this proved to be the case, the Americans' conception of 'Overlord' might have to be abandoned. The Joint Chiefs of Staff had therefore some cause to see

[1] His own phrase.

how the land lay at Teheran, and meanwhile not to commit themselves finally with the British.

On the other hand, the Americans wished to reach some firm decisions as soon as possible on the war in the Far East. This indeed had seemed to them from the first the main purpose of a preliminary meeting with the British; for since Russia was not at war with Japan, decisions could be taken in this field without considering her views. The most urgent necessity here was to define the rôle of China in the approach to Japan, which in turn seemed likely to depend on British action in south-east Asia. The Americans therefore wished to discuss operations in that theatre before going on to Teheran, leaving the main discussion on European operations—which might, of course, by then have been conditioned to some extent by the commitments in the Far East—to the later conference.

The British approached the conferences from a different position, the result of a different order of priority for the operations in 1944. Allowing for the presumed inviolability of the Pacific, where they could not hope to influence decisions, this was as follows:

(1) 'Overlord' and the Mediterranean. Pacific.

(2) A seaborne operation in south-east Asia.

The British therefore envisaged a full discussion with the Americans on the relation of 'Overlord' to the Mediterranean, unfettered by the presence of a Russian delegation or observer; followed by the conference with the Russians, which would settle finally the strategy for Europe; and thereafter by a further Anglo-American conference, at which the respective commitments for that strategy would be determined and the war in the Far East discussed, in that context, with the Chinese. In view of the likely shortage of assault shipping for all of these operations, the order of their debate was of considerable significance.

These divergent views were reflected in the arrangements for the conferences; and the outcome was of some importance for the subsequent course of events. Towards the end of October, the difficulties in the way of a meeting between the three Heads of Government seemed likely to prove insuperable. Stalin, owing to his military duties, could not agree to come further south than Teheran; while Roosevelt, owing to the nature of his constitutional duties, preferred North Africa or Iraq. On 27th October, the President therefore made his suggestion that a Russian military observer should attend the Anglo-American conference at Cairo. The Prime Minister, however, opposed this strongly; and a correspondence ensued on the detail of the arrangements. Mr. Churchill was anxious for a preliminary meeting of British and Americans at Malta, to discuss plans for the Mediterranean before the Russians and—as the Americans had suggested—the Chinese joined them at Cairo; but the President preferred to hold all meetings at Cairo, where the Western Allies could confer with each other before the others arrived. He was anxious, however, (as Chiang Kai-shek himself was anxious) to talk to the Chinese before the Americans and British met the Russians, and therefore wished to invite Chiang Kai-shek to Cairo to arrive by 22nd November, the date on which 'Sextant' was now due to start. The Prime Minister found that he could not but agree to these suggestions, and the invitation was sent accordingly. But the Russians, after a last complicated exchange, decided after all not to send a delegation to Cairo, and the President finally overcame the difficulties which had prevented him from going to Teheran.

So far as the British were concerned, 'Sextant' therefore opened unsatisfactorily. They had failed to persuade the Americans to come in advance to Malta for talks on the Mediterranean, and as soon as they met in Cairo the Combined Chiefs of Staff were confronted, in Chiang Kai-shek's presence, by the need to discuss the Far East. The result could be seen in the agenda for the conference, which was agreed at the first meeting of the Combined Chiefs of Staff on the afternoon of 22nd November.

> '1—Reaffirm Over-all objective, Over-all Strategic Concept and Basic Undertakings. . . .
> 2—South-East Asia Operations.
> 3—'Overlord' and the Mediterranean.
> 4—The War against Japan.
> 5—Progress Reports.'

The British Chiefs of Staff, who had earlier proposed a different agenda on their order of priority, noted that 'South-East Asia Operations have been placed second on the list, in view of the intention to bring the Generalissimo and Admiral Mountbatten into the discussions at the earliest stage.'

The plans for south-east Asia thus assumed the foremost, and a central, position in the first stage of 'Sextant'; and 'Culverin' or 'Buccaneer'[1] was the centre of those plans. In the view of the British Chiefs of Staff, either was a particularly unfortunate operation on which to concentrate so much interest. For whether or not either should be undertaken depended not so much on its own merits, as on its relation to the seaborne assaults in Europe and to the future British strategy in the Far East, as distinct from the strategy in Burma. Neither had as yet been decided, and both should be decided before the precise rôle of this apparently minor undertaking could be assessed. Provided that the date of 'Overlord' could be postponed from May to

[1] See pp. 150, 153 above.

July 1944[1], the British Chiefs of Staff estimated that the necessary assault shipping could be transferred between the Mediterranean and the Indian Ocean so as to allow 'Buccaneer' to be launched in March, after the operation in western Italy and the capture of Rhodes. But that possibility might be prejudiced in advance if a decision on 'Culverin' or 'Buccaneer' were taken first. It was moreover far from certain that the campaign of which 'Culverin' or 'Buccaneer' was to be a part, would prove correct or necessary in the context of the wider strategy for the war against Japan. At the beginning of 'Sextant', there were indeed two reasons for the British to think that it might not.

Both had appeared recently. The first concerned the action of the British themselves. On 25th October, the Combined Staff Planners produced a study, for which the Combined Chiefs of Staff had called at the end of the Quebec Conference, on the defeat of Japan within twelve months of Germany's defeat. Since it provided the basis for much subsequent Staff thought, and radically affected the existing British plans for south-east Asia, that part of it which concerned the British must be quoted in some detail. Its possibilities in the first instance concerned the British Fleet. Proceeding on the assumption that 'a plan which will ensure the defeat of Japan must provide for invasion', the Combined Planners considered four courses of action.[2]

> '*Course W.*—To aim at the invasion of Hokkaido in the summer of 1945 and, failing this, the capture of Formosa from the Pacific in the spring of 1945.
>
> The Japanese main islands might be invaded in the summer of 1946.
>
> *Course X.*—To aim at the capture of Formosa from the Pacific in the spring of 1945, retaining the option to undertake 'First Culverin' in the autumn (or possibly spring) of 1945 if the Formosa operation has to be postponed.
>
> The Japanese main islands might be invaded in the autumn of 1946.
>
> *Course Y.*—To aim at the capture of Singapore by the end of 1945 to enable Formosa to be attacked from both the Pacific and the South China Sea in the winter of 1945/6.
>
> The Japanese main islands might be invaded in early 1947.
>
> *Course Z.*—To undertake a major diversion in South-East Asia ('First Culverin') in the spring of 1945 (or possibly autumn 1944) and to aim at the capture of Formosa from the Pacific in the winter of 1945/6.
>
> The Japanese main islands might be invaded in early 1947.'

The consequences for the British Fleet varied in each of these four contingencies. Its presence was considered necessary to Course W and Course X, and, from the time needed for its transfer after the end

[1] See p. 114 above.

[2] See Map I, facing p. 11.

of the European war, ambitious seaborne operations in south-east Asia would accordingly be impossible. If, on the other hand, Course Y or Course Z were adopted, the Fleet might be used in the Pacific in the winter of 1944/45, subsequently carrying out an attack on northern Sumatra ('First Culverin') in the spring of 1945; or in the Indian Ocean, carrying out an attack on Malaya ('Culverin') in the spring of 1945, and thereafter aiming at the capture of Singapore and an entry into the Pacific by the end of that year; or at first in the Indian Ocean, carrying out an attack on northern Sumatra at latest by the spring of 1945, and thereafter entering the Pacific.

The preparations for the different possibilities themselves differed radically from each other. Course W would probably involve the establishment of bases for the British in Canada and the United States, with advanced bases in the Aleutians and in the south-west or central Pacific; Courses X and Z, the establishment of advanced bases in the south-west or central Pacific, which would be fed from India and perhaps from Australia; Course Y no new bases, but some help from the Americans in the Pacific.

The conclusions were as follows:

> '(a) We are unable to find a plan which offers any prospect of defeating Japan by October 1945.
>
> (b) *Courses W and X* are the only ones which offer any hope of defeating Japan in 1946.
>
> (c) *Course W* leaves open the greatest possibilities for exploiting an unexpected Japanese weakness or an unexpected entry of Russia into the war.
>
> On the other hand, it involves a big reorientation of our base preparations and risks the Japanese withdrawing forces from South-East Asia for the reinforcement of their "inner zone" before we have weakened them effectively.
>
> (d) *Course X*, by giving up the possibility of invading Hokkaido in the summer of 1945, involves less reorientation of base preparations and gives us the maximum flexibility between the main theatres in the Pacific and Indian Oceans, thereby leaving us an opportunity of exploiting a Japanese withdrawal from South-East Asia, though we risk being too late to prevent it.
>
> (e) *Course Y* rules out any hope there may be of defeating Japan in 1946, but provided we make sure of adopting the spring 1945 date for 'Culverin' and of capturing Singapore before the end of 1945, should prevent the Japanese from withdrawing into their "inner zone" by stretching them over the widest area. It therefore probably offers the surest way of defeating Japan in 1947.
>
> (f) *Course Z* has an advantage over Course Y in that it is not dependent on the timely capture of Singapore, but, on the other hand, being a compromise, is liable to prove to be a disadvantageous dispersion of forces.
>
> While Course Y is probably the surest way of defeating Japan

PLATE II. THE CAIRO CONFERENCE, NOVEMBER 1943

Back row, left to right: General Somervell, General Stilwell, General Arnold, Field Marshal Dill, Admiral Mountbatten, General Carton de Wiart.

Front row, left to right: Generalissimo Chiang Kai-shek, Mr. Roosevelt, Mr. Churchill, Madame Chiang Kai-shek.

eventually, we conclude that Course X is the best way of achieving our object in 1946, and should be adopted . . .

If . . . it is found impracticable or inadvisable to adopt Course X, we do not think Course Y should be adopted unless there is every prospect of providing the resources required to capture Singapore in time to enable the British Fleet to operate in the Formosa area by the Spring of 1946. In the absence of this prospect, Courze Z should be adopted.'

The adoption of Course X would raise important problems of supply and organization, which the British would soon have to consider if its timetable were to be maintained. At their first meeting at Cairo on 22nd November, the British Chiefs of Staff accordingly recommended that the naval planners should prepare an administrative plan 'as a matter of urgency', and the next day they followed this up with the suggestion that the Combined Chiefs of Staff should examine the policy for the Far East as soon as possible. But this had to await a further detailed study by the Combined Planners of the operations in the Pacific for 1944, which in the event was not ready by the end of the first stage of the conference. The British were therefore faced throughout that short period with the possibility that their participation in the Pacific campaign might mean the abandonment of operations against Malaya, a consequent revision of their strategy in south-east Asia, and thus a reconsideration of the scale of operations in Burma.

It was also not certain what part Russia might eventually play in the Far East. Hitherto, there had been no indication of her attitude, and the campaigns against Japan had naturally been devised without considering it. But three weeks before the Cairo Conference began, a most interesting development occurred. On 30th October, when the British and American Foreign Ministers were in Moscow, Stalin remarked suddenly and in passing to Mr. Cordell Hull that the Russians would join in defeating Japan when the Allies had defeated Germany. Moreover, a passage was included in the communiqué at the end of the conference, that

> ' this declaration provides for even closer collaboration in the prosecution of the war and in all matters pertaining to the surrender and disarmament of the enemies with which the four countries respectively are at war.'

The Prime Minister was inclined to think that the formula was designed to allow at least for an eventual break between Russia and Japan; and, if still a remote possibility, this must nevertheless constitute a further argument for postponing a decision on the operation in the Indian Ocean.

The Americans, however, viewed that operation in a different light. Distrusting the British proposals for the Mediterranean, and largely discounting the British strategy for the Far East, they looked on 'Culverin' or 'Buccaneer' solely for its importance to China, as a guarantee of Allied support whose abandonment must weaken Chiang Kai-shek, and thus in turn detract from the volume of Chinese support for the Western Allies. This concern for China, particularly since the Chinese would be present, disposed the Americans to press the claim for the British operation which their position in the Far East allowed them to make. On 18th November, the Joint Chiefs of Staff clarified their attitude.

> '(1) The United States Chiefs of Staff realise that it is undesirable for the Combined Chiefs of Staff to enter into the details of various operations, but do not agree, however, that only matters of grand strategy should be considered by the Combined Chiefs of Staff.
>
> (2) The 'Quadrant' decisions . . . state that the Combined Chiefs of Staff would exercise a general jurisdiction over strategy for the South-East Asia Theater. This is construed as requiring decision by the Combined Chiefs of Staff as to which of several courses of action are to be undertaken, and their sequence and timing.
>
> (3) Since the United States cannot furnish the required assistance for 'First Culverin' [attack on northern Sumatra], it is agreed that operation 'Buccaneer' [attack on the Andamans] should be mounted as early as practicable. However, we believe it may prove possible to conduct additional land, sea, and air operations in order to pin down Japanese forces in South Burma. We therefore recommend that the Commander-in-Chief, South-East Asia, [*sic*] be directed to explore this subject, and submit recommendations thereon to the Combined Chiefs of Staff.'

This threatened intervention alarmed the British Chiefs of Staff, for its effects on the South-East Asia Command and on the disposal of resources between that Command and other theatres. On the morning of 23rd November, a few hours before the first Allied meeting at Cairo began, they accordingly decided to recommend that the Joint Chiefs of Staff's paper on 'Buccaneer' should not be considered until after the main strategy for the war against Japan, that the Planners' relevant study should be presented as soon as possible, and that meanwhile 'it was undesirable to attempt to define too clearly the matter of the Combined Chiefs of Staff's jurisdiction in the South-East Asia Theatre'.

The British Chiefs of Staff, in fact, were now attempting to postpone consideration of the item on the agenda which they had only just agreed to take near the head of the list. Not unnaturally, they encountered considerable opposition. On the afternoon of 23rd November, they gained the consent of the Joint Chiefs of Staff to suspend a 'final decision' on 'Buccaneer' until it could be considered in relation to other operations; but this was not the same as postponing its 'consideration', and in fact it could not but be considered continuously over the next three days. All other interested parties—Mountbatten, the Chinese, and the Americans—were anxious to secure a firm assurance that, as the attack on Sumatra was now out of the picture, the attack on the Andamans would be launched in March, 1944; and in accordance with the agenda, the affairs of the South-East Asia Command—of which the operation was the centre—occupied the place of honour at the first Plenary Meeting on the 23rd, and at three of the remaining four sessions of the Combined Chiefs of Staff before the conference adjourned to Teheran.

The discussions on south-east Asia derived their form at this stage from three related demands, which Chiang Kai-shek and his advisers raised on 23rd and 24th November. They then insisted, first, that a lift of 10,000 tons a month over the 'Hump' must be maintained, irrespective of operations in Burma; secondly, that the proposed advance across the Chindwin (operation 'Tarzan') should aim at Mandalay instead of at the line Indaw-Katha,[1] to conform to the advance of the Yunnan force to Lashio; and thirdly, that a 'naval' operation must be launched to synchronize with the operations by land.

The first demand got short shrift from both British and Americans. Mountbatten, for the Command, and Marshall, on behalf of the Americans who supplied the aircraft, informed the Chinese that the ferry to China must undoubtedly suffer if larger operations in Burma were to be launched. The Chinese must therefore take their choice; and it was obvious what that choice must be. At the same time, Mountbatten was instructed to maintain the supplies over the 'Hump' if possible to a level of 8,900 tons a month for the next six months. The discussion then turned on the demands for the operations themselves. In a series of conversations with the Chinese, the British stated their position unambiguously. Mountbatten explained in detail that an advance to Mandalay could not be undertaken, for it would require at least five hundred more aircraft than he had at his disposal, and which he could not expect to receive. As a result, Chiang Kai-shek acceded to the original limits for 'Tarzan', provided that the Combined Chiefs of Staff still refused, on Mountbatten's specific request, to supply the aircraft necessary for the more ambitious plan.

At the same time, the British defined their attitude to 'Buccaneer'. Chiang Kai-shek had stated with particular emphasis at the first Plenary Meeting that

> 'the success of the operation in Burma depended, in his opinion, not only on the strength of the naval forces established in the Indian Ocean, but on the simultaneous co-ordination of naval action with the land operations.'

[1] See p. 153 above.

The Prime Minister replied immediately that naval operations would not necessarily be linked directly to the land campaign, as had happened, for instance, in the invasion of Sicily. It was not entirely clear, from the Generalissimo's use of the word 'naval', that the two men were referring to the same type of operation; but when they met privately on the afternoon of the 26th, there was no misunderstanding. The Prime Minister, while assuring Chiang Kai-shek that an adequate British Fleet (of which he gave details) would be available in the Indian Ocean by March 1944, could not promise that a seaborne assault would then be launched. Indeed, he seems to have gone further. 'The Prime Minister', he noted on 29th November,[1] 'wishes to put on record the fact that . . . he specifically refused the Generalissimo's request that he should undertake an amphibious operation simultaneously with the land operations in Burma.'

By 27th November, the British had thus stated their position to the Chinese. They also wished to put it on record to both Chinese and Americans. On Mountbatten's suggestion, the Combined Chiefs of Staff decided on the 25th that he should compose a paper of 'points on which the Generalissimo's approval should be obtained'; and this appeared on the same day. As finally amended the next day, it read:

> '(1) Since the Combined Chiefs of Staff are unable to find the 535 additional transport aircraft which are required for the Mandalay plan, it is agreed that the plan presented by Admiral Mountbatten at the first Plenary Session shall be accepted.
>
> (2) The stipulation which the Generalissimo has made that an amphibious operation is to be carried out in March is noted, and will be taken into consideration by the Combined Chiefs of Staff when amphibious operations in all parts of the world are reviewed in about a week's time. Meanwhile preparations are being pushed forward in the South-East Asia Theatre for an amphibious operation to meet this date, should approval be subsequently given.
>
> (3) A fleet of adequate strength to cover such an operation and to obtain command of the Bay of Bengal will be assembled by the beginning of March.
>
> (4) The Supreme Commander, South-East Asia Command, will be authorised to divert not more than an average of 1,100 tons per month from tonnage over the "Hump" to the requirements of the Burma Campaign. Diversions in excess of this figure may be made by him only to meet sudden and critical emergencies of the battle or by permission of the highest authority. The Air Transport Command will use its utmost energy to raise the efficiency of its operation and increase the "Hump" tonnage to a full 10,000 tons per month into China by the late winter and a further increase in the spring.[2]

[1] See Appendix X below for the complete text.
[2] For the results, see p. 127 above.

. . . (6) It is the intention to resume the offensive in October 1944, when the monsoon stops; it is however, too far ahead to decide the precise resources which will be available.'

This paper was explained verbally to Chiang Kai-shek before the conference adjourned. The British might therefore have concluded from these developments that they had successfully reserved their position over 'Buccaneer', in accordance with the Combined Chiefs of Staff's earlier agreement to postpone the decision until other operations had been discussed.

But in fact, though the British did not know it, that position had already been compromised. At some point in private conversation with Chiang Kai-shek, and almost certainly by 26th November, the President 'gave the Chinese the promise of a considerable amphibious operation across the Bay of Bengal within the next few months.'[1] The effect of this assurance was seen almost at once. At the same meeting on 26th November at which the paper for the Generalissimo was approved, the Joint Chiefs of Staff announced 'that they had direct orders from the President that 'Buccaneer' had got to be carried out at the appointed time,' and that the question of its abandonment or postponement could therefore be raised only between the Heads of Government; and by the 28th, when the delegates were in Teheran, the British Chiefs of Staff knew, what they had hitherto suspected, that the President had given a firm undertaking to the Generalissimo that the operation would take place. While the Combined Chiefs of Staff's formula in the paper of 26th November was not thereby invalidated, neither the Americans nor the Chinese were thus in any doubt as to the result.

Mr. Roosevelt's promise for south-east Asia effectively governed the result of the preliminary discussions on Europe. Considered by themselves, at first these went deceptively well. The British did not find the resolute opposition to their argument which they had expected, and indeed gained an apparently substantial measure of acceptance for it from the Joint Chiefs of Staff. But, as we have seen, the Americans' flexibility over European operations was more apparent than real at this stage. It awaited the verdict of the Russians, and was limited, and might be transformed, by the insistence on 'Buccaneer'.

Operations in Europe were not discussed until the second Plenary Meeting on the morning of 24th November, and were thereafter debated, in each case after the debate on south-east Asia, by the Combined Chiefs of Staff on the 25th and 26th. By comparison with the affairs of south-east Asia, which occupied nine items on the agenda of

[1] Churchill, *Closing the Ring*, p. 290.

the meetings from the 23rd to the 26th, those of 'Overlord' and the Mediterranean occupied four.

From their discussions in mid-November, the British Chiefs of Staff now produced a detailed statistical argument on the seaborne assaults proposed for the first half of 1944. It proceeded on three assumptions: that the retention of the sixty-eight L.S.T. in the Mediterranean until 15th January, 1944 would necessarily postpone 'Overlord' until about 1st July, 1944;[1] that the prevalent rate of American shipments of men and material to Britain could thereby be accepted; and that certain merchant vessels already in the Mediterranean could be used on assaults. If these conditions were met, the Chiefs of Staff estimated that the seaborne attack on the west coast of Italy[2] could take place in December, 1943 or early in January 1944, the operation against Rhodes[3] in February 1944, and 'Buccaneer' in March. But if 'Overlord' was not postponed until the beginning of July, only two of those three operations could take place. These conclusions formed the condition for the strategic argument, which the Prime Minister developed, along the lines already explained,[4] on the morning of 24th November. He ended by remarking:[5]

> 'To sum up, the programme he advocated was Rome in January, Rhodes in February, supplies to the Yugoslavs, a settlement of the Command arrangements and the opening of the Aegean, subject to the outcome of an approach to Turkey; all preparations for 'Overlord' to go ahead full steam within the framework of the foregoing policy for the Mediterranean.'

The Combined Chiefs of Staff discussed these possibilities on 25th November. Unfortunately, there is no record of the conversation, which was conducted in closed session; but from the minutes of the British meetings before and afterwards, it seems to have been concerned with the British Chiefs of Staff's aide-mémoire of 11th November.[6] Subject to some clarifying amendments, the paper was accepted on the 26th. The Joint Chiefs of Staff thereby agreed to accept the British proposal that the Mediterranean theatre should be placed under a single Command, to be effective forthwith; and 'tentatively accepted' the accompanying strategy 'as a basis for discussion with the Soviet Staff'. But, as it was then disclosed, this was only on the assumption that 'the British proposals . . . [for] the opening of the Dardanelles and the capture of Rhodes, for which the return of

[1] See p. 114 above.
[2] See p. 70 above.
[3] See p. 103 above.
[4] See pp. 105-15 above.
[5] See *Closing the Ring*, p. 295.
[6] See pp. 109-11 above.

landing-craft in the Mediterranean was essential . . . would in no way interfere with the carrying-out of Operation 'Buccaneer'.' The discussion accordingly turned on the relation of 'Buccaneer' to 'Overlord.' General Brooke explained that the operation in south-east Asia could be carried out provided that 'Overlord' was postponed; and General Marshall said 'he quite understood this point'. But he reiterated that in his opinion 'Buccaneer' was essential, and when the British raised the possibility that it might be postponed, the Americans revealed the President's personal interest in the operation. As Ismay reported to the Prime Minister, the American Chiefs of Staff seemed to accept the postponement of 'Overlord' 'with equanimity', but not of 'Buccaneer'; and 'it was therefore left at this, that if further discussions led the British Chiefs of Staff to the view that our proper strategy was to do 'Overlord' as quickly as possible and either to postpone or to abandon 'Buccaneer', they would have to take it up with the Prime Minister and request him to raise it on the highest level'. On the eve of the Teheran Conference, the position seemed to be that the Americans (given the appropriate Russian pressure) might accept the British strategy for Europe, if the British would accept the Americans' strategy for south-east Asia.

The Combined Chiefs of Staff also considered at this stage two problems of command, one arising from the character of the conference itself, the other from the strategic possibilities. The first was caused by the presence at an Allied conference of Chinese and Russians, for which the existing machinery of the Combined Chiefs of Staff did not provide specifically. On 23rd November, the Joint Chiefs of Staff, stimulated apparently by the Chinese, put forward a proposal for a committee of United Chiefs of Staff. Its purpose, as they stated, was to 'furnish adequate and satisfactory machinery for discussions by the principal Allies at the Chiefs of Staff level', while maintaining the exclusive character of the existing committee of the Combined Chiefs of Staff. 'The United Chiefs of Staff would function only when necessity arose, and would provide for attendance either by all members or by only those concerned in the problems to be discussed. This arrangement would give an "out" to China or Russia as the case might be. The proposed United Chiefs of Staff should consist of a single representative of the Chiefs of Staff of each nation. This representative would not necessarily have to be the same official at all meetings. . . .'

The British Chiefs of Staff, however, favoured a more flexible organization, whose relations to the Combined Chiefs of Staff need not then be defined. They feared the creation of a body which, while not exercising real power or holding a precise responsibility, might consider itself superior to that committee; and therefore preferred that the

Russians and the Chinese should be invited to attend those of its meetings in which they might be concerned. After some discussion, the Combined Chiefs of Staff accepted this view on the 24th; and the proposal of a United Chiefs of Staff was dropped.

The Joint Chiefs of Staff also raised officially the proposal for a Supreme Commander in Europe which had occasioned a preliminary skirmish three weeks before.[1] Their proposals were submitted on 25th November, the day on which the British proposals for the Command in the Mediterranean were being considered. An interesting exchange ensued.

'COMMAND OF BRITISH AND UNITED STATES FORCES OPERATING AGAINST GERMANY

Memorandum from the United States Chiefs of Staff

1. Current operations in the war against Germany and those approved for the immediate future are grouped geographically and functionally into three categories:

(a) Operations in the Mediterranean area involving combined forces with land, sea and air components.

(b) Operations in the North-Western part of Europe, also involving combined forces with land, sea and air components.

(c) Operations against interior Germany involving combined strategic air-forces based both in the Mediterranean area and in North-Western Europe.

2. Each of these operations is an entity, requiring unity of command over the forces which are engaged.

3. These operations are all intimately related to each other, with a common, over-all objective—Defeat of Germany . . .

4. The United States Chiefs of Staff now consider that the war in Europe has reached a stage where the necessity for command direction over all these forces, in conformity with general directives of the Combined Chiefs of Staff, is clearly indicated. This Command should be vested in a single Commander, and he should exercise command over the Allied Force Commanders in the Mediterranean, in North-West Europe, and of the strategic air forces. The immediate appointment of this Commander is, in our opinion, most urgently necessary. Even if he is appointed now, it is improbable that he will be able to organize his staff and begin to function before the end of January 1944. The situation which may develop in Europe by that time requires a more positive over-all command arrangement than that now functioning under the Combined Chiefs of Staff. Any delay in setting up such a command may lead to confusion and indecision at a critical time, thus delaying the attainment of early victory in Europe.

[1] See pp. 119-21 above.

5. In matters pertaining to strategic bombing, it is imperative that unified Allied command be established. The rapidity with which decisions regarding air operations must be made demands command control, as opposed to general directives or occasional direct action by the Combined Chiefs of Staff. We cannot escape the responsibility for adopting every means known to us to save the lives of our men and the planes they fly. The one effective method is to ensure the rapid co-ordinated employment, on a day to day operational basis, of United States Air Forces in both the United Kingdom and Mediterranean by day and R.A.F. bomber units by night in order to obtain the maximum dispersion of enemy air and anti-aircraft defence, and to take the greatest possible advantage of weather conditions in both theatres. This unified command must, therefore, be established without delay and must embrace all the strategic air forces engaged against Germany, including the United States Eighth and Fifteenth Air Forces and the British Bomber Command.

6. The British Chiefs of Staff have proposed the establishment of unified Command in the Mediterranean area. We are in accord with this proposal, with the proviso that the United States Fifteenth Air Force should be specifically excepted and commanded as in paragraph 5 above.

7. The United States Chiefs of Staff propose to the British Chiefs of Staff—

(a) That a Supreme Commander be designated at once to command all United Nations operations against Germany from the Mediterranean and the Atlantic under direction from the Combined Chiefs of Staff.

(b) That an over-all Command for North-Western European operations be appointed under the Supreme Commander.

(c) That a strategic Air Force commander be appointed under the Supreme Commander, to exercise command over the United States Eighth and Fifteenth Air Forces and the British Bomber Command.

(d) That the Commander of the Allied Forces in the Mediterranean shall come under the Supreme Commander.

8. The United States Chiefs of Staff further propose that the Supreme Commander be directed to carry out the agreed European strategy, and—

(a) be charged with the location and timing of operations;

(b) be charged with the allocation of the forces and material made available to him by the Combined Chiefs of Staff; and

(c) that his decisions on the above questions be subject to reversal by the Combined Chiefs of Staff.'

Their detailed proposals for the air Command, which derived a special force from the operations already under way in Italy, had been composed a week before.

The British Chiefs of Staff considered both papers at a meeting on

26th November. Both were regarded with suspicion. In the British view, a single command of the American and British strategic air forces throughout Europe, or of the Americans alone, raised serious disadvantages both of technique and of administration. The co-ordination of the convergent air attacks from different headquarters, although providing a superficially attractive nostrum for existing shortcomings, would in practice prove difficult to sustain; the re-organization would disturb relations in the Mediterranean between the air and the other Services, and might disturb those between the strategic and tactical air forces; while in London, whence the operations must be controlled, it might encroach seriously on the responsibilities of the Chief of the Air Staff, who alone could know, and already dealt with, the administrative and economic problems which warfare by bombing involved.[1] The proposal therefore seemed to them clumsy for the theatres involved, and possibly dangerous to the central conduct of the war.

The complementary larger proposal suffered from some of the same administrative disadvantages, heightened in this case by the constitutional and strategic difficulties which the British had raised with some vigour earlier in the month. They were explained in more detail in the British reply of 26th November.

> '(1) The British Chiefs of Staff have given careful consideration to the proposal put forward by the United States Chiefs of Staff . . . that "a Supreme Commander be designated at once to command all United Nations operations against Germany from the Mediterranean and the Atlantic." This proposal has an immense political implication and is clearly a matter for the most earnest consideration of the United States and British Governments. Nevertheless, the British Chiefs of Staff must say at once that, from the military point of view, they profoundly disagree with the proposal. Their reasons are set out in the paragraphs that follow.
>
> (2) Total war is not an affair of military forces alone, using the word " military" in the widest sense of the term. There are political, economic, industrial and domestic implications in almost every big war problem. Thus it seems clear that the Supreme Commander for the war against Germany will have to consult both the United States and the British Governments on almost every important question. In fact, it boils down to this, that he will only be able to make a decision without reference to high authority on comparatively minor and strictly military questions, such as the transfer of one or two divisions, or a few squadrons of aircraft, or a few scores of landing-craft, from one of his many fronts to another. He will thus be an extra and unnecessary link in the chain of command.

[1] See p. 20 above.

(3) There is no real analogy between the position of Marshal Foch in the last war and the position now contemplated for the Supreme Commander against Germany. Marshal Foch was responsible only for the Western Front and the Italian Front. His authority did not extend to the Salonika Front, the Palestine Front or the Mesopotamia Front. Under the arrangements now contemplated, the Supreme Commander will have not only 'Overlord' and the Italian Front under his authority, but also the Balkan Front and the Turkish Front if this is opened. There must be some limit to the responsibilities which Allied Governments can delegate to a single soldier, and the sphere now proposed seems to exceed these limits considerably.

(4) The United States Chiefs of Staff propose . . . that the decisions of the Supreme Commander should "be subject to reversal by the Combined Chiefs of Staff". If the main object of this new arrangement is to ensure rapid decisions, it looks as though the above proviso will lead to deplorable consequences. Instances will occur in which the Supreme Commander has issued orders and the troops have marched in accordance with these orders, only to be followed by a reversal of the order by the Combined Chiefs of Staff, and consequent confusion. Again it may happen that the British Chiefs of Staff agree with a decision taken by the Supreme Commander while the United States Chiefs of Staff totally disagree with it. What happens then? Or again, the Combined Chiefs of Staff may wholeheartedly support, on military grounds, a decision taken by the Supreme Commander, only to find that one or other of the Governments concerned is not prepared to ratify it. Then what happens?

(5) If the Supreme Commander is going to exercise real control, he will need to assemble the whole paraphernalia of Intelligence, Planning and Administration on an unprecedented scale. This staff will merely be a great pad between the theatre commanders and the Combined Chiefs of Staff.

(6) Finally, it is not admitted either that the existing machinery for the higher direction of the war has failed, or that the situation which now confronts us is so inherently different as to demand a revolutionary change.

(7) The conclusion to be drawn from the above arguments is that the Supreme Commander of the War against Germany will never have, under the system of Government which now obtains in the United States and the United Kingdom, authority to deal with anything but strictly military, and comparatively minor, problems. He will be boosted by the Press and public opinion as a Superman who is going to lead the two nations to victory. This is a mere delusion. His position will be a sham. In important matters, he will not be able to do anything more than is now done by the theatre commanders.

(8) If the well-tried machinery that has led us safely through the last two years has failed in the smaller problems, it would be

better to examine that machinery and see how it could be speeded up and adjusted, rather than to embark upon an entirely novel experiment, which merely makes a cumbrous and unnecessary link in the chain of command and which will surely lead to disillusionment and disappointment.'

The Prime Minister also composed a Minute on the subject, adding to the arguments of the Chiefs of Staff.[1]

'. . . 4. The principle which should be followed as far as possible between allies of equal status is that the command in any theatre should go to the ally who has the largest forces deployed or about to be deployed there. On this it would be natural that the command in the Mediterranean should be British and that the command of 'Overlord' should be American.

5. If the two commands are merged under a Supreme Commander, the British would have available against Germany in May decidedly larger forces than the United States. It would therefore appear that the Supreme Command should go to a British Officer. I should be very reluctant, as head of His Majesty's Government, to place such an invidious responsibility upon a British Officer. If, on the other hand, disregarding the preponderance of forces involved, the Supreme Command were given to a United States Officer and he pronounced in favour of concentrating on 'Overlord' irrespective of the injury done to our affairs in the Mediterranean, His Majesty's Government could not possibly agree. The Supreme Commander, British or American, would therefore be placed in an impossible position. Having assumed before the whole world the responsibility of pronouncing and being overruled by one Government or the other, he would have little choice but to resign. This might bring about a most serious crisis in the harmonious and happy relations hitherto maintained between our two Governments.

6. It is not seen why the present arrangement should not continue, subject to any minor improvements that can be suggested. Under this arrangement an American Commander would conduct the immense Cross-Channel Operation and a British Commander would conduct the war in the Mediterranean, their action being concerted and forces assigned by the Combined Chiefs of Staff, working under the heads of the two Governments. . . . More frequent meetings of the Combined Chiefs of Staff should also be arranged, and possibly monthly visits of one week's duration by the chairman of each Chiefs of Staff Committee alternatively to London and Washington.'

These papers were handed to the Americans before the delegates left for Teheran. They undoubtedly played their part in determining the final choice of the commander, as well as the arrangements, for 'Overlord'.

[1] See *Closing the Ring*, pp. 298-300.

(ii)

Teheran: The Decisions Taken

All was therefore still in the melting pot when, on 28th November, the Western Allies arrived at Teheran. When the Combined Chiefs of Staff left on 1st December, the shape of operations in Europe over the next six months had been settled, and the context provided within which their final balance, the detail of their command, and the shape of the operations in south-east Asia could be determined over the following weeks.

The Russians' contribution to the discussion, which was thus decisive, was contained in three important statements. The first was made at the outset of the conference. The President, who by general agreement acted as chairman of the Plenary Meetings, opened on the afternoon of 28th November with a survey of the Far East and of Europe. The Prime Minister having reserved his remarks, Stalin spoke next.[1]

> 'Marshal Stalin said that he would first address himself to the question of the Pacific. He welcomed the successes which the United States were having in that theatre; but, unfortunately, it was impossible for the Soviet to join the struggle against Japan at the present time, since practically all their forces were required to be deployed against Germany. The Soviet Forces in the Far East were more or less sufficient for defence, but they would have to be at least trebled in order to assume the offensive. The moment for their joining their friends in this theatre would be the moment of Germany's collapse; then they would march together.'

This categorical assurance—of which the Prime Minister later remarked that he thought it the most important statement made at the Conference—at once suggested new possibilities for the conduct of the war against Japan. It was indeed soon to be followed by detailed studies of its implications on the part of both British and Americans.[2] Meanwhile, it reinforced the conviction of the British that operations in south-east Asia must be examined further before their shape was finally decided. As the Joint Planners argued at the end of the following week, 'Stalin's declaration makes the early defeat of Germany and rapid progress in the Pacific of paramount importance. We could not choose a worse moment to open up a vacuum in South-East Asia.' 'Buccaneer' was now suspect on its merits, as well as for its possible effect on operations in Europe.

These operations occupied the rest of the first meeting. The Prime

---

[1] Quotations from the minutes of the meetings at Teheran are taken from the British version, which does not always correspond with the American version.

[2] See pp. 427-33 below.

Minister explained the British argument in three stages. First, 'Overlord' would definitely be launched, in the late spring or summer of 1944, with thirty-five strong divisions, of which sixteen would be British.[1] Secondly, it was impossible for the British, owing to their commitments elsewhere, to sustain more than these sixteen divisions in north-west Europe, and subsequent reinforcements must come from the United States. Seven British and American divisions were in the process of being removed from the Mediterranean for 'Overlord'. The problem was therefore how best to use the rest within the Mediterranean, and in support of the main operation. The first target was Rome, whose capture, owing partly to the external commitment which had just been mentioned, had already been postponed; but the city should be taken by January 1944, and it was necessary therefore to envisage the subsequent operations. The Western Allies intended to stand on a line Pisa-Rimini, and not to debouch into the Lombard plain. They might thereafter attack southern France, or might (as the President indeed had mentioned in his preliminary remarks) move from the head of the Adriatic north-east towards the Danube. But these possibilities lay in the future, and meanwhile the Mediterranean campaign must not stagnate. The Prime Minister therefore wished—and this was his third point—to bring Turkey into the war. It should then be possible to take the Dodecanese with two or three divisions, and, secure in the islands and in Turkey, to open the passage to the Russian ports in the Black Sea. The immediate necessity, therefore, was to consider the means and the implications of inducing Turkey to join the Allies.

Stalin questioned the Prime Minister closely, following the stages of his argument. He wished first to be clear on the division of forces between the two fronts. His questions on this have been called by Churchill 'the crucial point' of the discussion.[2]

> 'Marshal Stalin then addressed the following questions to the Prime Minister:
>
> Question 1—"Am I right in thinking that the invasion of France is to be undertaken by 35 Divisions?"
>
> Answer 1—"Yes. Particularly strong Divisions."
>
> Question 2—"Is it intended that this operation should be carried out by the forces now in Italy?"
>
> Answer 2—"No. Seven Divisions have already been, or are in process of being, withdrawn from North Africa to take part in 'Overlord'. These 7 Divisions are required to make up the 35 Divisions mentioned in question 1 above. After they have been withdrawn, about 22 Divisions will be left in the Mediterranean for Italy or other objectives. Some of these could be used either

[1] In fact, British and British-controlled.

[2] *Closing the Ring*, p. 312.

for an operation against Southern France or for moving from the head of the Adriatic towards the Danube. Both these operations will be timed in conformity with 'Overlord'. Meanwhile, it should not be difficult to spare 2 or 3 Divisions to take the Islands in the Aegean." '

Stalin then moved to the Mediterranean itself.

'In reply to a question by Marshal Stalin, the Prime Minister said that no operation against the South of France had as yet been planned in detail, but the idea was that it might be done in conformity and simultaneously with 'Overlord'. The assault would consist of troops now in Italy. He added that it would also be necessary to examine the President's idea of moving North-East from the head of the Adriatic.

Marshal Stalin asked how many Anglo-American troops would have to be allotted if Turkey came into the war.

The Prime Minister, observing that he spoke for himself alone, said that 2 or 3 divisions at the most would be required to take the Islands in the Aegean, and that, in addition, we should probably have to give Turkey about 20 squadrons of Air Force and several regiments of Flak to defend herself. Both the Air Forces and the Flak could be provided without prejudice to other operations.

Marshal Stalin thought it would be a mistake to disperse forces by sending part to Turkey and elsewhere, and part to Southern France. The best course would be to make 'Overlord' the basic operation for 1944 and, once Rome had been captured, to send all available forces in Italy to Southern France. These forces could then join hands with the 'Overlord' forces when the invasion was launched. France was the weakest spot on the German front. He himself did not expect Turkey to agree to enter the war.

The Prime Minister said that he was under the impression that the Soviet Government were very anxious to get Turkey into the war. We had tried once and failed. But was it not intended that we should renew the effort?

Marshal Stalin was all in favour of trying again. "We ought," he said, "to take them by the scruff of the neck if necessary."

The Prime Minister said that he entirely agreed with Marshal Stalin's observations about the undesirability of dispersion, but all that he suggested was that a handful of divisions—say, two or three—would be very well employed in making contact with Turkey, while the Air Forces which would come into play were those which were already defending Egypt and would merely be advancing their line. Thus, there was no appreciable diversion of effort either from the Italian front or from 'Overlord'.

Marshal Stalin intervened to remark that it would be well worthwhile to take the Islands if this could be done with three or four divisions. . . . Marshal Stalin repeated that 'Overlord' was a very serious operation and that it was better to help it by invading the South of France. . . .

The President suggested that the relative timing of operations required the most careful consideration. Any operation undertaken in the Eastern Mediterranean would probably put off 'Overlord' until June or July. He himself was opposed to any such delay if it could possibly be avoided. He therefore suggested that the military experts should examine the possibility of operations against Southern France on the timing put forward by Marshal Stalin, i.e. two months before 'Overlord', the governing factor being that 'Overlord' should be launched at the prescribed time.

Marshal Stalin said that the experience gained by the Soviet during the last two years of fighting was that a big offensive, if undertaken from only one direction, rarely yielded results. The better course was to launch offensives from two or more directions simultaneously. . . . He suggested that this principle might well be applied to the problem under discussion.

The Prime Minister said that he did not disagree in principle with the views expressed by Marshal Stalin. The suggestions that he had made for action in Yugoslavia and in respect of Turkey did not, in his view, conflict in any way with that general conception. At the same time, he wished it to be placed on record that he could not in any circumstances agree to sacrifice the activities of the armies in the Mediterranean, which included 20 British and British-controlled divisions, merely in order to keep the exact date of the 1st May for 'Overlord'. If Turkey refused to come into the war it could not be helped. At the same time he earnestly hoped that he would not be asked to agree to any such rigid timing of operations as had been suggested by the President. . . .

The President . . . suggested that the Staff should set to work the following morning.'

This suggestion was approved.

Stalin's interest in an attack on southern France took the Western delegates by surprise. They had not, indeed, even brought with them to Teheran Eisenhower's report on the possibilities which he had produced in October,[1] and the only available paper was an outline plan of 9th August, which by now was out of date. But there were in fact good military reasons for the Russians' interest in the operation. Their chief demand remained, as always and despite the Americans' recent doubts, that 'Overlord' should be launched in May, 1944. Operations in the south, while important, could not, in their opinion, absorb the same number of German divisions and thus assist to the same extent the operations on the Eastern Front. Their own campaigns, with 'Overlord', formed the most effective pincer on Germany that

[1] See p. 104 above.

PLATE III. THE TEHERAN CONFERENCE, DECEMBER 1943

Back row, left to right: Mr. Hopkins, M. Molotov, Mr. Harriman, Sir A. Clark-Kerr, Mr. Eden.
Front row, left to right: Marshal Stalin, Mr. Roosevelt, Mr. Churchill.

could be devised: if, as both British and Americans agreed, operations in the Mediterranean were necessary to help 'Overlord', they could therefore do so most effectively by acting, with it, as a preliminary pincer on France. Other operations, whatever their advantages, could be only diversions: it was for instance desirable—if difficult—to bring Turkey into the war; but not at the expense of the pincer in the west. This strategy must have received further support from the fact that the Western Allies themselves obviously disagreed on the implications of operations in the Aegean; and if there was any question of alternatives, as the Americans seemed to suggest, it must have appeared the more important to the Russians to throw their weight into the scales.

This indeed became clear when the Staff meeting, which had been suggested on 28th November, was held on the morning of the 29th. This meeting was attended only by the military advisers, and was thus unable to take decisions; the discussion itself appeared inconclusive; nevertheless, it may have been the turning point of the conference. For by that time the Russians had clearly gauged the positions of the British and the Americans, and from the tone of the minutes used the occasion to probe further. As a result, Stalin was able, at the second Plenary Meeting in the afternoon, to state the Russians' final position which determined the main issue.

The Staff meeting indeed was dominated by questions and statements from the Russians. Their principal delegate, Marshal Voroshilov, began by emphasizing the difference between the Americans and the British.

> 'Marshal Voroshilov . . . said that, before commenting on what had been said, he would like to ask certain questions: firstly, as regards 'Overlord'. From reports received and from the statements of Sir Alan Brooke and General Marshall, he understood that Operation 'Overlord' was being prepared for the spring, for about May 1944. Could information be given just as to what preparations were being made for 'Overlord'? . . .
>
> Secondly,—and this question was of great importance—Marshal Voroshilov said that he understood from General Marshall that the United States High Command and United States Government considered 'Overlord' to be an operation of the first importance. He said he would like to know whether Sir Alan Brooke considered this to be an operation of the first importance; whether he both thought the operation was necessary and that it must be carried out, or whether, alternatively, it might be replaced by another operation if Turkey were to come into the war.'

Marshall replied at length to the first question, explaining the critical position of the assault shipping. Brooke then replied to the second with a further statement of the British case, in which he stressed that operations in the Mediterranean were designed precisely to give 'Overlord' the best chance of success. Voroshilov, however, continued.

> 'Marshal Vorishilov asked Sir Alan Brooke if he could say a little more precisely whether he regarded Operation 'Overlord' as the most important operation, as he understood the United States to think so and, from the Russian point of view, it was an operation of vital importance.
>
> Sir Alan Brooke said that he considered the operation of vital importance, but he made one stipulation. He knew the strength of Northern France and of its defences and he did not want to see the operation fail. In his opinion, in certain circumstances, the operation would be bound to fail, i.e. if the circumstances were not right.
>
> Marshal Voroshilov went on to say that Marshal Stalin and the Russian General Staff attached the greatest importance to Operation 'Overlord'. Any other operation, whether in the Mediterranean or possibly in the South of France or Bay of Biscay, could only be regarded as being auxiliary.
>
> Sir Alan Brooke said that that was exactly the light in which we also regarded the operation, but unless some such auxiliary operation were carried out, the conditions necessary for 'Overlord' would not obtain. A pincer movement was already taking place in Europe.'

Voroshilov then turned to the Russian case.

> '. . . Marshal Voroshilov said that he entirely agreed with the opinion expressed by Sir Alan Brooke that some smaller operations in the Mediterranean were necessary for the purpose of diversion and for attracting troops, both from the Russian Front and from Northern France. The Russian view on this was broadly the same as the British. As a soldier, he thought that if 'Overlord' were considered to be the most important operation, other auxiliary operations must be so planned as not to interfere with Operation 'Overlord'. He referred to operations in Italy, Yugoslavia and elsewhere. It should be the object, he said, of the auxiliary operation, primarily to ensure the success of the main operation. Unfortunately he had heard that operations in other areas were to be undertaken which might interfere with or delay 'Overlord'. This should not be the case, because the auxiliary operation should be made to fit in with the main operation.
>
> He went on to say that the suggestion made yesterday by Marshal Stalin was that, at the same time as the operation in Northern France, operations should be undertaken in Southern France. Operations in Italy and elsewhere in the Mediterranean must be considered as of secondary importance, because, from those areas, Germany could not be attacked directly with the Alps in the way. Italy, he said, offered great possibilities for defence. Defence should be organised there with the minimum

of troops. The remaining troops could be used for the South of France in order to attack the enemy from two sides.

Marshal Voroshilov went on to say that Marshal Stalin did not insist on an operation against the South of France, but that he did insist that the operation against the North of France should take place in the manner and on the date already agreed upon.'

Nothing said thereafter during the meeting modified this statement.

By the afternoon of 29th November, the Combined Chiefs of Staff were therefore clear on the Russians' preference. The second Plenary Meeting served to underline it for the Heads of Government. When the military advisers had reported, Stalin opened the discussion with a further surprise. His first question was to ask the name of the commander for 'Overlord'. The President replied that this had not yet been decided: an officer was in charge of planning, with a combined Anglo-American staff, and plans and preparations were in fact far advanced; only the commander remained to be chosen. This, however, failed to satisfy Stalin. He observed that the commander might wish on his appointment to alter the existing plans, and should therefore be chosen at once, to be responsible for the design and for its execution. He added that the Russians should then be told his name. The Prime Minister agreed that the appointment must be made soon, and hoped that it would be settled within the next fortnight.

The Prime Minister then deployed his arguments again, in the new context which the Russian proposals had created. Three points now demanded study. First, what help could be given to 'Overlord' by the forces already in the Mediterranean? In particular, what were the possibilities and what should be the scale of the operation against southern France, which had not yet been examined in detail? Secondly, could landing craft be made available to take Rhodes and to open the Aegean when Turkey entered the war? Thirdly, could they be used later, in five or six months' time, for the attack on southern France? In his view, landing craft for two divisions should be held in the theatre, which meanwhile could assist the advance in Italy that remained the immediate commitment. But it was obvious that this would either postpone the date of 'Overlord' by perhaps six to eight weeks, or alternatively would mean recalling from the Far East the assault shipping sent there for operations against the Japanese. 'This placed us on the horns of a dilemma. It was a case of balancing one problem against the other. He would be grateful to hear the views of Marshal Stalin and Marshal Voroshilov on these points, since their military record inspired their British Allies with admiration and respect'. The Prime Minister finished by recapitulating the case for bringing pressure to bear on the Turks, and asked that Russia should assist them, if their action led to war with Bulgaria, by herself declaring war on Bulgaria.

Stalin assented to this last demand. He also agreed briefly that the

Allies should help the Partisans in Yugoslavia. He then—ignoring the Prime Minister's invitation to speculate on 'Buccaneer'—returned to his main argument.

> '. . . In his view there were three main matters to be decided. First, the date of the operation should be determined. This should be some time in May and no later. Secondly, Operation 'Overlord' should be supported by a landing in the South of France. If this could be carried out two or three months before 'Overlord' so much the better, but, if not, the South of France operation might coincide with 'Overlord'. If, however, owing to difficulties of shipping and landing-craft, the two operations could not coincide, it would still be advantageous if the South of France operation could take place a little after 'Overlord'. He regarded the assault on the South of France as a supporting operation which would be definitely helpful to 'Overlord'. The capture of Rome and other operations in the Mediterranean could only be regarded as diversions.
>
> The third matter to be decided was the appointment of a Commander-in-Chief for the 'Overlord' Operation. He would like to see this appointment made before the conclusion of the present conference. If this was not possible, at least within a week.'

Stalin had now made his three statements on strategy; and as the statement on the Far East had raised new possibilities for the war against Japan, so the two main statements on Europe decided the shape of the operations against Germany. He was followed at once by Roosevelt, who had hitherto refrained from committing himself, but who now inclined definitely to 'Overlord' in May. The problem for the British, however, was still not resolved. For even if 'Overlord', and an attack on the south of France, were accepted for May, the size of the second operation, and thus the provision of assault shipping, had still to be settled. Both, as Churchill had pointed out, must affect the other operations which the British wished to consider. Was the assault shipping for the attack on the south of France to come from the Mediterranean? If so, how could 'Overlord' be launched in May? If not, where was it to come from? These questions directly concerned the Aegean and 'Buccaneer'. The Prime Minister therefore returned to the eastern Mediterranean, in 'a final and, one must say, gallant attempt on behalf of Rhodes and Turkey.[1]' He ended by proposing that a military committee should meet the next morning, to consider the nature and the timing of the subsidiary operations in support of 'Overlord'. The President agreed to this, so long as the committee was instructed to present 'agreed recommendations' to the Heads of Government; and his proposal was accepted by Stalin, who however sought to clinch the matter before the Plenary Meeting closed.

---

[1] Sherwood, *The White House Papers of Harry L. Hopkins*, II, p. 791.

'Marshal Stalin said . . . he wished to pose a very direct question to the Prime Minister about 'Overlord'. Did the Prime Minister and the British Staffs really believe in 'Overlord'?

The Prime Minister replied that, provided the conditions previously stated for 'Overlord' were to obtain when the time came, he firmly believed it would be our stern duty to hurl across the Channel against the Germans every sinew of our strength.'

The military committee, which was in fact the Combined Chiefs of Staff, met at 9.30 a.m. on the morning of 30th November. The British Chiefs of Staff had already met three quarters of an hour before. After some discussion, they agreed to place before their colleagues the following list of suggestions and points.

'(a) An operation shall be mounted for the south of France. Timing and scope to be decided later—maybe after 'Overlord'.
(b) We advance in Italy to Pisa-Rimini line.
(c) We assist Partisans in Yugoslavia, but no forces other than Commandos to be used.
(d) Operations in Aegean are entirely dependent on the entry of Turkey into war. In any event no more landing-craft will be kept away from 'Overlord' for the specific purpose of operations in the Aegean.
(e) In view of (b), we must keep landing-craft in Mediterranean till 15th January,
(f) Because of (e) earliest date of 'Overlord' cannot now be before 1st June.
(g) Is 'Buccaneer' affected by Marshal Stalin's statement about Russia coming in against Japan once Germany is out?'

When the Combined Chiefs of Staff met immediately afterwards, General Brooke opened by developing these points. The debate then concentrated on the timetables for the assault shipping. According to the latest British calculations, the retention of the sixty-eight L.S.T. in the Mediterranean for the Italian operations must postpone 'Overlord' until 1st June (a significant reduction from the first estimate of 1st July):[1] according to those of the Americans, to 15th May. But even then, a prior or simultaneous assault on the south of France could be launched only with one division. In these circumstances, the British hinted that 'Buccaneer' might well be sacrificed to the Mediterranean; but whatever was decided later on this, it was recognized that the Russians must meanwhile be given a definite date for 'Overlord'. The discussion therefore hardened on this point. The British pointed out that 'Overlord' should benefit from the Russians' operations as they were to benefit from it, and that no Russian offensive had so far started in May of any year. The date of 1st May for 'Overlord', which still stood from the 'Trident' Conference, had moreover been selected

[1] See p. 114 above.

originally as a compromise, and had no validity in itself. British and Americans at length agreed that if they took 1st June as the closing date, it would be possible to inform the Russians that they would launch 'Overlord' in May without curtailing excessively the current operations in Italy, or the necessary margin within which to debate further the possibilities elsewhere. They therefore decided, after a long and circuitous discussion,

> '(a) That we should continue to advance in Italy to the Pisa-Rimini line. (This means that the 68 L.S.T. which are due to be sent from the Mediterranean to the United Kingdom for 'Overlord' must be kept in the Mediterranean until 15th January.)
> (b) That an operation shall be mounted against the south of France on as big a scale as landing-craft permit. For planning purposes D-day to be the same as 'Overlord' D-day.
> (c) To recommend to the President and Prime Minister respectively that we should inform Marshal Stalin that we will launch 'Overlord' during May, in conjunction with a supporting operation against the south of France on the largest scale that is permitted by the landing-craft available at that time.
> *Note:* The United States and British Chiefs of Staff agreed to inform each other before the Plenary Meeting this afternoon of the decisions of the President and Prime Minister respectively on the above point.
> The Combined Chiefs of Staff were unable to reach agreement on the question of operations in the Aegean until they had received further instructions from the President and Prime Minister respectively.'

Soon after these decisions had been reached, Churchill saw Stalin alone, and for the first time during the conference discussed military affairs in private. The talk did much to remove the impression, which the Russians had received, that the British wished to stop 'Overlord' in favour of an invasion of the Balkans. A full account of it, from the notes kept by the Prime Minister's interpreter, may be found in Volume V of Sir Winston Churchill's memoirs.[1] This meeting was followed by a luncheon of the three Heads of Government, when Roosevelt, as agreed with Churchill, informed Stalin that the Americans and British had decided to launch 'Overlord' 'during the month of May.' The meal thereafter went pleasantly, and after a brief interval the last Plenary Meeting began at four o'clock in the afternoon. General Brooke read to the assembled delegates the unanimous recommendations of the Combined Chiefs of Staff,

> '. . . that we will launch 'Overlord' in May, in conjunction with a supporting operation against the South of France on the largest scale that is permitted by the landing-craft available at that time.'

[1] *Closing The Ring*, pp. 332-6.

The three principals then agreed that their Staffs should in future concert their relevant plans, and should consult each other on the complementary plans of deception for the summer's operations. Lastly, a public communiqué was composed, on a note, as the Prime Minister suggested, of 'brevity, mystery and a foretaste of impending doom for Germany.'

> 'The Military Staffs of the three Powers concerted their plans for the final destruction of the German forces. They reached complete agreement as to the scope and timing of the operations which will be undertaken from East, West and South, and arrangements were made to ensure intimate and continuous co-operation.'

The military discussions were now over, and the day ended happily with a dinner for the three delegations in the British Embassy, at which Mr. Churchill celebrated his sixty-ninth birthday by acting as host. The last day was devoted entirely to diplomatic questions, while the Combined Chiefs of Staff and their advisers left once more for Cairo. Mr. Roosevelt and Mr. Churchill, with their staffs, followed on 2nd December.

(iii)

Cairo: The Details Reconsidered

Apart from the executive consequences of the agreements at Teheran, the Western Allies had two problems still to resolve on their return to Cairo: the relation, in assault shipping, of the Aegean and 'Buccaneer' to 'Overlord' and the south of France; and the choice of a commander for 'Overlord' or for operations throughout Europe, depending on whether the British or the American conception of command prevailed. All other unsettled business was related to these two questions.

The settlement of the first problem depended now on close statistical calculation of assault shipping, which, owing to the circumstances of the earlier discussions, remained exceptionally difficult. For the very short interval allowed between the decisions of principle and those which must now be taken on detail aggravated the problems, always awkward, of estimating with this type of material. The result may be seen in the tables shown in Appendix V below, which reveal the shifts to which the planners were put in this short and confused period, and illustrate, perhaps better than any account, the difficulties of forming plans from calculations of assault shipping which themselves proved unreliable without a firm plan. The difficulties were moreover aggravated by a fresh time limit imposed on the discussions. The British had hoped for at least another ten days in which to debate the outstanding decisions. But the President had been away from Washington for three weeks, and his presence was now required in the capital as soon as possible. On 4th December, to his allies' keen disappointment, he announced that he must leave Cairo on the 7th, and that the Combined Chiefs of Staff's Final Report must be ready for signature on the evening of the 6th. Much intricate calculation had accordingly to be compressed into a very short period.

The first question to be decided, in settling the first of the two main problems, was the lowest scale on which operation 'Anvil' could be launched against the south of France. On the basis of Eisenhower's report of 27th October, and of a necessarily sketchy report provided at Teheran, the British thought that this should be fixed at two divisions. As it was, after 15th January there would be an assault lift in the Mediterranean for only about $1\frac{1}{3}$ divisions. There would also probably not be enough aircraft carriers. The assault shipping must moreover be studied in relation to the size of the force eventually to be put into southern France, which might be as much as ten divisions, and which, under the plan for the Italian campaign, would have to be transported entirely by sea;[1] to the preliminary casualties anticipated from earlier operations in the central, and possibly the eastern, Mediterranean; and to the small but prior commitment to supply the Partisans in Yugoslavia. In these circumstances, the British Chiefs of Staff on 3rd December were inclined to place less emphasis than before on operations in the Aegean, which must now definitely conform to 'Anvil'. They recommended accordingly that Turkey should be invited to enter the war only in the middle of February 1944, instead of within the next few weeks; that meanwhile either 'Buccaneer' in south-east Asia should be cancelled, or its equivalent in assault shipping for the Mediterranean should be supplied by the Americans; and that in the first of these cases, the British assault shipping involved should leave the Indian Ocean at once, so as to allow a programme for the Mediterranean to be calculated more exactly. The British, moreover, should embark on a review of their assault shipping throughout the world, as the Chiefs of Staff understood the Americans were already doing.

The Combined Chiefs of Staff agreed that a new study of 'Anvil' must be the first step. The Combined Staff Planners were accordingly told to produce it, on the assumptions that the size of the initial assault should be at least two divisions, and that the resources must not be found at the expense of 'Overlord' in May.

But while this report was under way, the problem was complicated by developments in south-east Asia. Since his return from Cairo on

---

[1] See p. 104 above.

27th November, Admiral Mountbatten had been studying the detailed plans for 'Buccaneer' at greater leisure, and in company with his commanders. As a result, on 29th November he submitted a proposal for a more powerful assault. The chief weakness of the earlier plan had lain in its vulnerability to air attack. Mountbatten therefore intended first to remove the most immediate threat by air from the south, by attacking the most northerly of the adjacent Nicobar islands in greater strength, with a division instead of with a brigade; and secondly, to provide more ample air cover for the main assault, at least until the first airfield on the Andamans had been secured. The extra forces required would amount probably to two brigade groups (bringing the total strength of the land forces to about 50,000 men), a comparable addition in ocean and assault shipping, and 120 carrier-borne fighters. The brigade groups, and the shipping of all types, could be found from the resources already in the theatre; and Mountbatten had apparently received a verbal assurance from Admiral King at Cairo, that if necessary he could count on six American aircraft carriers from the south-west Pacific. He therefore claimed that no new British resources would be needed from elsewhere, and asked for permission to carry out 'Buccaneer' on this basis.

But coming at this precise moment, the revised plan for 'Buccaneer' was received with little favour in Cairo. The British Chiefs of Staff were now being asked to sponsor an operation, to which they had not agreed and of whose merits they were not convinced, on a larger scale than before, at a time when other agreed operations were demanding fresh resources. On 4th December they considered the new proposals. The difficulty lay not so much in providing extra men or ships for the operation (though this seems not as yet to have been entirely clear to the Chiefs of Staff) as in the fact that the ships already involved might well be needed elsewhere. The combination of so many converging developments—'Overlord' in May, 'Anvil' with two divisions, Stalin's declaration at Teheran on the war against Japan, its possible effect on the operations in Burma itself—which for the first time was being considered as a combination in these forty-eight hours, could scarcely bear a further complication. It was already uncertain how much of Mountbatten's assault and ocean shipping, and of the naval forces in the Indian Ocean, might not have to be removed for the Mediterranean; now he was proposing to use them all, and with more aircraft carriers. The British Chiefs of Staff therefore decided to recommend to the Combined Chiefs of Staff that 'Buccaneer' should be cancelled for the time being. At the same time, they thought that without 'Buccaneer' the operations in northern Burma could not stand on their own. Depending as they did largely on the Chinese, their fate was involved in that of the seaborne attack without which the Generalissimo had hitherto refused to move; and it was therefore agreed that the cancellation of 'Buccaneer' should be accompanied by the cancellation of operation 'Tarzan'.[1]

The Prime Minister, who by position, departmental experience and temperament was always suspicious of the increased demand, had been more keenly dismayed than the Chiefs of Staff by Mountbatten's new proposals; and, fortified by their decision, he argued with fresh vigour against 'Buccaneer' at the Plenary Meeting which followed immediately their session on 4th December. This meeting opened inauspiciously, with the President's announcement that the conference must end on the 6th. This, Mr. Roosevelt thought, should present no serious difficulty; for apart from the question of bringing Turkey into the war, only the distribution of some eighteen to twenty landing craft seemed to stand in the way of an agreed programme, and he was sure they could not be beaten 'by a small item like that'. The British, however, did not view the obstruction so lightly; and after voicing his apprehension at the date for the end of the conference, the Prime Minister developed their argument as it now appeared. Two new great facts had been recorded within the past few days. Russia would declare war on Japan after Germany had been beaten; and 'Overlord' was to be launched in May 1944, in conjunction with an assault on the south of France. The combination of these facts modified the emphasis, though not the shape, of the British proposals. An assault should now be undertaken on southern France, with at least two divisions. The capture of Rhodes, in consequence, could no longer be regarded as so important. But on the other hand, it was more desirable than ever to reconsider 'Buccaneer' in south-east Asia, particularly in view of the increased demands that had just reached him. The British Chiefs of Staff developed, one by one, different aspects of this argument, before the discussion became general. No decision could be reached, and finally the President,

> 'summing up the discussion, asked whether he was correct in thinking that there was general agreement on the following points:
>
> (a) Nothing should be done to hinder 'Overlord'.
>
> (b) Nothing should be done to hinder 'Anvil' [against southern France].
>
> (c) By hook or by crook we should scrape up sufficient landing craft to operate in the Eastern Mediterranean if Turkey came into the war.
>
> (d) Admiral Mountbatten should be told to go ahead and do his best with what had already been allocated to him'.

The Prime Minister, however, could not consent to (d) until the means had definitely been found for (a), (b) and (c); and since the President

[1] See p. 153 above.

ruled out the possibility of abandoning 'Buccaneer' in any form, the Staffs were instructed to discuss the issue further.

When they did so, on the same afternoon of the 4th, two more new factors had to be considered. First, at the Plenary Meeting itself, Admiral King had made a significant contribution to the pool of assault shipping. Since 'Overlord' had now been postponed from 1st May to some time in May, he had arranged for all new landing ships and craft, completed in the United States between 1st March and 1st April, to be sent to Europe instead of to the Pacific. This would in fact amount to some twenty-five L.S.T. and some sixty-six landing craft, of which twenty-four L.S.T. and twenty-six L.C.T. could be spared for the Mediterranean. Possibly because the figures were not mentioned at the Plenary Meeting, the British do not seem immediately to have given this offer the attention it deserved. In fact, it virtually met the shortage of assault shipping for 'Anvil' on a basis of two divisions, and thus might seem to have closed the most important gap, and to have rendered the cancellation of 'Buccaneer' unnecessary. But 'Anvil' was still only an outline plan, and the detail and possible casualties of earlier operations (on the west coast of Italy, and perhaps in the Aegean) had still not been considered closely enough to stipulate exactly the size of the necessary margin, and thus of the total requirements. The British therefore continued, despite King's welcome addition, to press for the abandonment of 'Buccaneer'.

Secondly, the Combined Staff Planners had now produced their long-awaited report on strategy against Japan, which had been called for early in the Cairo Conference,[1] and which was due to be discussed at the afternoon meeting on the 4th. This led to a review of 'Buccaneer' from another point of vantage. The paper had been completed while the Combined Chiefs of Staff were at Teheran. It accordingly still allowed for the possibility rather than for the certainty of Russia's eventual declaration of war on Japan. But with that important exception, the earlier conclusions held. The Americans now announced that:

> '. . . The advance along the New Guinea—N.E.I. [Netherlands East Indies]—Philippine axis will proceed concurrently with operations for the capture of the Mandated Islands. These two series of operations will be mutually supporting. . . . When conflicts in timing and allocation of means exist, due weight should be accorded to the fact that operations in the Central Pacific promise at this time a more rapid advance towards Japan and her vital lines of communication; the earlier acquisition of strategic air bases closer to the Japanese homeland; and of greatest importance, are more likely to precipitate a decisive engagement with the Japanese Fleet.
>
> The aim should be to advance along the New Guinea—N.E.I.

[1] See p. 161 above.

—Philippine axis and to complete the capture of the Mandated Islands in time to launch a major assault in the Formosa—Luzon—China area in the Spring of 1945, (i.e. before the onset of the typhoon season), from a distant base.'

The scale of these operations defined the 'concept within other areas'.

> '. . . Operations in the North Pacific, the South Pacific, China and the South-East Asia theatre should be conducted in support of the main operations in the Central and South-West Pacific. In the event of the U.S.S.R. entering the war, operations in the North Pacific may assume far greater importance, and may involve a major redeployment of forces.'

The 'general concept' therefore remained that 'the main effort against Japan should be made in the Pacific'.

A substantial effort, however, should also be made in south-east Asia. The Combined Staff Planners thought that operations in that area should aim first at the capture of Upper Burma in the spring of 1944, 'to improve the air route and establish overland communications with China', and at 'an amphibious operation at approximately the same time.' The land operations should be continued in the autumn of 1944 within the limits of the forces available. Should there be the means, other operations could be undertaken by land, sea and air, to disperse and wear down the enemy.

The British argued from the rest of the paper that these conclusions for south-east Asia should be reconsidered. General Brooke in particular feared 'that Burma would become a huge vacuum', which would not conform to the main strategic concept. But no agreement could be reached, and the issues were deferred until the next day. The paper on strategy against Japan was returned to its authors for review, and the Combined Chiefs of Staff agreed meanwhile to exchange papers on the relation of operations in south-east Asia to those in Europe, for discussion on the morning of the 5th.

The next day, 5th December, proved decisive. The threads were gathered together, and a pattern emerged. The Combined Chiefs of Staff met at 10.30 a.m. Both the British and the Americans had already prepared papers; and a brisk discussion ensued, which centred on south-east Asia. To the Americans, the idea that the main operation by land in Burma, to which they were committed by inclination and promise, must be cancelled because a contingent operation by sea could not take place, was naturally distasteful. Always alive to the diplomatic implications of the C.B.I. Theatre[1], the Joint Chiefs of Staff opposed the dropping of both 'Buccaneer' and 'Tarzan' on these as well as on military grounds, and pointed out further that the reduction of operations in south-east Asia might have serious repercussions

[1] See pp. 126-7 above.

on those in the south-west Pacific, where more Japanese could then be sent. To this argument the British, and particularly the C.I.G.S., replied that the creation of a vacuum in Burma, which they foresaw if an offensive were begun on the lines suggested, could not help and might endanger General MacArthur's operations, and 'would not fit in with the strategic concept set out in the plan . . . that the main effort should be made in the Pacific'. They therefore refused to modify their proposals.

A curious position had in fact now been reached, whereby the Americans seemed to be endangering the European attacks, which they had been advocating for so long and so persistently, for the sake of an operation to which they had initially been indifferent, while the British wished to postpone the plan which to them had originally seemed the most attractive feature of the campaign in south-east Asia, in favour of an attack on southern France about which they remained less enthusiastic than the Americans. The matter was referred to the next Plenary Meeting, which was due to be held at 11 a.m.; and the Combined Chiefs of Staff composed a composite memorandum accordingly.

'OPERATIONS IN THE EUROPEAN THEATRE

1. 'Overlord' and 'Anvil' are the supreme operations for 1944. They must be carried out during May 1944. Nothing must be undertaken in any other part of the world which hazards the success of these two operations.

2. 'Overlord' as at present planned is on a narrow margin. Everything practicable should be done to increase its strength.

3. The examination of 'Anvil' on the basis of not less than a two-division assault should be pressed forward as fast as possible. If the examination reveals that it requires strengthening, consideration will have to be given to the provision of additional resources.

4. Operations in the Aegean, including in particular the capture of Rhodes, are desirable, provided that they can be fitted in without detriment to 'Overlord' and 'Anvil'.

5. Every effort must be made by accelerated building and conversion, to provide the essential additional landing craft for the European Theatre.

GENERAL

6. The decision[s] made by the Combined Chiefs of Staff at the 'Quadrant' Conference covering the bombing of German industrial targets and the destruction of the German air force . . . are reaffirmed.

OPERATIONS IN SOUTH-EAST ASIA THEATRE

(a) *British Proposals*

7. We fully realise that there are political and military implications in the postponement of 'Buccaneer'. As regards the

political implications, we must leave these to be taken into consideration by the President and Prime Minister. As regards the military disadvantages, these are overridden by the far greater advantages to be derived from a successful invasion of the Continent and the collapse of Germany.

(b) *U.S. Proposals*

8. Political and military considerations and commitments make it essential that Operation 'Tarzan' and an amphibious operation in conjunction therewith should take place. Apart from political considerations, there will be serious military repercussions if this is not done, not only in Burma and China, but also in the South-West Pacific.

9. The Supreme Commander, South-East Asia Command, should be told that he must do the best that he can with the resources already allocated to him.'

The Plenary Meeting, though indecisive, proved important. All agreed to the paragraphs on the European operations. They then debated 'Buccaneer'. Americans as well as British had by now studied Mountbatten's revised proposals for the operation, which (justifiably or not) threw a shadow over the discussion. At the same time, both British and American Chiefs of Staff drew attention, for the first time officially, to the dissatisfaction which their paper expressed at the proposed scale of the two European assaults. In neither case, they argued, was there a reasonable margin of safety: neither assault amounted to the size of the assault on Sicily, and both might well be beaten back. These doubts may perhaps seem to have been expressed rather late in the day. But it must be remembered that the burden of decision had until recently lain on the operations in any form, and not in their ideal form; and it was only very recently, in the complex and hurried talks, that any consideration could be given to this problem. The effect, however, combined with that produced by Mountbatten's proposals, swung the Americans for the first time towards a reconsideration of 'Buccaneer', though not as yet of 'Tarzan' in northern Burma. The Combined Chiefs of Staff were invited, as a result, to look again at the detail of 'Overlord' and 'Anvil', to consult the force commanders for 'Buccaneer', and then to ask Mountbatten what alternative he could devise if the bulk of his assault shipping was soon withdrawn from south-east Asia. 'Thus', Churchill has recorded, 'we parted, leaving Mr. Roosevelt much distressed.'[1]

This ended the morning of 5th December. The Combined Chiefs of Staff met again at 3 p.m. They first talked to the force commanders from south-east Asia, whom Admiral Mountbatten had recently sent to argue in detail for a stronger 'Buccaneer'. The conversation brought out, perhaps more clearly than before, that the necessary resources could be

[1] *Closing the Ring*, p. 364.

provided from the theatre itself; but this did not of course solve the difficulties elsewhere, and the Combined Chiefs of Staff accordingly decided to send their telegram to Mountbatten, informing him that priority was now given to European operations and that 'Buccaneer,' 'as at present planned', might therefore have to be ruled out before the monsoon. 'But', they proceeded, 'the necessity would remain to stage, in conjunction with 'Tarzan', amphibious operations on a smaller scale. Do you consider operations of this kind feasible?'

The Combined Chiefs of Staff then considered the scale of the attack on southern France. They now had the report on the operation for which they had called two days before.[1] In the light of the strategic conditions likely to obtain in May 1944, and of Admiral King's redistribution of the new American production of assault shipping,[2] the Combined Staff Planners reported that an assault of two divisions could be launched, provided that various shortages could be met. The operation seemed likely on current estimates to be short of some ancillary troops, of troop and cargo shipping, of some naval escorts and aircraft, and of assault shipping including 26 L.S.T. and 31 L.C.T. But it also seemed that most of these could be supplied—the assault shipping, on which all depended, coming by 15th April from American production, apart from five L.C.T. earmarked for 'Overlord'. The two divisions could therefore probably be transported without disturbing 'Overlord' or any other operation. This of course still did not allow for any margin elsewhere, or for a margin in the operation itself; and in view of the doubts now felt as to its strength, the position could not be considered safe. On the other hand, the report provided an acceptable basis for detailed planning by the Mediterranean Command; and a directive was accordingly sent to Eisenhower on 6th December, instructing him to prepare an outline plan as a matter of urgency, on the assumption that the assault on southern France would be launched to coincide approximately with 'Overlord' in May 1944, with a strength of two divisions and from south of the line Pisa-Rimini in Italy.

The Combined Chiefs of Staff's meeting ended in the late afternoon of the 5th. By the evening, the deadlock had been broken. Since the end of the Plenary Meeting that morning, the President had been reviewing in private the position that had emerged in the last two days. He decided that the stalemate could be removed only by abandoning 'Buccaneer'. This could not, in the circumstances, have been an easy decision to take. It meant breaking his promise to Chiang Kai-shek,[3] and facing the consequences which, on expert advice, had led him to make that promise; and it meant reversing many of the arguments

[1] See p. 184 above.

[2] See p. 187 above.

[3] See p. 165 above.

which Marshall and King had been advancing since the conference began. Mr. Sherwood has stated, indeed, that this was probably the one occasion during the war on which Roosevelt arbitrarily overruled the unanimous decision of his Chiefs of Staff.[1] 'There was', he has remarked, 'plenty of bitterness over this reversal'.[2] But the decision held good. Before dinner, the President sent the Prime Minister the laconic message, 'Buccaneer is off'; the next day, he sent a telegram to Chiang Kai-shek, explaining that European commitments left no margin for a large operation in the Bay of Bengal. 'This being so', he continued, 'would you be prepared to go ahead with 'Tarzan' [in northern Burma] as now planned, including commitment to maintain naval control of Bay of Bengal coupled with naval carrier and commando amphibious raiding operations simultaneous with launching of 'Tarzan' . . . if not, would you prefer to have 'Tarzan' delayed until November to include heavy amphibious operation. Meanwhile concentrating all air transport on carrying supplies over the Hump to air and ground forces in China.'

The way was now clear, on the last day of the conference, for an agreed programme on the main issues. The Combined Chiefs of Staff had agreed on the commitments for Europe. They could now specify the limits, if not the exact commitments, that followed for south-east Asia. Only the plan for the defeat of Japan remained to be approved. This was finally considered by the Combined Chiefs of Staff on the morning of 6th December. The Americans would have liked to defer appraisal of the document until the future of both south-east Asia and the Chinese theatre had been decided more exactly; but the British now wanted to know where they stood. They proposed in turn that the Combined Staff Planners' formula, that 'the main effort against Japan should be made in the Pacific', should be adopted as a basis for further investigation; and after some debate this was accepted 'in principle'. The revised paper, which appeared on 23rd December, formed in practice an appendix to the Combined Chiefs of Staff's Final Report at the conference.[3]

At the same time, the Combined Chiefs of Staff agreed to accept the following programme for south-east Asia as put forward by the Americans.

'(a) Delay major amphibious operations in the Bay of Bengal until after the next monsoon and divert the landing craft now assigned to 'Buccaneer' to operations 'Anvil' and 'Overlord'.

(b) Make all preparations to conduct 'Tarzan' as planned, less 'Buccaneer', for which will be substituted naval carrier and amphibious landing operations simultaneous with the launching

[1] *The White House Papers of Harry L. Hopkins*, II, p. 799.

[2] *Loc. cit.*, p. 800.

[3] See pp. 422-5 below.

of 'Tarzan'; and carry out air bombardment of the Bangkok-Burma railroad and the harbour of Bangkok, in the meantime maintaining naval control of the Bay of Bengal, or, alternatively
(c) Postpone 'Tarzan', increase to a maximum with planes available the air lift to China across the "Hump", and intensify the measures which will enable the B.29's [very long-range American bombers] to be brought to bear on the enemy.[1]
(d) The choice between alternatives (b) and (c) above will be made at a later date by the Combined Chiefs of Staff after obtaining an expression of opinion by the Generalissimo and the Supreme Allied Commander, South-East Asia Command.'

The last Plenary Meeting was held at 7.30 p.m. that evening. The President read out the Combined Chiefs of Staff's Final Report paragraph by paragraph. It was then accepted and initialled, the Prime Minister remarking 'that when military historians came to adjudge the decisions of the 'Sextant' Conference, they would find them fully in accordance with the classic articles of war.' A telegram was composed, conveying the broad conclusions, to Stalin; complimentary remarks were exchanged; and the last Plenary Meeting closed.

One more meeting took place, on the morning of 7th December, between the Combined Chiefs of Staff. It considered, *inter alia*, the alternative operations to be undertaken in south-east Asia. By now, Mountbatten's reply had been received to the Combined Chiefs of Staff's telegram of the 5th.[2] In his view, seaborne operations smaller than 'Buccaneer' were not worth the effort involved. They would neither accomplish anything of importance, nor be likely to save 'Tarzan'; and he therefore proposed, in place of the previous plans, a limited advance as far as the Chindwin, to which he gave the code name 'Gripfast', accompanied by the operations already planned in Arakan[3]. The Combined Chiefs of Staff could not act on this information until, as they had agreed on the 6th, they knew the Generalissimo's reaction to the President's telegram of that date;[4] and the matter therefore awaited a decision after the conference came to an end.

In the European section of their Final Report, the Combined Chiefs of Staff referred to 'the rôle that Turkey might be called upon to adopt if she comes into the war.' Such a development, as an aspect of the larger theme, had by now become subsidiary. Nevertheless, it remained important to the British, and of interest to the Russians. The negotiations proceeded actively on the return of the Western Allies to Cairo, along the lines which had been settled with Stalin at Teheran.

[1] See p. 453 below.
[2] See p. 191 above.
[3] See p. 153 above.
[4] See p. 192 above.

On 1st December, the Prime Minister invited President Inönu of Turkey to join Mr. Roosevelt and himself at Cairo on the 4th; and the invitation was accepted, on the understanding that the visit was 'to afford opportunity of free, equal and unprejudiced discussion as to the best method by which Turkey can serve common cause.' The proviso, according to the British Ambassador, was made so as to preserve the Turkish President's position vis-à-vis the National Assembly. It served to point the warnings already received that war would not be popular in Turkey, and that, if only to preserve itself, the Government must ensure favourable terms for its intervention.

The British therefore, as the Russians had surmised, were likely to have a stiff task ahead of them. The Americans, for their part, were no more enthusiastic than before about the Turkish alliance. When the Combined Chiefs of Staff met on 3rd December to consider, in closed session, the military implications of Turkey's entry into the war, the British minutes noted that there was an 'undercurrent of feeling' throughout the discussion against operations in the Aegean, and that the Joint Chiefs of Staff were not prepared to accept them as an American, a British or an Allied commitment unless it was clear that they would not at any stage interfere with resources needed elsewhere. Mr. Roosevelt himself, while associating the United States with the Allies' demands, seems at the meetings with the Turks to have conveyed an impression of some sympathy with their hesitation.

The results of those meetings, however, were reasonably satisfactory to the Prime Minister. Two each were held on 4th, 5th and 6th December, and a further meeting between the British and the Turks on the morning of the 7th. The discussion turned, as it had turned a month before, on the extent of the damage which the Turks had to fear from the Germans on a declaration of war, and which they rated higher than did the British. While both sides accepted the form the preparations should take, they therefore differed on the manner of their execution. It was agreed that the measures should be divided broadly into two stages: the first comprising a period during which British technicians (to the extent of some 2,000) and supplies would be introduced; the second, the arrival of the seventeen R.A.F. squadrons which would coincide with the declaration of war. But the Turks feared that the infiltration of men would provoke war before the squadrons arrived, while the British were satisfied that the squadrons could not be put into the country unless the men had been put in first. On the morning of the 7th, it was finally agreed that British military experts should go immediately to Ankara for further talks, and that the Turkish President should place a detailed programme in secret before the National Assembly on his return.

This programme had been worked out by the Chiefs of Staff and the Prime Minister over the previous four days. The first stage, which would last until 15th February, would be occupied by the infiltration of supplies and specialists for the preparation of airfields and communications, and by discussions in Ankara and Cairo on war plans, on the import of munitions and on diplomatic questions. On 15th February, the Allies would ask the Turks for permission to send in air squadrons. If the Turks then refused, the Allies would abandon all plans for further co-operation. If they accepted, the Allies would open the sea route from Egypt and the Levant, would send in British anti-tank and armoured units and munitions for the Turkish Army and air force, and would bring into operation the plans already concerted.

The Turks left Cairo at mid-day on 7th December. Meanwhile the Prime Minister and the Chiefs of Staff, after studying the opinions of the commanders in the Middle East, exchanged papers on the British movements outside Turkey itself. The final result appeared in a Minute of the Prime Minister of 10th December. After Rome had been captured in January 1944, three groups of medium bombers were to be moved to Cyrenaica for preliminary bombardment of the enemy's airfields and shipping in the eastern Mediterranean, and to cover the later arrival in Turkey of the seventeen squadrons of fighters. Once these squadrons were established in Turkey, air operations would be conducted thence and from Cyrenaica against the enemy in the Aegean, while two divisions from the Middle East prepared to attack and garrison Rhodes. That attack would take place in March 1944, if enough assault shipping could be provided: if not, possibly Cos and Leros would be attacked. During the same period, supplies would be passed into Smyrna and if possible through the Dardanelles, while six or eight British submarines, with a depôt ship and stores, would stand by to sail for the Black Sea. The preparations were given the code name of 'Saturn', and the capture of Rhodes the code name 'Hercules'.

The result of the final conversation with the Turks was communicated to the Americans and the Russians, who accepted it equably. Churchill himself now hoped for a favourable outcome; and, while negotiation was still open, at the end of the Cairo Conference it seemed probable that he would have his way.

The Combined Chiefs of Staff's Final Report also referred to problems of command. As these had preceded the discussion of strategy, so their solution conformed to the strategic settlement. While the Combined Chiefs of Staff were at Teheran, the Planners had composed draft directives for the new commander in the Mediterranean, along the lines foreshadowed by the Combined Chiefs of Staff's agreement of 26th November.[1] But in the event, the promulgation of the directive had to await the discussion of three other problems during

[1] See p. 166 above.

the second phase of 'Sextant': first, the organization of support to Yugoslavia; secondly, and connected with it, the machinery for providing the new commander with diplomatic advice; thirdly, the proposed reorganization of the American strategic air forces throughout Europe.

The first question, it will be recalled, had provided one of the most effective reasons for a single Mediterranean Command,[1] and its solution had become the more necessary as the British Mission to Tito settled on its new basis. Brigadier Maclean's position as an agent not only of S.O.E. but of the Foreign Office and of the Prime Minister, was an incentive to reassess S.O.E.'s own position vis-à-vis the military and diplomatic authorities in the Mediterranean. The definition of the nature and limits of the Allied aid to Yugoslavia now provided a more satisfactory context for that task. But the process was complicated by simultaneous conversations in Cairo on the relation of S.O.E. to the comparable American agency, the Office of Strategic Services (O.S.S.), and on that of the British diplomatic authorities for Yugoslavia to the Middle East Command. When, on 3rd December, the British Chiefs of Staff came to consider the draft directive to the Mediterranean commander, they were therefore obliged to ask the Foreign Office for guidance on both aspects of this problem, and meanwhile to suggest to the Americans that discussion of the directive itself should be postponed. The representatives of the Foreign Office replied provisionally on 5th December that S.O.E., associated more closely with the Americans, would remain responsible to the Middle East Command for its operations, and that the machinery for proffering diplomatic advice would also, for the moment, remain unchanged. But they stressed that these arrangements must be regarded as temporary, and recommended that the directive to the new Command should be phrased accordingly.

It had also not been decided how diplomatic advice for the rest of the Mediterranean should be offered to the new commander. There were both British and American advisers for North Africa and Italy at General Eisenhower's existing headquarters. Their relations with the new headquarters must now be regulated in harmony with those of the diplomatic advisers in the eastern areas, while, in view of 'Overlord', advice on French affairs in North Africa must also be correlated with advice on the affairs of metropolitan France. These matters had not yet been settled, or indeed fully discussed. The immediate arrangements must therefore be provisional and in general terms.

Meanwhile, the reorganization of the strategic air command was under discussion. The American and British papers on this subject were first considered on 4th December.[2] Air Chief Marshal Portal then

[1] See pp. 106, 113-14 above.

[2] See pp. 169-70 above.

exposed the British case for leaving the arrangements as they were. He stressed particularly the danger to the position of the Chief of the Air Staff which the interpolation of the new command must involve. If closer co-ordination was thought desirable between the bombing from north and from south, Portal would therefore prefer to be responsible for it himself, and to include the necessary staff in the existing machinery. But he recognized that it was a matter for the Americans to decide, and assured them that, whatever his objections, he would do his utmost to see that the arrangements worked. General Arnold then explained the background to the Americans' paper. The high losses, and the consequent need for high reserves, which still marked the conduct of the air operations against Germany, could be lessened considerably, and possibly only, by a greater weight of attack from different quarters. This in turn could be provided only by a closer co-ordination between the areas whence the attacks were launched, which in his view could best be secured by the proposals under debate. But agreement proved impossible, and the Combined Chiefs of Staff decided to discuss the matter again later.

It was accordingly placed on the agenda for the morning of 5th December. By then, the Joint Chiefs of Staff had produced a revised arrangement to meet some of the British objections. The commander of the American strategic air forces would now be placed temporarily under the Chief of the Air Staff in London for the control of all American bombing operations against Germany, until the Combined Chiefs of Staff decided to transfer his allegiance, as was ultimately intended, to the Supreme Allied Commander for 'Overlord'. Better provision was also made for co-operation with the Mediterranean Command. Owing to the press of other business, this revised paper was not considered in detail until the morning of 7th December. Portal then agreed that it met some of the British objections, and, while repeating his disapproval of the arrangements, accepted them as an American decision. After final consultation on detail with the commanders in the Mediterranean, the directive was accordingly issued on 4th January, 1944.[1]

While the arrangements for the air were not settled until the end of the conference, allowance was made for them in framing the directive to the Mediterranean Command. The Americans submitted their draft on 4th December: the British submitted theirs on the 5th. Since it was generally accepted that the new commander would be British, the latter was substantially accepted. Apart from adding the necessary amendment to provide for the new air command, it was left entirely alone; and the final directive from the Combined Chiefs of Staff accordingly read as follows.

---

[1] See p. 292 below.

'(1) We have decided to set up a unified command in the Mediterranean theatre on account of its geographical unity and its dependence on all bases in the area.

(2) We have no intention of changing existing organisation and arrangements any more than is necessary to give effect to our main intention. You should assume, therefore, that all present arrangements continue with the exceptions outlined below, but you should report as necessary whether you consider any further changes are required in the light of experience.

(3) To your present responsibilities you will add responsibility for operations in Greece, Albania, Yugoslavia, Bulgaria, Rumania, Hungary, Crete and Aegean Islands and Turkey. The British and American forces allocated to you from Middle East will be determined by the British and United States Chiefs of Staff respectively. You will have full liberty to transfer forces from one part of your Command to another for the purposes of conducting operations which we have agreed. The Commanders-in-Chief, Middle East, will be under your orders for operations in these areas.

(4) You will provide United States Strategic Air Forces under separate command, but operating in your area, with the necessary logistical and administrative support in performance of Operation 'Pointblank' as the air operation of first priority. Should a strategic or tactical emergency arise, you may, at your discretion, utilise the 15th United States Strategic Air Force for purposes other than its primary mission, informing the Combined Chiefs of Staff and the Commanding General, United States Strategic Air Forces in Europe, if and when that command is organised.

(5) You will, in addition, assume responsibility for the conduct of guerrilla and subversive action in the territories in your Command and for setting up the necessary organisation for the despatch of supplies to resistance groups in occupied territories.

(6) The Commanders-in-Chief, Middle East will remain directly responsible to the British Chiefs of Staff for all the territories at present in Middle East Command situated in Africa, Palestine, Syria and the Lebanon, and for the operation and security of the Middle East base with such forces as the British Chiefs of Staff may allot for this purpose from time to time.

(7) You will be notified later of any adjustments which are thought necessary to the machinery by which you receive political guidance. In the meantime, in respect of the new territories in your Command you should obtain any necessary political advice from Commander-in-Chief, Middle East, through the channels he at present uses.

(8) The system of Command is shown on the attached diagram (Appendix A). You will note that the Mediterranean Air Command will now be known as Mediterranean Allied Air Forces.'

APPENDIX A OF THE DIRECTIVE

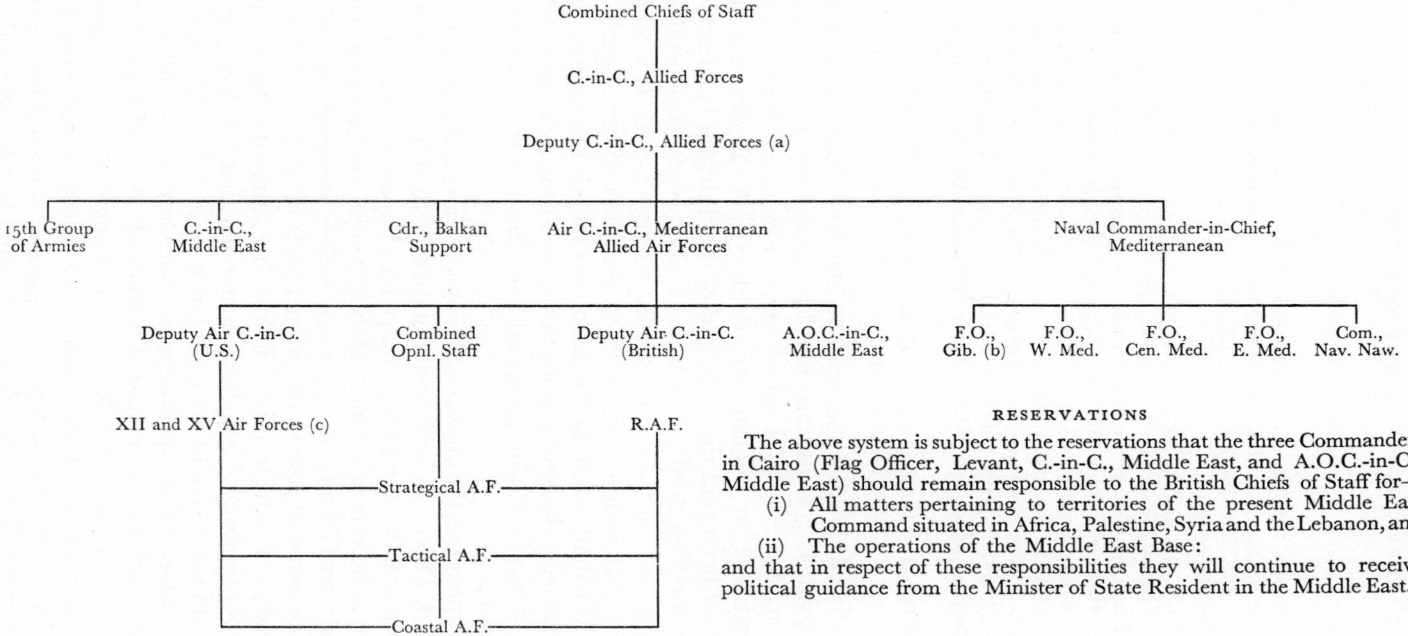

RESERVATIONS

The above system is subject to the reservations that the three Commanders in Cairo (Flag Officer, Levant, C.-in-C., Middle East, and A.O.C.-in-C., Middle East) should remain responsible to the British Chiefs of Staff for—

(i) All matters pertaining to territories of the present Middle East Command situated in Africa, Palestine, Syria and the Lebanon, and

(ii) The operations of the Middle East Base:

and that in respect of these responsibilities they will continue to receive political guidance from the Minister of State Resident in the Middle East.

NOTES:

(a) At present acts only as C.-in-C. 15th Group of Armies.

(b) Flag Officer, Gibraltar, is responsible to Naval C.-in-C., Mediterranean, for area between the longitude of Cape St. Vincent and longitude 3 W. For the remainder of the Gibraltar Command he is responsible direct to Admiralty.

(c) As from 1st January, 1944, Fifteenth Air Force will be placed under command of USSAFE for assignment of missions and for technique and tactics employed in their execution. [See p. 292 below.]

APPENDIX B OF THE DIRECTIVE

BALKAN SUPPORT

'It was agreed at the 'Eureka' Conference that our support of the Patriots in the Balkans, which now falls within the area in which you are responsible for Allied operations, should be intensified in order to increase their effectiveness.

You will be responsible for supporting them to the greatest practicable extent by increasing the supply of arms and equipment, clothing, medical stores, food and such other supplies as they may require. You should also support them by commando operations and by furnishing such air support as you may consider advisable in the light of the general situation.

You should examine the possibility of continuing to supply the Patriots with Italian equipment, in the use of which they are already experienced, making good deficiences in Italian formations to such extent as may be necessary with available British or American equipment.

We consider that this mission is of such importance that it would best be controlled on a regular basis by a special commander and joint staff.'

When this directive was approved, the identity of the commander was still unknown. It was assumed that Eisenhower would soon leave for Washington, that Marshall would come to England to command 'Overlord', and that an Englishman would go to the Mediterranean. But nothing had been said since the end of the Teheran Conference on the choice for 'Overlord', on which all arrangements depended. The President had not mentioned the subject ; and Churchill imagined, as he had indeed told Stalin at their last dinner together, that General Marshall would be the man. But on 6th December, just before they parted, Roosevelt informed the Prime Minister that Marshall would stay in Washington, and that Eisenhower would command 'Overlord'.

The appointment was the outcome of prolonged and severe reflection by the President. There can be little doubt that the British objections to a Supreme Commander for Europe played an important part in the result. Anxious as he was that Marshall should enjoy the greatest command that had ever fallen to an American soldier, Roosevelt was well aware of the consequent loss to the Joint Chiefs of Staff, and of the political disturbance which might follow his appointment to an apparently subordinate position. Both demanded that his disappearance from Washington should be, and should be shown to be, worth while. The command of all operations against Germany would have satisfied the demand: the command of 'Overlord' alone did not. The recent developments, moreover, had removed one of the main arguments for sending Marshall to London. 'Overlord' could now be regarded as safe, and it was presumably no longer necessary to choose as its commander the American soldier who could best be expected to protect it under attack. While the case for Marshall in Washington was as strong as before, the case for Marshall in Europe had thus become less important. The General himself, with Roman severity, declined to show his preference. On 5th December, the President therefore took the decision alone. 'I feel', he is said to have told Marshall, in informing him of the result, 'I could not sleep at night with you out of the country.'[1]

The President made his choice against the advice of Hopkins and of Stimson, despite the known preference of Churchill and Stalin, and against his own keen desire to give Marshall the command. Probably, of all those concerned at the two conferences, only the other Joint Chiefs of Staff wished the General to stay in Washington. 'It was', writes Mr. Sherwood, 'one of the most difficult and one of the loneliest decisions he [Roosevelt] ever had to make.'[2] In the field of appointments, it was perhaps one of his best.

The appointment of the commander for 'Overlord' was the signal for the necessary general post among the higher military appointments, to which both Governments addressed themselves in the weeks that followed. The results, which completed the structure erected at the conference, will be shown in the next chapter.

The last meeting of 'Sextant' took place on the morning of 7th December. The final remarks perhaps illustrate best the nature of the great conference.

> 'Sir Alan Brooke said he would like to express on behalf of the British Chiefs of Staff their deep gratitude for the way in which the United States Chiefs had met their views. . . .
>
> General Marshall said that he very much appreciated Sir Alan Brooke's gracious tributes. He felt that it was most important that during the next month or so the British and United States Chiefs of Staff should both study how best the magnitude of future Conferences could be reduced. They would undoubtedly in future have to take place at shorter intervals. . . .
>
> The Combined Chiefs of Staff—
>
> Agreed:
>
> (a) That it was desirable to cut down as much as possible the attendance at future United States—British Conferences.
>
> (b) That a study with this in view should be carried out within the next month.'

In fact, Brooke's and Marshall's observations were closely connected. 'Sextant' and 'Eureka' together formed an exceptional conference, and one whose complexities and length could scarcely have been avoided. Unlike earlier conferences, it was dominated by the shadow of irrevocable decisions, as the climax approached in Europe. British and

[1] Sherwood, *loc. cit.*, p. 801.

[2] Ibid.

Americans had now finally to make their choice in Europe, and to relate it, for the first time, directly to the Russians' plans. The conclusions, in these novel circumstances, would determine the future in the West, and would affect the foundations which were being laid for the offensive in the Far East. It was therefore perhaps not surprising that the discussions should have been close and intricate, the papers many and varied, and the staffs swollen beyond the normal size. The nature of the conference derived from the nature of the occasion; and when the occasion itself had passed, the normal machinery again sufficed for the guidance of events. Despite the general agreement that such meetings must in future be held more often, there was in fact a longer interval between 'Sextant' and the next Allied conference than there had been between any two Allied conferences since the United States entered the war.

CHAPTER V

THE DECISIONS FOR 1944: II, EPILOGUE TO CAIRO, DECEMBER, 1943–JANUARY, 1944

(i)

The Settlement of the European Commands

ON THE CONCLUSION of the Cairo Conference, the British could review its results with some confidence; and the gratitude with which the Prime Minister and the C.I.G.S. addressed their final audiences showed indeed the measure of their satisfaction. 'Overlord' would be launched in May, 1944. But this would not, as had been feared, rob the Mediterranean of the assault shipping needed in the near future for strokes in Italy and in the Aegean, owing to the decision to launch 'Anvil' also in May; 'Buccaneer', whose prosecution had seemed not unlikely to embarrass the British strategy in the East and the operations in Europe, was cancelled; and apart from the arrangements for the strategic air forces, the structure of command in Europe was settled much as the British had wished. These results had been achieved thanks to the Americans' concessions in accepting the abandonment of 'Buccaneer', and the conditions of command which partly prevented Marshall's appointment to 'Overlord'. But they did not conflict with the Americans' main purpose, whose achievement was regarded with relief in Washington, to secure 'Overlord' in May, 1944; and they met the Russians' demands. General harmony thus reigned among the Allies, and each could view the decisions as on the whole satisfactory for himself. Only the selection of the men for the various new appointments, the detail of the landing in Italy, and the negotiations with the Turks had still to be settled; and none of these, on 7th December, seemed likely to prove an insuperable, or even a serious, difficulty.

The first care of the Western Governments was to fill the outstanding appointments, and to complete the structure of command in the Mediterranean. The new commander in that theatre was to be a British officer; and the Prime Minister had assumed that, provided he remained there, General Alexander would be given the post. But he must then be removed from the command in Italy, for which he was admirably suited, on the eve of important operations. The Chiefs of Staff therefore suggested that General Wilson, whose experience in the Middle East had lain much in the diplomatic as well as in the military sphere, held particular qualifications for a post in which the military issues were connected so closely with the diplomatic, and largely affected the eastern Mediterranean which he knew intimately. The Prime Minister agreed, and Wilson's name was submitted to the President on 18th December as the new Allied commander in the Mediterranean.

The other appointments in the theatre depended directly on those made at the same time for 'Overlord'. Seven important posts had now to be filled in the latter Command, to accord with the balance of forces and with the preferences of the new commander. Following the pattern now generally accepted, the Deputy Commander was to be British. In view of the dominating position of the air before and in the early phases of the campaign, the British suggested that Air Chief Marshal Tedder—an experienced co-ordinator of Allied operations—should fill this appointment. Another critical air command to be filled was that of the American strategic air forces in Europe, which was destined to be placed at some stage under the commander for 'Overlord', and must meanwhile be linked with his preparations. Eisenhower was anxious that General Carl Spaatz, then commanding one of the American air forces in the Mediterranean, should be appointed to this post; and his views prevailed. The sea and air forces for 'Overlord' itself had already been placed initially under British officers: the naval forces under Admiral Sir Bertram Ramsay, and the air forces under Air Chief Marshal Sir Trafford Leigh-Mallory. The armies were to be divided eventually into two groups of American and British, but were placed for the period of the assault and build-up under a single, British, command. The choice for this post centred on Generals Alexander and Montgomery. Much could be claimed for either. Montgomery had been successful as an Army Commander, Alexander as an Army Commander and as a Commander-in-Chief; and in other spheres each had his own advantages. Montgomery was a war hero in a particular sense. He had never lost a battle, and the impression which he conveyed, of a commander dedicated to success, exercised a peculiar fascination over British troops and public. Alexander's virtues, particularly as a co-ordinator, had won him the respect of his staff, his superiors and his allies. The choice was eventually submitted to the War Cabinet; as a result, Montgomery was given the appointment, partly because it was thought that his reputation would instil a unique flavour of confidence throughout his British command and in the country, partly because, yet again, Alexander could scarcely be spared from the Italian scene. Meanwhile, the Americans had selected Lieut.-General Omar Bradley, one of Eisenhower's Corps commanders in the

Mediterranean, as the commander of their sector of the assault and later of the American group of armies. Lastly, the new Supreme Commander took with him to 'Overlord' his experienced and reliable Chief of Staff, Major-General Walter Bedell Smith.

These moves dictated the senior appointments in the Mediterranean. Now that the Command embraced the whole of that area, an officer was needed to administer the base in North Africa for which Alexander had hitherto remained theoretically responsible. On Eisenhower's recommendation, Lieut.-General Jacob L. Devers, commanding the American forces in England which would now fall under 'Overlord', was appointed to this post as Deputy Allied Commander. Alexander remained in command of the Allied Armies in Italy, with General Mark Clark in command of Fifth Army and reserved for the probable command of 'Anvil', while Lieut.-General Sir Oliver Leese relieved Montgomery in command of Eighth Army. Admiral Sir John Cunningham remained commander of the Allied naval forces; and Lieut.-General Ira C. Eaker, hitherto commanding Eighth U.S. Air Force in England, became commander of the Mediterranean Allied Air Forces, being himself relieved in England by Major-General James Doolittle. Air Marshal Sir John Slessor assumed, under General Eaker, the command of the British air forces in the Mediterranean; and Wilson selected as his Chief of Staff Lieut.-General Sir James Gammell. Wilson himself was relieved as the land Commander-in-Chief, Middle East, by General Sir Bernard Paget, who was also given the responsibility for future operations in the Turkish sphere.

These appointments were completed early in January, 1944. It was arranged provisionally that Eisenhower should hand over the Mediterranean Command to Wilson on the 1st of that month, though in the event he did so on the 8th; and that the most important of the changes should be announced publicly, with suitable reservations of title, before the end of the year. The President and the Prime Minister issued simultaneous statements accordingly.

The appointments marked the completion of a process which had been developing over the past two years, and which now culminated in the establishment of the Supreme Command as the pattern for all areas controlled by the Western Allies in combination. Every theatre now had, in fact or name, its Supreme Commander—Nimitz and MacArthur in the Pacific Ocean Areas and South-West Pacific, Mountbatten in South-East Asia, Wilson in the Mediterranean, and Eisenhower for 'Overlord'. The structure varied in each case, and each Command enjoyed its own relations with the Combined Chiefs of Staff; but, under different conditions and from varied experience, a type had emerged whose broad features were not to be altered significantly for the rest of the war. The period of the main Allied offensives was also the period of the Supreme Command.

The pattern of the Command for 'Overlord' was worked out over the next few months in England.[1] In the Mediterranean, it followed that already evolved. No change occurred in the relations between the main subordinate commanders or between them and the Supreme Commander. But there was one significant change, in his relations with higher authority. When General Eisenhower was Commander-in-Chief, the Mediterranean theatre was controlled directly by the Combined Chiefs of Staff. But on 4th January, 1944, the Joint Chiefs of Staff proposed that, since the new commander was British, the British Chiefs of Staff should assume 'the executive direction of affairs in that theatre'. This offer, as Field Marshal Dill reported privately, was made spontaneously by Marshall to 'ease a somewhat complicated and difficult set-up'. It was the more warmly appreciated by the recipients, who were thus able to assume direct control when General Wilson took over on 8th January. On that day, the Combined Chiefs of Staff issued the following directive:

> 'You, as Allied Commander-in-Chief, Mediterranean will be responsible to the Combined Chiefs of Staff through the British Chiefs of Staff, who will act as the executive of the Combined Chiefs of Staff in all matters pertaining to the details of operations with which you are charged, and will be the channel through which all directives will be given'.

Two ancillary questions, however, remained from the issue of the recent directive to the new Command: the machinery for exercising military responsibility in the Balkans, and the machinery for proffering and co-ordinating diplomatic advice throughout the theatre. The first question was not answered for some months, and must be followed in greater detail elsewhere;[2] but it is convenient here to treat briefly of the second, whose settlement falls beyond the chronological limits of this chapter.

Diplomatic authority in the eastern Mediterranean remained the same for the time being, pending a final solution to S.O.E.'s position in the Balkans and to the complementary position of the American agencies. But its relations with the central diplomatic authority of the new Command were settled in accordance with changes, that took place early in 1944, between the diplomatic authorities in the western and central areas. At the end of 1943, Mr. Harold Macmillan and Mr. Robert Murphy were responsible to the Commander-in-Chief, on behalf of the British and American Governments respectively, for all diplomatic questions in North Africa and Italy. But in November 1943, the British Government appointed Mr. Duff Cooper as its representative with the French Committee of National Liberation, holding the

[1] See pp. 292-3, 296-7 below.

[2] See pp. 274-5 below.

rank of Ambassador; and at the turn of the year he took up his post in Algiers. Wilson thus had three separate diplomatic advisers in the western and central Mediterranean, one of whom held responsibilities outside the theatre, and a committee of diplomatic advisers in the eastern Mediterranean, reporting through the medium of the Commander-in-Chief, Middle East. The ambiguities of this position were tackled by the Foreign Office during January 1944, and towards the end of that month the Prime Minister informed the Supreme Commander that he would in future receive 'political assistance and advice' in matters affecting the French Committee of National Liberation from Mr. Duff Cooper, in those affecting all other countries except Turkey from Mr. Macmillan, and in those affecting Turkey from the Minister Resident in the Middle East. He would also receive directions as required on matters 'of major importance' from the Foreign Office or from the Prime Minister himself. Early in March, detailed arrangements followed from the Foreign Office.

(ii)

Unsettlement in the Mediterranean and South-East Asia

But while the work of the conferences was thus being rounded off in the sphere of command, it was being threatened in the sphere of strategy. The programme for the Mediterranean, on which so much thought had been expended at Cairo, relied for its execution on the capture of Rome in January, 1944. This indeed had been taken for granted; but in fact, while the plans were under debate, their premises were being undermined.

In the second and third weeks of November, Fifth and Eighth Armies composed their plans for the offensive which General Alexander had ordered on the 8th.[1] Eighth Army aimed at the transverse road running inland from Pescara, some forty miles north of the Sangro along whose southern bank the Army lay. Mountainous country almost to the coast, the rivers Sangro and Pescara and intervening streams, lay between it and the target. Fifth Army, disposed in the mountains to the south of the winding Garigliano, aimed at the Liri valley and route 6 (Via Casilina) to Rome, between the massifs which stretched, to the east in a curve from the Garigliano to route 6 and thence to the peaks by Monte Cassino, and in the west for almost sixty miles from north of the Garigliano to the Alban Hills south of Rome. On both flanks the

[1] See p. 75 above; and Map V, facing p. 270.

country is difficult in the extreme, the weather is severe in winter, and the German defences were well sited in depth. Nevertheless, no alternative was possible for an approach to Rome, and Alexander relied on the seaborne assault in the west to relieve the frontal attack of much of its opposition.

Planning for this assault began on 12th November, by a special staff at Fifth Army's headquarters. The state of the reserves, and of the assault shipping in the theatre, limited its weight to one division with supporting troops. The German opposition was estimated at one division from the second to the fourth day, thereafter reinforced by possibly two more divisions from the north. The assaulting force must therefore join Fifth Army from the south within seven days of the landing. The necessary shipping would not be available from other tasks until 20th December. By that date, Alexander estimated that Fifth Army should have forced the passage of the Garigliano, and should have driven up the Liri valley to points within fifteen miles of Frosinone. It would then be threatening positions in the Alban Hills from which artillery could dominate the coastal plain to the south of Rome. The date for the seaborne assault was therefore settled at 20th December, and plans were made to provide a lift seven days beforehand for 24,500 men and 2,700 vehicles. The area selected for the assault was the coast between the small port of Anzio and the seaside resort of Nettuno, due west of the Alban Hills, some fifty-five miles from the estuary of the Garigliano and less than twenty miles from that of the Tiber. After capturing Anzio itself, the assault force was to move inland, to cut the longitudinal route 7 (Via Appia) at the foot of the Alban Hills and join Fifth Army advancing across the mountains from the Liri valley. The operation was given the code name of 'Shingle'.

On 27th November, in weather which had already delayed the operations by six days, Eighth Army attacked along a front of three divisions. The Germans had withdrawn one division earlier in the month; but the remaining two divisions were quickly reinforced by a further two recalled from reserve, and the attack found itself from the start confronted by strong opposition. By 2nd December, the whole line was across the Sangro; but it was unable to advance much farther, and after bitter fighting Eighth Army halted at the end of the month on a line running inland from Ortona, some twelve to fifteen miles north of the Sangro but over twenty-five miles south of Pescara. For the time being, it had clearly shot its bolt.

Throughout the second half of November, Fifth Army regrouped to the west of the Apennines. Two divisions were withdrawn, as planned, for 'Overlord', and replaced by the equivalent of three divisions; and a new American Corps' headquarters was formed to complement the two existing British and American Corps. The Germans also reinforced during the same period. One division was brought from reserve.

and one from Slovenia, during November; and a third division arrived from Russia in December. Early in that month, as a result, the defence disposed of a force equal to that of the attack.

Fifth Army's operations began on 1st December, on a front of three Corps. By the 9th, its left had cleared the southern bank of the Garigliano as far as the sea. Its right, meanwhile, was held in the mountains beyond route 6. The centre then attacked towards Monte Cassino itself, and after severe fighting captured the ridge of Monte Sammucro, a few miles south of that position, in the middle of the month. But it was then exhausted; and as no further advance was possible on the right, at the end of December the Army came to a halt. Meanwhile, the Germans had been constructing stronger defences, behind the main positions, around Monte Cassino.

The prospect of a stalemate in both sectors made it plain by the middle of December that the seaborne assault 'Shingle' could not be launched on the 20th. It seemed unlikely, indeed, that Fifth Army could be within supporting distance before 10th January at the earliest, and on 18th December General Clark reported that even that date could not be met. He therefore advised Alexander that 'Shingle' must be cancelled; and by the 20th, when the assault should have been launched, its planning staff had been largely dispersed.

This disappointment once more upset the careful allocation of assault shipping. If 'Shingle' was launched on its original scale some time after 10th January, when Fifth Army might be near supporting distance, the sixty-eight L.S.T., retained in the theatre largely for the operation, would be leaving or would have left for England; but if it was undertaken before or near that date, it must be on a larger scale for which the available L.S.T. might not suffice. In either case, the programme for the shipping would be upset. On the other hand, if that programme was allowed to take its course without any seaborne assault being launched, the campaign in Italy would probably degenerate into a slow and expensive slogging match, with the possible consequences envisaged by Alexander in October.[1] This in turn might well lead to further calls being made on assault shipping, and probably at equal or greater inconvenience. To avoid the prospect of an immediate reverse, and of a later drain on the limited resources, the necessary assault shipping must therefore be kept in the Mediterranean for longer than had been anticipated, or must be reinforced immediately; but in either case without damaging the preparations for 'Overlord'.

It was obviously by no means easy to tackle an obstacle of this nature only eleven days after the end of the Cairo Conference; and it may therefore have been fortunate, although it hardly seemed so at the time, that the Prime Minister should have been held in North Africa by ill-health until early in January, 1944. Throughout the recent conferences

[1] See pp. 69-70 above.

he had been feeling far from well, and on 12th December, when visiting Eisenhower at Tunis, he succumbed to a bad attack of pneumonia. The worst, however, was over by the 18th, and the ensuing convalescence, in Tunis and later in Marrakesh, did not prevent him from intervening with vigour and despatch in the hard and intricate discussion. His presence on the spot, indeed, with powerful support from Brooke in London after 19th December, was largely responsible for the result.

The first task was to ascertain the necessary scale for the assault on Anzio, assuming that it was launched before Fifth Army reached Frosinone. The authorities in London and those in the theatre considered that it should then be on a scale of two divisions, which was thought to require a lift of 246 assault ships and craft. The problem therefore was how to find these vessels within the next few weeks, without disturbing the date for 'Overlord'.

The 246 ships and craft comprised 96 landing ships and 150 landing craft. The Mediterranean theatre could provide 135 of the landing craft, and more would become available, after refit and repair, in the course of February. Of the landing ships, six out of the eight L.S.I. required would become available from south-east Asia for operations in the Mediterranean by 20th January. The critical shortage, as usual, lay in L.S.T., of which eighty-eight were thought to be needed. In December, there were 105 L.S.T. in the Mediterranean; but on and shortly after 15th January, sixty-eight would depart for 'Overlord'. This would leave only thirty-seven, of which ten would be refitting, and a further ten would be engaged in transporting air forces to Corsica in preparation for the later assault on southern France. Fifteen L.S.T. were on their way from south-east Asia, and would be ready for operations in the Mediterranean by 5th February; but they were destined for the attack on Rhodes ('Hercules'), if all went well with the Turks.[1] No more L.S.T. were then due to arrive in the theatre before the new American production appeared in April, 1944.[2]

There were four possible ways in which, singly or in combination, to meet the gap of seventy-one L.S.T. for Anzio. First, all or some of the twenty L.S.T. which would be in the Mediterranean after 15th January, but which were earmarked for refit and for Corsica, might in fact be made available by revised programmes for both those commitments. Secondly, some or all of the sixty-eight L.S.T. due to sail for England on 15th January, might be held in the Mediterranean for a further period. Thirdly, if 'Hercules' (against Rhodes) proved impossible in February, the fifteen L.S.T. from south-east Asia could be transferred to Anzio. Fourthly, more L.S.T. could be taken from

---

[1] See p. 195 above.

[2] See p. 187 above.

south-east Asia, if it was decided that no seaborne assault should be carried out in that theatre before the onset of the south-west monsoon.

At this point, therefore, we must follow the progress, over the previous fortnight, of the three contingent problems, in south-east Asia, in the Aegean, and in the plans for the assault on the south of France. Each remained open at the end of the Cairo Conference: each had developed since that date. The greatest potential change had taken place in south-east Asia. On 6th December, Admiral Mountbatten had informed the Chiefs of Staff, in answer to their inquiry of the 5th, that as 'Buccaneer' was to be postponed, he saw no useful purpose in pursuing smaller seaborne operations. He was then, of course, unaware of the size of the assault force he would be allowed to retain. But on the 7th, he was ordered to send to Europe the fifteen L.S.T. and six L.S.I. which comprised rather more than half of his landing ships, and he therefore reviewed the situation on the assumption that he could keep the rest. As a result, he submitted a new plan on 11th December, for a smaller seaborne attack (to which he gave the code name 'Pigstick') on the southern Mayu peninsula, behind the Japanese positions in Arakan. This, he thought, would prove a useful contribution to the operations along the coast, and might be regarded as an earnest of the Allies' obligations to the Generalissimo. But assuming that it failed to save 'Tarzan' in northern Burma, he requested that it might still be substituted for 'Buccaneer' as a complementary operation to the lesser operation 'Gripfast'.[1]

When the Combined Chiefs of Staff received Mountbatten's telegram, they had not yet heard Chiang Kai-shek's reaction to Roosevelt's message of 6th December, informing him of the cancellation of 'Buccaneer', and asking if he would be prepared to go ahead with 'Tarzan' in conjunction with raids in the Bay of Bengal. A negative answer appears to have been received in Washington on the 9th; but it does not seem to have been conclusive, and the British moreover were not aware of its existence until the 23rd. By the 17th, however, it seemed to them unlikely, from what they could learn in Chungking, that Chiang Kai-shek would move in the spring of 1944, and on the 18th he told General Carton de Wiart, the British representative attached to him, that he refused to advance on Burma until the following November unless the original seaborne operation was carried out. But meanwhile Mountbatten was doing his best to ensure that the combined plan should not disappear. Placing his hopes on the fact that the Chinese had never been told the exact scale and target of 'Buccaneer', and without asking permission from the Combined Chiefs of Staff, he instructed Carton de Wiart on 21st December to inform

[1] See p. 193 above.

Chiang Kai-shek that 'Pigstick' would be mounted, and asked him to accept this operation, with a target on the Burmese coast instead of the Andaman Islands, 'as the amphibious operation he had postulated'.

The news of this offer reached the British Chiefs of Staff only two days after they had resolved, with the Prime Minister, to work for a larger version of the seaborne assault on Anzio. They were correspondingly alarmed. The remaining L.S.T. in south-east Asia now formed one of the possible means of relief for the Mediterranean, and they were therefore anxious not to be forced into a premature acceptance of 'Pigstick' before they had settled the problem in Italy. Their anxiety was increased by the course of events affecting the eastern Mediterranean.

On 7th December, the British had looked forward with some confidence to bringing Turkey into the war in the middle of February, 1944. But on 12th December, the discussions took a turn for the worse. The Turkish Foreign Minister then informed the British Ambassador that, while his Government accepted the latest British proposals in principle, it remained convinced that Germany would attack when war was declared, and must therefore ask both for more help and for more protection than had been offered so far. The figures of 216 Spitfires, 500 tanks and 66,800 tons of petrol were mentioned in the first connexion, and the old disputed figure of forty-nine air squadrons in the second. The sudden change in the atmosphere was shown by the adverse terms in which the Foreign Minister referred to the conversations in Cairo; and when the detailed demands were received over the next two days, they confirmed the preliminary report.

This marked deterioration in the Turkish attitude reflected partly the widespread opposition to intervention, which became the more articulate as the event became the more likely, and partly an increasing apprehension by the Turkish Government of German troop movements in Bulgaria. But it was also the result of a thrusting British approach which the Turks were inclined to resent, and which, as it was later learned, they thought was not in any case supported wholeheartedly by the other Allies. The British were no more disposed than before to accept the argument or the demands; but they were equally not disposed to break with the Turks. After reviewing the new figures, they therefore instructed the Commanders-in-Chief, Middle East, to go to Ankara forthwith, and to offer more tanks and artillery, together with Spitfires and medium bombers, provided that the Turks adhered to the arrangements already devised. Meanwhile, they attempted to meet the diplomatic difficulties by reminding the Turks of Stalin's assurance in regard to Bulgaria,[1] and by asking the United States Government to join with the British Government in a further *démarche* to Ankara. At the same time, the British Ambassador was informed that

[1] See p. 179 above.

these measures were designed to ease the passage of the earlier arrangements, and not in any way to depart from them; and that if they were refused, the Turks should understand that British supplies would cease and that British diplomatic support could no longer be assured.

But the immediate result of this policy was disappointing. While the Turks now agreed to admit British technicians, they preferred not to receive the commanders from the Middle East, whose visit might arouse suspicion. The discussions were correspondingly delayed, and from the Ambassador's reports in the third week of December the outcome seemed uncertain.

The decline in the prospects for 'Saturn' (preparations for Turkey's entry into the war) could not but affect the prospects for 'Hercules' against Rhodes.[1] A further, if indirect, complication had also just emerged which affected the western Mediterranean. Following the instructions from the Combined Chiefs of Staff, the Mediterranean Command set to work on a fresh report on operation 'Anvil' against southern France, which it completed by 16th December. On the 17th, Eisenhower informed the Combined Chiefs of Staff that it would be submitted as soon as it had been discussed with the 'Overlord' authorities: meanwhile he gave its conclusions. The new plan, like its predecessors, envisaged that a force of ten divisions, of which two would be armoured, would finally be put ashore in southern France. But it differed from them in its demands for the assault itself.

> 'The appreciations on which plan is based,' Eisenhower reported, 'point definitely to a compelling need for a heavier assault force. The necessity for an initial broad and deep beach-head to accept at least two additional Divisions with necessary scale of supporting troops in a rapid follow-up, and the great advantage to accrue by firmly establishing strong forces ashore rapidly to cover our later relatively slow build-up, before the Germans can react in strength, make it imperative that 'Anvil' assault be launched by a force of three Divisions if craft can be made available from any source having a priority on resources lower than 'Anvil'.'

He accordingly asked 'urgently' that the necessary assault shipping should be provided, and that this should be confirmed if possible before the end of the month, since detailed planning should start by 1st January, 1944.

Eisenhower's new demand was no less awkward because it was not unexpected. ''Anvil',' as he remarked, 'has become an operation of major proportions'; and its growth within three weeks from a design which had been a mere possibility involving one division, to a commitment enjoying a priority second only to that of 'Overlord', and

---

[1] See p. 195 above.

demanding thrice its original strength, was particularly disconcerting in a period of such complexity.

Such were the circumstances in which the British sought to find the seventy-one extra L.S.T. for Anzio within the next few weeks. Their efforts are of considerable interest, apart from the result. For while the latter affected the conclusions of the Cairo Conference and the Italian campaign, setting the scene for the preliminaries to 'Overlord', the process by which it was reached provides, owing to its conditions, a test case which has no parallel in our period. Figures in plenty had been exchanged before; but the permutations had always been based on common assumptions, which themselves had passed unquestioned. Now, for the first time, those assumptions were examined, with results that may throw some light on their validity. For, when put to the test, it was found that timetables could be cut and programmes undertaken beyond the limits provisionally accepted; and the extent of the slack which is here displayed so precisely, provides at least a rough measure —and probably the best we can hope to have—of its extent in other less well-defined cases. This standard is the more valuable because, in the course of the discussion, the limits as well as the existence of the margin were clearly noted. For beyond a certain point, strategic planning gives way to planning for a crisis; and while the latter may be necessary on occasions, for a local or temporary emergency, it cannot be accepted as the norm by which to estimate in war. That point was clearly marked in the debate on ways and means for Anzio. The course of the discussion is therefore of particular interest: 'the military student', as Sir Winston Churchill has noted, 'may some day be interested to read the details of this tense and clear-cut argument'[1]; and an outline of the confusing but important episode will accordingly be given.

Of the four possible pools from which to extract the necessary L.S.T., the Mediterranean itself could be fished first. Of the thirty-seven L.S.T. in the theatre after 15th January, twenty were deemed not to be available for Anzio. But it was soon found that ten of them could be transferred from the Corsican run, provided that the estimated rate of supply could subsequently be doubled; and by 21st December, Anzio therefore had twenty-seven L.S.T., and a deficit of sixty-one.

The largest block of L.S.T. affected by the other possible measures,[2] comprised the sixty-eight ships destined to sail from the Mediterranean for 'Overlord' on 15th January, 1944. But there might well be serious consequences if many or all of them were held beyond that date. The programmes of refitting, assembly and training in Britain were exact

[1] *Closing the Ring*, p. 379.

[2] See pp. 210-11 above.

and delicate; allowance must now be made for greater casualties in the assault on Anzio; and, depending on those two factors, the return of the vessels from south-east Asia must be dovetailed carefully into an already complex timetable. When they first reviewed the position on 22nd December, the British Chiefs of Staff therefore preferred to withdraw the sixty-eight L.S.T. from the Mediterranean as already arranged, and instead to cancel 'Hercules' against Rhodes—whose prospects were in any case now affected by Turkish recalcitrance—, to allocate the L.S.T. already returning from south-east Asia definitely to Anzio, and if necessary to stop 'Pigstick' in south-east Asia[1] and add its assault shipping as well to that in the Mediterranean.

The Prime Minister saw two objections to this course of action. He agreed that the attack on Rhodes might have to be abandoned, although he was anxious not to be forced into a decision within the next few days. But he anticipated that the President would object strongly if 'Pigstick' were to share the fate of 'Buccaneer', and he pointed out that in any event most of its shipping could not reach the Mediterranean in time to participate in Anzio, even early in February. Unlike the Chiefs of Staff, he therefore favoured the retention in the Mediterranean until 15th February of as many L.S.T. as would be needed for Anzio. This would serve two purposes. It would enable the Italian operation to take place, and it would leave within the theatre, from the casualties needing immediate refit after that operation, more L.S.T. for the subsequent enlarged assault on southern France than would otherwise be available locally.

The Chiefs of Staff, however, held to their earlier opinion. There seemed indeed to be strong technical objections to the Prime Minister's alternative. The L.S.T. from the Mediterranean must train with their assault forces for 'Overlord' for at least one month, and if possible for almost two months, before that operation; and, even without considering their use in Anzio, many needed docking and refit, for which there were not the necessary facilities in the Mediterranean. The combination of these two factors made it necessary to adhere to the existing arrangements; and in these circumstances, only the assault shipping from south-east Asia could provide the necessary force. For while it was true that the L.S.T. from 'Pigstick' could not arrive in time for Anzio itself, they would relieve casualties, would add to the force available for the subsequent maintenance and reinforcement, and—now most important—would provide a part of the larger assault lift for the south of France which all agreed might have to be provided.

But even so, since 'Pigstick' could not help Anzio directly, the latter would still lack some of the lift for an assault of two divisions late in January. The Chiefs of Staff made detailed proposals to meet the deficit, based on the existing programmes for withdrawing L.S.T. from

[1] See p. 211 above.

the Mediterranean and for the movements of L.S.T. from south-east Asia and from American production. These figures reached the Prime Minister on 24th December. But meanwhile, he had himself been investigating the timetable for the L.S.T. due to leave the Mediterranean on 15th January, with the help of the naval Deputy Director of Plans in the Mediterranean, Captain M. L. Power, R.N. As a result, he was able to suggest that it could be modified without undue danger. Unlike the assault shipping in Britain, the Mediterranean L.S.T. were manned by highly-trained crews, and need not therefore join their assault forces for 'Overlord' more than three weeks before the date of that operation. They would also need four weeks for docking, whether in the United Kingdom or in the Mediterranean. Those that were to be docked at home must therefore arrive, at the latest, seven weeks before D-day for 'Overlord'. The passage home occupied about fourteen days. All L.S.T. could thus stay in the Mediterranean at least until 15th February, even if 'Overlord' itself took place early in May.

Captain Power also investigated afresh the facilities for docking L.S.T. in the Mediterranean over the next two months, and by a rearrangement of the programme was able to increase the number of ships that could be taken within the theatre. On 25th December, he flew to London to argue the case in person with the Chiefs of Staff. Meanwhile, on the night of the 24th the Prime Minister discussed the problem with Wilson, Alexander and Tedder. The commanders stated that, given a lift for two divisions, the assault on Anzio could be launched on 20th January, and that its immediate reinforcement should be complete by 5th February. If these dates were approved, and if Power's calculations were accepted, the attack on Rhodes should be abandoned, and the L.S.T. needed for Anzio until after 5th February should be found by keeping in the Mediterranean fifty-six of the sixty-eight ships due to leave the theatre on 15th January. These, with the twenty-seven L.S.T. already earmarked,[1] would give the assault eighty-three of the eighty-eight L.S.T. demanded initially. The L.S.T. from 'Buccaneer' could meanwhile, as the Chiefs of Staff had indeed suggested in their detailed proposals, carry on to England for 'Overlord' instead of coming under the Mediterranean Command. These conclusions were supported at a subsequent meeting, on Christmas Day, of the Prime Minister with the three British commanders, and Eisenhower and Bedell Smith. Churchill accordingly telegraphed to the Chiefs of Staff later on the same day:[2]

> '1. I am in agreement with your general line of argument, but facts are as follows: we cannot leave the Rome situation to stagnate and fester for the three months without crippling preparation

[1] See p. 214 above.

[2] See Appendix X below for the complete text.

of 'Anvil' [south of France] and thus hampering 'Overlord'. We cannot go to other task and leave this unfinished job behind us.

2. Today we decided in conference with Generals Eisenhower and Smith that orders should be issued immediately to prepare two divisions for 'Shingle' [Anzio] with target 20th January. . . . We required to have 88 [L.S.T.] in Central Mediterranean from 15th January to 5th February. Nothing must stand in the way of this.

3. It will therefore be necessary to stop whole of 56 L.S.T. due to sail for United Kingdom at different dates between 1st January and 5th February. The ex-'Buccaneer' S.L.I.[1] are an essential part. But the 15 ex'-Buccaneer' L.S.T. cannot possibly arrive in time. . . . They will, however, be invaluable to replace casualties to assist in later build-up for 'Anvil'.

4. Everything therefore turns on delaying returns to United Kingdom of remaining 56 L.S.T. for three weeks. . . . Every effort of ingenuity must be made to fill the gap. . . . The only point unprovided which I can see is reconstructing these craft on reaching United Kingdom which must be at a minimum rate of 25 a month. This should have priority over all Admiralty construction, whether merchant ships or anti-submarine craft. I am confident dockyards can achieve this and I ask directions to be given to that effect.

5. I recognise with great regret Aegean and 'Hercules' [attack on Rhodes] must be ruled out.

6. As to 'Pigstick' [in south-east Asia], nothing engaged in that can possibly reach Central Mediterranean in time for 'Shingle' [Anzio]. But, of course, it will all help the build-up of 'Anvil' [south of France].

7. The reason why it is essential that 'Shingle' shall be launched before end January is that this is the only way in which the position can be cleared so as to send home ear-marked in accordance with 'Overlord' landing craft in time and also to enable 'Anvil' to be set up in Mediterranean.

8. . . . I am also signalling the President [on these lines]. . . .'

The telegram to Roosevelt was despatched the same day.

A series of telegrams passed between London and North Africa over the next two days, on the detail of the various possibilities. The two sides, as the Chiefs of Staff noted on the 27th, approached the problem from slightly different points of view.

'(a) We have throughout approached the problem on the basis that nothing is done to jeopardise the execution of 'Overlord' and 'Anvil' at the agreed and most appropriate date. Subject to this consideration, as many landing craft should be provided for 'Shingle' as is practicable at the earliest possible date.

---

[1] i.e., L.S.I. See p. 210 above.

(b) Your approach appears to have been that the first requirement is to produce sufficient landing craft for what the Allied Commander-in-Chief in the Mediterranean regards as the minimum assault force for a successful 'Shingle'—i.e. two Divisions in the assault requiring 88 L.S.T.—and that this must be done in such a way as to make sure that a May 'Overlord' is not prejudiced thereby.'

Nevertheless, after much consideration, the Chiefs of Staff announced that, by accepting Captain Power's arguments (not all of which they approved) and by a considerable dislocation to other programmes 'which would be felt for many months', they could arrange a timetable that would allow eighty-four L.S.T. in all to stay in the Mediterranean until 5th February. Three special L.S.T. from south-east Asia might also reach the Mediterranean by 20th January, if the necessary orders were given at once, and in that case Anzio would be only one L.S.T. short. But even so, the Chiefs of Staff wished to stress that this was working without a margin. If the operation were postponed further, by weather or by unforeseen difficulties; if it did not go as well as expected, and if L.S.T. were held beyond 5th February; if more L.S.T. were lost than had been estimated, or if the programme for 'Overlord' were itself dislocated by enemy action; then there was a real danger that 'Overlord' would suffer decisively. 'From past experience', the Chiefs of Staff concluded, 'we feel that a programme so tight as this cannot be accepted unless we are prepared to face the probability of a postponement of 'Overlord' and 'Anvil'.' They did not like the prospect, and they did not expect the Joint Chiefs of Staff to like it.

This was, indeed, a good argument of the case. On the one hand, as Captain Power's calculations had shown, it always seemed possible to question accepted figures, and to extract more from a programme than had been anticipated. But on the other hand, it was dangerous to juggle to a fine limit when planning for campaigns. Ample programmes might constrict operations; but a series of improvisations might ruin them altogether. The point indeed seemed now to have been reached where no margin remained, and where strategic advantage must be balanced against limited resources.

The timetable, as worked out by the Chiefs of Staff in London, was finally as follows. Fifteen L.S.T. from 'Buccaneer' would proceed straight to England, arriving by 13th February. Twenty of the 104[1] L.S.T. in the Mediterranean would leave immediately, for docking in Britain. The other eighty-four would stay for Anzio. Thirty-three of those eighty-four ships would then sail for England, all to arrive there by early in March; the rest would stay in the Mediterranean, refitting there in time for the attack on the south of France.

The Prime Minister accepted the risks inherent in this programme.

[1] Compared with 105 a few weeks before. See p. 210 above.

There seems, indeed, to have been a new inducement for him to do so at this point. Over the past three days, he had been discussing the plan for 'Overlord' with Eisenhower for the first time in detail; and from the General's reaction, it seemed possible that the assault would have to be strengthened and, in that case, postponed until the suitable period of moon and tide just after the end of May. The Prime Minister therefore mentioned this possibility to the Chiefs of Staff on 28th December.[1] 'Our contract with Stalin would be fulfilled by any date up to the 31st May. It seems to me from what I have heard from Eisenhower that 3rd June, which is the corresponding moon phase, would be perfectly permissible, especially if it were asked for by the Commanders now nominated for the operation. There is no need to discuss such matters now, but here is something to veer and haul on.' This was the first, tentative reference to a date which was soon to become significant.

While these exchanges were proceeding, Roosevelt replied on 28th December to the Prime Minister's telegram of the 25th.[2] Somewhat to the latter's surprise, he agreed without demur to postpone the departure of the L.S.T. from the Mediterranean so that Anzio could be launched on 20th January, 'and on the basis that 'Overlord' remains the paramount and will be carried out on the date agreed to at Cairo and Teheran.' Operations in the Aegean must be 'side-tracked', and the attack on Rhodes itself abandoned at least until the attack on southern France had taken place. 'I thank God', replied Churchill within the hour,[3] 'for this fine decision which engages us once again in whole-hearted unity upon a great enterprise.' The next morning, Alexander informed the Prime Minister that he would agree to attack Anzio with eighty-four L.S.T. instead of the eighty-eight originally demanded.

In the event, the Admiralty and the Chiefs of Staff were better than their word. At the end of December, they sent the necessary orders to enable the three special L.S.T. from south-east Asia to reach the Mediterranean by 20th January, thus bringing the number in that theatre by that date to eighty-seven; and early in January, after further debate with the Prime Minister and with the naval authorities in the Mediterranean, they agreed to leave in that theatre another eight British L.S.T. Alexander therefore had ninety-five L.S.T. at his disposal.

But the exchanges that led to the retention of these eight L.S.T. heralded a last crop of difficulties. As so often occurred when detailed planning had to be undertaken simultaneously by local and central authorities, fresh allowances had constantly to be made for factors

---

[1] See *Closing the Ring*, p. 391.

[2] See p. 217 above.

[3] See *Closing the Ring*, p. 390.

that had just come to light. In this case, a new figure had to be taken for the number of L.S.T. likely to be out of order when the attack on Anzio was launched. At the turn of the year, two other difficulties arose. First, Alexander was forced to ask Eisenhower for permission to hold one parachute regiment of an American airborne division, which was now thought necessary for the assault and which was due to be shipped to England for 'Overlord'. Secondly, on 4th January he broke the startling news to the Prime Minister that, of the ninety-five L.S.T. which he had been given, only six would be available for maintenance and reinforcement after the landings at Anzio had been completed. The first difficulty was soon resolved. Supported by Eisenhower and Churchill, the demand for the parachute regiment was met by the Americans on 2nd January. The second, however, led to a further brief debate. Alexander's figures had been reached by processes which, allowing considerable margins of safety at every stage of the operations, reverted to the methods of planning that had only recently been overruled for the assault itself. The Prime Minister was obviously not likely to accept them without further examination, and he at once held a conference of those concerned. The result, as he informed General Ismay, was to show that the figures were 'all nonsense'. Some demands were excessive, and in other cases reasonable economies could be made by better management of dates and convoys. Instead of the picture painted by Alexander, the final result on 8th January was as follows:

L.S.T. available for operations in the Mediterranean until and including 3rd February	88[1]
L.S.T. available from 3rd–13th February	25
L.S.T. available from 13th–end February	12
L.S.T. available thereafter	0 Except by encroaching on the reinforcement of Corsica.

The meeting therefore agreed that the assault on Anzio could be carried out with two divisions. The date was settled finally for 22nd January. On the 12th, the Chiefs of Staff explained the decision to the War Cabinet, 'without, of course, mentioning dates'.

One comment may perhaps be quoted as a conclusion to the affair. On 6th January, reviewing the discussion of the past six weeks, Churchill remarked to Ismay, 'Generally speaking are we not all making too much of this L.S.T. business, which has become a kind

[1] Presumably taking the original minimum demanded, which now allowed seven ships out of ninety-five to be out of order on 20th January. See p. 210 above.

of obsession when we are told that the greatest operations of war turn on 3 or 8 kept here or sent there?' On the evidence of the previous fortnight, it was a legitimate question.

The decision to launch the attack on Anzio on 22nd January defined the action to be taken in the eastern Mediterranean and in the Indian Ocean. The assault on Rhodes was abandoned on Christmas Day, and its abandonment was confirmed on 28th December by the President. The negotiations with the Turks, which continued, thereafter lost much of their force.

We may therefore follow them briefly to their close. The Turks, who earlier in December had declined to see the Commanders-in-Chief from the Middle East, agreed towards the end of the month to receive a single emissary from that theatre; and on the 30th, Air Marshal Sir Francis Linnell arrived in Ankara. Long discussions proceeded throughout January, but without much satisfaction. Meanwhile, the possibility of a larger assault on southern France was leading General Wilson to consider afresh whether he could provide the air forces mentioned earlier for operation 'Saturn';[1] but as the reports continued to come from Ankara, revealing many difficulties, it appeared unlikely that he would be called on to reconcile his commitments.

By the third week of January 1944, it seemed probable that the deadlock would persist. The British therefore decided to bring strong pressure to bear, if possible without provoking an irreconcilable disagreement which both countries might later regret. On the 31st, they instructed Linnell to return at once to Cairo, and stopped all military supplies to Turkey without explanation. The Americans and the Russians agreed to both measures within the following week. Linnell left on 3rd February, and by the 4th the delivery of military stores to Turkey had stopped by land and sea. But the Turks seemed as much provoked as alarmed, and unlikely to sue for a renewal of negotiations; and the British (though not as yet the Turks) accordingly gave up all idea of their entering the war in the near future. On 7th February, following a request from General Wilson, the Combined Chiefs of Staff released the forces hitherto earmarked for all plans affecting Turkey, other than those for the maintenance and completion of existing measures of aid; and on the same day, the British Chiefs of Staff wrote the end of the story.

> 'We attach considerable importance to the maintenance of threat against Germany in South-East Europe and are discussing with Foreign Office the policy we should pursue in this area in view of virtual abandonment of effort to get Turkey into the war as soon as possible. . . .'

---

[1] See p. 195 above.

The effect of the developments in the Mediterranean on those in south-east Asia was equally decisive. 'Pigstick', as we have seen, was a significant factor in the discussions on Anzio and the south of France. They in turn dictated the fate of 'Pigstick', and with it that of the whole campaign in Burma. Admiral Mountbatten's proposal of the new assault,[1] as a suitable substitute for 'Buccaneer', was welcomed in Washington as it was feared in London. But the reaction of the Chinese, on which all depended, remained as cautious as before. At first, indeed, they seemed to waver, and on 28th December Carton de Wiart reported to General Ismay that the atmosphere was improving, and that the night before, for the first time, Chiang Kai-shek had been willing to attack without a seaborne operation. But in its place he had demanded that Mandalay and Lashio should be taken by the British before the monsoon of 1944, and this, though Carton de Wiart did not appreciate it in Chungking, was clearly impossible. Meanwhile, Roosevelt had been trying to persuade the Generalissimo to shift his position, but again without success. There seems, indeed, to have been some confusion over the way in which the President's last message was interpreted, and it is probable that this finally sealed the fate of Mountbatten's proposal in Chungking. But whatever the manner of its presentation, it no longer affected the issue outside the theatre, and the final uncertainty was only the last act in a drama of which the end had already been foreseen.

For on 28th December, as the implications of Anzio became clearer, the Prime Minister consented to sacrifice the seaborne assault in the East. 'I quite agree', he then telegraphed to the Chiefs of Staff, 'that it should be 'Pigstuck' and not 'Pigstick'.' The Americans were at first reluctant to accept the abandonment of the operation, which seemed to them to force the President again to break faith with Chiang Kai-shek, who at no time had replied directly to Mountbatten's proposal. But a potentially difficult situation was averted by Mountbatten himself. Starting on 30th December, the British Chiefs of Staff withdrew various categories of his assault shipping throughout the first week of January; and while the debate on the principle of 'Pigstick' was still under way, its resources were thus being steadily removed. On 6th January, Mountbatten therefore announced his intention of abandoning the operation, for which he no longer had enough assault shipping. Both sets of Chiefs of Staff agreed to this proposal, the one with relief and the other with reluctance, and the Supreme Commander was thereupon instructed to proceed with the planning of his suggested alternative, a limited offensive by land along the Arakan coast north of Akyab which had first been proposed in September, 1943 by General Auchinleck, and which now went by the name of 'Cudgel'. 'Tarzan' in northern Burma was finally dropped, and replaced by the less

[1] See pp. 211-12 above.

ambitious 'Gripfast'.[1] Finally, with all seaborne operations abandoned, the South-East Asia Command was ordered to return all of its assault shipping to the United Kingdom or to the Mediterranean.

On 6th January, the Prime Minister telegraphed to Mountbatten:

> 'I fully sympathise with your difficulties, which are caused by the clash of greater events.'

Their effect on the theatre may best be summed up in Mountbatten's own words.

> 'Our projected operations had now been reduced to four: an offensive without landing craft in Arakan, an advance from Ledo, operations by Long Range Penetration Brigades, and a limited advance across the Chindwin River. None of these could result in a big strategic victory; nor could they achieve any of the major objectives laid down in my original directive from the Prime Minister; since these operations alone could not open the road to China during 1944, and the possibility of our engaging large numbers of enemy troops at numerous points now depended largely on the initiative of the Japanese themselves. I could not help feeling anxious about the possible effects of continual procrastination; particularly as the Commanders-in-Chief were beginning to express concern at the obstacles that were being placed in the path of building up morale. It now seemed likely, however, that our operational effort in the first half of 1944 could not be reduced any further; and it was on this assumption that I issued a final directive to the Commanders-in-Chief on the 14th January, outlining their tasks in the operations to be undertaken.'

The issue of this directive set the scene for the campaign in south-east Asia during the first half of 1944.

---

[1] See p. 193 above.

CHAPTER VI

'OVERLORD' AND THE MEDITERRANEAN, JANUARY–MARCH, 1944

(i)

The Attacks on Anzio and Cassino

IN ONE SENSE, the history of the strategy for Europe in the last quarter of 1943 is the history of the successive abandonment of all seaborne operations which threatened to detract from 'Overlord'. 'Culverin', 'Buccaneer', 'Hercules' and 'Pigstick' had gone; only 'Shingle' and 'Anvil' survived. In the same sense, the history of that strategy in the first half of 1944 may be seen as the defence of 'Anvil' against the combination of 'Shingle' and its sequel with the claims of 'Overlord'.

The story of this defence is intricate. It takes its form at the outset from simultaneous developments in the plan for 'Overlord' itself and in the Italian campaign, later from the implications of that campaign for the Mediterranean, and finally from developments in Italy and in north-west France. The fate of 'Anvil' may indeed be regarded as a barometer of strategic thought, tracing the results of events elsewhere that impinged immediately upon it. Their effect was often expressed in, as it derived largely from, calculations of assault shipping, which even after the abandonment of the subsidiary operations remained the most critical shortage during the first half of 1944, and whose detail must accordingly be followed over much of that period if the shape of strategy is to be understood.

The discussions themselves may be divided into three distinct phases: from January to late in March 1944, when 'Anvil' was postponed from its original date; from late in March to early in June, when its cancellation was more strenuously urged and rejected, and alternatives were canvassed; and from June to the middle of August, when, under changing circumstances, its merits continued to be debated until the eve of its execution. These discussions provide the main strategic theme in Europe for the period which they cover. This chapter is concerned with their first phase.[1]

[1] For a good *résumé* of the principal incidents during this period, see Appendix VII below.

As the date for the assault on Anzio approached, its prospects seemed to improve. The force, placed under the command of VI U.S. Corps from Fifth Army, consisted of two strong divisions with a parachute regiment and Special troops, and with elements of a third division to follow. It would carry enough supplies for two days, further supplies being landed through Anzio and the beaches. The operation was preceded by heavy air operations, as far afield as Pisa and the valley of the Po, which continued for a fortnight. Substantial naval forces were reserved for the preliminary bombardment of the coast, and to cover the landings and the reinforcement.

The assault was to accompany a further offensive in the south.[1] At the end of December 1943, Eighth Army, now consisting of two Corps with a total of four divisions and two brigades, had been halted between the rivers Sangro and Pescara; and throughout January it confined itself, against an opposition of some five divisions, to minor operations. But Fifth Army, now consisting of three Corps (a British, an American and a French), of eight divisions with one in reserve, was able early in the new year to return to the attack against an opposition of equal strength. Between 3rd and 15th January, the Americans and the French drove the enemy back for some ten miles in the eastern sector of the Army's front, as far as the mountains around the river Rapido which formed the approach to the Gustav Line. This brought them within range of Monte Cassino, the gateway to the upper valley of the Liri which was the main approach to Rome. Alexander now intended to surround the mountain to the north and east, while the British on the left of the line moved across the river Garigliano, and through the mountains on the west of the valley south of Monte Cassino. The dual attack began on 17th January. The opening stages went well. By the 19th, the British on the left had reached the foothills beyond the Garigliano plain, and—of great significance at this precise point—by the 20th had drawn into the battle the Germans' immediate reserve of one division near Rome, as well as a further division from those opposing Eighth Army.

Fifth Army's advance had thus achieved its first object, by attracting to the main front some of the most immediate opposition to 'Shingle'. In the middle of January, that opposition was thought likely to consist of one division, with four parachute battalions, on D-day; a further division, and possibly a panzer regiment, on the next day; and possibly one more division on the fourth day. Further reinforcement was thought unlikely, owing to the Allies' air operations, before D+16, when two divisions might arrive from the north. But the first success of the offensive in the south led the Allied Command to hope that the immediate opposition might prove less than had been anticipated, and

---

[1] See Map V, facing p. 270.

that 'Shingle' would complete a general disintegration that now seemed a distinct possibility.

Early in the morning of 21st January, the assault task force sailed from Naples and the surrounding ports, with 50,000 men and more than 5,000 vehicles. The air operations over the past fortnight had effectively subdued the Luftwaffe, and no reconnaissance by the enemy was encountered. Five minutes after midnight on the 21st/22nd, the force arrived off Anzio, and at 2 a.m. on the 22nd the first troops landed on the beaches. Complete surprise had been achieved, and throughout that and the following day men and material were put ashore with little opposition. Anzio itself was taken, and used without delay; and by the night of the 23rd, 90 per cent of the cargo had been unloaded in the assault area. Alexander, and the authorities waiting tensely in London, were at once relieved and hopeful.

But the very success of the assault, coming on top of the recent change in the nature of the operation, brought its own dangers. 'Shingle' had been prepared, in some haste, on two assumptions: that the assault would at once encounter significant opposition, and that it must support itself for some weeks before relief could arrive from the south. Its commander therefore decided not to risk the rapid penetration which recent advice suggested was possible, and which in fact might well have led him, virtually unopposed, to Rome. Whether or not such a course would have proved ultimately successful, it was not attempted, and the assault force instead consolidated its position for the first two days. Meanwhile, Kesselring acted with despatch. Reserves were summoned from around Rome, and from northern Italy, France and the Adriatic. By the end of January, the equivalent of five enemy divisions faced the equivalent of $3\frac{1}{2}$ Allied divisions, the latter heavily equipped with armour and vehicles.

When the assault force tried to move further inland, it therefore found itself unable to do so. After probing unsuccessfully for a few days, it launched a heavier attack on 30th January. But by then the enemy had concentrated in strength, and on 3rd February he counter-attacked with some success. Within the next few days, it was clear that the perimeter was sealed off and that no further advance was possible for the time being. The only immediate hope therefore lay in relief from the south. But this now seemed unlikely for the next few weeks. For since the landings had taken place, the main battle had taken a turn for the worse. After its early advance, the British Corps of Fifth Army had been halted on the left of the line, while the Americans were held temporarily along the Rapido. The enemy disposed of strong natural defences, all his divisions on that front were actively engaged, and the defence was skilfully conducted. On 24th January, Hitler ordered that 'the Gustav Line must be held at all costs for the sake of the political consequences which would follow a completely successful defence. The Fuehrer expects the bitterest struggle for every yard.'

This struggle centred on Monte Cassino, crowned by the ancient monastery of St. Benedict; and a word is necessary here to explain its significance in the battle on which the campaign now turned. Cassino was the gateway to the Liri valley; but a gateway that was peculiarly difficult to open. No large force could move up the valley towards Rome except along route 6, which passed directly beneath the southern and western foothills of the mountain. But it was equally difficult to turn or to capture the mountain itself. An outflanking movement to the north and east encountered precipitous slopes, now under snow, and deep ravines; an attack from the north and east suffered from the same disadvantages; while an attack from the south must be launched, across the flooded Rapido and the neighbouring soft ground, beneath the eyes of the defenders and of the enemy in the mountains across the valley. It was clear that the fighting here must be fierce. Both sides accordingly reinforced at the expense of the Adriatic, the Germans by two divisions, the Allies by three (one Indian, one New Zealand, and, slightly later, one British) which were formed into a New Zealand Corps.

Alexander's first plan was to capture the heights to the north, and thence attack along the eastern flank of Monte Cassino from ground as high as the monastery itself. Against determined opposition, the Americans and French pushed into the mountains throughout the last week of January, and with such effect that at the end of the month the Allies expected the position soon to fall. In the first week of February, the main attack began. The American Corps soon reached the town of Cassino, where it was within striking distance of Monastery Hill and only a mile from route 6 beyond and below. But that mile was broken by ridges and gulleys, defended by troops of high morale. On 12th February, the Corps was forced to pass to the defensive, while the New Zealand Corps, which had been waiting to exploit the capture of the mountain by a rapid advance up the valley, now prepared instead to attack the mountain itself from the south on the 16th.

The operations were preceded by the bombardment of the monastery, which the enemy was thought to be using for military purposes. It was accordingly largely destroyed on 15th February, for the fourth time in its history, after the monks had been warned to leave. But the subsequent attack failed. The New Zealand Corps, like the Americans before it, was halted on the 16th by fierce resistance. Two attacks had now been made unsuccessfully on the mountain. Until it was captured, no further advance was possible.

The bridgehead at Anzio was itself in a critical state. On 15th February, the expected German counter-attack began. The Allied force in the area had now been brought to rather less than five divisions, two more divisions having been withdrawn from Fifth

PLATE IV.

Above: General Wilson
Left: General Alexander

Army's sector. The Germans, by further reinforcement, were thought to amount to no less than the equivalent of ten divisions. Stimulated by their superior strength, and by an order from the Fuehrer demanding the elimination of the 'abscess', they attacked with vigour. By the evening of the 17th, they had driven a deep wedge, and were approaching the Allies' last line around the beach-head. The next day was critical. But the Allied sea and air forces bombarded the enemy continuously, the defences held, and that night the Germans pulled back. On 19th February, the Allies in turn gained a little ground, and after another effort on the 20th the enemy was temporarily exhausted. He attacked again, on the 29th, but without success; and in the first week of March, after suffering heavy casualties, gave up the attempt. The trial of strength was over, and deadlock supervened.

By 20th February, it was clear that, whatever its secondary consequences, the Allied attack on Rome had failed. It was also possible to see, in outline, the shape of the immediate future. The force at Anzio must now be nourished, as a similar force had been nourished at Tobruk, until it could join the main advance to trap or pursue the enemy south of Rome. It remained a threat to the Germans, and a commitment to the Allies. The extent of this commitment would be measured by the course of events on the main front, where there now seemed to be two possibilities. Either, as Wilson and the air forces thought likely, intense and continuous air attack on the enemy's communications and bases, combined with the maintenance of a limited offensive on the ground, would compel him within the next two months to withdraw beyond Rome to the line Pisa-Rimini; or, as Alexander thought more likely, a further large offensive must be launched early in the spring, after due preparation, in enough strength to force him out of the mountains. In either case, a third attack should be made on Monte Cassino as soon as possible, to see if that obstacle could not be overcome before the end of the winter's operations. Plans were made for this attack to take place after three successive days of fine weather, so as to allow for the use of tanks, and to be accompanied by an exceptionally heavy air attack, by all the air forces in Italy, designed to 'whip out Cassino like an old tooth'. In the event, this had to wait until 15th March. Meanwhile, Alexander prepared to regroup for what he considered an inevitably hard struggle in the spring. The Germans were now thought to dispose of eighteen divisions south of Rome, with another five in the north. He himself had some twenty-one divisions, which he asked should be reinforced by a further $7\frac{1}{2}$ divisions by the middle of April. Meanwhile, he proposed to bring the headquarters of Eighth Army, whose operations on the Adriatic coast were of steadily decreasing importance, over the Apennines to take command of all British troops, leaving one Corps in the eastern sector. Eighth Army would then take over the attack on

Monte Cassino, thereafter advancing up the Liri valley. Fifth Army would attack simultaneously in the west, advancing (it was hoped more rapidly than Eighth Army) through the mountains towards Anzio, where it would be joined by the divisions in the bridgehead. Thus reinforced, it would turn inland to cut routes 7 and 6 in the enemy's rear. The plan was to destroy the German Tenth Army south of Rome, so that little remained thereafter to check a rapid advance to the line Pisa-Rimini.

Wilson examined and approved these plans on 22nd February. They involved three commitments. First, the *enclave* at Anzio must be supported until Fifth Army was within striking distance. Secondly, 7½ fresh divisions must be transferred to Italy in seven weeks. Thirdly, replacements must be provided for the divisions already weakened by the heavy casualties of the winter, and for the casualties anticipated in the spring. At the end of February, over 5,000 men were needed to bring to their proper strength the formations already engaged; while future operations were expected to demand the replacement of a further 15,000 men over the next four weeks, and thereafter of not less than 10,000 a month. The sum of these three commitments was likely to be heavy in men and shipping. In all, some 276,000 men and 34,000 vehicles might have to be moved to Italy and Corsica over the next two months; and while it was calculated that 225,000 men could be carried in troop shipping already available to the theatre, the rest must be taken in cargo shipping, which seemed likely to be short in March and April, and in assault shipping, most of which would already be engaged in sustaining the force at Anzio. But although the demand on shipping for March and April had thus increased, and exceeded in some respects the resources of the theatre, it was not so great as that on men. Some of the movements had already been envisaged; while the added burden on the assault shipping, which might have been thought to offer the greatest difficulty, was eased by simultaneous developments outside the theatre.[1] On the other hand, the demand for the 7½ divisions, together with the anticipated high rate of casualties, drained the theatre of its operational reserves.

As Wilson surveyed the scene on 22nd February, he was therefore led to an inescapable conclusion, which he communicated at once to the British Chiefs of Staff.

> '. . . 2. The offensive which opened on the night 17/18 January was designed to compel the enemy to withdraw north of Rome so as to establish satisfactory military position in Italy before we adopt a strategic defensive on that front in favour of other areas. . . .
>
> 3. Once main front has joined with Anzio bridgehead the main tactical object will have been achieved. . . . At this stage it

[1] See pp. 240-1, 244 below.

is impossible to say when such a junction can be effected but until it is achieved the withdrawal of forces cannot be risked from the Battle Front in Italy.

4. The Combined Chiefs of Staff instructed me to plan for an operation ('Anvil') against Southern France, with assault lift for at least two divisions.

The divisions necessary to make up the full force of 'Anvil' could be obtained only by drawing on those in Italy.

5. The effect of such a withdrawal on the battle in Italy will naturally vary in severity according to the size of the assault ordered. If an attack is to be made on Southern France against the opposition at present estimated at least a two division plus assault is needed. To make the necessary preparation for this operation on this scale we must start withdrawing service units from the battle in Italy now, United States divisions earmarked for the operation by 1st April and later the French troops for the build-up. We obviously cannot withdraw combat divisions now and I cannot state when circumstances will allow me to start training.

6. If it is decided to undertake a two or three divisional 'Anvil', the effect on operations in Italy will be most serious and cannot but prejudice their success. Moreover, air resources will not allow us to fight two battles at the same time, one in Southern France and another in Italy.

If on the other hand, the battle in Italy is continued and combined with feint operations which are already being planned, we may go far, now and after 'Overlord' is launched, towards keeping the enemy employed.

7. I recommend that 'Anvil' be cancelled and that I be given a fresh directive to conduct operations with the object of containing the maximum number of German troops in Southern Europe with the forces now earmarked to be placed at my disposal including an assault lift for one division plus.'

(ii)

New Demands from 'Overlord' and from Italy

The suggestion that 'Anvil' should be cancelled was not new to the British Chiefs of Staff. They had themselves been working for the past month, from a different background, for the same object. That background was provided by the development of the plans for 'Overlord'. Since August 1943, no significant change had taken place in the plan for the operation which had then been approved. It will be recalled that this postulated an assault of three divisions on beaches in the Caen sector, between the base of the Cotentin peninsula and the river Orne, through which two more divisions would be passed in the following two days.[1] Neither the weight of the assault, nor its reinforcement through the same area, was ideal; but the only means of overcoming both disadvantages lay in simultaneous landings on the east of the Cotentin peninsula, against which could be balanced arguments of geography and resources. Cossac[2] had stated in his report that an increase of at least 10 per cent in landing ships and craft was highly desirable to provide a greater margin within the existing plan, and that a further increase would open the possibility of an extra landing on other beaches. Both possibilities had been noted at the Quebec Conference; but there the matter rested for the time being.

Their experience in the autumn of 1943 taught the Allies, if they needed teaching, the dangers of a weak assault; and at Cairo the Combined Chiefs of Staff expressed their doubts of the existing plan. But owing to the delay in choosing the commanders for 'Overlord,' it was not until towards the end of December that it could be examined afresh. Eisenhower and Montgomery were able to read Cossac's report before they left the Mediterranean, and each decided at once that the front of the assault was too narrow and the assault itself two weak. Eisenhower was also perturbed by the intention to proceed without a major port for at least two weeks. Before he left the theatre on 1st January for a brief visit to the United States, he therefore told Montgomery of his reaction, and instructed him to review the plan as soon as possible in London.

This review opened on 7th January, 1944. By that time, and on the basis of his earlier talk with Eisenhower, Montgomery had a clear idea of what he wanted. The area of the assault should be extended in the west as far as Varreville, on the eastern side of the Cotentin peninsula, and in the east to Cabourg, beyond the river Orne.[3] British and Americans would take separate sectors, the Americans in the west, the British in the east. The Americans' task, as in Cossac's plan, would be to clear the Cotentin pensinsula and capture Cherbourg, thereafter developing operations to the south and west. The British meanwhile would operate to the south of their own area of assault, to pin down German forces which might interfere with the Americans' preliminary operations. The final 'lodgment area', from which the subsequent campaign would develop, should if possible extend, as Cossac had proposed, from Caen to Nantes on the Atlantic coast, the British being supplied through the Cotentin peninsula and the Americans through Brittany.

This defined the area of the assault. At a second conference on 15th January, Montgomery reviewed its strength. He wished if possible to

[1] See pp. 55-6 above.

[2] See p. 22 above.

[3] See Inset to Map VI, facing p. 279.

attack with eight brigades, drawn from either four or five divisions, and followed immediately by the essentials of two divisions, including one armoured division on the British front. One airborne division should if possible be dropped on the Cotentin peninsula ahead of the Americans, followed twenty-four hours later by a second airborne division at a place still to be determined.

While these conclusions could only be provisional until they had been examined by Eisenhower, Montgomery's review brought a welcome and overdue sense of urgency to a series of plans which had necessarily awaited the arrival of the commanders. For as the result of the instructions at Cairo to investigate the scale of the operation, and of the recent proposal from the Mediterranean for an increase in the scale of 'Anvil', Cossac had himself already been reviewing the prospects for 'Overlord'. On 6th January, he submitted the results to the Chiefs of Staff, in two papers which together provided a basis for much of the subsequent British argument.

Cossac began by urging, as was now common ground, that 'Overlord' should be increased from three to four divisions, each on a front of two brigades. There should be an immediate reserve of one division afloat at the time of assault, followed by another division, and the rate of supply and reinforcement from D-day to D+6 should be increased by 10 per cent, and thereafter by 20 per cent. All this would demand extra resources—some more beach groups and headquarters, at least three more cruisers, twenty-seven destroyers, and a variety of smaller ships, eight more squadrons of fighters and two hundred more transport aircraft, and an extra 64 storeships, 54 assault ships and 216 assault craft.

The Joint Planning Staff calculated that the extra naval forces could be provided, possibly in part from the Atlantic; that the ground and air forces could be found only from the Mediterranean; and that the assault and ocean shipping could come most easily, and possibly only, from the Mediterranean, but probably not in time for 'Overlord' in May. It reported therefore that Cossac's proposals were practical, provided that the bulk of the extra resources could be taken from the Mediterranean and that 'Overlord' itself, on its new scale, could be postponed for up to one month.

All this pointed to one conclusion, which Cossac drew on 6th January.

> '. . . 5. In the 'Overlord' plan there was a requirement for a diversionary threat against the South of France concurrently with the launching of 'Overlord'. The object of this threat was to tie down German mobile reserves and air forces in the South of France for as long a period as possible during the critical battle for the lodgment area in the North. . . .
>
> 6. The conversion of the threat as originally conceived to the

present plan[1] entails the provision in the Mediterranean of additional craft to lift at least one, if not two extra assault divisions, in addition to considerable extra shipping. Additional air forces would also be required.

7. It is for consideration, however, whether it would not be strategically sounder to employ these additional resources in strengthening Operation 'Overlord' rather than converting the threat into an assault. . . .

9. Operation 'Anvil' as at present planned, if successful, could do little more to assist the main operation than the pinning down of two or three divisions of the German mobile reserves. It is too remote from any German vital interests to be likely to cause a greater diversion.

I feel that the same effect could equally well be achieved, and with much less diversion of resources, by a threat. . . .

. . . 11. I realise that the abandoning of an assault in the South of France would be a bitter disappointment to the French who will, no doubt, demand participation in Operation 'Overlord'. Compensation for this could be made by the introduction of French forces through the Brittany ports after the initial phase of 'Overlord'. French forces would then have the opportunity of being present at the entry into Paris.

12. I recommend, therefore, that the whole strategical conception be reconsidered on the following lines:

(a) The assault against the South coast of France should revert to a threat on the basis of one assault division as originally conceived. . . .[2]

(b) The additional requirements in landing craft and other resources which would have been allotted to [the Supreme Commander, Mediterranean] to convert the threat into a two or three divisional assault should be re-allocated as early as practicable to strengthen Operation 'Overlord', and a reduction of air forces in the Mediterranean theatre in favour of the air forces in this country should be urgently considered.

13. In view of the shortness of time available in which to complete planning, I request the early concurrence of the Combined Chiefs of Staff to this proposal.'

On 7th January, the British Chiefs of Staff informed the Joint Staff Mission in Washington that they were considering this paper as a matter of urgency.

Other authorities meanwhile were coming independently to the same conclusion as Cossac. Early in the month, Montgomery informed Bedell Smith that 'Overlord' could be launched satisfactorily only at the expense of 'Anvil', and Bedell Smith informed Eisenhower and Churchill that he was inclined to agree. By 10th January, Montgomery was appealing direct to Eisenhower to 'hurl yourself into the

[1] See pp. 213-14 above.
[2] See pp. 104-5 above.

contest and what we want, get for us'; and Cossac's paper therefore arrived in Washington as the culmination to a series of similar rumours and communications.

The Joint Chiefs of Staff answered the British telegram on 12th January. In view of the fact that Eisenhower, the author of the plan for 'Anvil', would soon be in London to review 'Overlord', they suggested that he should be instructed to submit final recommendations for the size of both operations, in consultation with Wilson, by 1st February. Eisenhower himself, who was then in Washington and intended to reach England within a few days, thought that this could be done. Meanwhile, on 14th January, the British Chiefs of Staff informed the Prime Minister in Marrakesh of the position, pointing out that Cossac's increase in the size of 'Overlord', together with Eisenhower's recent increase in the size of 'Anvil', would demand an extra sixty L.S.T., two hundred merchant ships, two hundred transport aircraft and many long-range fighters, which on the present plans for Europe could presumably be found only from the Pacific. The relation between the two European operations must therefore be carefully considered. An addition to 'Overlord' might mean its postponement until June, and a new strategy for the Mediterranean if 'Anvil' were reduced to the proportions of a threat: an addition to, or possibly even the maintenance of, 'Anvil' on its present scale, might mean a further call on the Americans for the resources which 'Overlord' now seemed likely to demand. The Chiefs of Staff emphasized that they themselves had not reached any conclusion on the problem, and suggested that it should be discussed, with Eisenhower and possibly with Wilson, as soon as the former and Churchill himself were again in London.

Eisenhower set to work in London on 16th January. The discussions were conducted on the assumption that, somehow or other, the necessary needs of 'Overlord' would be met; and on this basis, the Supreme Commander was in a position by the 21st to examine the provisional recommendations. With some further additions to the naval forces—five cruisers instead of at least three, thirty-six destroyers instead of twenty-seven, and one or two old battleships or monitors—he accepted Cossac's figures for the increased commitments, and Montgomery's reasons for them. He agreed that the assault must be increased to a weight of five divisions, employing eight brigades, and the front extended to the limits now proposed. The problem, as he informed the Combined Chiefs of Staff on the 23rd, was then to find the extra forces.

> '. . . 14. I deem 'Anvil' to be an important contribution to 'Overlord' since I feel that an assault will contain more enemy formations in Southern France than a threat. The forces, U.S. and French, are in any case available; and an actual landing by them will increase co-operation from elements of the resistance in France.

> 15. 'Overlord' and 'Anvil' must be viewed as a whole. The ideal, if we could have sufficient forces, would be a five divisional 'Overlord' and a three divisional or, at worst, a two divisional 'Anvil'. But if there cannot be enough forces for this, I am driven to conclude that we should have 'Overlord' with five divisions and 'Anvil' with one division, the latter remaining a threat until the enemy's weakness justifies its active employment. But we should adopt this solution only as a last resort, after all other alternatives have failed to provide the strength for a five divisional 'Overlord' and a two divisional 'Anvil' by the end of May.
>
> 16. In regard to the target date, it is preferable for the Army to adhere to the early-May date if possible so as to obtain the longest campaigning season . . . But rather than risk failure on the earlier date with reduced forces, I would accept postponement of a month if I could then be sure of obtaining the required strength. . . .'

He asked for speed in reaching a decision.

The Combined Chiefs of Staff were now faced with two demands from Eisenhower, the first, in December 1943, for a rapid decision on 'Anvil' employing either two or three divisions,[1] the second for a rapid decision on 'Overlord' and on 'Anvil' employing either one or more divisions. The telegram of 23rd January accordingly inaugurated an urgent discussion of the problem, whose first phase lasted until towards the end of March.

The two questions which General Eisenhower had posed—the postponement of 'Overlord' and the reduction of 'Anvil' to one division—were distinct, if connected. For while the second necessarily involved the first, the first did not necessarily involve the second. The postponement of 'Overlord' to a date early in June, whether or not the scale of 'Anvil' was reduced, had much to be said for it. It would allow an extra month's British production of landing craft to be provided for the assault—to that extent, indeed, weakening the case for reducing 'Anvil'—, would improve the chances of a Russian offensive contributing to the first stages of the operation, and—although the Prime Minister alone seems to have attached weight to the point at this time—would meet the conditions of moon and tide which Cossac had postulated originally, and which could not be met in the second half of May.

But whatever its intrinsic advantages, the postponement of the operation was in practice linked from the first with the future of 'Anvil', and the attitudes of British and Americans towards the first question reflected, at least initially, their attitudes towards the second. By the time that Eisenhower had completed his review of 'Overlord', the

[1] Pp. 213-14 above.

British Chiefs of Staff had decided that 'Anvil' should be reduced to the scale of one division. The conclusions of Cossac's report, followed by Montgomery's review, had persuaded them—what they had earlier been inclined to doubt—that the increased scale of 'Overlord' could not be met from its existing resources, and that therefore, unless the Americans unexpectedly diverted assault shipping from the Pacific, there must be a transfer of resources from the Mediterranean. But at the same time, events in the Mediterranean opened the prospect of an acceptable alternative to 'Anvil' on the larger scale. The period from 10th to 23rd January, when Fifth Army's offensive was going well and when the assault on Anzio was launched, was a period of success and hope; and by the 19th, the authorities in London felt able to envisage a movement to the left from northern Italy in May, as the complement to a seaborne assault on southern France with one division, such as Eisenhower had envisaged in the previous October.[1] The Chiefs of Staff instructed the Joint Planners to study its possibilities 'on the assumption that our operations [in Italy] progressed favourably during the next few months'; while the Prime Minister was already contemplating a grand design, embracing guerrilla operations by the French in Savoy and the Alpes Maritimes, an Allied offensive by land from Italy, and a small but potent Allied assault from the sea.

The Chiefs of Staff conveyed the consequences to the Americans on 26th January. They regarded 'Anvil' as useful if undertaken with not less than two divisions, and 'if the necessary resources can be found by hook or by crook, so much the better.' But if not, they preferred to concentrate the main force in Italy, preserving a threat from the sea meanwhile. They therefore recommended that 'Overlord' should be increased to five divisions, whatever the cost to 'Anvil'; that it should be launched early in June instead of in May; that every effort should meanwhile be made to undertake 'Anvil' simultaneously with two divisions; but that if those efforts failed, the assault shipping in the Mediterranean should be reduced to a lift for one division.

The Joint Chiefs of Staff did not agree with any of the British recommendations. In the first place, unlike their British colleagues, they were not content with the figures submitted by the 'Overlord' Command. These were based on the rates of serviceability for assault shipping laid down at the Quebec Conference, of 90 per cent for L.S.T. and 85 per cent for L.C.T.[2] But the Americans were prepared—as it turned out, correctly—to accept a uniform rate of 95 per cent; and on that basis, they thought—incorrectly, in view of the special composition of the assaulting forces—that a force of six to seven divisions could be mounted for 'Overlord' in May, instead of a force of five divisions. Further to ensure success, the Americans announced that they would

[1] See p. 104 above.

[2] See Appendix IV (B) below.

provide an additional three landing ships and fifty-seven landing craft for the operation, with two hundred troop carrier aircraft; and while further requirements must be met by the British, they were confident that these extra allocations, with the revised rate of serviceability, would meet 'Overlord's' new demands. In any case, however, they were not prepared to reduce 'Anvil' to the scale of a threat. They doubted if it would then contain the necessary number of German divisions in southern France; they reminded the British that the Russians had been promised an attack, and not a threat; and they pointed out that the assault itself was part of a large operation, involving up to ten divisions, whose effect would be jettisoned if the first stage was abandoned.

Turning to the other British recommendation, the Joint Chiefs of Staff saw no reason to postpone 'Overlord' until June. Stalin had announced at Teheran that the Russians would synchronize their attack with that of the Western Allies; they themselves still thought that 'Overlord' could be undertaken, as then announced, in May; and a postponement would thus be both unnecessary and unwise. They recommended, therefore, that 'Overlord' should take place 'not later than 31st May'; that 'Anvil' should be launched, to coincide with 'Overlord', with an assault of two divisions; and that 'Overlord' should be mounted with as large an assault lift as American and British resources could make possible. In support of these views, they proposed further that all plans for operations in the eastern Mediterranean should be suspended finally, the resources being allocated to the two assaults or to the campaign in Italy, and that Eisenhower, after conferring with the Supreme Commander in the Mediterranean, should be allowed to redistribute the assault shipping in detail between 'Overlord' and 'Anvil' so as to conform with the Americans' recommendations.

The Prime Minister and the Chiefs of Staff discussed this reply over the next four days. They finally developed three objections to it. First, they were certain that a rate of serviceability of 95 per cent could not be sustained for the landing craft in 'Overlord.' Secondly, they could not ignore the moon and tide, which neither side had so far mentioned, but which dictated a period for that operation of early or mid-May or early in June. Lastly, they had again to consider a new situation in the Mediterranean, which seemed to militate strongly against 'Anvil'. For whereas the prospect of victory south of Rome, as envisaged less than a fortnight before, had provided an alternative to its more ambitious form, the prospect of a stalemate, with which they were now confronted, seemed likely to rule out the operation altogether.

At the beginning of February, Fifth Army was engaged in the bitterly-contested and costly struggle for Monte Cassino, whose outcome could not easily be foreseen, while the stroke at Anzio seemed to have failed in its object, and the troops were indeed in immediate danger of a heavy counter-attack. The British deduced from these events that a fundamental change had taken place in the Germans' strategy for the Mediterranean since 'Anvil' had been approved at Teheran. At that time, it was known that the enemy intended to resist in Italy for as long as possible. It now seemed clear that his conception of the possible embraced the indefinite reinforcement of the peninsula up to the limit required to stalemate his opponents. This strategy both committed and suited the Western Allies. It would occupy all of their available divisions in the theatre, from which the force for 'Anvil' must be drawn; but it would enable them in the most direct way to carry out their original intention in Italy, to contain as many German divisions as possible outside France. The British moreover had now come to the conclusion that a campaign in southern France held serious disadvantages. The distance between the scene of 'Anvil' and that of 'Overlord', the rugged nature of the intervening country, and the strength allowed to the defence by military thought, persuaded them that an attack up the Rhône valley could be contained by a small number of German divisions, or impeded by them sufficiently to prevent it from acting as a major diversion. They therefore no longer accepted, as they had accepted hitherto, that 'Anvil' would form an effective southern pincer with 'Overlord'. The maintenance of the offensive in Italy, on the other hand, would continue to attract, as it was already attracting, fresh German resources; while its success would later provide a larger force than 'Anvil' itself for an attack through France from the south. The British Chiefs of Staff, in fact, now regarded 'Anvil', for much the same reasons as they had regarded a landing in Yugoslavia in November 1943, as probably impossible and certainly unnecessary.

On 4th February, they answered the Americans along these lines, recommending as before that 'Overlord' should be increased at the expense of the Mediterranean, that only one division should be reserved for 'Anvil', and that 'Overlord' should be launched on about 2nd June. But while the recommendations remained the same, the British position was now different from their position in January. Then, it had been much the same as that of Eisenhower. Now, it differed both from his and from that of the Joint Chiefs of Staff. There were now in fact three well-defined points of view. The American Chiefs of Staff relied on finding ways and means, from the resources already assembled, to satisfy the demands of 'Overlord' without calling on 'Anvil', and were meanwhile, as always, reluctant to depart in any way from a strategy already debated and agreed. Eisenhower, who had advanced the claims of a strong 'Anvil' while in the Mediterranean, saw in it a genuine complement to 'Overlord' which he was anxious to retain if possible, but which he was prepared reluctantly to abandon for a threat if the genuine needs of 'Overlord' demanded. The British, on the other hand, while agreeing with Eisenhower on the demands for 'Overlord', no longer believed that 'Anvil' formed a better complement to that operation than did the campaign in Italy, and therefore preferred a threat on its own merits.

The result was a curious reversal of rôles. As Marshall wrote to Eisenhower on 7th February, of the British and American Chiefs of Staff, 'we have become Mediterraneanites and they heavily pro-'Overlord'.' Nor was either side likely to change its position until the British persuaded the Americans that a new situation obtained in Italy, or the Americans persuaded the British and Eisenhower that the calculations for the assault shipping in 'Overlord' were unsound. Neither succeeded throughout the first three weeks of February; and the deadlock persisted accordingly.

The British foresaw on 4th February that their proposals would not be well received in Washington; and at the meeting on that day, the Prime Minister suggested that it might be advisable soon to invite the Joint Chiefs of Staff to London. General Ismay, on his own initiative, had the same idea on the 5th. 'We are now', he remarked to the Prime Minister, 'within less than four months of decisive events and yet our plans are still indeterminate. Nor is the situation likely to improve unless there can be a meeting of minds.' On the 6th, Mr. Churchill accordingly asked the President if such a conference could be arranged. But the Joint Chiefs of Staff were fully engaged by a domestic debate on the strategy in the Far East, which representatives from both Pacific theatres were attending,[1] and they did not wish to leave for London, so soon after the recent Allied conference, to discuss a problem which they still considered turned largely on technical difficulties. Marshall suggested instead that General Eisenhower should act for them in conferences with the British, and sent a soldier and a sailor from the planning staffs in Washington to advise him on the technical questions involved.

Meanwhile, however, one issue was settled. The British arguments on 4th February for the postponement of 'Overlord' seem to have convinced the Americans. They proposed in turn that its target date should be taken as 31st May, on the understanding that this would give Eisenhower enough latitude for a few days on either side, and would thus satisfy consciences over the earlier assurance to the Russians. The British took this proposal for consent, and a day in the first week of June was now accepted as certain to be D-day. The British Chiefs of Staff were greatly relieved by the decision, which not only established firmly an essential factor for planning, but gave the commanders in the Mediterranean that 'something to veer and haul

---

[1] See pp. 431, 450 below.

on', in the disposition of their assault shipping, for which the Prime Minister had hoped when Anzio was being planned.[1]

The discussions in London began on 13th February. A series of plans for the assault shipping was presented over the next six days. The problem was to find a lift for 'Overlord' to carry an extra $1\frac{2}{3}$ assault divisions plus the equivalent of four extra armoured brigades, five regiments of self-propelled field artillery, some shore groups and some naval and air units, all needed within the first thirty-six hours. The solution depended partly on the tactical loading of the vessels, on which different ideas prevailed, and partly on the rates of serviceability accepted for the various types of shipping. Faced with the disagreement on this point between the two sets of Chiefs of Staff, the 'Overlord' Command distinguished in its plans between the two, allowing British rates to the British shipping, and the American rate to the American. On this basis, it finally produced a scheme whereby assault ships and craft from American production, including types not held by the British, would replace the equivalents in different types demanded in January. The exchange would still leave a lift for two divisions in the Mediterranean, and would almost satisfy 'Overlord's' demands for L.S.T. Eisenhower and, after some hesitation, Montgomery were prepared to accept the plan, with a small further demand on Washington for L.S.T.

The British Chiefs of Staff were not much impressed by these arrangements, which they were inclined to suspect would stint both 'Overlord' and 'Anvil'. But, as before, their main objection was not technical, but derived rather from the most recent developments in Italy. For by 19th February the British fears of a stalemate seemed likely to be realized. On the morning of the 16th, while the talks in London were in progress, the Germans counter-attacked in strength at Anzio and the New Zealand Corps launched its attack on Monte Cassino. By the morning of the 19th, when Eisenhower presented his proposals, it was clear that both had failed, and that while bitter fighting would continue the position was unlikely seriously to alter. If so, new plans would probably be needed before the stalemate could be broken, which would inevitably demand the full strength of the Mediterranean Command. After their meeting with Eisenhower, the British Chiefs of Staff put this issue plainly to their American colleagues, stating that 'the shadow of 'Anvil',' which was already cramping Wilson, should be removed, and all efforts concentrated wholeheartedly on 'bleeding and burning German divisions' where they had apparently determined to fight to the last.

The British arguments—or perhaps the developments in Italy themselves—had a certain effect. On 21st February, the Joint Chiefs of Staff replied that 'Anvil' should undoubtedly be launched with two

[1] See p. 219 above.

divisions, and that this should prove possible without interfering with operations in Italy. But they proposed meanwhile to protect those operations by notifying Eisenhower and Wilson, subject to the concurrence of the British, that 'all combat ground forces in Mediterranean should be considered available to Italian campaign, but United States and French units being rehabilitated should be re-equipped and trained for 'Anvil' as required.' Eisenhower himself, however, was now coming to agree with the British that 'Anvil' might prove impossible, although unlike the British he still considered it desirable. On the 19th he informed the Joint Chiefs of Staff, as he hinted on the same day to the British, that all of the troops earmarked for the south of France might have to be used for operations in Italy; and on the morning of 23rd February, he agreed with the British Chiefs of Staff to a formula which achieved a reasonable compromise between their positions. The campaign in Italy should have priority, until further orders, over all existing and future operations in the Mediterranean. Subject to that proviso, the Supreme Commander in the Mediterranean should make plans and preparations for seaborne operations in the theatre which would contribute to the success of 'Overlord', and of which 'Anvil', on a scale of two divisions and simultaneous with 'Overlord', was to be considered first. For this purpose, the Mediterranean Command could rely on keeping the assault shipping allotted to the theatre, apart from twenty L.S.T. and twenty-one landing craft, in lieu of which it would receive six large American assault ships. These arrangements would be reviewed on 20th March, in the light of the situation obtaining in Italy; and unless the Combined Chiefs of Staff then decided that 'Anvil', as already defined, could be undertaken, all assault shipping needed for 'Overlord', above a lift for one division, would be withdrawn at once from the Mediterranean.

Meanwhile, the Chiefs of Staff in each country had been trying to meet the most recent demands for assault shipping for 'Overlord'; and on 21st February, the two bodies announced that they could together provide enough to fill the gap, provided that the twenty L.S.T. and twenty-one landing-craft from the Mediterranean were also made available.

Such was the position when Wilson sent his request from the Mediterranean, on 22nd February, that 'Anvil' should be cancelled.[1] Coming on top of Eisenhower's telegrams, and followed immediately by the agreed recommendations of Eisenhower and the British Chiefs of Staff, it provided the connecting link in the chain. On the 25th, the President and the Joint Chiefs of Staff consented to the recommendations from London, and the two Supreme Commanders were notified accordingly.

[1] Pp. 230-1 above.

(iii)
The Postponement of 'Anvil'

As was its purpose, the agreement of 25th February governed the period to 20th March. But it did not lead to a pause in the debate. The pressure of events in Italy, coming at a time of active planning for 'Overlord', could not but continue to affect the disposition of resources so minutely considered; and in the three and a half weeks before final agreement was due, discussions of detail threatened the main intention.

In Italy, there were two immediate commitments: the maintenance and reinforcement of the troops at Anzio, and the capture of Monte Cassino. The size of the first commitment could be determined only by the fate of the second. Towards the end of February, Alexander planned to extend the area of the beach-head at Anzio during March, and to prepare for the subsequent breakout. For these purposes, he wished to relieve the two divisions which had borne the brunt of the fighting, to put three fresh divisions into the beach-head, and to increase the supply of arms and equipment. During February, some 3,000 tons a day had been unloaded in the beach-head; but 4,000 tons a day would now be needed, apart from such stores as were put in with the troops themselves.

These figures were based on the expectation of a stalemate in the south until the middle of April, and of the relief of the bridgehead at Anzio in the middle of May. But a third attack was nevertheless due to be launched on Monte Cassino as soon as weather permitted, to try to gain a bridgehead from which later to move in strength. Constant and heavy rain delayed the operation until 15th March. Very strong air support had been assembled, in the hope of numbing the defence immediately before the New Zealand Corps attacked; and on the morning of the 15th, bombers and artillery went into action. But when the New Zealand Corps moved forward, it found itself still confronted by fierce resistance. This was an extraordinary feat of survival on the part of the defenders; but the New Zealanders were nevertheless able to clear a large part of Cassino, and to move a certain way up the mountain. That night, contrary to the forecast, the weather again broke. On the next day, the Corps attacked the heights, and managed to gain a knoll not far below the monastery itself. But that marked the limit of the advance. On the 19th, the Germans counter-attacked with success; attacks by the New Zealand Corps between the 20th and 22nd produced no result; and on the 23rd the operation was called off. The knoll was abandoned, and after six weeks of gallant but frustrated effort the New Zealand Corps was dissolved on 26th March. At the end of that month, the Allies were thus left in possession of the greater part of the town of Cassino, of a bridgehead over the Rapido, and of a salient to the south-west of Monte Cassino formed by the earlier British attack in January. But the mountain itself had still to be taken, and a pause was now necessary to prepare for the operations later in the spring.

These developments, at Anzio and on the main front, gave rise to further debate in London and Washington. The first complication arose from the programme for the assault shipping for Anzio, which had undergone some changes since it had been settled, on 8th January, for 'Shingle'. At that time, only twelve L.S.T. were left available for Anzio after 13th February, and none after the 29th.[1] But the position had been relieved to some extent early in February, owing to the decision to postpone 'Overlord' until early in June. As soon as the Americans' agreement had been secured, the British Chiefs of Staff informed General Wilson that he might keep thirteen extra L.S.T. until 29th February, and another eight L.S.T. until 10th March. But on 28th February, twenty-four hours before the thirteen L.S.T. were due to leave the theatre, Alexander sent an urgent message through Wilson to the British Chiefs of Staff. The beach-head at Anzio was still under pressure, and a further counter-attack was expected; and at the same time it was essential to start putting fresh troops and supplies into the area, for its enlargement during March. Wilson stressed that this latter duty, even without the complication of the immediate threat, demanded more assault shipping than was, or would be, available. He had therefore postponed the departure of the ships for twenty-four hours, and now asked that, as a first measure, it should be postponed for nine days.

The Chiefs of Staff supported the immediate recommendation to Washington, 'in order to prevent the collapse of the bridgehead'; and the Joint Chiefs of Staff concurred on the same day. At the same time, the British proposed an alteration to the subsequent programme only recently agreed. By that, forty-one L.S.T. (13+8+20)[2] were due to leave the Mediterranean for England on or before 1st April. The Chiefs of Staff now suggested, in order to relieve Wilson of constant changes and of some temporary shortages in his assault shipping, that all should stay in the theatre, being replaced in Britain by the assault shipping from American production which Admiral King at Cairo had offered to 'Anvil', and by the six large American assault ships due to go out to the Mediterranean.[3] Elaborate discussion between London, Washington and the Mediterranean disclosed various obstacles to this solution. Instead, it was finally agreed that the L.S.T.

[1] See p. 220 above.
[2] See p. 242 above.
[3] Ibid.

from the Mediterranean should be sent to England, as already intended, but only as the last two-thirds were replaced by L.S.T. from American production. The Americans also undertook, at the conclusion of the negotiations on 10th March, to meet the deficit for 'Overlord' that might arise from further damage to any of the L.S.T. before they left the Mediterranean. These arrangements satisfied all parties, and met some difficulties of timing and in the allocation of particular vessels which the earlier programme had raised.

But, as so often happened, while the debate was proceeding the apparently inadequate forces on the spot were meeting the demand. In the first ten days of March, the naval command in the Mediterranean made a supreme effort, and the assault shipping landed an average of 7,000 tons a day in the bridgehead. Bad weather, and increased shelling by the enemy, then lowered the average to 4,225 tons, and later to between 3,000 and 3,500 tons a day. But thanks to the reserve built up by the earlier efforts, the result met Alexander's demands, and enabled the force at Anzio later to play its part in the operations of the spring. It is indeed an interesting commentary on the prolonged and complicated debate, that the vessels intended originally to land and support for under a month a force of 70,000 men, should have been able in the event—although under conditions of continuous crisis—to land and support for a full two months a force rising to 170,000, and to raise the original rate of unloading supplies by a third.

The time was now drawing near when a decision should be taken on 'Anvil', and on 13th March the British Chiefs of Staff turned to consider the nature of the recommendations that were due on the 20th. Some of the assault shipping had recently been tied more closely to the Italian campaign. It was now necessary to consider carefully the prospects of that campaign itself. On 14th March, the Chiefs of Staff accordingly asked General Wilson to submit a detailed appreciation of the position and of his plans; and his reply, delayed until the third attack on Monte Cassino had been launched, was received on the 22nd.[1]

Wilson expected that current operations would secure Cassino and a bridgehead for a fresh offensive towards Rome. But this offensive involved considerable preparations, which would probably not be complete before 15th April. The fighting moreover would almost certainly be hard, at least at the outset, and it was therefore unwise to count on reaching the force in the bridgehead at Anzio before 15th May at the earliest. It should then be possible to gain Rome within a month; and thereafter there seemed to be four possibilities:

---

[1] General Ismay's date, in para. 19 of his memorandum in Appendix VII below, is not correct.

'(a) 'Anvil'.
(b) A full offensive in Italy together with an amphibious "end run"[1] assault wherever the enemy line may be sited.
(c) Landings in the Gulf of Genoa or alternatively in the Po valley.
(d) A landing in Istria.'

Of these four possibilities, the Supreme Commander was inclined to discount 'Anvil'. It could not be launched, in his opinion, less than ten weeks after the bridgehead at Anzio had been relieved, and therefore until late in July. Moreover, once it had been launched the enemy would be relieved of any further seaborne threat in the Mediterranean, for its scale would obviously absorb all available assault shipping for some time. The second possibility, on the other hand, would enable full pressure to be maintained on the enemy and would aid the strategic bombers in their operations from the theatre, while the smaller scale of the seaborne operation neither removed the threat of landings elsewhere nor in fact rendered later landings to west or east impossible. But the advance up Italy might be slow, which would then affect the value of the third and fourth possibilities.

On balance, however, Wilson much preferred a full offensive in Italy, combined with threats and feints against the enemy's coast line elsewhere and support for the guerrilla forces, to 'Anvil' on the scale contemplated. He therefore asked for a directive from the Combined Chiefs of Staff:

'(a) To continue the battle in Italy to include the capture of Rome and its airfields.
(b) Thereafter to carry out intensive operations up Italy, the assault lift of 1 division plus . . . being allotted for this purpose.
(c) To cancel forthwith 'Anvil' as at present designed and to prepare for a landing in the south of France under approximate 'Rankin' conditions.[2]
(d) To be allotted resources for carrying out any Commando operations and feints that I may wish to implement.'

This report naturally carried great weight. Its effect was increased by a report on 'Anvil' which Eisenhower submitted on the same day, and of which he had already sent a copy to General Marshall. It was now his 'firm opinion' that the operation could not be carried out on the scale envisaged, in view of developments in Italy. This being so, he no longer had cause to limit his demands for more assault shipping out of consideration for the south of France. He drew attention to the narrow margin to which he was working, even after the recent additions which the American and British Chiefs of Staff had provided;

[1] A term used in American football. Here, it describes a complementary operation designed to support the main operation by attacking the enemy in the rear.

[2] Conditions obtaining if Germany should suddenly collapse or weaken considerably.

and recommended therefore that 'Anvil', 'in its present conception of a two division assault building up to ten divisions', should be abandoned, and assault shipping transferred accordingly from the Mediterranean to 'Overlord' by the end of April.

The British Chiefs of Staff discussed this and Wilson's paper on 22nd March. They accepted their conclusions and Eisenhower's request for assault shipping. Later on the same day they so informed the Joint Chiefs of Staff, recommending that 'Anvil' early in June should be cancelled, that the assault shipping specified by Eisenhower (with a slight reduction in L.S.T.) should be returned to the United Kingdom by the end of April, and that Wilson should be issued with a fresh directive.

The proposal that 'Anvil' should be abandoned, and the terms of the consequent directive, formed the subject of a further long and keen debate. But meanwhile the American Chiefs of Staff agreed that, in view of Wilson's report, 'Anvil' could not be launched early in June; and they therefore consented on 24th March to transfer the assault shipping as proposed, and suggested that the attack on southern France, with two divisions as before, should be postponed to a target date of 10th July. After the alarms and developments of the past two months, the Mediterranean Command was now assured of its forces for the critical battle for Rome; and the first phase in the debate on 'Anvil' was over.

CHAPTER VII

'OVERLORD' AND THE MEDITERRANEAN, APRIL–JUNE, 1944

(i)

The Debate on 'Anvil' Continued

THE POSTPONEMENT of 'Anvil' late in March, which might have been expected to lead to a pause in the discussion, served rather to emphasize the fundamental antagonism between the attitudes of the British and the Americans. These did not change over the next four months; and while stages may be marked in the debate which proceeded almost continuously throughout that time, the arguments themselves, which were constantly repeated with appropriate changes of emphasis, may therefore be stated here before we follow the debate to the end of its next phase in the middle of June.[1]

As the Joint Chiefs of Staff remarked on one occasion, the difference between the British and the Americans turned on their conception of 'the relative importance of 'Anvil' as compared to continued offensive operations in Italy'. This definition of the problem reveals three opportunities for disagreement, the third a consequence of the other two: first, the value to be attached to 'Anvil'; secondly, the value to be attached to the different stages of the Italian campaign; thirdly, the timing of preparations for 'Anvil' in the light of the Italian campaign.

The British Chiefs of Staff were by now convinced of the correctness of their earlier impression that 'Anvil' would not achieve its intended result. The obstacle, as they saw it, was not so much the fate of the assault itself as its immediate reinforcement, on which the rate of the subsequent operations must depend. On the latest intelligence, they estimated that nine German divisions would be available in central and southern France to block the advance of the stipulated ten Allied divisions, over five hundred miles of largely difficult country. No ultimate geographical target had been specified for the attack, and no detail provided as yet on the plans for the initial build-up of forces. In these circumstances, the British doubted if 'Anvil' would cause a major

[1] A good *résumé* of the principal incidents in the first part of this period, to the last week in April, appears in Appendix VII below.

diversion from 'Overlord'. So far indeed from benefiting 'Overlord', it might succeed only if that operation had already drawn off some of the potential opposition to 'Anvil'.

Moreover, once 'Anvil' had been launched on the scale intended, the enemy would appreciate that no other large stroke remained open to the Allies in the Mediterranean. The advantages of a threat would then disappear, and must be compensated by the advantages of the operation itself. Since the Chiefs of Staff discounted the latter, they preferred to retain the former.

The Americans, in contrast, expected 'Anvil' to achieve its object. Although separated by the length of France, the scene of the operation remained closer to that of 'Overlord' than any other that had been proposed; and if the assault itself was successful, which the British had not seriously questioned, they could see no reason why a further eight divisions should not be landed in reasonable time, nor why they should not then prove a sufficient threat for the enemy to ignore them at his peril. The attack in central Italy, unaccompanied by attacks elsewhere, had drawn, and was thought to be drawing, fresh German divisions into the peninsula. An attack on southern France, following an attack on northern France, might surely be regarded as equally grave, and, in the more critical circumstances, might exercise a decisive effect.

But secondly, the Americans favoured 'Anvil' because they disliked the alternative suggested by the British, the maintenance of the offensive in Italy for an indefinite period. The British argued that since the enemy was known to intend to stand south of Rome, and since eight of his divisions had already been brought from other areas and fronts for that purpose, the Allies should acknowledge that the Italian campaign was fulfilling its main purpose of containing as many Germans as possible, and should take full advantage of the fact. If the renewal of the offensive led to a further stalemate, that would be because more German divisions had arrived and were being tied down at the expense, now directly, of 'Overlord'. If it led to a further advance, the situation could be exploited as the occasion required, possibly by entering France from the south-east. But if the operations in Italy were to be weakened or broken off by the withdrawal of divisions for 'Anvil', the Allies would be sacrificing the one area where they held the initiative, and where they were containing large enemy forces in the critical period before and surrounding 'Overlord', for the sake of a putative offensive which might not succeed. If 'Anvil' on the larger scale were abandoned, and an active threat were prepared and maintained instead, they would have the benefit of that and of the campaign in Italy: if a large 'Anvil' were launched, they might well lose both.

The Americans disagreed. In the first place, they pointed out that the offensive in Italy could not be maintained precisely as the British suggested, for there would be a pause of at least a month (and, as soon became apparent, of almost two months) before it was renewed.[1] There would thus be a critical period before 'Overlord', during which the enemy might well redispose his forces so as later to impede the Allies without calling on further reinforcements. The British, in fact, were gambling on the continuation of the existing German strategy, regardless of a possible change of circumstances. But instead, there might be an Allied advance in Italy which would not contain the necessary enemy forces, and which would reach the northern plains only to find that a large proportion of them had slipped through the Alps. Meanwhile, the nine German divisions thought to be in central and southern France, secure from any serious assault, would remain disengaged, held in check only by a threat which must indeed be ingenious to contain them for long.

The enemy, in fact, might well call the tune in Italy, as the Americans hinted had happened before; and thereby, on this occasion, the tune in western Europe. This seemed the more likely to the Joint Chiefs of Staff, because they suspected that the terrain of Italy could in fact never offer a good opportunity for an offensive, and that the difficulties which it imposed could never foster an imaginative direction of the campaign. They feared therefore that they were being asked to abandon a seaborne operation in which they believed, for operations by land which they thought were not being conducted, and possibly could not be conducted, with sufficient boldness. It was thus the more necessary to strike outside the peninsula, in a potentially more sensitive area, and to adopt the flexible and mobile strategy on which the British themselves had laid such stress only a few months before. Each partner thus again saw strategic opportunity in a different area from the other.

Holding such different views on the alternatives, the British and American Chiefs of Staff naturally differed on the timing and nature of the preparations for 'Anvil'. The Americans wished to withdraw the necessary formations and shipping for the large-scale assault as soon as the troops at Anzio had been relieved, and thereafter to maintain a limited offensive in Italy. To ensure their objects, they also wished to associate the commander of 'Overlord' with the detailed allocation of assault shipping between that operation and 'Anvil'. The British, on the other hand, wanted to maintain the offensive in Italy which would then be in full spate, to prepare as far as possible for 'Anvil' with two divisions if the situation allowed, but meanwhile to mount a threat that would contain the enemy effectively in southern and central France over the critical period for 'Overlord'. In these circumstances, they saw no need to bring the allocation of assault shipping for 'Anvil' within the purview of the commander of 'Overlord'.

[1] See p. 245 above.

Underlying the arguments on both sides was the familiar difference of approach to policy on the part of British and Americans. The former were anxious, as ever, to avoid a rigid commitment some months before the event, which might detract from an intervening success that could not be promised or even clearly foreseen. They preferred to concentrate on the opportunity that offered, while preparing as best they could for the opportunity that had not yet come. The Americans, in contrast, were anxious not to depart from earlier agreements which had demanded careful preparation, for the sake of an opportunism whose consequences could not be foreseen, and in this instance at the possible cost of Russian confidence, which had been enlisted precisely by the threatened plans. This difference of approach, rather than the difference of opinion itself, was responsible for a certain heat entering the debate, particularly when concessions were made by one side to the other which were not, in its opinion, sufficiently appreciated. These concessions, it should be added, were made at first almost exclusively by the Americans, and later almost exclusively by the British; and the origin and nature of the resentment varied accordingly.

The second phase of the debate began in the very telegrams, of 22nd and 24th March, which brought the first phase to a close. This is not so surprising when the circumstances are considered. It was exactly a month since General Wilson had asked for a new directive;[1] and now that the immediate issue had been settled by the cancellation of 'Anvil' in May, the Combined Chiefs of Staff had to decide as soon as possible what to do in the course of the summer. The preparations must be set in motion within the next few weeks. Further discussion on 'Anvil' could thus not be evaded, but was rather precipitated, by the earlier decision.

In their message of 22nd March, the British had proposed a draft for a directive to Wilson. This instructed him to continue the battle for Rome, capturing it if he could by the first week in June; thereafter to attack up Italy, with the object of destroying as many German divisions as possible; and meanwhile to examine, and as far as possible prepare for, the use of his assault shipping in operations after D-day for 'Overlord'.

The Americans could not agree to this. They proposed in turn that the Allies should launch a 'co-ordinated, sustained, all-out offensive' as soon as possible in Italy, to link the bridgehead at Anzio with the main line; that they should then maintain as much pressure as possible from that line, while developing a threat against southern France in the period surrounding D-day for 'Overlord'; and should thereafter, on a target date of 10th July, launch 'Anvil' as planned with two divisions.

[1] Pp. 230-1 above.

In support of this strategy, they announced that they would send twenty-six L.S.T. and forty landing craft from the Pacific to the Mediterranean, to arrive during June. This was indeed a notable, and unexpected, concession. It marked the first occasion on which assault shipping had been withdrawn from the Pacific, where as elsewhere it was the critical factor, for operations in Europe;[1] and since the Administration remained under strong pressure to send more to the Far East, the decision was not taken lightly. It was not therefore surprising that the Joint Chiefs of Staff should have felt justified in insisting that these resources should be used in accordance with their policy. 'The U.S. Chiefs of Staff', they stated, 'can agree to the impact of this withdrawal on the Pacific operations only on condition that it is agreed by the British Chiefs of Staff that preparation for the delayed 'Anvil' will be vigorously pressed and that it is the firm intention to mount this operation in support of 'Overlord' with the target date indicated.' They proposed a directive to Wilson which would conform to this intention.

The British were prepared to agree that 'Anvil' should be postponed and not cancelled; but they declined to submit to a specific period for the postponement. They therefore answered on 28th March that Wilson could certainly prepare for the operation, but that the campaign in Italy should meanwhile proceed as they had suggested. This reply, which was curtly phrased, annoyed the Joint Chiefs of Staff. It came, moreover, at a particularly unfortunate moment, for the Combined Chiefs of Staff had just received a message from Wilson announcing that the offensive in Italy was now unlikely to start until 14th May, instead of in the middle of April as had hitherto been estimated. The delay, as the Americans pointed out with some force, seemed seriously to weaken the British case; and they insisted that a decision must be taken at once on 'Anvil' for a specific date if the operation were not to be abandoned by default. Their telegram in turn aroused the British Chiefs of Staff. 'The implication', they informed the Joint Staff Mission in Washington on 31st March, 'that in British view Mediterranean strategy is any less subservient to 'Overlord' than in the American view, is particularly painful to us on the eve of this the greatest of our joint ventures. We fully realise and equally deplore that time is being lost, but we think a right decision is even more important than a quick one.' A quick decision, however, could not in fact be avoided; and the British therefore decided over the next few days to seek agreement by concentrating on the wording of the directive to Wilson rather than by raising questions of principle. Warned by the Joint Staff Mission that the Americans, and particularly General Marshall—who was now handling the discussion almost

[1] As distinct from the occasions on which it had been sent to Europe instead of to the Pacific.

entirely on their behalf—insisted on a date, the Chiefs of Staff submitted a revised draft on 3rd April which met the Americans' wishes in this respect.

> '. . . 2. (a) Launch as soon as is practicable a co-ordinated, sustained all-out offensive in Italy so as to join the beachhead with the main line. Thereafter through offensive action contain the greatest number of German formations in Central Italy.
>
> (b) Develop a positive amphibious threat against the French Mediterranean coast and employ air forces as though in preparation for an amphibious assault so as to delay the movement of German forces in the Mediterranean towards 'Overlord'. This threat should be fully developed by 'Overlord' D-5 and fully maintained for as long as possible after D-day. The build-up of the threat should not start before D-31.
>
> (c) Prepare plans for 'Anvil' on a basis of at least a two divisional assault to be launched at the earliest practicable date. Target date 10th July.
>
> (d) 'Anvil' is the most ambitious operation that can be undertaken in the Mediterranean theatre, and plans for this operation should be pressed forward vigorously and wholeheartedly, together with all preparations that do not prejudice the operations specified in (a) above. The undertaking of these preparations for 'Anvil' will in no way preclude a change of plan by the Combined Chiefs of Staff if an undeniably better course of action should be presented by changing circumstances.'

This message was accompanied by another from the Prime Minister to Dill, stressing that General Eisenhower had approved its terms and that the British were only concerned not to be forced into an irrevocable commitment regardless of intervening circumstances. But the differences remained too great. On 4th April, the Americans accepted the revised draft, but only with four alterations which in fact threatened its purpose.

> '2(*a*) *last sentence:*
> *Insert* "maintain pressure to" after "thereafter".
> *Delete* "through offensive action".
> 2(*c*) *first sentence:*
> *Insert* "and preparations" after "plans".
> 2(*d*)
> *Delete* "together with all preparations that do not prejudice the operations specified in (a) above".'

On the 7th, the British replied that these alterations were 'quite unacceptable'.

Continued efforts on the part of the Joint Staff Mission in Washington failed to bridge the gap between the protagonists. The American

Chiefs of Staff were angry and hurt by the apparent nonchalance with which the British had accepted their offer of new resources, without any strategic concession in return. The British Chiefs of Staff, for their part, were annoyed by the apparent exploitation of an offer of resources to force a strategy of which they disapproved on a theatre in which they held the larger forces and the immediate operational responsibility. After further meetings had been held and telegrams exchanged between London and Washington, it was clear, as the Joint Staff Mission remarked, that the principals were 'poles apart'. Dill reported that 'only over his [Marshall's] dead body will you get a change of outlook'; and the feeling was the same in London. The American Chiefs of Staff accordingly informed the British on 8th April that, in view of the urgency of the matter, they would consent to the latest British draft of the directive, but that since in their view this removed the possibility of 'Anvil' as a complement to 'Overlord', they could not divert assault shipping from the Pacific to the Mediterranean. This seemed to settle the matter, and the British Chiefs of Staff prepared to make the last minor amendments to the document before its formal approval.

The Prime Minister, however, was not prepared to lose the American assault shipping, and possibly American interest in the Mediterranean, without a further effort. Hitherto, while following and approving the arguments of the British Chiefs of Staff, he had not entered the debate with Washington. But on 10th April, when the Combined Chiefs of Staff seemed to have reached a deadlock, he announced that he was not prepared to take the final decision on 'Anvil' without more thought. He wished to talk to General Alexander, who on 30th March had asked leave to come home for discussion early in April, and also to communicate with the President. At the Chiefs of Staff's request, however, he agreed to await the result of the first step before embarking on the second. Meanwhile, the draft of Wilson's directive was laid aside. The authorities in London welcomed Alexander's visit, for at the beginning of April they were still largely in the dark over his plans for the spring offensive. Wilson's recent message, announcing its postponement by a month, had 'staggered' the Prime Minister, had upset the Chiefs of Staff and, as we have seen, had been a potent factor in leading to the deadlock with the Americans. An outline of the revised plans was brought to England on 1st April by an officer from Alexander's headquarters, and Wilson sent a further appreciation four days later. But neither gave much detail, and the authorities in London were correspondingly glad to discuss the position fully with Alexander himself.

Their opportunity came on 11th April, when Alexander made a long statement. He dealt first with the state of the enemy. The Germans were now thought to dispose of twenty-three divisions in Italy, eighteen south of Rome. Most of them, after reinforcement at an average rate of 15,000 men a month throughout the winter, were up to strength, and were well equipped; they still held the Gustav Line, weakened in sectors by the Allies' attacks during the winter; and had constructed two more fortified positions in its rear, the Adolf Hitler and Caesar Lines, the first running east from the river Liri to the slopes of Monte Cairo north of Cassino, the second across routes 6 and 7 between Anzio and Rome and thence, through Avezzano, to positions west of Pescara.[1]

Alexander would thus encounter three defended positions, the most formidable of which had already been seriously weakened. His main problem was to decide at what point to use his force at Anzio, whether in the assault on the Gustav and Adolf Hitler Lines, or in the later pursuit towards Rome. He had decided to reserve it for the latter, mainly because he must otherwise split air support between two fronts at a time when its greatest effort would be needed in the south. Measures had therefore to be taken, of reinforcement, redeployment and deception, to enable Fifth and Eighth Armies to break the existing German positions, and thereafter the Adolf Hitler Line, by a frontal assault. The Allies estimated that they could maintain twenty-eight divisions at most in central Italy, which would give them a superiority over the defence of $1\frac{1}{4}$ divisions to 1, and would leave only four active divisions in the theatre not engaged in the campaign. Alexander intended to deploy the equivalent of eighteen divisions west of the Apennines, to leave the equivalent of three divisions in the Adriatic sector, and to concentrate six divisions, rising finally to seven, in the bridgehead at Anzio. The duties of the various forces remained the same as those outlined in February.[2] Eighth Army was to attack Monte Cassino, thereafter driving up the Liri valley along route 6 as far as Valmontone. Fifth Army would meanwhile advance through the western mountains to meet the force at Anzio, which would hold itself ready to attack inland on or after D+4 of the main offensive. Communications between and behind the enemy's lines would be bombed throughout April and early May, and for the last fortnight before the offensive would also be sabotaged by Italian guerrillas. The codeword for the offensive itself was 'Diadem'.

The date of attack had been governed by a combination of factors: by the length of time needed to transfer the necessary reinforcements and fresh divisions to their areas, and the bulk of Eighth Army secretly across the Apennines; by the subsequent redeployment of the two Armies, which involved difficult questions of supply and administration between forces differently grouped and equipped; and by a period

[1] See Map V, facing p. 270.

[2] See pp. 229-30 above.

for training Eighth Army in its new conditions. The extra weeks, moreover, promised better weather for the operations, and gave a longer period for the preliminary air attacks. On 2nd April, the local commanders had agreed that the preparations could be complete by 3rd or 5th May. Alexander therefore offered to attack on any date after 10th May on which the Chiefs of Staff might decide.

This statement, and subsequent questioning, convinced Alexander's audience that the offensive could not start until the middle of May. The implications for 'Anvil' therefore remained the same as before. The junction between the main forces and those at Anzio could not take place before early in June, and it would be impossible to prepare in time thereafter for 'Anvil' on 10th July. The Prime Minister, however, was still reluctant to forego the American assault shipping, which would add to the effectiveness of the necessary measures of deception in the Mediterranean at the time of 'Overlord', and would provide thereafter an additional pool from which to exploit success in Italy. He therefore decided to send a telegram immediately to General Marshall, followed possibly by one to the President.

The telegram to Marshall was sent on 12th April, after revision by the Chiefs of Staff. After repeating the main features of the British case, it continued:[1]

> '. . . 4. At the moment my own position is as follows. We should above all defeat the German army south of Rome and join our own armies. Nothing should be grudged for this. We cannot tell how either the Allied or enemy armies will emerge from the battle until the battle has been fought. It may be that the enemy will be thrown into disorder, and that great opportunities of exploitation may be open. Or we may be checked and the enemy may continue to hold his positions south of Rome against us with his existing forces. On the other hand, he may seek to withdraw some of his Divisions to the main battle in France. It seems to me we must have plans and preparations to take advantage of the above possibilities.
>
> 5. Regarding 'Anvil', . . . I believe that whatever happens on the mainland of Italy, the enemy forces now detached to the Riviera can in the meanwhile be fastened there by feints and threats. One thing that alarms me, however, is lest our Directive to General Wilson should make him fall between two stools. This would mean that we should be denied the exploitation of any victory gained south of Rome (and victories are wonderful things) or the power to pin down German Divisions in Italy, and yet on the other hand not be able to make a major operation out of 'Anvil'.
>
> 6. . . . I would not now rule out either a vigorous pursuit northward of the beaten enemy nor an amphibious cat's-claw higher

[1] See Appendix X below for the complete text.

up to detain him or cut him off. I should have thought we could contrive plans and preparations to render possible either this or 'Anvil' in one form or another. After all, the power to put men into ships is one thing and the question where to disembark them is another.

. . . 9. When you have reflected on the above, I ask you to consider the following formula:

(1) The prime duty of all the forces in the Mediterranean is to pin down as many German Divisions as possible away from 'Overlord'.

(2) Secondly, to achieve the above we must give the highest priority to operations to join the Anzio bridgehead and the main front, meanwhile making such preparations for 'Anvil' . . . as are practicable in consonance therewith.

(3) Thirdly, after joining the bridgehead we must survey the situation arising from the results of the battle in Italy, as well as the first results of 'Overlord' and the dispositions of the enemy.

(4) Fourthly, we must then decide whether to go all out for 'Anvil' or exploit the results of victory in Italy. It must be recognised that this option will not exist unless the L.S.T's from the Pacific are assigned now to the Mediterranean. . . .'

Marshall replied two days later.

'. . . We appear to be agreed in principle, but quite evidently not as to method. If we are to have any option as to what we can do when the time comes, preparations for 'Anvil' must be made now even though they may be at the partial expense of future operations in Italy after the beach-head has been joined to the main line. Unless this has been done, in our view there will be no option, whereas if preparations for an 'Anvil' are made Wilson will have an amphibious force available to carry out another and perhaps a less difficult amphibious operation than 'Anvil' should the circumstances at the time make the latter appear inexpedient.

Furthermore, the urgency of our need for these landing craft in the Pacific at this particular period is very great. . . . This sacrifice in the Pacific can be justified only with the assurance that we are to have an operation in the effectiveness of which we have complete faith.'

The Prime Minister and the Chiefs of Staff considered this telegram at a meeting on the same afternoon. They decided that the Prime Minister might approach Marshall once more, while the Chiefs of Staff approached their colleagues and showed them the final draft of the proposed directive to Wilson. Churchill accordingly telegraphed again on 16th April, in a last effort to sway the decision. But his message had no effect. Neither the Joint Chiefs of Staff nor Marshall showed any sign in their replies of giving way. The directive for Wilson was accordingly put into final order, and despatched.

'OBJECT:

1. To give the greatest possible assistance to 'Overlord' by destroying or containing the maximum number of German formations in the Mediterranean.

METHOD:

2. (a) Launch, as early as possible, an all-out offensive in Italy.

(b) Develop the greatest possible threat to contain German forces in Southern France. This threat should be fully developed by 'Overlord' D-5 and fully maintained for as long as possible after D-day. Process of building up the threat should not start before D-31.

(c) Make plans for the best possible use of the amphibious lift remaining to you, either in support of operations in Italy, or in order to take advantage of opportunities arising in the South of France or elsewhere for the furtherance of your object and to press forward vigorously and wholeheartedly with all preparations which do not prejudice the achievement of the fullest success in (a) above.

COMMAND AND CONTROL OF FORCES OPERATING IN FRANCE

3. If, in the course of operations, you should establish forces in France, you will continue to exercise operational control of these forces until the Supreme Commander, Allied Expeditionary Force, can assume this responsibility. . . .'

(ii)

The Capture of Rome and its Implications

With the issue of this directive, the British were both free and obliged to review the possibilities afresh; and in the three weeks before the offensive began in Italy, they went some way towards establishing an order of priority between them. The first stimulus came, three days after Wilson's directive had been issued, in a Minute from the Prime Minister to the Chiefs of Staff.

'1. It will be a scandal if, when the main battle [of 'Overlord'] is at its height, say the 20th to 30th day, we are found with two of our finest and most experienced armoured divisions, less in each case their motorised brigade, and six or seven fresh divisions all without employment. The essence of a battle like this is that everybody fights somehow somewhere.

2. What is the day when the bulk of transportation for the battle ['Overlord'] will be over? In what posture may we

reasonably hope to be on D+20? What will be the condition of the German Fighter and Bomber Air Force at that time? Will it not probably be shot to a standstill and largely annihilated? Will not divisions from the St. Nazaire–Bayonne coastal sector have been drawn upon? May there not be an opportunity for an important diversionary landing? Could not for instance an Anglo-French force with at least two armoured brigades and three or four French divisions be brought from Algeria and Morocco, having moved to their assembly points in secret, and be landed wherever is thought best on the wide front which is open? St. Jean-de-Luz, Bayonne, to the north or south of Bordeaux, La Rochelle, or Nantes—all require immediate study. Will not some of the shipping which has carried the army in 'Overlord' be available in time to reach Oran and Casablanca? Even a small force would be better than none. Cannot a dozen auxiliary carriers, no longer required in the narrow waters, and bombarding vessels which have done their part, be made available? There never was such a chance for a surprise descent into a population eager to revolt. It is a fine country for armoured cars and tanks. Look how the Germans overran it in 1940. The French ought to have a show in France and not merely be made to send more divisions to Italy. This would of course all have to fit in with General Wilson's plans for amphibious feints, etc., in the Mediterranean.

3. I am sure that even if as few as 50,000 troops were landed around Bordeaux by a surprise operation, they would liberate the city and enable reinforcements to sail up the Gironde. The effect upon the enemy would be profound. If this is neglected I am sure that we shall lay ourselves open to justifiable criticism. To hold the enemy tightly gripped at one point and to have nothing planned in either diversion or picking up easy gains is certainly difficult to defend.'

The idea of a landing on Bordeaux was not indeed a new one. Mr. Churchill had first raised it, with the code name of 'Caliph', at the beginning of February 1944, when he had envisaged a descent on the town by three armoured divisions at a similar stage of 'Overlord'. The assault force was to be assembled secretly in Morocco between March and May, and sailed in a wide arc to achieve surprise, while American reinforcements could be brought across the Atlantic. 'A force of this character,' in Churchill's view,[1] 'let loose in the south and centre of France, would instantly arouse widespread revolt and would be of measureless assistance to the main battle,' as the force put ashore by 'Anvil' might not. The British Chiefs of Staff, however, were not then greatly impressed by the idea. They admitted its attractions, but doubted if the assault could be launched without a complementary airborne attack, and thought that in any case there was little point in

[1] See *Closing the Ring*, p. 606.

examining the possibility in detail until decisions had been reached on the more urgent problems elsewhere. On 9th February, the Prime Minister accordingly agreed to defer consideration of his plan until the resources for the Mediterranean had been settled in the light of 'Anvil', of the campaign in Italy, and of the final demands for 'Overlord'.

Little more was therefore heard of the matter until 22nd April, when this condition had been largely fulfilled. There was now no reason why a landing on the west coast of France should not merit examination equally with landings elsewhere, and on the evening of the 24th the possibility was discussed at a Staff Conference attended by the Prime Minister, the Foreign Secretary, the Minister of War Transport and the Chiefs of Staff. Certain preliminary data had by now been assembled, as the result of an inquiry by Mr. Churchill in March. It seemed likely that the four divisions not required in 'Diadem'[1] (two French armoured, one French infantry and one American infantry), with assault shipping for one division and cargo shipping for another, could be spared from the Mediterranean by about D+20 for 'Overlord'. The operation would probably have to be mounted from Italy or from North Africa, for the ports of Britain would already be fully occupied. Air support could be provided by seven assault carriers, and naval bombardment would be forthcoming. The operation would be launched at a time when twenty-four Allied divisions should have landed in the north of France, and should have established a perimeter of some ninety miles on their area of assault. They were unlikely as yet to have attracted to the battle the enemy's coastal troops further south; but his mobile reserve in central France (thought to consist of some three divisions) might by then have moved to the north, and detailed examination would probably disclose gaps in the defences along the west coast where landings could take place. Opposition by air depended on events in the north, and it was impossible to tell as yet whether the seven assault carriers would suffice for the support of the operation. But on the data available, 'Caliph' was worth serious consideration, and the Staff Conference accordingly instructed the Chiefs of Staff to embark on a detailed study, and decided meanwhile to inform the American Chiefs of Staff and the two Supreme Commanders of the Prime Minister's original proposal.

A study of 'Caliph', moreover, could now be balanced against studies of other possible assaults which General Wilson, in pursuance of his directive, submitted during the last week of April. These depended on the results of his immediate commitments: operation 'Diadem' in Italy, the preparatory air operations and those forming part of the strategic bombing campaign, and the nourishment of the Yugoslav guerrillas. It would not be possible until early or mid-June to decide

[1] See p. 256 above.

whether the maintenance of these operations would themselves form the best complement to 'Overlord', or whether others, for which they might then have yielded the resources, would be better. But in the meantime, Wilson envisaged four possibilities. First, the Germans might stand successfully south of Rome, though not in their present positions. In that case no assault shipping could be spared. Secondly, they might retreat slowly to the line Pisa-Rimini, through country in which, unlike that south of Rome, the Allies could not deploy their full twenty-eight divisions. In that case all available assault shipping should be retained for outflanking strokes up the coasts. Thirdly, they might retreat fast to the same line. In that case it should be possible to launch a seaborne assault, or assaults, outside Italy, either on southern France or at the head of the Adriatic. Fourthly, events in France might make it possible and desirable to undertake a modified form of 'Anvil' to take advantage of a German collapse. Such a situation might occur under any of the other three conditions, in which case a balance must be struck between them. Wilson stressed, however, that anything less than an assault of three divisions had proved, by experience, unlikely to succeed except as a purely tactical operation in close support of other forces. Whatever happened, therefore, he considered that he should be given a further assault lift for $2\frac{1}{3}$ divisions over what he already held. Since assaults from the sea often included airborne operations as an integral part of the plan, he asked that his air transport should also be strengthened by at least the lift for one division.

By the end of April, therefore, the atmosphere had changed. The discussion on 'Anvil' was replaced by a wider debate, in which various possibilities could be compared. The Chiefs of Staff accordingly decided to take advantage of the lull in Italy to call Wilson home for conference. On 27th April they informed the Joint Chiefs of Staff, adding that they themselves were inclined to favour some form of 'Anvil' or 'Caliph', to be launched if possible some three weeks after 'Overlord'.

Their telegram had an unexpected result. On 28th April, at a meeting of the Combined Chiefs of Staff in Washington, Admiral King announced that if the conversations in London produced a definite recommendation for an assault on southern or western France, he would be prepared to send assault shipping for that purpose from the Pacific, up to the amount offered earlier for 'Anvil'.[1] This unexpected reprieve naturally delighted the British, and the Prime Minister was quick to convey their thanks to the President. It indeed seemed possible, as he then remarked, that the difficulties were clearing away; and when Wilson arrived in London on 1st May, the atmosphere was bright.

[1] See p. 253 above.

The talks took place from 3rd to 6th May. Wilson was asked to study four possibilities: an entry into western France after 'Overlord' was successfully under way, with the object of seizing a port; an entry into southern France, also after 'Overlord' was successfully under way; a seaborne 'left hook' in Italy, to accelerate or exploit the operations against Rome; and the seizure and development of air bases across the Adriatic. Before he gave an answer, Wilson in turn wished to know how soon, and in what strength, Eisenhower could release assault shipping and airborne forces from 'Overlord'. But this, not unnaturally, was difficult to determine, and he decided therefore not to count on any resources from that quarter by the end of June. In that event he was inclined to rule out an attack on western France, which moreover both he and Eisenhower considered should be launched, if at all, from Britain, on the detailed knowledge of conditions in the north which Eisenhower alone would possess. Wilson proposed instead to embark on detailed planning for four possible seaborne operations inside the Mediterranean:[1] an assault on the Gulf of Lions, probably on Sète, from which to develop operations mainly to the north-west; an assault to the east of Toulon, in the area already proposed for 'Anvil', whence to develop operations mainly to the north; an assault on the Gulf of Genoa, which in the right circumstances would combine a threat to the Germans still in Italy and to those in southern France; and an assault on the Italian coast north of Rome, possibly near Civitavecchia, if the course of the campaign demanded. The preparations would concentrate immediately on the four divisions not engaged in 'Diadem'.

The Chiefs of Staff supported these conclusions, which they agreed were as definite as was possible until 'Diadem' was under way; and on 7th May, they asked the Americans to accept them as fulfilling the conditions on which King had offered the extra assault shipping from the Pacific. On the 8th, the Joint Chiefs of Staff replied that the plans could be regarded as satisfactory, and that accordingly they would send to the Mediterranean nineteen L.S.T. each carrying one L.C.T. (instead of the twenty-six L.S.T. mentioned earlier), the first nine to arrive by 20th June, and the rest in batches up to about 20th July. So matters stood on the eve of the offensive in Italy, which would decide between Wilson's four possibilities.

'Diadem' had been timed to start on the night of 11th/12th May. By then, Fifth Army on the left of the line disposed of two Corps (one American, one French) containing six divisions, while VI Corps at Anzio had a further six divisions.[2] Eighth Army, immediately to the

---

[1] See Map IV.

[2] See Map V, facing p. 270.

east, comprised four Corps containing some 9½ divisions, with a striking force of one British Corps and one Canadian Corps on the left, a Polish Corps facing Monte Cassino, and a British Corps on the right. To the east of the Apennines, one British Corps disposed of three divisions. The Germans, leaving a holding force of three infantry divisions east of the Apennines, deployed some 6½ divisions to the west, three divisions facing Eighth Army in the mountains, another three defending the Liri valley and the coastal hills. Five German divisions contained the bridgehead at Anzio. These dispositions showed the success of General Alexander's measures of deception, which had led the Germans to expect a further reinforcement at Anzio or a fresh landing in the rear, rather than a fresh concentration of strength at points on the main front. Provided therefore that the enemy continued to stand for as long as possible in his southern positions, and did not gradually retire at once, the Allies might expect a rapid withdrawal once they had broken the crust of the defence.

Throughout April and the first ten days of May, the Allied air forces concentrated on the German communications between the main front and the line Pisa-Rimini, which they seriously disrupted; and on the night of 11th/12th May, preceded by a heavy artillery barrage, both Armies moved to the attack. After some hours of early success, proving that tactical surprise had been achieved, the familiar bitter fighting ensued for the smallest gains. But by 14th May, Fifth Army had moved forward to a point on the western bank of the Liri some seven miles due south of Cassino, threatening route 6 from the west, while Eighth Army had extended the bridgehead over the Rapido to the west of Monte Cassino, and had closed on the route itself. The heavy fighting during these two days, against a superior enemy, had weakened the German divisions facing Fifth Army; and in the next two days, it cleared the mountains west of the Liri valley almost as far north as the transverse road from Pico to the coast. On the 16th, after splitting the German front in this region, the French were shelling the road itself, and the German right flank seemed about to collapse. A further advance into the valley could now threaten route 6 to the north of Monte Cassino.

The attack on that position was entrusted to the Poles on 17th May. By nightfall they were just below the last height, and before dawn most of the enemy withdrew. On the morning of 18th May, the Poles raised their Eagle over the ruins of the monastery.

The fall of Cassino heralded the drive up the valley which the Allies had awaited since the previous November. The Germans had now to fall back on the Adolf Hitler Line,[1] whose defence they had already weakened by committing themselves so stubbornly to the south. Kesselring, moreover, had been misled until the 16th by the continued

[1] See p. 256 above.

measures of deception which still seemed to threaten a landing in his rear. He thus scarcely had time to garrison the Hitler Line before Eighth Army was upon it; but after an anxious day on the 18th he managed to stabilize the position, and Alexander was forced to pause for a deliberate attack.

Over the next few days, the enemy also managed to rally in the west. It was 22nd May before the French could take Pico, and make contact with the Canadians on the left of Eighth Army. On the coast itself, the Americans advanced as far as Terracina.

As soon as Cassino had fallen, Alexander ordered VI Corps at Anzio to prepare to break out from the bridgehead when the Hitler Line had been breached. On the 23rd, Eighth Army launched its attack on this position, and by noon on the 24th the main defences had fallen. The Germans, while still capable of delaying action, had now to retire towards the Caesar Line.[1] The time had come for the troops at Anzio to enter the battle. The disintegration of the main front had forced Kesselring in the past few days to remove most of his armour from the area, and to sacrifice his immediate mobile reserve. When VI Corps attacked on 23rd May, it therefore encountered only moderate resistance, and on the 25th it made contact with Fifth Army on route 7. By then, its armour was moving swiftly north towards the Alban Hills. Almost four months to the day since the assault on Anzio had been launched, the bridgehead was relieved and the two Allied Armies were advancing fast on Rome.

VI Corps was now geographically the spearhead of the attack. Alexander therefore directed it along route 7, while he drove to the east of the capital with Eighth Army, and with the rest of Fifth Army to the mouth of the Tiber. The capture of Rome itself, and of its communications with the sea, thus fell to Fifth Army. Eighth Army was to pursue the enemy up the valley of the Tiber towards the road and rail junction of Terni.

Eighth Army moved up the Liri valley with three Corps throughout the last week of May. By 1st June, the Canadians were in Ferentino, while two British Corps pushed to the north-east. Meanwhile, Fifth Army tackled the Caesar Line south and south-east of Rome. Encountering stiffer opposition west of route 6, VI Corps switched the weight of its attack to the north, and by 27th May had pushed the enemy back to his defended positions in the southern Alban Hills. There it was held until the 30th, while Fifth Army paused to regroup for a decisive attack. But by the night of 2nd June, the Germans began to give away along the front south of Rome, and the next day, while Eighth Army was trying to catch and maul the retiring troops to the north-east, Fifth Army pressed on towards the capital by every road. At 7.15 p.m. on 4th June, American troops drove into the Piazza

[1] See p. 256 above.

Venezia, the first conquerors of Rome for fourteen centuries to enter the city from the south. Thirty-five hours later, Allied troops landed on the beaches of Normandy.

Important and encouraging as it was, the capture of Rome was not the final object of 'Diadem'. As the Prime Minister telegraphed to Alexander,[1] 'The cop is the one thing that matters'. The delaying actions which the enemy had managed to fight in the Alban Hills had prevented his encirclement; but the Allies were now chasing hard up the Tiber valley and through the open country north of Rome. The pace was set in the western sector, where the terrain was easier and the enemy more disorganized. VI Corps moved swiftly up the coast, and on 7th June entered Civitavecchia, the most considerable port in the west between Naples and Leghorn and one of the possible objects, as considered a month before, of an assault.[2] By the 14th, the harbour was in use to support the further advance. Meanwhile, VI Corps had turned inland, its main forces capturing the Etruscan stronghold of Tarquinia on the 9th, and an advanced force seizing the airfield at Viterbo. At that point, it was relieved and returned to Naples. In the same period, Fifth Army advanced on Viterbo, Eighth Army up the Tiber, and the British Corps east of the Apennines to Pescara.

All of the enemy's divisions were now involved in a difficult and wearing retreat. Most had been badly mauled, and Alexander estimated that, unless considerable reinforcements were sent from elsewhere in Europe, the pace and weight of the advance should carry the Allies without pause through central Italy and, if required, through the line Pisa-Rimini into the valley of the Po. On 6th June, he formed his immediate plans. After reaching the area of Terni, Eighth Army was to move on Perugia and thence on Florence, while Fifth Army proceeded up the coastal plain to the west. On the next day, he sent an appreciation of the position to the C.I.G.S.[3] The Germans had been severely handled, and of the twenty divisions engaged in the battle they now probably disposed at the most of the equivalent of six. Unless reinforcements were received, they were unlikely to muster more than the equivalent of ten divisions in the near future to defend the line Pisa-Rimini, whereas its proper defence would need more than twelve. They must also, by that time, allow for the protection of the Ligurian coast in the west, and of Venice and Istria in the east. Alexander calculated that the enemy would therefore need ten fresh divisions from outside Italy to hold the north against serious attack. The Allied armies, in contrast, were now at the height of their strength and performance. The recent operations had proved their excellence, they had the measure of their opponents, and morale was

[1] See *Closing the Ring*, p. 536.

[2] See pp. 262-3 above.

[3] See Map VIII, facing p. 384.

'irresistibly high'. 'Neither the Apennines nor even the Alps should prove a serious obstacle to their enthusiasm and skill.' Alexander therefore considered that he should reach a line Perugia-Grosseto at the latest by the end of June, and a line Florence-Pisa in the west, and the port of Ancona in the east, during the second half of July. Within another fortnight he should be ready to attack the line Pisa-Rimini with a force of eighteen to twenty divisions, assembled and maintained partly through the ports of Civitavecchia and Ancona. If ordered to advance further, he would then develop his main thrust towards Pistoia and Bologna, whence he could turn either west towards Turin and Genoa, as bases for operations into France, or east towards Padua and Venice as bases for operations into Austria. Alternatively, he could stand on the line Pisa-Rimini, freeing substantial resources for operations outside Italy. If the first course were adopted, Alexander planned to attack Bologna not later than 15th August, using the land and air forces already at his disposal.

These proposals had to be compared with others for the use of the same forces, which by now had advanced further. On 17th May, Wilson submitted a preliminary report on the four possibilities which the Combined Chiefs of Staff had raised on his visit to London. As between the western and the southern coasts of France, and the Dalmatian coast, he favoured the southern coast of France; and as between an assault on Sète and an assault on the Riviera, he favoured the Riviera.[1] The entrance to Sète could be easily blocked, the beaches and their exits were poor, and the area was beyond effective range of fighter cover from Corsica or Italy. He had therefore reverted to 'Anvil' as his first choice, with a strength of two divisions for the assault, rising to five divisions by D + 10 and to ten divisions by D + 90. From the progress of operations in Italy, it seemed likely that an operation on this scale could be launched between the middle of August and the middle of September; but he intended in any case to prepare for smaller operations in the same area, or near Sète if conditions dictated or allowed.

While Wilson was elaborating the plans for southern France, the Prime Minister continued to press the claims of an assault upon Bordeaux ('Caliph').[2] The alternatives were due to be discussed at a Staff Meeting on 8th June, by which time Wilson had hardened on the date of 15th August for 'Anvil', and had provided his detailed demands for the merchant shipping required in that case from July to September. Alexander's appreciation now provided a third possibility for the meeting to discuss. Its effect was much as might have been expected.

---

[1] See Map IV, facing p. 263.

[2] See p. 260 above.

While still anxious to stage an assault from the sea, and in that event favouring 'Caliph' rather than 'Anvil', the meeting decided to seek the Americans' views, and to study the possibilities in the Adriatic afresh.

The debate with the Americans could take place at once; for, following a series of requests from the British, the Joint Chiefs of Staff had consented to visit England from 10th to 15th June, to discuss future strategy in Europe and to inspect the course of the battle in Normandy. Their first meeting was held on the 11th, at Stanwell Place in Middlesex. It did not seem that either side had as yet grasped the precise implication of Alexander's proposals; for while both considered that the armies in Italy must be left free to exploit their success, they also considered that a seaborne assault should be launched in support of 'Overlord' which did not conflict with that object. There was indeed a considerable measure of agreement on its detail. It should be mounted in the Mediterranean on a scale of three divisions, and directed, probably on France, before the end of July. This merely confirmed the trend of opinion before the capture of Rome, and did nothing to reconcile the earlier with more recent arguments.

It was indeed the Americans, and not the British, who at the next meeting on 13th June drew attention to the discrepancy between these conclusions and Alexander's proposals. The Joint Chiefs of Staff then pointed out that an assault on the scale recommended would probably leave no opportunity for an advance into the valley of the Po; and suggested that Alexander should be so informed. The British agreed, apparently without hesitation, that he should halt on the line Pisa-Rimini; but added as a rider that in that event he might launch a seaborne 'hook' against Istria, so as to maintain the offensive. Whatever the merits or the logic of this argument, neither side was then prepared to quarrel over the area of assault. The Americans seem to have been satisfied that they had preserved the idea of a seaborne operation, and the British that they had safeguarded the choice of manoeuvre. The Combined Chiefs of Staff accordingly sent a telegram to Eisenhower and Wilson on 14th June, which summed up the results of the meetings.

> '(1) The Combined Chiefs of Staff have reviewed the relation of 'Overlord' to operations in the Mediterranean in the light of the success of Operation 'Diadem' and of the progress of 'Overlord'. Their views are now as follows.
>
> (2) The overriding necessity is to apply all our forces to the enemy, at the earliest possible moment, in the way best calculated to assist the success of Operation 'Overlord'.
>
> (3) We must complete the destruction of the German Armed Forces in Italy south of the Pisa-Rimini line. No Allied forces should be withdrawn from the battle that are necessary for this purpose.

(4) When we have reached the Pisa-Rimini line, three possible courses of action will be open to us:

(a) An amphibious operation against the South of France;

(b) An amphibious operation against the West of France;

(c) An amphibious operation at the head of the Adriatic.

(5) We cannot make the final choice from among these three courses at the moment. Which will pay us best depends on several factors, at present unknown, such as:

(a) The progress of Operation 'Overlord' with the forces now assigned to it;

(b) The direction and degree of success of the forthcoming Russian offensive;

(c) The German reactions to (a) and (b) above.

The one factor common to all three courses is an amphibious operation, and the Combined Chiefs of Staff have decided to go forward forthwith with preparations on the greatest scale for which resources can be provided and at the earliest date.

(6) As to the scale of these preparations, the Combined Chiefs of Staff consider that the operations should be allocated greater resources than is contemplated at present. They have in mind an assault with three divisions to be made up from landing craft already in or allocated to the Mediterranean, such craft as Eisenhower can release without prejudice to 'Overlord' and such extra help as could be provided from the United States. The C.C.O.S. [*sic*] also propose to provide the lift for at least one full airborne division.

(7) The C.C.O.S. consider that 15th August is too late for the date of the amphibious operation and that we should aim at being ready to launch it by the 25th July so long as this does not limit the completion of operations south of the Pisa-Rimini line.

(8) The C.C.O.S. would observe, on the choice of a plan, that they are not inclined to favour landing in the area of Marseilles because of the strength of the coastal defences and the unprofitable line of advance up the Rhone Valley. The operation in France most likely to help Operation 'Overlord' appears to them to be either a landing initially at Sète designed to lead to the early capture of Bordeaux and to the support of the guerrillas in Southern France, or a direct descent on the West Coast of France so as either to open a port through which to achieve a direct build-up from the U.S.A. or if necessary to afford direct support to the 'Overlord' forces should they not be making sufficient progress.

(9) The planning and preparation of the above operations must evidently begin forthwith, since they will require the closest co-ordination between headquarters of the Mediterranean and 'Overlord' Commands who are requested to submit comments as a matter of urgency after mutual consultation.'

Such was the state of the plans for the development of the southern front, a week after 'Overlord' had been launched and ten days before the Russians' summer offensive began. The choice between them must now depend, no longer on hypothetical alternatives as affected by the fighting in Italy, but on the progress of three connected campaigns, in Italy, in northern France and along the Eastern Front.

(iii)

Developments in Yugoslavia

The retention of the Adriatic as a possible scene of operations focused attention, for the first time in nine months, on the prospect of their development inland. On 8th June, the British Chiefs of Staff asked the Joint Planners to report on the possibilities of exploiting a landing in Istria, and on the 15th this report was received. It had naturally to take account of the position in Yugoslavia.

This had changed in three important respects since the end of 1943. In the interval, the British had dropped Mihailovic, their relations with Tito and their aid to his forces had developed and had been substantially reorganized, and, partly as a result of this increased assistance, the Partisans, though sore pressed, were potentially more effective than before.

Throughout the last quarter of 1943, the British Mission with Mihailovic, strengthened by the arrival of Brigadier Armstrong,[1] pressed him continuously to act more vigorously against the Germans. But by the end of the year it was forced to admit that he seemed unlikely to do so. Mihailovic was in fact by this time in an inextricably confused position, the result of a vain attempt, in impossible circumstances, to oppose the occupying power on his own terms, which differed from those both of the Partisans and of the Western Allies. His aims remained honourable; his practice, thanks to their irrelevance, was tortuous and uncertain. Neither a consistent opponent nor a consistent supporter of the Germans, he was now regarded by them with a wary tolerance punctuated by armed reprisals, and by the Allies with growing irritation and suspicion. His followers began to melt away, particularly in the centre and the south; and by the middle of November 1943, Brigadier Maclean reported that Serbs actually predominated among the Partisans, although command was still exercised by Croats. The contrast between the two movements was becoming too acute for the British to continue satisfactorily the policy of 'equal assistance'.[2]

---

[1] See p. 79 above.

[2] See p. 78 above.

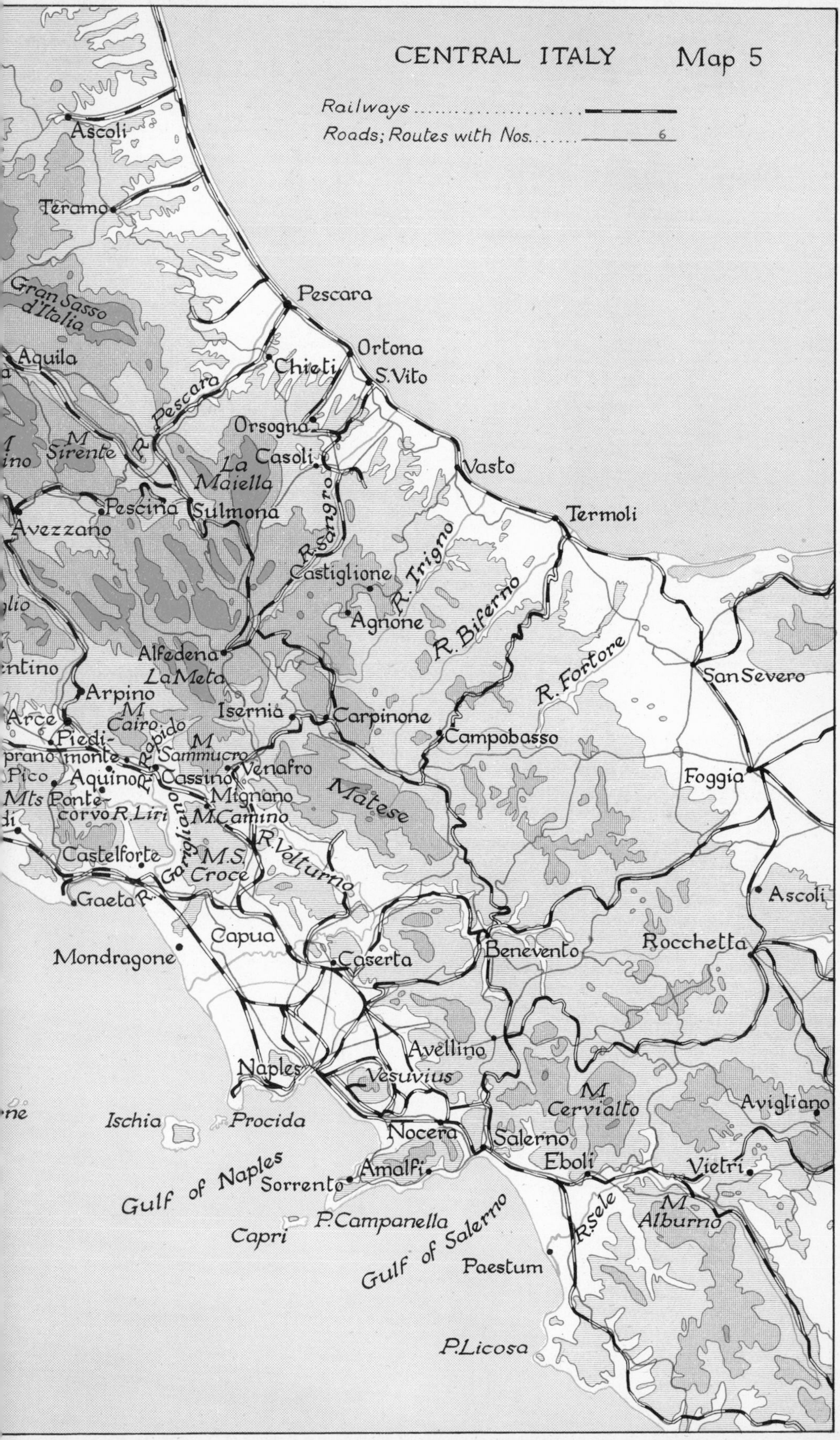
CENTRAL ITALY
Map 5
Railways
Roads; Routes with Nos.
6
Ascoli
Teramo
Gran Sasso d'Italia
Pescara
Ortona
S. Vito
Aquila
Chieti
R. Pescara
Orsogna
M. Sirente
Casoli
La Maiella
Vasto
Pescina
Sulmona
Termoli
Avezzano
R. Sangro
R. Trigno
R. Biferno
Castiglione
Agnone
R. Fortore
Alfedena
La Meta
San Severo
Arpino
M. Cairo
Isernia
Carpinone
Arce
R. Rapido
Campobasso
Piedimonte
M. Sammucro
Venafro
Pico
Aquino
Cassino
Foggia
Mts
Pontecorvo
Mignano
Matese
R. Liri
M. Camino
R. Garigliano
R. Volturno
Castelforte
M.S. Croce
Gaeta
Ascoli
Capua
Rocchetta
Mondragone
Caserta
Benevento
Avellino
Naples
Vesuvius
M. Cervialto
Avigliano
Ischia
Procida
Nocera
Salerno
Eboli
Vietri
Amalfi
Gulf of Naples
Sorrento
M. Alburno
R. Sele
P. Campanella
Capri
Gulf of Salerno
Paestum
P. Licosa

Either Mihailovic must be abandoned in favour of another leader of the Cetniks, or the Cetniks must be abandoned in favour of exclusive aid to the Partisans.

The British were not prepared to take the second course except in the last resort. The Cetniks still represented a significant movement in the country, and one which, under different leadership, might well contain substantial German forces. Moreover they supported the exiled King, to whom the British felt a particular responsibility. For these reasons, the British Government decided in December, 1943 to recommend to King Peter that he should replace Mihailovic as his Minister of War by a man 'of more moderate and balanced views'. Mihailovic himself was meanwhile given a last chance. Early in December, he was asked to destroy two viaducts on the main railway line from Belgrade to the south. But despite the usual assurances of action, accompanied in this case by an offer to renew discussions with Tito, nothing was done; and at the end of the year the British prepared to withdraw their missions as soon as possible.

But in the event the principal missions stayed for another five months, and by that time the break with Mihailovic involved a break with the Cetniks themselves. This was due, not to any further development in the relations between the British and Mihailovic, but to external developments, with which the latter was not concerned but which were intimately concerned with him, in the relations of the British with the exiled Royal Yugoslav Government on the one hand, and on the other with an increasingly powerful and self-conscious government of the Partisans. The Royal Yugoslav Government had cut a sorry figure from the first, and its influence in London rested on the prestige of Mihailovic and on British sympathy with the King. By the winter of 1943, Mihailovic was discredited and the King himself was tired of Ministers, who, under the leadership of the Pan-Serb M. Puric, successfully resisted all efforts to associate the Royal Government more closely with events. Its transfer to Cairo, in September of that year, did not, as had been hoped, induce a greater sense of reality; and the Ministers continued, throughout the subsequent winter and spring, to behave much as they had behaved before.

The sterile manoeuvres of the exiles excited the contempt of the Partisans, as their existence had long excited hostility. But it is likely that, even without this stimulus, the Partisans' own developing organization would have been forced to challenge an absent authority. The turning point, which came at the end of November 1943, was marked by a change of attitude towards the King, whom Partisan propaganda had hitherto conspicuously left alone. While this had no doubt been largely because his cause was thought to have been doomed by his absence, at least it had provided a possible opportunity for some form of reconciliation between the King and Tito, if necessary at the expense of Mihailovic and the exiled Serbs. But at the end of November, the Partisans set up a Provisional Government or National Committee, appointed a President, and formally deprived the Royal Government in Cairo of its powers in and for the country during the war. Tito himself, whose official title hitherto had been Secretary-General of the Yugoslav Communist Party, now became Marshal of Yugoslavia and acting Minister of Defence. As a necessary corollary to this assumption of power, King Peter was forbidden to return to Yugoslavia during the war, and his future was thereafter to be determined by national plebiscite.

All this made it more difficult for the British Government to force on the King the removal of his only champion in the country. Nevertheless, the military situation demanded that if possible Mihailovic should go. It was difficult to decide if his immediate dismissal should be urged on the King, in order to strengthen the position of the Crown, or if the position of the Crown should be strengthened before Mihailovic was dismissed. Events, assisted by the Prime Minister's efforts, favoured the first alternative. In January 1944, Mr. Churchill opened a personal correspondence with Tito, in an effort to reach a compromise which would protect the King. Perhaps not surprisingly, this met with a marked measure of success. Tito was delighted by such recognition of his movement, and flattered by the attention to himself. He replied in moderate strain, and early in February wrote to the Prime Minister that, after consulting the National Committee and others, they would co-operate with King Peter on condition that he and the British no longer recognized Mihailovic and the Government in Cairo, and provided that he accepted the laws promulgated by the National Committee and the result of a national plebiscite at the end of the war. The Prime Minister, encouraged by private reports from Maclean, replied in friendly terms; and on 22nd February, spoke warmly of the Partisans in the House of Commons and revealed the British Government's dissatisfaction with Mihailovic.

All this naturally had its effect, and in March it seemed possible that the Partisans might go so far as to deal with an exiled Royal Government which included two members not unsympathetic to them, the Croats M. Subasic and General Simovic. The British accordingly tried to persuade the King to dismiss the Puric Government, including Mihailovic, and to form a new Government including Subasic and Simovic, before Tito could seize the interval to act further on his own. But the King, though ready to rid himself of Puric, could not consent to work with Simovic, and not unnaturally remained anxious to have a Serb as his Prime Minister. The discussions dragged on, and by the end of April Mr. Churchill was fast losing patience. But on 15th May, the King announced that he was about to dismiss Puric and Mihailovic in favour of a new Government which would include Subasic and, if possible, both Serbs and Croats. Puric himself went on 18th May. But it soon became clear, as the King had feared but had not been sure, that no Serb would consent to succeed him unless Mihailovic remained Minister of War; and at the end of May, the King therefore turned to the Croats, and formed a new Government in which the Serbs were not represented. He had now complied with the first of Tito's demands. The British accordingly pressed for their reward. Churchill had already informed Tito of these developments, and had received his assurance that comment in Yugoslavia would be withheld until the situation had had time to clear; and on 1st June, when the changes were made public, Mr. Eden informed the War Cabinet that Subasic would probably soon go to Bari to establish contact with the Marshal.

Meanwhile, arrangements had been made to withdraw the British missions from Mihailovic as soon as the King had acted. Individual officers had slipped away from different areas between December and February, and the rest were ordered in March to concentrate on Mihailovic's headquarters. It was 20th May before all had assembled. Between the 28th and 30th, aircraft from Italy flew in and removed them all, together with some escaped Allied prisoners of war. By 1st June, when Mihailovic was publicly abandoned by King Peter and the British, no British remained with the Cetniks.

The removal of the British missions meant the removal of aid to the Cetniks at the very time when supplies for Yugoslavia had just been reorganized and greatly increased. During the first quarter of 1944, the amount of material carried by air, although more than double that of the preceding quarter, was still small, and most was carried by sea, largely to the islands off the coast. The weight of supplies by sea, indeed, was more than twenty times that of supplies by air, amounting to some 6,400 tons compared with between 230 and 320 tons. But in the second quarter of the year, the airborne supplies rose to between 2,600 and 3,100 tons, and for the first time large numbers of wounded Partisans were ferried out of the country, while seaborne supplies declined slightly to some 5,600 tons. This marked and sudden increase in the volume of the air traffic was the result of a reallocation of aircraft, and of a reorganization of their command, which proceeded throughout the first half of 1944.

In the summer of 1943, thirty-two bombers had been assigned to supporting the guerrillas in the central and eastern Mediterranean.[1] Compared with the same activities in other areas, this was generous: four aircraft were allowed for similar work in Italy and southern France, sixteen in western Europe, and six in central Europe. But

---

[1] See p. 79 above.

when the inevitable subtractions had been made for training and repair, when the inherent difficulties of weather and geography in south-east Europe are considered, and when the more urgent demands of the Italian campaign had been met, little enough remained for the tasks in hand. In December 1943, S.O.E.[1] accordingly asked the British Chiefs of Staff for a total of fifty-six operational aircraft in the Mediterranean and forty-four in England. The request came at a time when the merits of S.O.E. itself, recently shaken by a serious failure in Holland, were under debate; and it was not until the middle of January, 1944 that the figures were considered. The Chief of the Air Staff then stated that in fact these demands were likely to be met, mainly from production, by the end of February. The effectiveness of the Mediterranean force was also about to be raised, by the transfer of its bases from North Africa to the area of Brindisi; but in view of the doubts recently cast upon S.O.E.'s organization, Portal proposed that control of the aircraft should be placed in the hands of the theatre air forces.

This proposal had in turn to be considered as part of the general reorganization of subversive activities and diplomatic agencies in the eastern Mediterranean, on which there had been discussion since November, 1943[2] between the Prime Minister, the Foreign Office, the Chiefs of Staff and General Wilson. It was generally agreed that the Supreme Commander should exercise a more direct control over the affairs of that area than had been possible hitherto. But the interests of the Foreign Office and of the Americans, whose own chain of authority was under review, had to be considered; and it was not until March 1944, when the Americans appointed their own missions to Tito and Mihailovic, that the agencies could finally be reorganized to allow a settlement of command. S.O.E.'s administration was then left in Cairo, but operational control was transferred to General Alexander's headquarters in Italy, with an advanced force at Bari for activities 'across the Adriatic'.

This in turn made it possible to reorganize the control of all Allied operations in the Balkans. Wilson now proposed that a new headquarters should be set up at Bari for a Balkans Air Force, which under an air commander would co-ordinate all activities of whatever sort relating to that area. The Combined Chiefs of Staff soon approved the details, and on 15th June Balkans Air Forces were established under the command of Air Vice-Marshal William Elliot, to co-ordinate, subject to the concurrence of the respective Commanders-in-Chief, the planning and execution of 'all operations, Air, Sea, Land and Special, on and across the Dalmatian Coast.' Their liaison with Brigadier

[1] See p. 77 above.

[2] See p. 206 above.

Maclean's mission in Yugoslavia was carried out by a subordinate command known as Land Forces, Adriatic; and they received diplomatic advice from, and offered military advice to, a representative of the British diplomatic adviser to the Supreme Commander. In June 1944, Maclean's mission and S.O.E. had thus been brought satisfactorily within the aegis of the Mediterranean Command, although the former retained its right to communicate with the Foreign Office and with the Prime Minister.

While the British were overhauling their organization for Yugoslavia, the Americans and the Russians established their own organizations for the first time inside that country. American agents had been associated with the British missions since April 1943, and the authorities in Washington suggested in the autumn that they should be coordinated locally. The British, however, were not in favour, and the two organizations therefore continued to work together uneasily throughout the winter. But the prospect, in January 1944, of a transfer of military responsibility to Italy, precipitated the development which two months later was in fact to make it possible. The Americans decided to maintain their own mission with Tito, distinct from that of Maclean and responsible to its own authorities in Cairo; and this was inaugurated officially in March.

The arrangements in Cairo worked quite well throughout 1944, as far as the Partisans were concerned. Their weakness was revealed rather by a *contretemps* over Mihailovic. The American officers in Serbia had never been in close touch with the British, and when the latter prepared to leave Mihailovic, the former were ordered to stay. Early in April, indeed, the Americans prepared to send out a new intelligence mission, which there seemed reason to suppose that the President himself had approved. The Prime Minister was sufficiently perturbed to write to him, asking that the mission should be stopped. Mr. Roosevelt at once agreed; in May the British were withdrawn; but in August they discovered that, despite the President's undertaking in April, the American mission had reached Mihailovic, and that the latter was naturally making capital out of it. The Prime Minister again protested, pointing out the serious implications of pursuing two directly contrary policies in Yugoslavia; and early in September, the President agreed to withdraw the mission at once. After some resistance from the officers concerned, all Americans in Mihailovic's territory left at the beginning of November, 1944.

Russian policy throughout this period presented fewer difficulties for the British. The first, tentative proposal of a Russian mission to Yugoslavia seems to have been made in October, 1943; but despite a welcome from the British, it was not until December that it was raised seriously. At Teheran M. Molotov informed Mr. Eden that he favoured the establishment of a mission in Yugoslavia, based with the British on

North Africa and possibly divided, by some means, between the headquarters of the Cetniks and of the Partisans. But it seemed to the British that he had given the matter little thought; and when they explained the difficulties of such a course, and their own attitude to Mihailovic, the Russians agreed to reconsider the nature of their representation.

This apparent ignorance persisted for some time after the mission itself appeared in Italy, towards the end of January, 1944. Its members seemed amiable, but far from clear what they proposed to do. They were indeed still prepared to visit both Tito and Mihailovic; but in February, when they were flown direct to the former's headquarters, they abandoned the idea. For the next few months, they remained in the background with the Partisans, apparently exercising little influence on policy. They disposed of few supplies, although they later secured the lease of six American transport aircraft based on Bari; unlike the British mission, they seemed to take no part in the discussion of military operations or in the technical training of the Partisans; and, as far as Maclean could determine, did not venture to expound Communism to Tito. This appreciation may in fact have underrated the Russians' importance. There is certainly reason to suspect that they prepared the ground politically for a Partisan descent on Serbia in the spring. But in general they remained inconspicuous, content apparently to observe developments with which they did not interfere. Only on one significant occasion did they take the initiative, when one of their aircraft intervened early in June to rescue Tito and the Allied missions from a German attack.

In January 1944, the German Sixth Offensive, which two months before had retrieved the northern plains and most of the coast from the Partisans, died away in the mountains of Bosnia and Croatia;[1] and during the next two months the guerrillas rested and reorganized within the central massif, in preparation for the spring. Towards the end of March, better weather and fresh aircraft brought substantial supplies from Italy, the Germans were again subjected to the familiar raids and sabotage, and on the 18th the Partisans returned to the offensive with a strong attack on Serbia. This soon made headway against the local garrisons of satellite troops, and threatened further to disorganize the deployment of the German forces, already extended by the Russians, operations on the Eastern Front. At the end of the month, when all seemed to be going well, Tito suggested that he should send Maclean with a senior Partisan officer to Wilson's headquarters, to discuss arrangements for supplies and for concerting operations. Wilson at once agreed to receive the party, and on 15th April Maclean and the emissary arrived at Algiers. After satisfactory talks, they left on the 20th for London, where they saw the Prime Minister,

[1] See p. 82 above.

the C.I.G.S. and others. Towards the end of that month, therefore, the hopes of the Partisans were high. They had survived the fighting of the winter, and were now receiving considerable supplies from Italy; their rôle in the Allied strategy was clearly accepted; their representative was received in London by the highest authorities; and Mihailovic was in disfavour. In turn, British influence in Yugoslavia was at its height, and the British expected much of the Partisans.

But, as in the previous October, the picture changed dramatically within a few weeks. Early in April, the enemy succeeded in halting the Partisans in Serbia, and by the middle of the month they were on the retreat. Separate raids on German areas in Croatia were also repelled, and by the third week in April the Germans were able to renew the offensive in the central mountains. Determined now to crush the Partisans, they decided if possible to capture Tito himself. On 25th May, after several days of increasing air activity, mountain troops were dropped around the Partisans' headquarters in Bosnia. Tito, with his staff, escaped into the hills, where they joined the main Partisan forces and once again took to the woods. But the guerrillas were unprepared and disorganized, and for a week they were on the move. Substantial German forces now converged on the central mountains, and on 3rd June Tito decided to evacuate his headquarters to one of the islands off the coast. They were taken off by Allied aircraft from Bari, a Russian plane arriving first for Tito and the heads of missions. After a few days in Bari, the headquarters were transferred to the Yugoslav island of Vis, where they remained, under British protection, for the next three months.

As soon as they appreciated the scale of the German offensive, the Western Allies provided air support for the hard-pressed Partisans; and by the end of May, nearly three hundred medium bombers and some two hundred fighters were engaged on operations over Yugoslavia. The enemy, in consequence, soon lost control of the air and was unable to contain, or often to find, the elusive guerrillas. By the middle of June, the Seventh Offensive seemed likely to follow the Sixth, in the series which the Partisans had weathered successfully. The Germans had again cleared their communications in Serbia and Bosnia, thus strengthening their position in the event of an Allied landing in the Balkans; had captured some of the Partisans' most important landing grounds for aircraft, which however were soon replaced by others; and were still worrying the central forces. But they had failed to take Tito and the Allied missions, and to smash, or even to disperse, the hard core of the movement. In July, they were once more largely on the defensive, against an increasing weight of Allied air attacks and of guerrilla activities.

When the British Joint Planning Staff, therefore, was asked to consider the prospects of operations inland from Istria, it could count on the survival of the Partisans, and could expect a measure of co-operation from them. There seemed little danger of independent action from Tito which might embarrass the Western Allies, lodged as he was under their protection and on terms of increasing intimacy with the British. Diplomatic issues were temporarily quiescent, while the recent operations had disclosed the limits to the enemy's strength. If the Germans seemed unlikely to be defeated by the growing power of the Partisans, they in turn could not remove it, or prevent it from contributing to an Allied campaign. It was against such a background in the middle of June that the Joint Planners measured the possibilities in Istria, under the conditions likely to emerge over the next two months, as an alternative to those in southern or western France.

CHAPTER VIII

PREPARATION FOR 'OVERLORD', JANUARY–JUNE, 1944

(i)

The Revised Plan

'OVERLORD' has hitherto appeared in this account as the dominating element in strategy, whose needs determined the form of the intervening campaigns elsewhere. We must now examine some aspects of its own preparation, in relation to their progress.

The effect on the enemy of the Allies' strategy in the east and south of Europe, and its consequences for the 'Overlord' plan, may be gauged from the distribution of his forces throughout the first half of 1944, and of the British deductions from it. In January 1944, the Germans had some 179 divisions on the Eastern Front, 26 in south-east Europe, some 22 in Italy, just under 16 in Norway and Denmark, and 53 in France and the Low Countries of which 35 were north of the Loire. The figures did not alter greatly over the next five months; and on 6th June, there were some 165 divisions on the Eastern Front, 28 divisions in south-east Europe, 28 in Italy, 18 in Norway and Denmark, and 59 in France and the Low Countries of which 41 were north of the Loire. The Mediterranean strategy thus succeeded, within the context of the dominating Russian successes, in containing a rising proportion of the German forces throughout this period, but did not succeed in preventing the enemy from reinforcing north-west Europe. Indeed, in the winter of 1943/44, and again just before 'Overlord' was launched, the number of German divisions rose in France and the Low Countries at times when they did not fall, but rather rose slightly, in Italy and in south-east Europe. This increase in strength in the west is subject to severe qualifications. The extra divisions, which were not provided at the expense of the south, were also not provided at the expense of the extreme north, and only in one—though important—respect at the expense of the Eastern Front. In January 1944, there were twenty-four Panzer divisions facing the Russians, and eight in the rest of Europe: in mid-June, the figures were eighteen and fifteen. There was thus a significant transfer of armour, which took place mostly from the middle of April. Otherwise, neither the Russian front nor the garrisions in the north seem to have been weakened significantly on behalf of the western sector. Nor did its reinforcements come from a central reserve, for no appreciable reserve had existed since the summer of 1943. They came in fact partly from the increasingly muddy pool of German and satellite manpower—from troops used hitherto in home defence or on administrative duties, from a limited transfer of men from the other Services, from an ever widening demand on German civilians, and from an increasing dilution of German formations with troops from eastern Europe—and partly from the exchange and reorganization of formations between France and the active fronts. The western area, indeed, acted as the closest equivalent at the enemy's disposal to a central reserve. Within limits dictated by the Allies' operations and threats, the proportion of divisions forming, training or on the move was always considerably higher there than in other theatres, and for the same reasons many were always below strength or in a low state of readiness. Their material varied widely, only some were fully mobile, and morale varied with efficiency. The photographs of large groups of elderly men and youths of a low military category, and of horse-drawn vehicles and second-rate equipment, which surprised the British and American publics in the late summer of 1944, confirmed a state of affairs whose extent was known to their Intelligence in the previous winter and spring.

But while the value of the reinforcement may thus be qualified, it cannot be dismissed; and there was even a certain, last-minute improvement in some of the 'defensive' formations in France which had not been disturbed so gravely by the constant movements. The net effect was to be seen in the British estimates, over the first half of 1944, of the enemy's rate of reinforcement against the 'Overlord' assault. From the beginning of the year, it seemed doubtful if Cossac's initial figures of opposition, on which the plan had been accepted, would prove correct;[1] and as the months went by, the estimates tended to rise.[2] The strategy decided at Cairo thus seemed unlikely to enforce the conditions specified originally for 'Overlord'; and the British, as we have seen, did not expect 'Anvil' to supply the answer. The progress of the operations in Italy, in the late winter and spring, did not redress the balance; and by the end of April 1944, when the enemy's main dispositions seemed to have been made, the picture for June looked in some respects forbidding.

The more the estimates of opposition rose, the greater the emphasis that had to be placed on the other measures necessary to fulfil Cossac's conditions for invasion. These measures fell into two distinct categories. First, the effect of the greater opposition could be partly removed by a greater weight and area of assault. This was secured by

[1] See p. 57 above.
[2] See p. 281 opposite.

British Estimates of German Opposition to the 'Overlord' Assault (including coastal divisions and divisions from reserve.)

Time By	2nd January	February	30th April	17th May
Evening D day	3–4		3+	3+
Evening D+1		5–6	7–8	7–8
Evening D+2	8+		9	9
Morning D+4		12+		
Morning D+7			18	18
Evening D+7	11+			
Morning D+10		25		
Morning D+20		30		
Morning D+25			26+	30
Morning D+30			30–36	34–40
Morning D+35		37½		

the revised plan in January and February, 1944.[1] But secondly, the opposition itself must be reduced by delaying the enemy's movements and, if possible, by diverting his attention elsewhere. Throughout the six months before the invasion, a greater burden thus fell on the preparatory measures of attack and deception, as the limits of the complementary strategy of containment were revealed.

The Combined Chiefs of Staff issued their directive to General Eisenhower, through the Joint Chiefs of Staff, on 11th February, 1944. Its first four paragraphs read as follows:

'DIRECTIVE TO SUPREME COMMANDER, ALLIED EXPEDITIONARY FORCE

1. You are hereby designated as Supreme Allied Commander of the forces placed under your orders for operations for the liberation of Europe from the Germans. Your title will be Supreme Commander, Allied Expeditionary Force.

2. Task. You will enter the continent of Europe and in conjunction with other United Nations undertake operations aimed at the heart of Germany and the destruction of her armed forces. The date for entering the continent is the month of May, 1944. After adequate channel ports have been secured, exploitation will be directed towards securing an area that will facilitate both ground and air operations against the enemy.

3. Notwithstanding the target date above you will be prepared at any time to take immediate advantage of favourable circumstances, such as withdrawal by enemy in your front, to effect a re-entry into the continent with such forces as you have available at the time . . .

[1] See pp. 232-6 above.

CHAIN OF COMMAND

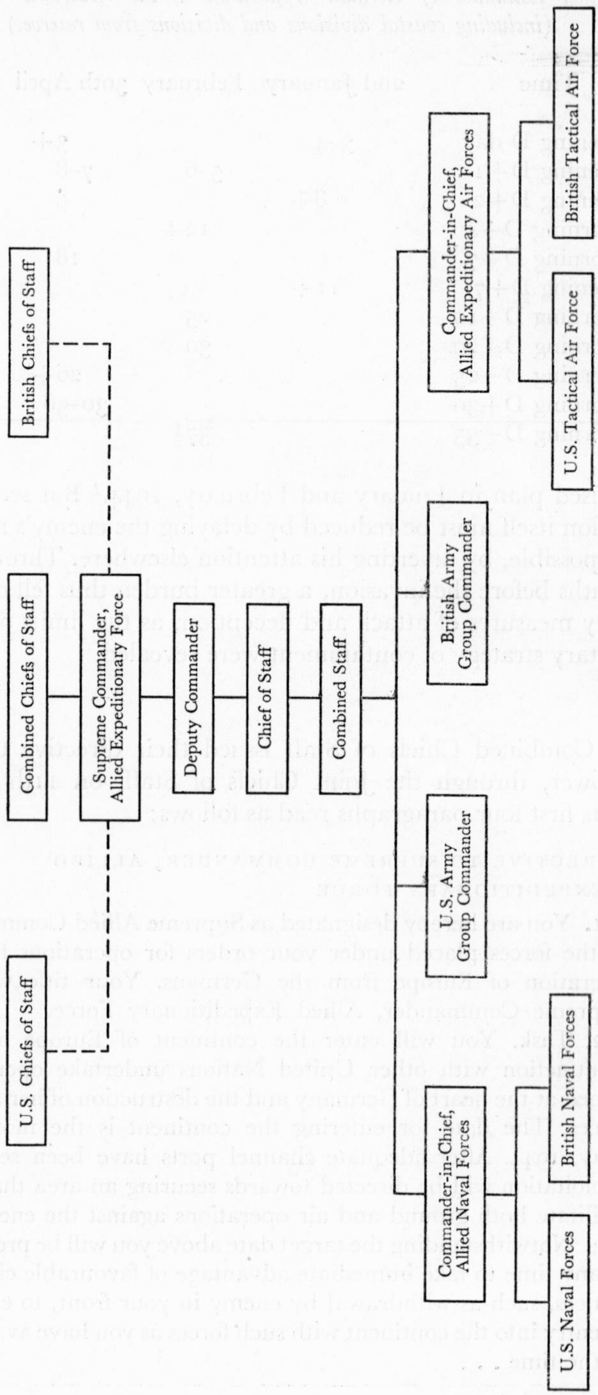

> 4. Command. You are responsible to the Combined Chiefs of Staff and will exercise command generally in accordance with [the chart shown]. Direct communication with the United States and British Chiefs of Staff is authorized in the interest of facilitating your operations and for arranging necessary logistic support.'

The outline of the revised plan for the assault and first phase of the campaign was ready in essentials on 1st February, and was thereafter amended in detail until the middle of April. The complementary administrative plan, which also suffered some detailed alteration later, appeared on 8th February. The design was as follows.[1] The first assault on D-day would be carried out by a force of five seaborne divisions with some additions. Two American divisions of First U.S. Army would land in the west, one at the eastern base of the Cotentin peninsula due west of the estuary of the Vire, one to the east of that river. Three British divisions of Second (British) Army would land at the same time on three beaches further east, between Carentan and the river Orne. Seven hours before these landings began, two American airborne divisions (increased later from one as specified in February) would drop behind the most westerly American beach, and one British airborne division would drop on the eastern bank of the river Orne, at its estuary north-east of Caen. Second Army was to develop the bridgehead to the south of a line Caen-St. Lo and south-east of Caen, so as to secure sites for airfields and to protect First Army's flank. First Army was meanwhile to strike north-west as fast as possible from the base of the peninsula towards Cherbourg, and to advance southwards towards St. Lo to conform to the pace of the British advance. This phase was to be complete on D+9, although Cherbourg might not be cleared finally for some days or weeks thereafter. By D+17, which was to mark the end of the first period of the 'build-up', the two Armies should stand on a line Cabourg–east of Caen–Condé–Vire–Granville.

The date and time of the assault were determined by the state of tide and moon. In order to preserve the shipping from underwater obstacles, and the troops from a long advance across exposed beaches, it was decided to attack when the tide was at half flood, and to accompany the disembarkation with armour fitted specially for the sandy approaches. While the state of the tide thus governed the seaborne landings, the state of the moon governed those from the air; for while the airborne forces should approach their targets in the dark, they must be able to identify them on arrival by moonlight. To reconcile these conditions to the tactical plan, the invasion must take place on a day when the tide was at half flood on the east coast of the Cotentin peninsula forty minutes after first light, following a night when the

[1] See Inset to Map VI, facing p. 279.

moon rose at between 1 a.m. and 2 a.m. This limited the suitable days in any month to three, the first of which in June was the 5th. Eisenhower accordingly chose that day for D-day.

After the assault, men, vehicles and supplies were to be landed through all five beaches, if possible on the remaining three tides of D-day and D+1. The rate of reinforcement now allowed for some nine divisions (excluding the airborne troops) to be ashore and effective by D+3, compared with 8⅓ as originally estimated, and just over twenty by D+14, compared with 19⅔.

These divisions would be landed across the beaches. But their maintenance, and that of the greater force which would follow immediately, presented a very difficult problem in the absence of a port or harbour. The Allies could not count on using any of the small harbours in the Baie de la Seine for several days after the assault, or a great port (Cherbourg, Nantes or Le Havre) for several weeks. Cossac had insisted in the summer of 1943 that eighteen divisions at least must be supported across the beaches within the first fortnight. In February 1944, it was laid down that arrangements for supplying the whole of the invasion force across the beaches must be complete within the same period, and must continue until Cherbourg and the ports of the Loire and Seine were all in working order. The answer was found in the most careful preparation for immediate supply, partly from a line of ships sunk off the beaches, and in the revolutionary idea of transporting across the Channel two large prefabricated artificial harbours, which were intended to serve the purpose of the docks at Cherbourg and Nantes for at least a month.

The revised estimate of operations after D+17 was as follows.[1] The main advance south and south-east was to begin on or after D+20. By D+60, the Allies were to have secured the lodgment area,[2] the Americans having reached a line from the Atlantic coast south of St. Nazaire, along the southern bank of the Loire to a point just beyond Tours, and thence north to a point mid-way between Alençon and Chartres; the British lying between that point and the estuary of the Seine. By D+90, the line should run from just south of the estuary of the Loire, along its southern bank to a point beyond Orléans, thence in a curve north-east to the Seine, and thence following the course of that river to the sea. Paris might fall soon after D+120, in October.

The numbers of men and quantities of material involved in the first phase, were impressive even for the Second World War. In the event, 185,000 men and 19,000 vehicles (some of revolutionary types) were carried across the Channel on D-day and D+1, in over 4,000 landing ships and craft, supported by some 1,300 merchant ships and ancillary vessels, and over 1,200 warships of all types, including seven battleships

---

[1] See Map VI, facing p. 279.

[2] See p. 232 above.

PLATE V. 'OVERLORD' COMMANDERS

Back row, left to right: General Bradley, Admiral Ramsay, Air Chief Marshal Leigh-Mallory, General Bedell Smith.
Front row, left to right: Air Chief Marshal Tedder, General Eisenhower, General Montgomery.

and twenty-three cruisers. Another 19,000 men were carried by air, by a force of 1,087 transport aircraft and 804 gliders. Some 10,000 Allied aircraft supported the landings in various operations. More ships and aircraft carried out measures of deception in the eastern Channel, and others again covered the operations to east and west, in the Western Approaches and in the North Sea. Within the next few days, two artificial harbours, capable between them of handling eventually 12,000 tons of supplies and 2,500 vehicles a day, were placed in position by a force of one hundred tugs and ferries. Before they were in working order, in the first five days alone, over 60,000 tons of ammunition and other supplies were brought ashore. At the end of the first eleven days, 641,170 British, Canadians and Americans had been landed in north-west France. The operation dwarfed all others hitherto undertaken—the invasions of North Africa and Sicily, the landings at Salerno and Anzio, the assaults on the Pacific islands. It was indeed the greatest conjunct operation in the history of war.

It was also, as it remained, the most complex. Within a year, indeed, plans were being drawn up for an invasion on an even greater scale, to take place in November, 1945 against Japan. But while the forces involved were then larger, their preparation and assembly, undertaken in lonely islands and ocean spaces far from the United States, were simpler than in Europe. The process was not imposed on a highly developed and intricate society, already strained and distorted by war and in continuing danger of attack from the air, nor was it mounted and launched within easy range and almost under the eye of the enemy. 'Overlord' was not only a vast and intricate operation; it provided both a complication and a climax for the British war economy, affecting in different degrees almost every aspect of the national life.

It is not our task to examine either the details of these preparations or their effects on the life of the country. The former are the concern of the historians of the campaign, the latter of the historians of the British war economy and production. Nor, therefore, are we concerned with the machinery of organization, which indeed in the six months before the invasion provides virtually a microcosm of the United Kingdom at war. For the climax of the grand strategy for 1944 had passed, by the beginning of that year, largely beyond the review of the strategic authorities, into the province on the one hand of the 'Overlord' headquarters and on the other of a nexus of military and civil committees. This is not to say, of course, that the central authorities were not concerned with the preparations, and that Ministers and the Chiefs of Staff retired, like Moltke on the eve of Sedan, to read French novels and await the result. On the contrary, they supervised the process closely and continuously; but in their individual capacities as Ministers and as the professional heads of the armed forces, rather than as a central committee. It was indeed typical that the War

Cabinet 'Overlord' Committee, set up in January, 1944 to act as the pivot for all this effort, should have met only eight times between the beginning of February and the end of April, while its sub-committees on transport and security, which were in fact typical inter-departmental organs, met often and prepared most of the decisions. The great operation itself was preparing in a thousand different ways throughout the country. The strategic authorities meanwhile were concerned more directly with ensuring that its necessary conditions should be achieved: with the strategy of containment whose progress we have already followed, and with the development and consequences of those other preparatory conditions which were becoming steadily more important. From the point of view of the commanders, their impact upon the operation may therefore seem uneven and indirect, now isolating for attention a single aspect of the preparations, now concentrating on the political or diplomatic effects. No valid pattern emerges, and the central authorities seem to be relegated to the fringe of events. But while the relation between the factors may not be clear from the vantage of the operation itself, in fact they enjoyed a strategic connexion which was essential to its success. Surprise, delay and containment provided the context for the assault; and it was in support of the first two elements of this strategy that Ministers and Chiefs of Staff debated the three main issues which we shall now examine: the employment and distribution of the air effort and the pattern of its command; the diplomatic consequences of the measures of security; and, affecting the first and affected by the second, the treatment and position of the French.

(ii)

The Rôle of the Air: 'Pointblank' and the Transportation Plan

'The strategic air arm', wrote General Eisenhower on 1st February, 1944, 'is almost the only weapon at the disposal of the Supreme Commander for influencing the general course of action, particularly during the assault phase'. 'It was all a question', von Rundstedt remarked later of the invasion, 'of air force, air force and again air force'. Both the critical importance and the success of the air effort for 'Overlord' cannot indeed be overestimated. Without the reduction of the Luftwaffe's fighting capacity, and the widespread delay of movement by land, the assault might well have failed; and the first result depended solely, and the second principally, on air operations. The air also played an important part in supporting the complementary measures of deception and subversion: by the substantial effort which it devoted to the Pas de Calais (partly caused, as we shall see, by its defensive commitments), and by the transport of agents and arms to the French Resistance. Its effect indeed was felt, as was necessary to the task and inherent in the exercise of air power, over many diverse and complementary aspects of the defence of north-west Europe. In the event, during the five months before D-day the Allied air forces from Britain cut the volume of rail traffic throughout north-west Europe significantly, and between northern France and Germany by about 70 per cent; did much to hamper the arrangements for new forms of long-range air warfare, whereby the enemy hoped to forestall the invasion; and finally, in the climax of the last fortnight, utterly disorganized his communications and activities throughout the north-west. By contrast, when an unprecedented assembly of material and men was concentrated on 6th June off the enemy's coastline, the German air force virtually failed to appear.

This satisfactory result was brought about by a particular combination of strategic and tactical bombing over a period of six months. But the effect, satisfactory in retrospect, seemed far from certain at the time. The combination, indeed, then seemed to one of the partners not to be a combination at all, but rather a compromise between two antithetical types of air warfare one of which was misconceived. A severe discussion accordingly took place in the winter and spring on which should receive the clear priority.

The causes and the background of this discussion derived from the Germans' disposition of aircraft throughout the first half of 1944. Three points emerged from the Allies' accurate intelligence. First, there was no great transfer of air strength between east and west over the period: indeed, the Eastern Front was steadily reinforced regardless of France and Germany. This was in fact largely due to the different functions of the Luftwaffe in the different areas: in the east, it was required mainly for close support of the armies and for tactical bombing; in the west, mainly for the defence of the Reich and of its communications with France and with the Mediterranean. The balance of the forces differed accordingly. The new bombers went to the Eastern Front, while the new fighters were divided between the Eastern Front and the west; and such transfers of air strength as took place, mostly in the late spring, were confined principally to the western area itself, between Germany and France. Secondly, there was a serious increase in the total number of German aircraft between July, 1943 and January 1944, from some 4,700 to some 6,700. Thirdly, a further slight rise, to some 7,100 aircraft by May 1944, was accompanied by a marked decrease in their effectiveness, as measured by the number of sorties flown.

These facts between them illustrate the German position, and its effect on the measures open to the Allies. In July 1943, contemplating the figures as they were then estimated, Cossac concluded that:

> 'The most significant feature of the G.A.F. [German Air Force] in western Europe is the steady increase in its fighter strength which, unless checked and reduced, may reach such formidable proportions as to render an amphibious assault out of the question. Above all, therefore, an overall reduction in the strength of the German fighter force between now and the time for the surface assault is essential. . . . This condition, above all others, will dictate whether the amphibious assault can or cannot be successfully launched on any given date.'

But by January 1944, so far from having been reduced or even checked, the numerical strength of the German fighter force had risen alarmingly. Strategic bombing, which had been given high priority at the Quebec Conference, had failed in the last quarter of 1943 to produce its anticipated effect. The high Allied casualties of the summer were reduced, but not to an acceptable figure; while the forecast of a dramatic loss in Germany's productive power, leading to the collapse of her war economy, proved unreal. German war production indeed continued to rise steadily in several vital sectors, including that of aircraft, throughout the year and for much of 1944. This disappointing result was due partly to an increase in the Germans' efficiency, and partly to the Allies' inevitable inexperience of air warfare on such a scale and with such objects. Both British and Americans had overestimated the immediate effect of heavy, scattered destruction on a powerful national economy which was not yet stretched to capacity. Their air authorities were rather in the position of weather prophets, who can forecast correctly the effects of a given situation still distant from them, but who have mistimed its rate of approach and are therefore liable to find that the situation itself has altered in the interval.

But in fact, the continued rise in the numbers of the Luftwaffe, which caused the Allies such anxiety at the turn of the year, was less depressing than the figures suggested. For, like sea power, air power cannot be measured by numbers alone. 'Air superiority', Lord Tedder has remarked,[1] 'is a subtle question; before one has seen the results which flow from it I think one can only sense it. You may say this is a nebulous basis on which to launch major combined operations such as the Sicily and Normandy landings—for which air superiority was an essential pre-requisite—certainly nothing like as satisfactory as an enemy order of battle! I could not help feeling a certain sympathy for my soldier and sailor colleagues in the earlier days who could not understand why, before their operations began, I could only say that I "thought" and "felt" the air situation would be all right . . .' And in

---

[1] *Air Power in War* (n.d., but 1948), p. 40.

fact, while the attacks on Germany were apparently failing to produce the necessary reduction in the numbers of German aircraft, they were inflicting on the Luftwaffe an effect which was revealed only in the period surrounding D-day. The fact that the operations took place over Germany, and that the Allies gained continuously in an offensive technique which their opponents were forced entirely to abandon, confirmed and greatly increased the superiority that the growing strength of the Allied air forces provided. If air power did not obtain the quick results originally postulated, the final effect was still decisive. While the figures of German aircraft available to oppose the assault remained higher than those on which Cossac had demanded a reduction, their value was less than anything for which he could have hoped.

Something of this feeling lay behind the contrary arguments advanced during the technical discussion early in 1944. They were represented by two plans, 'Pointblank'[1] and the Transportation Plan. Despite the recent disappointment, 'Pointblank' seemed to its supporters at the end of 1943 to be on the verge of success. The conditions they had posited, and on which so much effort and discussion had concentrated for the past two years, had at last been provided. Eighth U.S. Army Air Force in England had been brought to the necessary strength, co-ordination had improved between its daylight operations and the night operations of the R.A.F., and the acquisition of new bases in Italy promised for the first time convergent attacks on Germany which would divide the defences and reduce the heavy losses hitherto sustained from the United Kingdom. Both British and American bombing authorities were therefore confident that in the next six months they could justify their claims.

Their confidence was not lessened, but indeed was rather increased, by the demands of 'Overlord'. For if, as they insisted, they could inflict decisive damage on the enemy within the next six months, they would have proved conclusively that strategic bombing could dictate not only the long-term issue of the war, but also the short-term issue of invasion. This would indeed be a triumph for a particular theory of warfare. The strategic air commanders were the more determined that it should be given a fair trial.

The means by which they proposed to achieve their object were the same as before, but with a different order of priorities. 'Overlord' demanded the reduction of the German air force by June, 1944 to a state where it could not oppose the invasion effectively. At the end of January, the Combined Chiefs of Staff accordingly issued a new directive for 'Pointblank', which gave it a new emphasis.[2] Operations were to concentrate even more closely on the German fighter aircraft

---

[1] See p. 6 above.

[2] See p. 5 above.

industry, which had enjoyed the highest priority since June 1943, and attacks on the oil industry (though not begun in the event until May) were now given priority over the destruction of U-boat bases, formerly high on the list. Bomber Command and Eighth U.S. Air Force calculated that, given all the strategic air forces under their control at the end of 1943, they could meet the requirements of 'Overlord' from this programme by the middle of May 1944, and thereafter could switch their main effort to the tactical tasks called for by the invasion itself, while preparing without loss of time for the subsequent destruction of the German economy which remained their goal. But complete success could be achieved only by retaining complete freedom of action and control over all of their resources. Although they differed on the details of the programme itself, Air Chief Marshal Sir Arthur Harris of Bomber Command, and Generals Spaatz and Arnold for the Americans, were at one in stressing the importance of this issue; and Arnold indeed, early in January 1944, stated that its settlement must be regarded a 'major turning point in the war'.

The 'Overlord' authorities, while not disputing the advantages of 'Pointblank', insisted on the other hand that some at least of its forces must be devoted to a task of equal urgency for a given period. It was not enough, as they saw it, to paralyse the German air force by D-day. It was also necessary to ensure that the German army's reserves in the west did not reinforce the divisions in north-west France in time to defeat the invasion. While the reduction of the Luftwaffe was essential, it must therefore be followed or accompanied by the dislocation of the transport system throughout a given area of north-west Europe. This same dislocation, they claimed, would help—possibly better, even, than attacks on oil—to disrupt the German economy.

According to the air authorities for 'Overlord', the attack on communications was therefore a strategic, and not a tactical, task. The strategic air authorities argued that the dislocation of the German fuel industry, which would be achieved by 'Pointblank', would automatically reduce the mobility of the divisions in France, and that the task could then be completed by heavy and sustained attacks on their communications over a short period. Their opponents denied both assumptions. The German army in France already possessed large stocks of fuel; and experience in Italy proved that it was impossible to stop the movement of several divisions to a front by heavy attacks for a short time on a specific area. The only way to do so was to wage a campaign of attrition against the whole system of communications over a fairly wide area for a fairly long period, so that it was in a state of chaos by the time that it was called on to support the extra strain. Experience in Italy again suggested a possible means of success. The basis of movement was power: power must therefore form the main target of attack. The bombing of roads and bridges should be confined to critical points and occasions. The weight of the bombardment should fall rather on the railways, and particularly on the regulating centres which also included servicing facilities, and assemblies of rolling stock and locomotives. By dislocating these focal points continuously, the Allies would automatically disrupt the widespread system which radiated from them, and without obviously disclosing on which sector they wished particularly to concentrate. The area chosen for the main operations should extend from the Belgian and French northern coasts to a line through Reims, Paris and Tours to the mouth of the Loire. Secondary attacks should be delivered on the electric railway system of the south-west region at Tours, and on certain German railway targets within a radius of four hundred miles from England; and the French Resistance should collaborate by destroying as many locomotives as possible. In order to achieve their object, these attacks should be sustained without interruption for a period of three months before D-day.

It is important to appreciate what the Transportation Plan was not, as well as what it was; for it suffered throughout from several misapprehensions. First, it was not designed to satisfy the demands of 'Overlord' in or by itself. It did not claim to prevent all movement along the communications involved, but rather to reduce it to the point at which a given number of divisions could move only at a pace which would prove too slow to defeat the first stage of the invasion. It thus posited a particular degree of success, which could be measured theoretically with some accuracy, but in practice only with difficulty. Secondly, it did not claim to be more than a part, though an essential part, of a wider programme, whether for 'Overlord' or for the weakening of the German economy. It might delay the movement of the German reserves in France; but the necessary air operations must contribute to the initial deception whereby the enemy was disposed incorrectly. It might weaken them on their way to battle; but other operations were needed to weaken and harass the divisions already in the battle area. It might be a necessary preliminary to the assault; but it could still not be carried out without the prior or simultaneous reduction of the German air force which 'Pointblank' was designed to achieve. While therefore, as its proponents claimed, the Transportation Plan formed an integral part both of the air operations for 'Overlord' and of operation 'Pointblank', it was not in itself a complete answer to either.

Nevertheless, although 'Pointblank' and the Transportation Plan were not mutually exclusive, they could be regarded as antithetical, and they seemed, particularly to the strategic air authorities, to pose in classic form the theoretical alternatives open to air power: on the one hand, its use as an independent element of warfare, which could by itself decide the result and secure for the intervening operations the conditions they required; on the other, its use as a powerful and necessary factor in providing those conditions, but within the context of the other operations. The battle on the plans therefore lay at first among the air authorities themselves.

It was waged the more fiercely because it involved a problem of command. Indeed, as was so often the case, the problem of command preceded the strategic problem. In December 1943, the Joint Chiefs of Staff had decided to co-ordinate all American bombing operations against Germany, from the United Kingdom and from Italy, in the headquarters of Eighth U.S. Air Force in England.[1] The directive to General Spaatz, the new commander, provided for the formation of the United States Strategic Air Forces in Europe, from 1st January, 1944. Their relations with the 'Overlord' Command were defined as follows:

> '. . . 2. The United States Strategic Air Forces in Europe will come directly under the command of the Supreme Allied Commander at a date to be announced later by the Combined Chiefs of Staff. In the interim the Chief of the Air Staff, R.A.F., will continue to act as the agent of the Combined Chiefs of Staff, pending transfer of the U.S.S.A.F.E. to the Command of the S.A.C. [Supreme Allied Commander] and will be responsible under the Combined Chiefs of Staff for co-ordination of all 'Pointblank' operations. Under his direction the Commanding General, United States Strategic Air Forces in Europe, will be responsible for the determination of priorities of 'Pointblank' targets to be attacked by the Eighth and Fifteenth Air Forces[2] and for the technique and tactics employed, and is authorised to move the units of the Eighth and Fifteenth Air Forces between theatres within the limits of base area facilities available for his forces.'

Spaatz was also responsible for keeping the Supreme Commander in the Mediterranean informed of his intentions and requirements.

This directive had a dual purpose: to co-ordinate more effectively the operations of the two American bombing forces, from the United Kingdom and from Italy; and to bring them within the aegis of the 'Overlord' Command. To the Americans, they were successive steps in the same process. Both were intended to free the strategic air forces from the immediate control of the Combined Chiefs of Staff, which in the opinion of the Joint Chiefs of Staff was already hampering the conduct of air operations, and would in future hamper liaison between them and the 'Overlord' campaign. As General Marshall put it, 'a

---

[1] See pp. 196-7 above.

[2] See p. 72 above.

PLATE VI. AIR COMMANDERS

Left to right: Air Chief Marshal Harris, General Spaatz.

Committee cannot fight a battle'; still less, therefore, could it co-ordinate its battle with another authority which enjoyed a different and more direct pattern of command. The British Chiefs of Staff, on the other hand, did not admit the inevitable logic of the two steps. They were prepared, reluctantly, to acquiesce in a single command of the American strategic air forces, as a matter ultimately of domestic concern to their allies; but they did not agree that it then, and of necessity, involved the substitution of the Supreme Commander of 'Overlord' for the Combined Chiefs of Staff as the organ of direct control. They still considered, as they had always considered, that 'Pointblank' was a special case, and that it must enjoy a special pattern of command and special relations with other commitments.

This disagreement affected the structure of the 'Overlord' Command itself. Pending the appointment of the Supreme Commander, and the issue of his directive, the air forces allotted to his operations were formed, in November 1943, into the Allied Expeditionary Air Forces, under the Air Commander-in-Chief designate, Air Chief Marshal Sir Trafford Leigh-Mallory.[1] They then consisted of all the British, and a large part of the American, fighters and fighter-bombers in the United Kingdom, and of the necessary transport aircraft. But they did not include any heavy bombers, which remained under the control of Bomber Command and of Eighth U.S. Air Force. The headquarters of the Allied Expeditionary Air Forces thus could not exercise direct control over bombing operations on behalf of the Supreme Commander; and it was to remedy this defect that Air Chief Marshal Tedder was appointed Deputy Supreme Commander in December, 1943.[2] But Tedder's appointment in turn could not take effect until the 'Overlord' Command had been granted the necessary powers; and as the British Chiefs of Staff continued to withhold them, the form of the 'Overlord' air command remained provisional and partial. The Supreme Commander's directive had at last to be issued in February, 1944 without its completion; and the settlement of command, which the Americans had intended to force the strategic issue, in turn awaited its settlement.

The strategic debate itself began with the presentation of the Transportation Plan in January, 1944. This was based on a variety of reports, of which the most important emanated from the Mediterranean Command, where the advantages and detail of such a form of attack had been discussed for some time. As soon as the plan appeared, Leigh-Mallory recommended that, on its approval, Eighth U.S. Air

---

[1] See p. 204 above.

[2] See ibid.

Force should begin the necessary operations over France, Belgium and western Germany, and that S.O.E. should enlist the aid of the Resistance in destroying locomotives throughout France. After various criticisms had been met from the army and the security authorities, the Supreme Commander approved the plan in the middle of February. Leigh-Mallory then called a meeting with Tedder and the strategic air commanders.

Harris and Spaatz at once opposed the plan. They argued that, as an offensive with a precise and limited object, it was doubly open to failure if the degree of success that was either possible or necessary had been miscalculated. And in that case, the reduced form of 'Pointblank' could not compensate for such a failure, and a stronger German air force would be available to support the battle and the successful movement of reserves. A full 'Pointblank', on the other hand, should knock out the German air force and still leave enough time to attack the communications in France, if not with complete success at least without such a waste of effort as the alternative. The arguments turned on technicalities, and the meeting ended with no decision, but merely with the disagreement clearly defined.

Throughout the rest of February, the Transportation Plan was therefore again examined in detail; and on 2nd March, Leigh-Mallory submitted to the Air Ministry the list of targets which he wished the British bombers to attack. The Air Ministry, however, reserved its approval of most of them; and Leigh-Mallory, alarmed, approached the Supreme Commander. Eisenhower in turn forwarded his letter to the British Chiefs of Staff; and after discussion on 21st March, they asked the Chief of the Air Staff to examine the whole question forthwith.

By this time, the situation had changed in two respects. In the first place, General Spaatz had produced a detailed alternative to the Transportation Plan, which he claimed would meet the needs of both 'Overlord' and 'Pointblank'; secondly, Tedder, who had been associated with the Transportation Plan from its inception in the Mediterranean, had been asked to investigate the problem on behalf of the Supreme Commander, and had reaffirmed his earlier conviction that the plan offered the best solution. Spaatz's design 'for the Completion of the Combined Bomber Offensive' appeared on 5th March. After arguing against the Transportation Plan, it proposed a method of reconciling the terms of the most recent directive on 'Pointblank' with Eisenhower's needs. In the first stage, the strategic air forces would continue to bomb targets mainly in Germany, the petroleum industry receiving first priority, the fighter aircraft industry second, rubber third, bomber production fourth, and transportation targets—'last resort targets'—fifth. In the second stage, the strategic air forces would switch their main effort to helping 'Overlord' directly, by bombing the transport system and other tactical targets in the area affecting operations.

Here was the detailed alternative to the Transportation Plan. Meanwhile, that plan itself was coming under criticism from various quarters. The chief question at issue was whether or not a period of three months was necessary to achieve the precise degree of success envisaged. Was it too great a price to pay for what was promised? Or would the alternative of a shorter period of attack, even after the previous reduction of the German air force, merely draw attention to an invasion which it would fail effectively to support? It was on these two aspects of the question that Tedder concentrated throughout the first half of March. As a result, he concluded that while the Transportation Plan did not offer a perfect solution to the problem of the reserves, it offered a better solution than Spaatz's alternative, which he was sure could not achieve its object in the time allowed. He therefore considered that the Transportation Plan, with all the risks which he acknowledged, must be regarded as an integral part of 'Overlord'.

By the time that the discussion reached the Chiefs of Staff, it was thus both clearly defined and had attracted widespread attention; and on 22nd March, the Prime Minister decided to examine the problem himself. On learning, however, that the Chief of the Air Staff was about to do so, he consented to await the result. Meanwhile, Tedder and Spaatz submitted papers to Portal containing their respective cases.

Portal called a meeting on 25th March, which was attended by Eisenhower, Tedder and Leigh-Mallory, by Harris and Spaatz with members of their Commands, and by representatives of the Air Ministry, the War Office, the Ministry of Economic Warfare and the Joint Intelligence Committee. The result favoured the 'Overlord' authorities. After a long appraisal of the evidence, Spaatz's plan was rejected as failing to provide enough support for 'Overlord' during its first and critical stage. Portal therefore decided, with Eisenhower's concurrence, that it should be considered again as soon as the situation of 'Overlord' allowed, and that meanwhile the strategic air forces should be divided between operations against the German fighter aircraft industry and, with as great a strength as possible after conforming to that object, against the transport system of France and Belgium as defined by the Transportation Plan.

A detailed and comprehensive programme was proposed, within a new directive.

'OVERALL MISSION

1. The overall mission of the Strategical air forces remains the progressive destruction and dislocation of the German military, industrial and economic system, and the destruction of vital elements of lines of communication. In the execution of this overall mission the immediate objective is first the destruction

> of German air combat strength, by the successful prosecution of the Combined Bomber Offensive. Our re-entry on the Continent constitutes the supreme operation for 1944; all possible support must, therefore, be afforded to the Allied Armies by our Air Forces to assist them in establishing themselves in the lodgement area.
>
> PARTICULAR MISSION
>
> 2. The first prerequisite of success in the maintenance of the Combined Bomber Offensive and of our re-entry on the Continent is an overall reduction of the enemy's air combat strength and particularly his air fighter strength. The primary role of our air forces in the European and Mediterranean theatres is, therefore, to secure and maintain air superiority.
>
> 3. Our armies will also require the maximum possible assistance on the ground preparatory to the actual assault. This can best be given by interfering with rail communications, particularly as affecting the enemy movements and concentrations in the 'Overlord' area . . .
>
> 4. The particular mission of the Strategical air forces prior to the 'Overlord' assault is :
>
> (a) To deplete the German air force and particularly the German fighter forces and to destroy and disorganise the facilities supporting them.
>
> (b) To destroy and disrupt the enemy's rail communications, particularly those affecting the enemy's movements towards the 'Overlord' lodgement area. . . .'

Targets were then specified for the U.S. Strategic Air Forces in Europe and for Bomber Command: the former against the enemy's fighter aircraft industry and, secondly, his rail transport; the latter against German industry in general, the operations being 'as far as practicable' complementary to the Americans'. The whole programme would be subject to review 'after 'Overlord' is established on the Continent'.

The meeting on 25th March was followed immediately by another important development. While the strategic discussion had been under way, the Combined Chiefs of Staff had continued to debate the complementary issue of command. As the arguments hardened, both sides became the more determined to safeguard their authority; and by the middle of February 1944, Eisenhower had resolved to insist categorically on the control of the strategic air forces. So highly indeed did he rate its importance that he was prepared, as he informed the Prime Minister at the end of the month, to relinquish his command if it were refused. Early in March, the British accordingly gave way to the extent of allowing the Supreme Commander, as soon as he and Portal should have agreed on their shape, to assume 'responsibility for supervision of air operations out of England of all the forces engaged in the programme' for the support of 'Overlord'. The American Chiefs of Staff, however, were not entirely satisfied by this formula. They distrusted the implications of the word 'supervision', and preferred 'command'. The British in turn demurred to this proposal, which seemed to them to contain possible dangers to 'Pointblank' and to the Combined Chiefs of Staff's strategic responsibility for it; and after a last, somewhat confused struggle, a compromise was reached on 26th March on the word 'direction'.

The decision on command thus coincided with the strategic agreement which was to herald its execution; and Tedder, as Deputy to the Supreme Commander, was able to take over the co-ordination of air operations at the very time when events made it imperative. On 27th March, he assumed his powers of direction, and formally relieved Leigh-Mallory of responsibility for the Transportation Plan.

The interpolation of the Deputy Supreme Commander into the pattern of the air command for 'Overlord' proved quite successful. But this was due entirely to the dominating position which Tedder himself at once established with the tactical and strategic commands, and in theory the solution could not be considered particularly satisfactory. But in the circumstances which had evolved it, and which it had perforce to reflect, no other seemed possible; and despite the anomalies in the chain of command, it is no disparagement of Leigh-Mallory to say that Tedder's association with the air support of 'Overlord' provided it with a more effective champion in the discussion that still lay ahead.

For the decision of the air authorities by no means ensured the final approval of the Transportation Plan. When, on 29th March, Portal reported to the Prime Minister the results of the meeting of the 25th, he concluded:

> 'There is one point which I should mention to you now. In the execution of this Plan very heavy casualties among civilians living near the main railway centres in occupied territory will be unavoidable, however careful we may be over the actual bombing. Eisenhower realises this and I understand that he is going to propose that warnings should be issued to all civilians living near railway centres advising them to move. I hope you will agree that since the requirements of 'Overlord' are paramount, the Plan must go ahead after due warning has been given.'

This problem, which in its extent was unique to the Transportation Plan, gave rise to further debate.

The probable effect of the plan on the French and on the Belgians had already disturbed those Ministers who knew of its existence; and Portal had warned the meeting of 25th March that it could expect the War Cabinet to scrutinize the diplomatic implications. As he had forecast, a meeting for that purpose was called on 3rd April. The ensuing debate is significant, not only for its result, but because, so far as I can see, it marked the one occasion within the period covered by this volume on which the War Cabinet itself was consulted on a strategic issue, as distinct from an issue affecting or affected by strategy.

Before the meeting on 3rd April, there was a strong feeling among Ministers, and particularly on the part of the Foreign Secretary, that the loss of life and damage to property which the Transportation Plan might inflict, was likely to cause such intense and widespread anger among the French as to outweigh its military advantages. With memories of Oran and Dakar, no British authority wished, on the eve of invasion, to risk the goodwill that had been nurtured so carefully over the past three years. Ministers were therefore inclined to demand from the air authorities proof positive both that the object of the plan was well conceived and that the necessary degree of success could be attained. Only if both could be guaranteed, should the Allies risk alienating French sympathy, and possibly French help, at this time.

These feelings were expressed on 3rd April, when, as the Prime Minister informed Eisenhower,[1] the War Cabinet 'took rather a grave and on the whole an adverse view' of the plan. It decided that the question should be reviewed on its behalf by the Defence Committee—a body which, on this one topic and possibly as a reflection of the intervention of the War Cabinet, was preferred to the *ad hoc* Staff Meetings which had by now largely displaced it. Meanwhile, the War Cabinet instructed the air commanders to select only such targets in territories occupied by the enemy as could be attacked 'with relatively little risk of injury to the civil population.'

The Chiefs of Staff had meanwhile asked the Paymaster-General, Lord Cherwell, who already knew details of the Transportation Plan, to examine it afresh as an independent authority. By 5th April, and apparently largely on evidence produced by the Joint Intelligence Committee, he formed the conclusion that it was unlikely to achieve its object in the time available, even after a possible expenditure of 50,000 tons of bombs, and at the cost of perhaps 40,000 Frenchmen killed and a further 120,000 injured. The Joint Intelligence Committee itself stressed the need for accurate bombing if the diplomatic consequences were not to be disastrous. When the Defence Committee met on that day, Ministers, and the Prime Minister in particular, therefore remained highly sceptical of the merits of the plan.

The Prime Minister opened the meeting by developing four arguments against the air proposals. First, they seemed unnecessary. In order to hamper the movement of a limited number of divisions over a relatively small area, an air campaign of great magnitude was to be undertaken which would seriously restrict 'Pointblank'. Even so, some

[1] See *Closing the Ring*, p. 466.

authorities thought it would not succeed. In that case, a shorter period of intense attack should prove acceptable, which would allow the bombers meanwhile to proceed with their operations against Germany. Secondly, the diplomatic implications were serious; for even if, as he suspected, the estimates of civilian casualties had been exaggerated, the results might well cause an irreparable breach between France and the Western Allies. Thirdly, therefore, the plan could not be adopted without consulting the United States Government, a process which might impose further delay. Fourthly, it could scarcely be undertaken without first consulting General de Gaulle, who might then demand access to details of the 'Overlord' plan which the Western Allies were not prepared to divulge. For these reasons, a heavy onus of proof rested on the air authorities.

A long discussion ensued. The supporters of the plan succeeded in showing that many of the technical criticisms of its expense and of its results were ill-founded, and that the estimates of civilian casualties were highly questionable. But they could not produce convincing evidence—as was indeed difficult by the nature of the case—that it would command enough success to outweigh the diplomatic disadvantages. It was even possible that the latter would endanger the plan itself, by leading the French Resistance to abstain from the destruction of locomotives which formed an integral part of the operations. The Defence Committee remained divided, and could only confirm the War Cabinet's provisional decision temporarily to limit the attacks, while the air authorities examined the possibility of excluding from the plan those operations which might entail the heaviest civilian casualties.

The debate continued within the Defence Committee over the next three weeks, in an atmosphere of intense anxiety. For even in a period of grave decisions, this was a grave decision to take. Moreover, as evidence began to accumulate from the limited attacks, each side could claim support for its views: the air authorities pointing to good results, to lower casualties than had been expected, and to a possible modification of the plan itself; the civil authorities, to reports of the reactions from western Europe. Disagreement on principle thus remained; and as the critical weeks slipped by, it seemed likely that experience or the dictates of time alone would provide an answer.

The Defence Committee met again on 13th April. By that time, the air authorities had produced a revised list of targets, excluding two near Paris where casualties were expected to be particularly heavy, and including instead fifteen new targets in the south of France. Partly as a result of the new list, but largely as the result of sounder calculation, the estimate of the casualties themselves had also been drastically revised, from a maximum of 160,000 to a mean of 16,000 (10,500 killed, 5,500 seriously injured). The first information seemed likely to modify even these reduced figures. By 13th April, nine railway centres had been attacked, and so far as could be discovered 1,103 civilians had been killed, compared with an estimate of 2,540 on the revised basis. The military authorities were satisfied by the reports of damage, and since no conclusion could as yet be drawn from the first reactions in France and Belgium, the Defence Committee decided to continue as before for another week, and meanwhile to issue a warning to the French and Belgians that attacks must be expected by day and by night.

By the 20th, when the Committee met again, almost a third of the targets had been attacked, and while the figures of deaths were still apparently below the revised estimates, the ratio of casualties seemed to have risen. The air authorities reported that the attacks were yielding favourable results, and were inclined to think that, if allowed to proceed, they would prove as successful as had been claimed. On the other hand, while comment in the French press and on the radio was surprisingly small, and there was undoubtedly much sympathy for the Allies throughout the country, local resentment seemed to be spreading. The Belgian press and radio were vociferous. The Defence Committee, still divided, accordingly repeated its decision of a week before.

It met again on the 26th. By now, only six weeks remained before 'Overlord' was to be launched, and a final decision had to be taken. The arguments had been exposed from every aspect, and in every detail; over one-third of the plan had by now been carried out; and the series of limited targets was almost exhausted. 26,000 tons of bombs had been dropped on thirty-two targets, mostly by British aircraft, although the Americans were due to carry out the larger number of attacks in future. It was extremely difficult to gauge the number of civilian casualties, for as the number and variety of the targets increased the Allies had to rely increasingly on figures given by the enemy, which might well be exaggerated for the purpose of propaganda. But even accepting this source, it seemed that at most 4,000 had been killed, and the casualties had therefore amounted so far, at the worst, to rather less than 75 per cent of the number estimated. From photographic examination, it seemed likely that this was due largely to the fact that bombing had been far more accurate than some authorities had anticipated. Nevertheless, evidence was accumulating that the attacks were causing real and growing anger; and Ministers, while relieved that the casualties had not been worse, remained anxious to drop the plan if possible. The Prime Minister accordingly referred the question again from the Defence Committee to the War Cabinet.

Before the War Cabinet met, the Chiefs of Staff discussed the position. While all did not view the Transportation Plan with equal enthusiasm, they decided that there was now no feasible strategic alternative, and that on military grounds they must recommend its adoption. They did so therefore in a Minute of the 26th, concluding that 'the Plan should proceed unless political considerations are held to be overriding'.

The War Cabinet met on the next day, 27th April. The Prime Minister summed up the developments since the 5th. He remained perturbed by the weight of casualties, particularly as the British alone could so far be blamed for them; reinforced by Lord Cherwell's advice, he still questioned the merits of the plan in the short time available; and he was therefore disposed formally to advise the President that on balance it seemed likely to do more harm than good. He proposed, however, to discuss the matter with General Eisenhower before taking such a step. Other Ministers supported him, and Cherwell suggested that an alternative plan should at once be prepared, to include only those railway targets where the estimated casualties would not exceed one hundred, and, in place of the rest, vehicle parks, camps and supply dumps. In this case, the Americans should assume a full share of the responsibility for the operations. The War Cabinet accepted this advice. Churchill at once informed the Supreme Commander of these developments, and at the turn of the month Eisenhower again consulted his air advisers. As a result, he replied on 2nd May.

> 'I have throughout realised the political considerations arising from the inevitable casualties to French civilian personnel caused by the attack on the enemy's Rail Transport system. . . . although (the limitations previously accepted) inevitably affect the full efficacy of the Plan, . . . I feel this handicap can be accepted in view of the weighty political considerations put forward by the British Cabinet.
>
> I must point out that casualties to civilian personnel are inherent in any plan for the full use of Air power to prepare for our assault. . . . It applies to the present problem and will equally apply to the future. It applies particularly to the proposed program of attack on M.T. [Motor Transport] Depots . . . , and it will certainly apply to attacks on Headquarters and Communication Centres which will be of vital importance immediately prior to the assault. Railway Centres have always been recognised as legitimate military targets, and attack on them is clearly obvious to the general population as a strictly military operation.
>
> . . . I fear that there is still considerable misunderstanding regarding the nature of the object of my operations against enemy Rail transportation. It has never been suggested that these Operations by themselves will *stop* essential military movement. The object of the whole Operation is so to weaken and disorganize the Railway system as a whole that, at the critical time of the assault, German rail movements can be effectively delayed, and the rapid concentration of their forces against the lodgement area prevented. Time is the vital factor during the

period immediately following the assault. The delay which would be involved by enforced use of Motor Transport in place of Railway Transport would, in itself, be of inestimable value.

As regards alternative plans, at my Meeting [on 25th March] with C.A.S. at which all authoritative military and expert opinion was represented, it was clear, both to me and to the C.A.S., that there is no effective alternative plan. I have earnestly searched for these in my anxiety to avoid risking French antagonism towards the U.K.-U.S. Forces and Governments. . . .

As I said at the beginning of this note, I fully appreciate the gravity of the issues raised. I have modified my plan as far as possible without vitiating its value. If it is still considered that the political considerations are such as to limit the Operations to centres where the casualties are estimated at 100/150, such a modification would emasculate the whole plan. Moreover, such a limitation would logically apply to all Air operations prior to the assault, including essential tactical operations which must begin at least two or three weeks before the assault. It is not perhaps fully appreciated that from D-30 onwards there is an extensive program of bombing operations against military targets of diverse character over a wide area, extending over 150 miles from the coast. Attack on many of these targets, e.g. M.T. Depots, will inevitably involve considerable civilian casualties.

The 'Overlord' concept was based on the assumption that our overwhelming Air power would be able to prepare the way for the assault. If its hands are to be tied, the perils of an already hazardous undertaking will be greatly enhanced.'

The War Cabinet met on the same day to consider this letter. Only the most pressing sense of its disadvantages compelled Ministers still to maintain their opposition to the Supreme Commander's advice. But reports over the past few days had emphasized more strongly a rising hostility throughout western Europe, and they could not bring themselves to approve the plan without a last effort to mitigate its effects. They therefore referred the question once more to the Defence Committee, asking it on this occasion to consider the implications of limiting all air operations in support of 'Overlord', of whatever kind. A last, prolonged discussion took place on 3rd May. Some time was devoted to a new side issue, the use of delayed-action bombs on which the enemy's propaganda had recently been concentrating, and a special study of this point was ordered; otherwise, the arguments ranged the familiar ground. Finally, the Defence Committee agreed that, subject to approval by the War Cabinet, the Transportation Plan should be carried out in such a way that the total casualties did not exceed 10,000 (a higher figure than that favoured by the War Cabinet, but substantially lower than any estimate, and one which

Tedder thought, on the available evidence, could be accepted without unduly hampering the operations), and that the Prime Minister should approach the President forthwith, to explain the significance of the decision and to ensure that the United States Government would be identified with the consequences. Two days later, the restrictions on targets lapsed, and were not renewed; but the Supreme Commander ordered that those liable to involve the greatest casualties should still not be attacked until as near as possible to D-day.

On 7th May, the Prime Minister sent his telegram to the President.[1]

> '1. The War Cabinet have been much concerned during the last three weeks about the number of Frenchmen killed in the raids on the railway centres in France. We have had numerous Staff meetings with our own Officers and I have discussed the matter with Generals Eisenhower and Bedell-Smith. There were and are great differences of opinion in the two Air Forces not between them but criss-cross about the efficacy of the "Railway Plan" as a short-term project. In the end Eisenhower, Tedder, Bedell-Smith and Portal all declare themselves converted. I am personally by no means convinced that this is the best way to use our Air Forces in the preliminary period, and still think that the G.A.F. [German Air Force] should be the main target. The matter has been discussed in very great detail on the technical side and it would not be wise to dismiss lightly the arguments for or against.
>
> 2. When this project was first put forward, a loss of 80,000 French civilian casualties, including injured, say 20,000 killed, was mentioned. The War Cabinet could not view this figure without grave dismay on account of the apparently ruthless use of the Air Forces, particularly of the Royal Air Force, on whom the brunt of this kind of work necessarily falls, and the reproaches that would be made upon the inaccuracy of night bombing. The results of the first, say, three-sevenths of the bombing have however shown that the casualties to French civil life were very much less than was expected by the commanders, in fact Air Chief Marshal Tedder has now expressed the opinion that about 10,000 killed, apart from injured, will probably cover the job.
>
> 3. I am satisfied that all possible care will be taken to minimise this slaughter of friendly civilian life. Nevertheless, the War Cabinet share my apprehensions of the bad effect which will be produced upon the French civilian population by these slaughters, all taking place so long before 'Overlord' D-day. They may easily bring about a great revolution in French feeling towards their approaching United States and British liberators. They may leave a legacy of hate behind them. . . . It may well be that the French losses will grow heavier on and after D-day, but in the heat of battle, when British and United States troops will probably be losing at a much higher rate, a new proportion

[1] See *Closing the Ring*, pp. 466-7.

establishes itself in men's minds. It is the intervening period what causes me most anxiety. We are of course doing everything in our power by leaflets, etc., to warn the French people to keep clear of dangerous spots, and this may prove beneficial in the remaining interval. However both on technical and political grounds, which latter are very gravely involved, the War Cabinet feel very great distress and anxiety.

4. Accordingly they ask me to invite you to consider the matter from the highest political standpoint and to give us your opinion as a matter between Governments. It must be remembered, on the one hand, that this slaughter is among a friendly people who have committed no crime against us, and not among the German foe, with all their record of cruelty and ruthlessness. On the other hand, we naturally feel the hazardous nature of Operation 'Overlord' and are in deadly earnest about making it a success. I have been careful in stating this case to you to use only the most moderate terms, but I ought to let you know that the War Cabinet is unanimous in its anxiety about these French slaughters, even reduced as they have been, and also in its doubts as to whether almost as good military results could not be produced by other methods. Whatever is settled between us, we are quite willing to share responsibilities with you.'

The President replied on the 11th.

'. . . I share fully with you your distress at the loss of life among the French population incident to our air preparations for 'Overlord'.

I share also with you a satisfaction that every possible care is being and will be taken to minimise these civilian casualties. No possibility of alleviating adverse French opinion should be overlooked, always provided that there is no reduction of our effectiveness against the enemy at this crucial time. . . .

However regrettable the attendant loss of civilian lives is, I am not prepared to impose from this distance any restriction on military action by the responsible commanders that in their opinion might militate against the success of 'Overlord' or cause additional loss of life to our Allied forces of invasion.'

This settled the issue. On 16th May, three weeks before 'Overlord' was due to be launched, the Prime Minister informed the Chiefs of Staff and Eisenhower that, in view of the President's telegram, and of the fact that the casualties seemed certain to be kept below the lowest figure allowed, the War Cabinet would be content to let the matter rest. The directive proposed on 25th March was now officially adopted, and the air offensive on France and Belgium, reinforced by the heavy bombers, grew in intensity during the period that remained.

(iii)

The Rôle of the Air: 'Crossbow'

While the main offensive possibilities centred on 'Pointblank' and the Transportation Plan, the Allied air forces had also to ensure that the preparations for 'Overlord' were adequately defended. Defence of course might well involve attack on the enemy, which would concern the strategic as well as the tactical forces. But the emphasis lay on the latter, and the structure of the 'Overlord' air command, including as it did all British fighter forces in the United Kingdom, placed in the hands of the Supreme Commander direct control of the country's first line of defence, for which, with all measures of defence, the British Chiefs of Staff retained their traditional responsibility.

By the end of 1943, the greatest, and indeed the only serious, danger from the air seemed likely to come from some form of rocket or pilotless explosive aircraft, to all aspects of whose preparation and destruction the Chiefs of Staff allocated the code name 'Crossbow'. The development of such weapons had long been a particular study in Germany. Experimental work had begun in the late 1920's; the army had become interested, and had provided facilities, in 1930; and in the summer of 1934, the prototype of the V.2 weapon which appeared ten years later had been developed as a form of long-range artillery. In 1936, a research station was set up by the army and air force at Peenemünde on the Baltic, where the development of rocket weapons continued under the supervision of their main progenitor, the army officer Walter Dornberger. By that time, rockets had flown successfully for considerable distances, although the problem of their control in flight had still not been solved.

By the outbreak of war, two types of rocket – the A.4 (or, as it was known to the British in its final form, the V.2) and the smaller A.5 – had been developed in some detail, but the same problem of control remained. Research continued, under the direction of the army, during the next three years; and in June, 1942 the first A.4. was launched. After further experiment and modification, in October an A.4 was guided successfully to the target area at a range of 120 miles.

But meanwhile, the air force section of the establishment at Peenemünde had produced, with roughly equal success, a different type of pilotless weapon. At first, the two Services seem to have collaborated closely on the rockets for whose development the station had been set up. But by the beginning of the war, Peenemünde West, controlled by the air force, had drawn apart from Peenemünde East, controlled by the army, and was engaged on the development of pilotless missiles launched and guided from a parent aircraft. Various types were sponsored during the first three years of the war, two of which in 1943 were used with some success against shipping; but in the autumn of 1942, a more promising variant appeared in the F.Z.G.76 (at some stages of its development called the Fi.103), which was launched from the ground and guided by its own automatic pilot, and which the British knew eventually as the V.1. Under the direction of Colonel von Gyldenfeld, the first F.Z.G.76 to be so launched was fired from a ramp at Peenemünde in December 1942, and flew the scheduled distance of three kilometres.

In the spring of 1943, these experiments attracted the attention of the Fuehrer's headquarters; and, as often happens when the user of the weapon intervenes, research thereafter concentrated on one or two of the most promising developments to the exclusion of the rest. The High Command, and Hitler himself, were anxious to concentrate if possible on one weapon alone, with the consequent advantages of priority for research, and of simplicity and speed of production. The A.4 and F.Z.G.76 held the lead in their respective fields, and by May, 1943 work had virtually stopped on other types. But it was more difficult to choose between the two main weapons themselves, and in April Hitler called for a full report before deciding on a programme of production. The experts, however, could still not commit themselves exclusively to either; and work accordingly continued on both.

This decision, thanks to the recent personal interest of the Fuehrer, was accompanied by a high degree of attention to both projects. A programme of production for the A.4 had been drawn up in January, 1943; and in July, it was given exceptional priority. The scheme provided for a target of thirty rockets a month, rising to nine hundred a month by December 1943, and for final assembly in three factories, at Peenemünde, at Friedrichshafen on the northern shore of Lake Constance, and at Wiener Neustadt near Vienna. The programme for the F.Z.G.76 was set, after further encouraging tests in the Baltic which in turn attracted the volatile favour of the Fuehrer, at a target of sixty weapons a month in September, and three hundred a month in October 1943, rising to 5,000 a month by the end of the year. In the event, production began late in September at Fallersleben in Hanover. It was estimated – most optimistically – that these rates of production would enable a heavy and growing attack to be launched against England, beginning in December, 1943 or at latest in January 1944, with a stock of 2,000 A.4 and (as estimated in September) of 5,000 F.Z.G.76. Hitler himself, who placed the highest hopes on the new weapons, informed the military authorities in June, 1943 that by the end of the year London would be flat and the British Government forced to capitulate.

These target dates demanded the rapid construction of launching sites and their defences. The attacks from both weapons were aimed principally at London, with a secondary group of targets in the south and south-west, including Portsmouth, Southampton and Winchester, Aldershot, and Bristol. The firing sites had therefore to be placed in two areas, those for London in and near the Pas de Calais, and the others further west, many in the Cherbourg peninsula. But while the area in each case was the same, the installations for the two weapons were quite different from each other. The A.4 could be discharged from a small, mobile structure, which needed only a clear line of fire towards the target and a clear path from the firing point to its equipment. Advanced stores and testing stations were also needed at certain points, which must be served by their own communications with the mobile firing sites and with the rear. The F.Z.G.76 needed a more elaborate firing site, consisting of two long inclined rails bedded at their inner end in a concrete emplacement and pointing in the direction of the target. The necessary stores, testing facilities and accommodation had to be provided in advanced centres, and sites and centres required communication between each other and with the rear. Work began on the equipment for the A.4 in the spring of 1943. A plan was made to launch the rockets from forty-five sites of simple construction between the Pas de Calais and Cherbourg. A main forward base for the Pas de Calais, consisting of a large concrete bunker enclosing a firing emplacement, stores, repair shops and accommodation, was also begun at Watten near St. Omer, to be finished by mid-October. This was designed to serve both as an advanced base for the mobile firing sites, and as a supplementary site. In May 1943, work began on two other sites near Cherbourg, one of which however was converted before completion into a site for the F.Z.G.76. Positions for the F.Z.G.76 were begun only in August 1943, following the decision in July to manufacture the weapon. The original plan envisaged sixty-four main sites, with another thirty-two in reserve, in a belt from Cherbourg to St. Omer, and eight protected stores each containing about 250 weapons. All of these firing sites were to be ready by 1st November, and the supply sites by mid-December, 1943.

It is not surprising that, after an initial period of scepticism, Hitler should have been excited, at this particular stage of the war, by the possibilities of a rocket campaign. It promised the restoration of the offensive which he had lost with the decline of the German air force, enabling him to impede such measures as might be preparing for invasion, and to retaliate on the English towns for the damage to his own. The first object was not one for which pilotless missiles, in their then state of development, were particularly well fitted; but it could at least be supported, and at best rendered unnecessary, by the achievement of the second, for which they seemed admirably suited and which might be expected peculiarly to appeal to the

Fuehrer. For pilotless missiles, of whatever sort, were likely to attract Hitler on more intimate grounds than that of strategy. As a new and revolutionary weapon, capable of sudden and decisive attack, they would provide an incomparable proof of his unorthodox war-making genius and of German scientific supremacy; and, perhaps dearest of all, of his capacity to exact a just retribution from the 'authors' of the indiscriminate 'terror raids'. They may have offered to a twentieth-century war lord an emotional, as well as a strategic, release.

Intelligence of the German preparations increased, throughout the summer and autumn of 1943, with the preparations themselves. Rumours, and some information, had reached this country since before the war of German interest in pilotless missiles; but little detail was available on the miscellaneous experiments before 1942. By the spring of 1943, a clearer picture began to emerge, although only partly correct; and on 11th April, a report was circulated on the developments of the past five years. It reflected the Germans' emphasis on the rocket as opposed to the pilotless aircraft, of which indeed the British were not aware. The Vice-Chiefs of Staff discussed the paper, and agreed that it warranted a report to the Prime Minister and the Ministry of Home Security; and this was submitted on 14th April, with a note advocating the appointment of a single person to take charge of the investigations.

The Chiefs of Staff agreed with the proposal, and recommended to the Prime Minister that the work should be directed by Mr. Duncan Sandys, who as Joint Parliamentary Secretary to the Ministry of Supply had experience of weapon development, and from his earlier career in the army knew something of rocket anti-aircraft gunnery. The Prime Minister gladly concurred, and Mr. Sandys at once embarked on his investigations.

The evidence was difficult to assess with precision. Reports suggested that the rocket might carry between five and ten tons of explosive, and might have a range of between one hundred and two hundred kilometres (62-125 miles). Some scientists were inclined, on the evidence of the effort which the enemy was devoting to the project, to credit these figures, which were certainly astonishing on the basis of earlier technical knowledge. Others, of whom Lord Cherwell was the most important, did not believe that the Germans could have made such a revolutionary technical advance from their earlier known position, without producing an intermediate weapon of which something would probably have been heard. Cherwell in particular refused (and rightly) until the end to believe that a missile with this performance existed; and therefore maintained (wrongly) that the preparations were designed purely as an elaborate bluff to conceal another development, possibly that of a pilotless or jet-propelled aircraft. Faced by this division of scientific opinion, Mr. Sandys and the Chiefs of Staff deemed it prudent to anticipate the worst; and a special committee was accordingly set up to recommend the appropriate measures for civil defence. By the late summer of 1943 it had produced a comprehensive scheme, covering a system of public warning, evacuation on a large scale from the towns of south-east England, and the transfer of Government departments from London.

Meanwhile, British aircraft carried out reconnaissance over northern France, where the heavy structures at Watten and in the Cherbourg peninsula were closely observed. At the end of June 1943, Sandys decided that some action should be taken, and recommended that Peenemünde should be heavily bombed in August when the longer nights would first permit. The Chiefs of Staff agreed, and on the night of 17th August a large force of British bombers attacked the station. Despite the loss of forty-one aircraft the operation was a great success, causing heavy casualties among the scientific staff, destroying much of the research equipment, and seriously damaging the principal factory for the assembly of the A.4. It was indeed largely responsible for a major change in the production of that weapon, all components thereafter being produced and assembled in an underground factory in the Harz Mountains. Ten days later, American aircraft bombed the bunker at Watten, repeating the attack on 7th September, on both occasions with considerable effect. Extensive damage induced the enemy to abandon work on the site for four months, and thereafter only the oxygen plant was completed. But by this time, the British were faced with a new and perplexing problem, caused by the growing weight of reports throughout August on the development of an apparently new type of weapon. A culminating report of 27th August suggested strongly that this was some form of pilotless aircraft, and by the end of the month some observers thought that it offered a more immediate danger than the more familiar rocket. But there was now considerable confusion between the two, and indeed on the number of weapons that might exist; evidence which had formerly been thought to apply to the rocket was now re-examined for light on the pilotless aircraft; and the whole problem had to be reviewed afresh.

The debate, which continued with growing intensity into the autumn of 1943, was accompanied by some administrative confusion. For Mr. Sandys, feeling that the field of investigation was now being extended beyond his resources, arranged in September that he should concentrate as far as possible on rockets, while the Intelligence authorities of the Air Ministry took over the investigation of pilotless aircraft, which seemed to be associated with that of jet-propelled aircraft on which they were already engaged. But by the middle of October, it was plain that neither scientists nor administrators could work successfully on these lines; and early in November it was agreed that the Air Staff, which would soon have to plan counter-measures on a large scale against all forms of pilotless missiles, should assume full responsibility for 'Crossbow'. New machinery was accordingly set up, whereby all intelligence and operational work was co-ordinated under the Deputy Chief of the Air Staff, while Sandys continued to sit with the Chiefs of Staff whenever the subject was debated in committee. By January, 1944 the reorganization was complete. The Air Ministry was in direct control of 'Crossbow', co-operating with the Joint Intelligence Committee in the military field, and with the Ministry of Home Security and its agents in the civil field. These arrangements lasted satisfactorily throughout 1944.

With the recognition that possibly two main types of weapon were involved, and with the consequent administrative reorganization, the measures against 'Crossbow' entered on a new phase; and in the same month of November 1943, the establishment of the 'Overlord' air command gave to a single commander the immediate disposal of a substantial force which could be used, in due proportion to its use on other tasks, on 'Crossbow' operations. It was also hoped that the strategic air forces in England would be available to carry out attacks on request.

By December 1943, the targets were more clearly defined. During October and November, reports and reconnaissance showed the emergence in large numbers of the new type of installation which was now being built for the F.Z.G.76. From their appearance from the air, the sites were known as 'ski-sites', and by the middle of November some seventy to eighty had been photographed, all within a range of 140 miles from London and mostly in the Pas de Calais. By that time, too, the British had intelligence of the F.Z.G.76 itself, a small pilotless aircraft or 'flying bomb' with a wing span of some twenty feet. The identification of the installations and the weapon brought the issue to the fore. Some authorities anticipated an attack beginning possibly in December 1943, and Cossac was asked to report on the implications for 'Overlord'. In December he replied that, as the existing plan of invasion could be carried out only from bases on the south coast, the preparations should if possible continue as before, but if not should be transferred entirely to the West Country. In the latter case, a decision must be taken at once. The authorities, however, decided on reflection to leave things as they were, and to rely on the counter-measures that were then beginning.

Throughout December, the Allied Expeditionary Air Forces searched for all ski-sites within a radius of 140 miles of London and

Portsmouth. By the end of the year, ninety-three had been disclosed. Attacks were begun against the most advanced positions; but early in December 1943, it seemed unlikely that they would prove enough. The strategic air forces were therefore asked to collaborate, by carrying out regular attacks both on the firing sites and on the factories and assembly points. This was naturally not popular with the authors of 'Pointblank'; but they agreed to bomb firing sites by day and night when other operations allowed, and those factories producing pilotless weapons which also produced aircraft.

The burden, however, continued to rest mainly on the tactical air forces. The results, and the estimates of them by the British, did credit to the 'Crossbow' authorities. As a result of over 9,000 sorties in three months, the British calculated at the end of March, 1944 that two-thirds of the ski-sites had been seriously damaged and just under a quarter damaged; and early in April, they estimated that the enemy's programme of repair could be effectively contained. By that time, the Germans had decided to abandon most of the ski-sites for operations in the near future, and to confine themselves entirely to repair work and measures of deception.

While the concentration on the ski-sites was the key to the counter-measures, operations were also carried out against the heavy sites in northern France[1]. But these were not so successful; and the poor results, combined with the repairs to some of the ski-sites, raised again in April the more acute fears which had recently diminished. In spite of the growing demands of the Transportation Plan, a substantial proportion of the tactical air forces accordingly remained on 'Crossbow' operations, and in the middle of April the Chiefs of Staff called for more help from the strategic air forces. Despite the partial nature of the response, the weight of attack from both sources increased notably over the next four weeks, with some satisfactory results. Although the heavy sites remained a problem, the reconstruction of the ski-sites was stopped effectively; and by the end of May, when all attacks virtually ceased, eighty-six of those sites were thought to have been severely damaged, eight moderately damaged, and only two to be still intact. When the immediate needs of 'Overlord' brought the 'Crossbow' operations to an end, the Allies could reflect that 'Overlord' had survived the period of 'Crossbow'.

Meanwhile, the second line of defence had been prepared. In December 1943, a plan was composed for the defence of the country against flying bombs. It took as its point of departure the proposition that the missile was an aircraft, and thus vulnerable to traditional methods of destruction. The existing pattern of defence—fighter aircraft in collaboration with anti-aircraft artillery, searchlights and balloons, the whole depending on an elaborate system of radar stations

[1] See p. 307 above.

and observers—could therefore be retained with suitable changes of emphasis. It was essential not to conflict directly with the final preparations for 'Overlord', which were due to begin on 1st April; and as it was considered likely that the attacks would start at about the same time, the measures must be complete by the end of March. The plan, drawn up in consultation with the army's Anti-Aircraft Command, was ready in February 1944, and was not thereafter seriously modified before the attacks began. It was known as the 'Overlord-Diver Plan', 'Diver' being the code name for the measures during the period of attack, which the needs of 'Overlord' affected at every point. While not representing all that its authors had wished, it was the best that could be done at the time. The first object was the defence of London, the second that of the Solent area and of Bristol. The advanced defences for all three areas consisted of fighter aircraft. Behind them were two main groups of anti-aircraft guns and searchlights, the larger concentration on the North Downs in front of London, the smaller in front of Bristol. The protection of the Solent was already provided for by the 'Overlord' plan itself. Lastly, a balloon barrage was supplied for London. These measures provided the largest appropriation of material that could be spared for the task, and the smallest likely to be effective against the threat as it was then foreseen. All was ready early in April.

The British counter-measures were only one of the factors contributing to the delay in mounting the attack by pilotless missiles. Indeed, after the raid on Peenemünde they scarcely affected the preparations for the A.4 (V.2), and while they disrupted those for the F.Z.G.76 (V.1), it nevertheless proved possible to launch a sustained attack with the latter weapon from other sites from the middle of June.[1] Equally serious difficulties arose from design and production, and, in the case of the F.Z.G.76, from the form of operational control.

By the end of September 1943, sixty F.Z.G.76 a month were being produced, and early in November this seemed likely to be doubled. But such figures fell far short of the estimates, and moreover modifications of design were constantly being introduced which not only prevented a higher rate of production but rendered useless much of the stock already collected. In the middle of November, the target of 5,000 weapons a month, promised initially for December 1943, was put back to June, 1944. Meanwhile, the performance of the weapon was still imperfect. The automatic pilot was particularly unreliable, and the scientists at Peenemünde remained unconvinced of the wisdom of trying to produce that delicate mechanism in mass. A final complication appeared as late as the summer of 1944, when the extent and

[1] See p. 314 below.

density of the balloon barrage in front of London forced the designers to concentrate afresh on a device to 'shoot around the corner'—an object they never achieved. To these fundamental difficulties were added others—so often a feature of the German conduct of the war—of control. The operation of the F.Z.G.76 had been entrusted in August, 1943 to a special formation of the army. But as the preparations in northern France came increasingly to conflict with those against invasion, it found itself increasingly hampered by other formations and headquarters that had no real appreciation of its significance; and when the moment came to begin the attack, its facilities and communications remained inadequate, and the officers and men, exhausted by their efforts and disappointments, were not ready.

The same difficulties of production and design affected, even more seriously, the A.4. The raid on Peenemünde disorganized the programme of production until January 1944, when the new factory was ready in the Harz Mountains. Three hundred rockets were thereafter produced by 1st May; but at that point, a fundamental defect in design could no longer be disregarded. Experiments with live warheads over the previous five months had shown that the weapon was liable to burst in the air; and since no satisfactory solution to this failure had as yet been found, production was halted. It began again later in the month, after a partially successful demonstration of a modified warhead, and thereafter increased fast despite the persistence of various unsatisfactory features in the design. Meanwhile, sites for mobile firing parties were prepared in the Pas de Calais, and further south to the line of the Somme, and fourteen depots and plants were built, most of which escaped systematic air attack owing to the more urgent problem presented by the ski-sites. But on the eve of the invasion, there seemed no prospect of the A.4 being used before August, 1944; and in the event, the course of the Allied operations further postponed and radically altered the nature of the attack.

In the last weeks before 'Overlord', the enemy's interest therefore centred on the F.Z.G.76(V.1). Thanks to the success of the Allied attacks on the ski-sites, the Germans had now either to make alternative arrangements or to admit defeat. Unexpectedly, they devised new arrangements. Beginning, as it seems, in January or February, they managed to build a large number of 'modified sites'—on the same principle as the ski-sites, but ingeniously simple and easy to camouflage—over a large area; and by 12th June some sixty-four were manned, over forty in and near the Pas de Calais and over twenty in the Cherbourg peninsula. The British, rather tardily, followed these preparations; but because of the steadily growing demands on aircraft as the preliminaries to 'Overlord' were put in train, and the consequent difficulty of deciding which were the most important of the 'Crossbow' targets, the new positions were scarcely attacked. The flying bomb campaign was accordingly able to begin, in a state of some confusion and desperation, in the middle of June. In the early morning of the 13th, four V.1s landed in south-east England, and after a pause the main attack began on the evening of the 15th.[1]

The attack, on which Hitler had placed such high hopes, had therefore largely failed before it started. Not only was London saved from destruction, and the British Government from capitulation, at the end of 1943, but the invasion of France took place six months later, undisturbed by a single rocket or pilotless aircraft. The postponement of the operations was not the result of the British measures alone, although without them the other difficulties affecting the F.Z.G.76 might well have been overcome sooner. But that does not detract from the value of those measures, in their effect upon the enemy or, perhaps almost as important, in their effect on the other Allied measures then under way for 'Overlord'. Their value was indeed largely a negative value, to be seen in the absence of unfortunate developments elsewhere: in the fact that there was no lack of protection for the civil population, as devised on the knowledge available, in June 1944; and in the fact—of crucial importance to 'Overlord'—that there was no drastic demand, in the period immediately preceding that operation, for aircraft to bomb 'Crossbow' targets which were needed for other tasks in support of invasion. At the climax of the European war, when all forces and services in Britain were already extended, this extra strain was indeed borne with comparatively little disturbance, thanks to forethought and prompt action; and Sir Winston Churchill is justified in describing it as 'an example of the efficiency of our governing machine, and of the foresight and vigour of all connected with it'.[2] A more immediate tribute was paid by General Eisenhower on 28th March, when, reviewing the immediate threat that had not then disappeared, he was able to report:

> '(1) That 'Crossbow' attack would not preclude the launching of the ['Overlord'] assault from the South coast ports as now planned, and that the probable incidence of casualties does not make it necessary to attempt to move the assault forces west of Southampton.
>
> (2) Although some interference with the loading of shipping and craft must be expected, it is not sufficient to justify plans for displacement of shipping and craft from these areas.'

[1] The results of this attack did not affect strategy in the following months, and are not therefore discussed in this volume. A full account will be found in Basil Collier, *The Defence of the United Kingdom* (H.M.S.O.).

[2] *Closing the Ring*, p. 213.

(iv)

Deception, Security and the French

While preparing for invasion, the Allies had to mislead the enemy as to its nature. Positive measures of deception had to be set on foot, and the real measures concealed by these feints and by security.

The deceptive measures fell into two distinct classes, strategic and tactical. The former were designed to induce the enemy, until the preparations were in their later stages, to make faulty strategic dispositions in relation to the operations which the Allies had specified at Teheran; the latter to mislead him, when the preparations could no longer be entirely concealed, as to the date, strength and area of attack. While 'Anvil' as well as 'Overlord' was included in the plan, the emphasis fell on the larger operation, whose nature was the more important and the more difficult to hide.

The strategic plan of deception was known as 'Bodyguard', from the Prime Minister's remark at Teheran that 'truth deserves a bodyguard of lies'. Relying on the well-known principle that false deductions may best be fostered from true premises, it consisted of an ingenious assembly of true and likely facts, so presented as to suggest the wrong conclusions. Supported by some physical evidence, they formed indeed a remarkably persuasive argument, whose various aspects had in fact been debated, along lines already discussed in this volume, by the Combined Chiefs of Staff; but in every case with a result contrary to that implied in the 'Bodyguard' plan. They were moreover designed to allow for the subsequent tactical measures, so that the latter's indications of invasion should not invalidate all, but rather should support some, of the arguments originally offered to conceal its possibility. These later measures relied to a greater extent than their predecessors on physical deception, introduced in a variety of ways: by false concentrations of material, by misleading movements and exercises, by wireless and radar, and by other means. Their object was twofold: first, to persuade the enemy that the landings would take place in the north of France, but in the Pas de Calais and not in the Cherbourg peninsula; secondly, to suggest that the main blow was still to come even after the landings in the Cherbourg peninsula had taken place. They succeeded admirably.

Plan 'Bodyguard', which in essence was a British plan, involved action by the Americans and Russians. Their approval was sought at the end of January 1944, and, after the experts had met in Moscow, was obtained early in March. But it remained to safeguard 'Bodyguard' itself. False plans could not succeed unless the real plans were kept dark; and the scale of the preparations in England throughout April and May would be such that this would not be easy under the conditions prevailing in January and February. It seemed likely that movement and information must be, possibly drastically, curtailed, if the whole elaborate structure was not to be revealed; and this of course had implications beyond the military sphere.

The ideal of the military authorities was to shroud the preparations completely from view, and to prevent any comment from leaving the country except under their auspices. They were prepared to sacrifice to this positive gain in security, the normal, useful flow of miscellaneous and often misleading information which left the country, and to accept the effects of such a warning on the enemy. Such a policy would affect British subjects, allies and neutrals alike. The first provided the simplest problem. It was unlikely that the country would seriously resent any temporary restrictions imposed in such a cause on movement and mail, and the question was therefore how best to achieve their objects without unnecessary inconvenience. After some discussion in the 'Overlord' Committee and the War Cabinet, the latter decided on 10th March to impose a ban on all unauthorized travel, and to some extent on communications, to and from the coastal region between the Wash and the Cornish coasts in England, and to and from an area in Scotland adjacent to the Firth of Forth. From 6th April, all normal leave for the British armed forces was also stopped within the United Kingdom—a step taken the more readily for the relief it afforded to the heavily burdened transport system.

The movement of Allied troops was similarly restricted, in this case on the orders of the Supreme Commander. A more difficult problem was set by the control of the movement and mail of allies who were not under his authority, and of neutrals. For restriction here affected Governments and Embassies falling into several different categories of importance and confidence, some likely to deplore the ban as a significant precedent in diplomatic usage, others as a deprivation of their rights as allies. Two questions had to be answered: first, could restrictions be devised which could be applied usefully to all members of such a heterogeneous body? Secondly, if they could not, how were the restrictions to be graded?

There was a strong case for comprehensive restriction. It was conceded that military necessity must override any argument of convenience or tradition, and there seemed to be no satisfactory military alternative. If no ban were imposed, a flood of information and comment would continue and might increase; and while it would undoubtedly include much misleading rumour, it must also contain a number of pieces of accurate information, which, as the 'Crossbow' authorities could confirm, provided after a time the best guide to the truth. But any half measure suffered from the same defect, and from the added inconvenience that half measures usually cause. To impose restrictions on certain Governments and Embassies alone would be awkward and unsatisfactory: unreliable individuals were not confined to unreliable institutions, to watch some involved almost as much work as to watch all, and such a step would merely attract the greatest odium for the least result. It would be almost equally awkward to impose a series of sudden and comprehensive bans for short periods, as the Prime Minister suggested: information would still leave the country at intervals and after delay, and such an irritating embargo could not be imposed in practice on more than a very few occasions. After much debate in February and March, all therefore agreed that the ban must be continuous and comprehensive throughout a given period, which was to start on 15th April and to last until such time after D-day as was later considered necessary.

In its final form, the ban forebade the diplomatic representatives of all neutral and Allied Governments in the United Kingdom, apart from those of the British Dominions, the United States and Russia, to leave the country except in specially approved cases, to send or receive uncensored communications by telegram or diplomatic bag, and to receive couriers from abroad. The 'Overlord' Committee noted specifically that these restrictions applied equally to the French Committee of National Liberation. No ban was placed on the traffic of cypher telegrams to and from enemy, neutral or Allied representatives in Eire, although in practice these were subject to certain technical delays. Nor were there restrictions on the sailing of ships from Eire which had not called at a port in the United Kingdom, or on the use of their wireless after departure, although here again steps were taken to lessen the risk of leakages of information. Thus, no exception was made in the United Kingdom itself for the representatives of any but the three great Allies. The rest were subject equally to the ban, although all possible facilities were offered to ease the consequences. A special dispensation was, however, later allowed in strict secrecy to the Poles, to maintain an uncensored correspondence with their agents.[1]

The exiled allies in general received the restrictions well. But, as was bound to be the case, special difficulties arose with the French. For the French in London were in a unique position, in that, unlike the other exiles, they represented a sovereign Allied authority situated in its own territory, in the French North African Empire. They were therefore naturally anxious to keep their communications free and secret, and the ban was accepted only with great reluctance in London and with unconcealed anger in Algiers. Its imposition indeed marked a critical point in the relations of the Western Allies with the French, whose effects were to be felt increasingly in the short period that remained before the invasion. For the problem of security reflected in this case an important problem of policy; and its solution

[1] See p. 370 below.

served notice on the authorities in Algiers, not of a mere technical inconvenience, but of the decision of the Western Allies, hitherto not clearly expressed, to limit the rôle of the French in the projected liberation of their country.

French affairs form a side issue to the strategic argument, and in the history of the invasion itself. The Resistance in the event had a distinct effect on German movements in the summer of 1944, greater than the Allies had expected though less than itself had earlier claimed; and incidents such as the liberation of Paris, and General de Gaulle's activities in search of a Government, thereafter had specific military and diplomatic repercussions. But the Allies' main policy and conduct remained unaltered, and the subject may therefore seem of minor importance to the theme with which we are concerned. Nevertheless, it cannot be dismissed so lightly. To invade France was not the same as to invade Italy. With whatever limitations, the French were allies, whose contribution and whose Government could, and certainly should, not be determined simply by the invaders. The problem they posed was integral to the problems of 'Overlord', and in fact, particularly in the last few weeks before D-day, it occupied a large place in the discussions of the British Ministers and Chiefs of Staff. Its history must be examined in some detail if we are to appreciate the interaction of diplomatic and operational factors on a sector of this greatest of military ventures, and the anxieties that beset the authorities in London at a critical time.

In the four years before June 1944, the Western Allies' relations with the French followed the triangular pattern common to their relations with all those European nations, occupied by the enemy, which maintained a form of government in exile. They dealt on the one hand with the exiled representatives and forces, and on the other with the movements of resistance within the countries, according to the relations established between the former and the latter. The shape of the triangle therefore varied with the data. Sometimes, as in the cases of Norway, Holland and Poland, exiles and resistance were, or seemed to be, sufficiently in accord for the Western Allies to treat directly with the former in matters of policy affecting the latter. Sometimes, as in the cases of Greece and Yugoslavia, they had to maintain separate relations at all levels with exiles and resistance alike. But the case of France was unique, for there was at no time a central organization of resistance in that country to which the Allies sent representatives, and relations both with the Resistance and with the exiled authorities centred throughout on a single, controversial figure whose gradual domination of both was not accompanied by a settlement of his relations with the Allies themselves.

This figure was General Charles de Gaulle, who by the beginning of 1944 had established himself as the unchallenged head of the exiled French Committee of National Liberation, and as the effective symbol of resistance throughout the various movements inside France. It is therefore necessary to appreciate what was his purpose, and how he proposed to achieve it: the more so, as both his policy and his methods were and have remained the subjects of dispute. In the first place, it should be appreciated that de Gaulle had a policy. For it has often been alleged that the aims he expounded were merely, or largely, the result of his temperament, which his inspired decision in the summer of 1940 enabled him to impose upon French affairs. Certainly the personality was essential to the full prosecution of the policy; but there was nevertheless a policy which the personality supported. It was in fact logical and clear, and its premises, though not de Gaulle's conclusions from them, were largely common ground among exiled Frenchmen of whatever persuasion. France, de Gaulle argued with justice, unlike the other conquered nations of Europe, had been and remained a Great Power, with actual and potential assets that were of value to her allies. She still disposed of the second largest Empire in the world; and she provided a natural spring-board for the final attack on Germany which must presumably take place. Though conquered, she thus retained positions of strength from which to defend her integrity and to proclaim her value to the Allied counsels; and it behoved her representatives in exile the more rigorously to defend her rights.

De Gaulle insisted that the circumstances of 1940 placed the onus of this defence solely upon himself. Secure in his immediate and uncompromising hostility to the Germans, and assured of British support, he alone could concentrate on his person the free elements of France, and thereafter secure the recognition from his allies that was vital to her future. In the distance, but unwavering, dawned the prospect of a return to France, as a free, sole and potent authority by the side and not in the baggage of the conquerors.

The plausibility of this argument provided the obstacles to its success. The very fact that de Gaulle found it necessary to assume such a responsibility for France was likely to cause other Frenchmen to dispute it. For the French, scrupulous in their respect for legal authority, suffered throughout the war from the absence outside France of its obvious repository; and the deep divisions in national politics and traditions that remained in 1940, could only be expected over the next few years, and particularly while the Vichy Government endured, to underline the effects. De Gaulle was faced with the unpalatable fact that some of the most powerful interests outside France were indifferent or hostile to him; and while he was able in the early years to gain control over some parts of the French Empire—over

Indo-China and Equatorial Africa in 1940, and in Syria in 1941—he remained for a time excluded from, and later challenged in, its most important possessions in North Africa. Similarly, while he had his connexions from the start with some of the resistance movements, others, which opposed or stood apart from them, stood apart from him. The logic of his policy thus drove him, willingly enough, along a stormy route.

The fact that it was stormy naturally did not commend it to the Western Allies, who bore a definite responsibility for de Gaulle and viewed French affairs from a different point of vantage. Their disapproval was increased by the habitual acerbity which marked the General's dealings with themselves as well as with his fellow countrymen, and by his sudden *coups* in territories which they had occupied in the Allied cause, of which the most notorious occurred in Syria and in the Atlantic islands of St. Pierre et Miquelon. It was the more irritating that de Gaulle, secure in the logic of his case, regarded their disapproval as inevitable, and remained largely indifferent to it. He foresaw that an uncompromising stand in the name of French rights would not prove ungrateful to Frenchmen, and, provided he survived the Allies' displeasure, calculated that events would force them to accept his claims. Nevertheless, while both Governments joined in deploring de Gaulle's behaviour, their attitudes towards his position were not the same. The British, although driven eventually almost to breaking point, were not unsympathetic to his cause, which they had espoused before the Americans entered the war, and which they found both more attractive and more effective than that of any alternative authority. They therefore wished to retain de Gaulle at the centre of affairs, and to curb his more provocative ambitions by making him join forces with those of his opponents who were acceptable to London and Washington. The Americans, on the other hand, startled by the General's activities and, in this instance, more tolerant of the established authorities, saw him as a potential and unrepresentative dictator who was already an embarrassment, and might later prove fatal, to the interests of his country. This difference in attitude partly reflected, and partly accounted for, a difference between the British and Americans' estimates of de Gaulle's potential power, which by the end of 1943 the former rated higher than the latter; and while in the last resort the British Government would undoubtedly move with its ally against the General, it therefore tried constantly to postpone the occasion, which indeed as a result became increasingly undesirable.

For at the beginning of 1944 de Gaulle could face with some assurance the disfavour of the Western Allies, and could advance those further demands upon them which his policy made inevitable as the likelihood of invasion increased. He had survived dismissal in his weakness, and was now, as he had calculated, in a position of some strength. The critical year was 1943. After the Casablanca Conference in January, negotiations were begun to set up a new National Council (or Assembly) and a new National Committee (or Government) which would incorporate and replace the existing movements of de Gaulle and the North African authorities. After much discussion, the Conseil National de la Résistance was established in May; and in June the Comité National de la Libération (C.F.L.N.) was recognized by the Western Allies, Generals de Gaulle and Giraud being joint Presidents and Giraud Commander-in-Chief of the Armed Forces. At first it seemed that the main groups might now combine in a working, if not a particularly harmonious, alliance. But as the summer passed, it became clear that de Gaulle was in the ascendant, and was not reconciled to his partners. His steady and open accession of strength from the Resistance inside France, the appeal to national sentiment of his aggressive 'foreign policy', and the effective political superiority which he exhibited over Giraud, enabled and encouraged him to resume his march towards the seat of power. A turning point was reached in November, when at the instance of de Gaulle the Conseil National was reorganized as an Assemblée Consultative, half of whose members were 'resisters' brought out for the purpose from France. On the 9th, Giraud and his supporters resigned from the Committee, although Giraud himself remained Commander-in-Chief of the Armed Forces until April, 1944. De Gaulle became sole President, the Committee and its offices were overhauled and staffed entirely by his adherents, and Giraud was thenceforth virtually excluded from serious business. At the beginning of 1944, de Gaulle was thus effectively in charge of French affairs outside France. His future now depended on the extent of his support inside the country, and on the value which the Allies attached to it for their own purposes.

Despite its potential significance in the Allied strategy, the French Resistance was not treated as important until early in 1944, and at no time was it formally accorded the first priority among the resistance movements of Europe. This is not so surprising when we recall the functions and policy of S.O.E.—the British Special Operations Executive, dealing with subversion in territory occupied by the enemy. Once the decision had been taken, or had occurred, not to rely on subversion as an integral factor in strategy—as had happened by the summer of 1942—, it was neither possible nor desirable to afford much material aid to movements of resistance which could not be related directly and immediately to Allied operations. Even when they were so related, few ships or aircraft could be spared until late in 1943, and the difficulty of controlling scattered and often mutually hostile forces impressed on the British the importance of husbanding their effort until the critical moment. Throughout 1941 and 1942, the course of the war favoured support of the movements in the Mediterranean and the Balkans rather than of those in north-west Europe, a tendency which was confirmed at the end of the second year by the invasion of North Africa. In March 1943, the Chiefs of Staff provided S.O.E. with the following order of immediate priority for its operations.

(i) The Italian islands, Corsica and Crete.
(ii) The Balkans.
(iii) France.
(iv) Poland and Czechoslovakia.
(v) Norway and the Low Countries.
(vi) Far East.

And in November of that year, when 'Overlord' had been confirmed as the main operation for 1944, they revised it to read:

(i) The Balkans.
(ii) Enemy-occupied Italy.
(iii) France.
(iv) The Aegean islands and Crete.
(v) Poland, Hungary and Czechoslovakia.
(vi) Norway and the Low Countries.
(vii) Far East.

Only in 1944 itself, did north-west Europe in practice take first place in the necessarily short-range programme of S.O.E.

By that time, the resistance movements in France had developed to a point at which their main features were unlikely to alter. Their organization appeared impressive. The central direction was in the hands of a Conseil National de la Résistance (C.N.R.), composed of representatives from the various movements of resistance, from the political parties they had fostered, and from the Trades Unions; and exercising authority over a network of Liberation Committees, designed to take over national and local administration. The military organization was equally detailed. In January 1944, the various forces of the Resistance combined into the French Forces of the Interior (F.F.I.), including Gaullists, Giraudists and Communists, whose control again extended over a network covering large areas of the country. It thus appeared that the French Resistance embraced every aspect of the preparations necessary both to free and to govern France.

But impressive and important as it was, the development of this organization had been such as to limit its immediate value, at this late stage, to the Western Allies. For the growth of the French Resistance contained within itself a damaging paradox. Although directed to military ends, it was brought about by political means, which in the circumstances involved the mutual co-operation of different groups and movements with different types of membership and different associations. The larger, therefore, the central organization became, the less useful it or its parts seemed likely to be to the Allied strategy. While the British and American Governments looked for the most part with approval and sympathy on the creation of a comprehensive political centre of resistance, its very comprehensiveness made their military authorities wary of its military claims. In fact, the more these grew, the more cautiously they were received. It was one thing, the Western Allies felt, to control small, well-disciplined groups for particular operations: quite another to admit an extensive organization, containing many varied elements, to a knowledge of the plans for the most critical operation of the war.

This feeling, moreover, was the stronger because of the close and necessary association which the Resistance fostered with General de Gaulle. For while the British had from the first welcomed him as 'leader of all Free Frenchmen wherever they may be, who rally to him in support of the Allied cause', their support did not blind them to the limits of his position at that time, or subsequently to the implications of some of his demands. They therefore retained their own communications with France, their own organization as a part of S.O.E., and complete responsibility, on behalf of the Western Allies, for the policy of subversion; and although an arrangement was reached in 1941 regulating the interchange of information and the use of transport, the two separate organizations, of S.O.E. and de Gaulle, continued until the eve of 'Overlord' to work in virtually watertight compartments.

In 1943, indeed, it seemed possible that S.O.E. would become entirely separated from the main movements of the Resistance, which by then were rapidly extending and elaborating their machinery. For the British were by then concentrating—particularly in the north, where German activities and suspicions were most dominant—on a network of small independent groups, directly controlled by British agents, organized as far as possible (though not always successfully) against penetration by the enemy, and interested secondarily or not at all in politics. This tendency became the more marked in the course of the year, when the one large movement with which the British had been closely in touch, and which stood apart from the other elements in the combined Resistance, fell to pieces. Meanwhile, the main Resistance and de Gaulle had moved into an indissoluble, if latterly uneasy, partnership. From the start, indeed, the connexion had been close. When the first association of resistance groups in the unoccupied zone took place in the late summer of 1941, they sent a representative to London almost at once to see the General, and the latter soon managed to establish regular communication with, and some control over, their organization. By the autumn of 1942, he had appointed one of his officers to act as its military adviser and commander of its forces; and in the winter, he was acknowledged by a wider group of movements in the centre and south as 'the unchallenged leader of the Resistance'. Soon afterwards, the main movements in the north, and most of the smaller movements elsewhere, were brought into the alliance; and during 1943, as de Gaulle with this powerful support improved his position in Algiers, his improving position in Algiers supported the growth of his authority inside France. While a certain rivalry between the Resistance and 'le premier Résistant', and even parallel systems of command, developed as the former began to speak with greater assurance, the interests of both were too closely connected for them not to combine until the end as a single force in their claims on the British and Americans.

But the complete separation of the British organization from that of the main Resistance did not come about in the event, owing to a separate development in 1943. This was provided by the Maquis, which by the late spring of 1944 was to number perhaps 100,000 men, and was later to take over large tracts of territory in the centre and south of France. A movement on this scale naturally had a different origin from that of the earlier symptoms of resistance, based essentially on individual activity. It was in fact provided directly by German measures—by the calls for French labour which began in the late summer of 1942, and which were met by the disappearance into the woods and mountains of the young men whom they mostly affected. The rapid growth of these bands—some loosely organized and impermanent, some compact and disciplined, all known as 'maquis'—presented a serious problem both to the Resistance and to London. For while by the autumn of 1943 the former had established some measure of control over the assorted groups, effective control was impossible for such numbers without extraneous direction and support. There were not enough arms even for some of the maquis without large supplies from outside; while only the Allies could say how a force of this order should be used.

The Allies were not inclined to ask too much of the Maquis as a united force. In the first place, its direct control lay with the Resistance, to which they were not prepared to confide their intentions in detail. But secondly, even if they had been willing to do so, and even if they could have counted on the Resistance to control all of the maquis effectively, it seemed unlikely that the latter could be allotted an important part in 'Overlord'. The place of a guerrilla army within an intricate and exact military plan is extremely difficult to determine without considerable knowledge of its capacity, which in the circumstances was impossible; and it therefore seemed neither safe nor worthwhile to arm the Maquis on a large scale, even assuming the means to be available. In June 1943, Cossac had remarked that 'The assistance of the [resistance] groups should . . . be treated as a bonus rather than an essential part of the plan.' His conclusion was accepted fully by his successors.

The emergence of the Maquis did not therefore change the British attitude to the French Resistance. But it modified the practice of S.O.E., and substantially increased the supplies from England. For provided that the Resistance was not regarded as a necessary condition for 'Overlord's' success, its support along certain lines and within certain limits might prove of distinct value. If large operations were out of the question, specific types of sabotage and subversion were not; and if the Maquis as a whole could not be armed, some maquis could certainly be armed with limited but valuable objects. In the first six months of 1944, S.O.E. therefore co-operated as far as it could with de Gaulle in supplying and controlling certain groups and maquis, and made its own preparations for their direct leadership and support as soon as the invasion was under way. Its agents in the centre and south, with their compact organizations, were ordered to contact some of the local leaders, while others were sent from London, usually attached to the missions which de Gaulle was despatching for the same purpose. Meanwhile, a small body of British officers was trained to act as leaders to the guerrillas after the Allies had landed, and to ensure that their activities were co-ordinated as far as possible with the main operations.

All such activities depended on arms. Few had been sent in the last quarter of 1943, partly because the British were still concerned to support the guerrillas in the Balkans rather than in north-west Europe, and partly because S.O.E. itself was then going through a difficult time. The prospect in 1943 of campaigns on the mainland of Europe, which might have been expected to foster its importance, had in fact, thanks to that very prospect and to the familiar and apparently justified suspicions of its efficiency in some areas, led to the opposite result. Not only were S.O.E.'s representatives then placed firmly and finally under the direct supervision of the Supreme Commanders in the theatres, but its aircraft in western and southern Europe, which were redistributed in August, were placed respectively under Bomber Command and the Mediterranean Allied Air Forces. The central organization was also brought more closely within the aegis of the Chiefs of Staff. The immediate result was that S.O.E. lost much of its vigour, and that supplies to France declined even over those of the preceding quarter.

Early in 1944, however, the position was modified for western Europe. The new emphasis on 'Overlord' led to a review of S.O.E.'s operations in France, which was given a further impetus by the Prime Minister's sympathy for the guerrillas. As a result, a *modus vivendi* was established in February between S.O.E. and Bomber Command for the operational control of the aircraft based on England, which in effect returned to the former the powers it had recently lost. In March, S.O.E. received two fresh squadrons of British bombers, making a total of four in all, and two squadrons of American bombers. The increase in strength and efficiency, accompanied by a greater use of the aircraft from the Mediterranean over France, was soon reflected in the figures.

	Sorties from Britain to France			*Sorties from the Mediterranean to France*
	British	*American*	*Total*	*Total*
1943				
3rd quarter	327	—	327	1
4th quarter	101	—	101	4
1944				
1st quarter	557	52	609	91
2nd quarter	748	521	1,269	396

The material dropped to the Resistance, mainly between the beginning of February and the middle of May 1944, was of the following order:

	From General de Gaulle	*From S.O.E.*	*Total*
Sten guns	30,936	45,354	76,290
Pistols	10,385	17,576	27,961
Rifles	6,694	10,251	16,945
Bren guns	1,609	1,832	3,441
Bazookas	272	300	572
Piats	119	185	304
Mortars	17	143	160

This effort, distributed not unevenly between the Gaullist and Allied organizations, did not attempt, as it was not intended, to meet the demands of the Resistance. But it was a substantial effort at the peak of the air campaign, it came at the right time, and it did more than anything else to prepare its recipients, morally as well as materially, for what lay ahead. At the end of May 1944, according to the best estimates, there were 10,000 French men and women armed by London for more than one day's serious fighting, and 40,000 armed in some degree. All of these, and possibly another 60,000 unarmed men and women, belonged to formations that were in touch in some way with London. A further 350,000 unarmed men and women belonged to formations that were not directly in touch, and 350,000 again were probably in individual contact with them. There were also perhaps 500,000 railwaymen, and 300,000 Trades Unionists, under the control of their own authorities. Taking it in its widest sense, from the 40,000 armed men and women to those who might aid the Allies by passive resistance or by help if opportunity arose, the Resistance comprised perhaps some 3,000,000 people throughout the country.

Such numbers, with such weapons, made an accurate estimate of their contribution extremely difficult; and the forecasts ranged accordingly from very high to very low.

Against this background, the relations between the Western Allies and General de Gaulle developed fast over the first six months of 1944, until they reached a climax on the eve of 'Overlord'. De Gaulle's position, early in the year, contained elements of great strength and of weakness. He was by then supreme on the Committee of National Liberation, essential to the Resistance, and in direct contact with many of its forces. He had completely outstripped S.O.E. in establishing his influence inside the country, and was the recognized channel, to the French and to the Allies, for contact with each other. On the other hand, he was faced by the steadily growing organization of the Resistance itself, which now had a valid existence and power of its own and might try to act without him after the invasion. To prevent this, as well as to achieve his original goal, he must return with the Allies as an equal partner in the operation, and secure in their recognition of his Committee as the provisional Government of France. If they, in his view, needed him, he also needed them, and was moreover obliged to secure his demands at a time when he depended on them for greater supplies to the Resistance.

As the prospect of invasion increased, de Gaulle was thus driven by his policy and by the situation inside France to enlarge his claims. But in fact, having gained so much so far, he was unlikely now to gain more. The strong points in his position promised eventual success: its weakness was immediate. We have already seen why the Allies were not prepared to divulge their plans to the Resistance. Its own plans were first submitted to them in the late summer of 1943. It proposed to mount seven connected operations related to invasion, all to be directed from London: Plan Vert, a plan to attack the railways, Plan Tortue to attack German movements by road, Plan Violet to attack telecommunications, Plan Jaune to attack munition dumps, Plan Rouge to attack installations of oil fuel, Plan Noir to attack enemy headquarters, and Plan Grenouille to sabotage railway turn-tables. The Allies decided that Plans Vert and Grenouille might be of direct use during the last three months before D-day, and the rest during the last few weeks and days. But unfortunately, before the plans could be properly assessed in relation to the final Allied design, the French decided to try them out; and by January, 1944 only Plan Vert had survived the test. Violet, Jaune, Rouge and Noir were not heard of again, while Tortue and Grenouille in the event were put into effect raggedly though with some good results.

Plan Vert was accordingly adopted by the Allies as an integral part of the plan to delay movement by rail. It had a marked success in the hands of the railway workers and technicians—always one of the most highly organized elements in the Resistance—and aided effectively the British and American air operations.

The Resistance, however, did not remain content with these limited intentions; and at the end of 1943 it proposed a more ambitious design, based on the existence of the Maquis and known, in memory of the first Gaullist commander of the Resistance forces, as Plan Vidal. This postulated the seizure of large areas of France by the French themselves as soon as possible after D-day, to provide the British and Americans with 'ports of entry' for airborne supplies and possibly for troops, and the forces of the Resistance with bases from which to operate against the enemy. Such a plan, which must involve large supplies from Britain, close co-ordination with the Resistance, and at least its partial knowledge of the intentions for 'Overlord', did not appeal to the Allies, and they rejected it firmly in February, 1944. But, not unnaturally, the French did not abandon the prospect of redeeming their own territory, and the plan was in fact executed in places—on the Vercors Plateau and in the Massif Central—later that summer and independently of the Allies.

Denied a central place in the plans for invasion, the French representatives in London remained in much the same position as those of the other nations of north-west Europe until the eve of 'Overlord'. Plans for French action were transferred to the Supreme Commander in January 1944, and the relevant section of S.O.E. then amalgamated with its American counterpart to form a part of his headquarters. The French forces in Britain (one division for the later campaign in northern France) were placed at the same time under the Supreme Commander; but the Gaullist organization for the Resistance remained outside, in the same relation as before to its British and American counterpart. It was not until May 1944, when de Gaulle appointed General Koenig to London in command of all French Forces of the Interior,[1] that it was brought within the Allied Command. But the inclusion of de Gaulle's military representative, so eagerly awaited by de Gaulle himself, emphasized rather than mitigated the limits of his powers. Koenig was not admitted to the plans for 'Overlord', and indeed the security authorities used his headquarters in the service of the deception plan as well as to prepare the French for limited action. On 20th June, when the campaign was under way, he was finally placed in sole direction of all bodies concerned with the F.F.I., and the combined British and American organization was then brought within his own. But this was largely a diplomatic move, and had little immediate effect; and the eventual co-ordination, under de

[1] See p. 322 above.

Gaulle's representative, of the organizations for subversive warfare in France, was less important than the fact that they remained separate until after the invasion had been launched.

But in the first quarter of 1944, stimulated by his rôle in providing the growing volume of supplies to the Resistance, de Gaulle hoped for a more important place in the Allied counsels, and with it some definite recognition at least of his *de facto* jurisdiction in French affairs. In September 1943, following its recognition by both Western Allies, the French Committee of National Liberation had approached them on this subject, suggesting that it should be consulted immediately on the form of administration to be set up in liberated French territory. Its proposals were not acceptable as they stood; but they started a discussion between the British and the Americans, which by November, unknown to the French, had reached a position not unfavourable to them. There were three possible ways in which the Allies could administer French territory as it was reconquered. First, through a *de facto* French authority which would then provide the Allied forces with the facilities they required. Secondly, partly through the Supreme Commander, when and where military necessity required, and partly through a *de facto* French authority when and where it did not. Thirdly, through the Supreme Commander alone, until such time as the Allied Governments agreed to transfer control to a recognized French authority, which should if possible be *de jure* as well as *de facto*. The British were divided on, while the Americans on the whole disliked, the first course, which had been adopted in North Africa. The only possible *de facto* authority was the Committee of National Liberation, which was not considered sufficiently representative or sufficiently in accord with the Allies to be given such responsibility. The choice therefore lay between the other two possibilities. The British preferred the second, the Americans the third; but in October, 1943 they agreed upon a compromise, whereby a representative of the French Committee would be appointed under the Supreme Commander to take over the administration of reconquered territory until such time as the Combined Chiefs of Staff agreed to transfer the responsibility entirely to the French. 'If circumstances permit, [this] transfer . . . may be progressive'; meanwhile, 'in order to achieve the eventual aim of free and untrammelled choice by the French people of the form of Government . . ., the Supreme Allied Commander should do his best to hold the scales even between all French political groups sympathetic to the Allied cause.' As the Foreign Secretary remarked, this solution offered various theoretical difficulties; but it gave the French a good deal in practice, and provided a reasonable basis for further progress.

The Western Allies intended, in November 1943, to approach the French along these lines, after discussing their compromise with the

Russians at the Foreign Secretaries' conference in Moscow. But in the course of that month, developments in Algiers removed the opportunity. The elimination of General Giraud[1], and a fresh crop of indiscreet and unfriendly remarks by General de Gaulle, annoyed the two Western Governments, and particularly the President and Prime Minister. The discussion accordingly lapsed, and when Eisenhower was appointed to command 'Overlord' he had no instructions on the subject. Before the end of January 1944, he was asking either for a decision or for permission to negotiate with a representative of de Gaulle. A triangular correspondence ensued between himself and the British and American Governments. Eisenhower himself, with qualified support from the Foreign Departments, sought for a solution as near as possible to the North African model, which would limit his responsibilities to the area and the period of battle. The Heads of Government, on the other hand, preferred to await developments before granting any form of recognition. They were anxious not to repeat the experience of Italy, where the attempt to legislate in advance for the Allies' relations with the Italians had ended in failure and embarrassment; they did not trust de Gaulle; still doubted, more than most of their advisers, the extent of his influence in France; and feared that *de facto* recognition would give him a, possibly illegitimate, political advantage which would end by his extracting recognition *de jure*. They did not in any case believe that it would prove possible to free civil affairs from military supervision for some time; meanwhile they considered themselves the best guardians of the safety of their troops and the honour of the Allies, in a land still subject to severe fighting and inevitably torn by recrimination.

This difference of emphasis could not be bridged, and the Foreign Departments' proposals over the first two months of 1944 accordingly met with no response. But in March, the Supreme Commander insisted on some practical instructions, and on the 18th the President issued a directive, with Mr. Churchill's approval, which would enable Eisenhower to propose a working agreement to the French. This gave to the Supreme Commander 'supreme authority' in France, and the 'ultimate determination of where, when and how civil administration . . . shall be exercised by French citizens.' He might consult with the French Committee of National Liberation, and might authorize it at his discretion to select the men for the task. But this was not to be taken as conferring upon the Committee any recognition as the Government of France, 'even on a provisional basis'; and the same applied to any other French organization.

Such instructions were bound to offend the Committee of National Liberation, and indeed proved unpopular with many British and

[1] See p. 321 above.

Americans. But the balance was apparently redressed early in April 1944, in the course of a broadcast by Mr. Cordell Hull in which he stated that:

> '. . . The President and I . . . are disposed to see the French Committee of National Liberation exercise leadership to establish law and order under the supervision of the Allied Commander-in-Chief.
>
> . . . The Committee is, of course, not the Government of France and we cannot recognise it as such. . . . It has been a symbol of the spirit of France and of French resistance. . . .'

This speech was well received, and the Allies decided now to approach the French. There was indeed a last attempt to amend Eisenhower's directive so as to correspond more closely with the terms of the broadcast. But this proved impossible, the President and the Secretary of State maintaining that the speech and the directive were complementary and not contradictory; and on 19th April Bedell Smith accordingly handed to Koenig an *aide-mémoire*, based on the directive, on which discussions might proceed. This informed the French that civil affairs were regarded for the time being as of military importance, and that therefore the Allied headquarters wished to start talks at once with the French military authorities in London, with whom would be associated a civil representative from the Committee of National Liberation. The Supreme Commander's authority was made clear; but, provided that the Committee of National Liberation was prepared to accept the position, the proposals seemed to allow for an adequate treatment of practical problems during the earlier stages of the campaign.

But the approach was made at an unfortunate moment. Only a few days before, the British Government had imposed its ban on movements and communications;[1] and once he appreciated the full position, the effect on de Gaulle was immediate and severe. The growing attention paid to the Resistance, the increase in his own power, and the tone of Cordell Hull's recent speech, had led him to hope with some confidence for the attainment of his aims. The ban, followed immediately by the *aide-mémoire*, instead served notice of immediate exclusion. The Committee of National Liberation was now placed in the same category as the other exiled authorities—worse, it could not communicate freely, as they could, with its forces in England; while he himself could no longer hope to be associated in any way as an equal with the invasion, or to return to France as the head of a recognized provisional French authority. It seemed to him the denial of France's contribution to the war, and a blow to French pride that could not easily be forgiven; and in the few weeks that remained, which were so important to France, he brought his relations with the Western Allies to a dangerous climax.

[1] See p. 317 above.

(v)

The Last Weeks

In the last six weeks before D-day, the threads were drawn together, and the pattern emerged. While men and material continued to cross the Atlantic, the preparations for the first stage reached their peak in southern England. Troops, aircraft and supplies were distributed between their stations; naval, merchant and assault shipping assembled in the ports and off shore; advanced headquarters were set up; and the 'Overlord' Command adopted its preparatory organization. The Allied air forces, strategic and tactical, meanwhile embarked on the climax of their campaign, while across the Channel the Resistance was putting into effect Plans Vert and Grenouille, and preparing, with or without Allied direction, for the day that most believed must come soon.

In the same period, the pressure on Ministers and the Chiefs of Staff also reached a climax, only part of which was related directly to the operation. For apart from their responsibilities for the preparations, individually and in committee, they faced other serious problems demanding close attention. The long controversy on 'Anvil' was entering on a new and more hopeful phase;[1] an equally long debate on the strategy for the Far East seemed to be reaching a decisive point;[2] and in the first half of May there took place in London the only conference of Prime Ministers of the British Commonwealth that was held during the war. This meeting, planned the previous winter, was attended by the Prime Ministers of Canada, Australia, New Zealand, South Africa and Southern Rhodesia (Mr. Mackenzie King, Mr. Curtin, Mr. Fraser, Field Marshal Smuts, and Sir Godfrey Huggins) and by Sir Firoz Khan Noon and Lieut.-General H.H. The Maharaja of Kashmir for India. It began on 1st May, and ended on the 16th. The agenda included reviews of, and discussion on, the wars against Germany and Japan, reviews of and discussion on foreign affairs and economic policy in general, and detailed discussion on the post-war settlement, on colonial questions, on civil aviation and shipping, and on post-war employment and migration within the Commonwealth. There was in fact a comprehensive appraisal of the position and prospects of the Commonwealth which, important at any time, imposed on the British delegates the heavier pressure—if it also brought them the comfort of alliance and support—in view of the great developments of the past few years and of their simultaneous preoccupations with other dominant problems.

Upon this anxious and crowded scene was suddenly imposed at

---

[1] See pp. 259-63 above.

[2] See pp. 478-85, and Appendix XI, below.

the last moment a serious disagreement with the French, which, thanks largely to the personality of General de Gaulle and perhaps partly to the natural tension of the time, occupied a disproportionate amount of the Western Allies' attention on the eve of 'Overlord'. Indeed, French affairs occupied a greater proportion of the War Cabinet's agenda between 31st May and 7th June than any other topic, and the bulk of its discussion on the two days immediately before and after the landings.

The anger caused by the British ban on communications, and by the specifically *ad hoc* nature of the Allies' proposals for civil administration in France, produced two reactions in Algiers. On 15th May, the Assembly voted that the Committee of National Liberation should henceforth be styled the Provisional Government of the French Republic; and the next day General Koenig informed the 'Overlord' Command that the Committee had decided to suspend all negotiations, other than those concerning French forces in the Command, so long as communication with London remained impossible. At the same time, it suggested that Koenig himself, and its civil representative in London, should give personal guarantees that they alone would send cypher telegrams provided these were not subject to delay.

Such a relaxation of security could not be accepted, and the authorities in London were now faced with the fact that these two steps by the French had seriously lessened the possibility of useful consultation before 'Overlord' took place. Anxious as both British and Americans were to reach a practical agreement on civil administration before that event, they could not be expected, particularly in view of the President's keen antipathy to the idea, to recognize the Assembly's proclamation, or to reverse a decision on security that had been reached only recently and after considerable thought. At a Staff Conference on 18th May, at which General Bedell Smith was present, the Prime Minister and the Chiefs of Staff accordingly agreed that conversations with Koenig on civil administration should continue as far as possible, but that no relaxation of security should be permitted and no notice taken of the new style of the Committee of National Liberation. They also decided that de Gaulle, whom they had intended to invite to England in advance of 'Overlord', should now be asked to come only on D-day. At the end of May, however, he was invited to arrive on the preceding day.

In these circumstances, further conversations on civil administration proved, as had been feared, abortive, despite the efforts of both Allied and French officials to reach an understanding on specific points. The lack of agreement on principle, indeed, left a dangerously wide field for disagreement on detail, which was provoked in the event by three matters of immediate importance.

The disagreement arose on the very eve of D-day, when General de

Gaulle arrived in England. But the first and most important of the three problems had caused anxiety earlier. It concerned the currency to be adopted in liberated France. In January 1944, the Americans had reported that representatives of the French Committee of National Liberation in Washington had agreed to an Allied proposal that notes of various denominations should be printed for use in an invasion. These notes were not particularly satisfactory. They were to bear a serial number on the front, and on the reverse the French flag with the words '*Libérté, Egalité, Fraternité*'; but no indication of the redeeming authority, and no mention of either '*La France*' or of '*République Française*'. The former omission seems to have reflected the current indecision as to the financial arrangements between a future French Government and the British and Americans; the latter arose from the President's refusal to recognize a *de facto* French authority as in any way *de jure*. But it was hoped that both difficulties would be met by the issue of the notes on the authority of the Supreme Commander, and there the matter was allowed to rest until the last week in May. De Gaulle, however, then suddenly queried the look of the notes, which he thought should bear a reference to the French Republic. When he arrived in England, he raised the further objection that the currency should not be issued on the authority of the Supreme Commander alone; and, while consenting reluctantly to accept the notes as they stood, insisted that the Committee of National Liberation should be identified publicly with their issue. Until this question was settled, he refused to allow further talks to be held on civil administration.

By that time, the question of the currency had become involved in two other matters for disagreement. The lateness of his invitation, and the brief interval allowed him before the invasion took place, fanned the anger which de Gaulle had already displayed over the past few weeks; and he was not to be conciliated by the attention he received on arrival, or by the assurance, which the Prime Minister had been authorized to give him, that the President would welcome a visit to Washington once the invasion had taken place. A series of unfortunate incidents followed. After agreeing to broadcast on D-day in company with other national leaders, the General objected on 5th June to the omission of a mention of the Provisional Government, and refused to speak. At the same time, he forbade the 120 French liaison officers with the 'Overlord' Command to accompany the troops to France, on the ground that, as agents of a French authority which had not reached agreement with the Western Allies on civil affairs, they could have no functions to perform. The War Cabinet, informed of these developments on the late afternoon of the 5th, was pardonably annoyed. But there was little to be done. The next day, de Gaulle agreed to broadcast a brief statement, at a separate time from the series of broadcasts made by other Allied leaders, and omitting any reference to the Americans. He also agreed, on the 6th, to allow twenty of the 120 liaison officers to accompany the troops. But he still refused to sanction the currency which the Allies had proposed; and the War Cabinet on 7th June was therefore obliged to ask the Foreign Secretary to undertake discussions on the matter. Meanwhile, General Eisenhower was informed that he should act on his own authority as he deemed necessary.

The epilogue may soon be told, for once the invasion had taken place the French imbroglio became of less significance, and events dictated the result. As the Prime Minister and the President had forecast, hard fighting for some weeks restricted the area of Allied responsibility to a small corner of France, in which no great problem of civil affairs could arise until the military issue was determined. There was therefore time to debate an agreement in calmer circumstances than had prevailed before the landings. After discussions between London and Washington, the currency problem was settled at the end of June within the framework of a mutual aid agreement, which was formally approved by all parties in the middle of July. Over the same period, the President was persuaded—with less difficulty after a successful visit to Washington by de Gaulle—to recognize the Committee of National Liberation as the *de facto* authority for the civil administration of France. He announced American recognition publicly on 11th July. Allied recognition of de Gaulle's Administration as the Provisional Government awaited further negotiation, and a reorganization of the Assembly which could not take place immediately; and was granted eventually in October, 1944.

While these unhappy exchanges were taking place on the eve of 'Overlord', the operation itself was in the balance. The tale has been told of the sudden onset of bad weather, postponing the invasion by twenty-four hours and threatening its further postponement by at least two weeks; of how the meteorologists forecast on the evening of 4th June that a temporary improvement, lasting for perhaps thirty-six hours, would take place on the morning of the 6th; and of how the Supreme Commander then decided to invade on that day. The assault forces accordingly sailed on the 5th; and by dawn on the 6th the lull had come which the Allied, but not the German, meteorologists had foretold.

CHAPTER IX

THE ADVANCE ON THREE FRONTS, JUNE–SEPTEMBER, 1944

(i)

The Two Great Offensives

IN THE EARLY HOURS of 6th June, 1944, British and American airborne troops landed on the soil of France; and at 6.30 a.m., after a heavy bombardment from the sea and air, the first assault craft touched down on the beaches of the Cherbourg peninsula and the Baie de la Seine.[1] The first day proved the soundness of the preparatory measures. The German army lay dispersed along the coast, ignorant of the area of assault and undecided as to its own intentions. The dispositions and the structure of command pointed to a fundamental uncertainty. Two Armies and an Army Corps held northern France and the Low Countries, with one active and two static divisions in Holland, fourteen static, three active and five panzer divisions from the Dutch frontier to the river Orne, and six static, seven active and one panzer divisions thence to the Atlantic coast. One static division occupied the Channel Islands. The weight of these dispositions lay on the coast between the Belgian frontier and the Seine; but the defence was spread thinly over a large area, and there was no general reserve. This was due partly to a curious pattern of command. The Armies in the north, forming Army Group B, and two Armies in the centre and south forming Army Group G, were directed by Field Marshal Gerd von Rundstedt, the Commander-in-Chief, West. Army Group G was commanded by Colonel-General Johannes Blaskowitz, Army Group B by Field Marshal Rommel. But most of the panzer divisions, grouped for training and administration into a Panzer Group under General Leo Geyr von Schweppenburg, were placed directly under the control of the Fuehrer's headquarters; and moreover von Rundstedt, Rommel and von Schweppenburg all enjoyed direct access to those headquarters and to the Fuehrer himself. The navy and the air formed separate and sovereign commands, Navy Group West under Vice-Admiral Theodor Krancke, and Lufflotte 3

[1] See Map VI, facing p. 279.

under Field Marshal Hugo Sperrle. As might be deduced from this organization, the division of responsibilities in the West reflected and ministered to a centralization of responsibility in the Fuehrer's headquarters. Throughout the months preceding 'Overlord', as later, Hitler himself directly controlled and intervened in the affairs of the theatre, within and between the three Services and particularly within the Army Command. He thereby exacerbated and prolonged strategic differences of opinion that must, under the circumstances, in any case have existed.

For the Germans were sharply divided between alternative plans of campaign in north-west France. Von Rundstedt advocated a flexible defence with a strong mobile reserve, whose strength could be brought to bear, probably after an initial withdrawal from the coast, on ground not unfavourable to itself. Rommel, who suspected that the Allies' air supremacy would prevent the rapid movement of a general reserve, favoured a powerful and rigid obstruction, based on strongly fortified positions, along the whole of the threatened coastline, which would pin the enemy to the beaches for long enough to reinforce the sector of assault from reserves themselves held well forward. Each theory could be commended, given that its presumptions were correct. The difficulty was to choose between competing types of information. Hitler finally supported Rommel, but only after vacillation and delay; and since the enemy until the end remained uncertain of the direction and weight of the assault, the favoured design resulted in a fatal dispersal of force along a front of over five hundred miles. The indecision as to its use had in fact largely nullified the effect of the gradual increase in strength which had taken place, despite the Allies' strategy, over the past six months.[1]

In these circumstances, only timely and precise warning would have offered the Germans any chance of defeating the invasion. But the success of the Allied air operations and of the deception plans had its reward, and tactical surprise was achieved. Attacked continuously from the air and continually by the French Resistance, and beset by a fatal indecision within, the enemy's reactions were clogged and slow, in marked contrast to his reactions to the earlier Allied landings in Italy.

The first phase of the invasion accordingly went well. By the middle of June, the beach-heads had been linked up and both flanks had penetrated well inland. First U.S. Army, consisting by then of nine divisions, had thrust up the Cherbourg peninsula to within a few miles of Valognes, had pushed due west to within a few miles of the Atlantic coast, and stretched thence south-east through Carentan to the east of the river Vire. Second British Army, then consisting of some seven divisions, had pushed inland south of Bayeux, whence it stretched in

[1] See pp. 279-80 above.

a north-easterly direction astride the western and northern roads to Caen, at points ten and five miles from that town. The Allies were now through the coastal defences on a front of some sixty miles, and had beaten off several local counter-attacks. On 18th June, General Montgomery accordingly issued his orders for the next phase of the operations. First U.S. Army was to capture Cherbourg, to clear the peninsula, and to maintain a line some ten miles to the north of St. Lo. Second Army was to take Caen, and to reorganize beyond the town and the river Orne so as to contain the bulk of the enemy's forces. It was hoped that these movements would be complete on 25th June.

So far, the campaign had not departed substantially from the revised 'Overlord' forecast, except in one significant particular. The timetable will be recalled. The first phase should be complete on D+17, by which time the Allies should have occupied a line from the Atlantic coast north of Avranches, through Vire and Caen, to the eastern bank of the Orne. Cherbourg itself might, or might not, have fallen. Thereafter the Americans would advance south from the base of the Cotentin peninsula, while the British engaged the main weight of the opposition beyond Caen. It was hoped that the Americans might reach St. Nazaire, and lie along the Loire as far as Angers, by the middle of July. By D+90, when the forecast ended, the Allies should have reached, and in places have crossed, the northern Seine, and should be threatening Paris. On 18th June, it seemed possible that the first object would be gained in the manner and near the time anticipated. The rate of reinforcement and supply was falling behind schedule, and the key point of Caen had not been taken as expected; but the two artificial harbours were due to be completed in the next few days, and apart from Caen the operations were going well. At this point, however, there was an unexpected development. On 19th June, the Channel was struck by the worst June gale for forty years, followed by a week of severe weather. Convoys at sea were dispersed, and unloading on the beaches virtually stopped. Worse, the two artificial harbours, serving the American and British beaches, were so damaged that the former could not be used and the latter's capacity was severely reduced. In the week of 10th to 16th June, some 156,000 tons of material had been landed in the beach-head: in the following week, when it should have risen, the figure dropped to some 116,000 tons. As a result, movement on both flanks was immediately reduced. Meanwhile, the Germans managed to reinforce around Caen. By 25th June the number of divisions had risen to seven, including four armoured divisions, on a front of approximately forty miles. Second (British) Army, opposing them, mustered twelve divisions, mostly stronger than the enemy's.

Over the next fortnight, the pace of the advance accordingly slowed down. First U.S. Army continued to expand its hold on the Cherbourg peninsula, and on 26th June took Cherbourg itself. It had already reached the Atlantic coast opposite Carentan; but it was then held in the south of the peninsula by the equivalent of seven German divisions, while it built up its strength for further operations towards St. Lo. Second Army meanwhile attacked towards Caen on 25th June. It was immediately involved in close and heavy fighting.

The second half of June was an anxious, and at times seemed a critical, period; and it made a distinct impression on two figures in particular, General Eisenhower and Mr. Churchill. Montgomery's orders of 18th June had stressed the need to capture Caen, which 'is really the key to Cherbourg'. The fighting that ensued was interpreted differently by himself and by the Supreme Commander. Montgomery claimed that the battle conformed, though with a different timetable, to his final object: to contain and break the main strength of the enemy, while the Americans moved in the west. He therefore willingly accepted a tactical delay as a strategic gain, and welcomed the opportunity to decide the issue at this earlier stage. Eisenhower, on the contrary, was determined not to allow a stalemate to supervene so soon in the campaign and so close to the beach-head. Caen had always been regarded as the pivot of the immediate advance; and until it was taken, the Allies were not masters of the position, but in his view were fighting a critical battle on ground chosen by the enemy. His fear of a stalemate at this time was real and vivid; and it influenced his views on the strategy to be adopted elsewhere.

The impression of these events on Churchill was different, but important. His fear was not so much for the battle, on which Montgomery reassured him, as for the bridgehead. Supply was the key to the next stage in the operations; and supply had been badly threatened between 19th and 24th June. The ruin of the western artificial harbour left the Americans only with the beaches; nor did the capture of Cherbourg, though welcome, promise immediate relief. It was not indeed until the middle of July that the first ship could unload inside the port, and not until the second half of August that the quays themselves could be used. The British, though still possessing a damaged artificial harbour, had equally to rely on the beaches for the bulk of their immediate supplies, and for subsequent development could look only to a few small harbours in the Baie de la Seine. How, in these conditions, were the armies to be reinforced substantially? The storm underlined the possible dangers for the immediate future, and the obstacles to the more distant programme of reinforcement direct from the United States. These problems disturbed the Prime Minister more than they disturbed the Americans themselves. 'There was no sight in the war', General Eisenhower wrote later,[1] 'that so impressed me with the industrial might of America as the wreckage

[1] *Crusade in Europe* (1948), pp. 286-7.

on the landing beaches. To any other nation the disaster would have been almost decisive; but so great was America's productive capacity that the great storm occasioned little more than a ripple in the development of our build-up.' The crisis was in fact soon over, as the Americans later had occasion to point out. Unloading over the beaches, and within the port of Cherbourg, proved far more efficient than had been anticipated, and largely offset over the period the immediate loss from the artificial harbours. But coming so soon after the landings, when the enterprise was still vulnerable, the incident made a severe impression on the Prime Minister, and had some effect on his strategic thought.[1]

The battle for Caen ended only on 18th July. On the 9th, British and Canadians met in the centre of the town, but it was another nine days before they reached its eastern outskirts. By that time, Second Army controlled fifteen divisions, from which a new First Canadian Army was formed on 23rd July. The Germans mustered ten divisions, including six armoured divisions. Montgomery now planned to establish himself in positions beyond Caen from which to threaten Falaise and the open country to the east, while the Americans made the main advance in the west. Second Army pushed south and east, on the right towards the road from Caen to St. Lo, on the left from Caen itself and beyond the Orne. The scale and some of the details of the preparations, and the impression received by war correspondents attached to Montgomery's headquarters, suggested to the public that these limited operations were designed as the main advance; and their course was followed accordingly with some disappointment. But in fact they achieved their main object. By 21st July, Second Army had gained positions in which to regroup for the attack best calculated to aid First U.S. Army's forthcoming operations.

For meanwhile the Americans had gained their line through St. Lo, from which to prepare for a more rapid advance. Bad weather after 18th July delayed the offensive; but after a false start on the 24th, First Army attacked the next day. The unremitting pressure of the past five weeks, on land and in the air, had severely weakened and disorganized the enemy. On the 27th he began to retreat on the left, and over the next ten days the Americans drove rapidly through Brittany and Normandy. On 1st August, General George Patton took command of a new Third U.S. Army, and the two American Armies were formed into Twelfth U.S. Army Group under General Bradley. By the 6th, Third Army's front stretched from the Atlantic coast near Quiberon Bay inland to positions on the Loire east of Nantes, and thence north to positions near Chateaubriant, while First Army, moving at first more slowly, had reached a line Vire-Mortain in the east.

---

[1] See pp. 362-7 below; and *Triumph and Tragedy* (1954), pp. 656-9.

The Germans were now in a potentially dangerous position. Their line in the west had virtually gone, and in the north Twenty-First Army Group (Second British and First Canadian Armies) was preparing to attack towards Falaise. Early in August, the enemy therefore regrouped the bulk of his armour south of Falaise, and on the 7th counter-attacked with six armoured divisions towards Mortain and Avranches in an effort to cut the Americans' communications. The attempt failed. While elements of First U.S. Army met and contained the attack, the rest, combined with Second Army, formed the neck of a bag around it. The British pushed south from their positions between Vire and Caen, while the left flank of First U.S. Army moved south-east from Vire and its right in a northerly curve from south of Mortain towards Argentan. Meanwhile, Third U.S. Army to the south, leaving one Corps to attack the ports of Brest, Lorient and St. Nazaire, entered Mayenne and Le Mans on 8th August, whence the left flank curved through Alençon towards Argentan while the right moved due east parallel with the Loire. In the extreme north-east, the Canadians began their attack on Falaise. By 13th August, the shape of the bag was becoming clear. The Canadians were five miles north of Falaise, the British lay on their right in a south-westerly direction to join the Americans south-east of Vire, the line then turned to the south for fifteen miles, and thence irregularly to the north-east, the right of First U.S. Army stretching towards Argentan, and the left of Third U.S. Army lying on the outskirts of that town. Twenty miles separated the Allies in the north and south. The corridor was lined by nine German divisions, and another six lay within the neck of the bag. On that day, the battle began to entrap and destroy the whole force.

The course of the campaign, which the Allies had watched at times with anxiety, was fatal to the German Command. The early British and American successes had provoked the latent crisis between von Rundstedt and the Fuehrer's headquarters which previous disagreements had prepared. By the end of June, when all armoured counter-attacks had failed to carry out Hitler's plan, the Field Marshal was convinced that the Allies could not be held; and on 1st July, according to the pleasant account of his Chief of Staff, he met Keitel's query as to what should be done with the answer, 'Make peace, you fools'. He was relieved that night by Field Marshal Gunther von Kluge, a more pliable subordinate. But the *malaise* of the German system, inflamed by recent failures, was now about to take its toll on all fronts including the west. On 20th July, elements in the army made their long-prepared and hitherto frustrated attempt to assassinate Hitler; and its failure was followed by a relentless purge. Von Kluge, although not irrevocably committed, sympathized with the plot, and like many of the higher commanders was implicated in the subsequent inquiry.

On 16th August he was relieved by Field Marshal Walter Model, sent straight from the Russian front, and took his own life probably two days later. By then the Army Group Commander had also gone. On 17th July, Rommel was badly wounded from the air while surveying his dispositions round Caen. He had already, with von Rundstedt, informed Hitler that the battle could not be won; and he was involved in the aftermath of the plot of 20th July. He was nursed to recovery, to commit suicide in October. These serious changes of command did not hearten the German armies in the west; and the commanders themselves were henceforth more vividly aware that military decisions would always be viewed in the light of a murderous and implacable political suspicion.

While these events were taking place, the Eastern Front was on the move.[1] The elements of the two hundred-odd German and satellite divisions which faced the Russians at the beginning of June were divided into four main groups of armies, with a smaller front in the extreme north. In Finland, General Lothar Rendulic commanded eight divisions. From the southern shore of the Gulf of Finland, General Georg Lindemann commanded the Baltic front as far as the river Dvina with approximately thirty-eight divisions. Field Marshal Ernst Busch, with some fifty-four divisions, commanded the central or White Russian front, from the Dvina to the Dnieper and the Bug. Immediately to the south lay Field Marshal Model, who had recently replaced Field Marshal Erich von Manstein, with some forty-five divisions from the Dnieper to the frontiers of Czechoslovakia and Rumania. Finally, Field Marshal Ewald von Kleist commanded the Rumanian front, from the border to the line of the Danube, with approximately sixty-one divisions. Many of the German formations were well below strength, there were few reserves, and communications were partly interrupted between north and south. Nevertheless, the German army in the east remained a formidable opponent for the three hundred-odd Russian divisions that were now grouping to attack.

The Russians' programme for the summer was to demolish each German sector in turn, beginning in the north where their communications were shortest. On 10th June, they attacked from the Leningrad front, capturing Viborg on the 20th and precipitating the negotiations, which were already under way, to end the Russo-Finnish war. The main offensive then began on the 23rd. Over one hundred divisions under Marshals Chernyakovsky and Rokossovsky, and General Zakharov, attacked Busch in the sector Vitebsk-Mogilev-Zhlobin, with the target of Minsk. By the end of the month the three positions

[1] See Map VII.

had fallen, Busch had been replaced by Model, and Rokossovsky was threatening the White Russian capital. Minsk fell on 3rd July, and the next day the Russians crossed the Polish frontier to the north. In the next ten days, Chernyakovsky struck towards the Baltic States. While his right flank moved towards Riga, his left advanced on Vilna which he took on 13th July, and on the 16th broke into Brodno near the border of East Prussia. Chernyakovsky and Rokossovsky then paused to regroup, while another group of armies attacked immediately to the north from the region of Lake Peipus. They took Ostrov on the 21st, Pskov on the 23rd, and Narva, Dvinsk and Shavli on the 26th and 27th. On 1st August they reached Tukum near the Gulf of Riga, and a point some twenty miles south of Riga, cutting Lindemann's last railway communication with the rear. A fortnight later, after some partially successful counter-attacks, the Germans began to withdraw from Estonia and Latvia.

In the second half of July, Marshal Koniev opened the next stage of the offensive on the Lvov front. On the 17th, he took Kamenka and Zlochov, the eastern bastions of Lvov, while his right outflanked the city to the north, reaching the river San near Sandomierz in the last week of the month. Lvov itself was taken on the 25th. As Koniev continued to advance, the Germans then abandoned the line of the San due west of the city, and by the end of July the Russians were within thirty-five miles of the Czechoslovak border at Borislav. A few days later, Koniev forced the San near Sandomierz, and by the 3rd had reached the Vistula. Sandomierz itself fell on 18th August.

By that time, the Russians had resumed their advance in the centre. In the last week of July, Zakharov moved rapidly west on Bialystok, which fell on the 28th. On the same day, Rokossovsky took Brest Litovsk and his left flank advanced from Lublin towards Warsaw. On the 31st, when he was within fifteen miles of the city, Chernyakovsky forced the Niemen and took Kovno.

This was temporarily the high water mark of the Russians' advance north of the Carpathians. In the first half of August, the Germans managed to stabilize the front on the borders of East Prussia, on the Vistula and near Warsaw. They counter-attacked, indeed, in Poland with some success, halting Rokossovsky until the middle of September, and in the same period crushing a fierce and tragic rising of the Poles themselves in Warsaw.[1] But the respite, though valuable, could not disguise the general danger. In two months the Russians had advanced some three hundred miles in the centre and almost two hundred miles in the north, destroying some twenty-five divisions, ejecting the Germans from large areas in the Baltic States, threatening the frontiers of East Prussia and Czechoslovakia, and driving half-way across Poland. The anticipated blow on the Balkans, moreover, had

[1] See pp. 369-76 below.

still to fall. At the beginning of June, the Germans lay along the Channel and the Atlantic in the west, and the line in the east ran mostly through Russian territory. In the middle of August, thirty-six British and American divisions were attacking from Caen to the Loire, and the Russians were one hundred miles from the Reich at the nearest point excluding East Prussia.

(ii)

The Consequences for the Mediterranean

The course of these great operations in the west and east formed the background to the discussions on the development of the southern front, which proceeded continuously from the middle of June to the middle of August. When we last saw General Alexander's armies, they were moving swiftly north of Rome, Eighth Army towards the road and rail junction of Terni in the Apennines, Fifth Army up the west coast as far inland as Viterbo. On 7th June, Alexander himself proposed a plan of campaign, based on his retaining the forces then at his disposal, for a continuous advance into the Lombard plain, to be followed by a thrust either eastwards into northern Yugoslavia and towards Austria, or westwards into southern France. This in turn had to be weighed against four other possibilities already considered by the Combined Chiefs of Staff[1]: a descent on Bordeaux, to thrust into central France; a landing near Sète in the Gulf of Lions, to thrust mainly north-west; a landing ('Anvil') near Marseilles or Toulon, to thrust north up the Rhone valley; and a landing at the head of the Adriatic, to turn the Germans' flank in Italy and/or to aid the Yugoslav Partisans. Any of the last three operations must be mounted and manned largely from Italy, and it seemed unlikely that more than one could be undertaken in the course of the summer.

The importance of the choice was not to be underestimated, small though the chosen operation might be compared with operations elsewhere. For the southern front, which had hitherto served as the necessary prelude to 'Overlord', might now provide the extra pressure needed to secure its success, possibly in the only region where the Western Allies could combine their movements directly with the Russians. The possibilities were varied. A landing on Bordeaux, or in the Gulf of Lions, might set central France aflame, secure the southern flank of the advance further north, and gain a large port on the Atlantic for supplies from the United States; 'Anvil' might directly assist the northern advance, immediately by threatening

[1] See Map IV, facing p. 263.

the German flank between Burgundy and Switzerland, later by providing an additional, though distant, port; a landing in the Adriatic might help to contain and disrupt the large German forces already pinned in Yugoslavia; while the exploitation of victory in Italy might release a large and experienced Allied force, either for the same purpose as 'Anvil' or for operations, possibly in concert with the Russians, in the southern approaches to the Reich. Much would hang on the decision which limited resources imposed. It was therefore perhaps not surprising that strategic thought in the summer of 1944 should have centred on this problem, while the battle proceeded in France.

Throughout the second half of June, Alexander pushed steadily to the north.[1] By the 10th, Kesselring had partly reorganized his battered divisions, and was able to offer more effective opposition. But over the next ten days Fifth Army took Orvieto and Grosseto, whence French forces captured Elba by the 19th; Eighth Army approached Lake Trasimene, over half way from Rome to Florence; and in the east the Poles pushed towards the river Chienti, twenty miles south of Ancona. There Kesselring decided to stand if possible, on a line running from the Chienti through the high ground north of Perugia and Chiusi to the upper Ombrone inland from Grosseto. The defences, though long, were sited in hilly, cultivated country, and in a part of Italy where communications from the south were necessarily strained; and fresh drafts of German troops were arriving from the west and from the Reich. Nevertheless, provided the Allies retained all of their forces, there was no reason to doubt that they would soon force the position.

But in the same week that Kesselring decided to stand, it began to look as if those forces would be reduced. On 14th June, the Combined Chiefs of Staff decided against General Alexander's proposals of the 7th.[2] The armies in Italy were to halt, as agreed earlier, at the line Pisa-Rimini, and their task was limited to the destruction of the Germans south of that position. All forces considered necessary for that purpose should be retained in the battle: preparations should go forward meanwhile, 'on the greatest scale for which resources can be made available and at the earliest possible date', for a landing of three divisions near Bordeaux, or near Marseilles or Toulon (now preferred to Sète), or at the head of the Adriatic, if possible by 25th July 'so long as this does not limit the completion of operations south of the Pisa-Rimini Line.' The results soon began to show. On 14th June, Alexander was informed that VI Corps' headquarters would be withdrawn from Fifth Army at once, to join the headquarters for the landing, and that one division would follow on the 17th, a

---

[1] See Map V, facing p. 270.

[2] See pp. 268-70 above.

second on the 24th, a third on the 27th, and a fourth in the first week of July. Two days later, in response to a query, he was told that this programme must hold good.

The British Chiefs of Staff seem to have concurred in this decision without fully examining the implications. The immediate course of the campaign in Italy was safeguarded by formula; but it was not yet certain that the formula corresponded to the recommendations which followed, or that the connexion between them had been examined clearly. Possibly events across the Channel, and the current preoccupations with the Far East, were responsible: certainly the American Chiefs of Staff appeared to grip the problem more closely than their colleagues at the meetings from 11th to 14th June.[1] But over the next ten days, the British were forced to reconsider the position. Neither Wilson nor Alexander was prepared to accept it without complaint, and they soon pointed out forcefully, and with considerable effect, the implications for the Italian campaign. To Alexander in particular the alternatives were clear. Allowing for recent losses, he disposed of twenty-seven active divisions against, as he reckoned, the enemy's equivalent of fourteen. Even if Kesselring was reinforced by a further four to seven divisions, he estimated that the Allies could break the enemy's main Gothic Line between Pisa and Rimini in August, and could penetrate the valley of the Po, with eighteen divisions. Thereafter, they could swing either east or west. A move to the west now seemed to him likely to prove both difficult and unprofitable. It must proceed initially through the narrow and easily defensible coastal gap at the head of the Gulf of Genoa, and its effect on the 'Overlord' campaign, while no doubt useful, might be limited. A move to the east, on the other hand, would pass initially through easier country at the foot of the Julian Alps, would stimulate the Partisans in Yugoslavia, and might result in a common front with the Russians against Germany's sensitive south-eastern flank. It was therefore likely to affect the whole position in Europe more powerfully than the apparently more direct move into France. Alexander estimated that he could continue without pause from the Apennines to the river Piave, north-east of Venice, with eighteen divisions, and could carry the Ljubljana Gap with the same strength. But it would probably be impossible to use the same troops consecutively throughout all of these operations, and he must have a reserve of at least six divisions. In fact, given a minimum of twenty-four divisions he was prepared to conquer Italy in August, and to challenge the Ljubljana Gap immediately afterwards. But if he was deprived of the five, or possibly seven, divisions likely to be needed for an operation against the south or west of France, the Italian campaign must again be slowed down. For the armies would then be not only weakened, but temporarily

[1] See p. 268 above.

unbalanced. The loss would fall entirely on Fifth Army, and thus entirely on one flank of the operations; it would remove the most experienced mountain troops, thus unbalancing the composition as well as the disposition of the forces; and the ensuing disorganization, as formations were moved and plans adjusted, would probably postpone the date of the attack on the Gothic Line, thereby favouring any reinforcement of the enemy and leading possibly to a check in an advance whose final success might depend on maintaining its momentum. Alexander objected particularly to such a postponement because he believed, first that the Germans would soon reinforce the northern Apennines, so that fighting there would in any case afford a direct relief to the campaigns elsewhere; and secondly that they would in any case be driven back, even if more slowly, into the northern plain. There was thus every reason to proceed with the greatest strength towards an object that would eventually be achieved, and to derive an advantage from it which no alternative course appeared to offer.

General Wilson considered these proposals at a meeting with his commanders on 17th June. The navy and air agreed with Alexander, and the administrative staff confirmed his estimates: the American General Devers[1] continued to support 'Anvil'. Wilson himself inclined towards Alexander. But he pointed out that the French might not consent to use their divisions, which formed the main French army outside France, in south-east Europe instead of in their own country; and he therefore wished to investigate the possibility of confining the proposed operations to the British and American divisions not needed for 'Anvil', supported by an assault from the sea on the Istrian peninsula. In that case possibly Trieste and not Ljubljana should be the immediate target, at a date when 'Anvil' had taken place.

Wilson had a good opportunity to test these views on the Americans, for in the third week of June Marshall and Arnold visited the theatre for a few days, following their meetings in London and a visit to northern France. Later on the 17th, the Supreme Commander accordingly informed them of the proposals. They were not impressed. General Marshall, after repeating the familiar argument for 'Anvil', stressed the importance that was now attached to gaining a further large port in France as soon as possible, through which to pass the divisions waiting in the United States. The Americans could not therefore abandon the prospect of securing Toulon and Marseilles. A further meeting, on the 19th, served to confirm this point. Meanwhile, the Mediterranean commanders had decided that landings in the south of France and in Istria could not be launched consecutively, and Wilson had accordingly to choose between 'Anvil' and Alexander's proposed campaign.

[1] See p. 205 above.

On 19th June, he decided to support the latter, whose strategic importance seemed to him greater than that of 'Anvil'. He admitted the importance of another great port to operations in France; but he thought that those operations would be better served in due course by an advance into south-east Europe than by extra reinforcement from the United States through Marseilles and Toulon. The choice between the alternatives, in his opinion, would show 'whether our strategy in the coming months was to be aimed at the defeat of Germany in 1944 or in the first half of 1945.' Since the withdrawal of formations for 'Anvil' in mid-August must start at the latest on 28th June, he asked for a rapid decision. Two further telegrams on the same lines followed over the next four days from Alexander and from Smuts, who on 22nd June visited Italy on his way home after the Dominion Prime Ministers' Conference.

Smuts indeed was still in London when Wilson's telegram of the 19th arrived. He at once supported its argument, and on the 21st the Prime Minister called a meeting of the Chiefs of Staff to hear his views. This served effectively to reopen the question, which was pursued at a Staff Conference on the following day. It was then generally agreed, as had been foreshadowed earlier and as Wilson himself had argued,[1] that a landing in southern France was preferable to one on or near Bordeaux, which was far from any base and from the Allies' line in the north. But the old objections to 'Anvil' were revived, the old reluctance to abandon the Italian campaign at the moment of its success again found expression, and the Chiefs of Staff prepared to investigate the possibilities afresh.

On 23rd June, however, Eisenhower intervened strongly in favour of the Combined Chiefs of Staff's decision. The pace of his operations was then slowing down, and he had just been forced to postpone the second phase of the 'build-up' by the severe gale and continuing bad weather in the Channel. He was alarmed by the possibility of a stalemate; and as a landing on Bordeaux was no longer considered feasible, he returned to the case for 'Anvil' as against a landing in south-east Europe. If resources allowed—and the recent damage to his assault shipping by weather might mean that he could not help to meet any new demand from the Mediterranean—he recommended that the operation should be launched not later than 30th August, and preferably by the 15th: if they did not, all of the French and one or two of the American divisions earmarked for it should be transferred to north-west Europe as soon as possible.

> 'France', he summed up, 'is the decisive theater. The Combined Chiefs of Staff took this decision long ago. In my view, the resources of Great Britain and of the United States will *not*

---

[1] See p. 263 above.

allow us to maintain two major theaters in the European War, each with decisive missions.'

The Joint Chiefs of Staff entirely agreed.

'. . . 3. The essential requirement,' they telegraphed to London on 24th June, 'is the support of 'Overlord' and the earliest possible exploitation of the success which it has already attained. This demands a rapid concentration of maximum forces against the enemy in the decisive theater of France. Such a concentration can only be achieved by seizing another major port in France. We are convinced that the best use to which we can put our resources in the Mediterranean is to launch an 'Anvil' at the earliest possible date. . . .

4. General Wilson estimates he will reach the Pisa-Rimini line by the end of June. The commitment to 'Anvil' of the resources required for that operation will still leave large forces available to General Wilson to exert a very heavy pressure on the enemy in Italy.

5. General Wilson has a massive preponderance of air power, and overwhelming air pressure can be exerted both in Italy and in the support of the 'Anvil' operation.

6. . . . In view of the vital importance of the time factor to 'Overlord' General Wilson should make every effort to launch 'Anvil' by 1st August, having in mind that the German capability of resistance will, in all probability be considerably below the scale of May or June.

7. General Eisenhower should be directed to release the additional resources in assault shipping and landing craft required for a 3-division 'Anvil' to be provided from 'Overlord', in time to sail from United Kingdom not later than 1st July, and the remainder of naval support and bombardment forces not later than 10th July. . . . [He] and [General Wilson] should arrange between them the date of temporary release from 'Overlord' of the additional airlift required for one division.'

The British, however, were not prepared to endorse these proposals at once, and the Prime Minister telegraphed to the President that 'these very grave questions' must be examined immediately by the War Cabinet.[1] A series of arduous meetings followed, among the Chiefs of Staff and with the Prime Minister. While all recognized the force of Alexander's views, the Chiefs of Staff were concerned immediately not so much with the results of victory in Italy as with its achievement. There would be time later to argue the merits of a development to east or west: meanwhile, it was necessary to see the battle through to the end. The final message to Washington, which was sent

[1] The War Cabinet was in fact consulted, as a body, only to the extent of being shown a memorandum by the Prime Minister. Ministers were concerned in the discussions mainly through Staff Meetings or Conferences specially called.

on 26th June, was accordingly careful not to prejudice the immediate issue by an insistence on any particular set of consequences.

> '1. At the present stage of the war in Europe, our view of the overall strategic concept is to engage the enemy on the largest scale with the greatest violence and *continuity*. Only in this way can we expect to bring about his earliest collapse.
>
> 2. We agree . . .
>
> (a) That the essential requirement is the support of 'Overlord' and the earliest possible exploitation of the successes which it has already obtained;
>
> (b) that this demands a rapid concentration of the maximum forces against the enemy in France. We would add that "enemy in France" means to us those enemy forces in France which are or may be opposed to the 'Overlord' operation.
>
> 3. We are not, however, convinced that this can only be achieved by the seizing of another major port in France.
>
> 4. We are convinced that the Allied forces in the Mediterranean can best assist 'Overlord' by completing the destruction of the German forces with which they are now in contact, and by continuing to engage, in maximum strength, all German reinforcements deployed to oppose their advance. Any compromising of the prospects of the destruction of the enemy Armies in Italy at this critical phase in the war, without a compensation in the early destruction of equal forces elsewhere would in our opinion, be wrong. . .'

But even if they had felt more kindly towards 'Anvil', the British Chiefs of Staff now doubted if it could be carried out in August. The withdrawal of the necessary land and air forces from Italy in time for 15th August seemed to them impossible without ruining Alexander's current operations, and their withdrawal in time for 1st August impossible altogether. Moreover, the British certainly did not agree that the Allies had enough air forces for Italy and the south of France simultaneously.

As a result, they recommended that:

> '. . . 14. (a) We should continue to give absolute priority to the support of 'Overlord' and to the exploitation of the successes which it has already attained.
>
> (b) General Eisenhower should retain all the landing craft he needs to undertake further amphibious assaults, and to develop the intake capacity of the coastline as he captures it, and should have the first call on all divisions which can be received from all quarters from which they can be found.
>
> (c) General Wilson should direct General Alexander to continue to develop the full power of his offensive in Italy with the object of engaging and destroying all German forces opposed to him.
>
> (d) General Wilson should do everything possible to emphasise

the threat of an assault on the south coast of France, and to prepare to send General Eisenhower one or more American divisions and/or all the French divisions which General Eisenhower is capable of receiving and which our shipping resources will permit us to transport.'

This telegram had no effect. On 27th June, the Joint Chiefs of Staff repeated their arguments and conclusions. They added:

'The fact that the British and United States Chiefs of Staff are apparently in complete disagreement in this matter at this particular moment when time is pressing presents a most deplorable situation. We wish you to know now, immediately, that we do not accept statements in your paper in general with relation to the campaign in Italy as sound and as in keeping with the early termination of the war. The desire is to deploy as many United States divisions in France and as quickly as possible. A successful advance by Alexander's force in Italy does not promote this possibility.'

Since a decision was urgent, they proposed that the necessary orders should be sent at once.

The Americans' message in turn failed to move the British. On 28th June, the Prime Minister appealed again to the President, placing his own emphasis on the problem.[1]

'1. The deadlock between our Chiefs of Staff raises most serious issues. Our first wish is to help General Eisenhower in the most speedy and effective manner. But we do not think this necessarily involves the complete ruin of all our great affairs in the Mediterranean, and we take it hard that this should be demanded of us.

2. I am sending you in a few hours a very full argument on the whole matter which I have prepared with my own hands, and which is endorsed by the Chiefs of Staff. I shall consult the War Cabinet on the subject tomorrow 29th, and I have already circulated the paper to them. Those who have seen it completely endorse it, including those members who belong to the Defence Committee. I have very little doubt of unanimous support on this issue.

3. I most earnestly beg you to examine this matter in detail for yourself. I think the tone of the United States Chiefs of Staff is arbitrary and certainly I see no prospect of agreement on the present lines. What is to happen then? It was such a pity that they all separated before this issue arose, just like we separated before the Italian climax after 'Quadrant'.

4. Please remember how you spoke to me at Teheran about Istria, and how I introduced it at the full Conference. This has sunk very deeply into my mind, although it is not by any means the immediate issue we have to decide.

---

[1] See *Triumph and Tragedy*, pp. 55-6.

5. I am shocked to think of the length of the message that I shall be sending you tonight. It is a purely personal communication between you and me in our capacity as Heads of the two Western Governments.'

The memorandum followed the next day, developing forcefully and at length the whole British case against 'Anvil', and repeating the recommendations of the Chiefs of Staff. Its text may be found in Sir Winston Churchill's memoirs.[1]

The Chiefs of Staff themselves replied simultaneously to their colleagues' telegram of 27th June. They were supported in their argument by important intelligence, received in London on that day, that Hitler now expected the Allies to follow up their advantage in Italy as fully as possible, and had therefore decided definitely to hold the northern Apennines, whose breach would have 'incalculable military and political consequences', as 'the final blocking line'. Alexander's estimate[2] had thus proved correct.

The Joint Chiefs of Staff met the British representatives in Washington on 29th June, to consider these developments. Little new emerged as a result of an hour's discussion. 'It was perfectly clear at the end of the meeting that the United States Chiefs of Staff were quite unanimous in adhering to their views'. Meanwhile the President replied fully to the Prime Minister.

'1. I have given careful personal consideration to your [telegram] and I have had our Joint Staffs give the whole subject further consideration.

2. I agree with you that our over-all strategic concept should be to engage the enemy on the largest scale with the greatest violence and continuity, but I am convinced that it must be based on a main effort together with closely co-ordinated supporting efforts directed at the heart of Germany.

3. The exploitation of 'Overlord', our victorious advances in Italy, an early assault on Southern France, combined with the Soviet drives to the west—all as envisaged at Tehran—will most surely serve to realise our object . . . in this connection also I am mindful of our agreement with Stalin as to an operation against the South of France and his frequently expressed views favouring such an operation and classifying all others in the Mediterranean as of lesser importance to the principal objective of the European campaign.

4. I agree that the political considerations you mention are important factors,[3] but military operations based thereon must

---

[1] *Loc. cit.*, pp. 656-62.

[2] See p. 348 above.

[3] The Prime Minister's memorandum had stated:
'. . . 5. Political considerations, such as the revolt of populations against the enemy or the submission and coming over of his satellites, are a valid and important factor.'

be definitely secondary to the primary operations of striking at the heart of Germany.

5. I agree that the 'Overlord' build-up must receive continuing attention, but consider this to be definitely Eisenhower's responsibility. The forces we are sending him from the United States are what he has asked for. If he wants divisions ahead of service troops he has but to ask—the divisions will be ready.

6. Until we had exhausted the forces in the United States, or it was proved we cannot get them to Eisenhower when he wants them I am opposed to the wasteful procedure of transferring forces from the Mediterranean to 'Overlord'. . . .

7. My interests and hopes centre on defeating the Germans in front of Eisenhower and driving on into Germany, rather than on limiting this action for the purpose of staging a full major effort in Italy. I am convinced we will have sufficient forces in Italy with 'Anvil' forces withdrawn, to chase Kesselring north of Pisa-Rimini and maintain heavy pressure against his army at the very least to the extent necessary to contain his present force. I cannot conceive of the Germans paying the price of ten additional divisions, estimated by General Wilson, in order to keep us out of Northern Italy.

8. We can . . . immediately withdraw five divisions (3 U.S. and 2 French) from Italy for 'Anvil'. The remaining 21 divisions plus numerous separate brigades will certainly provide Alexander with adequate ground superiority. With our air superiority there is obviously sufficient air in the Mediterranean to furnish support both for operations in Italy and for 'Anvil', and to provide overwhelming air support during the critical moments of either operation. We also have virtual mastery of the sea in the Mediterranean.

9. I agree that operations against Bordeaux or Cette [Sète] with Mediterranean forces are out of the picture. As for Istria, I feel that Alexander and Smuts for several natural and very human reasons are inclined to disregard two vital considerations: the grand strategy firmly believed by us to be necessary to the early conclusion of the war and the time factor as involved in the probable duration of a campaign to debouch from Ljubljana gap into Slovenia and Hungary. The difficulties in this advance would seem far to exceed those pictured by you in the Rhone Valley, ignoring the effect of organised resistance groups in France and the proximity to 'Overlord' forces. I am informed that for purely logistical reasons it is doubtful if, within a decisive period, it would be possible to put into the fighting beyond the Ljubljana gap more than six divisions. Meanwhile we will be struggling to deploy in France 35 U.S. divisions that are now in continental United States plus an equivalent of corps and army combat troops not to mention the necessary complement of service troops. I cannot agree to the employment of United States troops against Istria and into the Balkans, nor

can I see the French agreeing to such use of French troops.

10. The beaches, exits, communications and cover in the Toulon area are most suitable. The Rhone corridor has its limitations, but is better than Ljubljana and is certainly far better than the terrain over which we have been fighting in Italy.

11. I am impressed by Eisenhower's statement that 'Anvil' is of transcendent importance . . . and by Wilson's statement that he can conduct the operation if given an immediate directive.

12. Wilson's plans for 'Anvil' are well developed and hence the operation can be launched with no delay.

13. Since the agreement was made at Tehran to mount an 'Anvil', I cannot accept, without consultation with Stalin, any course of action which abandons this operation. In the event that you and I are unable to agree to issue a directive to General Wilson by 1st July to launch 'Anvil' at the earliest possible date, we must communicate with Stalin immediately. Furthermore, I feel that if we are to abandon 'Anvil' we must at at once discuss with the French the use of their forces, which might by this decision be kept out of the battle in France, while taking losses in a secondary effort in Italy or the Balkans.

. . . 15. At Tehran we agreed upon a definite plan of attack. That plan has gone well so far. Nothing has occurred to require any change. Now that we are fully involved in our major blow, history will never forgive us if we lose precious time and lives in indecision and debate. My dear friend, I beg you let us go ahead with our plan.

16. Finally for purely political considerations over here I would never survive even a slight set-back in 'Overlord' if it were known that fairly large forces had been diverted to the Balkans.'

The deadlock was now complete, and feeling in London ran high. A telegram from Alexander to the C.I.G.S. on 29th June, asking urgently for a decision and informing him that the Americans had begun to withdraw some small units from the front line, further stoked the fires. But it now seemed inevitable that one side must give way; and on 30th June the Chiefs of Staff addressed a Minute to the Prime Minister, advising him that while they were 'completely unshaken' by the President's military arguments, they would defer to his views 'in the broadest interests of Anglo-American co-operation' if the Prime Minister thought this necessary. After a further meeting on that day, Churchill accordingly made a last appeal to Roosevelt on 1st July. It did not neglect the President's allusion to the political implications of a move to the east.[1]

'1. We are deeply grieved by your telegram. There are no differences whatever between my War Cabinet colleagues and the British Chiefs of Staff. The splitting up of the campaign in the

[1] See Appendix X below for the complete text.

Mediterranean into two operations neither of which can do anything decisive, is, in my humble and respectful opinion, the first major strategic and political error for which we two have to be responsible.

2. At Tehran you emphasised to me the possibilities of a move Eastward when Italy was conquered and mentioned particularly Istria. No one involved in these discussions has ever thought of moving armies into the Balkans; but Istria and Trieste in Italy are strategic and political positions, which as you saw yourself very clearly might exercise profound and widespread reactions, especially now after the Russian advances.

3. After Tehran I was made doubtful about 'Anvil' by General Eisenhower's dislike for it. . . .

4. Furthermore, I was impressed by General Montgomery's arguments when at Marrakesh . . . he explained that it would take ninety days for a Force landed at 'Anvil' to influence the 'Overlord' operation.

5. . . . It is no reflection on these officers that they should now express a different view.[1] But their opinions, expressed so decidedly, made me less confident about an 'Anvil' operation. Moreover in those days the date was to be early in June. . . .

. . . 7. I have considered your suggestion that we should lay our respective cases before Stalin. . . . I do not know what he would say if the issue was put to him to decide. On military grounds he might be greatly interested in the eastward movement of Alexander's Army, which, without entering the Balkans, would profoundly affect all the forces there and which, in conjunction with any attacks he may make upon Rumania or with Rumania against Hungarian Transylvania, might produce the most far-reaching results. On a long-term political view, he might prefer that the British and Americans should do their share in France in this very hard fighting that is to come, and that East, Middle and Southern Europe, should fall naturally into his control. However it is better to settle the matter for ourselves and between ourselves.

8. What can I do, Mr. President, when your Chiefs of Staff insist on casting aside our Italian offensive campaign, with all its dazzling possibilities, relieving Hitler of all his anxieties in the Po Basin, and when we are to see the integral life of this campaign drained off into the Rhone valley in the belief that it will in several months carry effective help to Eisenhower so far away in the North?

9. If you still press upon us the directive of your Chiefs of Staff to withdraw so many of your forces from the Italian campaign and leave all our hopes there dashed to the ground, His Majesty's Government, on the advice of their Chiefs of Staff, must enter a solemn protest. I need scarcely say that we shall do our best

[1] General Montgomery later pointed out to the Prime Minister that in fact his views on this subject had not changed in the same way as had General Eisenhower's.

to make a success of anything that is undertaken. We shall therefore forward your directive to General Wilson as soon as you let us know that there is no hope of reconsideration by your Chiefs of Staff or by yourself. . . .

10. It is with the greatest sorrow that I write to you in this sense. But I am sure that if we could have met, as I so frequently proposed, we should have reached a happy agreement. I send you every personal good wish. However we may differ on the conduct of the war, my personal gratitude to you for your kindness to me and for all you have done for the cause of freedom will never be diminished.'

The reply came on the 2nd.

'I appreciate deeply your clear exposition of your feelings and views on this decision we are making. My Chiefs of Staff and I have given the deepest consideration to these problems and to the points you have raised. We are still convinced that the right course of action is to launch 'Anvil' at the earliest possible date.

Perhaps I am more optimistic than you are, but I feel that our Commanders in Italy will, with the forces left to them continue to do great things and attain all the essential objectives there.

I do not believe we should delay further in giving General Wilson the Directive. . . . Will you ask your Chiefs to despatch it to General Wilson at once.

. . . At Tehran what I was thinking of was a series of raids in force in Istria if the Germans started a general retirement from the Dodecanese and Greece. But it has not happened yet, and Tito appears to be in a less strong position than he was then.

On the same lines, the country in Istria is bad combat terrain in the winter time, worse than Southern France.

Therefore I am compelled by the logic of not dispersing our main efforts to a new theatre, to agree with my Chiefs of Staff. . . .

I honestly believe that God will be with us as He was in 'Overlord' and in Italy and in North Africa. I always think of my early geometry: "A straight line is the shortest distance between two points".'

The Combined Chiefs of Staff's directive to Wilson was sent the same day.

'1. 'Anvil' will be launched at the earliest possible date. You will use every effort to meet a target date of 15th August. You will prepare for the operation on the basis of approximately a 3-division assault; an airborne lift of a strength to be decided later, and a build-up of at least 10 divisions as soon as the resources made available to you will permit: having in mind in your preparations the steady reduction of German capacity

> to resist and the vital importance of prompt support of the 'Overlord' operation.
>
> 2. You will use all available Mediterranean resources not required for 'Anvil' to carry out your present Directive with regard to operations in Italy.
>
> 3. By copy of this message S.C.A.E.F. [Eisenhower] is directed to release to S.A.C.M.E.D. [Wilson] as early as practicable the additional resources required for 'Anvil'. These resources and the dates at which they should be made available should be decided in consultation between the two Supreme Commanders.'

While these critical discussions were under way, four divisions had been removed from the Italian front, and another three were now due to go. All came from Fifth Army, which between 1st June and 1st August lost almost 40 per cent of its strength, including the most experienced mountain troops. Early in July, it also became necessary—as had been foreseen—to rest two British divisions of Eighth Army, in return for which two inexperienced divisions were brought from the Middle East. Throughout July, the Mediterranean Command searched for reinforcements to mitigate its loss. Wilson scoured North Africa and the Middle East, and asked permission of the Combined Chiefs of Staff to arm and employ some Italian formations. But the needs of security in Persia and Egypt prevented any substantial transfer from those areas, and while the Combined Chiefs of Staff agreed in August to equip Italians with captured material, this proved possible only on a small scale. From early in July, therefore, the armies in Italy were progressively weakened and unbalanced. At the same time Kesselring was reinforced by eight divisions (one from Denmark, one from Holland, one from Russia, two from the Balkans, and three from Germany which had hitherto been designed for Russia).

The plan of campaign had to be adjusted to these circumstances. On 5th July, Wilson issued a new directive to Alexander in accordance with the Combined Chiefs of Staff's orders of the 2nd. 'Anvil' now had first priority until its ten divisions had been landed. In return for the loss of probably seven divisions, the armies in Italy would receive two fresh divisions (one coloured American, one Brazilian) on about 15th September and 30th October respectively. No other reinforcement was as yet envisaged, and the air forces for Italy would be temporarily reduced by one group of bombers and twenty-three squadrons of fighters. The object of the campaign was now first to advance over the Apennines to the line of the Po, securing the area Ravenna-Bologna-Modena-west coast north of Leghorn; and subsequently to cross the Po to the line Venice-Padua-Verona-Brescia.[1]

[1] See Map VIII, facing p. 384.

'Anvil' itself should remove the necessity thereafter for any move to the west; and a further directive would be issued at that stage.

In the last week of June, the Allies forced the enemy out of his positions around Lake Trasimene.[1] At the end of the month, the left flank of Fifth Army had reached Cecina on the coast and its right was eight miles from Siena; Eighth Army lay from Montepulciano to the hills some ten miles north of Perugia; and on the Adriatic coast, the Poles had crossed the Chienti. Siena fell on 3rd July, and by the 5th Fifth Army faced Volterra, while Eighth Army was near Arezzo, the junction south of the river Arno thirty-five miles from Florence. The enemy then managed to stand on a line through Volterra and Arezzo to Osimo, ten miles south of Ancona, in positions dominating the broad valleys to the south. Kesselring had regained full control of his forces, and was conducting a skilful retreat, while the balance of the Allied line was being steadily disturbed and its air support reduced. Alexander therefore paused for a deliberate assault. After three divisions had been brought up central Italy to reinforce Eighth Army around Arezzo, operations began on 9th July. Limited but steady progress was made against strong opposition over the next four days, and on the 15th Arezzo itself was attacked. The next morning British armour entered the town, and by the evening Arezzo had fallen and Eighth Army had established a bridgehead across the Arno. Meanwhile, Fifth Army was pushing steadily through the hills near the coast, reaching the Arno east of Pisa on 18th July. In the east, the Poles took Osimo on 6th July, and thereafter developed their attack on Ancona. Stubborn fighting ensued against two German divisions, but the town fell on the 18th. On the next day Fifth Army took Leghorn, and the Allies again had two substantial if damaged ports at either end of the line. With Arezzo as an administrative base, with the prospect again of immediate seaborne supply, and with a foothold across the Arno south-east of Florence, they could now prepare to move on the city and thence towards the Gothic Line.

Preliminary operations for the capture of Florence proceeded over the next fortnight. By the end of July, Fifth Army lay along the southern bank of the Arno from the coast to a point some fifteen miles west of the city, while Eighth Army, having breached the main defences, lay thence to within a few miles of the suburbs, and in a curve to the south and south-east. The enemy now concentrated four and a half divisions south of Florence. But flanking attacks over the next few days drove him slowly back, until on the night of 3rd August he disengaged across the Arno. On the 4th, Eighth Army occupied the southern quarters of the city.

Florence was not finally cleared until the 13th. But on 4th August

---

[1] See Map VIII, facing p. 384.

the campaign in central Italy came to an end. The Allies had covered 270 miles from the Garigliano to the Arno in sixty-four days, breaking through three lines of prepared defences south of Rome and fighting two major battles to the north, destroying three and severely mauling a further eight German divisions, and capturing Rome, Florence and Leghorn. In the same period seven of their experienced divisions, including almost all of their mountain troops, had been withdrawn beyond the normal necessities for rest and change, while the enemy had gained eight divisions. They were now obliged to pause for three weeks before tackling the Gothic Line.

This had not been Alexander's intention, even at the end of July. His plan of attack at that time envisaged a main thrust at the centre of the German positions between Pistoia and Dicomano, to debouch into the Lombard plain at or near Bologna. This had obvious administrative and tactical advantages. It would allow the bulk of the Allied forces to be concentrated on Florence, thus reducing the administrative preparations, and would force the hinge of the enemy's line at a point which also led directly to the centre of his lateral communications. But the design depended for its success on preliminary operations in the mountains, and Eighth Army, which alone now had enough strength to carry them out, doubted increasingly if it could do so. The removal of the best mountain troops from Fifth Army, and the recent relief of some of its own experienced divisions, altered the nature of the attacking force, throwing a greater responsibility on its artillery and armour, which could not be fully developed in the central mountainous sector. The Army Commander was therefore unhappy about the plan, and on 4th August Alexander decided to change it. Instead of concentrating his main strength in the centre, he now proposed to deliver two complementary blows, in the east and in the centre, the first aiming, with nine divisions initially, up the Adriatic coast at Rimini and the area Ravenna-Bologna, the second, with five divisions initially, at Bologna and Ferrara. A small landing north of Ancona, to aid the eastern attack, had to be turned down through lack of assault shipping.

In the changed circumstances, the advantages of this plan were clear. But its execution demanded a major regrouping and reorganization. The bulk of Eighth Army must be transferred quickly and secretly from the centre to the east, while Fifth Army must be redisposed between the west and centre to help the central attack. The balance of supplies must be shifted correspondingly, with considerable administrative implications; and the enemy must be led to expect the main attack due north of Florence, rather than in the Adriatic sector. Plans were worked out at high speed, and the movements began on 15th August. On the 16th, Alexander issued his orders for the offensive. By the 23rd, the armies had been redisposed;

and on the night of the 25th the eastern attack began. Its preparation in that time was a remarkable feat of planning and organization; but the impetus of the advance had been lost, and the critical battle was launched with weakened forces at a time when Alexander had hoped to be across the Po.

The anger and foreboding with which the British had regarded the directive of 2nd July did not disappear with its acceptance. The Prime Minister composed, but did not send, several severe protests to Washington; and, as he put it privately to the Chiefs of Staff, 'an intense impression must be made upon the Americans that we have been ill-treated and are furious'. The fact, which the Joint Staff Mission in Washington pointed out, that the Americans had often given way to the British over the Mediterranean on earlier occasions, did not immediately lessen the distress, which was increased by a flying visit from Alexander at the beginning of the month, when he addressed the Defence Committee on the state of the Italian campaign. Throughout July, the Prime Minister and the Chiefs of Staff sought with Wilson to extract marginal forces from North Africa and the Middle East, and among themselves to reinforce Italy from the United Kingdom or the United States. But nothing could safely be spared from any quarter before the end of August, and little in September; air reinforcements were similarly impossible during the period of 'Anvil'; and the British were obliged to watch, with unconcealed regret, the anticipated slowing down of the Italian campaign.

The preparations for 'Anvil' were meanwhile put in hand. The landing was to be carried out by three American divisions, in company with French commandos, on the beaches between Cannes and Hyères, some thirty-five to forty miles from Toulon. Special forces, including American and British airborne detachments, would land the night before on the Iles d'Hyères and inland, to isolate the points of attack. On D+1, four French divisions would follow into the beach-head, which should be consolidated by D+6. The French would then move on Toulon, which should be captured by D+20. On that day, three more French divisions would begin to land in the area, making ten Allied divisions in all. Four French divisions would then move on Marseilles, to capture it by D+40, while the rest of the force probed up the Rhone Valley towards Lyon and Vichy. These operations would be sustained by eighty L.S.T., 240 landing craft and 130 merchant ships, and supported by some 230 naval vessels, including five battleships and nine escort carriers. Air support, at its height, would be provided from Corsica and Italy by a Tactical Air Force of ninety-three squadrons of fighters, bombers, transports and reconnaissance aircraft, and by a Strategical Air Force of ninety-four squadrons of heavy bombers. The troops, forming Seventh U.S. Army, would be commanded by the American Major-General Patch, under the direction of an advanced headquarters under General Devers. The operation would be served by Naples, Taranto and Brindisi in Italy, and by Oran in North Africa, with Ajaccio in Corsica as a forward staging post. At the end of July, its code name was changed, following the normal practice when a code word had been in use for several months, from 'Anvil' to 'Dragoon'.

The preparations were due to be complete by 12th August, D-day being the 15th. But while the British were active participants, they were no more reconciled than before to the purpose of the operation. As they had argued earlier, there were two possible ways in which to help the 'Overlord' campaign: first, by acquiring more ports in France, through which to pass, in the most direct way to the battle, the thirty or more fresh divisions waiting in the United States; secondly, by gaining and exploiting a final victory in Italy. The first alternative would directly strengthen the Allies: the second, although not so immediately, would weaken the enemy. The disappearance of the second possibility now threw a greater weight on the first. But 'Anvil', in the British view, would achieve neither object. It might well ruin the Italian campaign; and it was badly placed both for the early capture of an Atlantic port, and for relief to the main battle in France. It was in fact acceptable only because nothing else seemed possible. The Americans refused to exploit the possibilities in Italy, and the conditions prevailing in northern France offered no reasonable hope of attacking an Atlantic port from the sea.

These conditions lasted until the end of July. For as long as the deadlock endured around Caen, and the Americans were held in the Cherbourg peninsula, any landing on the west coast of France must involve a considerable risk to which 'Dragoon' should be preferred. But when, on 27th July, the German flank began to crumble south of St. Lo, the position suddenly altered; and by 4th August, when Patton had penetrated deep into Brittany, the British were speculating on the possibility of seizing a port or ports in the peninsula. Brest, Lorient and St. Nazaire were important prizes, the more so as the artificial harbours had been seriously damaged and Cherbourg could not operate fully for probably another three to four weeks. Together they could handle all the men and supplies required in the near future, and in an area where these could be deployed with least delay. Toulon and Marseilles by comparison seemed far from the centre of events. Now that the war of movement had begun, might it not therefore be feasible, even at this stage, to switch the forthcoming landings to the north, where there was at last a target worth the effort? The project appealed strongly to the Prime Minister, already seriously worried by the lack of ports in the north[1] and by the prospect of 'Dragoon'; and on the night of 4th August, he held a Staff Conference to discuss the new possibility. No details had been worked out; but the Chiefs of Staff were inclined to agree with him that it was worth approaching the Americans, and the Prime Minister at once despatched a personal telegram to the President.[2]

> '1. The course of events in Normandy and Brittany and especially the brilliant operations of the United States left [*sic*] wing give good prospects that the whole Brittany Peninsula will be in our hands within a reasonable time. I beg you will consider the possibility of switching 'Dragoon' into the main and vital theatre where it can immediately play its part at close quarters in the great and victorious battle in which we are now engaged.
>
> 2. I cannot pretend to have worked out the details but the opinion here is that they are capable of solution. Instead of having to force a landing against strong enemy defences we might easily find welcoming American troops at some point or other from St. Nazaire north-westward along the Brittany Peninsula. I feel that we are fully entitled to use the extraordinary flexibility of Sea and Air Power to move with the moving scene. The arrival of the 10 divisions assigned to 'Dragoon' with their L.S.Ts. might be achieved rapidly, and if this came off it would be decisive for Eisenhower's victorious advance by the shortest route right across France.
>
> 3. I most earnestly ask you to instruct your Chiefs of Staffs to study this proposal on which our people here are already at work.'

At the same time, Wilson was asked to report if such an operation could be carried out from the Mediterranean with the forces assembled for 'Dragoon'.

The Prime Minister's telegram, and another on the same lines from the British to the American Chiefs of Staff, were not likely to be welcomed in Washington. After a long and stubborn debate, which had lasted virtually without interruption for six months, the British had consented to prepare in detail for the landings in southern France, and had agreed to a specific date. Now, eleven days before the operation was due to begin, they were playing with the idea of transferring it to an entirely new area where conditions were still largely unknown, some 1,600 miles from its initial base, beyond the reach of air cover from the Mediterranean, and involving an unknown commitment for shipping. Hitherto, all assaults from the sea had been prepared in considerable detail. But no proper plan existed in this case, and no assessment had been made of its effect on current operations or on the

---

[1] See pp. 340-1 above.

[2] See *Triumph and Tragedy*, pp. 58-9.

subsequent campaign. The British were in fact proposing, for the sake of a hypothetically easier line of supply, to jettison a carefully planned operation on the eve of its execution, to alter the balance of the whole campaign in western Europe, and to abandon a strategy which they had worked out originally in concert with the Russians and had only recently accepted with every appearance of finality. It was not surprising that the Joint Chiefs of Staff should at once have re-affirmed their position.

> '. . . 2. We do not consider that the general situation has changed sufficiently to warrant such a radical change in our plans. The progress of 'Overlord' towards freeing ports in Brittany has been less rapid than the estimate current when we decided on 'Dragoon'. The time when we can make use of ports in Brittany and the communications leading therefrom cannot now be predicted with any degree of accuracy. General Eisenhower has always given us to understand that the forces he required and wanted for 'Overlord' build-up are determined by logistical factors in the lodgment area, such as port capacities. Our information is that General Eisenhower still has divisions in the United Kingdom which are available for use in France as soon as they can be moved and received. We are sending him four more this month and are preparing to send him the five in September, which are all he has asked for.
>
> 3. We are convinced that 'Dragoon' will be successful in its landing phase, and we anticipate a rapid advance up the Rhone Valley, aided to the fullest extent by the French Resistance Groups. This operation may well contribute the knock-out punch to the German Army in France. We consider that it would be extremely unwise to change our plans at this late date when all indications point to the complete success of the 'Dragoon' operation. . .'

Meanwhile, however, Wilson had been considering the details of the transfer, and his report on 6th August was not entirely hostile. A landing on the coast of Brittany would mean that the assault shipping from the Mediterranean could not take part, and extra merchant shipping would therefore be needed. But this might be provided, partly at the expense of the shipping reserved for Italy and partly from a convoy then in the Mediterranean, by 16th August; and in that case, so long as the supplies and troops already loaded in the cargo ships were not disturbed, three American divisions, four French divisions and the French commandos could be carried to Brittany to arrive at some time between 31st August and 2nd September. The airborne formations from the Mediterranean would presumably not be needed, and the other three French divisions and the supporting services must be sailed later. Formations would disembark, as in the south of France, with thirty days' supplies: thereafter they must be maintained from the United States or the United Kingdom. Reception facilities must be provided by Eisenhower, and also such small craft as might be necessary. All air support must come from northern France. Wilson stated that it would be impossible to carry out any form of 'Dragoon' as well as this assault; and if the target was to be changed, he must have his orders by the morning of 12th August.

These conclusions pleased the Prime Minister. For while they could not remove many of the difficulties facing the operation itself, they at least answered the objection that it could not be launched from the Mediterranean. The President was at this time in the Pacific, and Churchill accordingly addressed himself to Harry Hopkins, who had recently returned to the scene after seven months' illness, in an effort to influence Marshall.[1]

> '1. I am grieved to find that even splendid victories and widening opportunities do not bring us together on strategy. The brilliant operations of the American right wing have not only cut off the Brest Peninsula but in my opinion have to a large extent demoralised the scattered Germans who remain there. St. Nazaire and Nantes, one of your major disembarkation ports in the last war, may be in our hands at any time. Quiberon Bay, Lorient and Brest will also soon fall into our hands. It is my belief that the German troops on the Atlantic shore south of the Cherbourg Peninsula are in a state of weakness and disorder and that Bordeaux could be obtained easily, cheaply and swiftly. The possession of these Atlantic ports together with those we have now will open the way for the fullest importation of the great Armies of the United States still awaiting their opportunity. In addition the 10 divisions now mounted for 'Dragoon' could be switched into St. Nazaire as soon as it is in Allied possession, in this case American possession. Thus Eisenhower might speedily be presented with a new great port as well as with a new Army to operate on his right flank in the march towards the Seine.
>
> 2. I repeat that the above is additional to anything that has been foreshadowed in the schedules of transportation either from Great Britain or the United States. Instead of this we are to be forced to make a heavy attack from the sea on the well-fortified Riviera coast and to march westward to capture the two fortresses of Toulon and Marseilles, thus opening a new theatre where the enemy will at the outset be much stronger than we are, and where our advance runs crossgrained to the country which abounds in most formidable rocky positions, ridges and gulleys.
>
> 3. Even after taking the two fortresses of Toulon and

[1] See *Triumph and Tragedy*, pp. 59-60.

Marseilles, we have before us the lengthy advance up the Rhone Valley before we even get to Lyons. None of this operation can influence Eisenhower's battle for probably 90 days after the landings. We start 500 miles away from the main battlefield instead of almost upon it at St. Nazaire. There is no correlation possible between our Armies in the Brest and Cherbourg Peninsulas, and the troops operating against Toulon and Marseilles. When Marseilles is gained the turn round from the United States is about 14 days longer than the straight run across the Atlantic.

4. Of course we are going to win anyway, but these are very hard facts. When 'Anvil' was raised at Teheran it was to be a diversionary or holding operation a week before or a week later than 'Overlord' D-day in the hope of drawing about 8 German divisions away from the main battle. The decision to undertake 'Shingle' [Anzio] and the delays at Cassino forced us to continue putting off 'Anvil' until its successor 'Dragoon' bears no relation to the original conception. However out of evil came good, and the operations in Italy being persevered in drew no fewer than 12 divisions from the German reserves in North Italy and elsewhere and they have been largely destroyed. The coincidence that the defeat of Kesselring's Army and the capture of Rome occurred at the exact time of launching 'Overlord' more than achieved all that was ever foreseen from 'Anvil' and, to those who do not know the inner history, wears the aspect of a great design. Thus I contend that what 'Anvil' was meant for is already gained.

5. Bowing to the United States Chiefs of Staff under recorded protest and the overriding of our views, we have done everything in human power, including the provision of nearly one-half the naval forces about to be engaged. If nothing can be done to save the situation, I earnestly pray the American view may be right. But now an entirely new situation has developed through the victories that have been won in France and the greater victories that seem possible. It is in these circumstances that I have thought it right on the recommendation of the British Chiefs of Staff to reopen the question. There is still three or four days in which the decision to send to St. Nazaire the forces now destined and largely loaded for 'Dragoon' could be reconsidered. I admit the arguments against late changes in plans, but they ought to be fairly weighed against what seems to us to be the overwhelming case for strengthening the main battle, and thus possibly finishing up Hitler this year.

6. You know the great respect and regard which I have for Marshall, and if you feel able to embroil yourself in these matters I should be glad if you would bring my views before him especially the later paragraphs which are my reply to any complaint he may have that I supported 'Anvil' at Teheran and have turned against it since.

> 7. . . . I set the good relations of our Armies above everything else. . . .'

The message had no effect. Hopkins answered at once.

> '. . . While there has been no reply as yet from the President. . ., I am sure his answer will be in the negative. While I have seen no analysis of logistics involved, I am absolutely certain you will find the supply problem insurmountable. Divisions are already available for Eisenhower's immediate build-up which will tax the ports to the limit. Then, too, no-one knows the condition of the Brittany ports. It seems to me that our tactical position today in 'Overlord' is precisely as planned and as we anticipated it would be when 'Anvil' was laid on. To change the strategy now would be a great mistake and I believe would delay rather than aid in our sure conquest of France. I believe too the movement north from 'Anvil' will be much more rapid than you anticipate. They have nothing to stop us. . . . A tremendous victory is in store for us.'

On the 7th, the President replied briefly from the Pacific in the same vein; and on the next day Eisenhower formally recorded his dissent, as he had done verbally to Churchill on the 5th, using the same arguments as had the Joint Chiefs of Staff. On 8th August, the Prime Minister accordingly gave in.[1]

> 'I pray God that you may be right. We shall of course do everything in our power to help you achieve success.'

'Dragoon' was finally confirmed, a week before it was due to be launched. Two days later Churchill left on a visit, postponed for a few days by his recent efforts, to the Mediterranean. While there, he took the opportunity of watching the assault that he had hoped would never take place.

(iii)

Relations with the Russians

The later debate on 'Dragoon', although affected by developments on the Eastern Front, referred mainly to those in the west. But the course of operations in the east raised other and direct problems, which now began to shape, or at least to foreshadow, the new setting for the European war as the Allies closed on Germany.

The relations of the Western Allies with the Russians, which had received a notable fillip at Teheran, had again deteriorated to some

[1] See *Triumph and Tragedy*, p. 62.

extent over the first half of 1944. The strategic design had been settled, and no great events were then taking place to relieve or to influence the usual negotiations on minor points. But the invasion of France early in June, and the Russians' new offensive, at once evoked warmer feelings. A series of congratulatory telegrams flowed throughout June between Stalin and Churchill; and the marked improvement was reflected in a series of small but significant issues. In the second half of July, however, the atmosphere again began to change, and by the end of August the familiar gulf had reappeared. The explanation seemed to the British to derive in each case from the same cause, the success of the current operations. In June, the two main campaigns directly helped each other: in August, the campaign in the west could be seen as a rival to that in the east. The very success of the 'Second Front', which at first was so welcome, might later be held to lead to complications in central Europe.

If the Russians were chary of the future, they were not alone. Each of the three Allies regarded it with a mixture of misgiving and hope, and it would be difficult to say in what proportions the emotions were blended at this stage. The results were to be seen in the tentative exchanges during the summer to establish a practical division of responsibility for the Balkans. The proposals in this case came from the British, supported by the Dominions, and indeed stimulated in the first instance by Field Marshal Smuts. At the Conference of Prime Ministers in May, he had called attention to the military and diplomatic dangers of unco-ordinated action in south-east Europe, as a result either of the Allies' operations or of a sudden German withdrawal; and with the main offensive soon due to begin, Mr. Churchill and Mr. Eden agreed that some working arrangement was desirable in advance. Eden accordingly suggested to the Russians, as a basis for discussion, that they should take control in Rumania and the British in Greece. The proposal was well received, and at the end of May Churchill approached the President, pointing out that such an arrangement would be a natural development of the existing situation, which should tide the Allies over the immediate difficulties surrounding the end of the war. It did not seek to establish spheres of influence, or to prejudice the issue as presented to the subsequent peace conference. But some *modus vivendi* should be reached, for the sake of amity between the Allies and the welfare of the Balkan countries themselves.

The Americans, perhaps not surprisingly, were not happy about the proposal. The State Department disliked the prospect of a secret distribution of power, and the President was inclined to doubt if an immediate military agreement could be divorced so easily from far-reaching diplomatic implications. He recommended instead that some sort of consultative machinery should be set up, 'to dispel misunderstandings and restrain the tendency toward the development of exclusive spheres'; but after further correspondence with the Prime Minister, he agreed on 13th June to give the proposed arrangements a trial of three months. The British informed Moscow on the 19th. But the Russians, whose officials had meanwhile been in touch with their American counterparts, were anxious to gain a fuller measure of agreement than the President's assent seemed to imply; and in the middle of July, Stalin suggested that the arrangement had better await a more definite expression of approval from Washington. Early in August, agreement was made more difficult by the secret despatch of a Russian mission, in an aircraft flown from their small base at Bari, to the Communist guerrillas in northern Greece. The British objected strongly to a move of which they had not been informed, and which ran counter to the proposals under review; and those proposals, as a result, were tacitly abandoned. By the time that they were revived, circumstances had changed.

Such exchanges derive their interest largely from their subsequent fate. A far more serious development occurred in August and September, which directly influenced its form. It will be recalled that in the last three days of July the Russians advanced from Lublin towards the south-eastern suburbs of Warsaw.[1] Their aircraft were bombing the German garrison from airfields nearby, their guns could be heard in the city on the 29th, and on the 31st their tanks were rumoured to have broken into the last defences. A large underground movement, comprising most of the inhabitants of the capital, was ready to rise; on the 29th, Moscow broadcast an appeal to the people of Warsaw from the Poles in recaptured territory; and on 1st August, the Underground decided to strike. Commanded by General Bor-Komorowski, a well-planned attack opened that afternoon upon the Germans throughout the city. Within the hour, the population of Warsaw was entirely engaged.

The rising in Warsaw was the largest insurrection of the war, and it appeared to the watching world to occur at a critical moment in the Russians' offensive. The Germans seemed to be disorganized and in general retreat from an invincible tide, which was now for the first time lapping at the gates of an eastern European capital. The rising naturally roused deep sympathies throughout the West. In London it was watched with particular anxiety. For the British stood particularly close to the Poles, whose exiled Government they had sheltered since 1939, and whose relations with Russia they regarded as a test case for the alliance; and the circumstances of the Warsaw rising thrust a peculiar responsibility upon them.

---

[1] See p. 344 above.

From the start of the German occupation, the Polish Resistance had been dominated by the idea of a national rising, in which Poland would free herself by her exertions. The 'Big Scheme', as it was known, was never abandoned, and more limited sabotage and subversion were regarded as of secondary importance. A rising of this nature was of course the dream of most resistance movements; but in this case with more justification than usual. For Poland, like Norway though for quite different reasons, enjoyed a national solidarity under occupation which outweighed, if it could not overcome, domestic political differences. There were three separate movements of resistance, each grouped around a political centre: N.S.Z. on the Right, the Home Army (A.K.) in the Centre, and the People's Army (A.L.) on the Left. But neither the first nor the third could be compared with the second. N.S.Z., like so many right-wing movements, was suspected of partial collaboration with the Germans; and the People's Army, launched in 1943 by the Polish Communist Party, was not particularly effective, and was significant mainly as a potentially useful instrument for the Russians. Effective resistance centred on the Home Army, formed around the end of 1942 from a group of smaller, allied movements. Estimates of its numbers varied from 100,000 to 500,000, and only a small proportion was armed; but the movement commanded fierce and undivided loyalties, and soon established an efficient military and civil organization. The Home Army, moreover, owed a direct allegiance from the start to the Polish Government in London, which until his death in July, 1943 was dominated by General Sikorski. Under his remarkable leadership, relations between the Government and the Underground were cordial and close; and while the exiles' authority thereafter tended to decline, it remained direct and sufficiently effective for the Poles to be exempt in April, 1944 from the diplomatic ban on communications outside the United Kingdom. They thus enjoyed a peculiar measure of British confidence, as well as of British sympathy.

The practical limitations, however, were stressed from the first. The Poles first broached the 'Big Scheme' in October, 1942. But they were at once informed that they could not expect the necessary supplies from the West, and this decision held good throughout further talks between June and September 1943, which reached the President and Prime Minister. On 24th September, the Combined Chiefs of Staff finally resolved to support immediate and limited acts of sabotage with one squadron of S.O.E.'s heavy bombers, which had to be shared between several countries in central Europe. But while this meagre allocation of aircraft improved on the existing resources, which had hitherto been confined to six bombers manned by Poles, it brought no immediate result. Casualties proved heavy in the flight from England across Germany, and in October a more circuitous route had to be followed which reduced the operations to virtual impotence. In December, 1943 the aircraft were therefore transferred to North Africa, and a month later to Brindisi, whence they operated throughout 1944. In April of that year, when they were given a higher priority, they numbered fourteen aircraft manned by Poles, with the right to call for aid on S.O.E.'s other air resources in the Mediterranean. The operations thereafter increased. Whereas there were only twenty-three sorties from January to March inclusive, of which only two were successful, from April to July inclusive there were 318 sorties of which 174 were successful. 114 men, and 219 tons of stores, were dropped in the later period for the loss of eight aircraft.

But these improved figures were not such as to support the 'Big Scheme', for which the Home Army continued to prepare. Early in 1944, detachments amounting possibly to two divisions were mobilized, and fought the Germans in the north; and on 12th June, a senior emissary from Poland again approached the Combined Chiefs of Staff for help in the event of a general rising. He was again informed that assistance was impossible on a large scale, and that the Western Allies asked only for sabotage and diversionary action. But the Combined Chiefs of Staff did not prohibit a general rising, and the decision was left specifically to the Polish commander on the spot.

The Home Army, if it wished and dared, could therefore proceed with the 'Big Scheme'. The events of July provided it with powerful incentives. The Russians' swift advance across eastern Poland, against an apparently disintegrating enemy, seemed likely at the end of the month to carry them through and beyond the capital. Anything indeed might happen, and, particularly after the Russians' broadcast to the people of Warsaw, it seemed the moment to exploit the enemy's disorder. Moreover, if the Poles did not act soon, their chance might disappear; for a national rising would lose much of its force if a foreign army had already freed the capital. The appearance of the Russians in the approaches to Warsaw thus seemed to provide the military case for the insurrection. There was also a good political case, which applied equally to that moment. The Home Army was aware of the negotiations which the Polish Government in London had been conducting with Moscow on the settlement of the Polish frontiers, and which had temporarily failed in the spring of 1944. Indeed, its loyalty to that Government depended largely on the latter's treatment of the problem. But its case must be seriously weakened if the Russians could claim to have freed Poland by themselves, and if no independent Polish authority could maintain itself during their occupation. The danger, moreover, had recently grown. On 23rd July, the Russians took Lublin; on the same day they announced publicly the creation of a Polish National Committee of Liberation, composed of Polish Communists and supported by the People's Army. The 'Lublin

Committee' was promptly denounced by the Poles in London. But it could not be ignored, and on 27th July the exiled Prime Minister, M. Mikolajczyk, agreed to go to Moscow to negotiate for a combined Government. In these circumstances, action by the Home Army became the more urgent.

This combination of motives explains the tragedy of the Warsaw rising. For the political impulse led to a fatal military mistake. The Home Army wished to present the Russians with a *fait accompli*, which was however impossible unless the Russians were in close support. It therefore waited until Rokossovsky seemed to be on the point of entering the city, without informing him of its plans. On 1st August the moment seemed to have come; but in fact the Russian troops near Warsaw formed not a spearhead but an exposed flank, on which pressure might easily be applied. A successful rising would probably remove the danger; an unsuccessful rising might increase it, by attracting more German forces to the area. Only accurate information could decide the immediate prospects. The Home Army acted on what it deemed (thanks largely to the Russians' broadcast on 29th July) to be the most likely outcome, and because it could scarcely risk a decision not to act.

The Poles had dropped hints of the rising in the last days of July; but the moment was chosen, as the Combined Chiefs of Staff had approved, by the commander on the spot. The news reached London the next day. The Germans soon counter-attacked strongly, and on 4th August Bor-Komorowski asked the exiled Polish Government for help. Arrangements had in fact already been made for the Polish wing to fly supplies from Italy; but bad weather prevented an operation on the night of the 3rd/4th, and on the 4th the local authorities countermanded all flights to Warsaw in view of the ease of supply from the east. There were indeed good arguments against risking aircraft on a highly dangerous operation, involving a round flight of 1,400 miles, when ample and more defensible air supply lay so close at hand. Other air operations from Italy to Poland on the night of the 4th confirmed the nature of the hazard: fifteen aircraft left, two succeeded in their operations, and six were lost. The British therefore looked to the Russians. On 4th August the Prime Minister informed Stalin of the Poles' request, adding that their revolt might aid his operations. The reply on the 5th augured ill.

> '. . . I think the information which has been communicated to you by the Poles is greatly exaggerated and does not inspire confidence. . . . The Home Army of the Poles consists of a few detachments which they incorrectly call divisions. They have neither artillery nor aircraft nor tanks. I cannot imagine how such detachments can capture Warsaw, for the defence of which the Germans have produced four tank divisions. . . .'

It therefore seemed, whatever the Russians might decide, that the flight must be made from Italy after all; and on the nights of 8th, 9th and 12th August the Polish wing (with some British and Commonwealth crews) flew eighteen sorties to Warsaw. Three aircraft reached the city on the 8th, and a total of seven on the next two occasions. Larger sorties on the 13th and 14th resulted in twenty-three aircraft reaching their targets, but eleven were destroyed and eleven damaged. Such losses could not be sustained for such results, and the British and Americans accordingly examined the possibility of sending help from Britain. This would be possible only if heavy bombers were used from East Anglia, for it remained necessary, as in 1943, to make a long detour north of Germany, and the round flight was likely to amount to some 2,000 miles. It was also likely that a good many of the aircraft would be damaged over Warsaw, and that some might therefore have to land for fuel or repair behind the Russian lines. Since American aircraft would be involved, the Americans, after some consideration, asked Moscow if they could count on facilities being made available.

Meanwhile the insurrection was being slowly ground down. The Germans succeeded in splitting the city into separate sectors, in which savage street fighting gradually hemmed in the disconnected forces. On 12th August, a desperate appeal reached the Poles in London.

> 'We received from you only once a small drop. On the German-Russian front silence since the 3rd. . . . The soldiers and the people look hopefully at the skies, expecting help from the Allies. . . . They see only German aircraft.'

The sudden and complete absence of support from the east was indeed the most anxious feature of an anxious scene. Not unnaturally, it gave rise to the suspicion that diplomatic pressure was being applied. On 12th August, Mr. Churchill passed on the Poles' appeal to Stalin, accompanied by one from himself, and over the next few days the British and American Foreign Departments pursued inquiries in Moscow. The result appeared on the 16th, in a statement handed to the American Ambassador.

> 'In connection with your letter of August 14 . . . stating that a unit of American Air Forces has received an urgent directive to clear with Air Forces of the Red Army the question of the possibility of carrying out a shuttle flight from England so that the bombers and fighters should proceed across to bases in the Soviet Union and also a proposal regarding the necessity of concerting with Soviet Air Forces a similar attempt to drop arms in Warsaw if such an operation should be undertaken on that day from the Soviet side, I am instructed . . . to state that the Soviet Government cannot go along with this. The outbreak in Warsaw into which Warsaw population has been drawn

> is purely the work of adventurers and the Soviet Government cannot lend its hand to it. Marshal I. V. Stalin on the 5th August informed Mr. W. Churchill that it could not be supposed that a few Polish detachments, the so-called National Army, could take Warsaw, when it does not possess artillery, aviation or tanks at a time when the Germans had assigned for defence of Warsaw four tank divisions.'

Stalin sent a similar message to Churchill on the same day, remarking that the 'large sacrifices' of the population of Warsaw would not have occurred 'if the Soviet command had been informed before the beginning of the Warsaw action'.

The tenor of the replies alarmed the British Government. As the Prime Minister informed the President,[1] it constituted 'an episode of profound and far-reaching gravity'. For whatever the position on the ground east of Warsaw—and the Western Allies acknowledged that Rokossovsky could probably advance no further—there seemed to be no reason for the complete lack of air support from the east, and for the refusal to aid air support from the west, other than the most severe *realpolitik*. The military reasons seemed unconvincing. For if, as the Russians claimed, the rising was merely hampering their efforts by concentrating more German divisions in the area, the more important surely to enable the Poles to weaken those divisions. If Bor-Komorowski was not strong enough to capture or hold Warsaw, he was strong enough to defy five German divisions with armour (plus two more on the way). He was in fact containing an effective enemy force in an area and in circumstances where it could be severely mauled. Even if the rising had been ill-timed, there was now every military incentive to support it as far as possible. The impression therefore grew stronger that diplomatic advantage counted for more.

These suspicions alarmed the Americans as well as the British; and on 20th August the President and Prime Minister appealed together to Stalin. On the 22nd, their plea was rejected decisively. The Prime Minister then turned to more positive action. On the 23rd, he proposed to Mr. Roosevelt that the facts should be made public. On the 25th, he suggested that they should together inform Stalin categorically that American aircraft would supply Warsaw from England, landing for fuel or repair behind the Russian lines. The President, however, feared the consequences for the Americans.

> 'In consideration of Stalin's present attitude in regard to relief of . . . Warsaw . . . and his definite refusal to permit the use by us of Soviet airfields for that purpose, and in view of current American conversations in regard to the subsequent use of other Soviet bases,[2] I do not consider it advantageous to the long-range

---

[1] See *Triumph and Tragedy*, p. 119.

[2] This is discussed in my next volume, *Grand Strategy, October* 1944-*August* 1945.

general war prospect for me to join with you in the proposed message to Uncle J. I have no objection to your sending such a message if you consider it advisable to do so.'

The message accordingly was not sent.

Air support for Warsaw was thus confined to the flights from Italy. On 15th August, the Mediterranean Allied Air Forces again forbade flights directly over the city; but sorties continued to the neighbouring woods, where Polish guerrillas were in strength. The losses were still high, and on the 16th the operations were reduced. From 17th to 27th August the Polish wing flew alone, with partial success. Twenty-one of its forty-six sorties were successful; but by the later date, only three of its aircraft remained available for operations.

Meanwhile, Mikolajczyk in Moscow continued to discuss the formation of a new Polish Government. When he left on 31st August, he was prepared to suggest to his colleagues that the Lublin Committee should have fourteen seats in a combined Administration. His hand was strengthened by the assent of the Underground in Warsaw; but he could clearly go no further, and if the Underground was crushed the proposal might well disappear. The future stability of Poland, and Mikolajczyk's own position, might therefore depend on the issue of the battle.

The facts and implications of the case were not of course known to the British and American publics; but speculation was rife, and was growing with their anger. It was plain, as Mr. Churchill had forecast, that the fate of Warsaw must profoundly affect the feeling of the West for Russia, and that 'if . . . the German triumph. . . is followed by a wholesale massacre no measure can be put upon the full consequences that will arise.'[1] The strength of public emotion, combined with the distress and forebodings of the Governments, impelled Ministers in London again to consider tackling the Russians. The War Cabinet met on 4th September to discuss the possibilities. 'I do not remember any occasion', Sir Winston Churchill has since remarked,[2] 'where such deep anger was shown by all our members. . .' The only independent action open to the British seemed to be to stop the Arctic convoys, and the War Cabinet debated whether or not to take that step. But the results could not be foreseen, and in the interests of the alliance Ministers forebore. Instead, they resolved to try the Americans again, and that night the Prime Minister renewed his suggestion to the President that they should appeal together for permission to use the Russian airfields. But the Americans now calculated, from their most recent information, that the battle in Warsaw was virtually over; and the President replied on 5th September that no more could be done.

---

[1] See *Triumph and Tragedy*, p. 119.

[2] *Loc. cit.*, p. 124.

The story, however, was not entirely told. Destroyed as a homogeneous force, individual bands of Poles continued to resist for almost another month, and the Western Allies accordingly made further efforts to supply them. These were indeed more successful than the earlier measures. On the night of 10th/11th September, a further costly flight was made from Italy, which proved finally that no more could usefully be done from that quarter. But on the 12th an unexpected development occurred. The Russians, who had not been asked for help since 24th August, now 'grudgingly consented' to the Americans' proposal for a flight from England. Their reasons can only be inferred, without accurate knowledge, from the state of the battle in Warsaw and of sentiment in the West. The Americans at once sent a mission to Moscow to work out details, and on 18th September 110 heavy bombers of Eighth U.S. Air Force flew from East Anglia to Warsaw. They dropped 30 per cent of their supplies, for the loss of nine aircraft. But an operation on this scale demanded both preparation and fine weather, and there was no opportunity to repeat it. Meanwhile, as was not unexpected in view of the permission granted to the West, support suddenly appeared from the East. On 10th September, for the first time since the beginning of August, Russian aircraft flew over Warsaw, and on the 14th began to drop supplies. Few, however, could be used, for the parachutes failed to open. Polish Communist troops meanwhile fought towards the outskirts of the capital, reaching a suburb on 15th September. But this belated activity, like the last efforts from the West, served—in so far as it had any effect—only to prolong the epilogue. The Germans continued methodically to destroy the last remnants of resistance, and on 2nd October the tragic episode ended. The beginning of the last message from Warsaw deserves to be recorded.

> 'This is the stark truth. We were worse treated than Hitler's satellites, worse than Italy, Rumania, Finland. May God, Who is just, pass judgment on the terrible injustice suffered by the Polish nation, and may He punish accordingly all those who are guilty.'

So far as can be ascertained, some 200,000 men, women and children of the capital's population of a million were killed, including some 15,000 of the Home Army and of the less numerous Communist guerrillas. The Germans are thought to have suffered 10,000 killed, 7,000 missing and 9,000 wounded. Warsaw itself was virtually destroyed. The consequences were serious. The Polish question, always difficult, now became the conscience of the West, and relations between Britain and Russia suffered a shock from which they never fully recovered. As the European war entered on its last phase, the shadow of Warsaw lay over British strategic thought.

(iv)

Victory in Europe in 1944?

The three weeks from 15th August to 5th September were among the most dramatic of the European war, equalling in intensity those of May and June, 1940. Great events from every quarter followed in an unbroken series. In that short period, two enemy countries retired from the war and another tried to do so, Eisenhower advanced from Falaise to Brussels, Namur and Verdun, destroying eight German divisions and freeing two European capitals, the French and Americans landed in the south of France and drove rapidly to Lyon and beyond, Alexander attacked with early success in Italy, and the Russians drove from the Rumanian frontier to Yugoslavia and into Bulgaria, destroying twelve German divisions and routing the Rumanian army. Both in the west and in the east the crust seemed suddenly to have yielded, and at the end of the first week in September it was difficult to gauge if anything lay behind.

On the morning of 15th August, 'Dragoon' was launched on the south of France. Blaskowitz's Army Group G, south of the line Lyon—Bordeaux, comprised eleven divisions of varying quality, nine of which were disposed along or inland from the Mediterranean coast and three near the area of attack. The shore defences were strong, but there was virtually no opposition in the air, as was not indeed surprising after the preparatory operations by 2,000 Allied aircraft against the two hundred mustered by the enemy. By noon of the 16th the three American divisions were moving inland, one directly to the north, the other two to the north-west. Their appearance was the signal for the French Resistance to harass the Germans in the rear. Beginning with limited acts of sabotage against communications, and with the prevention of sabotage by the enemy in Toulon and Marseilles, the guerrillas soon enlarged their activities, blocking the lines of retreat through the Alps, taking over many small towns and villages in the south and south-west, attacking the Germans up the Rhone valley, and finally, early in September, freeing the great towns of Toulouse, Lyon and Bordeaux in advance of the Allies. Thus harried by the French and bombed by the Allies, the enemy withdrew rapidly, though in order, to the north. The assault on the Rhone valley soon became a procession. The right flank of General Patch's Seventh U.S. Army reached Sisteron on 20th August and Grenoble on the 24th, and its left entered Avignon on the 25th. Meanwhile, the French divisions were attacking Toulon and Marseilles against greater opposition. The enemy held out for twelve days, but both ports fell on 28th August, and First French Army then moved swiftly up the left bank of the Rhone. The pace of the advance quickened.[1] By 2nd September the Allies had taken 50,000 prisoners; on the 3rd, the French and Americans converged on Lyon, and the Americans moved swiftly on Bourg; on the 7th the Americans reached Besançon, whence they were directed towards the Belfort Gap; on the 8th the French took Beaune, and on the 11th were approaching Dijon. By that time, elements of Third U.S. Army from the north were only a few miles away, and on the 15th Eisenhower took control from Wilson of the southern armies, which were then formed into Sixth Army Group under General Devers.

For events on the main front had moved fast since the middle of August.[2] On the 13th, the battle opened to seal the Falaise gap and to destroy the fifteen divisions involved. By the 15th the gap had narrowed to sixteen miles. The enemy then began to extricate his armour, and fierce fighting ensued for two days along both walls of the narrowing corridor. Under intense attack from the air, some four divisions escaped with varying degree of loss; but the rest were now disintegrating, and on the 18th the Allies closed in for the kill. The battle ended on the 20th. Of the fifteen German divisions, the equivalent of eight had been severely mauled, with a serious loss of armour which may still be seen rusting in the fields of Normandy. Almost 30,000 prisoners were taken, including one Corps and three divisional commanders, and it was estimated that perhaps 15,000 Germans were killed. Destruction was not, as had been hoped, complete; but the German army had suffered its worst defeat since Stalingrad, and the way was open for a rapid advance.

The advance indeed was already under way further south. On 8th August, Third U.S. Army was in Le Mans. On the 16th, its left flank was approaching Dreux, its centre was in Chartres and its right in Orléans. After a brief pause, the advance continued on the 18th, and on the night of the 19th/20th an American division on the left crossed the Seine twenty miles north of Paris. On the 21st, the right was in Troyes, on the 23rd the centre crossed the Seine to the south of Paris, and on the 25th elements of First U.S. Army, which had followed Third Army through Dreux, reached the lower Seine eight miles from Rouen. These rapid movements proved the signal for the French in Paris. On the 19th, the Police rose and seized the Ile de la Cité, and by the morning of the 20th the French Resistance had gained control of the centre of the capital. After a brief armistice, fighting again broke out on the 21st, and on the 22nd the Americans despatched a Corps from First Army, including one French division, to aid the Resistance. French troops entered Paris on the morning of the 25th, and in the afternoon received the German surrender of the city.

---

[1] See Map VII, facing p. 343.

[2] See Map VI, facing p. 279.

Meanwhile, the British and Canadians advanced on the left of the line. After clearing up around Falaise, Second British Army moved with two Corps to join the Americans. On 23rd August, it reached the area north of Verneuil, where it halted while elements of First U.S. Army swung north down the Seine. First Canadian Army, with two Corps, drove north-east from Falaise towards Rouen and the lower Seine. Its right joined the Americans on the 25th; its left reached the river between Rouen and Le Havre on 27th August.

In the same period, one Corps from Third U.S. Army attacked the ports in Brittany. Determined German garrisons occupied the towns, and on the Americans' approach destroyed most of the facilities. St. Malo was reduced by 18th August, but Brest and Lorient held out, and a long siege followed before the Americans were able to enter the shattered harbours.

The battle of Normandy had cost the enemy in all perhaps 200,000 men killed, wounded and prisoner; he had lost over six hundred tanks, many guns, and large quantities of transport and equipment; and he was now in disorderly retreat. How was this great victory to be exploited? As is well known, Montgomery and Eisenhower had different ideas, whose merits may long be debated. They shared a common basis. The more rapid and extensive the advance, the harder it became to supply from the ports and beaches far in the rear. As it was, Third U.S. Army was being maintained almost entirely by air, and despite ingenious administration could not be so nourished for much longer; and as the front moved forward across the Seine, the system of supply was severely strained. This cardinal fact governed the strategic possibilities. Either the pace of the operations must be everywhere reduced, to conform to the supplies; or they must be concentrated on one sector and virtually halted elsewhere. The answer turned on the estimates of the enemy's position. General Montgomery believed that the Germans might well collapse, provided the current pressure could be maintained continuously. He therefore favoured a concentrated offensive on one sector. Two possible targets then offered: the Rhine on either side of the Ruhr, or the Rhine between Frankfurt and Karlsruhe. In Montgomery's opinion, the former should be preferred. An attack against the Ruhr must proceed by the Pas de Calais and Belgium, and would therefore, as he hoped, free the Channel ports and Antwerp; it would strike at the industrial heart of Germany; and in an area beyond the Rhine where armour could best be deployed. But whichever sector was chosen, whether the north or the centre, must enjoy absolute priority over the other, and enough forces must be massed and placed under a single command.

General Eisenhower, from a different position, reached a different conclusion. He was not so sure either that a concentrated offensive could be maintained or that the enemy was so near to collapse. If it was difficult to nourish the front on the Seine, what would be the difficulties when a more exposed attack approached the Rhine? And if the Germans did not collapse, what would be the Allies' position? They might be awkwardly deployed, and administratively unbalanced, for the subsequent operations, which must then demand a redisposition of forces and probably their reinforcement. It was, in his view, highly dangerous to gamble on a German collapse to relieve the limitations of supply. It would be better to accept them, and, while enlarging the capacity of the ports as fast as possible, to advance on a broad front towards the Rhine, at a pace and in an order which would conform to the administrative facts.

This was the general case. But a closer scrutiny of Montgomery's alternative revealed other serious difficulties. Eisenhower agreed that operations in the north should continue. The expansion of port capacity demanded the capture of the Channel ports and/or Antwerp; and he was also anxious to clear the Pas de Calais as soon as possible, to stop the V.1 attacks on southern England. But there were strong objections to halting the operations further south. As Supreme Commander, Eisenhower was concerned with factors which did not affect Montgomery. The course of the campaign had impressed on him the importance of sentiment within and beyond the Command. A bold strategy, as proposed by Montgomery, must carry the conviction, or at least the assent, of his fellow commanders; unfortunately, it was unlikely to do so. His relations with the Americans, and with important elements in the 'Overlord' headquarters themselves, were not particularly happy, although not yet as strained as they later became; and it was highly doubtful if those authorities would accept the northern thrust without severe opposition. The issue of command further complicated the problem, for feeling in Britain and in the United States, fanned by discussion at the time of Caen, was already sensitive on the subject. To perpetuate Montgomery's sole command of the land operations, for which the original plan had not allowed[1], to halt Patton in full spate, and to leave the armies from southern France with virtually nothing to do, might be to sacrifice the amity of the Command—possibly of the Alliance—to a controversial venture which might well not succeed. The same argument, in reverse, might apply if the advance were halted in the north. Such considerations, while not decisive, weighed the more heavily with Eisenhower because he was in any case sceptical of the military merits of Montgomery's plan.

The issue was discussed, and a decision taken, between 17th and 26th August. On the 17th, Montgomery presented his plan to Bradley, suggesting that Twenty-First and Twelfth Army Groups should move together towards the north-east, the former on the Pas de Calais

[1] See pp. 204, 282 above.

and Antwerp, the latter on Brussels and Aachen with its right flank on the Ardennes. He repeated the details to Eisenhower on the 23rd, and then proposed that either he or, if considered preferable, Bradley should command both forces so as to control the single plan. Eisenhower, who had already disagreed, remained unconvinced. He wished Twenty-First Army Group to secure the channel ports and Antwerp, and in order to concentrate the necessary strength lent it First U.S. Army until further notice. But he wished Third U.S. Army, supported as soon as possible by Sixth Army Group from the south, to move on Nancy and Metz; and in view of the fact that the two Army Groups would now be advancing along divergent lines, he decided that the time had come to put into effect the 'final system of command' of the 'Overlord' plan, whereby the Supreme Commander directed land operations himself. On 1st September, he accordingly assumed direct command of the Army Group Commanders. At the same time, General Montgomery was promoted to Field Marshal.

It is interesting to note that these differences were confined to the Command. Montgomery accepted the disappointment, and the Combined Chiefs of Staff were not called on officially to take notice of the divergence of opinion. Despite the size and gravity of the issue, it was not indeed by its nature a matter for their intervention. The alternatives referred solely to a plan of campaign whose object and shape they had already approved, and involved forces already within the theatre, which no action of theirs could reinforce immediately. While both sets of Chiefs of Staff, and the Prime Minister, were informed personally of the discussion, and while they both followed it with keen interest, they were not therefore in any way implicated in the result. It is indeed a good illustration, on the largest scale, of the type of circumstance dividing the responsibilities of a theatre from those of the central Command.

In the last days of August, Montgomery issued his orders to Twenty-First Army Group in accordance with Eisenhower's decision.[1] The two Armies were directed on north-east France and Belgium: First Canadian Army along the coast, initially to Bruges; Second British Army to the area Arras-Amiens, and thence, moving as fast as possible through Lille, to the area Ghent-Brussels-Malines. Bradley ordered First U.S. Army to move at a similar pace to the area Brussels-Namur. Third U.S. Army was meanwhile to advance towards Reims and Chalons-sur-Marne, where it would await the clearance of the Pas de Calais, and thence eastwards through Verdun to the area Nancy-Metz, joining Sixth Army Group[2] in the Vosges.

Third Army was in fact already nearing its first targets. On 29th August, its left flank crossed the Marne between Reims and Chalons,

[1] See Map VI, facing p. 279.

[2] See p. 378 above.

both of which it captured the next day. Its right moved beyond Troyes on the 27th, some elements towards Dijon and others towards St. Dizier. The advance further north began on the 29th. Progress was rapid. Second Army reached Amiens on the 31st, outflanked Arras on 1st September, and reached Lille on the 2nd. Early on the 3rd its right flank crossed the Belgian frontier, and by nightfall was in Brussels. On the 4th it entered Antwerp, and the port was secured largely intact within the next few days. Despite naval warnings, however, the Germans were left in control of the Scheldt to the north. The left flank, against greater opposition, meanwhile cleared the area between Lille and Ghent, which it took on the evening of 5th September. By that time, Second Army had advanced 250 miles in six days.

First U.S. Army moved at a similar pace immediately on the right. After a brief obstruction beyond Paris, it pushed rapidly towards the Belgian frontier, and by 3rd September had reached its area between Brussels and Namur. On Second Army's left, First Canadian Army fought its way up the Channel coast. After entering Rouen on 30th August, two divisions turned down the Seine to secure Le Havre and St. Valéry, one division moved on Dieppe, and another on Tréport and thence towards the Pas de Calais. The right moved towards Abbeville and St. Omer. It was soon clear, however, that the Channel ports would not be taken without a hard fight. Le Havre on 3rd September, Boulogne and Calais on the 5th, and Dunkirk on the 6th, demanded prepared assaults; meanwhile, like so many Tobruks, they remained inviolate on the flank of the advance. The rest of the Pas de Calais was cleared without great difficulty; on 6th September the right flank reached St. Omer, and crossed the frontier the next day. It then ran into stronger opposition around Ghent.

By 6th September, therefore, the picture in the west was entirely transformed. Eisenhower's line ran from the port of Antwerp, east of Brussels to Namur, thence across the frontier to the Meuse just north of Sedan, thence in an S-shape across the river to between Verdun and Nancy, and so back through Orléans to Nantes. A hundred miles to the south, and approaching fast, Devers was striking towards Besançon and Dijon. Only the uncaptured ports or their approaches remained to limit the results of this great achievement.

Developments on the Eastern Front were equally dramatic.[1] By the middle of August, the Russians' advance north of the Carpathians had lost much of its impetus.[2] They gained some further ground near East Prussia and beyond the Vistula; and on 25th August the final negotiations began which on 4th September ended the fighting in

[1] See Map VII, facing p. 343.

[2] See p. 344 above.

Finland, and on the 10th the Russo-Finnish war. But the Germans could also count some successes, halting the advance in Poland and re-establishing limited contact with their armies near the Baltic; and new Russian gains came mainly further south. Throughout the summer, the Germans had awaited with apprehension the assault on Rumania, where the Russians had earlier established two salients across the Dniester, towards Jassy and at Tiraspol. The enemy's position was indeed insecure. An Army Group of theoretically fifty divisions existed on the front south of the Dniester; but some twenty-one divisions belonged to the Rumanians and were largely unreliable, while the German divisions were mostly well below strength. In the rear was the Hungarian army, on which German formations had been quartered since April 1944, and in Bulgaria there was a mixed force of Bulgars and Germans. But the basis for effective co-operation no longer existed. Each of the three Governments was thoroughly frightened and disrupted. Each contained a peace party, which in Rumania and Hungary had already made contact with the Western Allies; Hungarians of all parties chafed beneath the German pressure and reinforcements; and Bulgaria, which unlike the others had never declared war on Russia, was the more anxious not to be involved. The Germans' weakness in the south-east was indeed shown early in August, when the Turkish Government announced that it had broken off diplomatic relations. A marked Russian success in Rumania might therefore be expected to lead to general disintegration in the Balkans.

When the offensive began, it was at once successful. On 20th August, an Army Group under Marshal Tolbukhin attacked from the bridge-head at Tiraspol, and within three days was driving fast to the south-west. Another Army Group under General Malinovsky advanced from the northern salient on Jassy, which it took on the 23rd. These successive blows were too much for the Rumanian Government. On 23rd August, King Michael arrested the dictator Antonescu, formed a new Government and pledged his loyalty to the Allies. On the 25th, Rumania declared war on Germany. On the same day, the last German pocket of resistance broke in northern Rumania; on the 27th, Tolbukhin reached the mouth of the Danube and occupied Galatz; on the 30th, Malinovsky took Ploesti and the oil wells; and on the 31st he entered Bucharest. These successes, as anticipated, affected the Bulgarians and Hungarians. On 26th August, the Bulgarians announced their withdrawal from the war, and on the 29th the Hungarian Cabinet resigned. The Russians, however, refused to recognize the Bulgarians' gesture, which would indeed have protected effectively the retreat of substantial German forces. They declared war on 5th September, and on the 8th Tolbukhin entered the country unopposed. On the 9th, the Bulgarians capitulated.

Meanwhile, on 6th September Malinovsky reached the Yugoslav frontier at Turnu Severin, ninety miles from Belgrade. Within three weeks, the Russians had entirely altered the situation in south-east Europe, had covered over half the distance from the Dniester to the Adriatic, and had opened the way to the northern frontier of Greece.

In Italy, too, this period brought promise of success. The enemy, confronted by the rapid advance in northern France and by the rising in Warsaw, and aware that the Allies had been weakened in the peninsula, had withdrawn four divisions since the middle of July. Kesselring therefore faced the equivalent of eighteen divisions with the equivalent of sixteen to seventeen in the line. On the night of 25th August, Eighth Army launched the attack on the Gothic Line in the Adriatic sector.[1] Alexander's measures of deception had achieved tactical surprise, and the coastal drive went well. On the 29th, it reached the Germans' advanced positions inland from Pesaro, and by 4th September was into the defences south of Rimini. Meanwhile, Fifth Army moved against the centre and west of the line. After four days' heavy fighting, the enemy began slowly to withdraw as his left flank retired along the Adriatic. In the west, the Americans occupied Pisa on 2nd September and Lucca on the 6th, while in the centre the Germans abandoned the northern bank of the Arno on 31st August, and pulled back to the hills in the first week of September. On the 8th, Alexander accordingly prepared to launch his main series of continuous and alternating attacks in the centre and east, Fifth Army leading in the mountains, while Eighth Army gained the open country by Rimini whence it could turn the line. The prospects, although closely balanced, seemed good; and on that day Wilson informed the Combined Chiefs of Staff of his confidence, 'from the progress of General Alexander's offensive from 26th August until the present date, that the enemy will be driven completely from the Gothic Line.'

Strategic thought moved and eddied with the movement of these great events. There was moreover the stimulus in August of another meeting in prospect between the British and the Americans. For, after several attempts on the part of the British, a conference (the 'Octagon' Conference) had been arranged to start on 11th September at Quebec, the first full meeting since 'Sextant' at Cairo nine months before. Both partners were therefore considering the subjects for discussion; and it was indeed partly to prepare for the event that the Prime Minister,

---

[1] See Map VIII.

with the C.I.G.S. and the Chief of the Air Staff, visited the Mediterranean from 11th to 29th August.[1]

For, as before, British strategic thought centred on the southern front. The 'Overlord' campaign, which dominated European strategy, was following the agreed strategic plan, and discussion on its conduct was confined to the Command. But the case was different in the Mediterranean. No agreed strategic plan existed for the development of operations in Italy from the point which they had almost reached; and while that development could not decide the main issue in Europe, it might seriously affect its form.

The British were faced by three problems in the Mediterranean, depending on the immediate outcome of events. First, the action to be taken if the enemy should soon withdraw from or surrender in Greece and Yugoslavia; secondly, the action to be taken if he should soon surrender, probably as part of a general capitulation, throughout south-east Europe; thirdly, the strategy to be followed if he did not surrender. In each case, military and diplomatic factors were closely connected with each other.

To judge from the signs in August, the Germans might begin to pull out of the southern Balkans at any moment. A redisposition of strength early in the month between Greece and Bulgaria, and within Yugoslavia, seemed to point—though falsely—to preparations for withdrawal; and further movements towards its close, when Rumania had collapsed, lent weight to this interpretation. The British prepared as far as they could to stimulate action by the guerrillas in that event. The plans for Greece ('Noah's Ark') had indeed been assembled in April 1944, not so much because the Germans were then likely to withdraw as to commit the indecisive and mutually hostile Greek forces. But the subsequent delay, and growing tension in Greece during the summer, robbed the preparations of much of their potential force, and by August relations between the headquarters of E.L.A.S. (commanding the guerrilla forces of the powerful Republican movement E.A.M.)[2] and the British Mission were so bad that the latter was concerned as much to survive as to direct operations against the enemy. The conversations with the Yugoslavs were more hopeful. Following their recovery from the Germans' Seventh Offensive,[3] the Partisans gradually regained the initiative in July 1944, and by the end of that month were again raiding communications in the north and threatening the enemy in Montenegro. At the beginning of August, the British Mission composed a plan to harass the German retreat through co-ordinated attacks on communications by the Partisans and the Allied air forces. Wilson immediately concurred,

[1] See p. 367 above.

[2] See pp. 83-4 above.

[3] See p. 277 above.

and urged acceptance of the plan on Tito; and on 12th August he was able to report that the Partisans would co-operate fully. The preparations were put in hand in the second half of the month. Yugoslavia was divided into sectors, each under a Partisan commander attended by a British officer who would specify the targets and arrange for the necessary air or sea support. The operations ('Ratweek') were to start on 1st September.

In the event of a German withdrawal, the British policy differed for the two countries. It was almost certain that troops would not be put into Yugoslavia: it was quite certain that they would be put into Greece. The Greek situation in August seemed likely indeed to demand their immediate despatch. From the spring of 1944, E.A.M.'s. relations with the exiled Government, and with the British representatives in Greece, had grown steadily worse, and another mutiny in the Greek forces in Egypt in July convinced the British Government that reconciliation was impossible. It decided, after some hesitation, not to accuse E.A.M. in public, and to maintain its missions in northern Greece. But it reduced severely the supply of equipment to E.L.A.S., and prepared to support the Royal Government, if necessary by force, as soon as circumstances allowed of its return. The arguments for such a course remained the same as in September, 1943;[1] only the issue had sharpened in the interval, and the necessary conditions seemed more likely to supervene.

The British had in fact never entirely lost sight of the possibility of landing in Greece since the Cairo Conference; and in May, 1944 the Minister of State in the Middle East had again raised it seriously. The Foreign Office then agreed that Greece must not be allowed to fall into a vacuum, which might lead to civil war and must affect the British strategic position in the Eastern Mediterranean. 'It is therefore of very great political importance,' Mr Eden informed the Prime Minister, 'that E.A.M. should not be allowed to seize power in Greece at the moment of a German withdrawal.' The question was how large a British force must be put in. As in September 1943, Mr. Churchill envisaged some 5,000 men with tanks; but the Chiefs of Staff and the Foreign Secretary, as before, thought this unrealistic, and in mid-July, when E.A.M. was showing its strength, the Chiefs of Staff proposed detailed alternatives. The first involved the occupation of Athens, Salonika, Morea and the west coast by four separate British forces, amounting to 80,000 troops with a small air contingent: the second, the occupation of Athens and Salonika alone by a British force of 10,000 men. The Chiefs of Staff favoured the first alternative, which naturally offered the greater chance of success; but Churchill and the Foreign Office preferred the second, which seemed to them a reasonable military measure by which to attain the specific diplomatic

[1] See pp. 86-7 above.

object. On 8th August, the Prime Minister ordered the C.I.G.S. to prepare a force of 10,000 men, while the Foreign Secretary informed the War Cabinet of the steps they proposed to take. The War Cabinet at once sanctioned the use of such a force, with some three squadrons of aircraft, and decided to inform the Americans. On 14th August, Wilson was ordered to prepare detailed plans, and on the 19th he submitted his report, including a proposal to drop a British paratroop brigade on Athens in advance of the main force. It seemed that the Middle East could raise a division for the operation without touching the forces in Italy, and in the last week of August the Prime Minister and the C.I.G.S. approved Wilson's plan ('Manna') at a meeting in Rome. If the Germans withdrew as expected, D-day was fixed provisionally for 11th September.

Meanwhile, on 17th August Mr. Churchill approached Mr. Roosevelt as the War Cabinet had asked, informing him of the British decision and, in view of Wilson's plan for an air descent, asking for the loan of American air transports in the Mediterranean. The President agreed, and the Prime Minister prepared for the assault on 11th September. Seized of its diplomatic importance, he seems indeed to have been under the impression that it would then take place whatever the circumstances, and whether or not the Germans had left. But neither the Chiefs of Staff nor the Mediterranean Command were willing to undertake a landing on those terms, and on 6th September Wilson informed Churchill that it must definitely await the Germans' disappearance. On the 8th, he received a directive accordingly from the Combined Chiefs of Staff.

The prospect of a landing on the mainland of south-east Europe led to a final reorganization of the administrative arrangements for the area, which had persisted uneasily since 1943.[1] The disadvantages of a separate direction of military and civil affairs, by two virtually separate Allied organizations in Italy and Egypt, were now recognized as excessive. The Mediterranean Command had been considering for some months the transfer of civil administration and relief for the Balkans from Cairo to Italy; early in September, the Combined Chiefs of Staff's directive instructed Wilson to make the necessary change, leaving only a 'rear link' in Egypt. Thereafter, the Supreme Commander's headquarters exercised direct control over all aspects of the Command.

The situation in Yugoslavia demanded different treatment from that in Greece. In the latter case, open disunity led to open British intervention. In the former, there was already some basis for reconciliation between the parties, which the British actively fostered. The formation of a new Royal Government by M. Subasic in May, 1944[2]

[1] See pp. 206-7, 274-5 above.
[2] See pp. 272-3 above.

was followed in June by talks between him and Marshal Tito under British auspices. They began very well. The Partisans' National Liberation Committee secretly consented to recognize the new Royal Government, and Subasic to recognize the National Army of Liberation; and in return for the exiled Government's agreement to try to enlist the co-operation of its supporters, the National Liberation Committee recorded that 'the question of the Monarchy is not an obstacle to the collaboration of the Committee and the Royal Yugoslav Government.' Liaison was established between the two authorities, their naval forces were allied in principle, and Tito was recognized as Supreme Commander-in-Chief. As was perhaps inevitable, these principles soon suffered in practice. It proved less simple than had been claimed to gain the co-operation of the Serbs, on the plea of a Royal Government in which Serbs were not represented; while Tito himself in July staged a sharp, and perhaps politic, reaction from his concessions in June. But Mr. Churchill's visit to Italy, when he held conversations with Tito and with Subasic, restored and indeed improved on the earlier position. The two sides were again drawn together, their land and air forces were amalgamated in principle as their naval forces had been earlier, King Peter called on the Serbs to support the National Army of Liberation, and on 21st August Tito and Subasic issued declarations of mutual amity and tolerance pending a settlement at the end of the war. The British, for their part, promised increased support to Tito under these conditions. They were indeed well satisfied with the results, in which, apart from the question of Istria to which the Yugoslavs laid claim from Italy, they had apparently obtained a large measure of agreement.

This was particularly satisfactory, because the British were by now strongly opposed to the idea of entering Yugoslavia when the Germans disappeared. No British force which could then be spared could affect the supremacy of the Partisans, or, it was thought, could hope to protect those whom they opposed. The Chiefs of Staff therefore did not intend to send troops into the country; and they hailed with relief the prospect of co-operation, or at least of tolerance, between the rival authorities.

Policy in Greece and Yugoslavia was thus clear and well prepared. But the Western Allies had also to consider their action further afield in south-east Europe, should the Germans collapse. This had hitherto been the study of the Post-Hostilities Planning Staff, a sub-committee of the Chiefs of Staff working in liaison with the Allied European Advisory Commission in London; and as such had received little active consideration or priority. Even so, by the summer the plans had reached a fairly advanced stage. It was generally assumed, even in the absence of an arrangement with the Russians, that they would be responsible for Rumania and for Hungary north and east of the

Danube. The most likely 'no man's land' was therefore the rest of Hungary, Austria and Bulgaria. Properly to garrison these areas, and to administer their relief, must involve a large commitment: the Post-Hostilities Planning Staff calculated that the garrisons alone, with those for Greece and the islands, would amount to 132,000 men. Even if the commitments were cut, the force must be considerable; and in May 1944, the Americans were therefore asked what responsibilities they would be prepared to assume. On the 28th, the Joint Chiefs of Staff replied that no American troops could be spared 'as occupational forces in southern Europe, including Austria, or south-east Europe, including the Balkans'. On the contrary, 'such United States forces as may be present in these areas due to military operations will be withdrawn as soon as practicable after the cessation of hostilities.' The Americans' administration of relief would be limited to 'procurement and shipment of supplies to Albania, Yugoslavia, and Greece', for which they would supply a few military officers until U.N.R.R.A. took over. These intentions, however, seemed to run counter to those expounded by the American representative on the European Advisory Commission, who stated on 31st May that the United States would participate in a tripartite occupation of Austria; and the domestic difference was solved early in July, when the President decided that American troops could be used for that purpose. Even so, as the Joint Chiefs of Staff made clear, the force involved was not likely to be large, and the British formed their plans on the assumption that British troops alone would be involved in south-east Europe, and must form the main Western garrison in Austria.

The details of these plans were settled provisionally by the end of July, 1944. In the event of a German collapse, the Chiefs of Staff recommended that Wilson should 'seize immediate control' of Greece with approximately one British division and small air forces, of the Dodecanese with 2,400 men, and of Austria with four divisions and a small tactical air force. He should not station forces in Yugoslavia or Albania, beyond guards for the distribution of supplies; nor should he send troops into Bulgaria, although British air forces might be used to see that the armistice terms were carried out. The problem of Istria awaited further consideration. The forces available for these objects were subject to the following considerations:

> '(a) . . . United States forces will be withdrawn as soon as practicable after the cessation of hostilities.
>
> (b) It will probably be the policy to withdraw Dominion forces as early as possible after the defeat of Germany for repatriation at an early date. . . . At the same time, there is no objection to the use of these forces for the early stages of 'Rankin'[1] if operations require it.

[1] Operations to be undertaken in the event of a sudden German collapse. (See p. 10 above).

(c) . . . Four British Indian divisions . . . will be withdrawn [from the Mediterranean Command] as early as possible and should not be used for 'Rankin' operations.

(d) French and Italian divisions will not be used.

(e) The internal security commitment in the Middle East after the defeat of Germany will require three divisions from forces at present in the Mediterranean and the Middle East.'

The British Chiefs of Staff intended to submit these proposals to the Americans as early as possible in the forthcoming conference at Quebec.

These plans for the remoter areas presupposed that the enemy would collapse. Meanwhile, it was necessary to settle the future of the armies in Italy assuming that he did not. The British position was put succinctly by the Prime Minister, at a meeting in Rome on 21st August with Brooke, Portal and Wilson.

> 'He was utterly opposed to the proposal that General Alexander's Army should move Westward. He was also determined that its operations should not be hampered by the withdrawal of further forces.'

These two points in fact covered two possibilities. First, Kesselring might weather Alexander's current attack, to the extent either of standing in the Gothic Line, or of withdrawing in good order and in his own time to the north. Secondly, he might be beaten decisively, and unable to control the pace of his retreat. In the first case, further operations would have to be mounted in full strength, and possibly including a flanking assault from the sea. This in turn meant that the Italian campaign must be granted priority over other Mediterranean operations if necessary until November 1944, a possible date, in Wilson's view, for an assault landing. But in the middle of August there were signs that this priority would be questioned. On the 7th, when the Joint Chiefs of Staff approved the Mediterranean Command's proposals for the forthcoming attack on the Gothic Line, they added that 'the campaign . . . will probably result in a weight of effort and forces on the east flank, thus pointing toward continued operations to the eastward. It is considered more probably that an advance to the westward would provide greater support for the two major operations, 'Overlord' and 'Dragoon' . . .' This passage alarmed the Prime Minister, not only because it favoured a subsequent development to the west, but also because it seemed to him to imply that 'Dragoon', as one of the two 'major' operations, meanwhile took preference over the Italian campaign. The Chiefs of Staff were less disturbed by this interpretation, which indeed, since 'Dragoon' had not yet been launched, was in a sense unrealistic. But they agreed to put the point to their colleagues, and after an exchange of views with the Joint Staff Mission in Washington, informed the Americans on 14th August:

> 'The British Chiefs of Staff note that the United States Chiefs of Staff refer to 'Dragoon' as a major operation on the same footing as 'Overlord'. They assume that this does not imply that 'Dragoon' is to be regarded, after its launching, as necessarily having priority over the Italian campaign. The relevant priority of the Italian and 'Dragoon' campaigns can only be decided when we see how these two campaigns develop.'

This clarification of the issue had an unfortunate result. The Americans replied on the 26th:

> '. . . The United States Chiefs of Staff consider 'Dragoon' to be a major operation rendering direct support to 'Overlord', and as such to have priority over the Italian Campaign. In this connection the United States Chiefs of Staff invite attention to an agreement at Sextant "that 'Overlord' and 'Anvil' ('Dragoon') would be the supreme operations for 1944 and that nothing would be undertaken in any other parts of the world to hazard the success of these operations".'

Such an attitude carried no guarantee that the Americans would remain in full strength in Italy over the next few months.

The British strategy in the second case, if Kesselring were decisively defeated, was equally clear, and was proclaimed unambiguously by the Prime Minister towards the end of August.

> 'My object now', he informed Field Marshal Smuts on the 31st,[1] 'is to keep what we have got in Italy . . . with this I hope to turn and break the Gothic Line, break in to the Po Valley and ultimately advance by Trieste and the Ljubljana Gap to Vienna. . . .'

Three days earlier, he had sounded Mr. Roosevelt.[2]

> '. . . 4. I have never forgotten your talks to me at Teheran about Istria and I am sure that the arrival of a powerful army in Trieste and Istria in four or five weeks would have an effect far outside purely military values. Tito's people will be awaiting us in Istria. What the condition of Hungary will be then I cannot imagine but we shall at any rate be in a position to take full advantage of any great new situation.'

The President was cautious.

> '. . . My Chiefs of Staff feel that a vigorous attack, using all the forces available, should force the enemy into the Po Valley. The

[1] See *Triumph and Tragedy*, p. 91.

[2] See *loc. cit.*, pp. 108-9.

> enemy may then choose to withdraw entirely from Northern Italy. . . . It is my thought that we should press the German Army in Italy vigorously and with every facility we have available and suspend decision of future use of General Wilson's armies until the results of his campaign are better known and we have better information as to what the Germans may do. We can renew our Teheran talk about Trieste and Istria at Octagon.'[1]

But the Prime Minister was not to be silenced in the interval.

> '. . . 3. As to the future,' he replied on 31st August,[2] 'continuous employment against the enemy will have to be found for the Eighth and Fifth Armies once the German Armies in Italy have been destroyed or unluckily made their escape. This employment can only take the form of a movement first to Istria and Trieste and ultimately upon Vienna.'

These were the same ideas as had appeared late in June,[3] which the interval had not weakened but had rather reinforced. In the first place, the alternative had now been tried, and its effect had been seen. The easy triumph of 'Dragoon', indeed, merely confirmed each side in its views. To the Americans, it vindicated their arguments in favour of the operation: to the British, it proved that the operation was superfluous. The pace of the advance, in the absence of serious opposition, suggested, as they had foretold, that 'Overlord' had already provided the conditions for 'Dragoon', instead of 'Dragoon' providing the conditions for 'Overlord'. As Churchill informed the King, on his return from watching the assault:[4]

> 'There is no doubt that Eisenhower's operations made a great diversion. The fact that this is the precise opposite of what was intended need not be stressed at the present time.'

The advance from the south, as an immediate contribution, had not affected the advance in the north; and the British saw no great purpose for the future in reinforcing Eisenhower's right flank from bases five hundred miles away. But if 'Dragoon' had been a waste of force and opportunity, any further move into France from Italy would be pointless. The very success of the landings seemed to the British to strengthen the argument for striking in another direction.

But apart from their opposition to the alternative, the British could now develop a strong case on its own merits for the move towards Vienna. If the military argument had been attractive in June, in August—particularly after the 22nd, when the Russians' advance

[1] See p. 384 above.

[2] See *loc. cit.*, p. 110.

[3] See pp. 347-8, 352-3, 356 above.

[4] See Appendix X below for the complete text.

through Rumania began—it seemed compelling. An Allied threat to the Balkans from the west, menacing then, might now prove fatal to the Germans. At the least, it must increase the growing disorder: at best, it would complete the ring around the Reich which the Russians' advance made possible. The most difficult phase of the operations, the passage of the Ljubljana Gap, should also prove easier now from the easier position in Yugoslavia, particularly if the Germans soon collapsed or withdrew to the north. But the military argument no longer stood alone. There were also strong reasons of diplomacy for an incursion into south-east Europe, which weighed with the Prime Minister and the Foreign Secretary. It was indeed at this point that the diplomatic argument came to the fore, which has often been assumed to have existed earlier. As we have seen, this was not so in 1943, when there was no question of operations by large Allied forces on the mainland beyond Italy; nor was it a necessary or explicit part of the case in May and June 1944, when such operations were first proposed. The diplomatic consequences could then be foreseen, and were acceptable; but the operations could be, and were, recommended without reference to the diplomatic consequences, and the Chiefs of Staff at least placed the emphasis not on the Ljubljana Gap but on Trieste.[1] There is in fact a valid distinction to be drawn between an advantage gratefully accepted as a result of other events, and a pressing necessity to secure that advantage. The first was the case at the end of June, the second at the end of August. The strong impression of growing Russian hostility, evinced in many different ways, and the evidence of activities by Communist agents in countries administered by the Western Allies, were then brought to the point by the shock of Stalin's behaviour over Warsaw; and as the Red Army entered eastern Europe, the British feared the Russians' intentions and their behaviour in the conquered territories. The war against Germany was entering on its last phase, whatever its duration: it was the more important for the West to gain a foothold in Europe beyond France, Italy and Greece.

These military and diplomatic arguments applied the more strongly if the war in Europe continued for more than a few months. As the Joint Planning Staff remarked, 'If operations in western Europe and in Russia are so decisive that it becomes clear that the German armies will not survive this year, then operations in Italy are of no great strategic significance except to pursue the retreating and disordered enemy.' But the longer Germany fought on, the more weight might attach to the southern front. The Prime Minister was the more attracted to its possibilities because it would be principally a British commitment. As he pointed out on 21st August, 'the Army in Italy was the most representative Army of the British Empire now in the

[1] See pp. 268, 350-1 above.

field', and the theatre enjoyed a British command. As British forces on the western front came in the winter to represent a progressively smaller percentage of the whole, it would be the more satisfactory if the British could make a significant contribution elsewhere in Europe, and in an area moreover where the Americans had announced they would not stay after Germany surrendered. The march on Vienna, as the Prime Minister saw it, thus met every demand at this stage of the war. It would provide the Western Allies, possibly in concert with the Russians, with a coherent strategy for the winter; it might lessen, or counter, the danger of excessive Russian ambitions; and it would form an appropriate contribution, within the limits of the British effort, to the common victory. From the vantage of his position, he could appreciate the importance of each factor.

There were two dangers to this strategy: that the Americans would refuse to support it, and that resources would be withdrawn over the next few weeks which might cripple the subsequent operations. In the first case, it might prove difficult for the British to carry on alone. Eighth Army in August disposed of nineteen divisions. But some would soon have to be rested, Wilson estimated that fifteen divisions at least must be used to penetrate into the Balkans, much specialized equipment for both Armies in Italy was supplied by the Americans, and assault shipping might be needed to hasten or force the passage of the Istrian peninsula. The debate on principle, however, could await the forthcoming conference, and there was moreover no real reason, as the C.I.G.S. told the Prime Minister, to suppose that the Americans would not support the operations if they were convinced of their military value.

The withdrawal of resources was a more immediate danger, and was not confined to the Americans. Throughout the past year, the Far East and the Mediterranean had alternately been regarded, according to circumstances, as a source of supply for the other; and as the odds lengthened against Germany, both sets of Chiefs of Staff looked the more closely to the war against Japan. The Americans had already announced the withdrawal of their troops from the Mediterranean theatre as soon as Germany collapsed: in the second half of August, they made plans to take four divisions over the next three months. At the same time, they informed the British that, 'Dragoon' having been completed, they intended from 1st October to withdraw eighteen L.S.T. a month from the Mediterranean, to refit in the United States before sailing to the Pacific. The British Chiefs of Staff also had their eye on the Mediterranean, in the interests of south-east Asia. Plans for an attack on Malaya in the spring of 1945 were now reaching a critical stage, and the operations would demand a further six divisions over those already in that theatre.[1] The Chiefs

[1] See pp. 492-5 below.

of Staff wished to take the first four, which were British/Indian divisions, from Eighth Army in Italy. There was no question of their doing so before the war in Europe allowed; but what the war in Europe would allow had still to be determined. At the end of August, therefore, the Prime Minister prepared to resist, from whatever quarter, a removal of resources which might cramp the opportunities in the Mediterranean.

But the prospects for the European war as a whole became increasingly difficult to assess as the 'Octagon' Conference approached. By 6th September, it seemed possible, even probable, that the enemy might surrender within the next few weeks. It had for long been generally assumed, despite the more enthusiastic advocates of strategic bombing, that Germany would collapse only after severe defeats by land. The question now was whether or not those defeats had been severe enough. There were three critical factors, on which the British Joint Intelligence Committee concentrated its attention during July and August: morale; the state of stocks and production, particularly of oil; and the decline of the armed forces.

While a definite picture could be drawn in August, it was still difficult to estimate the effects with any precision. The moral reserves of Germany were still unknown, even—or perhaps particularly—after 20th July. The plot against Hitler, indeed, while throwing light into some dark corners, tended to obscure the general scene. Such information as could be gained raised more problems than it answered. What elements were involved? How wide was their influence? What were the consequences for the Government, and for the people? What deductions could be drawn from those consequences? The symptoms seemed in some ways to contradict each other. Certain elements of the General Staff were known to be behind the attempt, and were thought to have their sympathizers in high positions on the fronts; but the army in the west, while shaken, remained intact. The administrative hierarchy in Germany was known to have been implicated, and to have been purged to some extent; but the wider public seemed apathetic. What did such a combination portend? Would the German army and people continue to support their leaders, now the more determined to suppress any revolt? Or did the general apathy suggest that leadership would fail? A week before the plot took place, the Joint Intelligence Committee thought that the occasion of a German collapse would be either a rout on the Eastern Front or a collapse of morale within Germany which might precede that rout; and that the end, though probably delayed by the Nazi Party's desperate measures of control, would be sudden when it came. Six weeks later, the plot had added nothing to these estimates. At the end of August, the Joint Intelligence Committee could only say that 'an underlying and potentially fatal weakness' ran through the German system, which 'may not show itself immediately in Germany's conduct of the war', but which had 'fundamentally weakened' her capacity to resist.

That capacity was thought to have declined seriously between the end of June and the end of August. Stocks and production of war material, particularly of oil fuel, were believed to be running down fast. Oil indeed was now considered to be the critical factor. It will be recalled that in March, 1944 General Spaatz had wished to give first priority in bombing operations to the petroleum industry, particularly petrol; but this proposal had been overruled by the decision to concentrate, as before, on the fighter aircraft industry in Germany, and also on the transport system of north-west Europe.[1] These priorities were subject to review 'after 'Overlord' is established on the Continent'. But some attacks on oil had already been made from both the Mediterranean and the United Kingdom: on three occasions in April, American aircraft from the Mediterranean bombed the oilfields of Ploesti, and in May Eighth U.S. Air Force for the first time bombed synthetic oil plants in Germany. From June to September, the attacks were persistent and almost continuous. Apart from many smaller raids, Eighth U.S. Air Force in that period made six large attacks on thirty-two plants and refineries, Fifteenth U.S. Air Force in the Mediterranean attacked forty-one plants and refineries, and Bomber Command made nine major attacks on eight targets. These operations seemed to the Allies almost to have achieved their object by the end of August. On 20th July, the Joint Intelligence Committee reported that 'Germany's shortage of oil has become the major factor limiting German strategy and operational efficiency.' At the end of that month, it estimated that output of finished products had fallen to 40 per cent of 'normal', that a drop of a further 15 per cent might be recorded by the end of August, and that Germany had consumed from the beginning of May to the end of July 188,000 tons of oil more than she had produced in that time. On 29th August, it calculated that Germany's shortage of oil as a result of Allied bombing attacks 'is for the first time threatening her with a potentially fatal situation', apart from the recent loss of the Rumanian oilfields to the Russians.

The quantity and variety of the evidence, and the difficulties inherent in assessing the relations between industries, made such firm deductions impossible for the rest of the German war economy. But the combination of bombing, loss of manpower and loss of raw materials —with the emphasis on bombing—was thought in London to have rendered the German industrial machine incapable of meeting the demands of the armed forces. They were believed to be particularly

[1] See pp. 294, 295-6, 304 above.

weak in heavy armaments and tanks, weak in motor transport, and embarrassed for certain items of equipment and for ammunition. The output of fighter aircraft, although rising steadily throughout the year, was achieved only under great difficulties, and was draining the industrial resources correspondingly faster than would have otherwise been the case. The disruption of industry, moreover, was increased by the general dislocation of transport which had begun in the spring. By the beginning of August, the Joint Intelligence Committee calculated that the damage to stocks and production was serious enough for it to become critical as further operations deprived Germany of her European resources. By 29th August, the Committee was therefore optimistic.

'. . . Battle wastage has continued on a heavy scale in Russia and on a substantial scale in Italy. In France the German losses (as yet uncounted) of supplies and all forms of equipment during the recent fighting have been catastrophic. . . .

It is impossible to estimate the extent to which these losses have further reduced the overall capacity of the German Armies to resist. It seems, however, clear that, in the time likely to be available to them, the Germans will be able to provide only very limited replacements, especially of heavy equipment and M.T. [Motor Transport], and that shortage of fuel and difficulties of transportation will make the task of bringing even these replacements up to the present battle fronts almost insuperable. . . .

Germany has been suffering from the loss of the raw materials which she once derived from her occupation of territory in Eastern Europe. Now, as the Allied Armies advance in Western Europe and Germany's paramount and rising need is equipment fit for immediate use in battle, she is losing the direct contribution to her fighting strength of the finished products, components and highly developed technical facilities of the Western occupied territories as well as the important supplies of foodstuffs from France. Although, particularly because of transportation difficulties caused by bombing, Germany has obtained less from France in recent months, she will be deprived of the varied products of value to her armed forces of French factories, and of a valuable source of bauxite and alumina. Simultaneously she is now cut off from all supplies from the Iberian Peninsula of which, since the great diminution in tungsten supplies earlier this year, the most important has been Spanish high-grade iron-ore. In the East the Russian advance is approaching the important industrial areas which Germany has greatly developed and to which with enormous effort she dispersed many of her own factories so as to be out of the range of Allied bombing. . . . Finally, the resources of Rumania, which included valuable minerals and foodstuffs as well as oil, appear likely to be totally

> lost to her, while her supplies from the rest of south-east Europe are increasingly in jeopardy as a result of Germany's weakening control of that area. . . .'

But while the German position seemed hopeless, it remained impossible to say at what point the decline in production would dictate the end of coherent resistance.

The German armed forces themselves were also steadily running down. By the middle of July, the last vestige of a central reserve had disappeared, and reinforcements for the two main fronts had to come either from the forces in Norway, Italy and the Balkans, or from formations newly recruited. As far as the Joint Intelligence Committee could tell, there was not much left in the barrel. On 20th July, it estimated that casualties in future could be replaced only by hastening the training of youths of seventeen, by combing the hospitals, and by using more foreigners. On 26th August, it reported that permanent casualties probably amounted to over 1,000,000 men in the first half of 1944, and that if the same rate of destruction could be maintained, the German army, which on 1st June was thought to have contained 7,100,000 men, would consist of 6,450,000 men at the end of the year, of whom only some 2,000,000 would be Germans of good calibre between the ages of nineteen and forty-six, 1,250,000 would be Germans of the same age group suffering from the effects of wounds or sickness, 1,000,000 would be foreigners, another 1,000,000 would be German boys of eighteen or less, another 750,000 German men of over forty-seven, and another 450,000 would be recruited from hospital. 'Germany's acute shortage of battle-fit manpower', the Joint Intelligence Committee concluded, 'is now taking direct toll of her fighting capacity in the field.' The navy and the air force were equally short of men, and were now largely ineffective. Both were starved of fuel, the surface fleet was confined to harbour except for coastal escort in the North Sea, and the U-boats could operate solely from bases in Germany and Norway. The air force, disrupted by the ceaseless attentions of the Allies, was limited in the west virtually to a night-fighter force.

The Joint Intelligence Committee therefore concluded as early as mid-July that 'all the elements for a collapse of Germany already exist'; and that though 'it is impossible to predict' when the collapse itself would come, 'it is . . . equally difficult to see how Germany can, if Allied attacks on the three major fronts are ceaselessly pressed home, prolong the struggle beyond December.' It was still not possible, late in August, to suggest an earlier date. But by 5th September, the Joint Intelligence Committee was prepared to hazard that the end would come quite soon, although no precise date could be given. The conditions for collapse, which already existed, now seemed likely to combine for the event. The Committee's report of that date is an interesting document.

'Since our last appreciation of German Strategy and Capacity to Resist, . . . Germany has suffered further catastrophic disasters. The process of final military defeat leading to the cessation of organised resistance has begun in the West. . . . We report as follows.

2. In France, the German front has virtually ceased to exist. The Germans have been unable, after our destruction of the greater part of their armies in Normandy, to hold any line, and the Allies have now entered Belgium and are advancing against very light opposition to the frontier of Germany and the Siegfried Line.

3. In Italy, the German defences based on the Gothic Line have been breached.

4. In the Balkans, the whole German position is crumbling. The bulk of the German Army in Rumania has been destroyed. The German front has virtually ceased to exist. Rumania has declared war on Germany, and Germany has lost her largest supply of natural oil. Bulgaria has deserted Germany and has announced her intention to withdraw from Serbia the divisions which protected Germany's communications with Greece and the Aegean. There are also indications of German plans to withdraw from Southern Greece. . . .

5. In the East, the Russians are preparing for what they may hope to be their final offensive to destroy the German Armies in Poland.

6. Finland has accepted the Russian conditions for the opening of Armistice negotiations. She claims to have secured Germany's agreement to the withdrawal of German forces from Finland.

7. The Allied advance in the West is rapidly driving the Germans from the areas from which flying-bombs or long range rockets can be launched against England and is thus destroying German hopes of influencing the course of the war by the use of these weapons.

8. The speed of events in the West and in the Balkans has taken Germany completely by surprise, and has left her without the resources, and apparently, without any co-ordinated plan, to meet her radically altered strategic position. The task of forecasting what, in these circumstances, Germany's strategy will be, is complicated by the fact that Hitler is increasingly out of touch with all reality. The object, however, of German strategy is to prolong the war, preventing for as long as possible the invasion of the Reich itself.

9. Germany's capacity to deal with her present situation is seriously reduced by her lack of oil. She has for practical purposes no free reserves and must, henceforth, limit her consumption to the much reduced figure of current production. Germany's losses in manpower and equipment have been enormous and she cannot now hope to replace them. She is, moreover,

faced with the imminent loss, in the Balkans and in the West, of natural resources which are essential to the maintenance of her war effort on any scale commensurate with its task.

10. The German Navy can no longer decisively influence the battle in the West, despite Germany's plans for carrying on the Atlantic U-boat campaign from Norwegian bases and the existing patrols in focal areas of shipping in the North Channel and St. George's Channel [at either end of the Irish Sea]. The greater part of the German Navy is now operating in the Baltic in direct support of Germany's Armies on the Eastern Front. . . .

11. In face of Allied supremacy in the air, the German Air Force has failed to have any material influence on the course of recent Allied advances in the East, in the West, in the Balkans and in Italy. Though the German Air Force is largely concentrated for the defence of the Reich itself, it cannot prevent the invasion of the Reich, or the final issue of the battle. Moreover, its operational activity is increasingly being reduced by Germany's acute lack of aviation spirit and her shortage of air crews. . . .

12. Until recently, German strategy was dominated by the determination not to give ground. We believe, however, that Hitler may now realise that his only hope of using some of his troops now in outlying parts of Europe for the prolongation of the war, and the defence of the Reich, lies in withdrawing them immediately before they are finally cut off. Even if he has so changed his strategy, however, he has left it too late. During September, he might be able to make available three divisions from Scandinavia and Finland, possibly a maximum of seven from Italy and the equivalent of ten new divisions from inside Germany, but the latter would be generally under strength, inadequately trained, short of artillery and only fitted for static defence. Any divisions which Germany can make available will today be sent to the West, so long as this front presents the most immediate threat.

13. There remains the question of whether Hitler will withdraw any divisions from the Eastern front. The Germans cannot be confident of holding their present line in Poland even with the forces which they now dispose there. It may be, therefore, that even though Anglo-American forces are on the point of invading Germany itself Hitler will not order any forces to be moved from East to West.

14. On the other hand, whereas the Germans have at the moment an organised front between the Russians and the German frontier, they have, at present, nothing in the West but disorganised remnants incapable of holding an Allied advance in strength into Germany itself. We therefore cannot exclude the possibility that Hitler may increase the risks in the East and transfer some divisions from there to the West.

15. However, whatever action Hitler may now take it will

be too late to affect the issue in the West where organised German resistance will gradually disintegrate under our attack, although it is impossible to predict the rate at which this will take place. . . .'

This estimate reflected well-informed opinion beyond the central Intelligence. The Allied Command in France was itself optimistic. As Field Marshal Montgomery has recorded,[1] 'at the end of August the current appreciation of the enemy's capabilities suggested that German resistance in Western Europe was on the verge of collapse'. This confidence spread from the Command to the armies and to the Western publics. Early in September, the greatest optimism prevailed in most quarters, and most of those in a position to judge, as well as those who were not, believed that Germany could not survive for long. The American and British Chiefs of Staff themselves inclined to the same opinion. On 6th September, the C.I.G.S. informed his colleagues that, although he considered the Joint Intelligence Committee's report to be slightly optimistic, he saw no reason to disagree with it; and the next day he told the Prime Minister that, while the Chiefs of Staff 'had not ignored the possibility that German resistance would be prolonged into the winter,' they were 'influenced by the optimistic Report which the Joint Intelligence Sub-Committee had just completed'. The American Chiefs of Staff apparently held much the same views, as a result of reports from their Intelligence.

Neither the President nor the Prime Minister, however, was convinced. The President is reported to have been sceptical. The Prime Minister gave his views to the British Chiefs of Staff on 8th September.

'1. I have now read [the Joint Intelligence Committee's] Report and have not noticed any fact in it of which I was not already aware. Generally speaking, I consider it errs on the side of optimism. Paragraph 2 already requires to be rewritten.[2] Paragraph 3 should also state that at the present time we are at a virtual standstill and that progress will be very slow.[3] Paragraph 6 has the effect of a reinforcement for Germany. I trust the assumption of a decisive Russian offensive on the Eastern front will be realised; but it is at present only an assumption.

2. On the other side, there are factors to be noted. Apart from Cherbourg and Arromanches, we have not yet obtained any large harbours. The Germans intend to defend the mouth of the Scheldt and are still resisting in the Northern suburbs of Antwerp. Brest has not been taken in spite of very heavy fighting, and at least two weeks will be needed after it is taken before it

---

[1] *From Normandy to the Baltic* (1946), p. 188.

[2] See p. 525 below.

[3] See pp. 529-31 below.

is available. Lorient still holds out. No attempt has been made to take and clear the port of St. Nazaire, which is about twice as good as Brest and twice as easy to take. No attempt has been made to get hold of Bordeaux. Unless the situation changes remarkably, the Allies will still be short of port accommodation when the equinoctial gales are due.

3. One can already foresee the probability of a lull in the magnificent advances we have made. General Patton's Army is heavily engaged on the line Metz-Nancy. Field-Marshal Montgomery has explained his misgivings as to General Eisenhower's future plan. It is difficult to see how the 21st Army Group can advance in force to the German frontier until it has cleared up the stubborn resistance at the Channel ports and dealt with the Germans to the North at Walcheren and to the North of Antwerp.

4. On the other side, the Russians have made no progress into East Prussia and the Germans have re-established contact with their armies cut off in the Baltic States. The turning-over of Rumania to the Allied cause has given the Russians a great advantage and it may well be that they will enter Belgrade and Budapest, and possibly Vienna, before the Western Allies succeed in piercing the Siegfried Line. However desirable militarily such a Russian incursion may be, its political effect upon Central and Southern Europe may be formidable in the last degree.

5. It would have been of great value had this report been accompanied by a table, showing the disposition of the various German Divisions as they are now and as they are expected to be at the end of September.

6. No one can tell what the future may bring forth. Will the Allies be able to advance in strength through the Siegfried Line into Germany during September, or will their forces be so limited by supply conditions and the lack of ports as to enable the Germans to consolidate on the Siegfried Line? Will they withdraw from Italy, in which case they will greatly strengthen their internal position? Will they be able to draw on their forces, at one time estimated at between 25 and 35 divisions, in the Baltic States? The fortifying and consolidating effect of a stand on the frontier of the native soil should not be underrated. It is at least as likely that Hitler will be fighting on the 1st January as that he will collapse before then. If he does collapse before then the reasons will be political rather than purely military.'

And if Germany did not collapse in 1944, the Western Allies, given the wrong strategy, might be badly placed in 1945. It was this fear that sharpened the Prime Minister's distrust of the general optimism. Until Germany actually surrendered, it remained as necessary as ever to ensure that the Italian campaign received due priority, and that, if successful, the consequences were properly understood. He was disturbed lest an easy assumption of sudden victory should rob the argument of its force; and despite the Chiefs of Staff's assurances, he did not believe that they could support that argument properly unless they acknowledged the real possibility that the war in Europe might continue into 1945. When the British party embarked for Canada on 5th September, Mr. Churchill's first anxiety was therefore to settle priorities firmly with his military advisers before meeting the Americans in a few days' time.

CHAPTER X

THE CAMPAIGN IN BURMA, JANUARY–JUNE, 1944

(i)

Arakan and the Central Front

AT THE BEGINNING of January 1944, a reduced programme of operations in Burma had to be accepted, when the basis of the more ambitious design was removed by developments in Europe. The South-East Asia Command was obliged to return to plans developed originally by its predecessor in September 1943, with the land and air forces, but without the sea forces, which had been anticipated.[1] Fourteenth Army was now to develop two complementary limited offensives: one in Arakan, with 15th Corps, to clear the coast and the Mayu mountains (operation 'Cudgel'); the other on the central front, with 4th Corps, to advance down the Kabaw valley and through the Chin Hills to Kalemyo and Kalewa on the Chindwin (operation 'Gripfast'). Meanwhile, General Stilwell's force in the north was to push down from Ledo to the area of Mogaung and Myitkyina.[2]

The operations in Arakan began early in the month, with some three divisions. Throughout January the R.A.F. steadily reduced the enemy's initial air superiority, until Japanese fighters were unable seriously to interrupt the operations on land or, later, their support from the air. Under this cover, 15th Corps moved steadily down both flanks of the Mayu range, driving the Japanese outposts back upon the main positions. The main attack was timed for 6th February, and preparatory operations began on 19th January. But on 4th February they were dramatically halted.

For while the Allies had been considering their plans for the reconquest of Burma, the Japanese had been putting the finishing touches to their plan for driving the Allies back on India. The design was divided into two initial phases: first, an attack in Arakan, to threaten the port of Chittagong and to involve the South-East Asia Command's reserves; secondly, about a month later, a major offensive against Imphal and Kohima, whence to attack the Assam line of communications and the airfields feeding the Hump.[3] A puppet government

---

[1] See pp. 222-3 above.

[2] Throughout this chapter, see Map III, facing p. 129.

[3] See p. 130 above.

would then appear in the captured territory under Subhas Chandra Bose, and the standard of revolt would be raised in north-east India. Throughout December and January the enemy reinforced and re-disposed his forward troops, until by the end of the latter month he had assembled some nine divisions—a total of nearly 200,000 men compared with 135,000 in November, 1943. In the early morning of 4th February the attack in Arakan began. By dusk, 7th Indian Division, which was the first British force to be involved, had been by-passed to the north, and within the next few days its communications were largely severed. But the front thereafter held under severe pressure, and by 13th February the first weight of the assault had slackened. The position now depended on the endurance of the encircled 7th Division.

The battle therefore turned on the air, and on 9th February the first supplies were dropped to the beleaguered troops. It was soon clear that air transport would be strained. By the second half of February, there were over seven hundred transport aircraft in India and Burma. But of these, some were reserved for the long-range penetration forces, while the whole of the American Air Transport Wing was reserved for the supply of China. This left 157 transport aircraft available for the support of Burma, and for the internal air communications of India and the Command; and, as always, the latter demanded a fair proportion of the total. At the same time, the commitments in Burma were growing. Not only did 7th Division have to be nourished entirely by air, but the time was approaching for the fly-in of General Wingate's groups to support Stilwell's operations on the northern front.[1] The only immediate source from which to draw more aircraft for the battle was the American Air Transport Wing, which by now was carrying some 14,000 tons a month to China. Admiral Mountbatten was not authorized himself to give orders to this force, but he had a useful, though abortive, precedent in a decision of the Combined Chiefs of Staff of 26th November, 1943, when 'Tarzan' was being discussed, allowing him to divert a maximum of 1,100 tons a month if necessary for his operations.[2] At Cairo, moreover, he had been assured that he would be permitted to cut into the Hump traffic[3] in an emergency. By 15th February, he decided that the emergency had arisen. The first of Wingate's three brigades had begun its march in the north a week before, and was now near the end of its land supply line; the other two long-range penetration brigades were due to be flown to their points of departure behind the enemy's lines in a fortnight; and the Arakan front, where the transports had already carried over a thousand tons of material and food, had

[1] See pp. 146, 223 above.
[2] See p. 164 above.
[3] See pp. 126-7, 164 above.

still to be supplied. Seventh Division, however, was still holding fast, and the enemy, who had counted on a swift break through to Chittagong, was finding his own communications badly strained, and might even be expected to crack. Victory over 'the invincible Jap' glimmered like a light in the distance. All depended on the air. The transfer had therefore to be swift.

But the procedure for a transfer was ill suited to the purpose. By paragraph 56 of the Final Report of the Combined Chiefs of Staff at the 'Quadrant' Conference, 'the organisation and command of the United States Army and Navy Air Transport Services in the South-East Asia area will remain under the direct control of the Commanding General, United States Army Air Forces, and of the Commander-in-Chief, United States Fleet, respectively, subject to such supply and service functions as may be by them delegated to the Deputy Supreme Allied Commander. Requests by the Supreme Allied Commander for the use of United States troop-carrier aircraft for operational purposes will be transmitted to the Deputy Supreme Allied Commander.'[1] The Deputy Supreme Commander was General Stilwell, who was at this time, as he had been for the most part since 20th December, with the Ledo force in the field, and whose consent to the transfer could not be quickly obtained. On 18th February, therefore, Mountbatten was forced to ask the British Chiefs of Staff to obtain permission from the Combined Chiefs of Staff to divert up to thirty-eight C.47 transports, or their equivalent in C.46's, from the Air Transport Wing. The American Chiefs of Staff were naturally reluctant to rob the Hump, but they consented to part with thirty C.47's 'to meet the emergency requirements of Admiral Mountbatten . . . with the understanding that these airplanes be returned to the Air Transport Command on termination of the emergency condition and with the understanding that further deficiencies in the transports for this requirement will be made up from British sources'. The balance of eight they estimated could come from R.A.F. reserves. After details had been worked out between the two bodies, Mountbatten was allowed on the 24th to divert these aircraft forthwith from the Hump, and to retain them for the period of the emergency.

Nourished continuously from the air, 7th Division held out in its defended positions, and the tide of the battle began to turn. The new Spitfires[2] had decisively defeated the supporting Japanese aircraft by the middle of February, and by the last week in the month the initiative had passed to the British on land. The enemy then began to withdraw, and in the second week of March was defeated in several important engagements. By its close he had retreated beyond his

---

[1] See p. 136 above.

[2] See pp. 146-7 above.

original line, with a loss of over 5,000 dead. His defeat had not only affected the second part of his plan: its effect on morale was immediate and significant, for the myth of 'the invincible Jap' had at last been exploded.

Early in March the transport aircraft were accordingly withdrawn from Arakan, and the Hump resumed its normal traffic. But almost at once a similar and greater emergency arose on the central front. Following preliminary moves on 8th March, on the 12th the Japanese launched their second and main attack with three divisions, designed to capture the small but important plain of Imphal and eventually to cut the Imphal-Dimapur road. As in the Arakan battle, the first British troops to be attacked were cut off from their rear, and their reinforcement affected the fate of the whole battle. 4th Corps' reserves were already engaged on this task, and General Slim, commanding Fourteenth Army, had already decided to support them with an Indian division from Arakan. In order to save time, he wished to transfer it by air. But the transports were again fully committed; as before, the remedy lay in robbing the Hump; and as before, Mountbatten had to obtain permission through Stilwell, who was in the field on the northern front, or from the Combined Chiefs of Staff. In February, a week had elapsed before this could be obtained. Now he acted without it. On 13th March, he gave verbal instructions to the local British air commander to request that thirty C.47's, or their equivalent in C.46's, might be transferred from the Hump; and he followed this up with written orders on the 16th. On the 15th he raised the matter, as one of urgency and of principle, with the British Chiefs of Staff. His first duty, as he recognized, was to protect the air ferry to China. He must therefore defend the Imphal plain, a bastion in the defence of Assam and the only base for an offensive by land into Burma. To fly in the necessary reinforcements, to maintain the front in that area, and at the same time to nourish Wingate's forces, now committed to the rear and on the flank of the Japanese, he needed thirty more C.47's. With them, he could defeat the enemy as decisively as, and on a larger scale than, in Arakan. Without them, his whole position was in jeopardy. Mountbatten then turned, in a second telegram, to the principle of the procedure. He had discussed with Stilwell the possibility of dealing with the latter's deputy, General Sultan, while Stilwell himself was in the field; but before they had reached an agreement this emergency had arisen, and he was forced to refer an urgent tactical question once again to London and Washington.[1] This, he submitted, was unworkable, and he considered that he should be given

[1] On 29th March, in a telegram to General Marshall, Stilwell claimed that in fact Mountbatten's proposed arrangement with Sultan 'has been in effect for some time.'

PLATE VII.

Above: Admiral Mountbatten
Left: General Stilwell

authority 'to divert aircraft for short periods in an emergency, reporting action to Combined Chiefs of Staff'. In the meantime, he had taken it into his own hands to order the transfer of the thirty C.47's, or their equivalent in C.46's, and unless countermanded they would begin to appear on 18th March and would be kept for about a month.

The two telegrams were considered by the Chiefs of Staff at their meeting on the following day. They at once agreed on the immediate issue, and a telegram was sent on the morning of 17th March to the British Joint Staff Mission in Washington, supporting Mountbatten's request for the thirty C.47's. At the same time, the Prime Minister addressed the President along the same lines, and Mountbatten was informed accordingly. On the evening of the same day the American Chiefs of Staff agreed to the diversion, adding 'these aircraft to be returned at the earliest possible time'. On the 18th, a few hours after the transfer had begun, Mountbatten knew of the decision.

The Americans' reply, while meeting the immediate demand, ignored Mountbatten's second request for authority to divert aircraft from the China ferry whenever he considered it necessary for his operations. The British Chiefs of Staff supported the Supreme Commander, but the Joint Chiefs of Staff were unwilling to delegate in any way their responsibility for the Hump. They consented, however, to modify the procedure so that Mountbatten's requests should reach them more quickly, and to this end instructed Stilwell 'to authorise Sultan to receive such requests from Mountbatten and transmit them to Washington whenever Stilwell is absent from New Delhi'. The British Chiefs of Staff did not accept this as a final answer; but, not wishing for the time being to press the point, they were prepared to give the revised arrangement a trial 'on the understanding that the question will be re-opened as experience proves this to be necessary'.

This agreement was barely three days old when Mountbatten was again forced to disturb the arrangements for the Hump. In the third week of March, the Japanese attack gained momentum. One division was pressing towards Kohima; another was in Ukhrul and threatening the Imphal-Kohima road; while a third was debouching into the Imphal plain. On the plain itself, the hinge of the whole front, preparations were under way for a siege: food and ammunition were sent in, non-combatants brought out as much as possible, and defensive positions built. The Japanese appeared to be within sight of their first goal, the Dimapur-Ledo lines of communication. To halt the advance, the British planned to fly in 7th Indian Division from Arakan to support a counter-attack in the north, and to supply the front itself by air. They already had to fly two more long-range penetration groups to support Wingate's operations; and in all, these commitments would require one hundred additional C.47's. Thirty of them, or rather their equivalent of twenty C.46's, were already available, and Mountbatten therefore telegraphed to the Chiefs of Staff on 25th March for permission to retain them beyond the month originally granted. The remaining seventy C.47's, or their equivalent, had still to be found.

Hitherto, the demands had been within the capacity of the Hump to supply; but the Americans could not remove any more aircraft without trouble from Chiang Kai-shek, and there did not seem to be a further reserve on which to draw. One possible source of supply had been opened a few days before. While the battle was at its height, discussions were proceeding in Washington about the future of operations in Burma, and it had been agreed that these were likely to be extended later in the year.[1] On 24th March, General Arnold accordingly promised to provide four hundred transport aircraft for south-east Asia, organized into four 'combat cargo groups', and these were designed to reach the theatre in groups of a hundred at monthly intervals starting on 1st July. On the receipt of Mountbatten's telegram, the British Chiefs of Staff inquired of the Americans if there was any chance of the first quota being advanced by three months. But this was most unlikely, and the Chiefs of Staff were therefore driven to suggest that the Hump should yet again be raided. The Americans, not surprisingly, refused, and suggested instead that British transports should be flown from the Middle East and India. At the same time, they informed Sultan that Mountbatten could retain the transports already transferred from the Hump for a further month beyond that originally allowed, as long as the situation required it. The British Chiefs of Staff thereupon looked round to see what they could provide. By raiding the reserve for 'Overlord' in Britain and the normal monthly quota of replacements for south-east Asia, they calculated that the gap of seventy C.47's could be reduced to one of thirty-eight. As an emergency measure, they still felt that the Hump should provide these thirty-eight aircraft immediately, while they proceeded to comb the Mediterranean for as many transports as they could find.

These measures did not satisfy Mountbatten. On 30th March, he telegraphed that the transports from Britain would not arrive in time, and that the normal monthly quota for the theatre was needed to replace normal wastage. Of the extra seventy C.47's, he required fifty by 4th April, and he hoped that some at least of these could come from the Mediterranean as the Chiefs of Staff had hinted. Meanwhile, however, events were moving fast at home. On 28th March, the Joint Chiefs of Staff announced that, since they could spare no more aircraft from the Hump, they would lend Mountbatten sixty-four American transports from the Mediterranean for a period not exceeding thirty days. They hoped that the British would supplement this with some of their transports from the same theatre. Any deficit could then be met by the American Air Transport Wing in India. On receipt of this offer,

[1] See pp. 455-6 below.

the British Chiefs of Staff asked General Wilson if he could spare twenty-five transports from the British strength, and could transfer the whole force as soon as possible to south-east Asia. Wilson agreed to provide fifteen transports, and to despatch all of the Mediterranean aircraft within a few days. In view of his existing commitments in Italy, the Chiefs of Staff agreed to this reduction; and on 1st April they informed Mountbatten that he would receive ninety-nine C.47's made up as follows:

From Britain:	20
From the Mediterranean:	64+15=79

Wilson added that the fifteen British aircraft should be in Karachi on 4th April, the first American échélon on the 5th, and the rest by the 8th.

Mountbatten had thus obtained his aircraft for the vital stage of the battle. He had done so only just in time. On 30th March the Japanese cut the Imphal-Kohima road and surrounded the Imphal plain, and by 4th April they were attacking the town of Kohima. But supplied continuously from the air, the Kohima garrison held out, while reinforcements gathered at Dimapur for the relief of the encircled troops both there and at Imphal. In the next two weeks the picture began to change. On 18th April the first relief reached the Kohima garrison, although the road to Imphal remained blocked; and by the end of the month the Japanese further north were being driven back slowly towards Ukhrul. Confronted, as in Arakan, by an enemy who no longer retreated when by-passed nor surrendered when encircled, but who continued to fight and to advance unsupported by land communications, the enemy's plan went awry and no adequate substitute could be found. By May, the first shock had been overcome. But great efforts were still needed to drive the enemy from the positions he had gained over the previous six weeks.

These efforts were likely to be prolonged, and it was difficult to foresee any marked reduction in the volume of air supply for some time. General Stratemeyer, commanding the air forces in the American C.B.I. (China-Burma-India) theatre,[1] had indeed already asked Mountbatten for the retention of the Mediterranean transports until at least 1st July, and had stated that if this was granted he could allow the transports withdrawn from the Hump to be kept for the campaign in Burma. But knowing the store which the Americans set by the ferry to China, Mountbatten decided to release these aircraft before making further demands; and on 20th April he informed the Combined Chiefs of Staff that half of them would be returned to the Hump that day and the other half as soon as possible. Since he had used them, however, for only part of the period for which they had

[1] See p. 126 above.

been promised initially, he wished to reserve the right to call on them again if necessary within the longer period. This limited demand was soon granted. Mountbatten thereupon signalled his future requirements. As the immediate threat receded these were becoming more complicated, for by now the later phases of the original Allied plan were dovetailing into the battle around Imphal. Besides the immediate commitment on the central front, where the monsoon was now delaying operations to recapture the roads, there was still one long-range penetration brigade to be flown in, while in the north Stilwell, who had been advancing slowly throughout the winter, was in need of greater air support. Towards the end of April, moreover, as will be seen, the Chinese had agreed to advance in Stilwell's support from Yunnan, and they were now asking for a small force of transports if their operations were not to be held up. Mountbatten therefore could not face the prospect of losing the seventy-nine Mediterranean aircraft, as already arranged, at the end of the first week in May, and on 25th April he asked permission to keep them indefinitely. In return, he proposed that seventy-nine of the first contingent of Arnold's four hundred transports for south-east Asia[1] should go straight to Wilson on 1st July, the balance coming to himself.

This demand placed the Combined Chiefs of Staff in the same quandary as they had been in ten days before, with the additional complication of supporting Stilwell and the Chinese. It was clear that Mountbatten must keep his aircraft until he had won the battle. It was also clear that the vital battle in Italy, which was planned for the second week in May,[2] should not suffer from lack of air transport. The first reaction of the British Chiefs of Staff, faced with this dilemma, was to suggest that the seventy-nine Mediterranean aircraft should be returned to that theatre as arranged, and that Mountbatten should make up his requirements from the Hump and from any further help that he might get from Stilwell or Sultan, 'who will refer to Washington'. This at once drew a strong protest from Mountbatten, who argued that any diminution of his existing force of transports might mean that Stilwell's troops would have to retire and that the long-delayed advance of the Yunnan Chinese would not take place. His message in turn aroused the Prime Minister, who signalled to Mountbatten on 4th May, 'Let nothing go from the battle that you need for victory. I will not accept denial of this from any quarter, and will back you to the full'.

Meanwhile, the Americans were doing their best to meet the demands of the two theatres. The trouble, as they stated, was that 'global air transport resources' were strained to the limit, and that there was simply not enough to go round. They could not agree to

---

[1] See p. 410 above.

[2] See p. 257 above.

send any of General Arnold's four hundred aircraft to the Mediterranean, for they had been specially fitted and their crews specially trained for operations in south-east Asia. Instead, after considerable difficulty, they proposed to despatch the first hundred of these aircraft to arrive in south-east Asia between 22nd May and 3rd June, instead of on 1st July; and this being so, they agreed with the British Chiefs of Staff that Mountbatten should return the seventy-nine transports to the Mediterranean in the middle of, instead of early in, May. If there was an emergency in the intervening period, the Supreme Commander was to draw upon the aircraft from the Hump already reserved for an emergency,[1] and if more were needed he was to apply to Washington 'through normal channels'.

The Prime Minister's message had strengthened Mountbatten's resolve to hold his transports, and on 5th May, before receipt of the Combined Chiefs of Staff's decision, he telegraphed that he had ordered the Mediterranean aircraft 'for the present to continue operating under Stratemeyer'. At the same time, General Wilson agreed to forego their return until 31st May, and on the 6th the Chiefs of Staff therefore informed Mountbatten that he could keep the seventy-nine transports until such a date as would enable them to arrive in the Mediterranean on that day. To the Combined Chiefs of Staff the gap seemed now to be bridged, and the British thanked the Americans warmly for their prompt and generous co-operation.

But to the commanders in south-east Asia, the gap seemed still to exist. For if the seventy-nine transports were to be in the Mediterranean on 31st May, they would have to leave south-east Asia on the 24th; and on the most optimistic assumption, the one hundred transports from America would not be available for operations in the Imphal battle before the middle of June. The interval could be filled only by robbing the Hump again, and Chiang Kai-shek was already pressing General Chennault[2] for increased support against a vigorous Japanese attack in China itself as well as to cover the Yunnan advance. 'Accordingly', Mountbatten signalled on 10th May, 'we have reached a point in our operations in this area where a readjustment of transport aircraft in the theatre or diversion from Air Transport Command is neither feasible nor sound'. He urged that a solution must be found which would prevent so many aircraft from flying in opposite directions at such a critical time. The next day he made the unwelcome announcement that, even with his existing resources, he had been compelled to call on the transports from the Hump to make up a deficit in deliveries to the Imphal front, arising from the increasingly bad weather.

On the night of 11th May, Alexander began the battle in Italy, and on the 12th the British Chiefs of Staff again sought to ensure that

---

[1] See p. 406 above.

[2] See p. 127 above.

neither theatre should suffer. As the first contingent of the four hundred new American transports was not considered suitable for the Mediterranean, they now asked if the Americans could not find seventy-nine aircraft direct from their resources in the United States. In view of the previous correspondence, this was clearly a counsel of despair. But the Joint Chiefs of Staff were now inclining towards the idea that Mountbatten should keep the Mediterranean aircraft for a further fifteen days beyond 31st May, releasing them individually before the later date if he found that he was getting the first of the new transports from America in time. At the back of this proposal lay the feeling, which the Americans had not conveyed officially, that Wilson already had enough transports in Italy to tide him over until the middle of June, and the Prime Minister himself raised this point specifically. The British Chiefs of Staff did not agree that there was any surplus in the Mediterranean. But the situation in Asia seemed meanwhile to be growing ever more critical. On 15th May, Mountbatten reported that Stilwell had been forced to ask the Joint Chiefs of Staff for permission to divert some aircraft to China for the support of the Yunnan force; and while the Supreme Commander agreed that this was vital if its advance were not to be retarded, it was likely to deprive the theatre of a further small but important force. In these circumstances, the Mediterranean had to suffer. On the 15th, the Americans decided finally to let the seventy-nine transports remain in south-east Asia until a date not later than 15th June, when they, or such as were left if Mountbatten could spare any in the interval, were to leave for the Mediterranean. Mountbatten thereupon transferred one squadron of transports to the support of the Yunnan force, in time to forestall a growing difficulty with Chiang Kai-shek.

Air supply was now assured until 15th June. It remained with the commanders on the spot so to frame their plans that Imphal could be relieved before the full force of the monsoon stopped large-scale operations at the end of the month. The scale of reserves on the plain was low, and there seemed a danger that, even at the rate of air supply in mid-June, they would be exhausted by about the 27th. All seemed therefore to turn on the speed with which the Kohima-Imphal road could be reopened. Throughout May, the Japanese had been held south of Imphal and driven back steadily in the north near Kohima. At the same time, the besieged troops were pushing north from the plain itself. But the fighting as always was stubborn, and progress in the first half of June was slow. The rate of air supply, despite the earlier fears, improved markedly after the middle of the month, and in the third week of June the Imphal plain was provided with some reserve; but while the position was improving, the monsoon was fast approaching. On the 22nd, however, Allied forces from Imphal met those from Kohima at a point twenty-nine miles north of Imphal, and the main road to the plain was open. On the same day the convoys began to roll in. The Japanese bid for India was over, and ahead lay the prospect of a major Japanese defeat.

(ii)
The Northern Front

The campaign had meanwhile proceeded well on the northern front, accompanied and in some measure developed by the operations of the penetration groups. General Stilwell had been instructed in November, 1943 to occupy northern Burma up to and including the area Mogaung-Myitkyina, so as to facilitate the construction of the overland route from Ledo through Myitkyina to China, and to cover more securely the bases of the air route to Kunming. He was confronted by one Japanese division, while on the eastern flank of his advance another faced the passes into China. His own force at the end of 1943 consisted of two Chinese divisions with a third in reserve, and American penetration groups, to which were added in February, 1944 some Burmese levies under British officers. In November, 1943 the difficult advance began; by the end of the year, when Stilwell himself—the first foreigner to be so honoured since Gordon—assumed direct command of the Chinese, he had negotiated the Patkai hills and was established at Shingbwiyang; and in February, 1944 he pushed on into the tangled country to the south. Here he encountered greater opposition, and the pace slowed down. Stiff fighting ensued throughout the month, but early in March the Japanese began to tire, and by the 20th, after outflanking moves on the part of the American penetration groups, the Ledo force had again begun to push ahead. Aided by a complementary attack by the Burmese levies, it passed into the Mogaung valley, and by the end of the month Stilwell was planning the capture of Myitkyina before the onset of the monsoon. Behind him, American engineers were toiling on the construction of the China road.

The plan for Stilwell's advance had included his support by British long-range penetration groups further south, designed to cut the Japanese communications and to dislocate their reserves. On 8th February, the first of these groups set off with its mules from Ledo, and throughout that month it wound its way south, supplied after the 10th entirely by air. In the third week of March, having traversed over 450 miles of mountainous jungle, it reached the enemy's lines of communication north of Indaw. Meanwhile, on 5th March, two other long-range penetration brigades were flown to the area of Indaw itself, where they could operate in support of both the central and the northern fronts. By the 11th, this force was operating actively. Later in the month, two more brigades were flown in, one for relief and the other to hold the airstrips and bases.

This is not the place to discuss the value of Wingate's operations.[1] From their nature and that of their progenitor, they attracted much attention at the time. To many, indeed, Burma spelt Wingate; and rather as in the case of the Zeebrugge raid, or the activities of Wingate's relation Lawrence in the First World War, the boldness of his exploits has magnified the importance of their contribution to the campaign. It is possible, as General Giffard[2] stated later, that 'the results achieved did not prove to be commensurate with the expenditure in manpower and material which had been employed'. But at the time the long-range penetration groups formed an integral and, as it seemed, an essential part of the Allied operations, and their curtailment was not suggested. In April, indeed, faced by the acute shortage of transport aircraft, Mountbatten considered the abandonment of one of the parent operations in order to maintain Wingate's forces. On 1st May, he telegraphed to the Chiefs of Staff that he might have to cancel Stilwell's attack on Myitkyina, with the loss of valuable months in the construction of the China road and the withdrawal of the Ledo force to a more secure front; but the provision of the aircraft from the Mediterranean saved him from reaching this unwelcome decision, which Stilwell himself might well have challenged.

The shortage of air transport was not the only possible deterrent to the later stages of Stilwell's advance. To force the Japanese back on Myitkyina, and to capture the airstrip and the town itself, he needed to be reinforced. By this time his three Chinese divisions were fully committed, and there was no British division to spare from either Arakan or the central front. Since January, 1944 he had been trying to extract a fourth Chinese division from the Generalissimo; but the threat of a new Japanese attack on the Peking-Canton railway, and the familiar threat of an attack against Yunnan, made any such reinforcement unlikely. Stilwell also needed help on his flank, to contain the Japanese division facing the Salween which might otherwise be expected to reinforce Myitkyina; and here again he had been trying without success to induce the Generalissimo to advance from Yunnan. In the middle of March, he agreed with Mountbatten to seek the support of their Governments in a further appeal to Chiang Kai-shek for both the extra division and the advance from Yunnan, and on the 17th Mountbatten requested the Chiefs of Staff to approach the President and Prime Minister. On the same day, Mr. Roosevelt sent a long and persuasive message to the Generalissimo, with which

---

[1] Wingate himself was killed in an air crash on 24th March, and was succeeded in command by Brigadier W. D. A. Lentaigne.

[2] See p. 144 above.

the Prime Minister was later associated. In this, the responsibility for victory in Burma was laid largely upon the Chinese. The enemy, it was argued, was already extended upon three fronts, and on one of them, in the north, he was in retreat; the provision of an extra division there, and the creation of a fourth front in the east, might well turn advantage into victory and hasten the reopening of land communications with Chungking by many months. It was an optimistic and a forceful document, and went far towards achieving at least one of its objects. For on 30th March, after a further visit by Stilwell, Chiang Kai-shek agreed to reinforce the Ledo front with one Chinese division from Yunnan.

This was perhaps as much as could have been expected for the moment, and local observers were not surprised that the Generalissimo ignored the second and the larger request. Mountbatten and Stilwell continued to raise the subject, and on 21st April they received their reward when Chiang Kai-shek agreed to attack with four divisions across the Salween. Within the next fortnight the force had grown considerably, amounting in the end to some 72,000 men. On the night of 10th/11th May the crossing of the river began, and a few nights later it was safely completed. By the third week in the month the Chinese were pressing forward over the border.

These operations raised a problem of command. In October 1943, Chiang Kai-shek had agreed to transfer to Stilwell the control of any Chinese Expeditionary Force which might cross the frontier into Burma;[1] and this had been confirmed at the Cairo Conference. But the frontier was ill-defined, and to avoid misunderstanding Mountbatten now proposed that the Yunnan force should pass under Stilwell's command on 1st June, on whichever side of the border it was then operating. On 21st May, he instructed General Carton de Wiart, attached to Chiang Kai-shek, to obtain the Generalissimo's views as a matter of urgency; but no answer was received for some months, and then only to the effect that the Generalissimo could not agree to the proposal. It was not indeed until January 1945, when a Chinese Army Group entered the undisputed frontier of Burma, that any Chinese came under Mountbatten's control.

The transfer of the Yunnan force to Stilwell's command was not the only difficulty which the operations raised at this time. Throughout April and early May, the Ledo force had been pushing slowly south towards Kamaing in preparation for the assault on Myitkyina. On 17th May a penetration column captured the airfield of Myitkyina, and substantial supplies, with gunners and technicians, were at once flown in. But the first attack on the town itself was a failure, and despite the landing by air of nearly 3,000 Allied reinforcements before the end of the month, the Japanese managed to hold out. By the beginning of

[1] See pp. 140, 149 above.

June, the forces under Stilwell's command amounted to some six divisions, and if, as at that time seemed likely, the Yunnan troops also were brought under him, he would be controlling what was virtually an army. It therefore seemed logical that the original chain of command, whereby he had been placed under General Slim, should be revised.[1] This was in any case likely to happen soon, for the capture of Kamaing, which was the occasion for the end of the arrangement, was unlikely long to be delayed. On 19th May the problem was raised by General Giffard, as Commander-in-Chief, Eleventh Army Group, and on the next day by Stilwell himself. Mountbatten wished, as he had wished from the start, to appoint an Allied Land Forces' Commander-in-Chief, on the lines of Alexander's appointment in the Mediterranean; but as his senior American staff officers pointed out, this was unlikely to be popular with either Stilwell or the Generalissimo. Nevertheless, in the third week of May the Supreme Commander sent his Chief of Staff to London to propose this solution, to arrange for a new commander to take over its duties, and to press for a revision of Stilwell's complex position.[2] Before any decision could be reached Kamaing fell on 16th June, and Mountbatten thereupon found himself directly responsible for the northern front.

In the middle of 1944, the problems of organization and command reflected the potential differences between the British and the Americans in south-east Asia. As long as operations were confined to the limits dictated at Quebec, or to the defensive as in the emergency of March to June, the differences remained potential, and could be expressed in terms of organization rather than directly of strategy. But the advance in northern Burma, and the prospect of victory on the central front, forced them into the open. As Stilwell approached Myitkyina, the question arose of what to do next. To the Americans, possession of the airfield and the town, apart from their value to the Ledo Road and its pipe line, seemed essential to provide a base for an easier air route to China than that over the Hump. To the British, it represented a further stage in the extension of the campaign in the north. Similarly, the victory of Imphal posed the question of the shape of future strategy. The two problems were naturally connected; for, without a greater use of air transport than had hitherto been possible, it was clear that the Allies' supply lines in 1944 could not carry the material necessary both for the full development of the air and land routes to China, and for substantial operations on the central and northern fronts. The ambiguities of the Quebec strategy were again

[1] See p. 146 above.

[2] See pp. 140-1 above.

revealed, and this time they could not be evaded. The preliminaries seemed to be almost over; but the preliminaries, it could now be asked, to what? Mountbatten's original directive of October, 1943[1] was clearly out of date. Since January, 1944 he had been asking for fresh orders, and in May both he and the Combined Chiefs of Staff felt that they could no longer safely be delayed. It is time, therefore, to turn to the debate in London and Washington, and to examine the policy for south-east Asia as it emerged over the first half of 1944, in its setting of the strategy for the war against Japan.

---

[1] See pp. 148-9 above.

CHAPTER XI

THE STRATEGY FOR THE PACIFIC AND SOUTH-EAST ASIA, JANUARY–APRIL, 1944

(i)

Growth of a British Strategy for the Pacific

APART FROM the campaigns in Burma and China, the war against Japan was a maritime war, and the British part in it therefore depended on the strength of the British Fleet. As long as Italy remained in the war, there was nothing to spare for the Far East; but with the surrender of the Italian navy the bulk of the Mediterranean Fleet was released for service elsewhere. At the time of that event the Prime Minister was still in the United States, whither he had gone at the close of the 'Quadrant' Conference, and his first thought was that the Eastern Fleet in the Indian Ocean could now be reinforced on the lines laid down later in the directive to Admiral Mountbatten. But to gain experience, and as a political deterrent to the Japanese, he suggested that the reinforcements should proceed by way of the Panama Canal and the Pacific, where they should spend at least four months under American control. This was accepted by the Americans, and Admiral King instructed the naval commanders in the Pacific to report on the possible use to be made of a British force.

At the same time, the employment of the British Fleet in 1944/45 was under more detailed consideration. Late in August 1943, the Combined Chiefs of Staff instructed the Combined Planning Staff to produce a study for the defeat of Japan within twelve months of the defeat of Germany, which was assumed for the purpose to have taken place by 1st October, 1944. On 25th October this study appeared.

Its contents have already been given in detail.[1] The conclusions may be recapitulated. The Planners recommended that the Western Allies should

> '. . . aim at the capture of Formosa from the Pacific in the spring of 1945, retaining the option to undertake 'First Culverin'[2]

[1] See pp. 159-61 above.

[2] See pp. 150-1, and note on p. 150, above.

[against northern Sumatra] in the autumn (or possibly spring) of 1945 if the Formosa operation has to be postponed.

The Japanese main islands might be invaded in the autumn of 1946.'

This course of action rested

'on the assumption that the bulk of the British Fleet, particularly in the aircraft-carrier category assists in the operation . . .

If . . . we decide to . . . deploy the British Fleet in the Pacific, major amphibious operations in South-East Asia requiring the support of an appreciable number of aircraft-carriers will be impracticable . . .'

After debate between the Combined Chiefs of Staff, this recommendation was accepted at the Cairo Conference. It was then agreed, as a basis for further investigation, that 'the main effort against Japan should be made in the Pacific'; and in the Combined Chiefs of Staff's Final Report, which was duly initialled by the Heads of Government, it was stated that 'we have approved in principle' the programme of operations which included that 'general concept'.

The relevant paragraphs of that programme were as follows:[1]

'OVERALL OBJECTIVE

3. To obtain objectives from which we can conduct intensive air bombardment and establish a sea and air blockade against Japan, and from which to invade Japan proper if this should prove necessary.

GENERAL CONCEPT

4. The main effort against Japan should be made in the Pacific.

CONCEPT WITHIN THE PACIFIC

5. The advance along the New Guinea – Netherlands East Indies – Philippine axis will proceed concurrently with operations for the capture of the Mandated Islands. These two series of operations will be mutually supported. . . . Transfer of forces and resources from one area to the other is contemplated. When conflicts in timing and allocation of means exist, due weight should be accorded to the fact that operations in the Central Pacific promise at this time a more rapid advance toward Japan and her vital lines of communications; the earlier acquisition of strategic air bases closer to the Japanese homeland; and, of greatest importance, are more likely to precipitate a decisive engagement with the Japanese Fleet.

The aim should be to advance along the New Guinea–N.E.I.–Philippine axis and to complete the capture of the Mandated Islands in time to launch a major assault in the Formosa–Luzon–

[1] See Map I, facing p. 11.

China area in the spring of 1945 (i.e., before the onset of the typhoon season), from a distant base.

CONCEPT WITHIN OTHER AREAS

6. Operations in the North Pacific, the South Pacific, China and the South-East Asia theatre should be conducted in support of the main operations in the Central and South-West Pacific. In the event of the U.S.S.R. entering the war, operations in the North Pacific may assume far greater importance, and may involve the major redeployment of forces.

SPECIFIC OPERATIONS IN 1944

. . . 8. . . . These operations are in accordance with the over-all concept. In brief they contemplate—

Central Pacific
(a) Capture of the Mandated Islands and conduct of V.L.R. [very long-range] strategic bombing of Japan proper from the Marianas (Guam, Tinian and Saipan).

South-West Pacific
(b) Continuing the advance along the New Guinea-N.E.I.-Philippine axis. Intensification of air bombardment of targets in the N.E.I.-Philippine area.

North Pacific
(c) Preparations to conduct very long-range strategic bombing against the Kuriles and Northern Japan.[1]

South-East Asia Theatre
(d) Operations for the capture of Upper Burma in the spring of 1944 in order to improve the air route and establish overland communications with China, and an amphibious operation at approximately the same time. Continuance of operations during the autumn of 1944 within the limits of the forces available . . . to extend the position held in Upper Burma.
(e) Should the means be available, additional ground, sea and air offensive operations, including carrier-borne raids, with the object of maintaining pressure on the enemy, forcing dispersion of his forces, and attaining the maximum attrition practicable on his air and naval forces and shipping.

China Area
(f) Conducting V.L.R. air operations from the Chengtu area in China against vital targets in the Japanese inner zone.
(g) Building up the United States Air Forces in China and the Chinese Army and Air Force with the object of intensifying land and air operations in and from China.'

In the following paragraphs the disposition of the forces required for these operations was given in detail. The British naval forces in the

[1] Preparations for the possible entry of Russia into the war were discussed in an Annex to the Report. See pp. 427-9 below.

Far East were to be allocated so as to provide enough strength in the Indian Ocean to maintain communications with the Andaman Islands if captured, and to carry out operations and threats against Japanese positions in south-east Asia. All other available units would be concentrated for the main effort in the Pacific. It was estimated that by June 1944, the British Pacific Fleet would consist of one battleship, nine or ten aircraft carriers (of which at least seven would be escort carriers), six cruisers, sixteen fleet destroyers, twelve frigates, and a number of repair ships and auxiliaries. By August 1944, it would be substantially reinforced. The Combined Chiefs of Staff considered that such forces could be supplied, and should operate, from advanced bases in the Bismarck and Solomon Islands, whence they could either cover operations in New Guinea, the Netherlands East Indies and the Philippines, or could co-operate with the American Fleet in the central Pacific.

On land, the plans contemplated the timely deployment in the Pacific of about forty American divisions and supporting troops. All British and Indian land forces which could be made available to the South-East Asia Command up to the end of 1944 were likely to be fully committed in that theatre. They might be reinforced after the defeat of Germany. Meanwhile, the target in the Pacific should be to provide four British divisions—at least two trained for 'combined operations'—based on Australia for service in that theatre as soon as possible after the defeat of Germany. Australian and New Zealand forces should be employed, as hitherto, on operations in the Pacific.

It was noted that it would probably be nine months after the defeat of Germany before the additional British troops could be trained and carried to the Far East.

The assault shipping required was given as a lift of twelve divisions for the Americans in the Pacific and at least one division for the British in south-east Asia, while as soon as the war with Germany was over the British should aim to provide in the south-west Pacific as large an assault lift as possible, probably for between two and three divisions.

In the air, British and American air forces were considered large enough for the existing plans. The substantial air forces which would be available when Germany was defeated, must be redeployed as quickly as possible. In principle, the air forces in the central Pacific would be American, those in the south-west and possibly in the north Pacific both British and American, 'predominantly British' in south-east Asia, and American in China.

Finally, the preparation of bases in India, needed for approved operations in south-east Asia and China, should continue as already planned.

The conclusions of the document, therefore, which affected the

British, were that all activities against Japan were to conform to the two main attacks through the central and south-west Pacific; that the final approach to Japan was not decided, although the central Pacific seemed to offer the greater attractions; that the British effort by sea, for which the forces were defined in detail, was to be mainly in the Pacific, although in which area was not yet certain; that the British should make their main effort by land in 1944 in south-east Asia, for which adequate bases were to be built in India, and should later provide a small contingent with its attendant assault shipping in the south-west Pacific; and that they should provide most of the air forces in south-east Asia, and, after the defeat of Germany, an air contingent in the south-west Pacific and possibly also in the north Pacific.

The final version of this document, which differed hardly at all from that available at Cairo, was produced on 23rd December, 1943. On the 15th, the Combined Planning Staff submitted a detailed appreciation of demands and resources for the various operations. By the end of 1943, the British Chiefs of Staff had therefore been furnished with an estimate of the strategy and the requirements for the Far East, and they now wished to confirm the first and further to investigate the second. It was indeed high time to get to work, for the lack of information was affecting diplomacy and delaying the administrative effort. Negotiations with the Portuguese over their position in Asia, which were proceeding at this time, were hampered by the uncertainty of the strategic demands upon them; an answer had to be made to a request from the Dutch to send Dutch troops to south-east Asia if the Netherlands East Indies were to be attacked; at home, the organs of supply, and particularly of manpower and ammunition, were clamouring for guidance in framing their programmes for the year; and, most urgent of all, the Admiralty wished to pursue the decisions reached at Cairo with questions to the Naval Boards of Australia and New Zealand. As yet, however, the Dominion Governments knew of those decisions only from a brief report sent through the British High Commissioners, and the Chiefs of Staff considered that Ministers should be fully informed of the consequences before their naval advisers were approached. They therefore drafted a telegram to the Governments of Australia and New Zealand, disclosing the programme for the Pacific, and sent it on 30th December to Mr. Churchill in Morocco for approval before transmission.

The despatch of this draft was the signal for a long and complicated debate which was to end only in September 1944, after involving the Prime Minister and the British Chiefs of Staff in perhaps their most serious disagreement of the war. It is difficult at times to trace a pattern in the discussion, for the arguments pursue many by-paths and the protagonists sometimes return to positions which they have previously abandoned. But, as in all mazes, a pattern must be established; and it is possible to divide the debate into three recognizable phases. The first, lasting from January until the middle of March 1944, may be called the period of principle, when each side presented and elaborated its point of view. The second, from the end of March to the end of July, was the period of fact-finding and the attempt at compromise. The third, in August and September, embraced the final solution. In this chapter we are concerned with the first and most dramatic of the three phases.[1]

The Prime Minister replied on 10th January, 1944, and his telegram showed at once that he was not in tune with the Chiefs of Staff. At Cairo, he had been concerned with the alternatives for action in the Bay of Bengal, and in the bustle of the last few days, with many questions still to be settled, the implications of the provisional strategy for the Far East had escaped him. With the subsequent collapse of 'Buccaneer' and 'Pigstick' his thoughts had reverted to his first love 'Culverin',[2] from which indeed they had never strayed far. 'This', he informed Mountbatten on 10th January, 'I am determined to press to the very utmost, day in day out'; and he therefore viewed the Chiefs of Staff's message to the Dominions in a different light from its authors. 'I have read this telegram', he replied, 'and see no objection to it being sent provided you are sure that it does not cut into 'First Culverin' on which I am increasingly resolved after the monsoon.' The Chiefs of Staff thereupon hastened to develop their views.

> 'Main feature [of the Cairo plan]', they informed Mr. Churchill on the 13th, 'is that instead of fighting slow war in south-east Asian jungles, British and U.S. efforts are concerted in Pacific, where a double thrust by combined navies and amphibious forces drives straight through to Formosa area in spring 1945. . . . If new strategy gains final approval 'First Culverin' requiring considerable naval and carrier-borne air support may well be inappropriate in early stages. . . . Prospects of undertaking 'First Culverin' in autumn 1944 are slender in any case, since necessary assault shipping cannot reach south-east Asia in time unless Germany collapses before 'Overlord'. If our Pacific advance should get held up agree with you that 'First Culverin' would definitely be best operation to undertake. . . .'

On receipt of this message, Churchill ordered the Chiefs of Staff to hold the draft signal to the Dominions until he had discussed 'the new plan' with them at home.

The discussion was accordingly held as soon as the Prime Minister

---

[1] For a good *résumé* of the principal incidents during this period, see Appendix IX below. Map I, facing p. 11, should be consulted throughout this chapter.

[2] For these plans, see Appendix I below.

returned, at a full meeting of the Defence Committee on 19th January. It was at once clear not only that Mr. Churchill disagreed with the plan for the Pacific, but that he was not conversant with it. He remarked that this was the first time he had heard of the proposals, and although the Chiefs of Staff pointed out that both he and the President had initialled the Combined Chiefs of Staff's Final Report in which reference to them was contained,[1] he continued to state that he had not been consulted on the plan, that he had not been aware of what had taken place, and that despite his initialling of the Report—which of course, on a document of that nature, did not commit him in the same way as a signature—he did not consider himself a party to the agreement.

The Prime Minister's vehemence arose from the fact that both he and the other Ministers on the Defence Committee were strongly opposed to the Combined Chiefs of Staff's proposals. Churchill's own objections, as developed over the next few days, were four-fold:

1. The plan did not seem to allow for the effect of Russia's entry into the war against Japan, which might enable the Allies to strike at the Home Islands from the Russian Maritime Provinces sooner than from across the Pacific.

2. The Americans themselves had not yet agreed on the shape of their final assaults upon Japan.

3. It was not yet certain that the American Fleet in the Pacific needed or desired heavy British support, although support of some kind would undoubtedly be sent.

4. The Pacific strategy provided no outlet in 1944, before the defeat of Germany, for the large British land and air forces now being assembled for south-east Asia. The remedy for this was 'First Culverin', for which the Americans could be asked to provide assault shipping in return for a reasonable measure of British naval support in the Pacific.

Mr. Churchill's first objection reflected his unawareness of the Cairo plan, for in fact that had covered the entry of Russia into the Japanese war as far as was possible at the time. In their studies in the autumn of 1943, the Combined Planners had not relied on such an event, but each of the proposed courses of action had taken its possibility into account. In the second half of the Cairo Conference, the plan was re-examined, in the light of Stalin's announcement at Teheran that the time for the Russian forces in the Far East to join 'their friends in this theatre would be the moment of Germany's collapse';[2] and one of the assumptions then was 'that the U.S.S.R. may enter the war against Japan early after the defeat of Germany'.

---

[1] See p. 193 above.

[2] See p. 173 above.

There was little enough for the planners to go on at the time, for at Teheran Stalin had made no mention of his military or diplomatic aims, and had confined himself to saying that his forces in the Far East must be trebled before they could attack. But his intentions could be guessed with some accuracy from the geography of the area. The long eastern sea-board of Russia was singularly badly served by harbours and communications. In the north, where Siberia adjoins the Bering Sea, there are no warm water ports. South of Siberia, where the peninsula of Kamchatka divides the northern Pacific from the Sea of Okhotsk, the one major port of Petropavlovsk had then no communications with the hinterland. There was no port of any size, nor were there proper communications, bordering the Sea of Okhotsk. There was no major port at its southern entrance, in the Russian part of Sakhalin; and in the southern Maritime Provinces, the large warm water port of Vladivostock could be approached only through waters held by the Japanese. The Japanese indeed, in the Kurile Islands, in southern Sakhalin and Hokkaido, in the Home Islands themselves, and in Manchuria and Korea, controlled all of the approaches south of Kamchatka. The natural ambitions of the Russians, therefore, centred in the south on Manchuria and Korea, and in the north on the Kuriles and southern Sakhalin. A campaign in either direction was agreeable to the Western Allies. The capture of the islands was a direct threat to Japan, while that of Manchuria and Korea prevented the enemy's formidable Kwantung army from being deployed elsewhere, and ensured that there was no last-ditch resistance from the Japanese on the mainland when all else seemed to be lost.

The Western Allies themselves looked on eastern Russia principally as a base from which to bomb Japan, closer to the enemy than south-east China, Formosa or the Marianas. It also provided an outlet for the large strategic air force which would be released for use against Japan after the defeat of Germany, and for which facilities might not exist elsewhere. At the time, however, there were few facilities in Russia, and their preparation was bound to be difficult. There were only two supply routes to the Maritime Provinces: from the west by the trans-Siberian railway, and from the east across the Pacific to Kamchatka. The railway was not of much use in its existing state, for although it boasted a double track for most of its 10,000 miles there were still long stretches of single track, and at its eastern end the rail-bed lay dangerously near the border of Manchuria and the depredations of the Kwantung army. In any case the length and complexity of the western approach, by convoy from America to Britain, by convoy again from Britain to Murmansk, and finally by rail across the breadth of Russia, was neither economical nor secret. The eastern approach across the Pacific was quicker but again not without hazard, for the last stage of the journey was threatened by the Japanese in the Kuriles. But it was clearly the preferable route, and the Combined Planning Staff accordingly submitted that preparations should be made by the spring or summer of 1944 to reinforce the Russian defences in the Kamchatka peninsula, to land forces (particularly air forces) if necessary for their support, and to supply as many aircraft and air units as possible. It might then be possible to develop air bases in Kamchatka and to seize the northern Kuriles, thus opening the route to the Maritime Provinces, and finally to build up air bases in the Maritime Provinces and Siberia. Staff conversations had of course to be held with the Russians before such plans could be developed.

The burden of these conversations fell on the Americans. At Cairo, the Combined Staff Planners had discussed the possibility of allotting control in the northern Pacific to the British, and of basing their main effort in Canada as suggested by Course W of their original study.[1] But this had not been accepted, and while the Combined Chiefs of Staff agreed that the strategic air force in eastern Russia might well be Anglo-American, the responsibility for its supply fell on the Americans alone. It was therefore for them to take up the running with Moscow. Before the end of the Teheran Conference, the President had decided to enter into details with Stalin, and on 29th November he asked five specific questions.[2]

1. Would Stalin agree to provide the United States with operational intelligence concerning the Japanese?
2. Should the United States expand its bases in Alaska and the Aleutians to harbour Russian destroyers and submarines which might be threatened in Russian ports by the Japanese?
3. Would the Russians be able to help, directly or indirectly, if the Americans attacked the northern Kuriles?
4. Would they furnish the Americans with data on Siberian ports which the latter might wish to use?
5. Would they furnish data to enable the Americans to set up air bases in the Maritime Provinces to accommodate up to 1,000 heavy bombers?

At first, despite the serious risk of antagonizing the Japanese, it seemed that the Russians might co-operate. On Christmas night, M. Molotov told the American Ambassador that his Government would provide such information about the Japanese as it could from its existing knowledge. Of the remaining questions, some would need further study, and others could not be answered yet in view of the fact that Russia and Japan were not at war. This was a promising start. The next day, the U.S. Military Mission in Moscow approached the question from the other end, with a proposal to the Russian General

---

[1] See p. 160 above.

[2] See *The Entry of the Soviet Union into the War against Japan, Military Plans*, 1941-1945 (U.S. Government, cyclostiled for public use, 1955), pp. 23-4; and John R. Deane, *The Strange Alliance* (1947), pp. 226-9, 255-60. Major-General Deane was head of the U.S. Military Mission in Moscow from October, 1943 to October, 1945 (See p. 24 above).

Staff that the Americans should start to build a secret supply depôt for the east near Lake Baikal, to be fed by the trans-Siberian railway and the Atlantic convoys to Murmansk.[1] Not surprisingly, this suggestion was turned down; but on 2nd February, to the Americans' joy, Stalin informed the Ambassador that they would be allowed to operate 1,000 bombers from Siberia after Russia had declared war on Japan. The existing bases would have to be expanded to allow for a further three hundred heavy bombers, and planning should therefore start as soon as possible with responsible Russian officers in the east. But, as in so many other cases, the hopes thus raised were not fulfilled. Despite the efforts of the Military Mission nothing more occurred, and it was not until January, 1945 that the first meeting took place.

Such was the background to Churchill's first objection. The British Planners therefore replied on 30th January that the Cairo plan held good. It allowed for preliminary action by the Americans in Kamchatka and the Kuriles; but this depended on Russian co-operation and on spring or summer weather, and in their view the combination was unlikely to appear before 1945. Valuable as the Russians' intervention might be at a later stage, its results could not affect the immediate future; and to maintain the existing pressure on the enemy, all available force must be assembled in the central Pacific against the Mandated Islands and Formosa, whence the bombing of Japan could proceed. This report had its effect, and it was in any case soon followed by a deterioration in the relations of the Western Allies with the Russians. As a result, the debate proceeded without further serious reference to the northern Pacific.

Whatever Russia might do in the Pacific towards the end of 1944, British plans were affected more immediately by American action in that area; and here the ambiguities to which Churchill drew attention were real enough. The Cairo formula, that 'the advance along the New Guinea-N.E.I.-Philippine axis will proceed concurrently with operations for the capture of the Mandated Islands', did not settle the inescapable question of which campaign was to be considered the more important. It was of course the case, as the British Chiefs of Staff liked to stress at this time, that the campaigns were complementary, that neither could be undertaken without the other, and that their interdependence might well lead eventually to a single Pacific Command. But however true this argument might be, it could not resolve the current rivalry between the existing Commands, or ease the decision where best to place the existing British resources. At the turn of the year the emphasis seemed to lie on the central Pacific, but General MacArthur's claims for the south-west had not been thoroughly considered, and it was still possible that the main axis of the advance might

[1] General Deane appears to have made this proposal on his own initiative (*loc. cit.*, p. 228).

be changed. The Chiefs of Staff knew that a vigorous discussion was under way in Washington on the future of the Pacific strategy and command; but their knowledge scarcely extended further. The campaign in the central Pacific had always been an exclusively American responsibility, and the British had never been told, nor had they wished to know, more than was necessary about its problems. Since the collapse of the first Allied Command in the Pacific in February 1942, there had also been little information on operational plans from the south-west area. This may seem strange, in view of the fact that MacArthur's headquarters were in Australia and that his Command and his staff included Australians as well as Americans. From November 1943, the British Government was also represented at his headquarters by Lieut.-General Herbert Lumsden, whom the Prime Minister sent as his personal representative, and in Australia by a liaison group and a military mission. But the Australians could supply information only on administrative facilities and on their own problems, while MacArthur himself was severely limited in his relations with authorities outside his theatre. As a subordinate of the Joint Chiefs of Staff, he was not empowered to correspond with the British Prime Minister; and even with the authorities in Washington, his relations were peculiar. For MacArthur occupied a unique position in the American military hierarchy. Unlike the other high commanders, he had not for some time had any direct connexion with the War Department; he was considerably senior to any other serving officer, having indeed retired as Chief of Staff of the U.S. Army in 1935, when Marshall held the rank of Colonel; since then he had been in the service not of the American but of the Philippine Government; his initial campaign in the Philippines had been an isolated and largely self-contained affair; and this background and his own self-confidence did not incline him to act as a subordinate in the manner of other senior commanders. A pronounced consciousness of his position, and of the political importance which it fostered, gave to his relations with Washington something of the flavour of an independent Power. He had not been to America since 1935, he did not meet any of the American Chiefs of Staff until December 1943, he had not received adirect communication from the President since assuming command of the South-West Pacific Area, and at the end of 1943 he had never met Admiral Nimitz, his colleague in the central Pacific.

While MacArthur's arguments and demands were therefore received with anxious care in Washington, they often, for the same reasons, met with a partial or an evasive response. In the autumn of 1943, he had submitted his views for the future to the Joint Chiefs of Staff. After neutralizing the Japanese air base in Rabaul by capturing the neighbouring base of Kavieng, and establishing himself further up the New Guinea coast at Hollandia and Aitape, he wished to strike north at

Mindanao in the southern Philippines, and thence if possible at Luzon. These operations would by-pass some of the Japanese possessions, and their success depended on a clear superiority of air and sea power over anything the enemy might assemble. They would in fact probably require the presence of the main American Fleet, as well as of the naval forces in the south Pacific. Given the necessary priority, MacArthur was confident that he could be in Mindanao in December 1944, and in Luzon in the following spring. From there he could attack Formosa, or if necessary strike at the Netherlands East Indies or at the mainland of Asia. With his existing resources, however, he seemed committed to a subsidiary rôle, and could not take advantage of his proven superiority in fighting efficiency and morale.

Admiral Nimitz and the navy were inclined to disagree with MacArthur's policy. As a result of their experiences in the Pacific islands, they considered it 'essential to avoid as long as possible fighting the Japanese army in any land area where they could delay . . . operations.' American strength, in the naval view, lay at sea and in the air. The most fruitful line of advance therefore lay through the Carolines and the Marianas, with Formosa as the eventual goal. Given the necessary priority, Nimitz was confident that he could capture the Eastern Carolines by the end of July 1944, and Guam and the Marianas in September or October. By the end of the year, he could begin to bomb Japan from the latter base.

The debate upon these two strategies, which followed a tortuous course, was complicated by the traditional rivalry between the American army and navy; and the clear alternatives of a predominantly land or sea advance were calculated to bring out the worst in the two Service Departments. The Joint Chiefs of Staff themselves were more immune from this internecine warfare, and early in 1944 they were thought as a body to favour the naval plan. Admiral King was its natural proponent, and Admiral Leahy as naturally supported it; but General Marshall, while concerned to give a fair hearing to MacArthur, was also thought to incline towards it. There was no sign as yet, however, of a final decision, and the British Ministers therefore did not wish to commit themselves too soon. It was clearly undesirable to abandon the more ambitious projects in south-east Asia for subsidiary operations in the Pacific; but it was also open to question if British forces would be required in a main Pacific campaign which had been decided by the Americans alone, presumably on the basis of American resources. There was, indeed, already reason to fear that they might not be welcomed in the central Pacific, despite the tenor of the argument in October. Even in September 1943, when the offer of a British squadron had been accepted as a temporary addition to the American Fleet,[1] it had been for political reasons, and the Prime

[1] See p. 421 above.

Minister had received the impression that the ships had not really been wanted. Early in January 1944, this impression was confirmed by Admiral King in a conversation with the head of the British Admiralty Delegation in Washington. He stated that in his view the British would have little to spare at sea from 'Overlord' and the Mediterranean, and that the rest could do more good in the Indian Ocean than in the Pacific, where the American Fleet needed no assistance for its immediate operations, but where on the contrary any additional strength would merely add to the difficulties of supply. If a force could still be spared for the Pacific, he thought that it might well be delayed until August or the autumn of 1944, and should then operate in the south-west. Despite a verbal denial a fortnight later that he wished to postpone the arrival of a British task force, on 25th January the Admiral confirmed in writing that he was anxious not to rob European operations for the Far East, and that anything which remained could do more service from the Indian Ocean against Japanese oil installations than anywhere in the Pacific.

The prospects in the south-west Pacific seemed more hopeful at first sight, for General MacArthur, with his naval weakness, was known to welcome the idea of a British contingent, and might be expected to do so, as a balance against the American navy, even if his theatre were given priority and the support of the American Fleet. It seemed doubtful, however, how far his authority would then extend at sea. For here again the domestic rivalry of the American Services intervened, and all the more strongly because a direct issue of command was involved. The idea that MacArthur might be entrusted with a British naval squadron was at once scouted by the American navy. Towards the end of January, King suggested that any British task force in the south-west Pacific should be placed under Nimitz's control, and 'rather hinted that the reason for this was because once it got joined up to General MacArthur's Command it might be difficult to move it freely.' Thus the British faced the possibility that MacArthur's Command might not be the best place for the Fleet, and that even if it were, MacArthur himself might not be in a position to control it.

American uncertainties bulked large at this stage because the British themselves were uncertain. In the weeks following the first meeting on 19th January, the Defence Committee remained divided and each side hardened in its views. The issue was still the future in south-east Asia, and this in turn centred on the Prime Minister's fourth objection to the Cairo plan, that it provided no outlet in 1944 for the forces now allocated to the theatre. Such an argument necessarily involved the staff of the South-East Asia Command itself, and Admiral Mountbatten had indeed been reconsidering his future strategy since the cancellation of

'Buccaneer' and 'Tarzan'. By 8th January, he was ready to present his views to the Chiefs of Staff. Basing himself on the Cairo plan, he considered that his main effort must be co-ordinated with the main Allied thrusts from the central and south-west Pacific. He had therefore re-examined the possibility of aiding China in the light of his reduced campaign for 1944. At present, even with the rival claims of the Ledo Road, the American Air Transport Wing in India was carrying some 13,000 tons a month over the Hump, and as a result Chennault's Fourteenth U.S. Air Force in China[1] was thought (with some exaggeration) to have inflicted severe losses on Japanese shipping and aircraft over the past few months. There seemed little chance of supplying a comparable tonnage by land for a long time to come. So far, the Ledo Road and its pipeline, which demanded 26,000 tons of material a month and were engaging 43,000 men, had progressed only some fifty miles. The road itself had originally been designed to take one-way traffic to Kunming by November 1944, and two-way traffic by March 1945, while the pipeline was supposed to be ready in November, 1944 and to reach its full capacity by the following July. Owing to the reduced scale of the campaign, and to unforeseen delays, Mountbatten now estimated that it would be January, 1946 before the road to Kunming was ready for any transport, and June, 1946 before it could take two-way traffic. With one-way traffic, some 8,000 tons could be delivered by road to China each month; at full capacity, some 20-30,000 tons. The pipeline was expected to operate from April 1946, and to reach full capacity in October of that year. It would start with a monthly capacity of 13,000 tons, and would later reach some 63,000 tons. On these calculations, the attempt to open a land line to China was a waste of time.

Mountbatten therefore considered that he should now be ordered to use the available labour and material to expand the capacity of the air route to China. While this alone might not meet the eventual needs of the theatre, it left him free to devote his remaining military resources to the establishment of a more profitable supply line elsewhere. For in default of the Ledo Road, the theatre's most valuable contribution to the Pacific campaign was to 'penetrate the enemy perimeter in the Malaya-Netherland East Indies area and push rapidly north from base to base along the Asiatic coast. . . . Such action would deny important raw material to the enemy and should facilitate the advance in the Pacific since the enemy are bound to divert some of their strength to block our advance. The forces of S.E.A.C. would then also be in a position, if necessary, to assist the main allied thrust', and to establish a supply route to China which should undoubtedly surpass, and without loss of time, the capacity of the Burma Road. An essential preliminary to this strategy would be the capture of Sumatra.

---

[1] See p. 127 above.

Throughout the rest of January, 1944 the Staff in south-east Asia prepared the detailed plan, and on the 31st Mountbatten held a meeting of himself, Stilwell, the three Commanders-in-Chief, and General Auchinleck from India. With some divergence of opinion over the timing of the operations, all except Stilwell agreed that the strategy was correct. He, however, regarded it as 'totally wrong in conception'. Judging by the less ambitious plans for 'Buccaneer' against the Andeman Islands, he thought that 'Culverin' against Sumatra would need very large assault forces, and that it would be unwise to count on them for November, 1944 even if, as was still entirely uncertain, Germany were defeated by October. On the other hand—and here lay the crux of the matter—he did not accept the Staff's schedule of progress for the Ledo Road, which he considered unduly pessimistic; and if, by means of the Road, the Allies could support a Chinese advance to Canton, the southern Japanese possessions, isolated from the north and outflanked by an American advance in the south-west Pacific, would fall into their hands without a struggle.

Stilwell's argument was that of the U.S. War Department, and Mountbatten had already decided that it must be debated in the presence of the Joint Chiefs of Staff. On 20th January he informed General Ismay that he was sending a mission, known as the 'Axiom' Mission, to London and Washington, with full details of his plans and authority to represent him. It was headed by the American Major-General Wedemeyer, Mountbatten's Deputy Chief of Staff, and included a number of experts familiar with 'Culverin'. On 5th February the Mission left Delhi, and on the 11th it arrived in England. General Lumsden also arrived on the 11th from MacArthur's headquarters, so that all seemed ready for a full-scale and informed debate. Meanwhile, without informing the Supreme Commander, Stilwell prepared to send a mission of his own to Washington, and this arrived before Wedemeyer's party had finished its talks in London.

The first Staff Conference was held on the night of 14th February, and was attended by the Prime Minister, the Foreign Secretary, the Chiefs of Staff with the Chief of Combined Operations, the 'Axiom' party and Lumsden. The pros and cons of 'Culverin' were fully debated and the various points of view maintained; but while the discussion was useful as an *exposé* of the different principles, it could be regarded only as a preliminary, for the 'Axiom' party and the Joint Planning Staff had not had time to consult on detail, and the consequences were thus difficult to assess. The Planners and the Mission were accordingly instructed 'as a matter of urgency' to examine the merits of the operations, either against Sumatra alone or against Sumatra and the Netherlands East Indies.

The debate upon the Far Eastern strategy can be assembled around a series of important meetings, for which information and argument were marshalled in the light of changing events. Three such meetings stand out in the course of the next few weeks: the conference of 14th February, the afternoon conference of the 25th,[1] and that of 8th March. In the intervals much work was done and the scope of the discussion thereby extended. The most significant result of the first meeting lay in the Joint Planners' report of 23rd February on the resources for 'Culverin', for this at last concluded the statistical uncertainty which had existed over the operation since it was first proposed. As has been seen,[2] the estimates for both 'Buccaneer' and 'Culverin' had varied continuously between August and November 1943, according to the nature of the authority responsible for the calculations. This continued, with more serious repercussions, after the end of the Cairo Conference. The principal reason was the familiar one which affects all planning, that those who plan in London are apt to see things differently from those who plan in the theatre, and that they again are apt to differ from the commanders on the spot. But it was perhaps aggravated in this case by two factors which were not present elsewhere. First, the South-East Asia Command was aware that it was operating in an atmosphere of inherited distrust, and was therefore eager to produce figures which would not appear excessive, particularly as the operation was known to be scrutinized closely by the Prime Minister. Secondly, its Staff organization, whereby until the autumn of 1944 the Supreme Commander's planners existed apart from the planners of the Commanders-in-Chief,[3] may have increased the opportunities for error and disagreement. Both factors had serious effects on an already complex problem. The planning authorities could not agree on their figures, while the Prime Minister was able to attack the discrepancies on the basis of the more optimistic figures which in fact had already been produced to forestall or evade such attacks. The result may be seen in a comparison between the figures produced from November, 1943 to February 1944, which, since their detail is unavoidably complicated, are examined in Appendix VIII below. Here it may suffice to say that the discrepancies persisted even after the 'Axiom' Mission had landed in England; and as late as 15th February, at a time when three separate calculations were produced in as many days, Wedemeyer was forced to inform the Prime Minister that 'the "bill of goods" for 'Culverin' is not considered firm.' In such circumstances, Churchill was naturally sceptical of the arguments of the Chiefs of Staff. But by the 23rd, the 'Axiom' Mission and the Joint Planning Staff had virtually closed the gaps, and the latter's report at

[1] There were in fact three meetings on the 25th between the Prime Minister and the Chiefs of Staff: at noon, at 3 p.m. and at 10 p.m. But the first and third were concerned chiefly with the reported movement of the Japanese Fleet to Singapore (see p. 440 below), and it was at the second meeting that the larger issues were again discussed.

[2] Chapters III, IV above.

[3] See pp. 562-4 below.

last represented an agreed demand for the operation.[1] It suggested that in November, 1944 the deficiencies would still amount to a large proportion of the naval and assault shipping required, to some 30,000 troops, and to almost half the air squadrons; but that, as long as Germany was defeated in October, all could probably be met by March, 1945 except for a small proportion of the naval shipping. The conclusions were therefore that 'Culverin' was impossible in 1944, and could be undertaken from British resources in March, 1945 only if Germany had been defeated in the preceding October. On this assumption, the alternative Pacific strategy would advance operations by six months.[2]

	Pacific Strategy		*'Culverin' Strategy*	
	Most favourable case	*Least favourable case*	*Pacific advance*	*South-East Asia advance*
Date				
1944—				
Spring	Bismarcks		Bismarcks	
Summer	Truk		Truk	
Autumn	Marianas.[1]		Marianas.[1]	
1945—				
Spring	Palaus and Formosa or	Palaus and Philippines	Palaus and Mindanao	'Culverin'.
Summer	Luzon[1] [2]			Malaya.
Autumn		Formosa[1] [2]	Sulu Sed, Luzon[1] [2]	
1946—				
Spring	Hokkaido?		Formosa[1] [2]	Singapore. Advance up China Sea.
Summer		Hokkaido?		
Autumn	Invade Japan?			
1947—				
Spring		Invade Japan?	Hokkaido?	
Summer				
Autumn				Invade Japan?

[1] Bombing of Japan should start 2-3 months later.
[2] Cut sea communications to S.E. Asia and open up sea route to China.

The Chiefs of Staff were thus confirmed in their answer to the Prime Minister's fourth argument,[3] and provided with a firmer basis than before for their alternative theory.

The validity of the Planners' conclusions rested, of course, on the margin of superiority over the enemy which they considered necessary. The Prime Minister had often chafed at the long odds allowed to the defence by contemporary military thought, and in this case his wrath had already been excited at the time of 'Buccaneer'. It appeared to him ridiculous that Mountbatten should then have asked for 50,000 British and Indian troops to meet 5,000 Japanese, and he remained far

---

[1] See Appendix VIII below.

[2] See Map I, facing p. 11.

[3] Page 427 above.

from satisfied by the answer that these numbers were needed to offset any possibility of failure, and that over 16,000 of the men would be administrative troops not engaged in the actual assault. 'By such standards', he signalled to Mountbatten, 'all amphibious operations are impossible'; and he complained that the Americans were able to attack the Pacific islands with a superiority of only $2\frac{1}{2}:1$. Mountbatten replied that in fact the Americans had used a margin of 6:1 at Guadalcanal, of over 4:1 against the Gilbert Islands, and of nearly 7:1 in the Munda operation; and that in operations such as 'Buccaneer' and 'Culverin', which depended entirely upon seaborne air support, a superority of 5:1 was the absolute minimum even if morale had not to be considered. This led Churchill into a technical discussion with the Admiralty on the rapidity with which aircraft carriers could be replenished during an operation; but he emerged with small satisfaction, and the Joint Planners' report on 'Culverin', with which the South-East Asia Command agreed, was based on the same margin of superiority as before.

It was not therefore surprising that Churchill should have objected to the figures at the meeting on 25th February. He then turned to the alternative. 'Culverin' might eat uncomfortably into the resources assembled for south-east Asia; but if it were not carried out, and if the campaign were confined to northern Burma, those resources were demonstrably too great for the theatre. In that case, what was to be done with the surplus when the initial campaign had ended? Presumably the troops, and their shipping and aircraft, should be used elsewhere; but if in the Pacific, the cost in shipping and material of transporting them from one theatre to another, and of constructing the necessary bases, must be weighed against any advantage that might accrue. Would it not be less wasteful to use the existing facilities of India, and the known capacity of shipping, in support of a strategy which, with a bolder vision and a proper scrutiny of requirements, could employ the forces already in the area?

The problem thus returned to its starting point, for before it could be answered the Chiefs of Staff needed more information on the facilities in Australia and New Zealand, with the consequent implications for shipping. They therefore again asked permission to open the question. But the circumstances were no more propitious than before, for in the meantime the discussion had been further complicated by two new factors, one diplomatic and one strategic, which the Prime Minister wished if possible to settle before the Dominions were admitted to the British counsels.

The diplomatic factor came to the fore a few days after the conference of 14th February, but it had been present since the first meeting of the Defence Committee on 19th January. So far, we have talked in terms of the Prime Minister and the Chiefs of Staff, because the

Prime Minister alone of the inner ring of Ministers was in full possession of the facts and in constant touch with the Joint Planners and the 'Axiom' Mission. He was, however, supported by his colleagues throughout. This clear-cut division between Ministers and their military advisers sprang largely from the diplomatic implications of the debate. On 14th December, 1943, the Foreign Secretary had stated in the House of Commons that 'the war with Japan is not one in which we in this country are playing the part of benevolent assistants. Even if we are compelled, for the time being, to devote the greater part of our human and material resources to the task of defeating Germany, we are still principals in the Far Eastern war.'[1] Ministers were now unanimous that the Chiefs of Staff's strategy might endanger this policy. On 21st February, the Foreign Office put its case to the Prime Minister. It rested on three assumptions: that the British rôle in the Far East was at present conceived merely as a contribution to the American; that such a rôle was not likely to appeal to the British people when called on to continue the war against Japan after the defeat of Germany; and that it was not likely to satisfy the Dominions. On this basis, the memorandum assessed the diplomatic value of the rival strategies. Of the Chiefs of Staff's strategy it remarked, 'The peoples of Asia are little interested in Pacific islands and to the mass of the Japanese people also they convey very little. A strategy which until a later date leaves the Japanese virtually unassailed in those regions which mean most to the peoples of Asia and to the Japanese themselves, will cast a considerable strain upon the already stretched endurance of the occupied territories and will materially retard their rehabilitation upon recovery.' In contrast, 'the strategy advocated by S.E.A.C. will . . . have immediate psychological and political effects which in themselves will contribute materially to the defeat of Japan. It will also do more than the Pacific strategy to discredit the Japanese Army, which is vitally important. . . .' It concluded that 'if the [Pacific] strategy . . . is accepted, and if there is to be no major British rôle in the Far Eastern war, then it is no exaggeration to say that the solidarity of the British Commonwealth and its influence in the maintenance of peace in the Far East will be irretrievably damaged.'

The Prime Minister and his colleagues shared this view throughout the first half of 1944, and laid great stress on the importance of the British reconquering the Malay Peninsula for themselves. At the same time, they had to consider the attitude of Australia and New Zealand. The Foreign Office's memorandum had discounted the effect of a British Pacific force on Commonwealth opinion; but it was by no means certain that it had judged the position correctly. Nothing had as yet been said officially; but towards the end of 1943 the Australian Prime Minister had told visiting British authorities that he would like

[1] *Parliamentary Debates*, (*Official Record of The House of Commons*), vol. 395, col. 1427.

to see the mother country represented in the Pacific, and had suggested to this end that a Commonwealth Command should be formed in the south-west Pacific to partner a revised American Command. If British troops could not be spared for the Pacific, the boundaries of the South-East Asia Command might be revised to include a part of the South-West Pacific Area, and Australian forces placed under Admiral Mountbatten's control. When therefore the Prime Minister raised the diplomatic issue at the conference on 25th February, the Chiefs of Staff drew attention to the Australian view, and suggested that here, as in the strategic field, further inquiries might well be made.

The other complication at the end of the month was provided by the Japanese themselves. On 24th February, a force of seven battleships, two fleet carriers, eight cruisers and eighteen destroyers was reported to be moving to Singapore. This meant that the main Japanese Fleet had left the central Pacific. The purpose of the move was uncertain. It might be purely defensive, the result of the American encroachment on Truk, where the Fleet had hitherto lain. In that case Singapore was a likely alternative, with its strategic position, its considerable facilities, and its proximity to the oil of the Netherlands East Indies. But whatever the cause, the possibility could not be ignored that the Japanese, with a clear surface superiority in the Bay of Bengal, might now attack British possessions or seek an encounter with the Eastern Fleet. If they stayed in Singapore for more than a few months, they also presented a new and serious threat to 'Culverin', which would then need greater naval support. The Prime Minister was seriously perturbed by the Japanese move, and used it on 25th February to argue against a hasty decision in favour of the Pacific strategy. But the Chiefs of Staff and the Admiralty were not unduly dismayed, for they considered that the strong force of shore-based aircraft and the small but balanced British Fleet could maintain essential communications in the Indian Ocean and deal with any sally by the enemy. A vigorous discussion developed over this conception of sea power, which died a natural death as the Japanese showed no sign of emerging and as other events overtook it. In the event, the enemy left Singapore in September, 1944 without disturbing or even challenging the increasing activities of the Eastern Fleet. The move did not cause either party to alter its mind; but it added to an already complex debate at a time when a decision was required.

Little therefore emerged from the discussions of 25th February, and indeed the extension of the argument merely confirmed each side in its views. It was now time for the 'Axiom' Mission to leave for Washington, and General Wedemeyer was therefore invited to explain to the Americans the British strategy for Burma, but to state that the general strategy for the defeat of Japan was still under consideration. The Prime Minister and the Chiefs of Staff then withdrew to consider the position, and to make a further attempt to convert their opponents. The Prime Minister was first in the field on 3rd March, with a memorandum to the members of the Defence Committee (dated 29th February) which was perhaps the best *résumé* of his argument that had yet appeared. The growing seriousness of the position was revealed in its opening sentence.

> '1. A question of major policy and strategy has now opened on which it may be necessary to obtain a decision by the War Cabinet. The two alternatives open are:
>
> A. To send a detachment of the British Fleet during the present year to act with the United States in the Pacific and to increase the strength of this detachment as fast as possible, having regard to the progress of the war against Germany. This Fleet would be followed at the end of the German war, or perhaps even before it, by four British divisions which would be based on, say, Sydney and would operate with the Australian forces on the left or southern flank of the main American advance against the Philippines, Formosa and ultimately Japan. Corresponding movements would be enjoined upon the Royal Air Force. For all these purposes it is necessary in the near future to begin the formation of a large Fleet train[1] to supplement any naval bases which may be available and to develop Australian bases for the use of a growing British Army.
>
> B. To keep the centre of gravity of the British war against Japan in the Bay of Bengal for at least 18 months from now and to conduct amphibious operations on a considerable scale against the Andamans, Nicobars and, above all, Sumatra as resources become available.
>
> 2. The British Chiefs of Staff favour 'A', and made an agreement at Cairo after brief discussions with the United States Chiefs of Staff that this should be accepted "as a basis for investigation". Neither I nor the Foreign Secretary was aware of these discussions, though I certainly approved the report by the Combined Chiefs of Staff in which they were mentioned.
>
> 3. Admiral Mountbatten and the South-east Asia Command are in favour of 'B', which is perhaps not unnatural since 'A' involves the practical elimination of the South-East Asia Command and the immediate closing down of all amphibious plans in the Bay of Bengal. They have submitted the plans for these operations, in particular for the last one, 'Culverin'. They ask for larger resources than we could supply by November without trenching upon the United States Pacific effort. By March 1945, however, the bulk of their demands properly pruned could probably be met by Great Britain and India, certainly if Germany had been knocked out by the end of this year. In pursuance of their theme the Chiefs of Staff express the

[1] See pp. 476-8 below.

view that the arrival of the British forces aforesaid in the Pacific and in Australia will be a valuable contribution to the United States main operations, that they will produce good results upon Australian sentiment towards the Mother Country, and that if, as and when they are successful these operations will compromise or even sever Japanese supply lines with Malaya and the Netherlands East Indies and that these places will fall easily into our hands, either as the result of decisive operations in the Pacific or by attacks launched at a later date from the direction of the Pacific. They accept unquestioningly the ample scales of attack asked for by the south-east Asia Command and dwell upon the difficulties of meeting them without serious detriment to the United States main operations in the Pacific even if, which is most unlikely, the United States Government were found agreeable to such dispositions.

4. On the other hand, the following considerations, some of which are urged by the south-east Asia Command, should be weighed. The side-tracking of the Indian theatre and the Bay of Bengal involves a division of our forces, naval, military and Air, between the Indian and Australian theatres. It throws out of offensive action permanently all the very large forces which must in any case be left in the Indian theatre either because they are needed for defence or because they cannot be applied to the enemy. It overlooks the diversionary and wearing-down value upon the Japanese Air and military forces which would be entailed by amphibious operations across the Bay of Bengal. It vastly lengthens our line of communication. It throws out of action all our bases in the Indian Ocean from Calcutta to Ceylon as well as those more distant bases in the Suez Canal and Red Sea which have been kept in being to supplement a large-scale south-east Asia campaign. The establishments of the Egyptian bases and the great workshops we have created there are largely immovable, though possibly some personnel and machinery could be transferred to aid in the development of the Australian bases.

5. A decision to act as a subsidiary force under the Americans in the Pacific raises difficult political questions about the future of our Malayan possessions. If the Japanese should withdraw from them or make peace as the result of the main American thrust, the United States Government would after the victory feel greatly strengthened in its view that all possessions in the East Indian Archipelago should be placed under some international body upon which the United States would exercise a decisive control. They would feel with conviction: "We won the victory and liberated these places, and we must have the dominating say in their future and derive full profit from their produce, especially oil." Against this last the British Chiefs of Staff urge that nothing in their plan excludes our attacking the Japanese in Malaya and the Netherlands East Indies in

due course from the Pacific, and they would like to obtain American agreement to setting up a British Command in the Australian theatre of war which would be independent of, though of course in close collaboration with, the main American Command in the Pacific.[1] The United States might well not view such a change with favour. It could not in any case be asked for by us with any show of reason until late in 1945.

6. Upon these competing arguments ('A' and 'B') has now descended a new and important event. The main Japanese Fleet has taken its station at Singapore. Whatever may be the Japanese motives, the fact remains that their main Fleet at Singapore deprives us of the command of the Bay of Bengal, threatens the whole East Indian coast including Ceylon with the possibility of raids or more serious attacks, and also enables powerful cruiser forces supported by battleships to range widely over the Indian Ocean menacing all our communications with Australia, which communications will become far more important if Plan 'A' is adopted. To my surprise, the Admiralty do not consider these dangers serious. They say that the British and American shore-based aircraft on the eastern shores of India and Ceylon are capable of defending India from attack without naval assistance; secondly, that, contrary to our former expectations, the Japanese have never yet sent out their cruisers to prey on our ocean convoys and that if they did the Catalina aircraft would discover the raiders and the convoys could be diverted. These are new doctrines for the Admiralty and if our experience should make them good it is evident that wholesale transference of Naval strength to Air strength should be made after the war. This is certainly increasingly the tendency of opinion and events. The Admiralty therefore would be prepared to divide our Fleet, leaving a certain force in the Indian Ocean and sending all the best ships on into the Pacific as they are tropicalised and modernised.

7. Before the War Cabinet could take responsibility for a decision of this novel character, it would be necessary to find out first whether the United States operations in the Pacific really required a detachment of our Fleet in those waters in 1944 or 1945 and which of their operations would be prevented by its absence. I propose therefore to ask this question of the President myself. Secondly, ought we to divide our Fleet and leave only weak forces in the Indian Ocean at a time when the main Japanese Fleet is concentrated at Singapore, before at any rate we know more clearly than we now do what the Japanese intentions are? Thirdly, will not a very great net loss in the application of our forces to the enemy be involved in the non-use of the Indian and Egyptian bases as compared with any additional servicing accommodation which we may set up in

[1] This is discussed on p. 481 *et seq.* below.

Australia and the south-west Pacific? On this we should have further information. At first sight it seems improvident to duplicate so many of our establishments instead of using those we have got to the highest advantage. Fourthly, what diminution of our striking power against the enemy is involved in the enormous lengthening of our lines of communication entailed by passing them south of Australia round into the south-west Pacific as compared with operating across the Bay of Bengal?

8. It is claimed that Plan 'A' would shorten the war by six months as against Plan 'B'; but no statement has been made as to the year from which this six months is to be deducted. I suggest that the time-table of future operations of such vast and speculative character cannot be accurately foretold. The United States plans stretch out to 1947. Many things may happen in the interval. For instance, the Japanese shore-based aircraft may prove as effective in the defence of the home lands of Japan, the Philippines and the China coast as the shore-based aircraft we now have in the Bay of Bengal are assumed by the Admiralty to be against the Japanese concentrated at Singapore. In this case the development of the American plans would have to be step by step, securing one shore-based air position after another. Again, the war with Germany may not end in 1944, or, again, Russia may enter the struggle against Japan and a very great recasting of our strategy may be required to meet their views and in consequence of their intervention. It may therefore be wise to concentrate upon practical steps which can be taken in a reasonable period of time—say 18 months, rather than to side-track and cast away the enormous facilities and opportunities which we now possess for the sake of a scheme of campaigns mapped out on paper for three or four years ahead. I deprecate, therefore, a hasty decision to abandon the Indian theatre and the prospect of amphibious operations across the Bay of Bengal.

9. Meanwhile, it seems that the Japanese are particularly sensitive about our possible attacks against the Western part of their south-east Asia co-prosperity sphere, and it may be more than a coincidence that the movement of our battleships through the Mediterranean and the Canal towards Ceylon should have been followed by the movement of the Japanese Fleet to Singapore. If this be so, we should certainly be rendering a great service to the United States by keeping up the threat and holding the Japanese Fleet at Singapore as long as possible, thus leaving the United States with no hostile naval forces worth speaking of before them in the Pacific. No greater service could be rendered to an Ally.'

Five days later, the Chiefs of Staff replied with a series of detailed comments, aimed particularly at Mr. Churchill's conception of the size of the forces in south-east Asia.

'We think that you would wish to have our comments on your unnumbered note of 29th February.

2. *Your paragraph* 1

Your definition of the Pacific strategy omits its first object, namely to obtain a footing in Japan's inner zone at the earliest possible moment; while your definition of the Bay of Bengal strategy does not bring out that it is contingent upon Germany's defeat and, therefore, cannot begin until about six months after that event. Nor does it mention the stages which must follow the capture of Sumatra. If we adopt the Bay of Bengal strategy, we will be committed to making our main thrust via Malaya to the South China Sea. We suggest that the definitions at Annex A give a more accurate presentation of the alternative strategies.

[Annex A read as follows :

A. To concentrate British and American forces for a combined main thrust from the Pacific to effect a lodgment in Japan's inner zone as early as possible. This will entail the despatch of a detachment of the British Fleet during the present year to the Pacific; and the increase of the strength of this fleet as fast as possible having regard to the progress of the war against Germany. This fleet would be followed at the end of the war with Germany by 4-6 British divisions and British air forces which, based on Australia, would operate with the Dominion forces on the left or southern flank of the main advances against the Philippines, Formosa and ultimately Japan.

B. To make an independent British contribution to the war against Japan from South-east Asia Command, building up the British Fleet in the Indian Ocean and, when resources become available after Germany's defeat, to capture Northern Sumatra, Malaya and eventually force an entry into the South China Sea.

In either alternative, it is necessary in the near future to begin the formation of a large fleet train to supplement any naval bases which may be available. For Course A, Australian bases must be enlarged for growing British land and air forces.]

3. You refer in your description of Strategy A to the need of a large fleet train. In fact, whether Strategy A or Strategy B is adopted, a comparable fleet train and an expansion of naval facilities will be required.

4. *Your Paragraphs* 3 *and* 4

Resources for 'Culverin'. We do not consider Admiral Mountbatten's requirements for 'Culverin' to be excessive. For example, he has asked for 30 carriers, which is a modest demand to meet strong shore-based air defence. For the projected Pacific operations we plan to use something of the order of 100 carriers. In any case, the resources required for 'Culverin' cannot be provided by the British until about six months after Germany's defeat. The Bay of Bengal strategy is, therefore, conditional upon the defeat of Germany and tied to that event in date. This does not apply to the initiation of the Pacific strategy.

5. *Rôle of South-East Asia Command*

With the exception of 4 to 5 divisions, all the available land forces will be needed to secure the air route to China by operations in Burma and to maintain internal security in India. There is no question, therefore, of large forces in South-East Asia Command remaining inactive if 'Culverin' is not undertaken. Of these 4 to 5 divisions, two could be moved to the South-west Pacific before the end of 1944. The remainder will provide a much needed reserve for South-East Asia Command and India. S.E.A.C. state that all the air forces now available will be needed to ensure the security of the air ferry route to China and in connection with Plan 'Drake' [long-range bombing from China] . . .[1] Thus, the strategy we advocate leaves a useful rôle to South-East Asia Command.

6. *Your Paragraph* 5

Political Considerations. Whatever strategy we follow, the major credit for the defeat of Japan is likely to go to the Americans. Their resources and their geographical position must make them the predominant partner in Japan's defeat. The first mortal thrust will be the Pacific thrust, upon which the Americans have already embarked. We should not be excluded from a part in this thrust. . . .

8. *Your Paragraph* 6

. . . We expressed the view [with regard to the Japanese Fleet at Singapore] that, with the strong shore-based air forces that will become available *and* with a small British Fleet, essential communications in the Indian Ocean could be maintained. . . . Our contention is that naval strength or air forces alone are incomplete in modern maritime warfare. The two are entirely complementary. This has been borne out by all our experience in this war. No amount of naval strength can hold the Japanese Fleet at Singapore.

9. *Your Paragraph* 7

We do not think that if the President says that the United States operations in the Pacific do not require a detachment of our Fleet in those waters in 1944 or 1945, the issue should be regarded as settled and that we should, in consequence, follow a Bay of Bengal strategy. We submit that the right approach is to consider what strategy is best calculated to bring about the early overthrow of Japan and what contribution we can make to that strategy, and then to go to the Americans and put forward our case.

[1] See p. 453 below.

10. The expansion of bases is necessary whichever strategy we adopt. The Middle East and India bases would never be idle. They would be required for the limited operations which will, in any case, be carried out by the South-East Asia Command, and ultimately for mopping up in south-east Asia. Moreover, the Middle East and Ceylon bases lie on the direct line of communication to the South-west Pacific and their usefulness would, therefore, be continuous. Should there be any duplication of effort in the establishment of a base in Australia, it will be amply compensated by other factors. The Australian base will be established in a white country, free from the vagaries of climate. The Indian base is always subject to monsoon conditions and to the other disruptive climatic, economic and political factors inherent in India.

11. The answer to the question whether we should suffer diminution of our power by going to the south-west Pacific is affected by certain considerations. The distance is certainly greater, but our part in the operations could begin earlier and involves the use of fewer land forces, though the navy and air commitment would eventually be much the same. Clearly more shipping would be required for the Pacific strategy than for the Bay of Bengal strategy, but in view of the diminution of sinkings, the very high rate of building and the fact that as soon as Germany is defeated we could go out of convoy, there should surely be enough shipping to support whatever strategy would be considered the most profitable.

12. *Your Paragraph* 8

Time-Table . . . We [have given] our estimate of the possible time-table of operations under each strategy. Although this is necessarily conjectural at this stage, we adhere to the date . . . given.

13. *The entry of Russia into the War*

Should Russia enter the war, additional supply lines to the Maritime Provinces must be opened if her geographical position is to be fully exploited. This may well necessitate operations in the Kurile-Kamchatka area. These would require strong fleet cover. If at this stage the British Fleet were committed to the support of the drive into the South China Sea via Singapore, the American Fleet is unlikely to be able to support these northern operations without severely hampering the momentum of the drive in the Central Pacific. We should then find ourselves forced to pull our punch at the heart and confined once again to operations in the outer perimeter of the Japanese Co-prosperity Sphere.

14. Finally, the Pacific strategy does not mean casting away facilities we now enjoy in the Bay of Bengal. The hard fact is that there are no practical steps we can usefully take in that

> theatre until six months after Germany is defeated. This means that forces placed there, over and above those required for operations in Burma, the air lift to China and Plan 'Drake' might remain idle throughout the whole period of 18 months foreseen by you.'

In addition to this reply, the Chiefs of Staff set out their position in a detailed memorandum of 1st March, which in turn drew the comments of the Prime Minister.

At the beginning of March, therefore, the deadlock seemed complete, and on the 4th General Ismay tried to find a solution. His note to the Prime Minister shows the effect of the disagreement on an experienced and level-headed staff officer with full knowledge of the course of the debate.

> 'There is complete agreement between the War Cabinet and the Chiefs of Staff on the conduct of operations in the European theatre. Tremendous events are impending in Europe and political and military opinion are completely in step.
>
> 2. The same cannot, however, be said about more distant lands in the more distant future. There is a clear-cut divergence of opinion between yourself and your Ministerial colleagues on the one side, and the Chiefs of Staff on the other, as to the plan that should be followed for the ultimate defeat of Japan. A number of papers have been written on the subject, and there have been a number of discussions. But no agreement has been reached. On the one hand it seems absolutely certain that you and your Ministerial colleagues will not agree to the "Pacific" strategy. On the other hand, the Chiefs of Staff, even if their faith in this strategy were shaken by the papers which you have written and the discussions which are to take place, are extremely unlikely to retract the military opinions that they have expressed.
>
> 3. Thus, we are faced with the practical certainty of a continued cleavage of opinion between the War Cabinet and their military advisers; nor can we exclude the possibility of resignation on the part of the latter. A breach of this kind, undesirable at any time, would be little short of catastrophic at the present juncture. 'Overlord' is, in all conscience, a sufficiently hazardous operation. It must be given every chance.
>
> 4. I suggest that you should call a meeting, or perhaps a series of meetings, of the Defence Committee next week to go exhaustively into the "Indian Ocean" and "Pacific" strategies. Both cases can be fully ventilated and argued. It is just possible that agreement can thus be reached. If so, well and good. If not, would it not be possible and right for you to take the line that the issue cannot be decided on military grounds alone, and that, apart from the military merits of the respective strategies, political considerations must be over-riding. I

> cannot but think that the Chiefs of Staff would accept this decision with complete loyalty and would set to work at once to make the best possible plans for implementing it. Their position vis-à-vis their United States colleagues would then be perfectly clear. They could say—"We are not authorised to discuss any plans for moving British land, sea and air forces into the Pacific. We should like to concert with you how best to implement the Indian Ocean strategy." If the U.S. Chiefs of Staff disagree, it would then become a matter for the Heads of Governments . . .'

The meeting which Ismay proposed was accelerated by a fresh development on 4th March. After the meeting on 25th February, the Chiefs of Staff had submitted another draft telegram to Churchill informing Australia and New Zealand of the consequences of the Cairo decisions; and on 3rd March this had been refused in favour of a further investigation of the facilities in those countries, to be made in London. But by now the Australians themselves were wondering about the fate of the Cairo plans, of which they had heard nothing for almost three months. On the 14th, Mr. Curtin inquired of the British Prime Minister if he could be told of their progress, and the next day Mr. Churchill called a Staff Conference for 8th March to decide on a suitable reply. In the meantime, he asked the Minister of War Transport to report on the shipping implications of the Pacific strategy. All parties were thus fully engaged on their preparations in the brief interval that remained.

The meeting of 8th March marked the end of the first phase of this prolonged debate. Once again Ministers and Chiefs of Staff aired their differences of diplomatic and military principle, but on this occasion, unlike the earlier meetings, both sides agreed that not enough was known about the implications of supply for them to reach agreement on strategy. The preliminary report by the Minister of War Transport showed that the Admiralty and the Ministry were far from happy on the nature of the shipping problem. Lord Leathers argued that to support a Pacific strategy he would have to supply $2\frac{1}{2}$-3 times the tanker tonnage which he contemplated at present for India, about one million tons of cargo for every 100,000 tons of stores and every 5,000 vehicles transported from India to Australia, a further half a million tons to maintain the new bases as compared with the cost of the bases already under way in India, and an unknown increase to meet the construction of the new bases, the transport of the necessary forces to Australia, and their transport and maintenance on the scene of operations. Over the whole project hung the shadow of the extra 6,000 miles from England, at a time when shipping seemed still to be strained and British production might well be on the decline. But these figures differed from those of the First Sea Lord, and it was clear that the two

Departments had not considered the problem together. On 14th March, the Prime Minister therefore asked the Minister and the Chiefs of Staff to examine the whole question as soon as possible. It also seemed clear that the available information on Australia and the south-west Pacific was inadequate, and the meeting therefore decided that a telegram should be sent to the Australian Government, asking for its co-operation in assembling the necessary data. With this conclusion, the second phase may be said to have begun in the formation of a Far Eastern strategy, in which the facts of the case were investigated and, as a result, a fresh solution was proposed.

(ii)

The Americans' Position

At the same time, the meeting agreed to tell the Americans of the position about the Pacific strategy, as Mr. Churchill had contemplated a week before. On 10th March, therefore, he sent a telegram to the President, outlining the divergent views held in London and inquiring[1] if 'there is any specific American operation in the Pacific (a) before the end of 1944 or (b) before the summer of 1945 which would be hindered or prevented by the absence of a British Fleet detachment.' This message arrived at an opportune moment, for the American Chiefs of Staff were coming to the end of the prolonged investigations into their own Pacific strategy, the later stages of which had been attended by Nimitz and by MacArthur's Chief of Staff. This was concluded on 14th March, and the Joint Chiefs of Staff thereupon issued a new directive to the two commanders which Field Marshal Dill was allowed to pass unofficially to London. As had been foreshadowed at Cairo, they decided that 'the most feasible approach to Formosa, Luzon, China area is by way of Mariana Islands, Caroline Islands, Palau, Mindanao area.' To this end, they envisaged the following operations:[2]

'(a) The cancellation of [MacArthur's plan to capture Kavieng in New Ireland]. Complete the isolation of the Rabaul—Kavieng area with the minimum commitment of forces.

(b) The early completion of the occupation of Manus and its development as an air or fleet base.

(c) The occupation of Hollandia . . . target date 15th April, 1944 . . . for the establishment of heavy bombardment aircraft for the preliminary air bombardment of the Paulaus and the neutralization of the Western New Guinea—Halmahera area.

---

[1] See *Closing the Ring*, pp. 509-10.

[2] See Map I, facing p. 11.

(d) The establishment of control over the Mariana Islands, Caroline Islands, and Palaus area by Pacific Ocean Area[s] forces:

(1) by the neutralization of Truk.

(2) by the occupation of the Southern Mariana Islands, target date 15th June . . .

(3) by the occupation of the Palaus . . . target date 15th September . . . to establish a fleet and air base and forward staging area for the support of operations against Mindanao, Formosa, and China.

(e) The occupation of Mindanao . . . target date 15th November . . . to reduce and contain Japanese forces in the Philippines preparatory to a further advance on Formosa—either directly, or via Luzon—and to conduct air strikes against enemy installations in the Netherlands East Indies.

(f) The occupation of Formosa, target date 15th February, 1945, or the occupation of Luzon should such an operation prove necessary prior to a move on Formosa, target date 15th February, 1945.'

Operations (a), (b) and (c) were assigned to MacArthur, to be followed by 'operations along the New Guinea Coast, and such other operations as may be feasible in preparation for the support of the Palau operation and the assault on Mindanao'. With the cancellation of the attack on Kavieng, he was to return to Nimitz by 15th May, 1944 all units of the American Pacific Fleet at his disposal. Operation (d), and support for operation (c), were assigned to Nimitz.

This programme clearly favoured Nimitz rather than MacArthur. The occupation of Kavieng was cancelled and its isolation, with that of Rabaul, allowed only the minimum of troops, while the capture of Manus served the purposes of the American Pacific Fleet. The capture of the Palaus now fell definitely to Nimitz, and MacArthur's major land operation against Luzon was listed as an alternative to the by-passing attack upon Formosa, which must involve the co-operation, and possibly the superior control, of the Pacific Ocean Areas Command. The implications for the British were clear. The basis of the original plan, whereby a British Fleet was required in the Pacific in the spring of 1945, had been removed by the increasing speed of advance of the American Fleet. Admiral King had stated that it would not be needed in the summer of 1944; it now looked as if it might not be needed for at least another year. On 13th March, the President therefore replied to the Prime Minister.

'(a) There will be no specific operation in the Pacific during 1944 that would be adversely affected by the absence of a British Fleet detachment.

(b) It is not at the present time possible to anticipate with sufficient accuracy future developments in the Pacific to be

> certain that a British Fleet detachment will not be needed there during the year 1945, but it does not now appear that such a reinforcement will be needed before the summer of 1945. . . . In consideration of recent enemy dispositions [by which he meant the move of the Japanese Fleet to Singapore] it is my personal opinion that unless we have unexpected bad luck in the Pacific your naval force will be of more value to our common effort by remaining in the Indian Ocean. . . .'

This argument might seem at first sight to have favoured Churchill's case. The original inducement to a Pacific strategy was removed, and the value of the Indian Ocean reaffirmed. But in fact the American idea of an Indian Ocean strategy was very different from that of the Prime Minister, and on 21st March the Joint Chiefs of Staff made this clear.

> 'In our opinion', they remarked, 'once United States forces have a strangle-hold on enemy communications in [the China-Formosa-Luzon] area, the strategic value of operations in Malaya and the Netherlands East Indies will be considerably reduced. Furthermore, the requirements for a major amphibious operation in the South East Asia Theatre this year are not in sight. We cannot, therefore, at this time agree to support Operation 'Culverin' or any similar operation involving large amphibious commitments in the South East Asia Command.'

This argument of course reflected the Americans' view of the function of the South-East Asia Command, which had not changed but had rather hardened since the disappointments at the end of 1943. There were two reasons for this: first, the effect of General Stilwell's operations in northern Burma; secondly, an increasing American commitment in China itself.

The Joint Chiefs of Staff had abandoned operation 'Tarzan' in northern Burma with reluctance in January 1944,[1] and the tactical success of Stilwell's force, which was to have formed an integral part of the plan, had meanwhile strengthened their belief in his strategy. Accustomed as they were to distrust British figures and sometimes British intentions in Burma, they were the more inclined to accept his statistical estimates because his operational estimates seemed to be proving correct. In February 1944, Stilwell's stock stood high with the American Government. In the course of that month it was raised even higher with the public, by a sudden Press campaign which broke into exuberant support of the General to the detriment of his British colleagues. By the time that the 'Axiom' Mission arrived in Washington, the future of the South-East Asia Command was a lively issue throughout the United States—a development that caused some embarrassment to the authorities in Washington and London.

---

[1] See pp. 222-3 above.

By now, also, the Americans were increasingly committed to the creation of a strategic air force in China for the long-range bombing of Japan and its approaches, and this seemed to be threatened by the diversion of resources to another area. At Cairo, one of the 'Specific Operations in 1944' had been the 'conducting [of] V.L.R. air operations from the Chengtu area in China against vital targets in the Japanese inner zone'; and the details of the plan were set out in an appendix to the Combined Chiefs of Staff's Final Report. The bombing force was to be composed of the new and very long-range B.29 aircraft, supplied, partly by their own efforts and partly by a force of long-range B.24 bombers, through India and Burma. The plan, known in its earlier form as 'Drake' and finally, when revised, as 'Matterhorn', fell into two parts. The former comprised the preparations to be made in India—the construction or modification of airfields in Bengal, their connexion by fuel pipeline with Calcutta, and the expansion of the port and its line of communications through Assam; the latter the preparations in China itself—the construction of new airfields near Kunming,[1] the diversion of at least twenty Chinese divisions to the protection of all American airfields in the country, and the further expansion of the air ferry over the Hump. If all went well, bombing of targets in the inner zone of the Japanese defences, to 'soften up' Japan and to assist the Pacific advance, could begin in the autumn of 1945.

But the plan, to which the Americans had been greatly attached since the autumn of 1943, depended on factors largely outside their control. Thanks to a preliminary investigation before the Cairo Conference, preparations in north-east India had begun, under the aegis of the India Command, in November, 1943; but the work was timed to start in earnest in January, 1944 with American skilled labour and supervision, and if these were not to be wasted their work in Calcutta and Assam must not be diverted to other purposes. The preparations in China were more exacting. Not only did they demand 7,000 tons a month from the Hump, the provision of Chinese labour and the diversion or raising of a large number of Chinese divisions, but also—in the Americans' opinion—the completion of the Ledo Road and its pipeline by the end of 1944. Like the British in Burma, in fact, the Americans preferred not to rely on the air alone when considerable operations were envisaged far afield. Their plans thus seemed to be threatened by the collapse of 'Tarzan' and the appearance of Mountbatten's new strategy. The work in India was likely to be robbed of much of the capacity of Calcutta, now devoted to the mounting of 'Culverin', while the preparations in China would have to rely solely on air supply. The plan for the bombing of Japan therefore combined with Stilwell's

[1] Airfields near Chengtu had already been developed by General Chennault.

operations to reinforce the Americans' belief in the possibilities of northern Burma.

It was thus not surprising that the Joint Chiefs of Staff should have reacted quickly to Mountbatten's new plans, the more so because they were already disturbed by the lack of orders to replace his original directive. On 17th February, they approached the British Chiefs of Staff in an effort to revive the plans of the previous November.[1] They considered that Stilwell should be ordered to capture Myitkyina before the monsoon, while the British 4th Corps on the central front crossed the Chin Hills and secured the area Shwebo-Monywa in his support. But this would need all the forces that could be assembled, and there now seemed a possibility that they might be diverted elsewhere. The Americans therefore proposed that the Combined Chiefs of Staff should issue a new directive, ordering the Supreme Commander 'to commence operations without delay to seize and hold Myitkyina and Shwebo-Monywa area using all means now at his disposal.' This would pave the way for a direct contribution by the South-East Asia Command to the Pacific strategy.

The British Chiefs of Staff could not agree with this proposal, for much as they disapproved of 'Culverin' their adherence to the Pacific strategy rested on an equal disapproval of ambitious operations towards China. They reserved their full reply until they had received Admiral Mountbatten's comments, which arrived on 21st February. After pointing out that he was already using all of his resources in Upper Burma and was withholding nothing for 'Culverin', the Supreme Commander stated that the Americans' targets could not be achieved. He doubted if he could reach the area Shwebo-Monywa before the monsoon; and even if he did so, he could not support himself there during the following months. Nor did he anticipate that Stilwell could reach Myitkyina by the same date, for in his view air supply could not match the Japanese advantages of interior lines of communication. The subsequent operations to reopen land communications with China were correspondingly prejudiced, and he preferred to abide by the existing plan, which would amply protect the air bases for the ferry to China. In conclusion, Mountbatten suggested—mistakenly, but with some justification—that the Joint Chiefs of Staff might have been influenced beforehand by Stilwell's representations; and it needed the repeated assurances of General Marshall to satisfy him, and the British Chiefs of Staff, on this point.

On 25th February, the President followed up the message from his Chiefs of Staff. After stressing that in the Americans' view the capture of Myitkyina was necessary to protect the air route as well as to advance the construction of the Ledo Road, he turned specifically to 'Culverin'.

---

[1] See Map III, facing p. 129.

'I am gravely concerned over the recent trends in strategy that favour an operation towards Sumatra and Malaya in the future rather than to face the immediate obstacles that confront us in Burma. I fail to see how an operation against Sumatra and Malaya, requiring tremendous resources and forces, can possibly be mounted until after the conclusion of the war in Europe. Lucrative as a successful 'Culverin' might be there appears much more to be gained by employing all the resources we now have available in an all-out drive into Upper Burma so that we can build up our air strength in China and ensure the essential support for our westward advance to the Formosa-China-Luzon area.'

It was not clear from this if the Americans appreciated the relative timing of the operations which the British envisaged in the north and south, and Churchill hastened to reassure Roosevelt, quite correctly, that nothing would be withdrawn or withheld on 'Culverin's' account from the campaign in northern Burma. This of course referred to the operations in progress, and not to the future on which British and Americans had not yet agreed. The Prime Minister took care, therefore, to reaffirm his belief that the Ledo Road could not be advanced in time to help the Chinese. On the same day, the British Chiefs of Staff replied to the proposed American directive on the lines suggested by Mountbatten, and suggested in turn that he should be ordered 'to develop, maintain and protect the air link with China.'

This signal was sent after the second Staff Conference in London on 25th February, at which General Wedemeyer was instructed to convey to the Joint Chiefs of Staff the British views on Burma. He left on the 26th, and appeared with the rest of the 'Axiom' Mission before the Combined Chiefs of Staff on 3rd March. A succession of meetings with the Planners and other authorities followed. It was at once obvious that Stilwell's figures and views, whether or not as advanced by Stilwell himself, prevailed in Washington. General Arnold opposed the argument that Myitkyina was not necessary for the protection of the Hump, while the American administrative staff contradicted the 'Axiom' Mission's date for the completion of the Ledo Road, and asserted that communications could be built in time to support Stilwell at Myitkyina, and the British at Shwebo, during the monsoon. The discussions continued over the next fortnight, and, according to Dill, Wedemeyer's opponents found it hard to contradict his arguments. But, as Wedemeyer himself revealed in a letter to Churchill, the alternative was likely to be too distasteful. On 21st March, after a last talk with the 'Axiom' Mission, the Joint Chiefs of Staff took their decision, and conveyed it to the British.

'Nothing that has developed during these conferences has caused us to alter our previous concept. . . . On the contrary, these meetings have more conclusively developed that the greatest contribution which can be made to the defeat of Japan by the South-East Asia Command, is to assist in providing timely direct support of the Pacific advance to the China-Formosa-Luzon triangle. . . . It is conclusive to us that the greatest accomplishment that can be achieved by Admiral Mountbatten is to secure Myitkyina with the object of providing an immediate increase of the air transport capacity to China. . . . The increased capacity of the Assam line of communication and the success of recent operations in Arakan and the Hukawng Valley, together with the brilliantly executed airborne operations of the L.R.P. [long-range penetration] Groups, indicate that the difficulties previously emphasised in Burma operations may have been considerably over-estimated. We are inclined to take a more optimistic view than has been previously expressed of the objectives that are possible of attainment by our forces in that Theatre. We urge again, therefore, that the necessary directive be issued to Admiral Mountbatten to undertake the most vigorous action to capture Upper Burma during the remainder of this dry season, throughout the monsoon, and next fall, in order to increase the capacity of the air transport line to China and expedite the laying of a pipeline to that country.'

Five days later the 'Axiom' Mission left Washington on their way to New Delhi, breaking their journey in London in accordance with a request from the Prime Minister.

(iii)

The Pursuit of Facts

When the 'Axiom' Mission landed in England on 29th March, the situation had apparently altered little since earlier in the month. In one respect, indeed, it appeared to have retrogressed, for on the 20th the Prime Minister rebuked the Chiefs of Staff in a personal note which, had it been followed up, might well have closed the door to further negotiation. There had been no further Staff Conference, or full dress meeting of the Chiefs of Staff's or Defence Committees, since the 8th, and the time had been used to gain further information and to clarify points of detail. On 11th March, following the decisions of the 8th, the Prime Minister replied to the Australians' inquiry for information, stating concisely the alternatives under discussion and suggesting, subject to their agreement and on the understanding that it involved no firm decision or commitment, that small parties of British administrative experts should proceed to Australia to study conditions on the spot with Australian officials. Steps were thereupon taken to settle the composition and terms of reference of the parties, and these were ready for discussion on the 21st. But on the same day, the War Office received a warning from the British Military Mission in Australia that the Australian Chiefs of Staff considered themselves competent to provide the information required, and were opposed to the despatch of any parties other than for liaison. This was confirmed the next day by a telegram from Mr. Curtin, and Churchill thereupon asked for a further appreciation of the material available in London before he would agree to send the mission. This study was undertaken at the end of the month, but it was the middle of April before it could be considered. The arrangements with Australia, which had at last seemed to be prospering, meanwhile continued to hang fire.

The discussion on shipping was also postponed, for the Chiefs of Staff and the Ministry of War Transport were at work on their detailed report until the third week in April. But while this fact-finding was proceeding, there was a significant development elsewhere. After the meeting on 8th March, the Prime Minister decided to delve further on his own into the possibilities of 'Culverin'. Indeed, from the middle of March until the middle of April he virtually directed the detailed planning of the operation, holding a series of meetings with the Joint Planning Staff and, later, the 'Axiom' Mission in London and at Chequers, as a result of which its nature was gradually modified. By the end of March, the Prime Minister had agreed not to count on any reinforcements from Europe for 1944, but on the other hand the ratio of superiority over the enemy had been settled at 3:1 on land and at $2\frac{1}{2}$:1 in the air. On this basis, the Planners considered what courses were open to them in the coming winter across the Bay of Bengal. By the time that Wedemeyer was again in London, the choice seemed to lie between a reduced assault upon the northern tip of Sumatra and an attack upon the chain of islands off Sumatra and in the Malay Barrier, either against Simalur, Nias or Batu in the west, or against Christmas Island or Timor in the east.[1] Such an operation represented a compromise between the Prime Minister and the South-East Asia Command, using the available resources more modestly in support of the strategy to which both inclined. But it had a further and significant consequence. On 8th April, when the Joint Planners were instructed to report on the new alternatives, they were also told to investigate, in connexion with the second operation, the possibility of establishing air bases in northern and western Australia, and 'the general strategic concept of an advance on the general line Timor-Borneo-Celebes.'[2] Eight days before, pursuing their own investigations into the resources of Australia, the Chiefs of Staff had also instructed the Joint Planning

[1] See Map I, facing p. 11.

[2] Presumably a misprint for Timor-Celebes-Borneo (see p. 458 below).

Staff to report on the proposal 'that the main British effort against Japan should take the form of an advance on the general axis Timor-Celebes-Borneo-Saigon.' There is no evidence to show that the Chiefs of Staff believed in this plan at this point; but, faced with resolute Ministerial opposition to the original Pacific strategy, it may well have seemed a reasonable second best. The two points of view were still by no means reconciled; but the possibility of a compromise, with whatever doubts and reservations, could at last be observed.

CHAPTER XII

THE STRATEGY FOR THE PACIFIC AND SOUTH-EAST ASIA, APRIL–JULY, 1944

(i)

The Middle Strategy and its Implications

THE FRUITS of the inquiries from the Prime Minister and the Chiefs of Staff appeared in a paper from the Joint Planners on 12th April. It was headed 'War Against Japan—Alternative Proposal', and took as its thesis the Chiefs of Staff's formula that 'the main British effort against Japan should take the form of an advance on the general axis Timor-Celebes-Borneo-Saigon'.[1] Taking a target date in March 1945, it proceeded on the assumptions that the advance would be based on northern and western Australia; that the Americans' operations would proceed in accordance with the latest plans, though possibly not so fast as the timetable suggested; and that they would not call on British resources. The scale of opposition was not expected to be large: one active Japanese division in Timor, with remnants of the forces from New Guinea and some garrison troops; two active divisions, plus garrison troops, in Borneo and the Celebes; and two active divisions with garrison troops in Java. The Japanese naval forces in the area were thought to be small. These forces could be attacked either in the west or in the east, but there was little to be said for a western advance, which would come within easy range of the enemy's main airfields and would be separated from the Americans' flank in New Guinea. Its only advantage seemed to lie in the capture and later use of the enemy's airfields in Java and the Flores Sea. The main disadvantage in the east lay in the island of Timor, where both the enemy's strength and the weather were uncertain. The Planners therefore suggested that the island should be by-passed by an initial attack on Amboina, which moreover would remove the operations even further from the orbit of the Java airfields and would rest them immediately on the flank of the Americans'

[1] See Map IX.

advance. The attack on North Borneo could then proceed either directly or via Menado in the Celebes.

The forces for the capture of Amboina in March, 1945 could probably be supplied in part. It seemed likely that the naval demands (six cruisers, twelve escort carriers, a number of destroyers and escorts, and a covering force) could be met in full, provided that the ships left Europe in November, 1944; that the land forces (one division for the assault) could come from south-east Asia if all went well in Burma, but that no further reinforcements could reach Australia at best before July, 1945; that the essential air forces (mainly naval) could be provided from south-east Asia, but that again no further reinforcements could arrive from Europe before June, 1945; and that the assault shipping would be available if it left Europe by September, 1944.

The capture of Menado, which might follow two or three months later, would require no further forces, but more would be needed for the attack on North Borneo in the late summer or early autumn of 1945. Depending on the line of the initial advance, the timetable seemed likely to be:

Amboina—March 1945	or	Timor—July 1945
Menado (if necessary) —May or June 1945		Menado—October 1945
North Borneo— July or August 1945		North Borneo— November 1945
Either Saigon/Malaya, or Hong Kong and the China Coast	End of 1945 or early 1946	End of 1946

The advance would have to be mounted, as the Chiefs of Staff had assumed, in north-west Australia. At first sight it seemed doubtful if this could be done. The timely provision of advanced bases depended on the speed with which the main bases and training areas could be established, with the obvious implications for shipping and for land transport. The Planners declined to commit themselves without further information, but they drew attention to the danger of assuming that the advance could be maintained on the existing facilities.

The Planners concluded that the 'alternative proposal' had three advantages: it would place British naval forces in the Pacific (although not on the scale envisaged by the full Pacific strategy), readily available to the Americans if required; it would enable the British to reach Borneo sooner than would otherwise be the case; and it would give them the option in due course of attacking Malaya from the east as well as from the west. The disadvantages were that its contribution to the main strategy for the Pacific would be negligible, for the Americans would probably have captured Formosa well before the operations began; and that it would be quicker and more economical to approach northern Borneo by passing north of New Guinea, using the Americans' communications and air support from Mindanao, than by the route proposed.

This last consideration worried the Joint Planners and the Chiefs of Staff over the next few weeks. At first, they continued to incline towards the Amboina operation, which would not involve as long a passage by sea as the alternative north of New Guinea. But by the end of April, the Planners were so convinced of the operational advantages of the New Guinea plan that they were prepared to accept the disadvantage of distance. As a result, they submitted a fresh report in which the two strategies were again compared.

> 'We think that the value of the Middle Strategy as originally conceived is so limited that we have considered a modified version which envisages a British /Dominion advance to North Borneo based on East Australia, proceeding direct to North Borneo, north of New Guinea. This we think should be quite practicable, since, by the date on which we are ready to start—in Spring or Summer 1945—the North coast of New Guinea, Pelews [Palau Islands] and Mindanao (and possibly Luzon or Formosa) should already be in Allied hands. Certain staging points will be necessary along this route, but we see no reason why these and the necessary shore-based air cover should not be made available to us. If they were not available it would be quicker and more economical in resources to seize staging points by-passed by the Americans along this route, in waters already under Allied control, than to expend time and effort in gaining control of a new area.'

This 'Modified Middle Strategy', as the Planners called it, would also contribute more than the Middle Strategy to the main Pacific advance. It might enable the British to participate in operations against Formosa, if the Americans' timetable proved too optimistic; and it should in any case make it easier for them to take part in the subsequent operations against Japan. This was due partly to the fact that the base for the Modified Middle Strategy would be in eastern, instead of in north-west, Australia. On the other hand—and for the same reason—the Modified Strategy would probably demand more shipping than the alternative.

The Chiefs of Staff decided to forward the Planners' views; and on 4th May, after some revision, their paper was sent to the Prime Minister.

The Prime Minister himself had meanwhile been examining the Middle Strategy from a different point of view. By 17th April, when he held the last of his meetings with the 'Axiom' Mission and the Joint Planning Staff,[1] he had, according to the latter, 'definitely

[1] See p. 457 above.

accepted the fact that 'Culverin' could not be carried out since it was unlikely that the necessary forces could be made available'. But he was still determined to undertake some seaborne operation in south-east Asia before the end of 1944, and he therefore proposed to attack in November the island of Simalur, where an air base could be developed in support of a further advance. Although this operation required fewer forces than the Chiefs of Staff's new plans, they were still large enough to make other operations impossible, and thus to confine the main effort, as the Prime Minister intended, to the Indian Ocean. But the compromise did not commend itself to the Planners, and they informed Churchill that it could be defended only on the assumption that some operation was necessary in south-east Asia before the end of the year. The Prime Minister was not inclined at the moment seriously to defend it, and the Planners thought that in the circumstances he would be prepared to agree to the 'Middle Course'. But it was significant that while the Chiefs of Staff approached that course from the east, as a modified version of their original Pacific plan, the Prime Minister approached it from the west, as an alternative to a modified 'Culverin' which would not remove the seaborne advance entirely from the area of his choice.

By the beginning of May, there were therefore four possibilities to consider: 'Culverin', the Pacific strategy, the Middle Strategy, and the Modified Middle Strategy.[1] The operational advantages in each case had been fully discussed; the decision now seemed to rest on the relative advantages of maintenance and supply. Inquiries were by now under way into three of these problems: the respective merits of India and Australia as the main base, the implications for merchant shipping, and the requirements for a Fleet Train under the various circumstances. Before we follow the debate further, we must therefore examine the material on which its solution apparently depended, and pause to consider first the problem of selecting the main base.

We have already seen the origins of the inquiry into the facilities of India and Australia.[2] The report on India was not long delayed. There was naturally a great deal of information already available in London, which was increased by the return at this time of a special military mission that had recently been visiting the sub-continent. The Planners were therefore able to reach their conclusions without much delay.

In September 1943, India had been asked to prepare a base for the following forces:[3]

[1] See Map IX, facing p. 459.

[2] See pp. 425, 449-50, 456-7 above.

[3] See p. 148 above.

20 divisions with 5 more in transit,
154 R.A.F. squadrons,
30 shore-based naval air squadrons.

To these was now added the possibility of a major Fleet.

The value of an area as a military base depends on three factors: the accommodation and communications available to the forces, the capacity of the area either to maintain them or to handle the necessary supplies for their maintenance, and the environment, political and economic, in which the base must operate. India's advantages lay mainly in the first category. The three Services were assured at once of a nucleus of established bases and communications, and of an experienced organization upon which to expand. The navy had a dockyard at Trincomalee in Ceylon, and docks and repair facilities at Colombo and Bombay, to which it now added new facilities at Bombay and on the east coast at Calcutta, Madras and Vizagapatam. Bases for assault shipping were also set up on both the west and the east coasts, capable by March, 1944 of maintaining sixty L.S.T. and some 1,000 landing craft. By the same time, the naval air stations in southern India and Ceylon could support thirty-four squadrons. Immediate facilities, therefore, were not inadequate. As in other fields, the limitations were of the more distant future.

These assault and air forces, with a Fleet of four battleships, six cruisers, four destroyer flotillas and one submarine flotilla, could be fed and maintained for eighteen months. But there was no immediate prospect of increasing this capacity, and the Chiefs of Staff accordingly concluded that a major Fleet could not be based on India without developing the facilities serving the Indian Ocean as a whole, in East and South Africa and in the Red Sea area and Egypt. But East and South Africa were found on examination to lack the necessary resources and organization, and their use, together with that of the well-organized and powerful centres of the Middle East, demanded a larger fleet of auxiliaries than had been anticipated.

India's military capacity was less than might have been expected, for her vast body was fed by a small mouth. There were plenty of cantonments and camps either in use or available, although the facilities for jungle training were inadequate for a campaign in Burma. The difficulty lay rather in the ports. It was estimated that four divisions could be handled simultaneously, three at Bombay and one at Madras; and while this was acceptable for 'First Culverin', there was little margin for error. Nor was supply easy. Apart from ordnance, of which there were ample stocks, most of the supplies would have to be imported from Britain and America. The expansion of the army, therefore, could proceed only within the strictest limits.

The air force, unlike the other Services, was not well supplied with existing bases. But in May, 1942 it began to build new airfields to support the campaign in Burma, and by the end of 1943, 140 of these had been completed and another 150 were under construction. Depôts and camps were also being built. The limitations to the air effort, in fact, now lay, as in the case of the army and navy, not so much in construction as in supply.

For, despite real improvement over the past few years, the industrial system of India was still not geared to war. As an American technical mission discovered in 1942, many of the plants were mere jobbing shops producing a variety of articles, and many of the new orders had to be placed on a jobbing basis. Nor was a drastic reorganization possible in a sub-continent where methods and machinery were largely obsolete, where labour was largely unskilled, sometimes unreliable and normally tied to the district, and where the industralists themselves were not always in sympathy with the Administration. As it was, the Government of India had done a good deal. The Chatfield Plan of 1938, for increasing the production of military weapons and stores, and the Eastern Group Plan, which practically doubled the production of small arms' ammunition, were both completed and indeed surpassed in 1943; while the effects of the Japanese conquests were met in the same year by the completion of the Transportation Plan, whereby many factories and workshops were transferred from eastern to central and western India. By 1944, military production, based largely on an increased steel output from the great Tata works, had risen considerably: eleven times as many rifles, twenty times as many bayonets, guns and gun-carriages, four times as much small arms' ammunition and thirty-five times as much gun and mortar ammunition, were being produced as before the war. The production of clothes and medical stores had also increased greatly. But much of this output went to supply an Indian Army which had grown since September, 1939 from some 237,000 (189,000 Indians) to some 2,000,000 men—and whose size indeed, accompanied as it was by a marked decrease in quality, was causing the Prime Minister and Chiefs of Staff some anxiety—and it was in any case inadequate to meet the needs of a single major campaign. As has been seen, 'Anakim' in 1943 had been frustrated largely by the lack of material:[1] 'Culverin' and its successors demanded far more than could be met by the intervening rise in production.

The gap had to be met from Britain and America. All depended therefore on the capacity of the Indian ports and transport. But this was far from satisfactory. The ports themselves were unevenly distributed, only Karachi and Bombay enjoyed a natural harbour, and none was capable of much expansion. Although by April, 1944 Britain had supplied almost all of the original demands for equipment, the authorities in London were thus still forced to conclude that port capacity fell short of the strategic requirements.

---

[1] Pp. 137-8 above.

The fact that the best ports lay in the west, and that stores and men had therefore to be transferred to the other side of the sub-continent before they could be assembled, placed a heavy burden on sea and land transport. Coastal shipping was scarce, and, as in other fields, much had been diverted elsewhere in the early years of the war. This shortage increased the need for adequate land transport, already of serious concern. The landborne traffic of India was carried almost entirely by rail; but approximately nine-tenths of the railroad had only single track, and there was a marked shortage of locomotives and rolling stock, much of which had been sent earlier to the Middle East and had not been replaced. In April 1944, the number of locomotives in India, with an area roughly the size of Europe, was less than that possessed by the L.M.S. Company in Britain. With a recent increase of some 40 per cent in military commitments, the position was obviously grave.

Another result of the large scale of military imports was to be seen in the size of the military 'tail'. The familiar lesson of other campaigns, that the proportion of administrative and supply to fighting troops depends directly on the degree of industrialization in the base, was again found to apply. Unskilled labour was abundant, but the administration of supply and transport, the repair of equipment, and the supervision of construction demanded a large number of uniformed technicians. Despite remonstrances from the Prime Minister, and constant inquiries into the strength of the formations, the 'tail' in India remained unavoidably high at a time when manpower had to be economically employed.

The difficulties of supply were greatly aggravated by the absence of a firm strategy for south-east Asia. The airfield programme suffered severely from the varying estimates for Plans 'Drake' and 'Matterhorn',[1] and in April 1944, when American plans were imprecise, the proportion of effort to be put into the American bases was still unknown. The larger programme also suffered from competing intentions. As early as January 1944, when the original plans for Burma had miscarried, General Auchinleck had asked for a fresh directive for the India Command, and his demand was supported in March by the Joint Administrative Planners in London. Admiral Mountbatten was also worried by the current uncertainty, and pressed for an interim decision at least on the administrative future. But nothing could be done, and it was not until October, 1944 that Auchinleck received his revised directive. By that time the original programme had been largely completed, and the Americans' demands had grown.

Viewed even in a vacuum, as an isolated base, India was therefore far from satisfactory. There was no margin for error or misfortune, for the programme of expansion rested on insecure foundations. But the

[1] See p. 453 above.

base, of course, did not operate in a vacuum. It was affected by the conditions of the country in which it was placed—by its climate, its politics and its prosperity. The climate, always unfavourable to white men, but less so when quarters could be moved by the season and when troops were conditioned by long service, was a serious operational factor for a conscript army in war. Hospitals and medical equipment were a substantial item on the list of military requirements, claiming both men and material in an already tight programme, and the weather formed a serious argument in the opposition to India as a base.

More serious, however, was the state of subdued political and active economic crisis. There had been little actual unrest since the Congress leaders had been imprisoned in the autumn of 1942, few British troops were held immediately as a deterrent to civil disorder, and the disaffected Indian National Army, operating in Burma and Malaya under the Japanese, had mustered only about 30,000 men. But the atmosphere was uneasy, the attitude of labour remained in doubt, and the military authorities, uncertain both of the Government's intentions and of their reception by Congress, could not discount the possibility of further violence.

In his first despatch as Commander-in-Chief, Auchinleck stressed the obvious connexion between political unrest and economic crisis; and it was indeed from the economic state of the country that the British had most to fear. The stability of the thirties had not survived the war. The drain on resources for supply to other theatres, which could not be matched by imports, aided by the dislocation of industry, started a rise in prices, which increased rapidly with the increase in the white population and with the failure of first the rice crop and later the wheat crop in 1943. By the autumn of that year, the Government of India was seriously alarmed. In August, the Viceroy warned the Secretary of State 'in the most solemn terms that unless the appropriate help was received the Government of India could not be responsible for the continuing stability of India now, nor for her capacity to serve as a base against Japan next year'. Equipped, as the Secretary of State in turn told the War Cabinet, 'with only a veneer of developed finance' and 'a mere skeleton of administration', it was unable to impose a system of controls such as was possible in the West, and the normal apparatus of restriction—reduction in capital expenditure and increased taxation, voluntary savings and sponsored loans—only partly met the case. The Government was driven to import large quantities of gold and silver to meet the increased demand for currency. In response to urgent representations, the War Cabinet agreed to make available some four and a half million ounces of gold for the first two quarters of 1944, and the United States Government half a million ounces of gold and one hundred million ounces of silver. These measures, the second of which was not put into force for some months, temporarily pegged the rise in prices for all commodities but food. But the problem still remained of establishing more normal methods of control.

The greatest inflationary pressure sprang from the failure of the basic crops in 1943-4. 'Before the war', stated the Viceroy on one occasion, 'we had secured India against famine'. If by this he meant famine on a national scale, he was right. But a serious dislocation either of transport or of trade was enough to turn a local failure into a widespread disaster, and when such a failure occurred with the rice crop in 1943, there was a famine in Bengal which, with deaths from contingent disease, was estimated to have cost some 700,000 lives. At the beginning of 1944 rice promised well—indeed there was a bumper crop—but wheat had now failed disastrously, and as the harvest came to an end it appeared that the normal civil requirements would be short by some 800,000 tons. To this had to be added 724,000 tons required by the military. The total deficit was thus some 1,524,000 tons. Some 1,040,000 tons—gained from estimated surpluses in some areas, by reducing the civil ration by two ounces a head a month, and by using barley grains and millet where possible in place of wheat—could be set against this figure, leaving a final deficit of 484,000 tons. A long and unprofitable correspondence arose on the subject of the gap. As early as 4th August, 1943, the Secretary of State for India asked the War Cabinet to ship 500,000 tons of wheat to India between September and the following February. The War Cabinet, in reply, agreed to make preliminary arrangements for the despatch of 50,000 tons of wheat from Australia, and of up to 100,000 tons of barley from Iran. But this plan suffered, on examination, from an apparent lack of shipping, and over the next four months a series of proposals emerged for making the best use of the available transport. By the third week in February 1944, it seemed that 50,000 tons of wheat could be shipped from Australia; but meanwhile the Viceroy and the Commander-in-Chief, India continued to stress the danger of chaos if larger supplies were not provided soon, and the Viceroy urged an approach to the Americans and if necessary to U.N.R.R.A. The War Cabinet did not approve these proposals, and in March Auchinleck and Mountbatten therefore decided to cut their military imports by 10 per cent in favour of food. This gesture impressed the British Government, and enabled the Chiefs of Staff to allocate twenty-five ships, with capacity for 200,000 tons of wheat, to the Australian run before the end of June, 1944. The War Cabinet then urged the Viceroy further to reduce the gap by exchanging 150,000 tons of his surplus rice for the same amount of wheat from Ceylon; but Wavell, mindful of the tension which already existed, refused to allow rice to leave the country until confidence had been restored. The War Cabinet was thus still faced by a deficit of at least 250,000 tons. At this point there was a chance disaster. On 14th April an ammunition ship exploded in Bombay harbour, sinking eleven other ships, damaging more, and causing the loss of 36,500 tons of grain. This misfortune compelled the British Government at last to appeal to the United States. A committee of the War Cabinet was formed to draft an appropriate telegram to the President in the Prime Minister's name, and this was sent, with the approval of the parent body, on 29th April. After explaining the situation, it concluded:[1]

> 'I have had much hesitation in asking you to add to the great assistance you are giving us in shipping but a satisfactory situation in India is of such vital importance to the success of our joint plans against the Japanese that I am impelled to ask you to consider a special allocation of ships to carry wheat to India from Australia without reducing the assistance you are now providing for us, who are at a positive minimum if war efficiency is to be maintained. We have the wheat (in Australia) but we lack the ships. I have resisted for some time the Viceroy's request that I should ask you for your help, but I believe that, with this recent misfortune to the wheat harvest and in the light of Mountbatten's representations, I am no longer justified in not asking for your help . . .'

The President replied on 1st June.

> 'Upon receipt of your telegram,' he stated, 'I immediately directed that the matter be taken under urgent consideration by the appropriate authorities of this Government. The appeal has my utmost sympathy and you may be sure that there is full realisation of the military, political and humanitarian factors involved. The American Joint Chiefs of Staff have reported, however, that they are unable on military grounds to consent to the diversion of shipping necessary to meet the request because of the adverse effect such a diversion would have upon military operations already undertaken or in prospect. Needless to say, I regret exceedingly the necessity of giving you this unfavourable reply.'[2]

Faced with this decision, the War Cabinet could only suggest that Wavell confer again with Auchinleck and Mountbatten. But the Chiefs of Staff were now seriously alarmed at the possible consequences of delay, and sought to hasten a decision. Convinced that the shipment of food to India must be regarded as a military commitment, they re-examined the shipping position in the course of June. As a result, they

---

[1] See Appendix X below for the complete text.

[2] It should be noted that the American shipping demanded in this instance was additional to American shipping already provided for the Australian-Indian run, as part of the general aid in shipping to the British (see pp. 27-8 above); and that the Australian-Indian run was, by agreement reached in 1943, a British commitment.

made cuts in other programmes allowing vessels to be diverted to the Australian passage for shipment of 200,000 tons of wheat to India in the third quarter of 1944. This was soon approved, and the India Office and the Ministry of War Transport set to work immediately. But the decision was too little and too late, India's immediate needs were too pressing, and in August, 1944 the Chiefs of Staff and the War Cabinet were again seeking for a more rapid means to deliver supplies. By the end of the month, moreover, a fresh difficulty had arisen, for the Australians were now reluctant to part with so much wheat at least until mid-November, in view of a recent spell of bad weather which was endangering the crop. Welcome shipments were eventually made to India in December 1944, and the provision of a further 70,000 tons a month was approved for the first four months of 1945. A greater domestic use of ground nuts, usually exported, also helped to ease the position. But an apparent shipping shortage again emerged, and the familiar series of complaints and evasions continued throughout the following year and into 1946. The disaster of complete famine, such as had overtaken Bengal in 1943, was narrowly averted; but a long period of semi-famine followed which threatened the stability of the country and the maintenance of a large British base. These did not seem to be the conditions in which to mount the main British effort against Japan. The history of the wheat crisis amply confirmed the Chiefs of Staff in the fear, which they expressed in March 1944, that 'India is subject to local catastrophes, such as famines and floods, liable to upset plans which have very little administrative margin.'

Their conclusion was therefore as follows:

> 'By the spring of 1945 India (supported by the Middle East) could undertake the following commitments in addition to meeting her internal needs:
>
> (i) operations in Burma
> (ii) the Hump lift to China
> (iii) Plan 'Drake' [bombing from China]
> (iv) Plan 'Culverin'
>
> That is the maximum capacity of the Indian base upon which we could rely.'

In the same report, the Chiefs of Staff drew some general and tentative comparisons with Australia.

> ' . . . (a) The problem of labour, and particularly of skilled labour, presents difficulties in both countries, but a potential shortage of labour probably makes it a worse problem in Australia.
>
> (b) Australia has considerable advantages of climate over India.
>
> (c) The fact that Australia is a Dominion with a white

population and that she is already organised for war, offer obvious advantages over an oriental country which is inherently slow to co-operate.'

These comparisons, however, were only provisional. For it proved impossible to present the Australian case at the same time as that of India. Australia had not been considered by the British as a major base since 1920-2, during the initial investigations into Singapore, and there was therefore little relevant information in London. Where figures were available, as in the case of the navy, they were by now largely out of date; for the continent had been placed in the American sphere in 1942, and many unknown developments had since taken place. The army and the air, with fewer pre-war connexions, knew even less than the navy. The Chiefs of Staff therefore continued to press for a mission to be sent to Australia, and indeed while the inquiry into the facts was proceeding in London the Admiralty was preparing for a small party to proceed to the south-west Pacific by way of America. The Prime Minister's decision at the end of March to delay the despatch of the mission,[1] was followed in April by two reports from the Chiefs of Staff's administrative advisers, which confirmed the necessity of such a step; the naval party, after consultations in the United States, had reached the south-west Pacific and was awaiting permission to enter Australia; and on 20th April, almost four months after the subject had first been raised, the Prime Minister informed the Australians that it would soon reach them, to be followed probably by a full mission of the three Services. The Australians still preferred, as they had from the start, to be responsible for the investigation; and the Chiefs of Staff therefore arranged to place their representatives under the supervision of the Australian Chiefs of Staff, on whose authority the full report was eventually made to the Australian Government. At the end of May, the larger mission left for the Pacific. But its investigations took some time; the final report was issued only in August, 1944; and meanwhile the discussion in London had to proceed on the basis of intermittent and provisional reports.

As a base, Australia in some ways could be contrasted with India. With only recent experience of large military forces, and only moderate facilities for their reception and accommodation, it did not appear immediately attractive; but the state of the country and the attitude of the population provided a healthier basis on which to construct a policy, and a more hopeful future, than could be offered by the discontent and famine of Asia.

The 'Middle Strategy' demanded that the following forces should be based on Australia, assuming that Germany was defeated by 1st October, 1944:

[1] See p. 457 above.

	Autumn 1944 (Phase I)	1*st January*, 1945 (Phase II)	1*st July*, 1945 (Phase III)
Navy.	2–3 Battleships	2 Battleships	4 Battleships
	2–3 Fleet Carriers	4 Fleet Carriers	10 Fleet and Light Fleet Carriers
		14 Escort Carriers	18 Escort Carriers
	10 Cruisers	10 Cruisers	12 Cruisers
	24 Destroyers	24 Destroyers	60 Destroyers
	12 Submarines	24 Submarines	46 Submarines
		60 A/S Escorts	100 A/S Escorts
		60 Minesweepers	100 Minesweepers
	43 Auxiliaries	62 Auxiliaries	115 Auxiliaries
	150 Carrier-borne aircraft	520 Carrier-borne aircraft	1000 Carrier-borne aircraft
	15 Shore-based aircraft	160 Shore-based aircraft	300 Shore-based aircraft
			200–300 Coastal craft

In 1945, *after the defeat of Germany* (Phase IV)

119 Landing Ships (88 L.S.T.)
310 Major Landing craft
1,100 Minor „ „
16 Amphibious Auxiliaries
38 Auxiliaries (34 small Tankers)

	October 1944	*January-February*, 1945	*May-June*, 1945
Army.	1 British Division	3 British Divisions	5 British Divisions
		1 British Armoured or Tank Brigade	2 British Armoured or Tank Brigades
		2 British Commandos	4 British Commandos
	British Base Troops	British Base Troops	British Base Troops
	6 Australian Divisions	6 Australian Divisions	6 Australian Divisions
	1 New Zealand Division	1 New Zealand Division	1 New Zealand Division

	1944	*End of* 1945
Air Force.	52 R.A.A.F. Squadrons	63 R.A.A.F. Squadrons (11 from Europe)
	16 R.N.Z.A.F. Squadrons	16 R.N.Z.A.F. Squadrons
		78 R.A.F. Squadrons

If the original Middle Strategy were adopted, these forces would have to operate from an advanced base in the north or north-west of Australia. The most likely place seemed to be Darwin, which possessed the best anchorage on the coast and had been developed as a defensive outpost since 1942. But although the harbour, after improvements, could accommodate the Fleet and its merchant auxiliaries, it seemed most unlikely that facilities could be provided ashore for a main base or reception point. Nor indeed could they be provided anywhere in the north or west of the country. Industry and administration were concentrated in the south and east; it was there alone that the towns and docks, the communications and the organization, were to be found for the forces required. The navy accordingly decided to base its effort on Sydney, with minor bases at Adelaide and Melbourne, Fremantle, Brisbane and Cairns. The army planned to disembark its troops at Perth and Fremantle in the west, to train them in the east, and to base them in the area Brisbane–Newcastle–Sydney. The air force intended to set up its reception points and its main bases in the south and east at Adelaide, Melbourne, Sydney, Brisbane and Townsville.

The navy had at its disposal the facilities of the small Australian Fleet. The total number of docks (including one graving dock for capital ships completing at Sydney) was slightly less than that of South Africa and India combined. Of the main ports, Brisbane and Newcastle had no proper anchorage, and Melbourne only limited space. Sydney was the obvious main base, with a splendid harbour and with labour and machinery to refit ships up to a large cruiser. The other ports could cope with a few smaller vessels, and Darwin with landing-craft. Food, fuel, ordnance and naval stores were available at the larger dockyards. There were naval airfields near Sydney and Brisbane, although none had extensive buildings or facilities for repair.

The facilities for the land and air forces seemed likely to be more adequate, provided that existing American installations could be transferred to British use. There were quite good depôts for the army at Brisbane, Newcastle and Sydney, and a smaller depôt at Darwin; and in general the organization provided a reasonable nucleus for expansion. In one respect alone it was entirely inadequate: the existing transport could not hope to handle the increased traffic.

In the spring of 1944, there was an air force of seventy-six squadrons in Australia, or eight more squadrons than appeared in the first stage of the British plan. Twenty-one were American, and would presumably be withdrawn if that plan came into effect. The existing facilities were thus adequate for the immediate future, but would need to be enlarged to meet the later demands.

Each Service, therefore, had sooner or later to enlarge its bases. Allowing for a major Fleet in the Pacific, the navy planned to send out nine floating docks (one for a capital ship) and to build three more in

Australia; to build enough victualling and store sheds, and ammunition, tool and repair shops, to maintain the Fleet with a reserve of 180 days; and to increase the number of airfields in the east and south. The army planned to maintain a reserve of sixty days for formations actively engaged, a working reserve of stores of 120 days, and a fuel reserve of ninety days for all forces in the theatre. New engineers' and transport stores and workshops, victualling, fuel and ordnance stores, training camps and hospitals, would have to be built. The air force, already well supplied with airfields, planned to increase accommodation and repair and store space.

The demands of the three Services came to an impressive total in men and material. The British mission estimated that new construction would need a labour force of 13,500 in October 1944, rising to 21,000 in November, to 25,000 in December, and to a peak of 26,000 in February, 1945. The navy would need another 20,000 men and the army some 82,000 for skilled repairs, base operations, transport and administration, while the air force would want an unknown, but lesser, number.

The Australian contribution to this effort was still unknown in August, 1944. The navy wanted some 4,000 Australians for repair work, and some 5,000 for the administration of supply; the army and the air force were less precise, but the former hoped for at least 3,000 engineers from the Australian army. All Services reckoned on a substantial amount of labour and stores being withdrawn by mid-September from American use. But while the Australian Government undertook to help as far as possible, the exact extent of that help could not yet be determined. Meanwhile the British were warned that, at least in the early stages of the programme, they must be prepared to supply 'a very considerable proportion of the total requirements' for both men and material.

Assuming that both could be sent in time, success still depended on two other factors: on transport, and on Australia's ability to absorb the influx of British labour and fighting men into an already strained economy. The ports themselves were capable of handling the estimated increase in traffic, apart from Darwin which would need to be enlarged; but the transport from the ports was already under pressure. The main burden would fall on the railways, which by 1944 had not much capacity to spare, and it seemed unlikely that much could be done in time to meet the first influx from abroad. The necessary material could not be imported, the attitude of organized labour made the importation of British railway staff unlikely, and a growing national shortage of coal was likely to affect even the existing traffic. The Australian Chiefs of Staff were therefore forced to conclude that only a small increase in capacity could be expected by the middle of 1945.

They therefore turned to coastal shipping. But the gap here involved between 50,000 and 100,000 tons, much of which, with a world shortage of shipping, might have to be built in Australia itself. Such a programme could not readily be absorbed in the time.

This was indeed only one of the effects which the programme would have on the Australian economy. The country's inability to provide the necessary labour merely shifted the burden elsewhere. The Australian Chiefs of Staff estimated that some 675,000 British men and women would arrive in the country by the end of 1945. Their maintenance was clearly a major problem for a nation with strictly limited resources, whose economy was already geared to a definite and carefully balanced programme. Out of a population of seven million Australians, 678,000 were already in the armed forces, or one out of every two men between the ages of eighteen and forty. This accounted for 26 per cent of the total male labour force of the country, and a further 14 per cent was engaged on the production of munitions, aircraft, and other equipment and construction for war. The total available for normal production and distribution was thus 60 per cent of the country's male labour. Employment of women, in war production and normal work, had accordingly increased by 26 per cent since 1939. Under these conditions, Australia was required to sustain her own effort, to supply the American forces in the South-West Pacific Area, numbering some 380,000 men, with 90 per cent of their needs, and to export food to Britain, America and India. She was in fact producing food for twelve million people in 1944. Her economy was strained to the limits, and the Government, with MacArthur's agreement, had already decided to release 20,000 men from the army and 20,000 munition and aircraft workers by June 1944, to increase normal production. This had political effects, for the Australian Government was nervous lest the reduction in fighting strength might affect its standing at the peace table; and in October, 1943 Mr. Curtin had unavailingly asked the British Government for a statement of its views on the future balance of the Australian war effort. The advent of some 675,000 men and women—almost one-tenth of Australia's total population—thus raised serious problems if their needs were not to be met entirely from overseas, with the obvious consequences for shipping. When Mr. Curtin visited London in May 1944, he was obliged to state that the eventual size of the Australian forces awaited a statement from Britain, and that the size of a British force in Australia must in turn depend on that contribution.

The Australian Chiefs of Staff therefore finally recommended that the Departments concerned should at once examine the British requests, and that the British Government should meanwhile be informed that it must give a decision by the middle of September if the timetable[1] were to be realized even with substantial British help.

[1] See p. 471 above.

These conclusions were not available until August, 1944. Meanwhile, the authorities in London had to rely on provisional reports from their mission.

The comparison between India and Australia had of course to include an analysis of the implications for shipping, and the study for which the Prime Minister had called in March was now under way.[1] The report, produced by the Joint Administrative Planners in consultation with the Ministry of War Transport, appeared on 25th April. Its conclusion occasioned some surprise.

> 'Our examination shows that there is little difference between the needs of the two strategies except for tankers, the requirements of which, although more than double in the case of the Pacific, are estimated to be within our resources.
>
> We conclude, therefore, that a decision on the adoption of either strategy need not be governed by considerations of shipping.'

This statement was based on three assumptions, the third of which at least was controversial: first, that cargo ships and tankers from Europe and America would proceed to Australia by way of the Panama Canal; second, as in all such studies, that Germany would be defeated by October, 1944; and third, that the forces to be deployed in the south-west Pacific would be considerably smaller than those in the Bay of Bengal, thus offsetting the greater distance involved. It soon came under severe Ministerial fire. The Ministry of War Transport, despite the help which it was alleged to have given in the preparation of the figures, questioned the basic assumption that smaller forces would be engaged in the south-west Pacific than in the Bay of Bengal, and remarked that in any case the plans for the Middle Strategy were still too nebulous to support serious calculations. A more severe attack was made by Lord Cherwell, the Paymaster-General, who conducted special statistical inquiries for the Prime Minister. He argued that the report was inaccurate, in that it averaged the figures up or down according to the case, and withheld the detailed statistics for its conclusion on cargo shipping; incomplete, in that it neglected the shipping implications of building the base in Australia; and unrealistic, in that it underestimated the British shortage of tankers. 'The brute fact remains,' he concluded, 'that if a given number of men have to be carried to Australia rather than to India, and if, as is admitted, the round voyage to Australia is two thirds longer than the round voyage to India, then the shipping cost must be greater; and no statistical calculations or assumptions can alter the fact.'

---

[1] See pp. 449-50 above.

The departmental squabble has been recounted because it was in fact the sole result of the investigation. For there seems to have been no further discussion after this brief exchange. Cherwell advised the Prime Minister that no decision could be reached on the basis of the report, and Churchill thereupon ordered it to be circulated to Ministers with the accompanying comments. But no further debate occurred, and it was not until much later, when the war with Germany was approaching its end, that the question of shipping reappeared in an altered context. The main debate was indeed already passing into different channels, where its fate could be settled without recourse to this particular problem. The controversy, however, was not entirely without result. It strengthened the Prime Minister's suspicion of the figures for the Far East produced by the military, and his dislike of a strategy—such as the Modified Middle Strategy—which in any way favoured a longer sea passage.

Closely related to the main shipping problem was that of the Fleet Train. This did not spring from the current controversy, for a Train was in fact necessary under either of the Middle Strategies. But it was soon concerned in the main discussion, for the nature of the Train affected the nature of the facilities to be provided ashore, and raised the familiar questions of supply and maintenance which it was designed partly to solve.

The object of a Fleet Train, as defined by the First Sea Lord, was 'to provide mobile ship-borne facilities for the maintenance, repair and supply of our naval forces, including aircraft, assault shipping and landing-craft, in areas where shore-based facilities are absent or inadequate.' Such facilities were clearly needed in the Far East, with its great distances, its lack of Allied bases, and the possibility of severe destruction when enemy bases were captured; and their provision had indeed been envisaged as long ago as 1923-4, during the investigations into Singapore. The subject was first raised, in the new conditions, at the Quebec Conference in August 1943, and the first estimates soon followed. Assuming that few of the vessels would be needed before the end of the war in Europe, they allowed for some 800,000 tons of merchant shipping. But with the proposal of new plans at Cairo the two navies examined the problem afresh, and the British part of the report appeared as a memorandum from the Admiralty early in February, 1944. In all, the Admiralty asked for 134 merchant ships for the Fleet Train, of about 1½ million gross tons. Nine ships were needed in the Indian Ocean before, and thirty after, the defeat of Germany: in the Pacific, four ships were needed before the defeat of Germany, and ninety-one thereafter.

It was estimated that twenty of these ships could be provided in due course. There seemed to be three possible sources of supply for the rest. The first lay in the United States. But Admiral King could offer only five large vessels, to be subtracted from the merchant tonnage already allocated to Britain for 1944, and it was unlikely that his offer would be increased. Secondly, the Admiralty might be able to provide largely for its own needs, for in March, 1944 it disposed directly of 560 merchant ships, amounting to some 2¼ million gross tons. The proposal, however, revealed the complexities of shipping figures, and the 560 vessels soon shrank, in the Admiralty's reply, to a handful. Many were on operational service, some were colliers or tankers, and there were problems in the conversion or refitting of many others which placed a considerable strain on the already burdened shipyards. The Admiralty therefore wished to draw on the third possible source of supply, the general pool of merchant shipping, particularly in view of the net increase in production over the past eighteen months. This proposal again raised a host of difficulties. For if more merchant ships were available, there were more demands upon them. Many were needed to support the approaching operations in Europe, with a consequent growth in the demands on the shipyards; others would be needed for trade after Germany was defeated; others again, perhaps, for the relief of Europe. The Admiralty's demands were therefore subjected to scrutiny by the Defence Committee (Supply).

This scrutiny was the more severe because, perhaps unavoidably, the naval demands continued to rise throughout the spring. The first estimate from the Admiralty, which appeared in January 1944, had been for eighty merchant ships totalling 590,000 tons, which itself had surprised and alarmed the Prime Minister. But this soon rose to 134 ships, and towards the end of March to 158. Against these demands, the Minister of War Transport had earlier allotted ten new cargo ships of 10,000 tons each, and he now agreed to provide a further ten such vessels as well as a number of smaller ships amounting to some 33,000 tons. With the five heavy ships from America, the navy thus received some 293,000 tons for the Fleet Train, all of which would become available in the course of 1944. Ministers now thought that no further concession could be made without appropriate compensation. For every ton of ocean-going shipping converted for the Fleet Train, the Admiralty should release a ton of the ocean-going shipping which it could not use in the Far East. Thus the needs of both trade and Train would be met in the most economical way. Early in April 1944, the Defence Committee invited the two Departments to produce an acceptable formula; but the Ministers could not agree, and the Prime Minister was obliged to decide between them. On 9th April, he issued a Minute which defined the limits of the Fleet Train within the wider programme.

> 'The Fleet Train is limited by the need of getting an absolute irreducible minimum of 24 million tons of imports this year and next. All Naval and Military requirements must be subordinated

to this decisive rule, without which the life and the war effort of Britain cannot be maintained. In working out your Fleet Train you must observe these requirements.

2. The Fleet which you could operate in the Indian Ocean or in the South-West Pacific, whether north or south of Australia, must be limited by the Fleet Train. It is not a question of making the Fleet Train up to your ideas of the Fleet. However a searching and austere examination of naval requirements will probably give you a good deal of margin. For instance, why should sailors have a great quantity of accommodation—ships as well as hospital ships when soldiers might be content with only the latter?

3. The priorities are as follows:

(a) 24 million tons of imports this year and next
(b) The Fleet Train permissible on this basis
(c) The fighting Fleet that can be carried by the said Fleet Train.

4. It follows from the above that the great concession made to the Navy, by allowing them to have 230,000 tons of brand-new merchant shipping available in about a year, must be made good by ton for ton replacements in ocean-going tonnage to the Ministry of War Transport, which in principle must be simultaneous. In practice, a little latitude may be given for individual ships, and any tonnage turned over by the Navy beforehand will give them something to veer and haul on. Please take this as a decision; but ask me if there are any points about it which are not clear.'

The provisions of this ruling were not kept, and indeed had to be invoked again early in 1945; but it was a significant step in the formulation of policy, for a direct relation was now established between the size of the Fleet and the nature of its facilities ashore, through the limits set for its facilities afloat.

(ii)

The Middle Strategy Discussed

Throughout the summer of 1944, therefore, the facts of the controversy were scarcely better known than in the spring. The exact scale of British assistance to Australia, and the precise implications for shipping, were still uncertain, and only the size of the Fleet Train had been determined in principle. The debate had nevertheless to proceed, and on a wider stage than before. For in May, 1944 there took place in London the Conference of Prime Ministers and representatives of the Commonwealth which has already been mentioned,[1] and this was

[1] See p. 332 above.

followed in June by the visit from the American Chiefs of Staff.[1] The British authorities, therefore, in the absence of much detailed information, had to try to reach an agreement between themselves which would serve as a basis for discussion with two different but equally interested groups of associates.

The war against Japan was first discussed at the Prime Ministers' Conference at two meetings on 3rd May. It was clear that little progress could be made until the Australians and New Zealanders had been relieved of their uncertainty over the future balance of their war efforts, and the subject was accordingly referred for examination to the Minister of Production with Mr. Curtin and Mr. Fraser, and to the Chiefs of Staff with General Blamey of Australia and Lieut.-General Puttick of New Zealand. The results were heard at a meeting with the Australians at Chequers on 21st May. Allowing for the continued export of food to Britain on the scale already agreed, and for the export of grain to India, the Australians then announced that they had undertaken if required to maintain the Australian navy at its existing strength plus construction already approved, to field an army of six divisions, and to attain an air force of fifty-three squadrons by December, 1944. The British Government promised to help the programme by returning to Australia as soon as possible the Australian ships, men and aircraft that had been sent to Europe. At the same time, the New Zealanders, whose economy was also severely strained by the provision of food and material for Britain and America, proposed to maintain their existing naval forces and their air force of twenty squadrons, and to regroup their land forces, after releasing 11,000 men for the further production of food, so as to provide one division in the Pacific in 1945.

These welcome commitments enabled the Chiefs of Staff to plan with more precision. The first calculations for the attack on Amboina had budgeted unconvincingly for the land and air forces, and a more recent examination, with a target date for the defeat of Germany of December 1944, had shown that the necessary aircraft from Europe were unlikely to be available for operations before the middle of May 1945, and the troops before the middle of August. But the Australians estimated that they could transfer three infantry divisions then resting after operations in New Guinea, and could provide the necessary air contingent, by October, 1944. This left only the assault shipping still to be found, for which American help would be required.

With this stimulus, the plans themselves advanced. General Blamey had brought with him more recent news of the Americans' intentions than was available in London; and the Chiefs of Staff now learned that after the conquest of New Guinea, MacArthur intended to occupy the island of Halmahera to the north-west, so as to secure the Malacca Passage and protect the direct route to the Philippines. The assault

[1] See p. 268 above.

would probably be staged in the late summer or autumn; if so it would clearly assist, and might even be assisted by, the Commonwealth operations from north-west Australia, which would then rest directly on the flank of the Americans' advance. The Chiefs of Staff therefore returned to the initial Middle Strategy, particularly as the modified version had not been well received either by the Australians or by Churchill. For Blamey preferred to base the advance on northern and western Australia, while the Prime Minister refused to countenance a policy which might involve a longer sea passage from England, 'either on my own behalf or on that of the War Cabinet'. On 23rd May, the Chiefs of Staff accordingly submitted to Mr. Churchill a revised edition of the Middle Strategy, with Amboina as the target, with Commonwealth land and air forces and a small British Fleet operating from northern Australia, and with the main fleet base in the east.

> 'During recent discussions with you about the war against Japan we have gained the impression that a "middle" strategy to some extent attracted you. We have, therefore, believing as we do that it is highly important to take a firm decision at the earliest possible date, re-examined the whole question. . . . We propose a course of action which we commend to you as offering the following advantages:
>
> (a) It provides an important and timely naval contribution as early as the autumn of 1944.
>
> (b) It provides for important operations by Dominion land and air forces this year also.
>
> (c) It provides for the use of advance operational bases on the north and west coast of Australia. It is true that the facilities of the ports of the east coast of Australia will still be required for major repairs, but it does not involve a procession of troopships and supply ships around the long coast of Australia which you envisaged and to which you took such strong objection.
>
> (d) It provides for the use at a later stage of substantial British land and air forces, in addition to the fleet, in important operations directly related to the main campaign for the defeat of Japan.
>
> (e) It provides for a substantial Imperial and Dominion contribution by forces under the command of their own British commanders, though subordinate to an American Supreme Commander receiving his directions from the Combined Chiefs of Staff.
>
> (f) It provides for flexibility in the use of the main British forces when they arrive, so that they may either be directed northwards in conjunction with the main operations against Japan, or westwards in the reoccupation of British and Dutch possessions now in Japanese hands.'

They then specified the forces likely to be available in Australia by October, 1944: three battleships, three fleet aircraft carriers, ten cruisers (with another four Australian and New Zealand cruisers in the South-West Pacific Area) and twenty-eight destroyers; three Australian divisions; and some sixty-eight Dominion, and three British, squadrons of aircraft.

The later stages of the advance were left vague.

> 'We cannot, at this stage, define the actual operations which the British forces should undertake during [the second] phase. With the foundations laid by the operations of our naval forces and Dominion land and air forces during the first phase, and by the preparations which could, by then, be made in Australia, we will be placed in a position in which our strategy will be flexible. Our forces may then be directed either northwards, leaving the Japanese in the south to wither, while we advance on the left flank of the Americans; or, alternatively, westwards in operations for the recapture of Borneo, the Celebes, or the Portuguese and Dutch islands in the Malay Barrier. . . .'

One feature of this paper figured more prominently than before. A reference to the problem of command will have been noticed in its preamble. This was developed more fully in the body of the report itself.

> 'At present General MacArthur as Supreme Allied Commander in the South-West Pacific Area, takes his instructions from the United States Joint Chiefs of Staff, and the British Chiefs of Staff have no say in the choice of his operations. Since it is one of our objects to ensure that the British Empire plays the greatest possible effective part in the operations for the defeat of Japan, we feel it is only right that the Command arrangements should be altered and that the South-West Pacific Area should become a theatre of joint responsibility, subordinate to the Combined Chiefs of Staff, so that we may share in the control of operations in that theatre. Recognising that the American contribution during the first phase will predominate, we suggest that we should be willing to accept General MacArthur as Supreme Commander over the Allied Forces, but that the British and Dominion forces should operate as a distinct Command with British Commanders under General MacArthur's supreme direction. We feel, however, that even this arrangement should be left open to reconsideration at a later date.'

This was by no means a new argument. Since the allocation of spheres of responsibility in 1942, the Pacific had become in fact if not in theory an exclusively American command on which the Combined Chiefs of Staff were not consulted. The 'general jurisdiction over grand strategic policy', of which they theoretically disposed,[1] was virtually meaningless when the operations were not related to operations elsewhere, and when their only connexion with world strategy was through material which the United States was alone able to supply. But the

[1] See p. 19 above.

problem naturally changed with the possible advent of British forces, and the accepted Allied formula, that command followed preponderance of numbers, was at once invoked. The British Chiefs of Staff had indeed considered the question at the very beginning of the debate. On 13th January, 1944, when they first explained their views to the Prime Minister,[1] they had suggested 'for your private ear alone' that the provision of strong British and Dominion forces in the south-west Pacific might be followed by 'an additional British area of command'; and thereafter they often returned to the point. It was indeed a natural argument for the proponents of a Pacific strategy, offering military and diplomatic attractions equal to those in south-east Asia, and the prospect of a more equal collaboration with the Americans in the formulation of strategy in the Far East. It also supported, paradoxically enough, the argument for the unity of command in the Pacific which the Chiefs of Staff were concerned to stress at the time. For if the two main lines of advance could be regarded as complementary, with the eventual sequel of a single American Command, there was a good case for a separate Command for the operations on the flank, particularly if they diverged from the main advance in the direction of Borneo and the Netherlands East Indies.

Whatever the merits of the case, the difficulties were obvious enough. As the Prime Minister remarked in March, when the argument was first seriously pursued, what was supposed to happen to General MacArthur, confronted by this new commander with powers uncomfortably vague? The Chiefs of Staff thereupon distinguished between the early stage before the defeat of Germany, when comparatively small British and Dominion forces would operate under an American Supreme Commander, and the later stage when a single Pacific Command, concentrated on the assault of Japan, might be accompanied by a reinforced British or Commonwealth Command in the south-west. In both stages, however, the Combined Chiefs of Staff would replace the Joint Chiefs of Staff as the authority responsible for operational policy.

As the Commonwealth talks proceeded, the issue became of practical importance. The idea of a British or Commonwealth Command attracted the Australian military authorities, particularly as the future of their troops was by no means clear if the campaign developed an increasingly American character. The British Chiefs of Staff therefore felt free to suggest the formula which appeared in their report. But questions of command are always delicate, and it was not surprising that the Prime Ministers stressed the need for deliberation. Mr. Churchill, who appears to have had in mind a possible revision of boundaries rather than of organization, as in other fields deprecated a hasty decision; while Mr. Curtin, who had himself suggested a revised

[1] See p. 426 above.

arrangement some months before as an inducement to the British to enter the south-west Pacific,[1] was not ready to pronounce on its detail and was in any case now well satisfied with the existing dispensation. While continuing to welcome the prospect of British forces in the area, he was clearly worried by the possible repercussions of the Chiefs of Staff's suggestion; but the latter decided nevertheless to raise the subject with the Joint Chiefs of Staff, as an integral part of the unofficial talks on the Far East which were soon to be held in London.

The Americans' visit to England had been arranged to consider the future of European operations, and they had declared in advance that they would not be prepared to hold official discussions on the war against Japan. But in view of the British anxiety they agreed to a series of informal conversations, and these took place on 10th, 11th and 14th June. The Americans saw two objections to the proposed British strategy for the south-west Pacific. First, their own operations were advancing so fast that a British contribution might not be required. The timetable was now:[2]

15th June, 1944:	Occupation of the Marianas.
15th September, 1944:	Occupation of the Palaus.
15th November, 1944:	Occupation of Mindanao.
15th February, 1945:	Occupation of Formosa, or failing that of Luzon followed by Formosa.

But this accelerated programme was itself being overtaken, for in the past few weeks the Joint Chiefs of Staff had come to consider the possibility of going straight for Formosa, leaving the Palaus and the Philippines to be cleared up later, or even for Kiushu itself. No British contribution could affect plans of this nature, unless they suffered a severe reverse. By the time that the Australians were in Amboina, the Americans from the central Pacific might be in Formosa or at least in Luzon. MacArthur's programme was now also more optimistic than when Blamey had left for London, and it seemed likely that he would be well beyond Halmahera before the Australians could begin to move. Operations from north-west Australia would thus contribute little to his advance, and the Chiefs of Staff were driven to reconsider the possibility of the Modified Middle Strategy, proceeding round the north of New Guinea through an area already captured by the Americans. But the distinction was of greater interest to the British than to the Americans, who considered—not without reason—that any advance which had still to begin could scarcely be of much use to themselves. They therefore advised their allies to abandon the prospect of joining MacArthur to the north, and instead to regard the capture of Borneo as a prelude to the clearance of the Netherlands East Indies. This would serve a useful purpose, and the operations

---

[1] See pp. 439-40 above.

[2] See Map IX, facing p. 459.

could moreover be undertaken from the Indian Ocean without having to shift the main effort to a new theatre. Ceylon might then replace Darwin as the base, and Sourabaya on the island of Java might be substituted for Amboina as an immediate target.

Secondly, the Americans were seriously perturbed by the growing weight of the Japanese attacks in China, which seemed possibly to presage a retreat to the mainland of Asia if all were lost elsewhere. As always, they considered it essential to keep China in the war, and it was indeed partly for this reason that they were considering the early capture of Formosa. In the meantime, they looked to the South-East Asia Command to provide immediate assistance. The measures which they proposed for this purpose are examined elsewhere, and naturally concentrated on northern Burma rather than on attacks to the south. But since the British seemed determined to deploy an assault force somewhere in the Far East, they preferred that it should be used in operations from the Indian Ocean towards the South China Sea, rather than that it should cause a diversion of strength from south-east Asia to the south-west Pacific. The means by which such operations were to be achieved were not their concern, and the British remarks on the difficulties of supply seem to have met with little response. With their eyes already on Japan, and on the Japanese threat to China, the Joint Chiefs of Staff seem indeed to have found it difficult to appreciate their hosts' acute interest in a campaign which involved comparatively small forces, and which could be regarded only as an indirect contribution to a war that was being decided elsewhere.

The British Chiefs of Staff therefore agreed with some reluctance to re-examine the Indian Ocean strategy, with an immediate target of Sourabaya as a prelude to an attack on Borneo. As they had anticipated, the prospect was unattractive. If North Borneo was to be attacked in the late summer of 1945, Sourabaya, which lay at the heart of the local Japanese defences, must be captured in the winter of 1944. The forces required would be greater than those for the capture of Amboina, while the date of the operation was advanced. The Chiefs of Staff therefore preferred their previous plan, to form a Commonwealth task force under MacArthur's supreme command for operations 'of which the general object would be:

(a) To secure oil installations and air bases in North Borneo.
(b) To co-operate on the left flank of General MacArthur's advance.'

The Joint Chiefs of Staff left England on 16th and 17th June. Their visit, although brief and inconclusive so far as the Far East was concerned, had in fact marked the turning-point in the long British debate. By the middle of June, an agreement on the Middle Strategy seemed by no means out of the question. The Australians and New Zealanders, who would be most directly affected, were disposed in its favour; the

British Chiefs of Staff, while claiming it only as a second best, supported it as the only solution to the deadlock; and Ministers, who in February and March had unanimously opposed the full Pacific strategy, were less critical of its successor. Despite the disadvantages and burdens of a major transfer of resources, they were now in general prepared to adopt the middle course in default of an apparently impossible 'Culverin', and the Foreign Office accepted it as a reasonable substitute for the reconquest of Malaya. The Prime Minister himself, apparently reconciled to the loss of 'Culverin', seemed by an unwonted silence at least to acquiesce in the trend of events. Apart from remarking that the Commonwealth authorities should be fully informed of his views, he did not object to the matter of the discussions in May, or to the Chiefs of Staff's deductions. But by the end of June the picture had changed. The Americans had remarked at once the weakest point of the Middle Strategy, the constant and wishful assumption that their own operations would not be unduly accelerated. More important, they had again focused attention on the strategy for the Indian Ocean, which had been largely ignored during the past two months. The setback for the Chiefs of Staff was by no means final; but it may well have been decisive. For while the issue was still in doubt, the Prime Minister apparently made up his mind. Possibly the Americans' objections had helped to revive his own, which had lain dormant during the Commonwealth conversations: possibly the discussion on the future in south-east Asia, which was taking a fresh turn at this time, revived his hopes for that theatre.[1] On 24th June, he emerged from his silence to criticize the Chiefs of Staff's latest proposals and to summon a Staff Conference; and when this was held on 6th July, with the Chiefs of Staff and selected Ministers, he returned to his earlier position and pressed for an operation against Simalur.[2] He refused to approve the Chiefs of Staff's request, which Ministers generally supported, for the official adoption of the Middle Strategy; and after a brisk discussion, referred it to another meeting. The compromise had failed after the efforts of the past three months.

Two meetings were held accordingly on 10th and 14th July, at the second of which the arguments were fully ventilated without any result. The prospect of further delay was now really alarming, and the Prime Minister therefore undertook to give a decision within a week. But three days later, thinking that Mountbatten's views should first be heard, he invited him to London and postponed his own statement. Mountbatten arrived with Wedemeyer on 4th August, and the debate began again on the 8th. Before we recount its further progress, we must therefore consider the developments in south-east Asia, which had thus to be related to the plans for the Pacific.

---

[1] See p. 486 *et seq.* below.

[2] See p. 462 above.

(iii)

Developments in South-East Asia

The position in south-east Asia by the time of Mountbatten's visit to London had altered considerably since April.[1] There seemed little prospect at that time of reconciling the British and American views on Burma. The Joint Chiefs of Staff's decision of 21st March, promising further support for the strategy of the Ledo Road,[2] disturbed the British authorities, and Mountbatten was asked to report his views. On 14th April he replied, in substantially the same terms as before. While now acknowledging for the first time that Stilwell might be able to take Myitkyina, he still could not guarantee its retention until he knew the outcome of the battle around Imphal. Similarly, he could not yet comply with the Americans' proposal to advance on the central front to the area of Shwebo-Monywa, for it might well be beyond his resources even to reach the line of Katha-Bhamo as he had hoped. But whatever the result of the current battle, Mountbatten was increasingly disposed to reject any plan designed to support the strategy of the Ledo Road. The mounting speed of the Americans' advance in the Pacific confirmed his belief that his only timely contribution lay in expanding the capacity of the air ferry to China. He therefore proposed to halt the northern advance in the area Mogaung-Myitkyina, which he would hold and develop as a refuelling and staging point for that purpose. The road and pipeline should reach the area within the next few months, and the monthly capacity of the ferry might then soon be raised by at least a thousand tons. His other forces would meanwhile complete the vital battle at Imphal and the consolidation of Arakan, and, freed from the encumbrance of continued operations towards China, might then be available for a more rewarding attack further south. He therefore proposed that his directive 'in regard to North Burma should continue to be to develop, maintain, broaden and protect the air link to China'.

The stimulus of the Pacific advance, unfolding at a pace of which Mountbatten was not fully aware, was also affecting American opinion, but with somewhat different results. Both British and Americans were determined to improve the timetable in Burma; but where the former wished to change trains, the latter sought to overhaul the engine. Mountbatten wished to abandon the Road beyond Myitkyina; the Joint Chiefs of Staff, in response to the same situation, demanded a more ambitious campaign. Their efforts to this end were indeed considerable. They continued—and at last with success—to press the

---

[1] Throughout this section, see Map III, facing p. 129.

[2] See pp. 455-6 above.

Chinese to advance from Yunnan;[1] and they tried to stimulate Allied operations through the medium of supply. In March, Arnold had allocated four groups of transport aircraft, of a hundred planes each, to the South-East Asia Command, apparently without conditions.[2] But in the middle of April, Stilwell was informed privately that their allotment to the theatre would now be 'ill-advised' unless 'operational requirements' really justified it, and that he was to consider carefully whether these did so or not. At the same time, there were indications that the four groups would in any case be reduced to two. Mountbatten, who had learned of these exchanges only through the courtesy of General Sultan, was upset by the decision and by the manner of its communication; but he was obliged to abide by it in forming his plans.

But despite these efforts, and on the most hopeful assumption, the pipeline to Kunming could not be ready before July 1945, and in the meantime the capacity of the air ferry must be enlarged. For there was now a real danger that supply by air would prove inadequate as well as supply by land. Since the introduction of Plan 'Drake',[3] the ferry was being used principally to build up an air base in China; but at the current rate of progress that plan seemed likely to fail. If Formosa was to be attacked in February 1945, the preparations in Asia could scarcely be ready in time. The first assault on the Japanese inner zone of defence would proceed without the promised air bombardment from the west, and the South-East Asia Command's contribution, 'to assist in providing timely direct support of the Pacific advance to the China-Formosa-Luzon triangle', would thus have failed.

The Americans planned to avoid this misfortune by simultaneously increasing the capacity of the airlift and reducing the scale of the operations it was designed to serve. This was made the easier by the very speed of the Pacific advance. For if the Marianas were captured in June, 1944 they could be used as a base for B.29 bombers by the winter, and those which could not be accommodated in Asia could then operate instead from Guam and Saipan. It was indeed becoming possible to envisage a co-ordinated air offensive on Japan. The perimeter of the target was steadily shrinking, fresh bases were becoming available at various points along it, and in the spring of 1944 the aircraft themselves were coming off the assembly lines. The plans of the previous winter had been confined to eight groups of B.29's, all eventually to be based in Asia. But by April 1944, Arnold was able to produce a grand scheme for the employment of a strategic air force of some eighteen groups of B.29's. The first four groups were to be sent in the next few months, as before, to south-east Asia; a further four to the Marianas in the autumn; a further eight to the Marianas as soon as

[1] See pp. 416-17 above.

[2] See p. 410 above.

[3] See p. 453 above.

possible; and a further two thereafter to the Aleutians or, if circumstances allowed, to Siberia. At the same time, a revised plan of command was produced to ensure the proper co-ordination of these widely separated, but homogeneous, operations. The B.29's, unlike other American bombers, were not to be controlled by the local commanders, but directly by General Arnold as the agent of the Joint Chiefs of Staff. The area commanders would of course remain responsible for their sustenance and protection. The force would be known as Twentieth U.S. Army Air Force, and that part of it which lay in south-east Asia as Twentieth Bomber Command.

These proposals, which were approved by the Joint Chiefs of Staff at the beginning of April, were followed at the beginning of May by new instructions to Stilwell as the first American commander affected. Air forces from China, including the B.29 bombers, were to support the advance on Formosa which would take place early in 1945. Plans were to be submitted for this purpose to the Joint Chiefs of Staff through General Arnold, and were later to be co-ordinated with Nimitz and MacArthur.

> '. . . 4. It is recognised,' the instructions ended, 'that major curtailment of "Hump" support to ground forces in China and such other activities as do not directly support an air effort will be required.
>
> 5. Pending submission and approval of your plans, the Joint Chiefs of Staff consider it necessary to commence immediately the progressive stockpiling in China.'

These plans closely affected the South-East Asia Command and India, and the British authorities were accordingly disturbed by the proposals for command. Mountbatten had known of the exchanges on Stilwell's instructions, as he had known of the exchanges on the four groups of aircraft, only through the courtesy of Sultan, and he hastened to protest at a situation in which matters affecting his theatre could be discussed without reference to himself. The British Chiefs of Staff were equally disturbed at an arrangement which denied them any say in the control of Plan 'Drake' or its successor, and which might later affect the participation by British air forces in the long-range bombing of Japan. They therefore suggested that Arnold should act, as Portal had acted until recently with the Allied strategic air forces in Europe, as the agent of the Combined Chiefs of Staff. But as the Americans alone were at present concerned in the operations, their proposals were finally accepted, with the proviso that they could be reviewed if British forces were later involved. Stilwell meanwhile was directed to consult fully with Mountbatten on any aspects of the air affecting the interests of the South-East Asia Command.

At the beginning of May 1944, the precise nature of those interests was increasingly difficult to ascertain. Both British and American intentions, as seen from south-east Asia, were thoroughly obscure. The Americans were calling for detailed plans which they themselves, with their recent reservation of transport aircraft and their modified bombing plan, had thrown into confusion; while the British, who towards the end of April were occupied with the genesis of the Middle Strategy, had not yet replied to Mountbatten's message of 14th April,[1] so that their views were officially unknown. The 'Axiom' party,[2] however, had now returned to the theatre with the news that no British resources could be expected until six or nine months after the defeat of Germany, and Mountbatten therefore decided to plan on this basis. All seaborne operations seemed to be ruled out, and on 3rd May he accordingly asked to be informed if the Combined Chiefs of Staff wished him, on completion of the current battle around Imphal, to 'continue operations in North Burma with all . . . available forces and at the expense of any other operations in South-East Asia Command.'

This telegram aroused the Prime Minister. 'What with our own differences,' he remarked on 5th May, 'and the uncertainty of American opinion, we are not unveiling a creditable picture to history.' He therefore met the Chiefs of Staff on the 8th to discuss the action to be taken. The result was conveyed to Washington on the following day.

'The problem is to reconcile:

(a) The fact that operations by land in Burma must be carried out with land and air forces now available or earmarked for India and South-east Asia.

(b) The importance, on which we are agreed, of getting maximum supplies into China, particularly for the Air Force build-up.

(c) The time factor in relation to Pacific advance which indicates that maximum amount should be in China by early 1945.

2. In regard to (a) we must bear in mind that British sources can supply no more reinforcements for land and air forces until after Germany has been defeated. This being the case, Admiral Mountbatten should not be directed to undertake operations which call for extra forces. According to [Mountbatten's telegram of 14th April], he will have considerable difficulty even in reaching and certainly in holding Myitkyina, and will not be able to advance to and hold the Bhamo-Lashio line.

3. We appreciate that the result of the present operations may alter the situation, particularly if a severe blow is struck at the Japanese. Moreover, we do not know yet what influence the recently ordered advance of the Yunnan Chinese will have. But,

[1] See p. 486 above.

[2] See p. 435 above.

we must take into account the necessity for relieving certain units that have been operating in Burma for a considerable period.

4. In regard to (b) and (c), of the three ways of increasing the flow of oil fuel and stores to China, the direct Calcutta/China air route will go furthest towards the achievement of our object, because it does not seem to depend on the early capture and holding of Myitkyina and may prove to be the only way of gaining substantial results in time for the attack on Formosa. Nevertheless, the capture of Myitkyina, if achieved in time, should be of some help since it provides another and better air route to China.

5. In the light of the above, we therefore consider that Admiral Mountbatten should be given the directive he suggests in regard to operations in Burma:—"to develop, maintain, broaden and protect the air link to China in order to provide a maximum flow of P.O.L. [petrol, oil and lubricants] and stores." We would add, "operations to achieve this object must be dictated by the forces at present available or firmly allocated to S.E.A.C. and related in time to the Formosa operation." Mountbatten will then be free to seize and hold Myitkyina if he considers that he can do so with the forces allocated to him.

6. . . . we consider that operations in Burma should have priority for such forces as they need over any other operations in S.E.A.C. . . .'

The British proposal, with its specific mention of Formosa, satisfied the Americans in its definition of the immediate task. But it ignored the policy for the Ledo Road, which they regarded as complementary to it and which they were determined to retain. The Joint Chiefs of Staff therefore suggested a revised directive, designed to place greater emphasis on the land operations. This in turn was amended by the British, and the final version read as follows:

'To develop, maintain, broaden and protect the air link to China, in order to provide maximum and timely supply of P.O.L. and stores to China in support of Pacific operations; so far as is consistent with the above to press advantages against the enemy by exercising maximum effort ground and air, particularly during the current monsoon season, and in stressing such advantages, to be prepared to exploit the development of overland communications to China. All these operations must be dictated by the forces at present available or firmly allocated to S.E.A.C.'

The British Chiefs of Staff were satisfied that they had at any rate obtained agreement on the immediate task; and the Combined Chiefs of Staff accordingly sent the new directive to Admiral Mountbatten on 3rd June, 1944.

The Supreme Commander himself was not entirely happy with his orders; but they at least provided him with a clear indication of priority on which to plan with more assurance. In the course of the next few weeks, moreover, the situation began to clear. By 8th June, the effect of the Americans' new bombing plan could be foreseen with some precision, for Stilwell's air representatives had now produced a detailed estimate of their requirements. The programme was divided into two phases. Phase 1 would consist of the capture of the area Mogaung-Myitkyina, the further expansion of the air bases in India to raise the capacity of the Hump traffic to 29,000 tons a month by December 1944, and, if in July this object seemed unlikely to be realized, the diversion of one group of bombers to the Hump from July, 1944 until fifteen days before the attack on Formosa. In phase 2, American heavy bombers from south-east Asia, with two medium bomber groups, a substantial number of fighters and one photographic reconnaissance group, would be diverted to China fifteen days before the attack on Formosa. The American air forces directly available to the South-East Asia Command would then consist of one fighter bomber squadron, one fighter squadron, two reconnaissance squadrons and some air commando groups.

Mountbatten fully supported phase 1 of this plan, although he still could not guarantee to advance as far as the line Katha-Bhamo. But he reported that phase 2 would leave him weak in the air, and he therefore asked that all of the forces affected should be replaced so as to be available for operations in Burma by January, 1945. He also drew attention to a possibility which was not mentioned in the programme, but which he foresaw, of Allied land forces being removed from south-east Asia to China to protect the air bases there in case of a growing threat from the Japanese; and he stressed that in that event he must be given adequate replacements by the autumn of 1944, if Myitkyina was to be held while an active offensive was pursued.

By the end of June, the shape of this offensive could also be more clearly foreseen. Mountbatten had ordered General Giffard on the 9th,

> (a) To re-establish communication on the road Dimapur-Kohima-Imphal not later than mid-July;
>
> (b) To clear Japanese forces from the area Dimapur-Kohima-Imphal plain-Yuwa-Tamanthi; and
>
> (c) To prepare to exploit across the Chindwin in the Yuwa-Tamanthi area after the monsoon.

Task (a) was accomplished on 22nd June, and the sequel followed at once. The Japanese withdrawal, which had begun early in the month, was by now showing signs of becoming a rout. At the end of June, the British 33rd Corps assumed control of operations to the north and north-east of Imphal, while 4th Corps controlled those to the south and south-east; and throughout July the former drove the demoralized enemy out of and beyond Ukhrul, while the latter slowly cleared the southern approaches to the Imphal plain. At the end of that month, when 4th Corps' headquarters withdrew to India, the Japanese were back near the Chindwin in the north and in the south were retreating down the Tiddim road. Mountbatten could now count on the forces of the central front in planning his offensive after the monsoon, and could embark with certainty on operations which he had hitherto been unable to accept.

Two possible plans were already in preparation. The first (Plan 'X') provided for simultaneous advances by Stilwell's force, with American air support, from the area Mogaung-Myitkyina to the line Katha-Bhamo, and by the British 4th and 33rd Corps, with British air support, to the line of the Chindwin. These operations, if successful, would clear the mountains of northern Burma. The second plan was more ambitious. While Stilwell advanced as in Plan 'X', the British were to launch airborne attacks on Kalewa and on the entrance to the Mandalay plain, thereafter advancing beyond the Chindwin to Yeu and Shwebo, and thence to Mandalay. These operations would clear northern Burma to a depth which would adequately protect the bases for the China ferry, and would establish positions from which to clear central Burma as soon as possible. Mountbatten preferred this plan to Plan 'X', and decided to place it before the Chiefs of Staff under the code name of 'Champion'. But it had three disadvantages. First, it demanded more air forces than were then in the theatre, in the shape of three combat cargo groups—which formed, however, three of the four groups allocated by Arnold to the theatre in March, 1944[1]—and a second air commando.[2] Secondly, an advance across the Chindwin involved serious difficulties of supply, and might prove more expensive than had been anticipated, or might fail to reach the necessary targets before the ensuing monsoon. Thirdly, it raised very serious administrative problems, for it envisaged the clearance of central Burma, where an army could not be maintained throughout the monsoon on supplies from the north alone. If an advance beyond the Chindwin was to be rapidly exploited, it must therefore be accompanied by an attack on the port of Rangoon. Otherwise, it must aim only at limited targets until such an operation could be launched in 1945 after the end of the south-west monsoon.

Mountbatten was anxious to avoid delay if possible. He therefore submitted a third plan, hinging on a seaborne and airborne attack on Rangoon, to which the gave the code name 'Vanguard'. Although such an operation admittedly did not comply directly with his orders, the Supreme Commander urged that it might in fact prove more effective than 'Champion', by forcing the enemy to withdraw to the south and

---

[1] See p. 410 above.

[2] See p. 147 above.

thereby enabling the Allies to clear northern Burma with less difficulty and to engage in central Burma without delay. Rangoon itself would be attacked by an airborne assault, followed by a seaborne assault on the coastal and river defences. The forces would then move to the north, to cut the enemy's communications with the front and eventually to meet Stilwell and the remaining British. Meanwhile, Stilwell himself would advance as in 'Champion'. 'Vanguard', in fact, reproduced in different conditions the first and third phases of 'Anakim', thanks to an air superiority which had not existed earlier.[1]

'Vanguard', however, had one serious disadvantage. It demanded substantially larger forces than either Plan 'X' or 'Champion'. At the lowest estimate, it was likely to need four combat cargo groups, a second air commando, two more divisions, and additional naval and assault forces. The plan thus conflicted with Mountbatten's directive that 'all . . . operations must be dictated by the forces at present available or firmly allocated to S.E.A.C.'[2] In view of the advantages, the Supreme Commander resolved to press for its adoption; but whatever the outcome, he asked for a firm decision by 1st September.

These plans were submitted to the Chiefs of Staff in outline on 23rd July, by which time the future in south-east Asia, as visualized by the Prime Minister, had regained its importance in the main debate. Mountbatten's proposals had therefore to be compared with the plans for Sumatra or Simalur, and he was asked to consider and report on the latest conditions for 'Culverin'. He accordingly brought with him to London appreciations of 'Champion', 'Vanguard' and 'Culverin', together with other possibilities—for the capture of Sabang off the northern tip of Sumatra, and for the occupation of the Cocos Islands—which might be preferred as seaborne operations. When the conversations opened on 8th August the future was open, and the various plans provided for every likely possibility.

(iv)

The Final British Proposals

The new plans for south-east Asia differed in one important respect from their predecessors. For with the introduction of 'Vanguard' it was at last possible to envisage a satisfactory connexion between large-scale operations in the north and in the centre of Burma. Hitherto, they had seemed incompatible. The clearance of Burma from the north, which would release the forces required for a substantial campaign further

[1] See pp. 137, 146-7 above.

[2] See p. 490 above.

south, was rejected as too costly and too slow; while seaborne assaults further south, designed to relieve and accelerate the campaign in the north, could not in fact succeed without the forces they were supposed to assist. 'Champion' and the latest version of 'Culverin' did nothing to change the situation. The former, which like its predecessors 'offered the gloomy prospect of eating the porcupine quill by quill',[1] could scarcely achieve its object, even if assisted by a complementary attack on the flank, before the winter of 1945/46; while the latter, again as always, demanded more troops than could be spared. The Joint Planners therefore rejected both plans with the familiar objections. But a successful 'Vanguard', leading to the clearance of central Burma during the summer of 1945, provided the proper connexion between the two, removing the necessity for the later stages of 'Champion' and paving the way immediately for a large-scale variant of 'Culverin'.

The programme, however, had only a narrow margin of time. For the British rôle in south-east Asia to be effective, Malaya—including Singapore—and Burma must have been recaptured by the spring of 1946, before the anticipated end of the war against Japan. The Joint Planners estimated that some six months must elapse between the launching of 'Culverin' and the recapture of Singapore, which provided the final justification of the operation. 'Culverin' must therefore begin immediately after the south-west monsoon of 1945. Similarly, the clearance of Burma and the reassembly of the resources for 'Culverin' was reckoned to take six months from the time that 'Vanguard' was launched against Rangoon. The date for 'Vanguard' must therefore be in or before March, 1945. If that programme could be maintained, the British rôle in south-east Asia would be justified. If not, there was a strong case for transferring the main effort to the Pacific before it was too late.

The timetable might not have seemed unduly rigorous at first sight. But it was complicated, and possibly endangered, by the situation in Burma itself. In the late summer of 1944, the enemy, elsewhere on the retreat, offered his most stubborn opposition in the north around Myitkyina. The Japanese were thought to be reinforcing the area, and Mountbatten expected a serious attack in November which Stilwell with his existing resources would not be strong enough to withstand. Assuming this appreciation to be correct—and it could not be controverted at the time—Stilwell must therefore be reinforced to the detriment of operations elsewhere, or those operations must be mounted so as to forestall or relieve the threatened assault in the north. 'Vanguard' was timed for January, 1945 with a force of five divisions, plus one tank, one glider and two parachute brigades. Two of the divisions, the tank and glider brigades, and one parachute brigade were to be taken from Burma, and one division—the only division in reserve

[1] The C.I.G.S.' phrase.

—from India. This represented the utmost that could be spared in the theatre until 'Vanguard' itself had drawn the enemy towards the south, and it therefore left two divisions and a parachute brigade to be found elsewhere. But the Chiefs of Staff—and indeed the Supreme Commander himself—suspected that an assault on this scale was too light to achieve its purpose, and they decided finally that seven divisions were needed. In that case, four infantry divisions must be found from outside the theatre, or in other words from Europe. But even assuming that Germany was defeated by October 1944, the aftermath in Europe, the claims of demobilization and leave, and the problems of reassembly and transport to India, made it unlikely that the four divisions would be available for operations in south-east Asia before March, 1945. This delay led to a vicious circle. For if the operation took place in March, the two divisions from the South-East Asia Command would probably have been drawn into the battle in the north, and six divisions instead of four would then have to be found from Europe. In the meantime, the enemy must be engaged elsewhere.

'Vanguard', therefore, could not be considered on its own, but rather as a complement to preliminary operations further north. The Chiefs of Staff were thus led to reconsider the merits of 'Champion'. Mountbatten's plan had provided for four distinct stages in this operation:[1]

'(i) Mid-November to end of January.

Airborne operations to seize Kalemyo-Kalewa while ground forces advance down the Kabaw Valley and Tiddim road.

(ii) February to mid-March.

An airborne operation to seize the gateway to the Mandalay Plain at Yeu. Land forces secure the Kalewa-Yeu road to allow armoured forces to deploy in the Yeu-Shwebo area, which is dry and suitable for all arms.

(iii) Capture of line Mandalay-Pakokku.

(iv) Consolidation of line reached in Phase 3 and exploitation southwards.

Throughout the operations Northern Combat Area Command and Yunnan forces are to co-operate by advancing southwards on the eastern flank, eventually exploiting to Loilem.'

It therefore looked as if phases 1 and 2 of 'Champion' could usefully be undertaken. But phase 2 involved considerable engineering work, which would soon have to be put in hand, and it was necessary to decide whether in fact it should be carried out. The Chiefs of Staff were anxious not to get too deeply involved in the north, and they were therefore reluctant to proceed beyond phase 1 of the plan. After conferring with Mountbatten on 5th and 7th August, they recommended to the Prime Minister that preparations should be put in hand for phase 1 of 'Champion' and for 'Vanguard' in March, 1945; that the

[1] See Map IX, facing p. 459.

final decision to embark on these operations should be taken by 1st September, 1944 if resources then seemed to permit; and that if they did not, the Allies should proceed with the whole of 'Champion', meanwhile preparing to launch 'Vanguard' as soon as possible after the south-west monsoon of 1945. In the latter case, the reconquest of Burma could not be expected until the winter of 1945/46.

These recommendations were discussed at an important series of meetings with Ministers on 8th and 9th August. Churchill, who had so recently revived the prospect of an early variant of 'Culverin', regarded them without enthusiasm. He was 'horrified' that nothing should be done outside northern Burma until March 1945, and that the attack on Rangoon should then be followed directly by operations to the north. 'Vanguard' to him was the direct prelude to the reconquest of Malaya. He disliked the prospect of fighting up from Rangoon as much as that of fighting continuously down from Imphal. Both involved 'the laborious reconquest of Burma swamp by swamp', with all that that involved. Why should we not, like the Americans in the Pacific, leave the enemy to rot and starve behind us, while we concentrated our resources elsewhere? Rather than agree to the Chiefs of Staff's proposals, he preferred to attack the northern tip of Sumatra in the winter of 1944, holding northern Burma as lightly as possible and reinforcing the main attack later from Europe. This familiar argument met with the familiar response. Churchill thereupon developed a revised and more defensible version. As he recognized, the critical factor governing the choice of the operation to be carried out was the date of Hitler's defeat. If this occurred in the autumn of 1944, why should 'Vanguard', against Rangoon, be carried out at all? Why not proceed with 'Champion' in central Burma until March 1945, and use the fresh forces from Europe directly in a variant of 'Culverin' against Sumatra? We should then be strong enough to stand in the north, while we attacked in greater strength in the south. The Japanese would either be left in the remainder of Burma, isolated and eventually weakened by the weight of our operations against Malaya, or—as he anticipated—they would be largely withdrawn to reinforce the south. On the other hand, if Germany was not defeated in time and if the forces were thus not available from Europe, neither 'Culverin' nor 'Vanguard' could be staged on the necessary scale in March 1945, and in that case 'Vanguard' should be suitably revised so as to be mounted before the end of 1944. In any case he was anxious not to make a premature decision which would be overtaken by events.

The Chiefs of Staff and Mountbatten saw three objections to these proposals. First, 'Culverin' might not have the effect which the Prime Minister anticipated. The Japanese in Burma could not be bypassed as in the Pacific islands; they must remain a threat to the north until they were defeated there in battle. 'Culverin' in fact would not render large-scale operations unnecessary in the north, by drawing the enemy to the south: as the C.I.G.S. put it, 'only 'Vanguard' can kill 'Champion'.' Secondly, the proposals would not satisfy the Americans, who had to be convinced that northern Burma could be cleared more economically by attacking from Rangoon than solely by developing the existing operations. If 'Vanguard' were presented merely as an alternative to 'Culverin', they would almost certainly support 'Champion'. Once again, 'only 'Vanguard' can kill 'Champion',' and 'Vanguard' would be accepted only if it were seen to include the subsequent campaign to the north as well as the initial attack on Rangoon. Thirdly, it was impossible to delay the choice for much longer. A decision was necessary by 1st September if any preparations were to be made; and whereas those for 'Vanguard' could later be included if necessary in the more ambitious preparations for 'Culverin', the latter were such in scale and in type as to kill any hope of 'Vanguard'. The flexibility which the Prime Minister desired could in fact be achieved only by deciding to plan for 'Vanguard' immediately.

These views were canvassed at three long Staff Meetings on 8th August, and in papers exchanged the next day between the Chiefs of Staff and the Prime Minister. Two more meetings followed; and at length on the 9th, 'the Conference reached the following conclusions on the subject of the British rôle in the war against Japan:

(i) The necessary steps must be taken to contain the Japanese in northern Burma.

(ii) Proposals to plan and prepare for Operation 'Vanguard' should now be made to the American Chiefs of Staff. Extreme efforts should be made in conjunction with the United States Chiefs of Staff to launch this operation at the earliest moment whether Germany has surrendered or not. Search must be made in every direction, including, if necessary, Australia, for the extra resources, over and above those now at the disposal of the Supreme Commander, S.E.A.C., which, on detailed examination, are found to be required.

(iii) Plans should also be made for the recapture of Malaya in readiness for the time when the necessary forces become available.

(iv) Plans and arrangements should be made forthwith so that 4 British/Indian and 2 British divisions can be moved without delay into the war against Japan as soon as they can be spared from the European theatre. The movement of British troops further away from their homes will be attended by grave difficulties which must be faced and solved.

(v) If German organised resistance collapses early, it will be necessary to review the situation and decide between the operations against Rangoon and other operations, principally 'Culverin' or a variant thereof, which may then seem more profitable . . .

(x) The above conclusions should form the basis of a telegram in a form suitable to be sent forthwith to the United States Chiefs of Staff.'

Whichever operation was adopted, the new policy for south-east Asia affected decisively the British plans for the Pacific. Either 'Vanguard' or 'Culverin' would absorb the first British troops which might otherwise be sent to the south-west Pacific, although it would still be possible to send a British naval force there by the autumn of 1944, and an air contingent as soon as it could be spared from Europe. In these circumstances, Ministers were less inclined to support the Middle Strategy. Its diplomatic prospects declined as those in south-east Asia brightened, while its military advantages were less apparent if the Australians were unlikely to be reinforced until late in 1945. As the scale of the immediate British contribution shrank, it became the more important to exploit it to the full. A minor campaign on the flank of the main advance was not worth the effort involved. The main British contribution in the Pacific now seemed likely to be by sea; the Fleet must therefore be sent to the area of the main operations, and the Prime Minister, who had earlier asked and received Mountbatten's consent to a transfer of ships from his theatre, voiced the feelings of his colleagues when he proposed to make 'the greatest offer of naval assistance which is within our power to the United States, ascertaining from them in what way it can be most effective.'

It was decided to accompany this offer with a clear indication of the British preference. There was little doubt at the time where the main naval operations would lie. The Americans had referred in June to the possibility of invading Japan, and this was confirmed by a telegram on 11th July in which the Joint Chiefs of Staff announced their wish to restate the terms of the 'overall objective' against Japan as follows:

'to force the unconditional surrender of Japan by

(i) lowering Japanese ability and will to resist by establishing sea and air blockades, conducting intensive air bombardment and destroying Japanese air and naval strength;

(ii) invading and seizing objectives in the industrial heart of Japan.'

General Marshall added privately that this formula was designed to allow for an invasion of the Home Islands, which now seemed both feasible and certain. Ministers were therefore anxious to see the British Fleet in action with the American in the central Pacific.

The Chiefs of Staff, however, were still reluctant to abandon the prospects in the south-west. The fact that British troops would not be available immediately did not affect the first stage in the proposed operations there, or the diplomatic advantages to be gained from the presence of the British navy and air force. Irrespective of the achievements elsewhere, the introduction of some British forces into the area was the most direct contribution that could be made to the re-establishment of British prestige in that part of the Pacific, and since the conversations in May it was undoubtedly expected by the Australians and New Zealanders themselves. This had indeed been confirmed by a telegram from Mr. Curtin on 4th July. The Australian Prime Minister now calculated that the growing pace of MacArthur's advance might remove the necessity for large Commonwealth military operations, but he stressed the General's weakness at sea which could be made good only by the British. This presented an ideal opportunity for the employment of a naval task force which could worthily represent Britain in the Pacific, and which would be received with enthusiasm in Australia. The necessary resources would be made available, but action was required at once if it was to be effective. The Chiefs of Staff were impressed by this telegram, although they doubted if MacArthur could in fact advance as fast as Curtin suggested, and still preferred to view the naval contingent as the spearhead of a Commonwealth task force of all Services. They therefore proposed to Churchill, in conjunction with their suggestions for south-east Asia, that all units of the British Fleet not needed in that theatre should be sent at once to the Pacific, where they should form such a task force with the Australians and New Zealanders. Possibly appreciating that opinion was not on their side, the Chiefs of Staff hastened to point out that this move was not entirely at variance with the Prime Minister's suggestion. For the establishment of a British naval force in Australian waters might prove the best means of introducing it later to the central Pacific, while if that offer were refused we were well placed to make our distinctive contribution elsewhere. Their point of view was accepted in the final decision on 9th August, but only as an alternative.

> '. . . (vi) The greatest offer of naval assistance should be made at once to the U.S. Chiefs of Staff, it being impressed upon them that it is our desire to share with them in the main operations against the mainland of Japan or Formosa.
>
> (vii) If this offer is declined in favour of support by the British fleet to General MacArthur's operations, we should propose the formation of a British Empire task force under a British commander, consisting of British, Australian and New Zealand land, sea and Air forces, to operate under General MacArthur's supreme command.
>
> (viii) In the latter event, we should propose that control of operations in the South-West Pacific area should be on the same footing as the control of operations in the South-East Asia area, with this difference that the American Chiefs of Staff should be the channel of communications for the South-West Pacific and the British Chiefs of Staff for South-East Asia.

(ix) The decision as to what proportion of the British forces which become available after the defeat of Germany should be used for the main operations under the South-East Asia Command, and what proportion sent to the Pacific, should be left open for the present. Preparations should proceed for the reception, in either theatre, of these forces, and of the necessary landing ships and craft.

(x) The above conclusions should form the basis of a telegram in a form suitable to be sent forthwith to the United States Chiefs of Staff.'

The telegram was accordingly sent to Washington on 18th August, after further discussion of its detail.

'(i) As agreed at the 'Sextant' Conference we have devoted prolonged study to the strategy for the war against Japan. We have considered how best our forces can be disposed and what operations they should carry out, taking into account the undertakings given by H.M. Government at the Casablanca Conference that on the defeat of Germany we should assist the United States to the utmost of our power in defeating Japan.

(ii) Several important developments have taken place since the 'Sextant' Conference.

(1) The advance of the United States forces across the Pacific has been accelerated.

(2) The Japanese have strongly reinforced Burma, and their strength in that country has risen from $4\frac{1}{2}$ to 10 divisions.

(3) The capture of Myitkyina rules out, as was always foreseen, any purely defensive policy in North Burma.

(4) The likelihood of aggressive action by the Japanese fleet in the Bay of Bengal is now remote.

(5) Progress of the war against Germany on all fronts has been such as to render possible the partial or total collapse of Germany which might free forces from the European theatre in the coming months.

(6) We now have overwhelming air superiority in the South-East Asia Theatre.

The following paragraphs contain our proposals in the light of the above developments.

OPERATIONS IN SOUTH-EAST ASIA THEATRE

(iii) The present Directive to South-East Asia Command prescribes as a first task the protection of the air link to China, and so far as is possible, the support of the further construction of the Burma road (which cannot be completely opened until 1946), and of the pipelines to Yunnan (which are also progressing slowly). In addition, we have, of course, to defend the frontiers of India. We are thus committed to a long drawn out struggle in the jungles and swamps against an enemy who has superior lines of communication to those which we possess. The wastage from sickness and disease amounted during the campaign of 1944 up to 30th June alone to 282,000, in addition to a loss in killed, wounded and missing of approximately 40,000. Clearly, therefore, we should make every effort to liquidate this highly undesirable commitment, if it can by any means be done.

(iv) Admiral Mountbatten has put forward two plans. First plan ('Champion') is to continue to engage the Japanese in North Burma. This, in our opinion, will merely lead to a continuation of the present unsatisfactory state of affairs, and we feel bound to reject it.

(v) The second plan ('Vanguard') put forward by Admiral Mountbatten is to capture Rangoon by an airborne operation, to be followed by the opening of the port of Rangoon and the maintenance of the expedition by sea. This plan is now rendered practicable by the large measure of air superiority which we enjoy in this theatre and by the Japanese inability any longer to dispute our sea lines of communication to Rangoon.

(vi) The capture of Rangoon and Pegu (20 miles distant) will at a stroke sever the enemy's main lines of communication to the interior of Burma by road, river and rail. This will give us the opportunity of liquidating once and for all, under the most favourable military conditions, our commitments in Burma by the destruction of the Japanese forces.

(vii) Until such time as the Rangoon operation can be launched it will be essential to contain the Japanese by offensive action south of Myitkyina.

(viii) The bulk of the necessary resources for Rangoon are already available and we now ask the Combined Chiefs of Staff to agree to the above plan in principle, and that every effort should be made to provide from our combined resources the balance of the forces required . . .

(ix) We are now building up a strong fleet in the Bay of Bengal, the bulk of which, including our newest battleships, will not be required for the operations outlined above in the South-East Asia Theatre. It is our desire in accordance with H.M. Government's policy that this fleet should play its full part at the earliest possible moment in the main operations against Japan wherever the greatest naval strength is required, and thereafter its strength should be built up as rapidly as possible.

This fleet by mid 1945 will probably comprise 4 battleships of the King George V class, 6 fleet carriers, 4 light fleet carriers, 15 escort carriers, 20 cruisers, 40-50 fleet destroyers, 100 escorts and a considerable fleet train, the whole constituting a force which could make a valuable contribution in the crucial operations leading to the assault on Japan. This fleet built up as fast as possible would operate under United States command.

(x) If for any reason United States Chiefs of Staff are unable to accept the support of the British fleet in the main operations (which is our distinct preference) we should be willing to discuss an alternative. The suggestion that we would make in this event is the formation of a British Empire task force under a British Commander, consisting of British, Australian, and New Zealand land, sea and air forces, to operate in the South-West Pacific area under General MacArthur's supreme command. This alternative, if decided upon, would still enable the British fleet to be well placed to reinforce the U.S. Pacific Fleet if this should later be desired.

(xi) We ask for an early expression of the views of the United States Chiefs of Staff on all the above proposals. The urgency is dictated by the need to work out as soon as possible the logistic problems involved, including the development of the necessary base facilities.'

This telegram was despatched three and a half weeks before the 'Octagon' Conference was due to begin at Quebec.[1] The British were anxious that the Americans should be fully acquainted by then with the reasons for their proposals for south-east Asia, and Mountbatten therefore sent General Wedemeyer to Washington for the second time in six months. The Chiefs of Staff anticipated strong opposition to a campaign which was not confined to the north of Burma, particularly as Stilwell had already disapproved of the attack on Rangoon as involving an unacceptable risk. But in the event the Joint Chiefs of Staff were not unfriendly. As had been expected, they were eager to develop a campaign in the north, where operations were already in progress and where existing resources could be adapted more easily to the task. They therefore preferred to embark on 'Champion' and to leave 'Vanguard' until more troops were available, rather than to decide immediately on 'Vanguard' only to find later that it could not be carried out. But they did not on this account exclude the possibility of an attack on Rangoon as a complement to the northern advance. Arnold seemed willing to provide the extra aircraft involved, while Marshall was reported to have remarked that 'he did not think there would be any great difficulty in resolving this matter'. The Americans in fact seem to have felt that 'Vanguard' was a British affair, to which they had no objection as long as their own interests were safeguarded. The British Joint Staff Mission therefore thought that the Joint Chiefs of Staff would insist on phases I and II of 'Champion' being carried out,[2] but that if this was done, and if the situation elsewhere allowed the necessary forces to be concentrated, they would agree to 'Vanguard'. Their estimate proved correct, when on 1st September the Joint Chiefs of Staff stated that:

[1] See p. 384 above.
[2] See p. 495 above.

'. . . (ii) Provided operations [in Burma] do not militate against requirements of operations in European theatre and in Pacific, United States Chiefs of Staff propose that Admiral Mountbatten's plan ['Champion'] be accepted. They consider the objective of the operation should be attainment of line Kalewa-Shwebo-Mogok-Lashio, and exploitation toward Pakokku-Mandalay-Kyaukme . . . United States Chiefs of Staff are agreeable to minor modifications of this plan provided basic concept of severing Japanese lines of communication through Mandalay area is retained and plan vigorously implemented.

(iii) Assuming that German resistance collapses or that situation in Europe develops in such a manner as to permit allocation of resources for a strengthened plan ['Vanguard'] to be undertaken in mid March 1945, this plan might be initiated at that time, provided that objectives as envisaged in ['Champion'] are maintained and provided further, that preparations for an execution of ['Vanguard'] do not jeopardise early attainment of objectives of Phase I and Phase II of ['Champion'].

(iv) In view of Admiral Mountbatten's request that a directive be issued him prior to 1st September, 1944 the United States Chiefs of Staff urge that he now be directed to execute ['Champion'] with objective of attaining line set forth in paragraph (ii) above . . .'

This reply was made on the day on which Mountbatten had asked to be informed of the Combined Chiefs of Staff's decision, and the British were anxious to resolve any differences as soon as possible. The Joint Staff Mission, in consultation with Wedemeyer, therefore asked the Joint Chiefs of Staff to include in the proposed directive definite instructions 'to initiate planning and preparation for ['Vanguard'] in mid March', as long as this did not conflict with the prior commitments of 'Champion'. Their request was considered favourably on 8th September, after the British party had left England for Quebec, and the way was therefore open for the discussion of a draft.

The British proposals for the Pacific did not have such a smooth passage. The Joint Chiefs of Staff did not reply to the telegram of 18th August until 9th September. When they did so it was merely to remark:

'The United States Chiefs of Staff accept the British proposal . . . for the formation of a British Empire Task Force under a British Commander, consisting of British, Australian and New Zealand land, sea and air forces to operate in the South West Pacific Theatre under General MacArthur's supreme command.

It is noted that this will enable the British Fleet to be well placed to reinforce the United States Pacific Fleet if this should later be desired.'

This ignored the main British offer of a Fleet for the central Pacific, and it was therefore decided to press the point as soon as possible at Quebec. The alternative which had been accepted was in any case now raising difficulties which both the Prime Minister and the Chiefs of Staff would be glad to avoid; for the issue of command posed grave problems for the Commonwealth Powers in the Pacific, and as it seemed increasingly likely that the British would propose new arrangements, both the Australian Government and General MacArthur became increasingly upset. The matter was further complicated by personalities within the existing Command; and as anxieties grew with speculation, Mr. Churchill was forced early in September to dispel the exaggerated rumours that had arisen. The British themselves, moreover, were still uncertain if they could eventually spare a land contingent for the proposed task force, and the Prime Minister was not happy about the offer that had been made. But it might prove difficult to withdraw, and all parties would thus be relieved if the first alternative were accepted and the main British contribution were confined to the central Pacific.

The first alternative, moreover, received a fresh stimulus on the eve of the 'Octagon' Conference. On 12th September, the Chief of the Air Staff raised the possibility—for the first time at this level—of British participation from the Pacific in the long-range bombing of Japan. This was a new idea. When the Combined Chiefs of Staff had met in London in June, they had noted that British aircraft would be available in due course for long-range operations from south-east Asia; but by the end of August, the possibility of a German collapse seemed likely to free between six hundred and eight hundred heavy bombers, only some of which could be employed from the existing Indian bases. By turning half of this force into tankers, which could refuel their consorts in mid-air, the other half could be given a range of 1,500 miles, not unequal to that of the B.29's; and with bases in Formosa or on the Chinese coast near Amoy, it could thus cover the Japanese Home Islands. Some forty squadrons might well be provided by the early summer of 1945, if the first could be withdrawn from Europe by October, 1944. The project attracted the Prime Minister, and he promised to raise it at the forthcoming conference as a complement to the main offer of the British Fleet. With the possibility of a bomber force as well as of a Fleet in the central Pacific, the Middle Strategy declined still further in favour.

Thus, when Mr. Churchill and the Chiefs of Staff sailed for Quebec early in September, the proposals for the shape of the British effort in the Far East had at last been settled. It remained to find the resources for operation 'Vanguard', which linked those for south-east Asia with those for the Pacific.

CHAPTER XIII

THE SECOND QUEBEC CONFERENCE AND THE AFTERMATH, SEPTEMBER 1944

(i)

The Conference

THE SECOND Quebec Conference ('the 'Octagon' Conference), whose opening date had been settled in July 1944, was held at a difficult moment. It was necessarily much concerned with the relations between the war against Germany and the war against Japan; but the outcome of the first, on which the immediate future of the second partly depended, was highly uncertain when the delegates assembled, and remained uncertain until after they had dispersed. Some of their decisions, therefore, soon proved unrealistic; and indeed 'Octagon', like its predecessor 'Quadrant' thirteen months before, pointed the difficulty of arranging large military conferences, demanding ample preparation, to coincide with a decisive moment in a rapidly changing situation.

But this very fact marks the 'Octagon' Conference as the turning point in the last phase of the war. Early in September, it seemed likely to form the climax of the year that had begun with 'Quadrant', a year dedicated to the proposition that Germany would be defeated by the end of 1944. This hope, as we have seen, had grown in London and Washington, and had formed the basis for many of the plans for the Far East. It persisted throughout the conference itself, though with some diminution. But by the end of September, it had disappeared. The Allies were by then virtually certain that Germany would survive into the winter, and possibly into 1945; and the war in Europe, which for most of 1944 had seemed to progress towards a triumphant conclusion in accordance with a strategic plan, in October entered on a last stage that was in a sense an epilogue, whose inevitable end could no longer be affected significantly by strategic choice.

The interest of the last eight months in Europe is indeed of a different order. The result of the war against Germany had been decided by September, 1944; but it had not been decided in time. The consequences did not seriously affect the main strategy for the West, which unrolled at a slower pace and with minor divagations. But they profoundly affected the relations and the balance of power between the victors. The process was particularly serious for Britain. For the British had planned to reach the climax of their effort in 1944, and thereafter could only decline within an alliance whose own foundations were shifting. 'Octagon' is the last of the great series of Anglo-American conferences which formulated the grand strategy. In 1945, the meetings of the three Allies were concerned increasingly with diplomatic affairs, in which, as in the conduct of the war, the British influence was no longer so great.

When the British left for Quebec on 5th September, they were occupied by three main strategic problems: the future in Italy; the transfer of forces, depending partly on that future, from Europe to south-east Asia; and the British rôle in the Pacific. The first and third of these problems awaited discussion with the Americans; but the data at least for the second could be provided by the British themselves. It will be recalled that the Prime Minister was anxious early in September to investigate this question,[1] and he accordingly embarked upon it during the voyage to Quebec. The plans for 'Vanguard'[2] had been severely re-examined in London between 9th and 18th August, when Admiral Mountbatten left for Ceylon, and it had then been estimated that all of the naval and assault forces, and 190 out of the 552 transport aircraft required, could be supplied by Britain, leaving some 360 transport aircraft and some 550 gliders to be extracted from the Americans. The critical shortage lay on land, for of one airborne and six infantry divisions now thought to be needed, it seemed certain that only one infantry division could be found from the South-East Asia Command itself. Three factors had to be considered in providing the rest: the capacity of India as a base, the time to be allowed between their withdrawal from Europe and their commitment to the operation, and the dates at which they could be released from their existing duties.

Conditions in India had not changed appreciably since earlier in the year. The Command, despite continuous diversions and uncertainties, was working steadily towards its goal of providing a base for twenty divisions,[3] and General Auchinleck was able to report at the end of July, 1944 that this seemed likely to be achieved in April or May,

---

[1] See pp. 394-5 above.

[2] The code name 'Vanguard' was thought by 23rd August to have been compromised, and was then changed to 'Dracula', by which name the operation will henceforth be known. The code name 'Champion' was changed, at the same time and for the same reason, to 'Capital'.

[3] See p. 148 above.

1945. But however much the facilities of the hinterland might be enlarged, it seemed impossible radically to alter the capacity of the ports. Auchinleck stated that by March, 1945 he would be able to handle five divisions simultaneously for operations overseas, but only if he had five months' warning and if the troops were sent to India complete with stores of every type for three months and with all assault stores packed. They should moreover be allowed five months in India itself, for training and reorganization. The Chiefs of Staff did not agree with this estimate, and reduced the period to two months; but with that alteration, and assuming that Auchinleck's other conditions could be met, his programme would probably be accepted, for of the seven divisions contemplated for the assault on Rangoon only four would be carried to the operation by sea, of which only one Special Service (commando) brigade followed by one brigade group would take part in the assault itself.

The greatest difficulty in fact lay not in the rate of output but in the rate of intake at the ports. In August, 1944 this was limited to 50,000 men every twenty-one days, which, allowing for the normal reinforcements for the theatre, amounted to one complete infantry division. This was clearly inadmissible for an operation involving six divisions working to a very strict timetable, and Mountbatten asked Auchinleck to re-examine the situation. After making very considerable exertions, Auchinleck announced in the middle of September that, accepting certain risks and subject to certain conditions, he could probably take 100,000 men a month; but in the meantime the plans had to proceed on the earlier figure, which until then had seemed the most that could be expected, and which in fact could be exceeded only at considerable risk.

At the beginning of September a timetable was therefore drawn up, based on the withdrawal of three British divisions and two brigades from north-west Europe, and of three British/Indian divisions from the Mediterranean, all between mid-September and mid-November. Allowing for two months in India before re-embarkation for 'Dracula' against Rangoon, this just met the operation's demands for assault troops and reinforcements. But the programme was based on two assumptions, besides the capacity of the Indian base: first, that the shipping implications could be accepted; secondly, that the British troops could be withdrawn from Europe in time to enjoy the full quota of embarkation or home leave and the relevant measures of demobilization. The troop shipping for 'Dracula' was likely to absorb the entire British troopship lift from early in October, 1944 until the following February, thus placing the whole burden of reinforcing Europe on the Americans alone. But if conditions in Europe allowed troops to be withdrawn for the Far East, reinforcement on the agreed scale would be unnecessary, and the Chiefs of Staff therefore accepted the assumption that shipping could be spared.

But in the first ten days of September, it was by no means certain whether or not conditions in Europe would allow of a withdrawal of troops. We have seen the reasons which led the Joint Intelligence Committee, and with it the Chiefs of Staff, to expect an early German collapse, and the Prime Minister's reasons for disagreement;[1] and if Mr. Churchill was right, the fate of the British/Indian divisions in Italy might be of considerable import. The withdrawal of three of them over the next few weeks might conceivably decide the fate of the current battle, or if decided might prevent it from being exploited on the appropriate scale. The Prime Minister was therefore determined that they should stay in Italy for at least another six weeks, and hoped that if possible their transfer to the Far East would be postponed until 15th December.

Churchill thereupon embarked with the Chiefs of Staff on a detailed examination of the means to achieve this end. As he himself remarked, success depended 'on the making of a key fitted to open a particular lock'; and this was by no means easy even in a calmer atmosphere than prevailed at the time. It was therefore perhaps not surprising that the constantly changing calculations, made at high speed for high stakes against an uncertain background, should have been accompanied by misunderstandings, and should at times have aroused a feeling, in the week before the 'Octagon' Conference began, at least equal to that at the beginning of March when Ismay had tried to bring about an accommodation.[2]

The Prime Minister first attacked the assumption that the British elements of the divisions in Italy should be given a month's home leave before embarking for India. This should be eliminated, if possible, by replacing those who had served for three years abroad by men from other units whose leave was not yet due, or else by withholding the privilege of leave altogether. Allowing for the time spent in going to and from leave, a full two months would thus be saved. But the proposal did not meet the case. Apart from the dissatisfaction it might arouse—and which officers on the spot and at home feared might lead to serious trouble—it would not in fact achieve its object. For while all of the divisions in Italy could then be left at the front until the first half of November, their subsequent arrival in India would fall too near that of the divisions from north-west Europe, thus placing an excessive strain on the Indian ports. Their place in the programme would therefore have to be taken by those other divisions, the first of which must be ready to sail at the end of September instead of, as planned, in November. This meant cancelling its embarkation leave, with the possible undesirable consequences, and would merely delay by a fortnight the decision to withdraw the first troops from Europe.

[1] See pp. 398-402 above.

[2] See pp. 448-9 above.

The Prime Minister thereupon turned to the size of the operation itself. If the chief difficulty lay in the capacity of the Indian ports, the only remedy was to reduce the number of men and stores that must pass through them. The Chiefs of Staff stated on 9th September that 'the fundamental problem stated in its simplest terms is the movement of 370,000 men and 24,000 vehicles from the European theatre to India in the shortest time.' The Prime Minister fell on this remark. A lively debate followed, of the familiar and complicated kind which statistics are apt to produce; but though subjected to considerable pressure, the Chiefs of Staff, faced with demands not only for the operation itself but for the relief of sick and wounded and of men due to return home, would agree only to reduce the total slightly, to 352,000 men. This by no means satisfied Churchill, who embarked with Wilson and Alexander on a detailed inquiry into the composition of the British/Indian divisions in Italy; but despite his interpretation of the figures he received, the Chiefs of Staff, after further vigorous debate, could see no way to a greater reduction by the time that the party arrived at Quebec. The difficulties therefore remained to be solved in the light of the discussions at the conference.

The conference itself occupied five days, from 12th to 16th September. As the Prime Minister reported to the War Cabinet on the 13th, it opened 'in a blaze of friendship'.[1] The victories of the past three months, prepared and achieved in combination, warmed the atmosphere and stimulated resolve. The Prime Minister's opening remarks to the first Plenary Meeting on the 13th convey the impression.

> 'Since 'Sextant' the affairs of the United Nations had taken a revolutionary turn for the good. Everything we had touched had turned to gold, and during the last seven weeks there had been an unbroken run of military successes. The manner in which the situation had developed since the Teheran Conference gave the impression of remarkable design and precision of execution. First there had been the Anzio Landing, and then, on the same day as the launching of the great operation 'Overlord', we had captured Rome, which had seemed the most perfect timing. He wished to congratulate the United States Chiefs of Staff on the success of 'Dragoon', which had produced the most gratifying results.[2] . . . He was firmly convinced that future historians would say that the period since Teheran had shown the successful working of an extraordinarily efficient inter-Allied war machine.'[3]

---

[1] See *Triumph and Tragedy*, p. 137.

[2] Cf. p. 392 above.

[3] Cf. his remark on p. 193 above.

The conference, indeed, had already recorded its first success. At their first meeting at noon on the 12th, the Combined Chiefs of Staff had discussed the situation in the Mediterranean. The British were anxious lest the Americans should refuse to consider their proposal that, in certain circumstances, the Allies should move north-east on Austria once the Germans had yielded northern Italy; or lest they should in the meantime withdraw some of the American forces from the peninsula.[1] Admiral Leahy's opening remarks did not remove, though they met, some of their fears.

> 'Part or all of the Fifth Army should be transferred to France, if it can be used effectively in the attack on Germany. The timing of the transfer and the route, whether over land or by sea, is dependent on the progress and outcome of the present offensive in Italy.
>
> If General Eisenhower indicates that he does not require a part or all of the United States forces now in Italy, they should then be utilised to clear the Germans from Italy and to assist British forces in operations to the north-eastward toward Vienna.
>
> The transfer of part or all of the Twelfth [U.S.] Air Force [supporting the Armies] to France should be dependent on the progress and outcome of the present offensive in Italy, and more particularly on the disposition of the Fifth Army. The Fifteenth [U.S.] Air Force can best perform its mission [long-range bombing operations] by remaining at its Foggia bases.'

Field Marshal Brooke then put the British case. He thought that the Germans might well fail to disengage successfully from the Gothic Line into the Alps, but might rather be severely mauled in the northern plain. In that case, and if they also withdrew from Greece and Yugoslavia, the way might be open to the Ljubljana Gap, and thence to Vienna in the course of the winter. Even if that proved optimistic, the Western Allies might soon be able to seize the Istrian plain as a base for a further advance, or for a swift move into Austria should the enemy capitulate. He therefore asked that all elements of Fifth Army should be retained in Italy. He also asked what the Americans intended to do with their assault shipping supporting the recent landing in the south of France, which if held in the Mediterranean might be used for an attack on the Istrian peninsula.

The second question was answered at once. Admiral King stated that the assault shipping, although earmarked for 'other operations' (in the Far East), was not yet under orders; and 'he too had in mind the possibility of amphibious operations in Istria'. But an early decision was desirable, and the Combined Chiefs of Staff agreed that it should be taken by 15th October. Meanwhile, the Americans would withdraw from the theatre, as already planned, those L.S.T. which were not being used for the supply of Allied troops in the south of France.[2]

---

[1] See pp. 391-4 above.

[2] See p. 394 above.

PLATE VIII. BRITISH MILITARY ADVISERS AT THE SECOND QUEBEC CONFERENCE, SEPTEMBER 1944.
Left to right: Field Marshal Dill, Admiral Cunningham, Field Marshal Brooke, Air Marshal Portal, General Ismay.

The Americans were also not disposed to press for the transfer of their land forces to France. Marshall explained that any such move was contingent both on General Eisenhower's reception of the idea and on the Germans having first withdrawn from Italy, in which case there might not be immediate employment on the southern front for so large an Allied force. They had no intention of removing American troops from the current battle (except possibly a few small units) as long as there were Germans to fight; and successive statements by three of the four Joint Chiefs of Staff amply confirmed the position.

> 'Admiral Leahy re-emphasised that the United States' proposal was contingent on the destruction or withdrawal of a large part of the German Army.
>
> General Marshall said that there was no intention in the mind of the United States Chiefs of Staff to effect the withdrawal of forces from Italy at the present time.
>
> Admiral King confirmed that an option on the United States landing craft now in the Mediterranean could be retained provided the decision was reached by the 15th October.'

The Combined Chiefs of Staff thereupon agreed, and the British so informed General Wilson two days later, that no forces should be withdrawn from Italy until they knew the outcome of 'the present offensive'; that they could then consider further the withdrawal of formations from Fifth Army; and that Wilson should submit by 10th October plans for capturing the Istrian peninsula with the assault shipping already in the Mediterranean. When, on the 14th, the Prime Minister queried the meaning attached by the Americans to 'the present offensive', Marshall and Leahy assured him that it included 'the invasion of the Po Valley'; and the agreement of the 12th was then incorporated in the Combined Chiefs of Staff's Final Report.

The immediate future in Italy thus seemed safe. Nor, though both partners had concentrated on the immediate future, did the British encounter any opposition to their subsequent strategy. Whatever the forces to be employed (and this was not discussed), the Joint Chiefs of Staff, as the C.I.G.S. had indeed forecast in August,[1] did not object in principle to a move to the north-east after victory in Italy, but rather recognized it as the proper alternative to a further move into France. According to the Prime Minister on 13th September,[2] 'The idea of our going to Vienna, if the war lasts long enough and if other people do not get there first, is fully accepted here'. Moreover, on 16th September the Americans accepted the British proposals made in the summer for action in central and south-east Europe should Germany suddenly collapse,[3] with the addition that Wilson was now ordered to

[1] See p. 394 above.

[2] See *Triumph and Tragedy*, p. 137.

[3] See pp. 388-90 above.

seize control in Venezia Giulia (the western part of Istria) with approximately one division. In contrast to its prominence over the past year, the Mediterranean indeed now proved an uncontroversial topic, and occupied comparatively little of the conference's time.

There was also little to say on other strategic developments in Europe, whose future must depend on the outcome of the current operations. The delegates confined themselves to three questions, arising from those operations: the machinery for military co-ordination with the Russians; the relations of the strategic air forces to the 'Overlord' Command; and the British and American zones of occupation in Germany.

The possibility of closer and more regular co-operation with the Russians, as an extension of the Combined Chiefs of Staff's machinery, had been raised and rejected at the Cairo Conference.[1] For the next six months, there was no reason to allude to it again. But once the Western Allies had landed in France, and the Russian offensive had been resumed, the existing arrangements were likely to be questioned sooner or later. On this occasion, the Russians took the initiative. On 1st July, 1944, Major-General M. B. Burrows, who in February had succeeded Lieut.-General Martel as head of the British Military Mission in Moscow,[2] reported that Stalin had told the American Ambassador that he thought the time had come to form a military committee in Moscow, 'to co-ordinate matters of military importance concerning the Allies'. Although there was later some reason for suspecting that Stalin might have been referring to the Far East, the Russian Chief of the General Staff, Marshal Vassilievsky, made the same suggestion, referring specifically to Europe, later in July. The British and Americans agreed in principle, and during August exchanged views on the form the machinery should take. The Americans were anxious to establish liaison in the field, so as to take the greatest advantage of any rapid development. They therefore favoured the appointment of a senior Russian liaison officer to Eisenhower's and to Wilson's headquarters. But the British, while prepared to accept such officers if reciprocal arrangements were granted, were not anxious, from their experience of the Russian Mission already with the Mediterranean Command, to accept them as an alternative to a combined committee in Moscow. On the eve of the 'Octagon' Conference, the British Chiefs of Staff accordingly submitted proposals for the creation of a 'Combined British, United States and Soviet Committee in Moscow', to advise the Combined Chiefs of Staff and the Russian General Staff on all matters demanding combined planning or action in the military sphere. The Russian representative should be a senior member of the Russian General Staff: the British and Americans might

---

[1] See pp. 167-8 above.

[2] See p. 24 above.

well be represented by the heads of their Military Missions. While the Americans still wished to establish liaison in the field, they agreed that this might follow from the working of the committee; and on 14th September, the Combined Chiefs of Staff instructed their representatives in Moscow to propose the creation of such a body to the Russians.

The other two questions affected Eisenhower's Command. His control over the strategic air forces, which in all its aspects had given rise to so much discussion between November, 1943 and March 1944, had been subject to review after 'Overlord' had been established on the Continent.[1] At the end of August, the British thought that this review was due. On the one hand, 'the preparatory and critical phases of 'Overlord' have now passed': on the other, 'experience of the present method of control has shown it to be unsatisfactory as a long-term arrangement', and it was likely soon to be made more unsatisfactory by new factors. The physical separation of Tedder's headquarters in France from those of Spaatz and Harris in England already offset to some extent the original advantages of the machinery; it was no longer necessary to reserve a large proportion of the heavy bombers continuously for close support; the bombing of German oil and industry might soon be co-ordinated with air operations by the Russians, which perhaps should be done from London; and the marked decline in Germany's position demanded immediate control by the Combined Chiefs of Staff of a weapon with so potent an effect on morale. The British therefore recommended that the Combined Chiefs of Staff should resume control of the strategic air forces, associating the Americans with the machinery more directly than before, and safeguarding the position of the Supreme Commanders in north-west Europe and the Mediterranean should their operations suddenly demand support by heavy bombers.

> '. . . Before the 14th April 1944, the control of the strategic bomber forces was exercised on behalf of the Combined Chiefs of Staff by the Chief of the Air Staff as their agent. The arrangement proposed for the future is that control should be exercised jointly by the Chief of the Air Staff and the Commanding General U.S.A.A.F., who will respectively be represented for the purposes of local consultation by Deputy Chief of the Air Staff and the Commanding General U.S. Strategic Air Forces in Europe.'

After discussion on 12th September, the Joint Chiefs of Staff accepted the proposed machinery. The Combined Chiefs of Staff then addressed a directive to the Deputy Chief of the Air Staff and the Commanding General, U.S. Strategic Air Forces in Europe. The final version was approved on the 14th, and appeared in the Combined Chiefs of Staff's Final Report two days later.

---

[1] See p. 296 above.

'. . . 3. The overall mission of the strategic air forces is the progressive destruction and dislocation of the German military, industrial and economic systems and the direct support of land and naval forces.

4. Under this general mission you are to direct your attacks, subject to the exigencies of weather, and tactical feasibility, against the systems of objectives and in the order of priority now established by the Supreme Commander, Allied Expeditionary Force. When you decide that changes in objectives or priorities are necessary, you will issue the necessary directives and inform the Chief of the Air Staff, R.A.F., and the Commanding General, United States Army Air Forces.

5. Objectives other than those covered in paragraph 4 above will be attacked in accordance with the following:

(a) Counter Air Force action. As the result of air action against the production, maintenance and operation facilities of the German Air Force (G.A.F.), its fighting effectiveness has now been substantially reduced. At the same time, our combined air strength has been vastly increased. In these circumstances we are no longer justified in regarding the G.A.F. and its supporting industry as a primary objective for attack. Our major effort must now be focussed directly upon the vital sources of Germany's war economy. To this end policing attacks against the G.A.F. are to be adjusted so as to maintain tactical conditions which will permit of the maximum impact on the primary objectives. No fixed priority is, therefore, assigned to policing attacks against the G.A.F. The intensity of such attacks will be regulated by the tactical situation existing.

(b) Direct support. The direct support of land and naval operations remains a continuing commitment upon your forces. Upon call from the Supreme Commanders concerned either for assistance in the battle or to take advantage of related opportunities you will meet their requirements promptly.

(c) Important industrial areas. When weather or tactical conditions are unsuitable for operations against specific primary objectives, attacks should be delivered upon important industrial areas by both Bomber Command R.A.F. and U.S.St.A.F.E. (using blind bombing technique as necessary).

(d) S.O.E. operations. All S.O.E. /O.S.S. [U.S. Office of Strategic Services] operations undertaken by units of R.A.F. Bomber Command and United States Strategic Air Forces in Europe will be in accordance with the requirements of the Supreme Allied Commanders, who will issue the requisite orders from time to time, under existing procedure.

(e) Attacks in support of the Russian armies. Attacks in support of operations by the Russian armies should be delivered as prescribed from time to time by the Combined Chiefs of Staff.

(f) Fleeting targets. There may be certain other targets of great but fleeting importance for the attack of which all necessary plans and preparations should be made. Of these, an example would be the important units of the German Fleet in harbour or at sea.

6. You are responsible that the operations of the Strategic Air Forces are co-ordinated with the operations of the Tactical Air Forces in the theatres.'

The Combined Chiefs of Staff had hithero been concerned only intermittently with the allocation of zones of occupation in Germany. Cossac's plan in July, 1943 had tentatively assigned north-west Germany, Belgium, Luxembourg, Holland and Denmark to the British; southern Germany, France and Austria to the Americans; and had proposed that the Russians should take 'the sphere to the East of the British area'. The possibility of French participation had not been mentioned, and awaited further developments. The problems affecting and affected by this proposal were the concern of the Foreign Office and of the committees dealing with post-war affairs; and, as the Prime Minister and the Chiefs of Staff agreed, the latter 'should be kept as clear as possible' of them. But at Cairo, the Joint Chiefs of Staff put forward counter-proposals virtually reversing the British and American zones, which the British suspected came from the President. Subsequent inquiry in January, 1944 confirmed that this was so, and that the Joint Chiefs of Staff could not be expected to enter into details; and early in February the President himself approached the Prime Minister on the matter. His argument was political. Cossac's proposal for the American zone placed American forces in the centre of Europe, and dependent on communications across France; and 'I am absolutely unwilling to police France and possibly Italy and the Balkans as well'. The British, however, did not wish to exchange zones. The 'Overlord' plan of campaign placed the British forces and supply lines on the left and the Americans on the right, and while the Chiefs of Staff agreed that if Germany collapsed at an early stage a transfer of troops and material might prove possible, at a later stage it would involve great difficulties, which indeed in some circumstances might prove insuperable. Moreover, the British were particularly anxious to occupy northern Germany, so as to guarantee that the German navy was properly disarmed and investigated, and would be glad to maintain their association with Holland, whose forces with the Allies were their responsibility. They had also to consider the vacuum—which Britain herself probably could not fill—that would arise in these zones of particular interest, should the Americans withdraw from Europe soon after the war. While recognizing its political force, the Prime Minister therefore could not accede to the President's proposal.

Further exchanges followed between the Heads of Government

between May and July. But neither felt able to give way, and on 10th August the Prime Minister counselled the British Chiefs of Staff not to enter into a detailed discussion until the 'Octagon' Conference took place. The President, for his part, gave notice of his intention to settle the question personally with the Prime Minister. But by the time that the conference began, the position had altered to some extent. For the Americans now knew of the British intention to garrison the relevant areas in south-east Europe, and to accept the main responsibility for Austria;[1] while investigations in London had shown that it would be feasible to supply American forces in southern Germany through the Low Countries and northern Germany.

The Prime Minister and the President discussed the problem on 15th September. In the light of recent developments, the President no longer objected to the original proposals, and the Heads of Government agreed that the British should occupy 'North-Western Germany and a strip stretching right up the right bank of the Rhine', and the Americans 'Southern-Western Germany extending Northwards roughly to a line due East of Coblenz'. In order to ensure their communications to this zone, it was also agreed that the Americans might be given control of a northern German port.

The Combined Chiefs of Staff made more detailed arrangements the next day.[2]

> 'Upon the collapse of organised resistance by the German Army the following sub-division of that part of Germany not allocated to the Soviet Government for disarmament, policing and the preservation of order is acceptable from a military point of view by the Combined Chiefs of Staff.
>
> For disarmament, policing and preservation of order:
>
> The British forces under a British Commander will occupy Germany west of the Rhine and east of the Rhine north of the line from Koblenz, following the northern border of Hessen and Nassau to the border of the area allocated to the Soviet Government.
>
> The forces of the United States under a United States Commander will occupy Germany east of the Rhine, south of the line Koblenz-Northern border of Hessen-Nassau and west of the area allocated to the Soviet Government.
>
> Control of the ports of Bremen and Bremerhaven, and the necessary staging areas in that immediate vicinity will be vested in the Commander of the American Zone.
>
> American area to have in addition access through the Western and North-Western sea ports and passage through the British controlled area.
>
> Accurate delineation of the above outline of the British and American areas of control can be made at a later date.'

---

[1] See pp. 388-9 above.

[2] See Map VII, facing p. 343.

These arrangements provided the basis for later negotiations with the Russians and with the French.

The greater part of the conference was devoted to the affairs of the Far East. Agreement on south-east Asia, as we have seen, had virtually been reached early in September, and the British Chiefs of Staff and the Joint Staff Mission in Washington exchanged drafts for a proposed directive to Mountbatten while the former were on their way to Quebec. By the time they arrived, the following had been approved.

> '1. Your primary object is the recapture of all Burma at the earliest date. Operations to achieve this object must not, however, prejudice the security of the existing air supply route to China, including the air staging post at Myitkyina, adequate protection of which is essential throughout.
>
> 2. The following are approved operations:
>
> (a) The stages of Operation 'Capital' [formerly 'Champion'][1] necessary to the security of the air route;
>
> (b) Operation 'Dracula' [formerly 'Vanguard'].[2]
>
> The Combined Chiefs of Staff attach the greatest importance to the vigorous prosecution of Operation 'Capital' and to the execution of Operation 'Dracula' before the monsoon in 1945, with a target date of the 15th March.
>
> 3. If 'Dracula' has to be postponed until after the monsoon of 1945, you will continue to exploit Operation 'Capital' so far as may be possible without prejudice to preparations for the execution of Operation 'Dracula' in November 1945.'

This was discussed by the Combined Chiefs of Staff on 14th September. The Americans accepted the formula, as long as it was understood that their interests must not be threatened by any possibility of lack of resources. They were also anxious, as always, to insert a reference to the Burma Road, and in the final version the words 'and the attainment of overland communications with China' were added to paragraph 2(a) of the British version. The Combined Chiefs of Staff's Final Report to the President and Prime Minister repeated the terms of these orders, which were sent to Admiral Mountbatten on 16th September to supersede the directive of 3rd June.[3]

It was less easy to obtain agreement on the Pacific, where the British were anxious to place a Fleet and air force with the Americans. The Prime Minister lost no time in pursuing the theme. He discussed the matter of the Fleet with Admiral Leahy on the day of his arrival, when he was told that its offer had been accepted; and on the morning of

---

[1] See p. 506, n.2. above.

[2] Ibid.

[3] See p. 490 above.

13th September he raised the issue at the first Plenary Meeting of the conference.

'There were elements inimical to Anglo-American good relations which were putting it about that Great Britain would take no share in the war against Japan once Germany had been defeated. Far from shirking this task, the British Empire was ardent to play the greatest possible part. We had every reason for doing so. Japan was as much the bitter enemy of the British Empire as of the United States. British territory had been captured in battle and grievous losses had been suffered. The offer he, the Prime Minister, now wished to make, was for the British Main Fleet to take part in the major operations against Japan under United States supreme command. We should have available a powerful and well balanced force, including, it was hoped, at the end of next year, our newest 15″ battleship. A fleet train of ample proportions had been built up, which would render the fleet independent for a considerable time of shore base resources.

The President intervened to say that the British fleet was no sooner offered than accepted.

The Prime Minister, continuing, said that the placing of the British Fleet in the Central Pacific would not prevent a detachment being made to work with General MacArthur in the South-West Pacific if this was desired. There was, of course, no intention to interfere in any way with General MacArthur's command. As a further contribution to the defeat of the enemy, the Royal Air Force would like to take a part in the heavy bombardment of Japan. A bomber force of no mean size could be made available for this purpose and would be honoured to share with their American colleagues the dangers of striking at the heart of the enemy. . . .

Sir Charles Portal said that he hoped to have available between 600 and 800 heavy bombers for operations against the mainland of Japan.

The Prime Minister asked that he could have a more definite undertaking about the employment of the British fleet in the main operations against Japan.

The President said that he would like to see the British fleet wherever and whenever possible.

Admiral King said that a paper had been prepared for reference to the Combined Chiefs of Staff. The question was being actively studied.

The Prime Minister said that the offer of the British fleet had been made; was it accepted?

The President replied in the affirmative.

The Prime Minister enquired whether an undertaking could be given for the British Air Force to participate in the main operations.

General Marshall said that he and General Arnold were trying to see how best to fit in the maximum number of aircraft for these operations. It was not so long ago that we were crying out for aeroplanes—now we had a glut. He suggested that if the British were heavily engaged in South-East Asia and in Malaya that would require a large proportion of their air forces for these operations. Was there a distinction between these latter operations and the operations envisaged by Sir Charles Portal for heavy bombardment of Japan?

Sir Charles Portal replied that there was a distinction. The Lancaster bomber, if refuelled in the air, had a range nearly approaching that of the B.29. Without refuelling in the air these aircraft had a range of 800 or 900 miles.

The Prime Minister remarked that for the future good relations of the two countries, on which so much depended, it was of vital importance that the British should be given their fair share in the main operations against Japan. The United States had given the most handsome assistance to the British Empire, in the fight against Germany. It could only be expected that the British Empire in return should give the United States all assistance in their power towards the defeat of Japan.'

The British thus seemed to have gained their main point, the offer of the Fleet for the central Pacific. But the matter was not to be settled without further discussion. Later in the same day, the British Chiefs of Staff received a memorandum from the Joint Chiefs of Staff which had been composed before the morning session.

'1. The United States Chiefs of Staff would welcome a British naval task force in the Pacific to participate in the main operations against Japan. They consider that the initial use of such a force should be on the western flank of the advance in the South-West Pacific. They assume that such a force would be balanced and self-supporting.

2. The United States Chiefs of Staff repeat their acceptance of the British proposal to form a British Empire task force in the South-West Pacific. It is realised that the time of formation of such a force depends to a considerable extent on the end of the war in Europe as well as on 'Dracula' and on the requirements of projected operations in the South-West Pacific.'

When the Combined Chiefs of Staff met the next morning, the British raised the matter. While recognizing that the paper represented a view which presumably had been overtaken by events, they wished to be quite certain that the Prime Minister's proposal had been fully accepted. The ensuing conversation settled once and for all the nature of the British participation in the Pacific war. For this reason it will be given in full.

'Sir Alan Brooke said that the British Chiefs of Staff were disturbed by the statement of the United States Chiefs of Staff... with regard to British participation in the war against Japan. He realised that this paper had been written before the plenary session on the previous day. He felt that it did not entirely coincide with the proposal put forward at that conference and accepted by the President. For political reasons it was essential that the British fleet should take part in the main operations against Japan.

Admiral Leahy asked if Sir Alan Brooke's point would be met by the elimination of the words: "they consider that the initial use of such a force should be on the western flank of the advance in the South-West Pacific." It might be that the British fleet would be used initially in the Bay of Bengal and thereafter as required by the existing situation.

Sir Andrew Cunningham said that the main fleet would not be required in the Bay of Bengal, since there were already more British forces there than required. He agreed to the deletion proposed by Admiral Leahy.

Admiral King also agreed to the deletion of these words, which he felt were not relevant to the general case.

Continuing, Sir Andrew Cunningham asked the United States views as to the meaning of the term "balanced forces" in the final sentence of paragraph 1 of [the Joint Chiefs of Staff's memorandum of 13th September]. He said that the British Chiefs of Staff had in mind a force of some 4 battleships, 5 to 6 large carriers, 20 light fleet carriers and C.V.E.'s [convoy escort carriers] and the appropriate number of cruisers and destroyers. This he would regard as a balanced force.

Admiral King stressed that it was essential for these forces to be self-supporting.

Sir Andrew Cunningham said that, if these forces had their fleet train, they could operate unassisted for several months provided they had the necessary rear bases—probably in Australia. The provision of bases would be a matter for agreement.

Admiral King said that the practicability of employing these forces would be a matter for discussion from time to time.

Admiral Leahy said that he did not feel that the question for discussion was the practicability of employment but rather the matter of where they should be employed from time to time.

Sir Andrew Cunningham referred to the Prime Minister's statement that he wished the British fleet to take part in the main operations in the Pacific. Decision with regard to this was necessary, since many preliminary preparations had to be made.

Admiral King suggested that the British Chiefs of Staff should put forward proposals with regard to the employment of the British fleet.

Sir Andrew Cunningham said that the British wish was that they should be employed in the central Pacific.

Admiral King said that at the plenary meeting no specific reference to the central Pacific had been made.

Sir Alan Brooke said that the emphasis had been laid on the use of the British fleet in the main effort against Japan.

Admiral Leahy said that, as he saw it, the main effort was at present from New Guinea to the Philippines, and it would later move to the northward.

Admiral King said that he was in no position now to commit himself as to where the British fleet could be employed.

Sir Charles Portal reminded the Combined Chiefs of Staff of the original offer made by the British Chiefs of Staff, which read:

> "It is our desire, in accordance with His Majesty's Government's policy, that this fleet should play its full part at the earliest possible moment in the main operations against Japan wherever the greatest naval strength is required."

When the British Chiefs of Staff spoke of the main operations against Japan they did not intend to confine this meaning to Japan itself geographically but meant rather that the fleet should take part in the main operations within the theatre of war wherever they might be taking place.

Sir Andrew Cunningham stressed that the British Chiefs of Staff did not wish the British fleet merely to take part in mopping up operations in areas falling into our hands.

Admiral Leahy said that he felt that the actual operations in which the British fleet would take part would have to be decided in the future. It might well be that the fleet would be required for the conquest of Singapore, which he would regard as a major operation.

The Combined Chiefs of Staff then considered paragraph 2 of [the Joint Chiefs of Staff's memorandum of 13th September], referring to the use of a British Empire Task Force in the South-West Pacific.

Sir Charles Portal said that the Prime Minister had offered the British fleet for use in the main operations against Japan. By implication this paragraph accepted a naval task force for the South-West Pacific, and was therefore contrary to the intention he had expressed.

Admiral King said that it was, of course, essential to have sufficient forces for the war against Japan. He was not, however, prepared to accept a British fleet which he could not employ or support. In principle he wished to accept a British fleet in the Pacific but it would be entirely unacceptable for the British main fleet to be employed for political reasons in the Pacific and thus necessitate the withdrawal of some of the United States fleet.

Sir Charles Portal reminded Admiral King that the Prime Minister had suggested that certain of the newer British capital ships should be substituted for certain of the older United States ships.

Sir Andrew Cunningham said that as he understood it the

Prime Minister and President were in agreement that it was essential for British forces to take a leading part in the main operations against Japan.

Admiral King said that it was not his recollection that the President had agreed to this. He could not accept that a view expressed by the Prime Minister should be regarded as a directive to the Combined Chiefs of Staff.

Sir Charles Portal said that the Prime Minister felt it essential that it should be placed on record that he wished the British fleet to play a major role in the operations against Japan.

Sir Alan Brooke said that, as he remembered it, the offer was no sooner made than accepted by the President.

Admiral King asked for specific British proposals.

Sir Charles Portal referred once more to the offer . . . which he had previously quoted.

Admiral Leahy said that he could see no objection whatever to this proposal. He could not say exactly where the fleet could be employed at this moment but there would be ample opportunity for its use provided it was self-supporting.

Admiral King said that the question of the British proposal for the use of the main fleet would have to be referred to the President before it could be accepted.

Admiral Leahy said that if Admiral King saw any objections to this proposal he should take the matter up himself with the President. It might not be wise to use the term "main fleet".

Sir Andrew Cunningham said that the British fleet had been offered by the Prime Minister and the President had accepted it. He was prepared to agree to the deletion of the word "main" from paragraph 1 of [the Joint Chiefs of Staff's memorandum].

Admiral King said that the Prime Minister had also referred to the use of British air power in the Pacific.

General Arnold said that a definite answer with regard to British air help in the war against Japan could not be given now. The amount which could be absorbed would depend on the development of suitable facilities.

Sir Charles Portal said that it was, of course, impossible to be definite at the moment since the forces available would depend on the length of the war with Germany. What he would ask for was air facilities available in the bases in the Pacific so that the British could play their part. He would put forward a proposal for consideration.

General Marshall said that the best method would be a statement of numbers of aircraft and dates at which they would be available.

General Arnold agreed that this would be preferable.

Referring to paragraph 2 of [the Joint Chiefs of Staff's memorandum] Sir Alan Brooke pointed out that this paragraph dealt with the formation of a British Empire task force which was the second alternative put forward by the British Chiefs of Staff if for any reason the support of the British fleet in the main operations could not be accepted. Since this support had been accepted there would be no British naval forces available for the task force and British land forces could only arrive at a later date. He suggested therefore that this paragraph should be deleted.

Admiral King asked if it was intended to use the British fleet only in the main operations and to make no contribution to a task force in the South-West Pacific.

General Marshall said there were certain objections to forming a British Empire task force under General MacArthur's command at the present time.

This had been proposed by General Blamey, but if it were carried out between now and February of next year it would cause considerable difficulties from the point of view of land forces since the grouping of formations and the sequence of their movement had already been scheduled in accordance with future operations. The position would be different after March.

Sir Alan Brooke agreed that since British land forces would not be available until after Operation 'Dracula' it would be of no particular value to form a British task force now. The British fleet could, of course, play a part in operations in the South-West Pacific if they were required.

Sir Andrew Cunningham confirmed that there would be no objection to the British fleet working from time to time under General MacArthur's command.

General Marshall requested that, in order to safeguard his position with regard to the immediate formation of a task force, paragraph 2 of [the Joint Chiefs of Staff's memorandum] be deleted.

Sir Alan Brooke agreed. General MacArthur's plans had already been made and since no British land contribution could at present be made there was no object in retaining this paragraph.

The Combined Chiefs of Staff

(a) Agreed that the British fleet should participate in the main operations against Japan in the Pacific.

(b) Took note of the assurance of the British Chiefs of Staff that this fleet would be balanced and self-supporting.

(c) Agreed that the method of the employment of the British fleet in these main operations in the Pacific would be decided from time to time in accordance with the prevailing circumstances.

(d) Took note that in the light of (a) above, the British Chiefs of Staff withdraw their alternative proposal to form a British Empire task force in the South-West Pacific.

(e) Invited the Chief of the Air Staff to put forward, for planning purposes, a paper containing an estimate in general terms of the contribution the Royal Air Force would be prepared to make in the main operations against Japan.'

These decisions were repeated in the Combined Chiefs of Staff's Final Report, in which, for planning purposes, the date for the end of the war against Japan was set at eighteen months after the defeat of Germany. The shape of the British effort in the Far East had now been settled, and after nine months of continuous discussion at last seemed likely to bear fruit.

(ii)

Arnhem, the Gothic Line and the Consequences

While the conference was sitting, the 'Overlord' Command had decided the plans for the next, and as it hoped the final, phase of the campaign in Europe. On 9th September, General Eisenhower reported the position and his intentions to the Combined Chiefs of Staff.[1] He was confident that the enemy would concentrate on defending the Ruhr and the Saar; and since he intended 'to destroy the German Armed Forces and occupy the heart of Germany', he proposed to strike at those areas. It would first be necessary to break the Siegfried Line and seize crossings over the Rhine; and 'the main effort here will be on the left'. The northern Group of Armies, with that part of the central Group operating north of the Ardennes, would capture Antwerp, break the Siegfried Line where it covered the Ruhr, and seize the Ruhr. An Airborne Army, formed and now ready in Britain, would support the operations across the Rhine. Meanwhile the central Group of Armies, less that part operating north of the Ardennes, would take Brest, breach the Siegfried Line where it covered the Saar and seize Frankfurt, protect the Allies' southern flank, and where possible destroy German forces withdrawing from southern France.

When these operations were complete, Eisenhower saw three possible lines of advance across Germany: from the Ruhr to Hanover, Hamburg or Berlin; from Frankfurt to Leipzig, Magdeburg or Berlin; or a 'combination of both'. The possibility of secondary operations, for instance in the area Nuremberg-Munich, would depend on the state of transport and supplies.

These plans confirmed, as they derived from, the 'broad front' policy of August. The Supreme Commander could claim that it had brought the Allies almost to the frontier of Germany, and had weakened the German armies in the west possibly to the point of disintegration. On the other hand, the next stage of the operations, involving the

[1] See Map VII, facing p. 343.

breaching of the Siegfried Line, demanded plans for a further effort which the policy itself had possibly endangered. The shape of the picture emerged in the second week of September. In the south, Third U.S. Army's headlong advance still met with little opposition, and its forces were able to thrust onwards into the area between Nancy and Metz. In the centre, First U.S. Army likewise moved, though against growing resistance, on the right into Luxembourg and on the left from the area of Namur to the German frontier at Aachen, where on the 13th it paused before the Siegfried Line. The British and Canadians moved more slowly. For the Germans, once more under the supreme command of von Rundstedt, who was reinstated as Commander-in-Chief, West on 4th September, and still commanded north of the Loire by the skilful Model, now made desperate efforts to block the gap in the north, which they regarded as the chief danger. In the first week of September, they collected a large improvised force of paratroopers and airmen to hold the right flank east of Antwerp, while the formations along the coast clung stubbornly to their positions. These measures enjoyed some success. The enemy continued to hold out in Le Havre, Boulogne and Calais, although on 8th September the Canadians took Ostend; occupied, in positions difficult of access, both banks of the Scheldt, thus denying the use of Antwerp; and, after the 6th, managed to impose some delay on the British in the belt of canals north of Ghent. Thus, at the time when the Allied armies must prepare for a further assault, they were in some danger of being unbalanced. Immediate freedom of movement remained greatest in the south and centre; but the difficulties of supply, which had dictated the 'broad front' policy in August, had been increased by its consequences, and unless the impetus of the southern advance itself brought sudden victory, could now be relieved only by the capture of deep water ports in the north.

Nevertheless, the continuation of the same policy, with its emphasis now on the capture of Antwerp and subsequent pressure in the north, seemed to Eisenhower best to meet the possible contingencies. If, as he expected at the time, German resistance had declined enough for the Allies soon to breach the Siegfried Line, a general advance upon it, and the plan for a two-handed attack, were best calculated to bring about its fall; while the capture of Antwerp would provide the necessary port for the subsequent, and possibly contested, advance into Germany. If on the other hand (as the Supreme Commander argued after the war) the Germans managed to reinforce and contest the Siegfried Line, an approach on a broad front was necessary before the planned assault could begin. It is not clear how much emphasis Eisenhower placed on each alternative at this point; but it seems likely that his argument of August, overlaid by even if not reconciled with the more optimistic forecasts of early September, combined to present the 'broad front' policy, in its modified version, as the most suitable under all circumstances.

The Combined Chiefs of Staff approved Eisenhower's recommendations on 12th September, underlining the importance of securing Antwerp and Rotterdam, and the advantages of the northern over other routes of advance into Germany. Montgomery, however, opposed them and developed his own alternative. Where the difficulties of supply led Eisenhower twice to favour the strategy of the broad front, they caused the British commander twice to advocate a single thrust in the north. In his view, the recent successes had merely postponed, and made the more necessary, the moment for decision between the two policies. The supply of a general advance, difficult in August, must soon prove critical; meanwhile, a strong attack in the north could, in his opinion without doubt, throw the Germans back over the Rhine north of the Siegfried Line, and, given enough support, could penetrate the Ruhr and the northern plains to Berlin. If the armies embarked on a further general advance, a general pause might well ensue west of the Rhine whereby the enemy might survive into the winter. But if the advance was halted at once in the south and its supplies were devoted to the north, or if at the very least the forces in the centre were thrown into the flank of the northern battle, he believed that the impetus of the advance could be maintained, and that the war could be won 'reasonably quickly'.

To gain a foothold over the lower Rhine, Montgomery must first force the passage of the Dutch rivers Maas and (if striking in the extreme north) Waal, which lay, beyond flat country, some sixty miles from Antwerp.[1] Alternative plans were designed for this first, crucial step: the first involving an attack by Second British Army from the Dutch frontier through Eindhoven to the Maas, combined with a series of airborne attacks up to and on the bridges across the three rivers at Grave, Nijmegen and Arnhem; the second involving an attack by Second Army in a north-easterly direction, while airborne attacks were made on the Maas and Rhine at Venlo and at Wesel. On the morning of 10th September, elements of Second Army forced the last obstacle east of Antwerp, the Maas-Escaut canal, and the way seemed open for an advance across Holland. The Airborne Army of para- and glider-borne troops, under the American Lt.-Gen. Lewis H. Brereton, was ready for operations, and its aircraft, hitherto used largely to supply the advance, had been placed at Montgomery's disposal a few days before. On the 10th, Montgomery therefore decided to propose to Eisenhower that the attack should be carried out on Grave, Nijmegen and Arnhem, with priority over all other operations: a task demanding the capture of nine bridges over three large and five small

---

[1] See Inset to Map VII, facing p. 343.

waterways, but less likely than the alternative to suffer from air or anti-aircraft opposition, and involving a shorter advance by Second Army.

This is not the place to examine the validity of Montgomery's full plan. Eisenhower, however, was not convinced, and on 10th September refused to support it at the expense of Twelfth Army Group. But on the 12th, in view of the favourable development east of Antwerp, he agreed to allow Twenty-First Army Group to carry out the first stage. Instead of securing the seaward approach to Antwerp before attacking towards the lower Rhine, the Supreme Commander now consented to attack the lower Rhine before securing the approach to Antwerp. For this purpose, he allocated to Montgomery 1,000 tons of supplies a day, taken largely from First U.S. Army, and confirmed that he could use 1st Airborne Corps, of three divisions, from the Airborne Army. But the object of the operation, as the Supreme Commander made clear, was 'merely an . . . extension of our eastward rush to the line we needed for temporary security.'[1] There was no question, as his directive of 17th September showed, of a further exploitation of the bridgehead across the Rhine with support or supplies from the Armies further south.

> '. . . 6. My plan of manoeuvre is to push hard over the Rhine in the north with Northern Group of Armies, First U.S. Army and First Allied Airborne Army, while Third U.S. Army, except for a limited advance as explained below, is confined to holding and threatening action until the initial objectives are attained on the left.
>
> 7. Northern Group of Armies, swinging generally Northward from present position, will advance promptly to seize a bridgehead over the Rhine and prepare to seize the Ruhr. For this purpose, additional maintenance will be provided, until about 1st October, if necessary . . .
>
> 8. Central Group of Armies must push its right only far enough, for the present, to hold adequate bridgeheads beyond the Mosel thus creating a constant threat to the enemy and preventing him from reinforcing further North by transferring troops from the Metz area. As soon as this is accomplished all possible resources from Central Group of Armies must be thrown in to the support of First U.S. Army's drive to seize bridgeheads near Cologne and Bonn, in preparation for assisting in the capture of the Ruhr.
>
> 9. After Northern Group of Armies and First U.S. Army have seized bridgeheads over the Rhine, Third U.S. Army will advance through the Saar and establish bridgeheads across the Rhine. This advance will be initiated at an earlier date, if maintenance of Third U.S. Army becomes possible. . . .'

[1] Eisenhower, *Crusade in Europe*, p. 336.

The attack on Arnhem in mid-September (operation 'Market Garden') was thus a tactical change of plan, designed to meet a favourable local situation within the main plan of campaign. Its object was limited, and its strength confined to the attainment of that object. The story of the operation is well known. On 17th September, elements of 1st Airborne Corps, comprising a British airborne division with a Polish parachute brigade, and two American airborne divisions, were flown to the three targets. The two American divisions achieved their objects, to the north of Eindhoven and at Grave and Nijmegen. But the British division at Arnhem, which formed the spearhead of the attack, was doomed to misfortune from the start. The German Field-Marshal Model himself happened to be near the town when the troops landed, and he at once took command of the battle and summoned the slender German reserves to the critical sector. By the time that the British, dropped seven miles from their main target, had approached the bridge, he had organized its defence. The fight raged over the next eight days. But bad weather interrupted the reinforcement of the division, while Second Army, after reaching Nijmegen on the 20th, encountered fierce opposition and took four days to cover the last eight miles. By that time, the last elements of the British division had been driven from the vicinity of the bridge, and on the night of the 25th/26th its survivors were withdrawn across the Rhine. It was not until April, 1945 that British troops again set foot in Arnhem.

The significance of the result exceeded the planned rôle of the attack. It at once, and finally, dispelled the hope that the enemy would be beaten before the winter. First and Third U.S. Armies had already been checked, the former at Aachen and in the Ardennes, the latter at Metz and south of Nancy. The failure to outflank the Siegfried Line in the north finally dictated that pause in the general advance which Montgomery had feared. 'The interest in that battle,' General Eisenhower has remarked,[1] 'had its roots in something deeper than pride. We felt it would prove whether or not the Germans could succeed in establishing renewed and effective resistance—on the battle's outcome we would form an estimate of the severity of the fighting still ahead of us. . . . When, in spite of heroic effort, the airborne forces and their supporting ground forces were stopped in their tracks, we had ample evidence that much bitter campaigning was to come.'

The results appeared at once. Eisenhower turned to Antwerp, which despite the long-delayed capture of Le Havre on 12th September, of Brest on the 18th and of Calais on the 30th, remained, as the closest, largest and best-preserved of the ports, the necessary solution to the difficulties of supply. On 29th September, he reported to the Combined Chiefs of Staff. His intention remained the same, to seize

[1] *Loc. cit.*, pp. 340-2.

the Ruhr and the Saar. The main effort for the time being would be put into operations against the Ruhr by Twenty-First Army Group with First U.S. Army. But first, the northern Armies must open Antwerp 'as a matter of great urgency', reducing for that purpose the islands of Walcheren and South Beveland. This would be a major operation. Twelfth Army Group, less First U.S. Army, would meanwhile continue to thrust towards Cologne and Bonn as resources permitted, and would prepare to attack the Ruhr from the south when conditions allowed. Sixth Army Group further south would move towards Mulhouse and Strasbourg, containing the forces opposite it. These plans took account of a position where 'except in the Low Countries, the enemy has now succeeded in establishing a relatively stable and cohesive front, located approximately on the German frontier'. It was even possible that 'the enemy may attempt an attack south of Nancy using his armour with the object of relieving pressure on the remainder of the front. . . . It is also likely that he will attempt by counter-attack to eject penetrations of the West Wall [Siegfried Line], and to restore the situation in Holland.'

The battle in Italy reached its climax over the same period. On 7th September, after successful preliminary operations, General Alexander issued his orders for the main assault on the Gothic Line.[1] Eighth Army in the east was to capture the Coriano ridge which it was then attacking, and thence to move with two Corps (one British and one Canadian) over the river Marano on Rimini, and against the eastern sector of the Gothic Line to the south-west. A third, British, Corps would guard the left flank by San Marino. Fifth Army, which had reached the mountains some ten miles north of Florence, was to secure a line beyond the river Sieve whence to advance with two Corps (one British and one American) along the three main axes Dicomano-Forli, Borgo S. Lorenzo-Faenza, and Florence-Firenzuola-Imola. A third, American, Corps would guard the left flank around Pistoia.

After severe fighting, Eighth Army took the Coriano ridge, and crossed the Marano, on 14th September, while further west it made contact on the 13th with the Gothic Line. Meanwhile, Fifth Army reached the neighbourhood of Dicomano and of Borgo S. Lorenzo on the 12th, where it encountered the central defences. On the 13th, it launched its attack. The British Corps on the right met comparatively light opposition, and was soon well into the prepared positions. The Americans in the centre had a harder task, but on 18th September they cracked the defences south and south-west of Firenzuola, and by the 22nd lay from positions north of that town across the hills to the main Florence-Bologna road, and thence in a curve south-west to Vernio. By the same

[1] See Map VIII, facing p. 384.

date, the British Corps on the right had reached a point five miles north-east of Dicomano.

Eighth Army meanwhile pushed slowly towards Rimini. After three days of attack and counter-attack, its right flank reached the air-port of the town on 19th September, while its centre penetrated the defences to the south-west and its left conducted a holding operation west of Coriano. Two days later, Greek troops with the Canadians entered Rimini. But a further advance along the road to Ravenna soon met heavy opposition, and Eighth Army was forced to halt, in worsening weather, a few miles north and west of the town.

The situation on 23rd September therefore seemed promising. Eighth Army had reached Rimini, its twelve divisions having severely mauled eleven German divisions and, as Alexander wrote to Churchill, having 'smashed their way through . . . a system of defences the enemy has been working on . . . for over a year, and one which German prisoners had said was impregnable.' Fifth Army, with ten divisions, had likewise breached the main positions in the mountains on a front of thirty miles. The enemy had committed most of his divisions, and, should they crack, was unlikely to muster a balanced reserve to cover their retreat. 'At this stage of the battle', General Wilson has since stated, 'the enemy might have been expected to withdraw his forces behind the next major obstacle—the River Po—on which he could regroup while using every possible delaying device in front of it.'

However, he elected to stand; and thereby exposed the main weakness of the Allies. On 26th September, in acknowledging Wilson's congratulations on the course of the battle, Alexander stated:

> 'The trouble is that my forces are too weak relative to the enemy to force a break-through and so close the two pincers. . . . To put it briefly, we shall have to continue the battle of Italy with about twenty divisions, almost all of which have had long periods of heavy fighting this year, and some for several years, against the twenty German divisions committed to the battle front, with the prospect of four more German divisions, and probably two Italian divisions, joining in the battle at a later stage. We are inflicting very heavy losses on the enemy and are making slow but steady progress, but out losses are also heavy and we are fighting in country where, it is generally agreed, a superiority of at least three to one is required for successful offensive operations. It will be small wonder, therefore, if we fail to score a really decisive success when the opposing forces are so equally matched.'

The consequences of earlier strategic decisions were indeed now being felt, and on the critical occasion. Eighth Army had lost over 14,000 men during the past three and a half weeks, and the Americans in Fifth Army nearly 7,000 men. The British formations had indeed to be reorganized down to their battalions, in order to remain effective. Nor was there any prospect of immediate reinforcements to offset the withdrawals of the summer. While the tactical situation was good, victory therefore depended on the capacity of severely strained troops soon to force back a numerically equal enemy over ground suited to the defence, before their endurance or the weather declined.

At the end of September, it was still too soon to tell the outcome. Eighth Army was still held near Rimini, but Fifth Army made some more ground in the centre, and Wilson was inclined to think that the battle might be won. Alexander, on the other hand, expressed his fears on 2nd October that 'we may not be just quite strong enough to carry it through.' But whatever the result, two possible consequences had to be envisaged. It was unlikely that any troops could be spared from the line in the immediate future; and the possibility of a landing in Istria, to assist or to exploit victory, might well prove necessary soon.

The turn of events in Europe brought immediate disappointment to the British in south-east Asia. The disappointment was the greater, because in the interval since the end of the 'Octagon' conference a solution to their needs had seemed possible. During the conference, the Prime Minister, faced with what he considered disproportionately high figures for British troops to be moved from Europe,[1] had turned to the other two possible sources of supply for the assault on Rangoon, the South-East Command itself and the Americans. On 11th September, he inquired of Mountbatten if he could not after all provide more forces from his own theatre. On the 13th, the Supreme Commander replied that by taking certain risks he could probably spare three divisions, one of which must be replaced as soon as possible by a division from Europe; but the detail of the message was obscure, and it was not until the evening of the 16th that it was finally resolved. Meanwhile the Prime Minister tried the Americans. On 16th September, he stated that the British could probably withdraw two divisions from Europe in the near future and that Mountbatten had undertaken to provide a further two divisions without replacement in south-east Asia. He therefore asked the United States to release two divisions for south-east Asia which would otherwise be sent to Europe. This request was examined with care, but on the 23rd, in response to a further British inquiry, General Marshall could only reply that he saw little possibility of meeting the demand. It was indeed unlikely that the Americans would be prepared at this time to divert troops to an operation which they had always regarded as a British commitment, favouring purely British interests; and as the Joint Staff Mission had anticipated, no more was in fact heard from Washington on the matter.

---

[1] See p. 509 above.

But meanwhile the position was changing in London. On 16th September, the Chiefs of Staff asked the Vice-Chiefs to re-examine the timetable in the light of the discussions of the past ten days; and as a result they were able to issue a fresh report on the 26th. This was considerably more hopeful, for the Vice-Chiefs of Staff had been able to reduce the number of men involved by almost 100,000, from 352,000 to 253,000.[1] This had been achieved by allowing for the extra divisions from the South-East Asia Command which Mountbatten had promised on the 13th, by reducing headquarters' staff, and by drastically cutting India's additional base requirements. The Vice-Chiefs of Staff had also decided, after weighing the evidence, to send the divisions from Europe intact without any form of demobilization—'the only method,' as they reported, 'which, in the circumstances, would ensure efficient fighting units for 'Dracula', though the risks from the point of view of morale and discipline are real and serious.' They accordingly produced a new timetable, whereby an extra division was taken from north-west Europe, while the three divisions from the Mediterranean were reduced to two;[2] and the withdrawal of the first division (which was from north-west Europe) was delayed until early in November, although headquarters' staff would have to move earlier. The programme had thus come to depend mainly on the situation in north-west Europe. Two of the divisions from that theatre (one airborne) were now in England, re-forming for operations against Germany, and the Chiefs of Staff hastened to ask Eisenhower, Bradley and Montgomery if they could be spared directly for India without returning to the Continent. The commanders agreed to let them go; and with their consent, on 26th September a solution seemed to be in sight.

But the Chiefs of Staff's report had been overtaken by events before it was circulated. The failure of the attack on Arnhem, confirmed on the night of the 25th/26th, at once removed the resources for 'Dracula' against Rangoon. On 28th September, the First Sea Lord reported to the Chiefs of Staff that the landing craft on which they had hitherto relied for that operation might now have to be retained for operations up the Scheldt. This was confirmed by the end of the month, and a new factor therefore entered into the already complex calculations. The transfer of an airborne division to south-east Asia had now also to be reconsidered in the light of the loss of the airborne division at Arnhem, and by the end of the month it seemed probable that the other divisions would also be needed in the new circumstances that had arisen. The uncertainty in Italy, moreover, seemed likely to hold the two British/Indian divisions, possibly beyond the date at which they must be withdrawn.

---

[1] See p. 509 above.

[2] See p. 507 above.

When the Chiefs of Staff again met Mr. Churchill on 2nd October, the issue was no longer in doubt. After a brief discussion, 'The Prime Minister said that in these circumstances he thought it would be wrong to weaken our effort in France, which was and must remain the main theatre of operations until Germany was finally defeated. He therefore reluctantly concluded that 'Dracula' must be postponed until after the monsoon in 1945, and that in the next dry weather season we should devote all our strength in south-east Asia Command to the vigorous execution of 'Capital' . . .' There was general agreement with this, and the necessary measures were taken accordingly. On 5th October, a long explanatory telegram was sent to the British Joint Staff Mission in Washington for the American Chiefs of Staff, while the Prime Minister addressed Mountbatten in words remarkably like those he had been forced to use nine months before.[1]

> 'Defence Committee have been forced to conclusion that March 'Dracula' is off and Chiefs of Staff have made this proposal to United States Chiefs of Staff. You will receive official instructions in due course. Meanwhile, you should know that postponement of Operation is due to the working of far larger forces in the Western Theatre rather than to any attitude which you or S.E.A.C. have adopted. You have now to address yourself to the problem of bringing 'Dracula' on in November [1945]. I am very sorry indeed that we have not been able to carry out this operation, on which I had set my heart, but the German resistance both in France and Italy has turned out to be far more formidable than we had hoped. We must clean them out first.'

A bare three weeks after the British strategy for the Far East had been settled, an integral part of its foundations has thus apparently been removed.

The campaign in south-east Asia was the most immediate casualty of the disappointment in Europe. But the results affected every theatre and, behind the theatres, the plans and production of the Western Allies. In the first half of October 1944, both British and Americans therefore turned to consider the problems which the new conditions imposed, and which for the British at least held serious implications.

---

[1] Cf. on p. 223 above. See *Triumph and Tragedy*, pp. 147-8.

Appendices

APPENDIX I

Code Names Mentioned in the Text

(c) denotes a Code Name used and later cancelled

Accolade .	Operations in the Aegean
Anakim .	Recapture of Burma
Anvil (c) .	Landing in the south of France
Avalanche .	Landing at Salerno
Bodyguard	Strategic Deception Plan for 'Overlord'
Bolero .	Transport of men and stores from the United States to the United Kingdom, in preparation for 'Overlord'
Buccaneer .	Operation against the Andaman Islands
Caliph .	Landing in the west of France
Capital .	Replaced 'Champion'
Champion (c)	Plan for advance into central Burma from the north
Crossbow .	Preparations for, and Allied measures against, attacks by rockets and pilotless aircraft
Cudgel .	Land operations along the Arakan coast
Culverin .	Operations against northern Sumatra/Malaya
Diadem .	Operations to capture Rome
Diver .	Attacks by, and defensive preparations against, V.1 pilotless aircraft
Dracula .	Replaced 'Vanguard'
Dragoon .	Replaced 'Anvil'
Drake (c) .	Bombing of Japan from China
Eureka .	The Teheran Conference, November 1943
First Culverin	Operation against northern Sumatra
Gripfast .	Modified 'Tarzan'
Hardihood .	Assistance to Turkey
Hercules .	Operation against Rhodes
Jupiter .	Operations in northern Norway
Manna .	Plan to attack a German withdrawal in Greece
Market Garden	Attack on Arnhem
Matterhorn	Replaced 'Drake'
Noah's Ark	Plan for the occupation of Greece on the Germans' withdrawal
Octagon .	The Second Quebec Conference, September 1944
Overlord .	The liberation of north-west Europe
Pigstick .	Landing in the Mayu Peninsula
Pointblank .	Bombing of Germany
Quadrant .	The First Quebec Conference, August 1943
Rankin .	Operations to exploit a German collapse
Ratweek .	Plan to attack a German withdrawal in Yugoslavia

Saturn	.	Introduction of an Allied force into Turkey
Sextant	.	The Cairo Conference, November-December 1943
Shingle	.	Landing at Anzio
Symbol	.	The Casablanca Conference, January 1943
Tarzan	.	Advance on Indaw/Katha area
Torch	.	Invasion of North Africa
Trident	.	The Third Washington Conference, May 1943
Vanguard (c)		Plan to capture Rangoon from the sea

APPENDIX II

Ministerial Appointments, August, 1943 – September, 1944

(*Members of the War Cabinet are in italics*)

Prime Minister and First Lord of the Treasury, Minister of Defence	*Mr. Winston S. Churchill*
Admiralty, First Lord of the .	Mr. A. V. Alexander
Agriculture and Fisheries, Minister of	Mr. R. S. Hudson
Air, Secretary of State for . .	Sir Archibald Sinclair
Aircraft Production, Minister of .	Sir Stafford Cripps
Burma, Secretary of State for .	Mr. L. S. Amery
Chancellor of the Duchy of Lancaster	(a) Mr. A. Duff Cooper (b) Mr. Ernest Brown (appointed 17th November, 1943)
Chancellor of the Exchequer .	(a) Sir Kingsley Wood (b) *Sir John Anderson* (appointed 28th September, 1943)
Colonies, Secretary of State for the	Colonel Oliver Stanley
Dominion Affairs, Secretary of State for	(a) *Mr. Clement Atlee* (b) Viscount Cranborne (appointed 28th September, 1943)
Economic Warfare, Minister of .	The Earl of Selborne
Education, President of the Board of.	Mr. R. A. Butler (By the Education Act, August 1944, the title of the office was changed to "Minister of Education")
Food, Minister of . . .	(a) Lord Woolton (b) Colonel J. J. Llewellin (appointed 12th November, 1943)

Foreign Affairs, Secretary of State for	*Mr. Anthony Eden*
Fuel and Power, Minister of	Major G. Lloyd George
Health, Minister of	(a) Mr. Ernest Brown (b) Mr. H. U. Willink (appointed 17th November, 1943)
Home Department, Secretary of State for the	*Mr. Herbert Morrison*
India, Secretary of State for	Mr. L. S. Amery
Information, Minister of	Mr. Brendan Bracken
Labour and National Service, Minister of	*Mr. Ernest Bevin*
Law Officers:	
Attorney-General	Sir Donald Somervell
Lord Advocate	Mr. J. S. C. Reid
Solicitor-General	Sir David Maxwell Fyfe
Solicitor-General for Scotland	Sir David King Murray
Lord Chancellor	Viscount Simon
Lord President of the Council	(a) *Sir John Anderson* (b) *Mr. Clement Attlee* (appointed 28th September, 1943)
Lord Privy Seal	(a) Viscount Cranborne (b) Lord Beaverbrook (appointed 28th September, 1943)
Minister of State	Mr. R. K. Law (appointed 25th September, 1943)
Minister without Portfolio	Sir William Jowitt
Paymaster-General	Lord Cherwell
Pensions, Minister of	Sir Walter Womersley
Postmaster-General	Captain H. F. C. Crookshank
Production, Minister of	*Mr. Oliver Lyttelton*
Reconstruction, Minister of	*Lord Woolton* (appointed 12th November, 1943)
Scotland, Secretary of State for	Mr. Thomas Johnston
Supply, Minister of	Sir Andrew Duncan
Town and Country Planning, Minister of	Mr. W. S. Morrison

Trade, President of the Board of .	Dr. Hugh Dalton
War, Secretary of State for .	Sir James Grigg
War Transport, Minister of .	Lord Leathers
Works, Minister of . . .	Lord Portal
MINISTERS OVERSEAS:	
Middle East, Minister of State Resident in the . . .	(a) *Mr. R. G. Casey* (until 23rd December, 1943) (b) Lord Moyne (appointed 29th January, 1944)
Washington, Minister Resident for Supply in	(a) Colonel J. J. Llewellin (b) Mr. Ben Smith (appointed 12th November, 1943)
Allied Force Headquarters, Mediterranean Command, Minister Resident at	Mr. Harold Macmillan
West Africa, Minister Resident in	Viscount Swinton
Middle East, Deputy Minister of State Resident in the . .	Lord Moyne (until 29th January, 1944, when office lapsed)
House of Lords, Leader of the .	Viscount Cranborne
House of Commons, Leader of the	*Mr. Anthony Eden*

APPENDIX III

A. British and United States Chiefs of Staff; British Vice-Chiefs of Staff; British Joint Staff Mission in Washington; August, 1943 – September, 1944

BRITISH CHIEFS OF STAFF

Chief of the Imperial General Staff (Chairman of the Chiefs of Staff's Committee)	General Sir Alan Brooke (Field Marshal from January, 1944)
Chief of the Air Staff . .	Air Chief Marshal Sir Charles Portal (Marshal of the Royal Air Force from January, 1944)
First Sea Lord and Chief of the Naval Staff	Admiral of the Fleet Sir Dudley Pound (until September, 1943) Admiral of the Fleet Sir Andrew Cunningham (from October, 1943)
Deputy Secretary (Military) of the War Cabinet and Chief of Staff to the Minister of Defence .	Lieut.-General Sir Hastings Ismay (General from May, 1944)
Chief of Combined Operations[1] .	Major-General R. E. Laycock (from October, 1943)
Secretary	*Major-General L. C. Hollis*

BRITISH VICE-CHIEFS OF STAFF

Vice-Chief of the Imperial General Staff	Lieut.-General A. E. (later Sir Archibald) Nye
Vice-Chief of the Air Staff . .	Air Vice-Marshal Sir Douglas Evill (Air Marshal, 1944)
Vice-Chief of the Naval Staff .	Vice-Admiral Sir Neville Syfret

[1] Attended those meetings of concern to him.

UNITED STATES JOINT CHIEFS OF STAFF

Chief of Staff to the President and Commander-in-Chief of the U.S. Armed Forces . . . . (Chairman of the Joint Chief of Staff's Committee)	Admiral William D. Leahy
Chief of Staff of the U.S. Army .	General George C. Marshall
Commander-in-Chief of the U.S. Fleet and Chief of Naval Operations	Admiral Ernest J. King
Commanding General, U.S. Army Air Forces	General Henry H. Arnold
Secretary	*Brigadier-General J. R. Deane* *Colonel A. J. McFarland* (from October, 1943. Brigadier-General from June, 1944)

BRITISH JOINT STAFF MISSION IN WASHINGTON

Head of the British Joint Staff Mission	Field Marshal Sir John Dill
Head of the British Admiralty Delegation	Admiral Sir Percy Noble
Head of the British Army Staff .	Lieut.-General G. N. Macready
Head of the R.A.F. Delegation .	Air Marshal Sir William Welsh
Secretary	*Brigadier H. Redman* *Brigadier A. T. Cornwall-Jones* (from August, 1944)

B. Allied Commands, August, 1943—September, 1944

I ALLIED EXPEDITIONARY FORCE, NORTH-WEST EUROPE

(Appointments made at different dates in 1943)

Supreme Allied Commander	General Dwight D. Eisenhower (U.S.)
Deputy Supreme Allied Commander[1] . .	Air Chief Marshal Sir Arthur Tedder (Br.)
Commander-in-Chief, Allied Naval Expeditionary Forces	Admiral Sir Bertram Ramsay (Br.)

[1] And co-ordinating tactical with strategic air operations.

I ALLIED EXPEDITIONARY FORCE, NORTH-WEST EUROPE—(*continued*)

Commander-in-Chief, British Group of Armies (Twenty-First Army Group) . .	General Sir Bernard Montgomery (Br.) (Field Marshal from September, 1944)
Commanding General, U.S. Group of Armies (Twelfth Army Group) . . .	General Omar Bradley (U.S.)
Commanding General, Sixth Army Group (from 15th September, 1944) . .	General J. L. Devers (U.S.)
Commander-in-Chief, Allied Expeditionary Air Forces .	Air Chief Marshal Sir Trafford Leigh-Mallory (Br.)

II ALLIED EXPEDITIONARY FORCES IN THE MEDITERRANEAN

(To December, 1943)

Commander-in-Chief of the Allied Expeditionary Forces	General Dwight D. Eisenhower (U.S.)
Commander-in-Chief, Allied Naval Expeditionary Forces	Admiral of the Fleet Sir Andrew Cunningham (Br.) Admiral Sir John Cunningham (Br.) (from September, 1943)
Commander-in-Chief, Fifteenth Army Group . .	General Sir Harold Alexander (Br.)
Commander-in-Chief, Allied Air Forces[1] . . .	Air Chief Marshal Sir Arthur Tedder (Br.)

III MEDITERRANEAN COMMAND

(From December, 1943)

Supreme Allied Commander	General Sir Henry Maitland Wilson (Br.)
Deputy Supreme Allied Commander . . .	Lieut.-General J. L. Devers (U.S.) Lieut.-General J. T. McNarney (U.S.) (from September, 1944)
Commander-in-Chief, Allied Naval Forces . . .	Admiral Sir John Cunningham (Br.)
Commander-in-Chief, Allied Armies in Italy . . .	General Sir Harold Alexander (Br.)

[1] And of Middle East Air Forces after December, 1943.

III	MEDITERRANEAN COMMAND—(*continued*)	
	Commander-in-Chief, Mediterranean Allied Air Forces	Lieut.-General Ira. C. Eaker (U.S.) (Lieut.-General from December, 1943)
IV	MIDDLE EAST COMMAND	
	(Subordinate to Mediterranean Command for operations in Mediterranean from December, 1943)	
	Commander-in-Chief (Army)	General Sir Henry Maitland Wilson (Br.) (until December, 1943)
	Commander-in-Chief, Levant (Navy) . . .	Admiral Sir Henry Harwood (Br.)
	Commander-in-Chief (Air)	Air Chief Marshal Sir Arthur Tedder (Br.) (until December, 1943)
V	SOUTH-EAST ASIA COMMAND	
	Supreme Allied Commander	Admiral Lord Louis Mountbatten (Br.)
	Deputy Supreme Allied Commander . . .	Lieut.-General J. W. Stilwell (U.S.)
	Commander-in-Chief, British Eastern Fleet . . .	Admiral Sir James Somerville (Br.) Admiral Sir Bruce Fraser (Br.) (from August, 1944)
	Commander-in-Chief, Eleventh Army Group .	General Sir George Giffard (Br.)
	Commander-in-Chief, Allied Air Forces . . .	Air Chief Marshal Sir Richard Peirse (Br.)
	Commanding General, U.S. Army Air Forces in the (U.S.) China-Burma-India Theatre	Lieut.-General G. E. Stratemeyer (U.S.)
VI	SOUTH-WEST PACIFIC AREA	
	Commander-in-Chief[1] .	General Douglas MacArthur (U.S.)
	Commander-in-Chief, Australian Land Forces . .	General Sir Thomas Blamey (Aus.)
	Commander, U.S. Seventh Fleet[2]	Admiral Carpenter (U.S.) Vice-Admiral T. C. Kinkaid (U.S.) (from December, 1943)

[1] And in operational command of Allied land forces.

[2] Under orders of C-in-C., S.W.P.A. from C.-in-C., U.S. Pacific Fleet.

VI	SOUTH-WEST PACIFIC AREA—(*continued*)	
	Commanding General, Fifth U.S. Army Air Force and Allied Air Forces, South-West Pacific Area . .	Lieut.-General George C. Kenney (U.S.) (until June, 1944)
	Commanding General, U.S. Far East Air Forces and Allied Air Forces, South-West Pacific Area .	Lieut.-General George C. Kenney (U.S.) (from June, 1944)
VII	PACIFIC OCEAN AREAS	
	Commander-in-Chief, and Commander-in-Chief, U.S. Pacific Fleet[1] . . .	Admiral Chester Nimitz (U.S.)
	Commanding General, U.S. Forces, Central Pacific[2] .	Lieut.-General R. C. Richardson (U.S.) (until July, 1944)
	Commanding General, U.S. Army Forces, Pacific Ocean Areas	Lieut.-General R. C. Richardson (U.S.) (from August, 1944)
	Commanding General, Seventh U.S. Army Air Force[3]	Major-General W. H. Hale (U.S.) Major-General R. W. Douglass (U.S.) (from May, 1944)
	Commanding General, U.S. Army Air Forces, Pacific Ocean Areas, and Deputy Commander, Twentieth U.S. Army Air Force . .	Lieut.-General M. F. Harmon (U.S.) (from August, 1944)
	Commander, South Pacific Area[4]	Admiral W. F. Halsey (U.S.)
	Commanding General, U.S. Army Air Forces, South Pacific Area[3] . . .	Lieut.-General M. F. Harmon (U.S.) (until July, 1944)

[1] In direct command of all Allied forces in Central and North Pacific.

[2] Brought under the direction of the C.G., U.S. Army Forces, P.O.A., in August, 1944.

[3] Brought under the direction of the C.G., U.S. Army Air Forces, P.O.A., in August, 1944.

[4] In direct command, under C.-in-C., P.O.A., of all Allied forces in South Pacific until December 1943, when South Pacific land forces transferred to the command of C.-in-C., S.W.P.A.

VIII ALLIED STRATEGIC AIR FORCES IN EUROPE

Commander - in - Chief, Bomber Command . .	Air Chief Marshal Sir Arthur Harris (Br.)
Commanding General, Eighth U.S. Army Air Force[1]	Major-General Ira C. Eaker (U.S.) (until December, 1943)
Commanding General, Fifteenth U.S. Army Air Force[1]	Major-General J. H. Doolittle (U.S.) (November-December, 1943)
Commanding General, U.S. Strategic Air Forces in Europe	General Carl Spaatz (U.S.) (from December, 1943. General from December, 1943)

IX ALLIED NAVAL FORCES IN THE ATLANTIC

British Zone	
Commander - in - Chief, Western Approaches . .	Admiral Sir Max Horton (Br.)
U.S. Zone	
Commander-in-Chief, U.S. Atlantic Fleet . . .	Admiral R. E. Ingersoll (U.S.)

[1] Brought under the direction of the C.G., U.S. Strategic Air Forces in Europe, in January, 1944.

APPENDIX IV

A. Certain Types of Assault Shipping Estimated to be Available for Theatres Over the First Half of 1944

	L.S.T.		L.C.T.‖‖		L.S.I.††		L.C.I. §	
	British†	United‡ States	British†	United‡ States	British†	United‡‡‡ States	British†	United‡ States
UNITED KINGDOM								
Total 1.9.43	5	—	376	6	7	10	34	—
1.1.44	53	48	580	77	20	11	106	31
1.5.44	53*	110	687* (623)	146	29* (23)	11	106*	58
MEDITERRANEAN								
Total 1.9.43	71	73	168	88	18	—	144	90
1.1.44**		17		25				45
1.3.44	12	15	26	21	3	—	45	41
1.5.44**		14		20				39
INDIA								
Total 1.9.43	—	10	—	—	—	—	—	—
1.1.44	8	9	5	—	—	—	12	—
1.5.44**		8		—		—		—
PACIFIC‡								
Total 1.9.43	—	67	—	103	—	22	—	62
1.1.44	—	117	—	130	—	30	—	101
1.5.44	—	125	—	150	—	40	—	115

** British figures not given.

† British figures are totals of ships and craft under the British flag (i.e., including American production transferred to British control): figures in brackets, in L.C.T. and L.S.I. columns, are those available for operations.

‡ United States figures, except for the Pacific, are of ships and craft available for operations. Those for the Pacific are totals in the theatre.

‖‖ British L.C.T. comprise L.C.T.(2)-(6) and L.C.T.(R): United States, L.C.T.(5) and (6).

†† British L.S.I. comprise L.S.I.(L), (M), (S) and (H): United States, the equivalents of A.P.A. and A.K.A.

§ British L.C.I. comprise L.C.I.(L) and (S): United States, L.C.I.(L).

* British figures for United Kingdom on 1.5.44 comprise figures of 1.1.44 plus new British production. Additions from Mediterranean are included, with British production since 1.9.43, in figures for 1.1.44.

‡‡ United States figures given as total for 'Atlantic' (i.e. 'Overlord' and Mediterranean).

B. Estimated Rates of Casualties and of Serviceability

	'Overlord'		Mediterranean		Indian Theatre		Pacific Theatres	
	Casualties	Serviceability	Casualties	Serviceability	Casualties	Serviceability	Casualties	Serviceability
	%		%		%		%	
L.S.T.	45	90	15	85	15	85	10	85
L.C.T.	45	85	30	75	30	70	20 } +40% of remainder damaged for one month	75
L.C.I.(L)	45	85	30	80	30	70	10 }	80
Minor Landing Craft	50	85	30	70	30	70	30	70

Some Calculations of Assault Shipping

		1. 26.8.43	2. MID-NOVEMBER
L.S.T.	Culverin	—	72*
	Buccaneer	—	18*
	Overlord	53+110=163	—*
	Anvil	12+ 14= 26	—*
L.S.I.(L)	Culverin	—	30*
	Buccaneer	—	10*
	Overlord	14+ —= 14	—*
	Anvil	3+ —= 3	—*
L.C.T.	Culverin	—	120*
	Buccaneer	—	4*
	Overlord	646+146=792	—*
	Anvil	22+ 20= 42	—*
L.C.I.(L)	Culverin	—	—*
	Buccaneer	—	—*
	Overlord	66+ 58=124	—*
	Anvil	45+ 39= 84	—*
Notes			
1. Source of figures.		1. C.C.S.' estimate of availability for 'Overlord' on 1.5.44, and for 'Anvil' on 1.3.44.	1. Figures produced by Mountbatten for 'Sextant' (later reduced for 'Culverin' on 26.11.43).
2. Shipping estimated as serviceable.		2.	2.
3. Additions and subtractions.		3.	3.
4. Other notes. Figures of British shipping placed first, of United States shipping second, throughout.		4. A preliminary estimate only.	4. Figures with * denote requirements, as calculated by the relevant Theatre.

Required for Operations in 1944

3. 3.12.43	4. 5.12.43	5. 7.12.43
—*	—	—
18*	—	—
—*	62+133=195	62+133=195
—*	10+ 22= 32	15+ 45= 60
—*	—	—
9*	—	—
—*	14+ 7= 21	14+ 7= 21
—*	3+ —= 3	9+ 3= 12
—*	—	—
15*	—	—
—*	512+146=658	560+146=706
—*	30+ 30= 60	47+ 77=124
—*	—	—
—*	—	—
—*	70+ 40=110	78+ 40=118
—*	45+ 55=100	72+ 63=135
1. Figures for new scale of 'Buccaneer' submitted by Wedemeyer.	1. C.C.S.' estimate for 'Overlord' and 'Anvil' in May 1944.	1. C.C.S.' estimate for 'Overlord' and 'Anvil' in May 1944.
2.	2. All shipping assumed to be serviceable in figures for 'Anvil'.	2. Of the totals for 'Overlord', 176 L.S.T., 14 L.S.I.(L), 601 L.C.T., 102 L.C.I.(L) estimated as serviceable: for 'Anvil', 51 L.S.T., 12 L.S.I.(L), 81 L.C.T., 100 L.C.I.(L).
3.	3.	3. Extra shipping for 'Anvil' provided by 'additional shipping and craft promised by the Americans and the estimated number of ships and craft that will be withdrawn from 'Buccaneer'.'
4. The increase was felt mainly in other categories of amphibious shipping, in ocean shipping and in naval forces. Figures with * as in Col. 2.	4. Figures of American L.S.I.(L) are those of A.P.A. or X.A.P. Shipping for 'Anvil' to be available in part for earlier operations in Aegean and Italy if required; but not at expense of 'Buccaneer'.	4. Figures of American L.S.I.(L) as in note 4 of Col. 4. Shipping for 'Anvil' available in part for earlier operations in Aegean and Italy if and as required.

Some Calculations of Assault Shipping

		6. 15.12.43	7. 15.12.43
L.S.T.	Culverin	—	—
	Buccaneer	—	—
	Overlord	62+133=195	3+ 23= 26
	Anvil	17+ 20= 37	5+ 36= 41
L.S.I.(L)	Culverin	—	—
	Buccaneer	—	—
	Overlord	14 }+7= 21	—
	Anvil	9 } 16	6+ 3= 9
L.C.T.	Culverin	—	—
	Buccaneer	—	—
	Overlord	560+170=730	45+ 19= 64
	Anvil	40+ 35= 75	—+ 31= 31
L.C.I.(L)	Culverin	—	—
	Buccaneer	—	—
	Overlord	46+ 64=110	—+ 24= 24
	Anvil	67+ 55=122	—

Notes

1. Source of figures.	1. C.C.S.' estimate for 'Overlord' and 'Anvil' in May 1944.	1. C.C.S.' calculation of additional shipping allocated to 'Overlord' and 'Anvil' since estimates of 26.8.43 (see Col. 1).
2. Shipping estimated as serviceable.	2. All shipping assumed to be serviceable throughout. Attrition rates for 'Anvil' (not included in figures) as follows: L.S.T.—British 18%, U.S. 15%; L.S.I.(L)—22%, —; L.C.T.—35%, 20%; L.C.I.(L)—29%, 15%.	2.
3. Additions and subtractions.	3. American figures do not seem to include extra allocation for Europe from United States production in March 1944. Additions in American shipping for 'Overlord' from Col. 5 may possibly be result of reallocation of assault shipping throughout theatres, following investigation by Marshall after 7.12.43.	3. Difference of 6 British L.S.T. for 'Overlord' (c.f. with Col. 6) unexplained. American figures include United States production in March 1944 allocated to Europe, and equivalent of releases from South-East Asia (as adjusted with British), as well as reallocation referred to in note 3 of col. 6. Figures of American L.C.T. comprise allocations already agreed from United States March production, minus 5 from 'Overlord' and plus 5 for 'Anvil'.
4. Other notes. Figures of British shipping placed first, of United States shipping second, throughout.	4. Figures of American L.S.I.(L) as in note 4 of Col. 4, and given only as total for Europe. Shipping for 'Anvil' available in part for earlier operations in Aegean and Italy if and as required.	4. Figures of American L.S.I.(L) as in note 4 of Col. 4. Shipping for 'Anvil' available in part for earlier operations in Aegean and Italy if and as required.

Required for Operations in 1944

8. 20.12.43	9. 22.12.43	10. 30.12.43
—	—	—
—	—	—
—	—	—
71 corrected to 74	76 corrected to 77	75 corrected to 76
—	—	—
—	—	—
—	—	—
—	—	—
—	—	—
—	—	—
—	—	—
118 corrected to 118	120 corrected to 139	130 corrected to 128
—	—	—
—	—	—
—	—	—
122 corrected to 122	137	—
1. British Joint Planning Staff's figures for 'Anvil' in May 1944, as corrected by same body on 3.1.44.	1. Mediterranean Command's figures for 'Anvil' in May 1944 (on a basis still of 2 divisions) as corrected by British Joint Planning Staff on 3.1.44.	1. Americans' figures for 'Anvil' in May 1944, as corrected by British Joint Planning Staff on 3.1.44.
2. No figures given on 20.12.43. Corrected figures of 3.1.44 estimate serviceability of L.S.T. at 85%, and of L.C.T. at 75%, on totals given above, apart from 14 out of 21 British L.C.T. for 'Anvil', for which see note 3 of this Col.	2. Mediterranean Command estimates serviceability of L.S.T. at 91%, of L.C.T. at 68%, and of L.C.I.(L) at 80%. Joint Planning Staff estimates serviceability of L.S.T. at 92%, and of L.C.T. at 68%, all on totals given above.	2. Americans estimate serviceability of L.S.T. at 92%, and of L.C.T. at 68%. Joint Planning Staff estimates serviceability of L.S.T. at 83%, and of L.C.T. at 75%, all on totals given above.
3. 71 L.S.T. for 'Anvil' = 37 L.S.T. in Col. 6 plus 26 from United States March production plus 10 from south-east Asia, as in Col. 7, minus 2 since allocated instead to 'Overlord'. 118 L.C.T. for 'Anvil' = 75 L.C.T. in Col. 6 plus 26 from United States March production plus 5 American retained in Mediterranean minus 2 American diverted to 'Overlord' plus 14 serviceable British out of 21 retained in Mediterranean, all since Col. 6.	3. Mediterranean Command gives a more optimistic estimate of rate of casualties than Joint Planning Staff's first figures in Col. 8, but its figures do not include 21 British L.C.T. retained in Theatre (see note 3 of Col. 8). Corrected figures for L.C.T. include these 21 craft minus 2 American L.C.T. diverted to 'Overlord' (see note 3 of Col. 8).	3. Americans' figures for L.C.T. based on comparable figure of 40 L.C.T. for 'Anvil' in Col. 6, plus 21 British L.C.T. since retained in Mediterranean (note 3 of Col. 8) and omitted by Mediterranean Command in Col. 9., but do not allow for Mediterranean Command's estimated lower rate of casualties as given in Col. 9. Corrected figures for L.C.T. follow those in Col. 9, without allowing for Mediterranean Command's estimated lower rate of casualties.
4. Shipping for 'Anvil' available in part for earlier operations in Aegean and Italy if and as required.	4. Shipping for 'Anvil' available in part for earlier operations in Italy and Aegean if and as required.	4. Shipping for 'Anvil' available for earlier operations in Italy.

APPENDIX VI

The Prime Minister and the Balkans late in 1943

There are three statements by the Prime Minister on the subject of an entry into the Balkans which, taken singly or together, might suggest at first sight that he was advocating a campaign in that area towards the end of 1943.

1. At a meeting of the Chiefs of Staff's Committee on 19th October, 1943,

'Summing up, the Prime Minister said that it was clear that if we were in a position to decide the future strategy of the war we should agree

(i) To reinforce the Italian theatre to the full.
(ii) To enter the Balkans.
(iii) To hold our position in the Aegean Islands.
(iv) To build-up our air forces and intensify our air attacks on Germany.
(v) To encourage the steady assembly in this country of United States troops, which could not be employed in the Pacific owing to the shortage of shipping, with a view to taking advantage of the softening in the enemy's resistance due to our operations in other theatres, though this might not occur until after the spring of 1944.

Unfortunately, we could not take a unilateral decision regarding the future strategy of the Allied nations. A further meeting with the Americans would therefore be necessary . . .'

2. On 20th November, 1943, the Prime Minister circulated to the British Chiefs of Staff a Minute on 'Future Operations in European and Mediterranean Theatre' which he had composed over the previous week. Its last paragraph read as follows:

'The following are my proposals for action, in their order of priority:

(a) Stop all further movement of British troops and British and United States landing craft from the Mediterranean. Stop in particular the move of the British 1st Airborne Division and the various Commandos.
(b) Use all possible energy to take Rome.
(c) Bring Turkey into the war, making the necessary Air detachments for the purpose. Meanwhile prepare an expedition to take Rhodes before the end of January, using the Turkish airfields.
(d) Seize a port or ports and establish bridgeheads on the Dalmatian coast, and carry a regular flow of airborne supplies to the

Partisans. Use the British 1st Airborne Division and all the Commandos available in the Mediterranean, together with the "Plough" force [a British force specially equipped and trained for mountain warfare], to aid and animate the resistance in Yugoslavia and Albania and also to capture islands like Corfu and Argostoli. Establish air domination of the Southern Adriatic, and maintain sea superiority there.'

3. At the Conference of Dominions' Prime Ministers in London in May 1944, the Prime Minister remarked, at the fourth meeting on the morning of 3rd May,

'He was bound to admit that if he had had his own way, the lay-out of the war would have been different. His inclination would have been in favour of rolling up Europe from the South-East, and joining hands with the Russians. However, it had proved impossible to persuade the United States on this view. They had been determined at every stage upon the invasion in North-West Europe . . . He himself had opposed the opening of this campaign in 1942 and 1943, but now he was in favour of it, and all his military advisers supported him in this. Russian pressure, too, had been very severe. Meanwhile, in Italy we must strike and prevent the enemy drawing his forces away . . .'

In answer to a query later in the same meeting:

'. . . Mr. Churchill said that there had never been any question of major action in the Balkans. It was merely a question of assistance by Commandos and air action. Due priorities must prevail in the application of resources . . .

Mr. Churchill said that the Americans had all along said that we were leading them up the garden in the Mediterranean. His reply had been that, in return, we had provided them in the garden with nourishing vegetables and refreshing fruits. Nevertheless, the Americans had remained very suspicious, and thought that he was entertaining designs for dragging them into the Balkans. This he had never contemplated doing. He had merely hoped to be able to give adequate help to Tito, and he had viewed the whole Mediterranean problem from a purely military point of view.'

On examination, the force of the first two statements, and of the opening remarks on the third occasion, is weakened by the circumstances in which they were made. The statement of 19th October (No. 1) was made at the start of the investigation, before the possibilities had been examined in any detail, and before the campaign in Italy had clearly reached a stalemate. The entry into the Balkans was not defined at all exactly, but would depend on the implications of reinforcing Italy 'to the full'.

By the time that the Minute appeared on 20th November (No. 2), those implications, and accordingly the conditions for a landing in the

Balkans, had become clearer. The Prime Minister's proposals for Yugoslavia had settled at the fourth priority, and represented, in a more ambitious form, the design outlined in the first draft of the British Chiefs of Staff's *aide-mémoire* of 11th November (para. 6(3). See p. 111 above). But the last sentence of that paragraph ('if necessary, we might form a limited bridgehead on the Dalmatian or Albanian Coasts') was deleted on 23rd November (see p. 111 above), and when the British Chiefs of Staff discussed the Prime Minister's Minute on that day, they informed him that:

> 'We do not favour the establishment of a bridgehead on the Dalmatian Coast, because it would take up too much of our resources. It was the one point in our Mediterranean proposals which General Alexander did not like. We think that we can do just as much, and, at the same time, avoid an unlimited commitment by smuggling in material at many points on the coast and by air. The successful prosecution of operations in the Balkans depends much more on good organisation . . .'

The Prime Minister thereupon amended his Minute, which was not in fact used further and which appears, in its modified form and with the 'proposals for action' deleted, in Volume V of his memoirs (*Closing the Ring*, pp. 291-4).

The Prime Minister's remarks in May, 1944 (No. 3) reflect this background; the opening paragraph, like the statement of 19th October, 1943, voicing an ideal which the reality, as recognized in November and in the later remarks in May 1944, never supported. While the Prime Minister was undoubtedly anxious to increase our aid to the Partisans in the last quarter of 1943, it was within the context of the British strategy for the Mediterranean; and once this was settled early in November, his proposals related, like those of the Chiefs of Staff and subject to their correction, only to the means for achieving that end.

APPENDIX VII

Memorandum from General Ismay to the Prime Minister on 28th April, 1944, concerning the Discussion on 'Overlord' and 'Anvil', January – April

'Although the 'Anvil' project first came into prominence at the 'Sextant' Conference (at 'Eureka' in November, 1943) the idea had its birth at the 'Quadrant' Conference in August 1943, as a result of which General Eisenhower (then Supreme Allied Commander, Mediterranean) was in August 1943 requested to prepare an appreciation and outline plan. This he produced in October, and this plan was in process of examination when the 'Sextant' Conference started.

2. At the final Plenary Meeting at 'Eureka', the following decisions were recorded:

(a) 'Overlord' and 'Anvil' are the supreme operations for 1944. They must be carried out during May 1944. Nothing must be undertaken in any other part of the world which hazards the success of these two operations . . .

(c) The examination of 'Anvil' on the basis of not less than a two divisional assault should be pressed forward as far as possible. If the examination reveals that it requires strengthening consideration will have to be given to the provision of additional resources.

3. On the return to Cairo, the Combined Chiefs of Staff instructed the Supreme Allied Commander, Mediterranean Theatre, in consultation with C.O.S.S.A.C., to submit, as a matter of urgency, an outline plan for 'Anvil' on the assumption that he would be given the assault shipping and craft for a lift of at least two divisions.

4. During December and January planning proceeded, and while on the one hand General Wilson favoured a larger scale 'Anvil' with a three divisional assault, C.O.S.S.A.C. put in a memorandum in which he argued cogently against the strategical advisability of 'Anvil', other than as a threat on the basis of a one divisional assault. C.O.S.S.A.C., moreover, advocated strengthening the 'Overlord' assault from three to four divisions. At this period the Chiefs of Staff were steadily moving towards the opinion that everything should be done to support the biggest possible 'Overlord', and that this would inevitably put 'Anvil', as originally contemplated, out of court.

5. On the 14th January the Chiefs of Staff sent you their views, broadly speaking to the above effect, while you were at Marrakech. At the same time Field Marshal Dill was sent a copy of the Chiefs of Staff telegram, warning him of what was afoot. In reply, Field Marshal Dill's telegram showed the first reaction of the United States Chiefs of Staff after they had consulted General Eisenhower, who was at that time in Washington. It was clear from the outset that the United States Chiefs of Staff would not budge from the 'Sextant' decisions. In the meanwhile, the United States Chiefs of Staff were pressing for firm orders to be issued about 'Overlord' and 'Anvil'. On this the Chiefs of Staff replied that it would be a mistake to issue definite orders as to the exact proportions of 'Anvil' until the 'Overlord' plan, which was then being overhauled, had taken firm shape.

6. In a telegram on the 23rd January General Eisenhower telegraphed the Combined Chiefs of Staff his views on the revised 'Overlord' and 'Anvil', in paragraph 15 of which he said that if there were not sufficient forces for a two divisional 'Anvil' he would prefer to have a five divisional 'Overlord' and a one divisional 'Anvil', the latter being maintained as a threat. He still earnestly hoped that a two divisional 'Anvil' would be possible.

7. On the 26th January, the Chiefs of Staff telegraphed to Washington their agreement with General Eisenhower's conception.

8. On the 1st Feburary, the United States Chiefs of Staff telegraphed saying that they considered it would be practicable to mount a five divisional assault 'Overlord' and that a successful 'Anvil' was essential to the success of 'Overlord'. For this they reckoned that a two and two-thirds divisional assault lift was available.

9. On the 4th February the Chiefs of Staff returned to the charge. They said that the fundamental consideration in weighing the problem was the success of 'Overlord'; that once 'Overlord' had been catered for there would only be a balance of a one divisional lift remaining in the Mediterranean. This lift was only sufficient to mount a threat. They took the view that even if resources could be found for a two divisional lift, they were not convinced that the most profitable use of the forces would necessarily be the South of France. In this telegram for the first time the Chiefs of Staff emphasised the prime importance of prosecuting the Italian campaign with the utmost vigour. The Chiefs of Staff also expressed the view that Marshal Stalin would not take the change of plan unduly hardly. (This was borne out by events.) The attitude of General Marshall at this time can best be gauged by Field Marshall Dill's telegram [of 5th February].

10. On the 6th February the United States Chiefs of Staff came back with a reiteration of their previous view. They made no new points, but emphasised the importance of using French troops for 'Anvil'.

11. During this time attempts were being made to get agreement on a directive to General Wilson, who was more or less in the dark as to what

he had to do about 'Anvil'. While the main fundamental disagreement remained, however, no decision on General Wilson's directive could be reached. You and the Chiefs of Staff were anxious that the United States Chiefs of Staff should come to England to discuss the matter, but the United States Chiefs of Staff declined.

12. The next move was by General Marshall, who on the 9th February suggested that General Hull and Admiral Cooke should come to London to put their point of view to the British Chiefs of Staff, and that General Eisenhower, for the purposes of this conference, should represent the United States Chiefs of Staff. This procedure was agreed to and adopted.

13. On the 16th February you sent a telegram to the President on the contributory question of the despatch of two groups of fighter aircraft which the Americans wished to send from the Mediterranean to China. This elicited a non-commital reply from the President.

14. On the 19th February the Chiefs of Staff, after discussing the question with General Eisenhower, sent [a] telegram in which they stated frankly that the shadow of 'Anvil' was already cramping General Wilson, who required all the resources on which he could lay hands in order to nourish the battle and replace tired troops in Italy. They strongly advocated ending the uncertainty by the cancellation of 'Anvil' forthwith.

15. On the 21st February the United States Chiefs of Staff replied, saying that as in their view a two divisional lift could be made available for 'Anvil' it should be carried through; but that if the campaign in Italy had not developed favourably by 1st April the situation could be reviewed again.

16. On the 22nd February General Wilson, in a long telegram summarising the operations in Italy, recommended that 'Anvil' be cancelled and that he be given a fresh directive to conduct operations with the object of containing the maximum number of German troops in Southern Europe with the forces at his disposal, including an assault lift of one division. (This was in effect the directive which he ultimately received.) At this time several signals were exchanged with Washington which showed that General Eisenhower had come right round to the British point of view about 'Anvil' and the importance of nourishing the battle in Italy.

17. On the 26th February General Wilson was informed of the agreement which had then been reached between the Combined Chiefs of Staff and approved by the President and Prime Minister, which assigned overall priority for all existing and future operations in the Mediterranean to the campaign in Italy, but left General Wilson with an option to do 'Anvil' if he could manage it.

18. From the 26th February till the 18th March discussions took place about shipping and the allocation of air forces in the Mediterranean. On the 18th March the Chiefs of Staff called upon General Wilson for an appreciation in order that firm decisions could be reached.

19. This was received on the 20th March, in which he asked for the cancellation of 'Anvil' forthwith and for permission to prepare for a landing on the south coast of France under approximately 'Rankin' conditions.

20. On the 22nd March the Chiefs of Staff telegraphed to Washington saying that they agreed with General Wilson's views. The rest of the telegram followed the previous line taken by the Chiefs of Staff . . .

21. On the 24th March the United States Chiefs of Staff replied, saying that 'Anvil' should be delayed but not cancelled and the new date should be the 10th July. It should have a two divisional assault, and to make this possible they offered 26 L.S.T.s and 40 L.S.I.(L)s to be sent to the Mediterranean from the Pacific.

22. On the 28th March the British Chiefs of Staff replied saying that they entirely agreed with the United States Chiefs of Staff's view that we must not be caught unprepared to meet the possibility of the Germans holding our Armies in Italy by delaying action with small forces, while they moved considerable forces from Italy to the 'Overlord' theatre. They advocated the planning of an operation on the South coast of France, but that we should not commit ourselves to mounting it until it was clear that this was the best card to play.

23. On the 30th March the United States Chiefs of Staff summarised the points on which agreement had been reached, but went on to say that they were only offering the landing craft ex Pacific on the condition that preparations for the delayed 'Anvil' would be vigorously pressed, and that there should be the firm intention to mount this operation on the target date already indicated. To this the Chiefs of Staff replied, taking up the various points made by the United States Chiefs of Staff and saying that the latter's conception of consolidation in Italy once the bridgehead and the main front had joined and a rigid 'Anvil' would, in their view, risk the loss of initiative both in Italy and in the South of France.

24. A note of petulance now entered the controversy—see Field Marshal Dill's telegram of 1st April.

25. An exchange of drafting amendments to the directive then ensued, but on the 4th April the United States Chiefs of Staff telegraphed emphasising the same fundamental viewpoint about 'Anvil'.

26. On the 7th April the Chiefs of Staff telegraphed that in their view the continuance of the offensive in Italy was likely to be the greatest help to 'Overlord', and that if we had to switch over to preparing for 'Anvil', there might be a period of six weeks comparative inactivity throughout the Mediterranean coinciding with the six critical weeks at the beginning of 'Overlord'. They went on to say that everything would turn on whether the Germans decided to fight it out in Southern Italy after the bridgehead was joined, or whether they would then withdraw their forces and retire. The Chiefs of Staff thought it prudent, therefore, to retain an option on what type of 'Anvil' operation would suit our book best.

27. On the following day, 8th April, the United States Chiefs of Staff replied disagreeing with the British Chiefs of Staff's view as to the relative importance of 'Anvil' as compared with continued offensive operations in Italy. They stuck to their point that after the bridgehead had been joined highest priority should be given to *preparations* for 'Anvil'.

28. On the 12th April you sent a long telegram to General Marshall which advocated in general terms the policy which the Chiefs of Staff had been pressing for. This, however, fell on deaf ears.

29. On the 16th April the Chiefs of Staff put forward a revised directive which incorporated their own point of view, and this was accepted by the Combined Chiefs of Staff on the 18th April. The directive was issued to General Wilson on the 19th April . . .'

APPENDIX VIII

Estimates of Forces required for Operation 'Culverin', October, 1943 – February, 1944

1. JOINT PLANNING STAFF'S ESTIMATE, 6TH OCTOBER 1943

Against present estimate of opposition (see below)	Against greatest estimate of opposition (see below)
4 Divisions, including 4 assault Brigades	4 Divisions, including 6 Assault Brigades
2 Infantry Battalions (Garrison)	2 Infantry Battalions (Garrison)
1 Armoured Regiment	1 Armoured Regiment
6 Commandos	6 Commandos
1 Long Range Penetration Group	1 Long Range Penetration Group
5 Beach Groups	6 Beach Groups
4 Airfield Construction Groups	4 Airfield Construction Groups

The two scales of opposition were defined as follows:

	Present estimate of opposition	Greatest estimate of opposition
Nicobar Is.	3,000	5,000
Sabang	6,000	9,000
N. Sumatra	10,000	30,000
S. Sumatra	5/10,000	10,000

2. ADMIRAL MOUNTBATTEN'S ESTIMATE, 26TH NOVEMBER 1943

Divisions	$4\frac{2}{3}$, including 8 Assault Brigades
Beach Groups	8
Airfield Construction Groups	4

These were described as 'specially reduced demands'.

3. JOINT PLANNING STAFF'S ESTIMATE, 12TH FEBRUARY 1944

Divisions	$5\frac{1}{2}$, including 5 Assault and 2 Follow Up Brigades
Tank Brigade	1
Long Range Penetration Groups	2
Commandos	6
Beach Groups	7
Corps Headquarters	2
Force Headquarters	1

4. GENERAL WEDEMEYER'S ESTIMATE, 13TH FEBRUARY 1944

For 'Culverin' in November 1944, 'the requisite ground forces can largely be found from within the Command . . . The shipping and craft to launch 5 to 6 Brigades in the assault, with a follow up of 3 to 4 Divisions, must . . . be provided.'

5. GENERAL WEDEMEYER ON 14TH FEBRUARY 1944

'The total lift must be for 31,000 men in two lifts.'

6. GENERAL WEDEMEYER TO MR. CHURCHILL, 15TH FEBRUARY 1944

'The "bill of goods" for "Culverin" is not considered firm.'

7. BRITISH CHIEFS OF STAFF'S APPRECIATION, 23RD FEBRUARY 1944

Forces as in 3 above, but 'there is a requirement amounting to some 30,000 personnel for ancillary and administrative units which cannot be found from Indian Command . . . We consider that the overall requirement in ancillary units could well be halved . . . For a November 1944 date we are unable to make good the deficiency . . . from British resources.'

These estimates and statements raise three problems : the meaning of the figures themselves, the relations between S.E.A.C.'s statements and those produced by the authorities in London, and the relations between the statements produced by the different authorities in S.E.A.C. The last two problems are directly connected.

1. In the figures given in 1 above, the number of divisions do not include the forces specified separately, which must be added to them.

The lift given in 5 above may correspond with the figures given in 3 above, assuming that by 'Brigade' is meant 'Brigade Group' and that the strength is calculated at 'Assault Scale'. It seems doubtful, however, if the 6 commandos specified in 3 have been included in the 31,000 men specified in 5.

No part of the figure of 30,000 given in 7 is included in 3 above, or in the lifts specified in 4 or 5.

2. There are thus clear discrepancies between the figures produced by S.E.A.C. and by the Joint Planning Staff and Chiefs of Staff. The figures in 1 are the product of preliminary planning; those in 2 were assembled by Admiral Mountbatten at Cairo, without the assistance of a staff and in order to provide a basis on which acceptance of the plan might be possible; while those in 3 are the product of more detailed planning in conjunction with the Commanders-in-Chief's Planners in S.E.A.C., and possibly with a revised estimate of the enemy's strength.

The Chiefs of Staff's addition of 30,000 men in 7 above also reflects the argument of the Commanders-in-Chief's Planners in S.E.A.C. that the administrative 'tail' for 'Culverin' could not be provided from that already employed in Burma. Admiral Mountbatten's Planners, on the other hand, were inclined to think that it could; hence the discrepancy between the figures.

3. It appears, therefore, that the figures from S.E.A.C. itself did not always represent the same interests or points of view. Admiral Mountbatten's estimate in 2 above was 'specially reduced' from earlier demands, and was considerably lower than the figures of the Joint Planning Staff in 3 above, which took cognizance of the estimates provided by the Commanders-in-Chief's Planners in S.E.A.C. General Wedemeyer's figures

in 4 and 5 are those of the 'Axiom' Mission, representing Admiral Mountbatten's Planners, which again are lower than those of the Commanders-in-Chief's Planners in the theatre. The uncertainty produced by the system may be seen in General Wedemeyer's statement in 6 above.

There were thus three sets of authorities engaged in estimating the size of the forces for the operation—one in London and two in the theatre. Their changing relations over a period when the plans themselves were inevitably becoming more detailed, explain the inconsistencies between their figures.

The figures produced finally by the 'Axiom' Mission and the British Joint Planning Staff on 23rd February were as follows:

Forces required	*Deficiencies, November* 1944	*Deficiencies March* 1945 (If Germany defeated in October 1944)
NAVAL[1]		
3 Battleships 6 Fleet Carriers 22 Escort Carriers 29 Cruisers 5 Fighter Direction Ships 208 Destroyers and Escorts	5 Fleet Carriers 13 Escort Carriers[2] 19 Cruisers 3 Fighter Direction Ships 152 Destroyers and Escorts	2 Fleet Carriers 9 Escort Carriers[3] 13 Cruisers 1 Fighter Direction Ship
ASSAULT SHIPPING AND CRAFT		
101 Landing Ships (of which 67 are L.S.T.(2).) 682 Landing Craft	74 Landing Ships (of which 67 are L.S.T.(2).) 94 Landing Craft	Nil if released from Europe by 1st October 1944
SHIPPING		
47 Personnel Ships	Nil, provided spare lift elsewhere allowed to drop from some 250,000 to some 150,000 men, after meeting 'Overlord' and 'Anvil'.	Nil.
142 M/T Store Ships	Impossible to estimate extent of certain deficit.	Unknown.
ARMY		
5½ Divisions 1 Tank Brigade 2 L.R.P. Groups 7 Beach Groups 4 Commandos Administrative and Ancillary Units	Possibly 1 Division only, if operations successful beforehand in Burma. Only 2 Divisions will then be left in reserve for Burma. Some 30,000 men	Nil.
AIR		
39 Squadrons[4]	17 Squadrons[5]	Nil.

[1] Including the cover force.

[2] Or 9 Escort Carriers if the Americans provided fighters and crews for 4 of the British Escort Carriers.

[3] Or none if the Americans provided fighters and crews.

[4] Including Bombers, Fighters, Fighter-Bombers, Torpedo and Reconnaissance.

[5] Including Bombers, Fighter-Bombers, Torpedo and Reconnaissance.

APPENDIX IX

Memorandum from General Ismay to the Prime Minister on 29th April, 1944, concerning the Strategy for the War against Japan, January – April

'1. On the 19th January, 1944, there was a meeting of the Defence Committee at which the Joint Planners expounded the Long Term Plan for the defeat of Japan which had been "approved in principle" at SEXTANT as a basis for investigation and preparation.

2. On the 24th January you addressed a Minute saying that neither you nor your Ministerial colleagues were in agreement with the Plan, and emphasising that the operation which gave the greatest promise of being effective was CULVERIN. You added that we should await the arrival of Admiral Mountbatten's Staff Officers before going into the matter again.

3. On the 1st February, you wrote a further minute saying that you could not consider yourself bound by the SEXTANT agreement.

4. On the 5th February, the Chiefs of Staff submitted a minute to you covering a résumé of the strategical considerations that had led them to select the Pacific Plan for the Defeat of Japan.

5. On the 14th February, there was a Staff Conference on the subject of the war against Japan, with particular reference to operations in South-East Asia. General Wedemeyer and other members of Admiral Mountbatten's Staff were present and expounded their proposals; and General Lumsden gave a brief outline of General MacArthur's Plan.

6. On the 16th February, you circulated a paper containing your observations on the report mentioned in paragraph 4 above.

7. On the 23rd February, you addressed a minute to the Chiefs of Staff covering a Memorandum . . . on the political implications of Far Eastern strategy.

8. Also on the 23rd February, the Chiefs of Staff submitted a report in which they reviewed the requirements for CULVERIN and the availability of resources to meet these requirements. At the end of this report they set out their conclusions as to the relative merits of CULVERIN and the PACIFIC strategies.

9. On the 24th February, you had a preliminary discussion on the above paper with the British Chiefs of Staff, and the same afternoon you held a Staff Conference for its consideration. Mr. Attlee, Mr. Lyttelton, General Wedemeyer (and party) and General Lumsden were present. The Conference agreed as to the line that General Wedemeyer should take when he reached Washington.

10. On the 1st March, the Chiefs of Staff issued a further paper in which they tried to clear up some of the misunderstandings which they felt had been disclosed in the previous discussion.

11. On the 3rd March, you circulated a paper to:

Mr. Attlee
Mr. Eden
Mr. Lyttelton
Lord Leathers
The Chiefs of Staff.

12. Also on the 3rd March, you addressed a Minute to General Ismay saying that you wished an examination to be made on the Staff level of the facilities in the Indian Ocean and Australia. You also wished the Admiralty to prepare programmes and time-tables for the development of the Fleet Train at each stage in either case, both in scale and time.

13. On the 5th March, you addressed a Minute to the Chiefs of Staff asking a number of questions on their report [see paragraph 10 above].

14. On the 7th March, you circulated a note by the Minister of War Transport suggesting that the basing of the Far East Strategy on Australia would involve demands for shipping so heavy that they could not be accepted by the Combined Shipping Authorities.

15. On the 8th March, the Chiefs of Staff replied to your Minute [see paragraph 13 above] with a paper and attached a separate report on the Base and Maintenance Facilities in India and Australia.

16. On the 8th March, the Chiefs of Staff submitted a commentary on your paper at [paragraph 11].

17. On the 8th March, you held a Staff Conference (attended by Mr. Attlee, Mr. Eden, Mr. Lyttelton, Lord Leathers and the Chiefs of Staff) which concluded that no decision on strategy could yet be made, but that reconnaissance on bases in Australia should be arranged; that preparations for CULVERIN in spring 1945 should be continued and the United States Chiefs of Staff should be informed of our present position on this subject.

18. On the 10th March, you cabled to the President asking what would be the effect in the Pacific of the absence of a British Fleet detachment and received the reply that such a reinforcement would probably not be needed before the summer of 1945.

19. On the 11th March, you sent a cable to Mr. Curtin suggesting the sending to Australia of small parties of administrative experts to study the base potentialities there. The final despatch of these parties is awaiting the agreement of Mr. Curtin on his arrival in London.

20. On the 14th March, Field Marshal Dill sent a cable outlining a much accelerated programme for the U.S. advance in the Pacific.

21. On the 13th March, you held a meeting with the Directors of Plans at which you discussed a revised plan for CULVERIN, making use of artificial harbours and floating air strips.

22. On the 14th March, you sent a minute to the Chiefs of Staff outlining your question to the President and his reply as shown in paragraph 18.

23. On the 16th March, the Chiefs of Staff sent a reply to your minute referred to in paragraph 22, stating that the opinion of the President on the requirement for a detachment of our Fleet in the Pacific should not be

taken as final, but that our decision should be determined by the contribution which we could make to the strategy best calculated to bring about the early overthrow of Japan.

24. On the 20th March, you addressed a personal minute to each Chief of Staff reviewing the differences between yourself and the Chiefs of Staff and stating that you felt it your duty to give certain rulings, including the maintenance of the BAY OF BENGAL policy and the sending of a reconnaissance mission to Australia.

25. On the 21st March, the United States Chiefs of Staff stated that they could not agree to support CULVERIN and urged that Admiral Mountbatten should be instructed to undertake the capture of Upper Burma in order to increase the capacity of the air ferry route to China and to expedite the laying of a pipe line to that country.

26. On the 24th March, this suggestion was referred to Admiral Mountbatten for his comments. His reply dated 14th April is still being examined.

27. On the 28th March, you sent a personal cable to Field Marshal Dill emphasising that there was no question at present of diverting forces from Upper Burma for CULVERIN.

28. On the 28th March, the Chiefs of Staff sent a reply to your personal minute referred to in paragraph 24, explaining that they had not committed themselves to any fixed strategy in the Far East and restating their reasons for preferring the SOUTH WEST PACIFIC to the BAY OF BENGAL policy.

29. On 8th April, you held a Conference (attended by General Wedemeyer and South East Asia Command officers and the Directors of Plans) at which it was decided that reports should be prepared on:

(a) Simalur and other islands of the Malay Barrier as air bases.
(b) Various implications of the capture and maintenance of these islands.
(c) The general strategic concept of an advance on the general line Timor-Borneo-Celebes.

30. On the 17th April, you held a meeting with General Wedemeyer and the Directors of Plans at which you discussed the projects referred to in paragraph 29 above and instructed General Wedemeyer to submit the Simalur proposal to Admiral Mountbatten, while examinations were proceeding here on the MIDDLE COURSE Strategy outlined in paragraph 29 (c).

31. On the 21st April, the Chiefs of Staff circulated a paper concluding that risks were involved in using India as a base for the full programme required by the BAY OF BENGAL Strategy.

32. On the 27th April, the Chiefs of Staff expressed their agreement with the report concluding that an examination on the shipping cost showed it to be approximately the same for either strategy, although the PACIFIC strategy was more costly in tankers.

33. On the 27th April, the Chiefs of Staff despatched to you a minute suggesting the line to be taken in the discussions on the Far East Strategy with the Dominion Prime Ministers.'

APPENDIX X

Some Prime Minister's Minutes and Telegrams, Hitherto Unpublished, of which Extracts are quoted in the Text

Memorandum on Man-power, 1st November, 1943[1]

Important issues of policy are raised by the Man-power position as set out in the following Memoranda:

(i) Memorandum by the Minister of Labour and National Service on the Estimated Supply of Man-power in 1944.

(ii) Memorandum by the Secretary of State for Air on the Man-power requirements of the Royal Air Force.

(iii) Memorandum by the First Lord of the Admiralty on the Man-power requirements of the Navy and Admiralty industries for 1944.

(iv) Memorandum by the Secretary of State for War on the Man-power requirements of the Army for 1944.

2. The estimates of requirements in 1944, as shown in these memoranda, are as follows:

Forces—		
Navy	288,500	
Army	345,850	
R.A.F.	142,000	
		776,350
Munitions—		
Admiralty	71,000	
Ministry of Supply	—	
M.A.P.	97,000	
Other requirements	6,000	
		174,000
Other Industries and Services— (e.g., coal, agriculture, transport, etc.)		240,000
Total (in round figures) ..		1,190,000

In addition, as was forecast at the time of the last survey, unavoidable wastage from industry now exceeds the intake from all sources; and it is estimated that in 1944 there would be a net decrease of 150,000 in industry as a whole, even if there were no recruitment for the Forces.

To meet present plans and programmes, therefore, the Forces and industry need an expansion of 1,190,000. And, apart from any call-up for the Forces, our industrial man-power will shrink by 150,000 in 1944. Thus, on present plans, we are faced with an overall deficit of 1,340,000.

[1] See p. 44.

3. If we continued, regardless of the effect on industry, to operate the administrative machinery for the call-up, we could get about 260,000 men for the Forces—i.e., under 40 per cent, of their demand. About 190,000 of these would be the new class of 18-year-olds.

But this intake into the Forces could only be secured at the expense of the munitions industries; since (a) industries supplying the civil population have been cut to the bone, and there is no other source of supply; and (b) it is only in the munitions industries that there are still any substantial numbers of fit men of military age. And the munitions industries have already carried substitution (of women for men) to such a point that the withdrawal even of these numbers would be apt to have more than a *pro rata* effect on output. If still larger numbers were withdrawn, the effect on output would be progressively more serious; for we should then be calling mainly on the skilled key men, whose withdrawal would cause dislocation out of proportion to their numbers.

We could get about half of the women required by the Forces; but these also would be obtained largely at the expense of munitions.

4. Thus, the problem is no longer one of closing a gap between supply and requirements. Our-man power is now fully mobilized for the war effort. We cannot add to the total; on the contrary, it is already dwindling. All we can do is to make within that total such changes as the strategy of the war demands.

If we had to carry on the war against Germany and Japan for several more years, the scale of our war effort in terms of man-power would have to decrease progressively. This fact had not been taken into account by the Departments in estimating their requirements. We have now reached the point at which it must be taken into account. For the question how we should use our man-power in 1944 depends on what assumption we are prepared to make about the duration of the war with Germany.

5. There seem to be two broad alternatives:

(a) We can assume, *for the purpose of our man-power plans*, that our maximum effort must be made in 1944, and that Germany will be defeated by the end of that year. On this assumption we could (after allowing for the munitions and men required for the war against Japan) cut back substantially the requirements for munitions which could not be delivered until after 1944 and for men who could not be trained in time to fight in 1944. We could also cut down the training organisations and ancillary formations which would otherwise be kept up to the strengths required if the Forces were to be maintained at their present level after 1944. All Departments could be directed to concentrate on the measures necessary to bring our greatest striking power to bear in 1944. On this basis the present man-power demands for the Forces and munitions could be substantially reduced.

(b) Alternatively, we can say that our man-power plans must be based on the assumption that war with Germany will continue well beyond the end of 1944. In that event we must face the fact that our Forces and munitions industries have been built up to levels which it is impossible for us to maintain over a prolonged period. And we must plan now for a progressive reduction in the scale of our effort. Unless it can be assumed that this shrinking process could be applied equally to all claimants, it would be necessary to determine on what other principles the cuts should be apportioned.

6. Whichever of these alternatives is now chosen, if the war with Germany continues after the end of 1944 we shall have to rely increasingly on United States resources to make up for the declining scale of our own effort. Our choice between these two alternatives will, however, determine the form which this American assistance must take. If we have chosen alternative (a), we shall have unbalanced our war effort and shall have to look to the United States to provide a larger proportion of the equipment for our Forces. If, on the other hand, we have chosen alternative (b), the additional help from the United States will have to come in the form of more fighting units with their equipment.

7. The Departments' estimates of requirements have not yet been subjected to the usual detailed scrutiny; but it is not thought that the broad issues set out above would be materially affected by any process of paring and pruning. It is suggested, therefore, that before work is started on a detailed scrutiny of the figures, Ministers should decide whether our Man-power Policy for 1944 is to be based on either of the two alternative assumptions set out in paragraph 5, or on some different assumption.

Prime Minister's minute of 29th November, 1943[1]

1. The momentous declaration by Marshal Stalin that Russia would enter the war against Japan the moment Germany was defeated requires that the strategy of the United States in the Pacific should be reviewed so that all possible aid is given to 'Overlord' and to operations in the Mediterranean.

2. If the United States will provide the landing-craft for operation 'Buccaneer', the British landing-craft already in the Indian Ocean can provide for 'Accolade', for strengthening amphibious operations during the Italian campaign and for any operation against the South of France.

3. The Prime Minister wishes to put on record the fact that although operation 'Buccaneer' is at present to be carried out solely by British forces, he has never been consulted upon it, and that he specifically refused the Generalissimo's request that he should undertake an amphibious operation simultaneously with the land operations in Burma.

4. Cannot also more landing-craft, etc., be sent across the Atlantic to increase the "lift" for 'Overlord' and keep the May date?

---

[1] See p. 164.

Prime Minister to the Foreign Secretary and the Chiefs of Staff, telegram of 25th December, 1943[1]

1. I am in agreement with your general line of argument, but facts are as follows: we cannot leave the Rome situation to stagnate and fester for the three months without crippling preparation of 'Anvil' and thus hampering 'Overlord'. We cannot go to other task and leave this unfinished job behind us.

2. To-day we decided in conference with Generals Eisenhower and Smith that orders should be issued immediately to prepare two divisions for 'Shingle' with target 20th January. For this 88 L.S.T. are required in the Mediterranean until 5th February, when a proportion can leave by convoy MKS 39. Nothing less than two divisions will suffice and it is better to risk the withdrawal of landing craft from subsequent build-up than to stint the initial stroke. Taking 45 L.S.T. (the bottle-neck) as lift for one division of three Brigade Groups, we required to have 88 in Central Mediterranean from 15th January to 5th February. Nothing must stand in the way of this.

3. It will therefore be necessary to stop whole of 56 L.S.T. due to sail for United Kingdom at different dates between 1st January and 5th February. The ex-'Buccaneer' S.L.I.(I) are an essential part. But the 15 ex-'Buccaneer' L.S.T. cannot possibly arrive in time. Their present dates are—unmarked (? 2nd January), 14th January, and unprepared 2nd January, 22nd January. They will, however, be invaluable to replace casualties to assist in later build-up for 'Anvil'.

4. Everything therefore turns on delaying returns to United Kingdom of remaining 56 L.S.T. for three weeks. How foolish it would be after having kept 75 so long to take them away at the very moment and for the very three weeks in which they can render supreme service. Every effort of ingenuity must be made to fill the gap. Admiral John Cunningham says that if 56 start leaving Bizerta by 5th February convoy there will be time enough to bring them in for May 'Overlord' and Captain Power has furnished me with proposals, endorsed by naval Commander-in-Chief, to achieve that end. The only point unprovided which I can see is reconstructing these craft on reaching United Kingdom which must be at a minimum rate of 25 a month. This should have priority over all Admiralty construction, whether merchant ships or anti-submarine craft. I am confident dockyards can achieve this and I ask directions to be given to that effect.

5. I recognise with great regret Aegean and 'Hercules' must be ruled out.

6. As to 'Pigstick', nothing engaged in that can possibly reach Central Mediterranean in time for 'Shingle'. But, of course, it will all help the build-up of 'Anvil'.

7. The reason why it is essential that 'Shingle' shall be launched before end January is that this is the only way in which the position can be cleared so as to send home ear-marked in accordance with 'Overlord' landing craft in time and also to enable 'Anvil' to be set up in Mediterranean.

[1] See p. 216.

8. I shall be greatly obliged if you will recast your telegram to Combined Chiefs of Staff on these lines. I am also signalling the President as in my immediately following.

9. The case for finishing up Rome job is not the capture of City, important though that be, but the violation of portion of enemy's army in Italy and securing of a line protecting Naples-Foggia airfields from counter-attack. General Eisenhower, while reserving his opinion on 'Overlord' Operation, expresses himself strongly in this sense, as you will see from Hollis's notes of our conference. General Bedell-Smith is confident that matter can be adjusted by drastic arrangement. Tedder and Wilson concur, and General Alexander is fully prepared to carry out operation.

Telegram from Prime Minister to Field Marshal Dill for General Marshall, of 12th April, 1944[1]

Prime Minister to Field Marshal Dill for General Marshall. Personal and Most Secret.

1. Although the fighting at the bridgehead and on the Cassino front has brought many disappointments, you will I trust recognise that at least 8 extra German divisions have been brought into Italy down to the south of Rome and heavily mauled there. If at Teheran we had been told that the ANVIL there suggested would detach 8 divisions from the German front against OVERLORD, we should have rejoiced. [Intelligence] shows that Hitler has been saying that his defeats in South Russia are due to the treacherous Badoglio collapse of Italy which has involved 35 German divisions. At any rate I believe that our action in Italy has played a large part in rendering possible the immensely important advances made in South Russia, which as a further benefit are convulsing the satellites.

2. I have not hitherto intervened in the intricate and lengthy correspondence which has been proceeding between the United States and British Chiefs of Staff about ANVIL. Seven German divisions with two in reserve, equals nine, have already been assigned to the defence of the Riviera front. I do not believe an advance up the Rhone Valley is practicable in any period which will influence our main operations this summer. On the contrary, I am sure the German General in the west will concentrate on winning his battle there and will fight merely delaying actions in Southern France. Were we to succeed in landing by some variant of ANVIL, it would be better to move westwards towards Bordeaux than northwards up the Rhone Valley. In either case a two-division assault supported by 8 follow-up divisions, mostly French, would be good so far as it went, but could not go far enough in time to sway the main battle. The fact, however, that nine enemy divisions have been assigned to the Riviera defence and that 25 are now in Italy, of which 18 are south of Rome, a total of 34 divisions, acquits the Mediterranean armies of not playing their part.

[1] See p. 257.

3. I gather from the correspondence between the two Staffs that we are all agreed upon priority for joining the main army with the bridgehead army. Naturally we are all grieved that the opening date of this battle must be postponed till 14th May. General Alexander has arrived home, and has convinced us that an all-out sustained major offensive cannot be launched earlier. Moreover the timing of this great battle in the South will accord harmoniously with the date of OVERLORD. All available forces British, American and Allied, will be in heavy action on both fronts simultaneously.

4. At the moment my own position is as follows. We should above all defeat the German army south of Rome and join our own armies. Nothing should be grudged for this. We cannot tell how either the Allied or enemy armies will emerge from the battle until the battle has been fought. It may be that the enemy will be thrown into disorder, and that great opportunities of exploitation may be open. Or we may be checked and the enemy may continue to hold his positions south of Rome against us with his existing forces. On the other hand, he may seek to withdraw some of his Divisions to the main battle in France. It seems to me we must have plans and preparations to take advantage of the above possibilities.

5. Regarding ANVIL, hereinafter called ANVIL Z, I believe that whatever happens on the mainland of Italy, the enemy forces now detached to the Riviera can in the meanwhile be fastened there by feints and threats. One thing that alarms me, however, is lest our Directive to General Wilson should make him fall between two stools. This would mean that we should be denied the exploitation of any victory gained south of Rome (and victories are wonderful things) or the power to pin down German Divisions in Italy, and yet on the other hand not be able to make a major operation out of ANVIL.

6. Taking paragraph 6 of CCS.465/19, I agree with the first proposition but do not think the second proposition can be judged until we see the result of the battle. For instance, I would not now rule out either a vigorous pursuit northward of the beaten enemy nor an amphibious cat's-claw higher up to detain him or cut him off. I should have thought we could contrive plans and preparations to render possible either this or ANVIL in one form or another. After all, the power to put men into ships is one thing and the question where to disembark them is another.

7. I am sorry that we are not to have the additional landing craft you thought of deducting from the Pacific effort. We should all like to see them in the Mediterranean. But if you judge there is too much vagueness and option to justify their employment there so must it be. The consequence will be to reduce all amphibious possibilities to a one division scale.

8. Finally, I repeat that if we can keep 34 German divisions in the Western Mediterranean theatre, the forces there will have made an immense contribution to OVERLORD. I have hardened very much upon OVERLORD and am further fortified by the evident confidence of Eisenhower, Brooke, and Montgomery.

9. When you have reflected on the above, I ask you to consider the following formula:

Begins

(1) The prime duty of all the forces in the Mediterranean is to pin down as many German Divisions as possible away from OVERLORD.

(2) Secondly, to achieve the above we must give the highest priority to operations to join the ANZIO bridgehead and the main front, meanwhile making such preparations for ANVIL Z as are practicable in consonance therewith.

(3) Thirdly, after joining the bridgehead we must survey the situation arising from the results of the battle in Italy, as well as the first results of OVERLORD and the dispositions of the enemy.

(4) Fourthly, we must then decide whether to go all out for ANVIL or exploit the results of victory in Italy. It must be recognised that this option will not exist unless the L.S.T's from the Pacific are assigned now to the Mediterreanean.

Ends.

10. Every good wish to you, King, and Arnold. How I wish we were all together, but I trust we shall be reassembled before the supreme struggle begins.

Telegram from Prime Minister to President Roosevelt, of 1st July, 1944[1]

PERSONAL

1. We are deeply grieved by your telegram. There are no differences whatever between my War Cabinet colleagues and the British Chiefs of Staff. The splitting up of the campaign in the Mediterranean into two operations neither of which can do anything decisive, is, in my humble and respectful opinion, the first major strategic and political error for which we two have to be responsible.

2. At Tehran you emphasised to me the possibilities of a move Eastward when Italy was conquered and mentioned particularly Istria. No one involved in these discussions has ever thought of moving armies into the Balkans; but Istria and Trieste in Italy are strategic and political positions, which as you saw yourself very clearly might exercise profound and wide-spread reactions, especially now after the Russian advances.

3. After Teheran I was made doubtful about ANVIL by General Eisenhower's dislike for it. You will remember his words at Cairo when (quote) General Eisenhower stressed the vital importance of continuing the maximum possible operations in an established theatre since much time was invariably lost when the scene of action was changed, necessitating, as it did, the arduous task of building up a fresh base (unquote).

[1] See p. 355.

4. Furthermore, I was impressed by General Montgomery's arguments when at Marrakesh, after he had been nominated to the OVERLORD command, he explained that it would take ninety days for a Force landed at ANVIL to influence the OVERLORD operation.

5. Both these opinions are in contrast to SCAF. 54. It is no reflection on these officers that they should now express a different view. But their opinions, expressed so decidedly, made me less confident about an ANVIL operation. Moreover in those days the date was to be early in June. There is no doubt that an advance up the Rhone Valley begun at the end of August could easily be blocked and stemmed by a smaller number of German troops, who could come either through the tunnels from Italy or from Southern Germany. I doubt whether you will find that three American Divisions, supported by seven French 80 per cent. native divisions from Morocco, Algeria and Tunis, will have any important strategic effect on the tremendous battle which Eisenhower and Montgomery are fighting 500 miles away to the North. It seems more likely to prove a cul-de-sac into which increasing numbers of United States troops will be drawn, and I fear that further demands will be made even upon what is left to us in Italy. It would no doubt make sure of de Gaulle having his talons pretty deeply dug into France.

6. I should not be frank if I did not assure you that I fear a costly stalemate for you unless far more American divisions, at the expense of Eisenhower, are thrust into ANVIL to make it good at all costs by the great power of the United States. Little account is to be taken of Alexander's operations. The last decision given by the British and American Chiefs of Staff here a fortnight ago was: (quote) The destruction of the German Armed Forces in Italy south of the Pisa-Rimini line must be completed. There should be no withdrawal from the battle of any Allied forces that are necessary for this purpose (unquote) However, I received from Alexander on 28 June a long distressing telegram in which the passage occurs: (quote)

The ghost of ANVIL hangs heavily over the battlefront. For example, the Americans have been ordered to send 517 RCT and 117 CAV Recce squadrons which are actually in contact with the enemy. They are also required to release now an engineer regiment and other service units required for the conduct of battle. The French do not appear to be putting their hearts into the present operations and reason is undoubtedly because they have their eyes turned in another direction.

The air effort will shortly be curtailed owing to moves of fighting units to Corsica. Eighth Army are not directly concerned with ANVIL, but as long as there is doubt and uncertainty about the future so long will there be a moral weakening. Armies have a very delicate sense and they are beginning to look over their shoulders. You will no doubt remember the Biblical quotation (quote) For if the trumpet give an uncertain sound, who shall prepare himself to the battle (unquote). If the momentum of my offensive is to be kept to its maximum, I must receive confirmation that Italian campaign is to be backed. If on the other hand it is decided to go all out for ANVIL, then I must know so that I can recast my present plans. In the event of the latter decision I have proposed to General Wilson that I should fly home and table certain proposals aimed at producing best results my emasculated forces will be able to achieve in support of the war effort (unquote).

7. I have considered your suggestion that we should lay our respective cases before Stalin. The passage in the very nice telegram I have received from him yesterday (bracket) which follows this immediately (bracket) seems to suggest that he does not underrate the Italian front. I do not know what he would say if the issue was put to him to decide. On military grounds he might be greatly interested in the eastward movement of Alexander's Army, which, without entering the Balkans, would profoundly affect all the forces there and which, in conjunction with any attacks he may make upon Rumania or with Rumania against Hungarian Transylvania, might produce the most far-reaching results. On a long-term political view, he might prefer that the British and Americans should do their share in France in this very hard fighting that is to come, and that East, Middle and Southern Europe, should fall naturally into his control. However it is better to settle the matter for ourselves and between ourselves.

8. What can I do, Mr. President, when your Chiefs of Staff insist on casting aside our Italian offensive campaign, with all its dazzling possibilities, relieving Hitler of all his anxieties in the Po basin, and when we are to see the integral life of this campaign drained off into the Rhone valley in the belief that it will in several months carry effective help to Eisenhower so far away in the North?

9. If you still press upon us the directive of your Chiefs of Staff to withdraw so many of your forces from the Italian campaign and leave all our hopes there dashed to the ground, His Majesty's Government, on the advice of their Chiefs of Staff, must enter a solemn protest. I need scarcely say that we shall do our best to make a success of anything that is undertaken. We shall therefore forward your directive to General Wilson as soon as you let us know that there is no hope of reconsideration by your Chiefs of Staff or by yourself. Our Chiefs of Staff are letting yours know the corrections on points of detail which they think necessary in the previous draft.

10. It is with the greatest sorrow that I write to you in this sense. But I am sure that if we could have met, as I so frequently proposed, we should have reached a happy agreement. I send you every personal good wish. However we may differ on the conduct of the war, my personal gratitude to you for your kindness to me and for all you have done for the cause of freedom will never be diminished.

Letter from Mr. J. M. Martin to Sir Alan Lascelles[1]

16th August, 1944

My dear Lascelles,

The following message for the King has been received this evening from the Prime Minister, who is now in Naples:

"With humble duty.

Have just returned from watching the assault. Everything seems to be progressing with great precision. The shore batteries were easily silenced. Your Majesty knows my opinion about the strategy, but the perfect execution of the plan was deeply interesting. There is no doubt that Eisenhower's operations made a great diversion. The fact that this is the precise opposite of what was intended need not be stressed at the present time.

Am off to Alexander's Headquarters tomorrow 17th."

Yours sincerely,

J. M. MARTIN

Personal telegram from Prime Minister to President Roosevelt, of 29th April, 1944[2]

I am seriously concerned about the food situation in India and its possible reactions on our joint operations. Last year we had a grievous famine in Bengal through which at least 700,000 people died. This year there is a good crop of rice, but we are faced with an acute shortage of wheat, aggravated by unprecedented storms which have inflicted serious damage on the Indian spring crops. India's shortage cannot be overcome by any possible surplus of rice even if such a surplus could be extracted from the peasants. Our recent losses in the Bombay explosion have accentuated the problem.

Wavell is exceedingly anxious about our position and has given me the gravest warnings. His present estimate is that he will require imports of about one million tons this year if he is to hold the situation, and to meet the needs of the United States and British and Indian troops and of the civil population especially in the great cities. I have just heard from Mountbatten that he considers the situation so serious that, unless arrangements are made promptly to import wheat requirements he will be compelled to release military cargo space of S.E.A.C. in favour of wheat and formally to advise Stilwell that it will also be necessary for him to arrange to curtail American military demands for this purpose.

By cutting down military shipments and other means, I have been able to arrange for 350,000 tons of wheat to be shipped to India from Australia during the first nine months of 1944. This is the shortest haul. I cannot see how to do more.

---

[1] See p. 392.

[2] See p. 468.

I have had much hesitation in asking you to add to the great assistance you are giving us with shipping but a satisfactory situation in India is of such vital importance to the success of our joint plans against the Japanese that I am impelled to ask you to consider a special allocation of ships to carry wheat to India from Australia without reducing the assistance you are now providing for us, who are at a positive minimum if war efficiency is to be maintained. We have the wheat (in Australia) but we lack the ships. I have resisted for some time the Viceroy's request that I should ask you for your help, but I believe that, with this recent misfortune to the wheat harvest and in the light of Mountbatten's representations, I am no longer justified in not asking for your help. Wavell is doing all he can by special measures in India. If, however, he should find it possible to revise his estimate of his needs, I would let you know immediately.

Appendix XI : Chronological Table

This Table makes no attempt to provide a complete chronology of

N.W. EUROPE	MEDITERRANEAN	EASTERN FRONT	WAR AT SEA
1943 August	**1943 August**	**1943 August**	**1943 August**
17 FIRST QUEBEC CONFERENCE BEGINS			
17. 'Overlord' adopted as 'primary ground and air effort' in Europe in 1944; target date, 1st May.		Russian offensives under way from area of Smolensk to Sea of Azov.	
	18. C.C.S. approve plan for landings at Salerno and in southern Italy. Operations approved in principle for 'elimination of Italy . . . capture of Sardinia and Corsica . . . and creation of the conditions required for 'Overlord' and for an eventual re-entry' into southern France. Guerrilla forces in Balkans to be supplied.	18. Russians complete elimination of German salient around Orel. 23. Russians take Kharkov.	
September	**September**	**September**	**September**
	3. Italian military plenipotentiaries sign terms of surrender. British land in southern Italy.		
	8. Italian surrender announced.		
	9. Allies land at Salerno. Partisans attack in Yugoslavia. British party lands in Rhodes.		10-13. Italian battle-fleet reaches Malta, under surrender.

August 1943—September 1944

events or planning dates. It is designed only to illustrate the text.

	AIR WAR IN EUROPE	S.E. ASIA AND CHINA	PACIFIC	GENERAL
	1943 August	**1943 August**	**1943 August**	**1943 August**
17	FIRST QUEBEC CONFERENCE BEGINS			
		Operations approved in principle for increasing air supply to China, for establishing land communications with China through northern Burma, and preparatory to 'an amphibious operation in the spring of 1944.'	Operations approved in principle against Gilberts, Marshalls, Ponape and Eastern Carolines in central Pacific, and against eastern New Guinea, Admiraltys, Bismarcks, Palaus and Guam in south-west Pacific.	Morgenthau Plan approved in principle.
		25. Announcement of new South-East Asia Command, with Mountbatten as Supreme Allied Commander.		
	27. Report suggesting existence of a V1 rocket in Germany.			
	September	**September**	**September**	**September**

N.W. EUROPE	MEDITERRANEAN	EASTERN FRONT	WAR AT SEA
1943 September	**1943 September**	**1943 September**	**1943 September**
	12. British withdraw from Rhodes.		
	13-17. British land in Aegean islands.		
	16. Germans retreat from Salerno.		
	21. Alexander's first plans for winter in Italy.		
		23. Russians take Smolensk.	
	26-27. British adopt plan to take Rhodes.		
			29. British midget submarines damage *Tirpitz*.
	End. British consider passing force into Greece on Germans' withdrawal.		
October	**October**	**October**	**October**
	1. Allies enter Naples.		
	3-4. Germans recapture Cos.	3. Russians cross river Dnieper around Kiev.	
	4. Hitler orders stand in Italy south of Rome.		
	8. Guerrillas attack each other in Greece.		
	9. Conference in Mediterranean rejects plan to attack Rhodes.		

AIR WAR IN EUROPE	S.E. ASIA AND CHINA	PACIFIC	GENERAL
1943 September	**1943 September**	**1943 September**	**1943 September**
October	**October**	**October**	**October**
	7. Mountbatten arrives in India.		

N.W. EUROPE	MEDITERRANEAN	EASTERN FRONT	WAR AT SEA
1943 October	**1943 October**	**1943 October**	**1943 October**
			12. Announcement of use of Azores as naval and air base, by agreement with Portugal.
	Mid. German 'Sixth Offensive' in Yugoslavia.		
	21. Alexander's revised plans for winter in Italy.		
	24. Eisenhower's first directive for winter in Italy.		
		25. Russians cross Dnieper at Dniepropetrovsk.	
	27. Eisenhower's study of threat to southern France.	27. Russians break through between lower Dnieper and Sea of Azov.	
	31. Eisenhower asks for retention of L.S.T. in Mediterranean.		
November	**November**	**November**	**November**
		1. Russians cut German land communications with the Crimea.	
	2. British propose unified Command in Mediterranean.		
	5-7. Talks with Turks in Cairo (see *General*).		
	6. C.C.S. approve retention of L.S.T. in Mediterranean.	6. Russians capture Kiev.	

AIR WAR IN EUROPE	S.E. ASIA AND CHINA	PACIFIC	GENERAL
1943 October	**1943 October**	**1943 October**	**1943 October**
14. Raid on Schweinfurt, with heavy American losses.			
			19. Foreign Ministers' Conference begins in Moscow.
	23. Prime Minister's directive to Mountbatten for operations in S.E. Asia.		
		25. Combined Staff Planners' study of strategy in Pacific.	
November	**November**	**November**	**November**
Early. New machinery set up for study of action regarding German pilotless weapons.			1. Prime Minister's Minute on a 'double ending' to war.
			2. Foreign Ministers decide to ask Turkey to enter war.

N.W. EUROPE	MEDITERRANEAN	EASTERN FRONT	WAR AT SEA
1943 November	**1943 November**	**1943 November**	**1943 November**
	8. Eisenhower's second directive for winter in Italy.		
	11. British proposals for strategy in Mediterranean.		
	12-16. Germans recapture Leros.		
			Mid. Arctic convoys resumed.
22-28. CAIRO CONFERENCE, FIRST STAGE			
25. Americans propose a Supreme Allied Commander for all British-American operations in Europe.			
	27. Allies begin attack on German positions in Italy.		
28-1st December. TEHERAN CONFERENCE			

AIR WAR IN EUROPE	S.E. ASIA AND CHINA	PACIFIC	GENERAL
1943 November	**1943 November**	**1943 November**	**1943 November**
			9. Giraud resigns from French Committee of National Liberation. De Gaulle becomes President of Committee.
	10. Mountbatten submits plans for winter, including operations 'Tarzan' and 'Buccaneer'.		
	Mid. Advance begins in extreme north of Burma.		
18. Americans' proposals for unified Strategic Air Command against Germany.			
22-28.	CAIRO CONFERENCE,	FIRST STAGE	
	By 26. President promises Chiang Kai-shek 'an amphibious operation' in S.E. Asia 'within the next few months'.		
	26. Allies' intentions in S.E. Asia explained verbally to Chiang Kai-shek.		
		28. Stalin announces Russia will enter war against Japan when Germany has collapsed.	
28-1st December.	TEHERAN	CONFERENCE	

N.W. EUROPE	MEDITERRANEAN	EASTERN FRONT	WAR AT SEA
1943 December	**1943 December**	**1943 December**	**1943 December**
1. Western Allies agree to invade N.W. France 'in May, 1944'.	Western Allies agree to advance in Italy to line Pisa-Rimini, to retain L.S.T. in Mediterranean until mid-January, and to mount an operation against southern France if possible simultaneously with 'Overlord' (operation 'Anvil').		
3-7. CAIRO CONFERENCE, SECOND STAGE			
'Overlord' and 'Anvil' accepted as 'the supreme operations for 1944'.			
	Operations in Aegean accepted as desirable 'if they can be fitted in'.		
	4-7. Talks with Turks in Cairo.		
	12. Deterioration in relations with Turks.		
		14. Russians attack around Vitebsk.	
	Mid. Allied attack halted in Italy.		
	17. Eisenhower asks for bigger assault lift for 'Anvil'.		
		24. Russians renew attack beyond Kiev.	

AIR WAR IN EUROPE	S.E. ASIA AND CHINA	PACIFIC	GENERAL
1943 December	**1943 December**	**1943 December**	**1943 December**
3-7. CAIRO CONFERENCE, SECOND STAGE			
	President cancels promise of 'amphibious operation' to Chiang Kai-shek. C.C.S. cancel 'Buccaneer', and transfer assault shipping to Europe.	C.C.S. agree that 'main effort against Japan should be made in the Pacific.' British Fleet in Pacific to be part of that strategy.	
Early. Operations begin against pilotless weapons ('Crossbow'), and plan of defence drawn up.			
		15. Combined Planning Staff's paper on demands and resources for Pacific.	
	21. Mountbatten proposes operation 'Pigstick' to Chiang Kai-shek, instead of 'Buccaneer'.		
		23. Final version of C.C.S.' paper on Pacific (see Dec. 3-7 above).	

N.W. EUROPE	MEDITERRANEAN	EASTERN FRONT	WAR AT SEA
1943 December	**1943 December**	**1943 December**	**1943 December**
			26. H.M.S. *Duke of York* sinks *Scharnhorst.*
	28. President agrees to launch attack on Anzio ('Shingle') on 22nd January.		
		31. Russians recapture Zhitomir.	
End. Appointments announced of senior commanders for 'Overlord' and Mediterranean.			
	End. British prepare to withdraw missions from Mihailovic in Yugoslavia.		
1944 January	**1944 January**	**1944 January**	**1944 January**
	3. Allied attack resumed in Italy.		
6. Cossac reviews plan for 'Overlord', and requests cancellation of 'Anvil'.			
7. Montgomery begins review of plan for 'Overlord'.			
	8. Wilson, new Supreme Allied Commander in Mediterranean, to receive orders through British C.O.S. Programme of assault shipping settled for 'Shingle'.		
		15. Russians open offensive around Leningrad and Novgorod.	

AIR WAR IN EUROPE	S.E. ASIA AND CHINA	PACIFIC	GENERAL
1943 December	**1943 December**	**1943 December**	**1943 December**
	28. British propose cancellation of 'Pigstick'.		
	30. Assault shipping starts to leave for Europe.	30. British C.O.S. ask Prime Minister's permission to inform Australia and New Zealand of plans for Pacific.	
1944 January	**1944 January**	**1944 January**	**1944 January**
	Early. Allies start attack in Arakan.		
4. Directive to American strategic air forces in Europe, setting up unified command.			
	6. 'Pigstick' cancelled, followed by 'Tarzan'.		
		10. Prime Minister refuses permission asked above.	
	14. C.C.S.' directive to Mountbatten, following reduction of operations.		

N.W. EUROPE	MEDITERRANEAN	EASTERN FRONT	WAR AT SEA
1944 January	**1944 January**	**1944 January**	**1944 January**
16. Eisenhower begins review of 'Overlord' in relation to 'Anvil'.			
		20. Russians take Novgorod.	
	22. Allies land at Anzio.		
23. Eisenhower asks for rapid decision on strength of 'Anvil'.			
	24. Hitler orders stand in Apennines south of Rome.		
26. British recommend strengthening of 'Overlord' and its postponement to June, and reduction of 'Anvil' accordingly.			
		27. German blockade of Leningrad lifted.	
	31. British stop military supplies to Turkey.		
February	**February**	**February**	**February**
Early. 'Overlord' t ken as postponed.	Early. Allies attack Monte Cassino. Allied bridgehead at Anzio sealed off. Guerrilla civil war stops in Greece.		
		3. Russians cross Estonian frontier.	

AIR WAR IN EUROPE	S.E. ASIA AND CHINA	PACIFIC	GENERAL
1944 **January**	**1944** **January**	**1944** **January**	**1944** **January**
18. Transportation Plan presented by 'Overlord' Air Command. Discussion begins with strategic air commanders.			
	19. Discussion begins in London on British strategy in Far East.		
	31. Mountbatten and Stilwell disagree on strategy for Burma.		
February	**February**	**February**	**February**
		2. Russians inform Americans they will be allowed later to base bombers in Russia for attacks on Japan.	
	4. Japanese counter-attack in Arakan.		

N.W. EUROPE	MEDITERRANEAN	EASTERN FRONT	WAR AT SEA
1944 February	**1944 February**	**1944 February**	**1944 February**
8. Final administrative plan for 'Overlord'.			
11. C.C.S.' directive to Eisenhower.			
	12. First attack on M. Cassino fails.		
13. Staff discussions begin in London on relation of 'Anvil' to 'Overlord'.		13. Russians clear eastern shore of Lake Peipus.	
	16. Second attack on M. Cassino fails.		
	22. Wilson's plans for Italy, and request to cancel 'Anvil'.		
23. Eisenhower and British C.O.S. recommend that campaign in Italy should have first priority in Mediterranean, and that 'Anvil' be considered first of possible assaults in that theatre subject to such priority.			
			24. Main Japanese Fleet moves to Singapore.
25. C.C.S. approve these recommendations, to be reviewed on 20th March.			
	28. Revision of assault shipping programme in Mediterranean raised.		
	29. Last, unsuccessful German counter-attack at Anzio.		

AIR WAR IN EUROPE	S.E. ASIA AND CHINA	PACIFIC	GENERAL
1944 February	**1944 February**	**1944 February**	**1944 February**
	11. 'Axiom' Mission from S.E. Asia reach London.		
	14. Discussions begin in London on strategy for S.E. Asia and Pacific.		
	18. Mountbatten asks permission of C.C.S. to divert transport aircraft from China ferry to Arakan.		
24. First big combined Anglo-American offensive by day and night on one target, Schweinfurt.	24. C.C.S. grant this permission.	24. Main Japanese Fleet moves to Singapore.	

N.W. EUROPE	MEDITERRANEAN	EASTERN FRONT	WAR AT SEA
1944 March	**1944 March**	**1944 March**	**1944 March**
		6. Russians begin spring offensive in, and south of, Ukraine.	
	10. Revised assault shipping programme settled for Mediterranean.		
		13. Russians take Kherson, at mouth of Dnieper.	
Mid. Allies reject French Resistance's plan 'Vidal'.	15. Third attack launched on M. Cassino.		

AIR WAR IN EUROPE	S.E. ASIA AND CHINA	PACIFIC	GENERAL
1944 March	**1944 March**	**1944 March**	**1944 March**
	3. 'Axiom' Mission begins talks in Washington		
5. Strategic air commanders' alternative to Transportation Plan.			
		8. British decide to investigate facilities in Australia and New Zealand, and shipping problems involved in a Pacific strategy.	
	12. Japanese attack on central front in Burma.		
	13. Mountbatten again transfers transport aircraft from China ferry to Burma.		
		14. Americans announce next stage in Pacific operations, culminating in occupation of Formosa by mid-February, 1945.	
	17. President asks Chiang Kai-shek to advance from Yunnan into northern Burma.		

N.W. EUROPE	MEDITERRANEAN	EASTERN FRONT	WAR AT SEA
1944 March	**1944 March**	**1944 March**	**1944 March**
18. President's directive to Eisenhower on civil affairs in France.	18. Partisans attack in Yugoslavia.	18. Germans enter Hungary.	
22. Eisenhower's and Wilson's separate reports, the former on 'Overlord' and 'Anvil', the latter on Italy and 'Anvil'.			
	22. British C.O.S. propose new directive for Wilson.		
	23. Third attack on M. Cassino fails.		
24. C.C.S. agree to postpone 'Anvil' to target date of 10th July, and meanwhile to transfer some assault shipping to Britain.			
		30. Russians take Cernauti in Rumania.	

AIR WAR IN EUROPE	S.E. ASIA AND CHINA	PACIFIC	GENERAL
1944 March	**1944 March**	**1944 March**	**1944 March**
	18. C.C.S. sanction Mountbatten's transfer of transport aircraft.		
	Third Week. Japanese approach Imphal Plain. Discussion begins between C.C.S. on ways of finding more transport aircraft for battle in Burma.		
	21. 'Axiom' Mission completes talks in Washington.		
25. Meeting of air authorities on Transportation Plan. Plan accepted in principle. Limited operations to begin.			
26. C.C.S. give Eisenhower 'direction' of all air operations from Britain for support of 'Overlord'.			
30-31. Biggest British losses on bombing so far, on Nuremberg.	30. Japanese besiege Imphal Plain. Chiang Kai-shek agrees to reinforce northern front in Burma.		

N.W. EUROPE	MEDITERRANEAN	EASTERN FRONT	WAR AT SEA
1944 April	**1944 April**	**1944 April**	**1944 April**
	Early. German 'Seventh Offensive' in Yugoslavia.		
	10. C.C.S. reach deadlock on new directive to Wilson.	10. Russians capture Odessa.	
	11. Alexander's report on future in Italy. Prime Minister appeals to Washington on directive.	11. Russians enter the Crimea.	
		Mid. Russian spring offensive eases.	
15. Restrictions imposed on Allies' and neutrals' movements and mails.		15. Russians take Tarnopol.	
	16. Directive issued to Wilson, on lines favoured by Americans.		
19. Western Allies' *aide-mémoire* to French on civil affairs. Prime Minister proposes to British C.O.S. a landing in western, instead of southern, France.			

AIR WAR IN EUROPE	S.E. ASIA AND CHINA	PACIFIC	GENERAL
1944 April	**1944 April**	**1944 April**	**1944 April**
	1. C.C.S. agree to transfer transport aircraft from Mediterranean to Burma.		
	1. C.C.S. approve creation of Twentieth Bomber Command against Japan.		
3. War Cabinet begins discussion of Transportation Plan and its effect on French.			
	4. Japanese attack Kohima.		
5. Defence Committee begins examination of Transportation Plan.			
		8. First appearance of British 'Middle Strategy' for Pacific.	
		9. Prime Minister's Minute on size of Fleet Train, limiting initial size of British Pacific Fleet.	
	18. Kohima relieved. Japanese contained.		

N.W. EUROPE	MEDITERRANEAN	EASTERN FRONT	WAR AT SEA
1944 April	**1944 April**	**1944 April**	**1944 April**
May	**May**	**May**	**May**
	3-6. Discussions on future in Mediterranean with Wilson in London.		
	8. Americans agree to send more assault shipping to Mediterranean.		
		9. Russians capture Sevastopol.	

AIR WAR IN EUROPE	S.E. ASIA AND CHINA	PACIFIC	GENERAL
1944 April	**1944 April**	**1944 April**	**1944 April**
	21. Chiang Kai-shek agrees to advance into Burma from Yunnan.		
	25. Mountbatten asks permission to keep transport aircraft from Mediterranean indefinitely.	25. Report on shipping required for different strategies in Far East.	
	29. Prime Minister asks President for help in shipping wheat to India.		
May	**May**	**May**	**May**
			1-16. Dominions' Prime Ministers' Conference in London.
		3-21. Conversations with Australians and New Zealanders, at Dominions' Prime Ministers' Conference in London, on war against Japan.	
	6. C.C.S. allow Mountbatten to keep transport aircraft from Mediterranean until later in May.		
7. Prime Minister consults President on Transportation Plan.			
	10-11. Chinese begin to advance from Yunnan.		

N.W. EUROPE	MEDITERRANEAN	EASTERN FRONT	WAR AT SEA
1944 May	**1944 May**	**1944 May**	**1944 May**
	11. Allied attack begins in Italy (operation 'Diadem').		
16. French suspend talks on civil affairs.			
	17. Fourth attack launched on M. Cassino.		
	18. M. Cassino taken.		
	23. Allied force at Anzio joins in offensive.		
	End. King Peter of Yugoslavia forms new Government. British missions withdrawn from Mihailovic.		
June	**June**	**June**	**June**
	3. Tito evacuated from Yugoslavia to Vis.		
	4. Americans enter Rome.		
5. De Gaulle forbids French liaison officers to accompany Allies to France.			

AIR WAR IN EUROPE	S.E. ASIA AND CHINA	PACIFIC	GENERAL
1944 May	**1944 May**	**1944 May**	**1944 May**
11. President accepts Transportation Plan.			
Mid. Americans begin new campaign against German oil.	15. C.C.S. allow Mountbatten to keep transport aircraft from Mediterranean until 15th June.		15. French Assembly in Algiers votes that Committee of National Liberation be styled Provisional Government of French Republic.
16. Directive on Transportation Plan adopted.			
	17. Allies begin attack on Myitkyina.		
	22. Imphal Plain relieved. Japanese withdrawing on central front. Chinese over border of Burma.		
		23. British C.O.S. propose 'Modified Middle Strategy' for Pacific.	
		End. British missions leave for Australia, to investigate facilities.	
June	**June**	**June**	**June**
	3. C.C.S.' new directive to Mountbatten.		

N.W. EUROPE	MEDITERRANEAN	EASTERN FRONT	WAR AT SEA
1944 **June**	**1944** **June**	**1944** **June**	**1944** **June**
6. Allies land in Normandy.			
	7. Alexander's report on future plans in Italy.		
10-15. C.C.S. meet in England. Discussion on Europe.		10. Russians' summer offensive begins in extreme north.	
	14. C.C.S.' message to Wilson, leaving open choice of 'Anvil' or other assaults to assist 'Overlord', but forces to be withdrawn at once from Italy to prepare for such an operation. Operations in Italy to continue to line Pisa-Rimini.		
	15. Allied Balkans Air Forces set up, to co-ordinate all operations 'on and across the Dalmatian Coast.'		
	17. Wilson protests at C.C.S.' instructions of 14th (above). Lebanon Conference opens on Greek affairs.		
18. Montgomery issues first general orders for armies after landings.			
19. Gale in English Channel, damaging artificial harbours.			
	21-26. Conferences in London on future in Italy.		

AIR WAR IN EUROPE	S.E. ASIA AND CHINA	PACIFIC	GENERAL
1944 June	**1944 June**	**1944 June**	**1944 June**
	9. Mountbatten's directive for operations in Burma. Allies advancing on central front.		
	10-15. C.C.S. meet in England. Discussion on Far East.		
13. First V.1 lands in England.			13. President agrees to temporary allocation of military responsibilities in S.E. Europe between British and Russians.
Mid. British join Americans in new campaign against German oil.			

N.W. EUROPE	MEDITERRANEAN	EASTERN FRONT	WAR AT SEA
1944 June	**1944 June**	**1944 June**	**1944 June**
23. Eisenhower supports C.C.S.' instructions of 14th, and asks for 'Anvil' in August.		23. Russians' offensive begins north of Pripet Marshes.	
25. British launch attack on Caen.			
26. Americans enter Cherbourg.			
	27-2 July. Discussions with Americans on future in Italy.		
July	**July**	**July**	**July**
1. von Runstedt relieved of his command in France.			
	2. Allies decide to launch 'Anvil' in August, target date 15th. Directive sent to Wilson.		
		3. Russians take Minsk.	
	5. Wilson's new directive to Alexander.		
		13. Russians take Vilna.	
	15. Allies take Arezzo.		
		17. Russians' offensive begins south of Pripet Marshes.	

AIR WAR IN EUROPE	S.E. ASIA AND CHINA	PACIFIC	GENERAL
1944 June	**1944 June**	**1944 June**	**1944 June**
		24. Prime Minister rejects 'Modified Middle Strategy'.	
	End. Japanese routed south and east of Imphal Plain.		
July	**July**	**July**	**July**
		11. Americans inform British of new 'overall objective' against Japan, allowing for invasion of Japanese Home Islands.	11. President announces recognition of de Gaulle's Administration as *de facto* authority for civil affairs in France.

N.W. EUROPE	MEDITERRANEAN	EASTERN FRONT	WAR AT SEA
1944 **July**	**1944** **July**	**1944** **July**	**1944** **July**
18. British and Canadians meet in Caen.			
	19. Allies take Leghorn.		
25. Americans launch attack from base of Cherbourg Peninsula.		25. Russians take Lvov.	
27. Germans begin to give way on Americans' front.			
		28. Russians take Brest Litovsk.	
		29. Russians broadcast appeal to Poles in Warsaw to rise.	
August	**August**	**August**	**August**
		1. Poles rise in Warsaw. Russians' advance near Warsaw checked.	
		3. Russians reach Vistula near Sandomierz.	
4. Prime Minister suggests to Americans switching 'Dragoon' (formerly 'Anvil') from south of France to Brittany.		4. Poles appeal to West for help.	
	4. Allies enter Florence.		
		5. Russians refuse help to Warsaw.	

AIR WAR IN EUROPE	S.E. ASIA AND CHINA	PACIFIC	GENERAL
1944 **July**	**1944** **July**	**1944** **July**	**1944** **July**
			20. Attempt on Hitler's life.
	23. Mountbatten submits plans for future operations in Burma, including 'Vanguard' against Rangoon.		
August	**August**	**August**	**August**

N.W. EUROPE	MEDITERRANEAN	EASTERN FRONT	WAR AT SEA
1944 August	**1944 August**	**1944 August**	**1944 August**
8. Prime Minister's suggestion turned down.			
	11-29. Prime Minister, C.I.G.S. and C.A.S. visit Mediterranean.		
13. Falaise battle begins.	13. Florence cleared.		
	15. 'Dragoon' launched on south of France.		
17-26. Discussion on future operations between Eisenhower and Montgomery.			
	19. Wilson submits plans for entering Greece.		
20. Falaise battle ends.		20. Russians launch attack on Rumania. President and Prime Minister appeal to Stalin to help Poles in Warsaw.	
19-25. Paris freed.			
21-27. Allies reach and cross Seine.			
		22. Appeal rejected.	
	24. Americans enter Grenoble.		
	25. Alexander launches preliminary operations against Gothic Line in Italy.	25. Rumania declares war on Germany.	

AIR WAR IN EUROPE	S.E. ASIA AND CHINA	PACIFIC	GENERAL
1944 August	**1944 August**	**1944 August**	**1944 August**
	8. Talks begin again in London on future British strategy in Far East.		
			14. War Cabinet adopts date of 30th June, 1945, as end of war in Europe, for production planning.
	18. British send proposals for their future strategy in Far East to Washington.		

N.W. EUROPE	MEDITERRANEAN	EASTERN FRONT	WAR AT SEA
1944 August	**1944 August**	**1944 August**	**1944 August**
	28. French take Toulon.		
29. Americans cross Marne.		29. Hungarian Cabinet resigns.	
30. Canadians enter Rouen.		30. Russians take Ploësti.	
31. British enter Amiens.		31. Russians enter Bucharest.	
September	**September**	**September**	**September**
1. Eisenhower assumes direct command of Allied armies on Western front.	1. 'Ratweek' begins in Yugoslavia.		
	2. Allies enter Pisa.		
3. British enter Brussels.			
4. British enter Antwerp	4. Allies approach Rimini.		
5. Joint Intelligence Committee's report on possibility of German surrender.		5. Russians declare war on Bulgaria.	
6-13. German resistance stiffens in France and Low Countries.		6. Russians reach Yugoslav frontier.	
	7. Americans take Besançon.		
8. Allies take Ostend.	8. French take Beaune. Alexander launches main attack on Gothic Line in Italy. C.C.S.' directive to Wilson to enter Greece on Germans' withdrawal.		
9. Eisenhower submits plans for future operations in N.W. Europe.		9. Bulgaria surrenders.	

AIR WAR IN EUROPE	S.E. ASIA AND CHINA	PACIFIC	GENERAL
1944 August	**1944 August**	**1944 August**	**1944 August**
September	**September**	**September**	**September**
			4. War Cabinet accepts date of 31st December, 1944 as end of war in Europe for production planning.
	5-12. Discussion between Prime Minister and British C.O.S. on movement of troops and material from Europe to S.E. Asia.		

N.W. EUROPE	MEDITERRANEAN	EASTERN FRONT	WAR AT SEA
1944 September	**1944 September**	**1944 September**	**1944 September**
		10. Finland surrenders.	
		12. Russians agree to allow Americans to fly supplies to Warsaw from England.	
12. SECOND QUEBEC CONFERENCE BEGINS			
Allies take Le Havre.	Americans agree to leave American troops in Italy for present.		
		14. Russians fly some supplies to Warsaw.	
15. Eisenhower assumes control of 'Dragoon' forces.			
	16. Americans accept British proposals for action in S.E. Europe should Germany collapse.		
17. Attack launched on Arnhem.			
18. Allies take Brest.		18. Americans fly supplies to Warsaw from England.	
	21. Allies enter Rimini.		
	23-30. Climax of attack on Gothic Line.		

AIR WAR IN EUROPE	S.E. ASIA AND CHINA	PACIFIC	GENERAL
1944 September	**1944 September**	**1944 September**	**1944 September**
		12. C.A.S. proposes British long-range bomber force for Pacific.	
12. SECOND QUEBEC CONFERENCE BEGINS			
14. C.C.S.' directive on command of strategic air forces in Europe.		14. Americans accept British Pacific Fleet in 'main operations against Japan in Pacific', and possibility of British long-range bomber force.	14. C.C.S. propose establishment of Combined Military Committee in Moscow.
			15. President and Prime Minister settle provisional zones of occupation for Americans and British in Germany.
	16. C.C.S.' directive to Mountbatten on future operations in Burma.		

N.W. EUROPE	MEDITERRANEAN	EASTERN FRONT	WAR AT SEA
1944 September	**1944 September**	**1944 September**	**1944 September**
25-26. Attack on Arnhem fails.			
29. Eisenhower reports future plans: opening of Antwerp first priority.			
30. Allies take Calais.			

AIR WAR IN EUROPE	S.E. ASIA AND CHINA	PACIFIC	GENERAL
1944 September	**1944 September**	**1944 September**	**1944 September**
	26. Timetable agreed for movement of troops from Europe to S.E. Asia.		

Index

INDEX

Wt 2694—3/56—K40—CB&S Ltd G1246

S.O. Code No. 63-111-25-5*

COMBINED CHIEFS OF STAFF'S
October

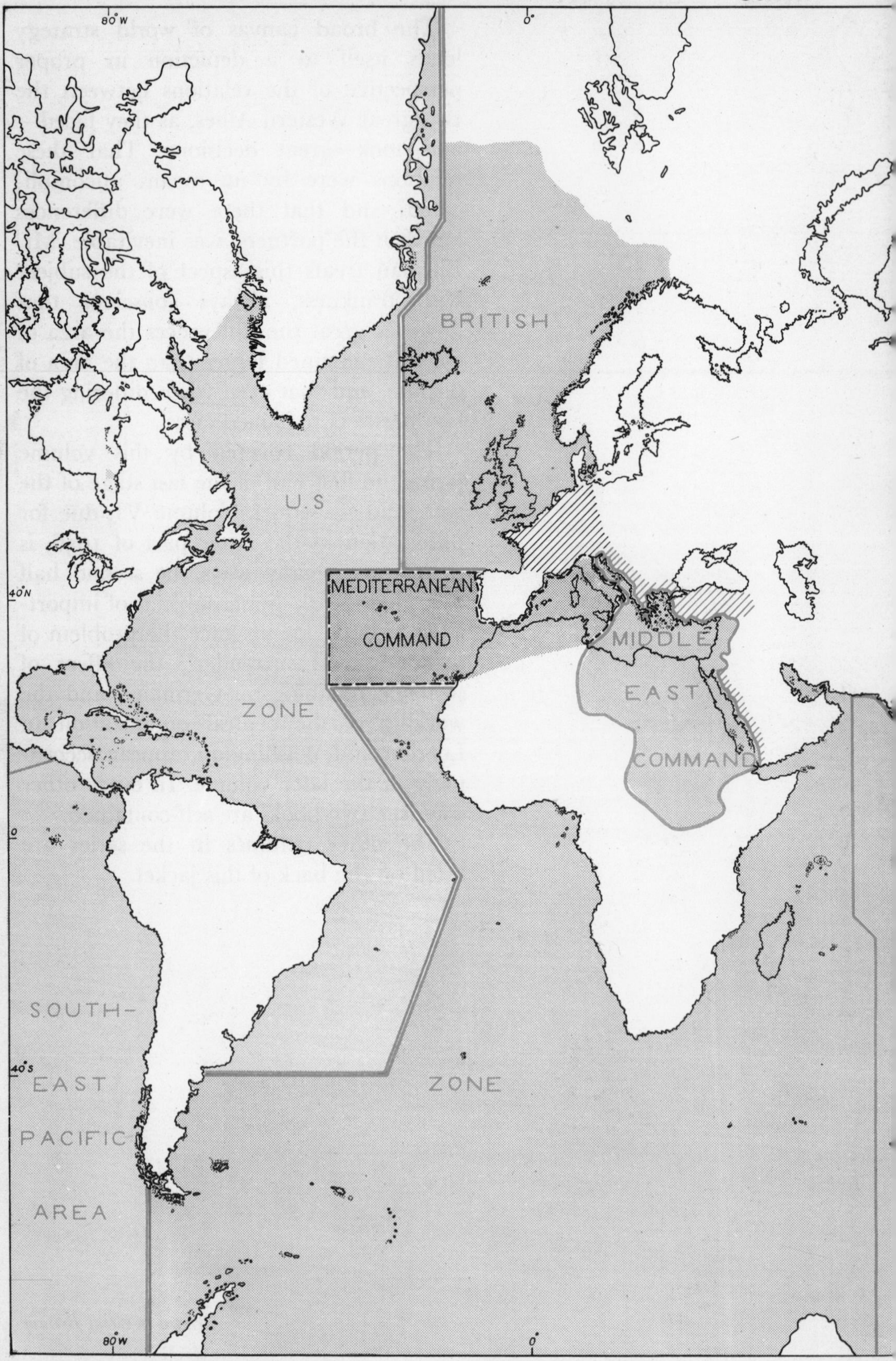